The City of God
(*DE CIVITATE DEI*)

Abridged Study Edition

Augustinian Heritage Institute

Board of Directors:

+John E. Rotelle, O.S.A. (1939–2002), founding director

Joseph L. Farrell, O.S.A. Jane E. Merdinger
David Hunter Boniface Ramsey
Joseph T. Kelley James Wetzel
Patricia H. Lo Jonathan Yates

Translation Advisory Board

Allan D. Fitzgerald, O.S.A. Edmund Hill, O.P.
Joseph McGowan Boniface Ramsey

THE WORKS OF SAINT AUGUSTINE
A Translation for the 21st Century

The City of God
Abridged Study Edition

THE WORKS OF SAINT AUGUSTINE
A Translation for the 21st Century

The City of God
Abridged Study Edition

introduction and translation
William Babcock

notes
Boniface Ramsey
(general editor)

abridgment
Joseph T. Kelley

Hyde Park, New York

Published in the United States by New City Press
202 Comforter Blvd., Hyde Park, New York 12538
©2018 Augustinian Heritage Institute

Library of Congress Control Number: 2018943935
Augustine, Saint, Bishop of Hippo.

    The City of God, Abridged Study Edition
    The Works of Saint Augustine.

    "Augustinian Heritage Institute"

ISBN 978-1-56548-660-7 (paperback)
ISBN 978-1-56548-661-4 (e-book)

Printed in the United States of America

CONTENTS

Preface to the Abridged Study Edition xi

Introduction xiii

    The Text..xiii
        The Sack of Rome and The City of God (Book I) — xiv; Rome's Gods and
        Earthly Happiness (Books II-V) — xviii; Rome's Gods and Happiness in Life
        after Death (Books VI-X) — xxi; The Origins of the Two Cities (Books XI-XIV)
        — xxvi; The Eternal Destinies of the Two Cities (Books XIX-XXII) — xxxviii

    The Translation... li

    A Select Bibliography lviii

    Revisions II,43 (70)... lix

Book I.. 1
    Barbarian Respect for Christ's Churches as Places of Sanctuary — 2; Rome's
    "Conquered Gods" — 3; Divine Providence, Human Suffering, and Temporal
    Goods and Evils — 5; Why the Good also Suffered in the Sack of Rome: Failu-
    re to Correct the Evil — 7; Forms of Christian Suffering: Loss of Riches — 8;
    Forms of Christian Suffering: Torture and Famine — 9; Forms of Christian
    Suffering: Dreadful Types of Death and Death without Burial — 10; Forms of
    Christian Suffering: Captivity — 12; Captivity: the Example of Regulus and
    His Loyalty to His Gods — 12; Forms of Christian Suffering: Rape; Moral
    Purity and the Issue of Suicide — 13; Rape and Suicide: the Example of Lucre-
    tia — 15; Suicide: the Example of Cato — 16; Is Suicide Permissible to Avoid
    Sin? — 18; The Perils of Unfettered Prosperity: Scipio Nasica against Roman
    Extravagance — 21; The Theaters and the Gods — 22; The Intermingling of
    the Two Cities in this World — 23; Study Questions for Book I — 25

Book II 27
    The Disasters that Afflicted Rome Prior to the Coming of Christ — 27; The
    Failure of the Gods to Provide Moral Guidance: the Rites of the Mother of the
    Gods — 28; Did the Gods Sponsor any Public Teaching of Virtue? — 29; The
    Fables of the Poets and the Shows in the Theaters — 30; The Greeks and the
    Romans on Poets and Actors — 31; Plato on the Poets — 33; The Natural "Jus-
    tice and Goodness" of the Romans — 34; Roman Morality, the Constraint of
    Fear, and the Destruction of Carthage — 35; The Issue of Justice and Scipio's
    Definition of a Republic — 38; Scipio's Definition of a Republic — 39; Cicero:
    the Republic Has Perished — 40; Had the Gods Withdrawn? — 41; The Gods
    and the Civil Wars: Marius — 42; Christianity's Public Teaching — 44; An
    Exhortation to the Romans to Abandon their False Gods — 44

Book III 47
    The Fall of Troy: the Gods and Laomedon's Perjury — 48; The Fall of Troy: the
    Gods and Paris's Adultery — 48; Troy and Adultery, Rome and Fratricide — 49;

The Peace of Numa's Reign — 50; The Seizing of the Sabine Women — 52; The War with Alba — 54; The Deaths of the Kings — 55; From the Expulsion of the Kings to the Second Punic War: the First Consuls — 56; From the Expulsion of the Kings to the Second Punic War: Conflict between Patricians and Plebeians — 56; From the Expulsion of the Kings to the Second Punic War: Famines, Plagues, and Wars — 57; The Second Punic War: Hannibal — 58; The Second Punic War: the Destruction of Saguntum — 58; From the Second to the Final Punic War: the Maltreatment of Scipio and the Cultivation of Luxury — 60; From the Punic Wars to Augustus: the Massacre of the Romans under Mithridates — 61; Evils Internal to the Republic: Civil Strife and Civil War — 62; Civil War: Marius and Sulla — 63; Civil Wars in the Time of Augustus — 64; These Evils All Occurred Prior to Christianity, when the Gods Were Still Worshiped — 65; Study Questions for Book III — 67

Book IV 69
The Basis for Rome's Expansion — 70; The Evaluation of Empire — 70; The Gods and the Rise and Fall of Assyrian Rule — 72; Which of the Gods Aided the Expansion of Rome? — 73; The Greater Gods: Jupiter and the Elements of the Universe — 74; Jupiter as the One God in All — 75; Why not Worship the One God Alone? — 77; God as the Soul of the World, the World as the Body of God — 78; Victory, Just War, and Foreign Iniquity — 79; The Goddesses Felicity and Fortune — 80; Virtue and the Virtues: not Goddesses but Gifts of God — 81; Virtue and Felicity — 82; The Naming of Gods for Their Gifts and the God Who Gives Happiness — 82; Three Views of the Gods — 84; Rome's Gods Incapable of Extending or Preserving Rome's Empire — 85; Cicero and Varro on Superstition, Images of the Gods, and the Religion of the Populace — 86; The One True God Is the God Who Gives Earthly Kingdoms — 89; Study Questions for Book IV — 91

Book V 93
Neither Chance nor Fate Caused Rome's Greatness — 94; Against Astrological Fatalism: the Case of Twins — 94; Against Astrological Fatalism: "Auspicious" Days — 97; Fate as the Chain of Causes — 98; Cicero's Argument on Foreknowledge and Free Will — 98; Divine Foreknowledge and Human Freedom — 100; The Giver of Empire is the True God — 104; Roman Love of Glory and Roman Virtue — 105; The Divine Gift of Empire to Rome: an Earthly Reward for Earthly Virtue — 107; The Roman Example: an Antidote to Christian Pride — 109; The Difference between the Desire for Glory and the Desire for Domination — 110; God Is the One Who Grants Power both to Kingdoms and to Individuals — 112; The Good Christian Emperor — 113; The Emperor Theodosius — 115; Study Questions for Book V — 118

Book VI 119
The Issue: Are the Gods to Be Worshiped for the Sake of Eternal Life? — 120; Varro and His Work on Roman Religion — 121; Varro's Three Types of Theology — 122; The Intertwining of the Mythical and Civic Theologies — 125; The Implied Aim of Varro's Account of Civic Theology — 126; Seneca's Boldness and Varro's Timidity — 129; Seneca on the Jews — 130; Neither the Mythical nor the Civic Theology Holds the Promise of Eternal Life — 131; Study Questions for Book VI — 132

Book VII 133
   The Select Gods and Their Functions — 134; The Absurdities and Inconsistencies in Varro's Account of the Select Gods — 135; The Indecent Acts Attributed to the Select Gods — 136; Varro's Naturalistic Interpretations of the Select Gods — 137; To Worship the World or the World's Soul Is not to Worship the True God — 139; The One True God and His Works — 140; Numa's Explanations of the Rites that He Instituted — 143; Study Questions for Book VII — 146

Book VIII 147
   Plato's Predecessors — 149; Socrates — 150; The Superiority of the Platonists — 153; The Closeness of the Platonists to Christianity — 157; The Issue: the Worship of Many Gods — 161; The Platonists on the Demons: Apuleius — 162; Hermes Trismegistus on the Demons: the Art of Making Gods and the Coming Abolition of the Gods — 163; Hermes's Lament and the Memorial Shrines of Christian Martyrs — 168; Christians Do not Worship the Martyrs — 168; Study Questions for Book VIII — 170

Book IX 171
   Apuleius on the Demons and the Passions — 172; Philosophic Views of the Passions — 173; Scripture on the Passions — 175; The Demons' Mind, the Highest Part of the Soul, Is Subject to the Passions — 176; The Demons: Immortal Body, Vice-Ridden Soul — 177; Evil Mediators and the Good Mediator — 178; God, the Gods, the Demons and the Issue of Contamination by Human Contact — 179; Good Angels Are not Good Demons — 181; The Pride of the Demons, the Humility of Christ, and the Good Angels — 181; Good Angels and the Gods — 183; Conclusion: neither Angels nor Demons Are Mediators to Be Worshiped for the Sake of Eternal Life — 183; Study Questions for Book IX — 185

Book X 187
   The One Source of Happiness, both Human and Angelic — 189; The Significance of the Sacrifices Commanded under the Old Law: the Self Directed to God in Love — 191; Porphyry on Theurgy and the Purification of the Soul — 194; The Visible Miracles and Visible Appearances of the Invisible God — 195; Divine Providence, the Education of Humanity, and the Giving of the Law — 196; Angels, Miracles, and the Worship of God — 197; Sacrifice, the Angels, and the Worship of God — 199; Porphyry on the Principles and the Purification of the Soul — 200; Christ: the True Mediator and the True Principle of Our Purification — 202; Porphyry on the Angels and the Theurgic Arts — 203; Porphyry's Failure to Recognize the Truth: Pride and Humility — 204; Corrections of Plato — 207; The Soul Has not Always Existed — 208; The Universal Way of the Soul's Liberation — 209; Study Questions for Book X — 213

Book XI 215
   Faith, the Mediator, and the Authority of Scripture — 217; Creation, Time, and the Immutability of God — 218; The Days of Creation and the Forms of Knowledge — 221; The Creation of the Angels — 222; The Divine Simplicity — 223; The Angelic Fall — 224; The Case of the Devil — 226; The Separation of the Holy Angels from the Fallen Angels — 228; The Goodness of God and the Goodness of Creation — 228; Traces of the Trinity in Creation — 232; The

Holy Angels and Their Knowledge — 235; Alternative Views of the Creation of the Angels — 236; Conclusion — 237; Study Questions for Book XI — 238

Book XII 239
The Difference between the Good and the Evil Angels: not Nature but Fault — 240; The Cause of the First Evil Will — 243; The Cause of the Good Will of the Good Angels — 245; The Origin of Humankind — 246; The "Date" of Man's Creation — 248; Against Theories of World Cycles — 249; Eternity and Time — 250; Time, Infinity, and the Divine Knowledge — 252; Ultimate Happiness: the Refutation of the Theory of World Cycles — 254; God's Creation of the Human Race from One Man — 255; God the Sole Creator — 257; Humanity's Social Character — 259; Study Questions for Book XII — 261

Book XIII 263
The Meanings of Death — 264; Death as Punishment — 265; The Death of the Saints — 267; "Before Death," "after Death," and "in Death" — 268; The Threat of Death — 270; The Body and Ultimate Blessedness — 271; The Issue of the Eternity of the Body — 273; Against the View that the Earthly Body Cannot Be in Heaven — 274; Self-Contradictions in the Platonic View of the Body — 274; The Body in Paradise — 277; Spiritual Interpretations of Paradise — 277; The Resurrected Body — 279; The Animal Body and the Spiritual Body — 279; The Question of Human Sexuality before the Fall — 281; Study Questions for Book XIII — 282

Book XIV..283
Living according to the Flesh and Living according to the Spirit — 285; The Meaning of "Flesh" — 286; Living according to Man, or Self, and Living according to God — 287; The Flesh, or the Body, Is not Evil — 288; The Will, the Passions, and Love — 288; The Passions in the City of God — 291; The Emotions and the Future Life — 293; Emotion in the First Human Beings — 295; The First Evil Will — 296; The Human Fall — 298; The Evil Will Precedes the Evil Act — 299; Humility and Pride — 300; The Punishment of Sin — 302; Lust, Human Sexuality, and the Sense of Shame — 303; Human Procreation Prior to the Fall — 305; Sexuality before the Fall — 306; The Happiness of Paradise — 308; Man's Sin and God's Foreknowledge — 309; Two Loves Have Made Two Cities — 310; Study Questions for Book XIV — 311

Book XV 313
Cain and Abel, the Earthly City and the Heavenly City — 314; Israel: the Earthly Image of the Heavenly City — 315; The Earthly City and the Heavenly City, Born of Nature and Born of Grace — 316; The Goods of the Earthly City and the Conflicts to Which They Give Rise — 317; Conflict between the Two Cities: the Flesh and the Spirit — 319; The Presentation of the Two Cities in the Lines of Descent from Cain and Seth — 320; The Long Lives of the Ancients — 321; The Intermingling of the Two Cities: the Sons of God and the Daughters of Men — 323; The Flood, Noah, and the Ark — 324; The Flood: History and Allegory — 326; Study Questions for Book XV — 328

Book XVI..329
   The Prophetic Significance of Noah and His Sons — 329; The Tower of Confusion and the Diversity of Human Languages — 332; Are Monstrous Races Descended from Noah and thus from Adam? — 333; The Line of Descent from Shem — 335; The City of God among the Peoples of Earth — 336; Heber and the Hebrew Language — 337; A Turning Point: Abraham — 338; The First of God's Promises to Abraham — 339; The Second Promise to Abraham — 340; The Third Promise to Abraham — 342; Abraham's Vision at Mamre — 343; Abraham's Sons: the Birth of Ishmael and the Promise of Isaac — 347; God's Appearance to Abraham at Mamre — 349; The Birth and the Sacrifice of Isaac — 350; Abraham's Marriage to Keturah — 352; The Twins Born to Isaac — 353; God's Promise to Isaac — 354; The Blessing of Jacob — 355; Jacob and Joseph — 357; From Moses to David — 360; Study Questions for Book XVI — 363

Book XVII 365
   The Age of the Prophets — 365; The Types of Prophecy — 368; The Prophecy of Hannah, Mother of Samuel — 370; The Transformation of the Priesthood: the Prophecy to Eli — 372; The Transformation of the Kingship: Saul and Samuel — 373; David, Solomon, and the Prophetic Anticipation of Christ — 376; David's Prophecies of Christ and the Church: the Psalms — 378; Solomon's Prophecies of Christ and the Church — 380; Prophecy after Solomon — 381; Study Questions for Book XVII — 384;

Book XVIII 385
   The Divisions in Human Society — 386; Assyria as the "First Rome" and Rome as the "Second Babylon" — 387; The End of Assyria and the Founding of Rome — 388; Sibyline Prophecies of Christ — 389; The Antiquity of Prophetic Wisdom — 394; The Superiority of Divine Wisdom over Human Philosophy — 398; The Translation of Hebrew Scripture into Greek: the Septuagint — 400; The Coming of Christ in Fulfillment of Prophecy — 403; The Spreading of the Church: Persecutions and Consolations — 405; The Persecutions of the Church — 407; Study Questions for Book XVIII — 410

Book XIX 411
   The Ends of the Two Cities: the Supreme Good and the Supreme Evil — 411; Varro: Possible Positions on the Supreme Good — 412; Varro's Position on the Supreme Good and the Life of Happiness — 414; The Supreme Good and the Supreme Evil according to the City of God: Eternal Life and Eternal Death — 419; Happiness, the Supreme Good, Cannot Be Found in this Life — 419; The Struggle of the Virtues against the Vices: Temperance, Prudence, and Justice — 420; Fortitude and the Question of Suicide — 421; The Miseries of Social Life: the Household and the City — 424; The Miseries of Social Life: the World — 426; The Miseries of Social Life: the Angels and the Demons — 428; The Meanings of Peace — 429; The Universal Desire for Peace — 430; Peace and Order — 434; Earthly Peace and Eternal Peace — 436; Sin and Slavery — 437; Earthly Peace and the Two Cities — 440; The Issues of Certainty and Style of Life — 441; The Definition of a Republic — 443; Justice and the True God: against Porphyry

— 445; An Alternate Definition of a People — 451; Earthly Peace and the City of God — 452; The Supreme Evil: Eternal Misery — 454; Study Questions for Book XIX — 455

Book XX   457

The Day of Judgment — 458; God's Inscrutable Justice — 459; Testimonies to the Last Judgment from Scripture — 460; Testimonies from the Gospel of Matthew: Judgment and Resurrection — 461; Testimonies from the Gospel of John: the First and the Second Resurrection — 461; Testimonies from the Book of Revelation: the Binding of the Devil for a Thousand Years — 462; The Releasing of the Devil — 467; The Thousand-Year Reign of the Saints — 467; The Last Judgment, the Second Resurrection, and the Book of Life — 470; The New Jerusalem — 472; Testimonies from the Apostle Paul: the Coming of Antichrist — 473; Paul on the Resurrection of the Dead — 476; Testimonies from the Prophet Isaiah: the Separate Ends of the Good and the Evil — 477; Testimonies from the Psalms: the Perishing of the World and Christ's Coming as Judge — 478; Testimonies from Malachi: the Purification of the Saints and Their Pure Offering to God — 478; How the Old Testament Points to Christ as Judge — 480; The Events of the Last Judgment — 484; Study Questions for Book XX — 486

Book XXI   487

The Body and Eternal Fire — 488; The Issue of Eternal Pain — 489; The Issue of Survival in Eternal Fire: Natural Wonders and the Power of God — 490; The Issue of the Nature and Properties of Human Flesh — 496; The Worm and the Fire: Eternal Punishment of Both Body and Soul — 497; The Issue of the Just Correlation of Temporal Sin and Eternal Punishment — 499; The Issue of Remedial or Purgatorial Punishment — 500; All Human Life on Earth is a Trial — 501; The Warfare of Flesh against Spirit and of Spirit against Flesh — 502; The Question of Divine Mercy and Eternal Punishment: Erroneous Views — 504; Reply to Error: the Devil and His Angels Will Suffer Eternal Punishment — 507; Reply to Error: Eternal Punishment is Eternal — 508; Reply to Error: the Intercession of the Saints and the Prayers of the Church — 508; Reply to Error: Who It Is That Is Saved as through Fire — 509; Reply to Error: the Issue of Works of Mercy — 511; Study Questions for Book XXI — 515

Book XXII   517

The Will of God and the Fulfillment of the Divine Promise — 519; The Miracle of the World's Belief in the Resurrection — 520; Miracles of the Present — 522; The Witness of the Martyrs — 529; Questions about the Character of the Resurrected Body — 529; Response to the Questions — 531; The Resurrection of Women's Bodies — 532; The Meaning of Complete Manhood — 533; Further Responses to Questions about the Resurrected Body — 534; The Gift of the Life to Come — 536; The Evils of this Life — 537; The Struggles of the Righteous: the Battle against the Vices — 540; The Goods of this Life — 540; The Goods of the Life to Come — 545; Against Philosophical Objections to the Resurrection of the Body — 546; The Eternal Life of the Saints: the Vision of God — 548; Will the Saints See God with the Eyes of the Spiritual Body? — 549; The Felicity of the Saints: Seeing, Loving, and Praising God — 551; Study Questions for Book XXII — 555

PREFACE TO THE ABRIDGED STUDY EDITION

Saint Augustine's classic work *The City of God* has endured sixteen centuries of study and scrutiny, enriching a great variety of readers across many eras and different cultures. Any intent to abridge such a text might seem the height of hubris. However, the hope is that a shorter, more manageable edition will invite the reader to subsequent engagement with the full text.

The last such edition appeared in 1958, abridged by Vernon Bourke. It included four different translators. This present edition depends entirely upon William Babcock's 2012 superb translation. His excellent introduction and the summaries preceding each of Augustine's twenty-two books are an important part of his scholarly bequest. The introduction and summaries are kept in their entirety.

Two criteria were used to reduce the almost one thousand pages of Augustine's text to around six hundred. Long sections comprising several chapters have been omitted when they constitute an excursus or digression, a popular rhetorical device of Latin orators. These long omissions are noted in the text by brief, bracketed summaries of their contents.

Shorter sections of one or several paragraphs within or across chapters have also been omitted. These are passages in which Augustine elaborates, illustrates, or explores logical variations of a point already made — fine-tunings of the rhetoric advancing his argument. These omissions are noted by ellipses in the text. An unfortunate casualty of both the longer and shorter omissions is the loss of Boniface Ramsey's excellent footnotes for those sections.

This abridged study edition provides several open, thought-provoking questions for each of the twenty-two books. These questions encourage the reader to probe Augustine's text for ideas that continue to inform religious and moral critique of political power, and for themes that remain fundamental to peace and social justice within and across nations and cultures today.

"Love and do what you will — *dilige et quod vis fac*," Augustine exhorts in his *Commentary on the First Epistle of John* VII,8. That advice steadied my hand as I excised almost half of Augustine's text. If this abridged classroom resource edition helps readers — especially new readers — understand the "two loves that made two cities," then it will have been worth the many dilemmas it entailed.

This effort is dedicated to and inspired by the Austin Scholars of Merrimack College.

Joseph T. Kelley
Merrimack College
August 28, 2018

INTRODUCTION

THE TEXT

"Two loves," Augustine writes, "have made two cities. Love of self, even to the point of contempt for God, made the earthly city; and love of God, even to the point of contempt for self, made the heavenly city." (XIV,28) For all its vast scale and intricate complexity, then, *The City of God* is a story of love. It is, however, a love story played out in a cosmic setting, across an immense historical range, and within complicated patterns of social order. It is important to note at the outset that the two cities that Augustine has in mind cannot be equated straightforwardly with any political units or social entities. While it is true enough that he does at times identify the heavenly city, the city of God, with the Christian Church and the earthly city, the city of the devil, with the Babylonian or the Roman empire, he insists that the Church inevitably contains some members of the earthly city and that the great empires contain some members of the heavenly city who are not yet known to the Church. The two cities will only be separated out and appear in unmixed form at and after the final judgment when each attains its ultimate destiny. In the meantime, in the span of human history, they are not and cannot be sociologically or politically defined. They are formed, rather, by the deepest orientations of the human heart, by its desires and its loves; and, for Augustine, it is never possible in this life to read the innermost direction of the heart. That is one of the most heartrending features of life in this world. There is always a veil of darkness that finally separates one person from another and makes it impossible to penetrate into the inner regions of another person's self. Augustine's tale of two loves, therefore, does not reduce or eliminate the ambivalence and ambiguity of human history and society. It does not allow us to cut through the uncertainties of human interrelationships and declare with complete assurance that we have found the true, the just, and the good society or, in contrast, the false, the unjust, and the evil society in any specific social or political grouping. Rather, it creates a context — an immensely complex context — within which we can interpret the modes of human behavior and the forms of human society without ever being able to assure ourselves that any one group is all right or all wrong. It is not a context that prevents or prohibits moral judgment. In fact, it might well be called a guide to moral judgment and a charting of the way of virtue. But it does undercut all self-righteousness in moral judgment. Within this context, it is clear that we cannot discern the ways of God (except where they are revealed in Scripture, which rests on God's authority, not ours), cannot plumb the depths of the human heart, and can find no morally pure community on earth. God alone, then, can see who does and who does not finally belong to each city, and God alone can achieve the separation of the one from the other.

The Sack of Rome and The City of God (Book I)

The immediate occasion for the writing of *The City of God* was the sack of the city of Rome by Alaric and his Gothic army in August of 410. The Goths occupied and pillaged the city for three days and left considerable destruction in their wake when they withdrew. But the political import of the city's fall was probably not as significant as its psychological impact. After all, the capital of the Roman empire had been transferred from Rome to Constantinople almost a century earlier, and the seat of imperial government in Italy had long since been removed from Rome to Milan and then to Ravenna on the Adriatic coast.[1] The symbolic import of the event, however, was immense. The news rippled out across the empire, like an earthquake's aftershocks, calling into question an ideology of Rome that was shared, in one version or another, by Christians and pagans alike. Far away in Palestine, Jerome would write, "When the brightest light of the world was extinguished, when the very head of the Roman empire was severed, the entire world perished in a single city."[2] According to Virgil's *Aeneid*, written late in the first century B. C., Jupiter had set no spatial or temporal limits on the Romans' power and had given them "empire without end."[3] Jupiter's promise was not erased when Christianity became the empire's dominant religion under Constantine or even when, in the late fourth century, increasingly stringent imperial edicts were issued against the rites and practices of Greek and Roman traditional religion. In some ways, it was even reinforced, since Rome seemed now to have acquired the backing of the Christians' all-powerful God, the creator and ruler of all. These "Christian times," it seemed, should be understood as the realization of God's providential direction of history to its culmination: Roman imperial rule as the vehicle for the triumph of true religion.[4] In the light of Rome's fall to the Goths, however, it seemed that Rome had suddenly and disastrously lost its invulnerability and that, against all expectation, Jupiter's promise had failed.

To the empire's remaining pagan population — especially in the Latin West where the traditional accounts of Rome's founding and its rise to greatness were still strong[5] — the reason for the failure was all too obvious. Rome had abandoned

---

1. A good, brief history of the period is Averil Cameron, *The Later Roman Empire, AD 284-430* (Cambridge, Mass.: Harvard University Press, 1993). For more detail, see Averil Cameron and Peter Garnsey, eds., *The Cambridge Ancient History,* vol. 13: *The Late Empire, A. D. 337-425* (Cambridge: Cambridge University Press, 1998).
2. Letter 126,2. The translation is from J. N. D. Kelly, *Jerome: His Life, Writings, and Controversies* (New York: Harper & Row, 1975) 304.
3. *Aeneid* I,278.
4. For discussion of the way in which the "Christian times" of the late fourth century were celebrated by some Christians, and for a treatment of Augustine's own brief dalliance with and ultimate rejection of this triumphalist view, see R. A. Markus, *Saeculum: History and Society in the Theology of St Augustine* (Cambridge: Cambridge University Press, 1970) 22-44.
5. For discussion of the lingering strength of paganism in the Latin West, see Gerard O'Daly, *Augustine's City of God: A Reader's Guide* (Oxford: Oxford University Press, 1999) 1-26 (on

her gods and banished the sacrifices that earned their favor; and, as a consequence, her gods had abandoned her and withdrawn their protection. The city had fallen to the onslaught of the Goths. And in the event, the new Christian God, for whom they had traded their traditional religion, had provided no defense at all. Not only had he proved powerless against the Gothic army, he had not even been able to defend his own devotees. Like their pagan counterparts, Christians too had been taken captive, tortured, raped, looted, and killed. Their prayers for protection had fallen on deaf ears, or had been no more than pleas to a God without power.

In North Africa, as his sermons show, Augustine was already responding to such complaints in 410, in the immediate aftermath of the calamity at Rome.[6] When he began writing *The City of God* in 412, then, he already had an arsenal of answers to the critics of Christianity on which he could draw; and, in fact, the first book of the work makes many of the same points that he had made in his preaching. He starts by reminding the pagan critics that they would never have survived to lodge their complaints if it had not been true that the Goths themselves, although Arian heretics, were Christians and, against all the traditional rules and customs of war, had treated Rome's churches as places of sanctuary where all — pagans quite as much as Christians — could gather in safety. In this regard, he insists, the treatment of Rome stood in stark contrast to pagan practice. The Romans themselves, in all their wars of conquest, had never treated the temples of the gods as places of sanctuary or allowed those who fled to them to gain the security of a safe harbor against the threats of death or captivity. Nor had their own gods ever offered such protection. Rome's own gods were, in fact, "conquered gods," who had been defeated when the Greeks had taken Troy.[7] They survived only because Aeneas had carried them off on the voyage that would ultimately lead to the founding of Rome. They were gods who, far from defending their defenders, had been defended by them; and when their defenders fell to their enemies, the gods fell with them, escaping final defeat only because a few survivors were able to escape from fallen Troy and take their gods with them.

From the outset, however, Augustine had a larger plan in mind for *The City of God*. His aim was not to chronicle a competition between gods on the dubious scale of success or failure at the level of historical events. It was rather to confront — and to counter — the entire religious, cultural and political tradition of Rome on an entirely different set of issues, the issues clustering around the question of religion

---

the Christianization of the empire) and 30 (on paganism in North Africa in particular). On the learned literary and philosophical culture of Latin paganism, see Peter Brown, *Augustine of Hippo: A Biography*, new edition (Berkeley and Los Angeles: University of California Press, 2000) 297-311. The literary account of Rome's origins most prominent in the Latin West was, of course, Virgil's *Aeneid*.

6. For a brief account of Augustine's preaching in the immediate aftermath of the sack of Rome, with the relevant citations, see Gerard O'Daly, 28-31.
7. *The City of God* I,3. Augustine takes the phrase "conquered gods" from Virgil's *Aeneid* II,320.

and the ultimate attainment of human happiness. Even in the first book of the work, then, he turns the question of Rome's fall into a confrontation between alternate ways of assessing human suffering and relating it to the role of the divine. The real issue, he argues, is not a supposed failure of divine protection but rather the enigmatic workings of divine providence. Why is it that God extended his mercy to some of the evil as well as to some of the good? Why is it that God imposed his severity on the good as well as on some of the evil? The answer, it turns out, has to do with the ways in which divine providence makes use of historical events to shape human character. It sometimes spares the evil as well as the good in order to provide opportunities for repentance; and it sometimes afflicts the good as well as the evil in order either to punish them for their moral failures or to test them in their perseverance in the good. Thus the sufferings of Christians at the hands of Alaric's Goths can be understood either as punishment for their failings, even if their failing was no more than the relatively minor fault of being afraid to rebuke and correct the powerful for their misdeeds, or as a way of putting them to the test in order to confirm them in their goodness. In neither case, however, does their affliction affect what genuinely counts as their true good. It does not separate them from God, nor does it rob them of the promise of ultimate happiness with him.

Thus, any Christians who lost their wealth in the pillaging of the city lost only what is transient and vulnerable, not what is enduring and invulnerable to loss. Any Christians who loved their riches as if they were of supreme value discovered, through the training of experience, how badly they had misplaced their devotion. Any Christians who were tortured by the enemy to force them to hand over their earthly goods neither could nor did hand over the good by which they themselves were good; and, if they preferred to be tortured rather than to hand over their possessions, they were not actually good and should have learned to love Christ, who offers eternal felicity, rather than gold and silver. Again, Christians who were taken into captivity by the Goths did not fall outside the realm of divine consolation, as indicated by the captives recorded in Scripture who were sustained by God. And the Romans themselves venerate the example of Marcus Regulus, a general who was defeated and taken captive by the Carthaginians. Regulus was sent back to Rome to negotiate an exchange of prisoners, having first sworn by his gods that he would return if he failed in his mission. In Rome, he argued against the exchange and, keeping strictly to his oath, returned to Carthage where he was put to a horrible death by torture. The episode shows, Augustine claims, that the Romans themselves honored one taken captive; and, in addition, it proves that Regulus's own gods, the very gods to whom he remained loyal even to the point of death, could neither protect him from his fate nor give him happiness in this life. If the Romans felt no hesitation about honoring gods who failed to protect Regulus, what grounds did they have for dishonoring the God who apparently failed to protect Christians but actually preserved them in the ways that really count?

Finally, in this catalogue of Christian sufferings in the sack of Rome, Augustine considers the case of Christian women who were raped by the Goths. What is inflicted on the body by someone else, however, does not affect a person's virtue, which is a function of the mind rather than the body. And here again, he sets his point against the counterpoint of a Roman example: Lucretia, who was raped by the son of the Roman king Tarquin and, overwhelmed by her sense of shame at what had happened to her, committed suicide. Like Regulus, Lucretia was held in high regard by the Romans as an example of moral excellence. But, Augustine argued, if she had truly not consented to the rape, then she had no reason to feel shame and, in committing suicide, she had in effect murdered an innocent person; or, if her shame was justified, then she must in some way have consented in her mind to the rape, and in that case she cannot be considered an paragon of feminine virtue. Here again, then, the Romans face a dilemma: either Lucretia's virtue was not damaged by the rape and she was wrong to put herself to death, or her shame was justified and she should not be honored as an exemplar of virtue. In either case, it is the Roman and not the Christian tradition that has gone astray in its moral reckoning.

Augustine then turns from his catalogue of Christian sufferings — which might be interpreted as a kind of preliminary intimation of what counts as true virtue and where real human happiness is to be found — to an abbreviated account of what he considers Rome's moral decline from the early years of the republic to the unfettered vice and viciousness of the period of the civil wars. Two events stand out in this first version of what will be a major theme throughout *The City of God*. The first is the fall of Carthage, Rome's traditional North African enemy; and the second is the introduction into Roman life of theatrical plays demanded and authorized by the gods. The first, in Augustine's view, brought to an end the external threat that had kept the vices of the Romans in check and introduced an era of prosperity that gave them full play in unrestrained greed for wealth and lust for power, tearing apart the fabric of Roman society and eventuating in the disaster of wars of Romans against Romans. The second put the immoralities of the gods on public display, making them central to the worship of the gods in the temples as well as in the theaters and establishing them as the dominant form of the gods' public presence in Roman life. The story of Rome's decline is, then, a story of the loss of all externally enforced moral restraint and, at the same time, a story of the gods' contriving of demonic control — for, Augustine will insist, the gods are really demons — over the religious and moral life of Rome in a vast deception of a whole society.

Despite the sharp contrast he has drawn between the intimations of true virtue in the Christian sufferings in the sack of Rome and the Roman decline into raw greed for wealth and power, however, Augustine closes the first book of his massive work with a reminder that in this world the two cities are always intermingled and intertwined. Included among the enemies of the city of God, there are some who are its friends and members; and, similarly, included among the Christians who bear Christ's sacrament, there are some who will not be joined with the heavenly city in the eternal destiny of the saints. Some of the latter, he states, are hidden, while some are out in the open and do not hesitate to mutter their complaints against God. Thus Augustine has used Book I to set the stage for what will be the master plan governing the structure of the work as a whole. His intended audience is not merely the pagan critics of Christianity and "these Christian times"; it is also the Christians who have, in one degree or another, turned against their faith as well as those Christians who stand in need of a wider vindication of their belief over against the accumulated weight of the Roman religious and political tradition which represented Christianity as a betrayal of all that had made Rome great and, most especially, as a betrayal of its gods.

Rome's Gods and Earthly Happiness (Books II-V)

It is against this background, then, that Augustine elaborates the wider argument of *The City of God*. The basic structure and pattern of the argument is relatively clear. It consists of two main parts. The first, set out in Books II-X, argues that Rome's traditional gods were neither able to provide happiness in this life (Books II-V) nor in the life to come (Books VI-X). The second, consisting of Books XI-XXII, offers an opposing vision of the divine and of the true character of humanity's relation to God, which it presents by tracing out in turn the origins of the two cities (Books XI-XIV), the course that each has followed through time (Books XV-XVIII), and ultimately their final destinies (Books XIX-XXII). Within this broad structure, however, the argument is more complex; and its themes require some unraveling in order to discern how it functions as a story of two loves that are played out on a cosmic scale and within complex patterns of social order and disorder. It is a story that is meant, at every stage, to counteract Rome's own account of its greatness — although without totally erasing Rome's claim to a special place in human history — and at the same time to offer an alternative account of what makes for genuine human virtue and what truly counts as ultimate human happiness, which is to be found not in the exercise of power and dominion but rather in the sheer love and enjoyment of God.

The initial stage of the argument is designed, then, to discredit the gods of Rome's traditional religion by showing, first of all, that, long before Christianity came upon the scene — and therefore long before there was any question of prohibiting the forms of worship offered to these gods — they had failed, time after time, to protect Rome from disaster and calamity.[8] In part, Augustine's argument is an argument by ridicule. At various points he dwells upon the sheer multiplicity of the Roman gods, each assigned to its own tiny little task as if none had the power to control or to direct any wider sphere of human life and history. But his main

---

8. For an excellent account of Roman religion (with illustrative documents), not as seen through Augustine's — or any Christian — eyes, but as it was practiced in its own right, see Mary Beard, John North, and Simon Price, *Religions of Rome*, 2 vols. (Cambridge: Cambridge University Press, 1998).

points are more significant and more far-reaching. The failure of the Roman gods, he insists, is most especially a failure in the moral arena. Far from offering moral guidance or providing instruction in virtue, the gods have, in fact, introduced into Roman life egregious examples of immoral behavior and have given them the weight of their own supposed authority, demanding that the tales of their own misdeeds be enacted in the theaters and in other public rituals. In this way, they have made it seem that the favor of the gods can only be attained and sustained by providing them with rites that instantiate the worst features of human immorality. And what this shows, Augustine argues, is that the traditional gods of Rome, far from being true divinities acting for the benefit of their adherents, are actually malicious demons bent on bringing humans into submission to themselves by deceiving them into treating the evil as if it were the good.

But there is more to Augustine's argument. The Romans' gods not only failed them in the moral sphere but also failed to protect them from such natural disasters as famines, floods, and plagues, or from such political catastrophes as civic conflict and all the horrible sufferings of war. Here again, Augustine wants to stress the malicious character of the demons, their eagerness to do harm. And because — for Augustine, as for the Roman tradition generally — religion is never a merely private matter, cut off from the public realm, the failure of the gods has deep political and social consequences. In fact, the celebrated civic virtue exemplified in the early years of the Roman republic, following the expulsion of the kings, was not a function of any moral guidance provided by the gods or of any loyalty to Rome's presiding deities. It was rather the result of fear, fear of external enemies, which constrained the Romans' love of praise and desire for glory, directing them to genuine service of the republic rather than unleashing them in a brutal quest for dominion over others. Following Rome's conquest of its enemies, however, the constraint that fear had imposed evaporated, and Rome's history became a history of internal strife and bloody civil war as one faction after another sought to gain control, eliminate its enemies, and secure its domination of the city and its growing empire. Augustine even suggests that the Roman republic never actually counted as a true republic. For a republic represents a people cohering in "a common sense for what is right and a community of interest" (II,21); and the Romans, untutored by their gods, lacked any true sense of justice and thus lacked any genuine "sense for what is right." Thus the failure of the gods to offer instruction in morality and virtue had a devastating social and political outcome. It undercut and undermined the very core of the Roman social order and left the Roman polity vulnerable to the destructive disorder in which it was torn apart by civil war.

Augustine's purpose, however, was not simply to disqualify the Roman tradition as a whole or to deny that Rome's rise to greatness deserves any special recognition. In fact, his account of Rome's slide into civic disorder and ultimately into self-destructive civil war draws heavily on Sallust, one of Rome's own historians, and the definition of a republic that he uses to discount the Roman claim to have been a republic is taken from Cicero, one of Rome's most prominent statesmen and political thinkers. It is not so much that Augustine is merely disparaging the Roman tradition, then, as that he is transvaluing it and, in fact, is transvaluing it from within as well as from without. In effect, he is transposing the role of the gods in Rome's history from a positive to a negative key. Far from being the ones who guided it to greatness and secured it against its enemies, they are the ones who bear responsibility for directing Roman morality away from virtue into vice and for transforming its internal politics from a politics of service to a politics of cruelty.[9] But if the gods do not account for Rome's rise to greatness, what does?

Augustine does not shy away from this issue. His answer to the question has several dimensions. In the first place, he argues — in Book IV — that empire should not be construed as if it were some great human good. It comes at the expense of war and bloodshed; and it is an expression of human greed for power and dominion. In addition, it is the kind of good that is given both to the good and to the evil in this life; and so it is clearly inferior to those goods that are reserved for the good alone. It is clear, then, that imperial rule should be downgraded on the scale of goods and should not be counted as one of the goods that genuinely contributes to ultimate human happiness. In fact, Augustine argues, a multiplicity of smaller kingdoms, each enjoying internal harmony and external peace with its neighbors, would be a better way of ordering political society than a vast empire imposing its rule on others by means of bloody conquest and harsh dominion. Beyond this, Augustine stresses that none of Rome's gods, whether minor or major, have the kind of reach and power that could control and direct the course of kingdoms. The spheres of their agency and the arenas of their concern are too small and too restricted to expand outward to guide and govern the full extent of human history and society. On the other hand — as Augustine argues in Book V — Rome's greatness, the wide extent and long duration of its rule, is not to be understood as a function either of fate or of mere chance. Instead we must understand that the gift of empire is given only by the one true God; and we should recognize that, in the Roman case, it was given on the basis of the Romans' virtues. Although these virtues rest on a false foundation — the love of praise and the desire for glory — they are nevertheless better to have than not to have in the political sphere of life on earth; and Augustine even goes so far as to cite several examples of Roman virtue which stand out strongly enough to prevent Christians from taking any special pride in their own virtue, even though their virtues may rest on the true foundation of true religion. Thus Augustine does not leave us helpless when it comes to making judgments about various forms of political order and discriminating between better and worse types of human government. He enables us to interpret Rome's

---

9. Augustine does not assign the sole or even the primary responsibility for Roman immorality to the gods. In his view, the Romans were vulnerable to the gods' misdirection precisely because their virtues, since they were rooted in love of praise and desire for glory rather than in worship of the true god, were not true virtues. Thus the ultimate responsibility for the Romans' moral failure lies with the Romans themselves. But the gods did nothing to instruct them in morality and, in fact, did everything they could to deceive them into yet more vice-ridden immorality.

empire as a divine reward for Roman virtue, such as it is (and, even with its false foundation, it is better than moralities that are worse), a gift given by the God who does guide and govern the full stretch of human history. But this interpretation comes with caveats. First, it may be true that God has some other hidden reason, not visible to human sight, for giving Rome the gift of empire; and we should not suppose that we can be confident that we have discerned the hidden purposes of God. And second, we must recognize that the gift of empire is no more than an earthly reward for a kind of virtue in the earthly context. We must not confuse it with the ultimate reward of true happiness, which is given for true virtue not in this life but in the life to come.

Rome's Gods and Happiness in Life after Death (Books VI-X)

On this note, Augustine turns to the second element in his argument against the traditional gods of Rome. He has adequately demonstrated, he believes, that these gods cannot and do not give happiness in this earthly life; and, in particular, he has shown that the gift of empire, which he is willing to count as a low-level human good, comes not from the gods but from the one true God who alone directs the course of history and the rise and fall of human kingdoms. Now he turns — in Books VI-X — to a further question: whether the gods can or do give happiness in the life to come after death. Once again his strategy is to challenge and to counter the Roman religious tradition not only from without but also from within. To this end, he takes the Roman scholar and antiquarian Varro — and, in particular, Varro's now lost work on Roman antiquities — as the basis for his discussion. In the first place, he criticizes Varro for treating "human matters" prior to "divine matters" in this work. Varro justified his approach by claiming that, just as the painter comes before the painting, so the human crafters of religion come before the religion that they craft. But Augustine construes this imagery as a tacit admission that the Roman gods were, in fact, created by the human beings who worshiped them — and thus a tacit admission by Varro himself that Rome's gods were actually all human inventions rather than real beings existing in their own right.

He then turns to Varro's classification of "divine matters" under three headings: the mythical theology of the poets, the natural theology of the philosophers, and the civic theology of the cities. Reserving natural theology for later discussion, Augustine reports that Varro himself discredits and condemns the poets' mythical theology, the theology of the theaters, with its tales of the disreputable acts and moral atrocities committed by the gods. On the other hand, Varro appears to approve and commend the civic theology, the theology of the temples and of public worship. But, Augustine argues, Varro presents the gods of Rome's civic religion in such a way that they are, for all practical purposes, indistinguishable from the disreputable gods of the poets' mythic tales. It would seem, then, that in identifying the gods of the temples with the gods of the theaters, Varro was obscurely hinting that the former were no better than the latter, but he lacked the courage and boldness to make any forthright declaration of his opposition to Rome's public religion in the face of prevailing tradition and custom. In contrast, the philosopher Seneca was quite open in his denunciation of Rome's traditional gods. But Seneca still held that the gods should be worshiped as a matter of law and custom rather than of truth. In effect, then, Augustine has used Rome's own intellectual tradition, as represented by Varro and Seneca, to undermine Roman religion and to bolster his own claim that the gods of Rome cannot possibly be understood as givers of eternal life but instead must be interpreted as malignant demons who have deceived humanity into taking them as gods. Their worship is sustained only by custom, not by truth.

Varro's treatment of civic theology, as Augustine represents it, includes a discussion of the "select" gods, that is, of the major and most prominent gods of the Roman religious tradition. In this case, however, Varro interprets the gods by correlating them with processes in the natural world and with the forces that underlie and govern these processes. But this interpretation, Augustine argues, results in all sorts of incongruities and absurdities in Varro's account of the gods. For instance, in the area of human sexuality and reproduction, it is the select god Janus who opens the way for the seed, the select god Saturn who provides seed, the select god Liber who delivers the male of the seed he ejaculates, the select goddess Libera — supposedly identified with Venus — who delivers the female of the seed she emits, while the select goddess Juno governs the menstrual flow in women. But, Augustine points out, it is two minor gods, the mere nonentities Vitumnus and Sentinus, who provide the really important gifts of life and sensation to the child that is to be born. Thus we have the ridiculous situation of a division of labor among the select gods that makes it look as though no one of them has the power to govern the whole process of reproduction, while, at the same time, the critical functions of providing life and feeling are assigned to minor deities who are not ranked among the select gods at all.

Beyond this, and on a larger scale, Varro associates Jupiter, the king and ruler of the Roman gods, with the world-soul, the force underlying and directing the world as a whole. Augustine insists, however, that no such interpretations, whether of Jupiter or of any of the select gods, can justify or compensate for the moral atrocities contained in the tales about the gods and in the rites by which they are worshiped; and in any case, he maintains, no worship of forces operative in the world, of the world itself, or even of the governing world-soul can possibly count as worship of the one true God who is no part or feature of the world but rather transcends this world and is alone responsible for all the forces and functions that Varro has assigned to the major (and minor) gods of the Roman pantheon. It is from this God, and only from this God, that human beings can truly attain ultimate happiness, not from the multiplicity of gods with their separate assignments and discrete functions which serve, in the end, only to show that, on Varro's own account, their range is limited and their power constricted. In Augustine's view, then, the best explanation of the gods of Rome's civic theology is that they were not gods at all, but rather were originally human beings who were honored for their strictly human accomplishments, and that their elevation to divine standing is actually the result of demonic deception.

The central core of Augustine's argument that the traditional gods of Rome cannot provide happiness in the life to come, however, lies neither in his discussion of the theology of the poets nor in his discrediting of the theology of the cities but rather in his more extended consideration of the theology of the philosophers. Here he leaves Varro aside and instead takes the Platonic tradition and, in particular, the Platonists of the imperial period as his conversation partners. He selects the Platonists on two grounds. In the first place, he says, they are the most renowned and preeminent of the philosophers; and, in the second, they are the philosophers whose views stand closest to Christianity itself. Their conception of the divine, in particular, mirrors the Christian view in that they maintain that there is one supreme God, who is not a part of or a force in the natural order but rather transcends the universe and governs its course. In addition, with Christianity, they hold that the supreme good for human beings rests in ultimate union with the supreme deity. Augustine even finds intimations of Christianity's triune God in the views of Plotinus and Porphyry. But, if the Platonists stand close to Christianity in their conception of the divine and the human good, they go astray — Augustine argues — in insisting that, along with the one supreme God, human beings should also worship the many gods of the Greek and Roman religious traditions. As the first stage in his counter-argument, Augustine takes up the views of Apuleius, the North African Platonist of the second century A.D., and specifically his views on the demons.[10] Apuleius presents the demons as superior to human beings in that they have lighter bodies and inhabit the air, above the earthbound habitat of humans. Their role, as Apuleius portrays it, is to serve as intermediaries between human beings and the gods — who would be contaminated by direct contact with their lowly human supplicants — carrying men's prayers up to the gods and bringing the gods' responses back down to men. Augustine counters, however, that it is neither character of body nor place in the hierarchy of the universe that makes for true superiority among rational creatures. It is rather capacity for moral goodness; and it is ridiculous to think that the demons, who are morally evil, could possibly serve as intermediaries between the good gods and human beings who, in fact, have a higher capacity for moral goodness than do the demons themselves. There is, then, no good reason to worship the demons as gods and, still less, to worship them for the sake of any benefits that they might confer after death.

This argument, however, leaves open the question as to whether there might be good as well as evil demons and, if there are, whether the good demons might be worthy of worship. In this connection, Augustine takes as his starting point Apuleius's own characterization of the demons. The demons, according to Apuleius,

---

10. On Apuleius and his philosophical views, see John Dillon, *The Middle Platonists, 80 B.C. to A.D. 220* (Ithaca: Cornell University Press, 1977) 306-338.

are subject to the passions — that is, they feel joy and anguish and all forms of human emotion — and they are subject to the passions in the mind itself, the highest and best part of the soul, the part which gives them their status as rational creatures. If this is true, however, they lack the moral qualities of wisdom and virtue by which some human beings — the "wise" — keep the passions under control and prevent their emotions from carrying them off in any direction that is inconsistent with moral goodness. It is important to note that Augustine's argument here is not an argument against all emotion, as if only the person completely lacking in emotion could be considered truly good. It is rather an argument for the moral control of the passions on the part of the mind, such that the mind will only consent to the pull of passion when the passions themselves are rightly directed, that is, when they function in conformity with and in support of what is morally good (when, for example, hatred is directed at the evil and desire is directed at the good). And it is precisely because the demons, in their lack of virtue and wisdom, lack the control of mind that rightly orients the passions that they cannot count as good. Furthermore, if the demons were truly intermediate between gods and human beings, and thus genuinely in a position to serve as intermediaries between them, they would need to share some characteristics with the gods and some characteristics with human beings. On Apuleius's account, however, the most important characteristic that they share with the gods is immortality of body and the most important characteristic that they share with human beings is a mind caught up in the turbulence and turmoil of unruly passions. In this sense, Augustine points out, they are somehow turned upside down: they are superior in the part of the rational creature that is inferior, the body, and they are inferior in the part that is superior, the mind. And what is more, characterizing the demons in this way amounts to a denial that they are actually able to serve as intermediaries between gods and human beings. For they share with the gods a feature that has nothing to do with goodness and thus cannot actually bring them into contact with the gods, who are all to be counted as good; and they share with human beings a feature that plunges them into misery, the misery of misdirected passion ungoverned by virtue. They are, therefore, in no position to be of real help to human beings by freeing them from that very misery. What human beings actually need is a mediator who is, so to speak, turned right side up, a mediator who is not immortal in body and miserable in soul but rather is mortal in body (at least for a time) and blessed in soul. And this mediator is the very Word of God, who becomes subject to death in his incarnate mortality and who, as God, is incontrovertibly good and blessed. This true mediator, unlike the Platonists' gods, is not contaminated by contact with human beings and, unlike the demons, is genuinely able to offer them a path to true happiness. Thus none of the demons can actually be considered good; and none of them can actually serve as real mediators between the distant gods and lowly human beings. It is plain, then, that the demons should not be worshiped for the sake of happiness in life after death.

As the final step in Augustine's disqualification of Roman religion, and specifically of the theology of the philosophers, he takes up the question of whether the gods themselves, as opposed to the demons, should be worshipped for the sake of benefits in the life that follows death. Here he interprets the gods as good — that is, unfallen — angels; and he starts with a definition of what is to count as true happiness for rational creatures: participation in the one God by clinging to him in love. This is a definition, in Augustine's view, which is common to both Christians and Platonists and, thus, which establishes common ground between them. At the same time, it illuminates the true meaning of worship, which is to devote the self to God in love. In this light, Augustine presents an extended argument, drawn from and based on his interpretation of the sacrifices commanded in the Old Testament, to show that the sacrifices offered to God did not represent or arise from any need on God's part, as if human beings could provide him with something he would otherwise lack. They served rather as signs of the true sacrifice required from human beings, namely, an offering of the self that is realized in love for God and others. The commands of the Old Testament, as confirmed by the miracles of the Old Testament, make it clear that sacrifice — the offering of the self in love — is due only to God and to none other. The good angels, therefore, do not want sacrifice offered to themselves but only to God. Unlike the demons, they do not want to be worshipped in their own right; they want worship to be directed to God alone.

But even at this late stage in the argument, when Augustine is drawing more fully on the authority of Scripture than he has at any earlier point, he continues to use the Roman tradition against itself. Over against the form of devotion represented by the biblical account of sacrifice, there is the practice of theurgy, a supposed means of purification that is discussed by the Platonic philosopher Porphyry.[11] Porphyry presents theurgy as a way of appealing to the gods to purify the lower part of the soul and, in this way, to bring about a moral purification that will raise human beings into contact with the divine. Appealing to examples of the practice, however, Augustine construes it as a form of manipulating the gods which can be and sometimes is blocked by more powerful deities that oppose any operations designed to achieve human goodness — which only goes to show, once again, that these gods are not truly gods but rather malicious demons plotting to keep human beings in subjection to themselves. And in any case, by Porphyry's own admission, theurgy serves only to purify the lower part of the soul and cannot provide a true way of return of the rational soul to God. Thus Porphyry himself maintains that a higher form of purification is required to restore a person to God and to attain the ultimate happiness of clinging to God in love. It is not theurgy, then, but rather what Porphyry calls the one "principle" that genuinely purifies the rational soul

---

11. On Porphyry and the intellectual context to which he belonged, see Andrew Smith, *Porphyry's Place in the Neoplatonic Tradition: A Study in Post-Plotinian Neoplatonism* (The Hague: Martinus Nijhoff, 1974) and Pauliina Remes, *Neoplatonism* (Berkeley: University of California Press, 2008).

and, in fact, the entire human person. In giving this one "principle" divine status, Porphyry has brought Platonism closer to Christianity and has even attained a kind of murky and unclear inkling of Christianity's triune God. Augustine asserts, however, that Porphyry is blinded by his intellectual pride from discerning and accepting the humility of the incarnation in which this "principle" — which is, in truth, the Word and Son of God — has taken flesh in order to enact the way of return that actually leads to God and to ultimate happiness. Porphyry reports that he has not been able to find the universal way of the soul's liberation in any of his own inquiries and investigations. Nevertheless, he maintains that there is such a universal way; and Augustine argues that, if only Porphyry had not been blinded by his pride, he would have recognized that Christianity does provide this universal way, which was realized in the coming of Christ and in the life of the Church.[12] There is, then, no reason at all to worship the gods for the sake of happiness in life after death. If the gods are interpreted as good angels, their concern is not to draw human worship to themselves but rather to direct it wholly to the one true God, to whom alone it is due. And if they are interpreted as demons, they not only can offer no help to human beings but, in their malice, are striving to keep humans away from the true God and subject to themselves. The Word incarnate is, then, the one true mediator who purifies the human person and opens the way to the ultimate happiness of clinging to God in love. Without him, this love lies wholly beyond human reach.

The Origins of the Two Cities (Books XI-XIV)

Augustine's alternative to the Roman religious, political, and philosophical tradition that he seeks to discredit in Books I-X is the story of two cities that he tells in Books XI-XXII. In the definition of true happiness that he had proposed at the beginning of Book X, he had already intimated that this story would center on the motif of two loves, a rightly directed love that clings to God (and thus attains true happiness) and a wrongly directed love that turns away from God (and thus plunges the lover into misery).[13] At the same time, intertwined with the motif of two opposing loves, there is a correlated motif of two opposing orientations of the self, one defined by pride and the other by humility, the first exalting the self as if it could be its own foundation and the other taking God as its foundation and relying solely on him.[14] But these two motifs, of course, are actually variations on

---

12. In the *Confessions*, written most probably in 397, Augustine presents a similar picture of the Platonists kept from embracing Christianity by their intellectual pride and their disdain for the lowliness of Christ. See *Confessions* VII,18,24-21,27.
13. For a study of the development on these themes in Augustine's early thought, see William S. Babcock, "*Cupiditas* and *Caritas*: The Early Augustine on Love and Human Fulfillment," in *The Ethics of St. Augustine*, ed. William S. Babcock (Atlanta: Scholars Press, 1991) 39-66.
14. For an extended discussion of Augustine's understanding of humility, see Otto Schaffner, *Christliche Demut: Des hl. Augustinus Lehre von der Humilitas* (Würzburg: Augustinus Verlag, 1959). On his view of pride, see D. J. MacQueen, "*Contemptus Dei*: St Augustine on the

a common theme. For the love that turns away from God is the root of the pride that is expressed in self-assertion; and the love that clings to God is the basis for the humility that recognizes the self's dependence on God and on God's grace.

Augustine presents the story of the two cities, the heavenly and the earthly, in three phases. The first tells of the origins of the two cities, first at the angelic and then at the human level (Books XI-XIV). The second tracks, in somewhat uneven fashion, the course followed by each city through time (Books XV-XVIII). And the third displays their final destinies, realized at the last judgment and culminating in eternal punishment for the earthly city and in eternal life for the heavenly city, the city of God (Books XIX-XXII). At each stage Augustine not only relates the story that he has to tell but also addresses the theological issues that it raises, replying to possible objections and offering support for the positions that he takes. Rather than a straightforward narrative, then, this second main part of *The City of God* consists of a complex argument designed not only to replace the Roman tradition with a new account of humanity's relationship with the divine but also to answer the critics — whether pagan or Christian — who might take offense at one aspect or another of that account.

At the outset, it is important to note that Augustine adopts a new basis for this phase of his work. He is going to speak, he says, of things that lie beyond the reach of human reason; and so he must take divine authority — specifically, the authority of divinely given Scripture — as the ground for his discussion. This does not mean, of course, that he is simply going to repeat passages of Scripture in his delineation of the two cities, as if all the workings of the human mind were now to be reduced to silence. Scripture itself requires interpretation, which is an enterprise of human reasoning; and, in addition, there are arguments to be made in support of what Scripture says and against those who deny either its authority or its content. His point, then, is not that divine authority displaces or disqualifies human reason, leaving it with no role to play. It is rather that, with regard to things that reason cannot grasp on its own (especially reason that has been darkened by "inveterate faults" [XI,2] brought on by its turn away from God), it requires guidance and direction from an authoritative source outside itself; and it is God's authority, expressed in the Scripture through which God addresses human beings, that provides the necessary guidance and direction. Here too, then, Augustine is drawing a sharp contrast between the Roman tradition, on the one hand, which even at its best, in his view, is based on the resources of a human reason operating on its own without knowledge of what constitutes true religion, and, on the other hand, a Christian account which rests on a knowledge of the divine that is supplied by God himself. Even at this preliminary point, the motif of humility and pride as two opposing orientations of the self is already at work. For it requires humility to submit to the authority of God and to follow its dictates, while it is an expression of arrogance to insist upon the independence of human reason and to assert its self-sufficiency.

Disorder of Pride in Society, and its Remedies," *Recherches Augustiniennes* 9 (1973): 227-293.

The story of the origins of the two cities begins at the level of the angels. Its setting is provided by the account of creation that is given by the opening verses of the Book of Genesis; and so, in Augustine's approach, it largely takes the form of a commentary on those verses, an explication of what they mean and what they imply with regard to the creation of the angels and their division into two companies, the holy angels and the fallen or apostate angels. Almost immediately, however, issues arise that go beyond the text of Genesis itself and require discussion in their own right. In the first place, there is the question of how the act of creation can be compatible with the immutability of God, the fact that God is a constant who is not subject to variation through time and thus undergoes no change whatsoever in his enduring eternity. For, if God were changeable, he would be, in Augustine's view, less than God, a variable thing like all created things, and thus an item within the created order rather than a being who transcends it and is its creator and governor. Right away, then, Augustine must provide an argument in support of his view that the act of creation does not compromise the immutability of God, his unchanging self-identity as God. He must show, that is, that it involves no change in the divine plan and no new act of will on God's part.

Beyond this, there is the hard fact that the opening verses of Genesis do not actually mention either the creation of the angels or their separation into two groups. Faced with this obvious difficulty, Augustine correlates the creation of the angels with the creation of light and their separation with the separation of the light from the darkness. At the core of Augustine's account is his insistence that all the angels were created good in nature. The distinction between the good and the evil angels is not a distinction between two different natures, one created good and the other created evil. Even the devil, who according to Scripture *sinned from the beginning* (1 Jn 3:8), was not created evil; he sinned from the beginning of his own primal pride, his own turn away from God and to himself, but not from his first creation. Like all the angels, he was created good; and his evil is a function not of his created nature, provided by God, but rather of his own act of will, his abandonment of the highest good, God, for a lesser good — himself — in an act of self-assertion. It is this act, an act followed and replicated by all the fallen angels, that plunges him and them into darkness and defines the point at which the light (representing the good angels who persisted in their orientation to God rather than to themselves) was separated from the darkness (representing the evil angels who turned away from God and to themselves).[15]

---

15. Echoing a Platonic theme, Augustine insists that the reason for creation is that a good God might create good things. Therefore nothing in the world is to be construed as evil by nature. Evil has no substantial reality. It is entirely due to the misdirection of the will. The question of evil, therefore, does not arise because some things are inherently evil — i.e., evil by nature — but rather because rational creatures turn away from the highest good to lesser and lower goods, treating them as if they were the supreme good and thus investing them with a value that they do not have (although even the lowest goods, because they were created by the good God, have value and

But this account of creation poses a difficult and delicate issue with regard to the fallen angels. If all the angels were created equally good, both in nature and in their original orientation toward God, how is it that some fell away while others did not? How did the first evil will arise? Augustine insists that, while an evil will is the efficient cause of an evil act, there is no efficient cause of an evil will. The evil will, Augustine argues, is not an effect — that is, is not the result of some force operating on it — but is rather a defect, a defect due to and identical with the will's own defection from God. Thus the first evil will cannot be explained by reference to any prior evil operating on it but only in terms of its own turn away from God in pride. This turn is possible because the angels, like all beings created out of nothing, are mutable and are thus capable of change. But it is not caused and cannot be explained by their mutability. Otherwise the evil will would be a function of their created nature, and their created nature could not be counted as unambiguously good. Instead, the evil will of the fallen angels must be construed as a function only of their own defection from God and toward a lesser form of good, as if this lesser good were the supreme good. Here, then, we have the origin of the two cities at the level of the angels. All the angels were created equally good and equally oriented toward God, by whose light their reason was illuminated and to whom they clung as their highest good. Some angels persisted in their orientation to God as their highest good, attaining the ultimate happiness both of enjoying God and of knowing that their happiness never could and never would be lost. Others, in contrast, defected from God, turning away from the highest good and valuing a lesser good — themselves — as if it were the highest good. This defection represents an expression of pride and an act of self-assertion; and, as its result, their understanding was plunged into darkness and their love was misdirected. Already at the angelic level, then, the story of the two cities is marked out as a story of two loves, love of God and love of self,[16] which are expressed in two different orientations, one of humble submission to God and the other of arrogant self-assertion in opposition to God and to the hierarchy of values he has established.

Augustine now takes up the origin of the two cities at the human level. In this case, unlike that of the angels, he does not face the problem of scriptural silence on the topic. There are texts in Genesis that deal explicitly with the creation and fall of human beings. But once again there are complicating issues and questions that he needs to address. He needs, for instance, to vindicate the biblical chronology — according to which, in Augustine's view, humans have not existed for more than six thousand years — against alternate chronologies that ascribe much longer historical spans to human existence and especially against views

---

are to be counted as good, not evil). For more extensive discussion of Augustine's views on evil, see G. R. Evans, *Augustine on Evil* (Cambridge: Cambridge University Press, 1982); J. Patout Burns, "Augustine on the Origin and Progress of Evil," in *The Ethics of St. Augustine* 67-85.

16. For a superb study on Augustine on love of self — and on love in general — see Oliver O'Donovan, *The Problem of Self-Love in St. Augustine* (New Haven and London: Yale University Press, 1980).

that posit a succession of world-cycles in which the world comes into being, runs its course, and then undergoes destruction, only to come into being again in an unending sequence in which its history is exactly repeated over and over again. This sequence of repeated worlds is not required, Augustine insists, in order to make the creation of humanity compatible with the immutability of God.[17] For God creates according to an eternal and immutable plan which does not change and is not altered when the world actually comes into existence. Nor does it make any sense to ask why man was not created at some earlier point in time. Time itself was created, and created at the same point as the world as a whole. Thus there was no time prior to creation, and so there is no temporal meaning to the word "earlier" prior to creation. Most tellingly, Augustine finds that the notion of repeated world-cycles is refuted by the saints' attainment of ultimate and unending happiness, an event that occurs in time and is never repeated again because their happiness is permanent and stable. In fact, if their happiness were impermanent and subject to loss, it would not be true and undiluted happiness. Instead, it would either be grounded in ignorance (as to its upcoming loss) and thus less than full happiness for a rational creature,[18] or it would be tinged with anxiety (about its upcoming loss) and thus compromised by fear of the future. To accept an unending sequence of repeated worlds with repeated histories would be, then, to undercut the very concept of eternal happiness that will ultimately give the story of the heavenly city its conclusion and its climax.

Having dealt with the issue of God's eternity in relation to creation at the human level, Augustine next turns to the creation of man in particular. It is noteworthy that Augustine begins by stressing the point that God did not create humanity, as he did the animals (as well as the angels), by making many individuals all at once. Instead he created a single individual, from whom all humanity would be propagated. God's purpose, however, was not to leave humans in isolation, each alone and bereft of human society. It was rather, and specifically, to underscore and to commend man's social character by insuring that they would be linked to one another not only because they have a common nature but also by a deeply rooted sense of kinship with each other, grounded in the fact that they were all derived from a single common ancestor. God knew, of course, that man was going to sin and that humans would go to such lengths in sinning that even the most savage beasts would live together more peacefully with their own kind than would the humans who were produced from a single individual precisely in order to encourage social harmony among them. But God also foreknew that, by his grace, some humans would be joined together as a godly people and would ultimately be united with the

---

17. Since an endlessly repeated succession of worlds would have no initial starting point (just as it has no **final** ending point), it would nowhere present a new beginning — so the argument would have gone — and thus would require no new decision or action on God's part, and thus would not involve any change in God.
18. For Augustine, it is not true that "ignorance is bliss." Any bliss based on ignorance is based on a false foundation and thus does not count as true bliss at all.

holy angels in eternal peace. In this sense, we can say that already in the first man, the man created at the beginning, there arose — if not in plain sight, then certainly in the knowledge of God — two societies, "like two cities" (XII,28), one destined to be joined with the evil angels in eternal punishment and the other destined to be joined with the good angels in eternal happiness.

It is clear, then, that Augustine is going to treat man's primordial fall as in some sense a rending of the social fabric, a breaking of the harmony and unity for which humans were created by God. Before he fully develops this theme, however, he has other points that he wants to make. The first has to with death, which is a consequence of the fall and a punishment for human sin. As first created, humans were capable of attaining immortality. They were not immortal in the sense that the angels are, who are wholly beyond the reach of death. But, if they had not sinned, they would not have died. Death, however, is a more complex notion than might at first appear. Relying heavily on Scripture, Augustine distinguishes four meanings of death: the death of the soul, when God abandons the soul (because the soul has first abandoned God); the death of the body, when the soul abandons the body, no longer giving it life; the death of the whole person, when soul and body are separated from each other so that the body is no longer enlivened by the soul and the soul only survives without its body; and, finally, the second death, which is the eternal punishment in which the soul, eternally separated from God but reunited with its body, is eternally tormented not only by its own anguish but also by the unending agonies that the body suffers in the fires of hell. All four forms of death were included in the death with which God threatened the first human beings in paradise if they ate of the tree of the knowledge of good and evil; and all four were brought into force in the wake of the first human sin. When the first human beings turned away from God, they were in turn abandoned by God; and, unless divine grace intervenes, that death, the death of the soul, is followed by the whole disastrous sequence of deaths which culminates in the second and final death of eternal punishment.

At the same time, if death in all its senses is a punishment, the body itself is not; nor is it an obstacle to the attainment of ultimate happiness.[19] Against the Platonists, Augustine cites Plato's own claim that the celestial gods are, by divine will, forever joined to their celestial bodies and thus are both immortal and eternally blessed precisely in their embodied state. Even on Platonic grounds, therefore, it is not true that happiness can only be attained by escape from the body. Furthermore, despite the Platonic argument against it, there is no reason why the body cannot exist in heaven, even though it is made from earth, the lowest and heaviest element,

---

19. For a study of Augustine's views on the body, see Margaret R. Miles, *Augustine on the Body* (Missoula: Scholars Press, 1979). See also Paula Fredriksen, "Beyond the Body/Soul Dichotomy: Augustine on Paul against the Manichees and Pelagians," *Recherches augustiniennes* 23 (1988): 87-114. For a more wide-angled study of the body in early Christianity, see Peter Brown, *The Body and Society: Men, Women, and Sexual Renunciation in Early Christianity* (New York: Columbia University Press, 1988).

which naturally sinks downward rather than rising upward. Just as people can make vessels that float on water even though they are manufactured from materials that ordinarily sink in water, so God can cause bodies to exist in heaven even though they are made of an element whose weight ordinarily carries it downward toward the lowest regions of the universe rather than upward to the highest. And, in any case, it is not the body *per se* but rather what Scripture calls *the corruptible body* that *weighs upon the soul* (Wis 9:15) in its present existence. This is the body not as it was created, but rather as it has become after sin, subject to death and resistant to the soul's direction. But the body of the resurrected saints will be perfectly attuned to the soul, no longer in conflict with it but rather expressing and supporting its desires and purposes. In the words of St. Paul, it will be a *spiritual body* in the sense that, unlike the *animal body* of the first parents,[20] it will be totally unable to die and will no longer require food and drink in order to ward off the pangs of hunger and thirst. In effect, then, Augustine has proposed a revisionist view of the body in which it is seen neither as antithetical to true happiness nor as alien to the human person. It is not the cause of the human plight, and the story of the two cities and their loves is not going to be a tale of escape or flight from the body.

Augustine now reiterates the point that humanity was created from a single human being and was meant to be joined in the bond of peace not only by virtue of sharing a common nature but also by virtue of the ties of kinship, making it clear that he will interpret the human fall as a rending of the social fabric and as the point of origin, on the human level, of the heavenly city and the earthly city. He also makes it clear that these two cities are not to be equated with any of the various socio-political units into which human society is organized at any given time, each with its own customs, language, dress, and religious rites. What he has in mind is a far deeper and more devastating division of humanity. Beneath all the civil polities in which humans live, he insists, there are actually only two types of human society. One consists of those who wish to live according to the flesh, the other of those who wish to live according to the spirit. One might expect, Augustine says, that to live according to the flesh would be to take bodily pleasure as the highest good for human beings and to make sensual delights one's highest goal in life. Similarly, one might expect that to live according to the spirit would be to locate the highest human good in the soul or mind and to make the cultivation of the mind the chief goal of life. But that is not how Scripture uses the word "flesh." Taking his cue from a passage in Paul, Augustine explains that, in Scripture's usage, *the works of the flesh* include not only such bodily pleasures as fornication, drunkenness, and carousing, but also such things as idolatry, enmity, jealousy, and dissension, which are all vices of the mind rather than of the flesh.[21] Thus, even a person who restrains and suppresses all fleshly desires for the sake of serving an idol or feeding his jealousy is still living according to the flesh as

---

20. See 1 Cor 15:44-46.
21. See Gal 5:19-21.

Scripture understands the term. It is clear, then, that the distinction between living according to the flesh and living according to the spirit cannot be mapped onto the distinction between the body and the soul; it has rather to be interpreted in a very different way: in terms of two orientations of the self at its deepest levels. This point is crucial for Augustine — and it coheres with his previous discussion of the body — because it cuts the ground from under any claim that it is the flesh that is the cause of human sin and immorality. While it is true enough that the flesh, in its corrupted state after the first human sin (*the corruptible body*), occasions and even produces some incitements to sin, yet that is not a function of the body in itself. It is rather an outcome of the misdirection of the self which is the result of sin. The flesh cannot be blamed for the fact that humanity has gone wrong.

The true contrast underlying the distinction between living according to the flesh and living according to the spirit, then, is not the contrast between the body and the mind; it is rather the contrast between two forms of life: living according to man and living according to God. At the same time it is a contrast between a lie and the truth. To live according to the self is to live a lie. It is to take as the highest good something that is not the highest good for human beings; and, as a result — even though its aim is to attain happiness — it is to live in such a way as to make the attainment of happiness impossible. To live according to man is to try to make oneself the source of one's own happiness. It is, therefore, an expression of human pride. And, in the end, it is doomed to fail. For the true highest good, and therefore the true source of human happiness and human fulfillment, is God. What is at issue, then, is not any supposed opposition between the body and the mind; it is rather the basic orientation of the will, the direction of the self. And, in this context, Augustine offers once again what might be called a Christian vindication of the passions or emotions.[22] Against the Platonic notion that the passions arise from the body or from the lower part of the soul and afflict the mind, which is at its best when it is passion-free, Augustine argues that the passions are rather a function of the will. On his interpretation, the passions are all modes of willing, modes in which the will either consents to the things we want or dissents from the things we do not want. Thus, when the passion of desire is an expression of a will for the good, it is good; and when it is as expression of a will for something evil, it is evil. Just as Augustine had previously displaced the false opposition between the body and the mind, here he is displacing the false opposition between the passions and the will and replacing it with what he considers a true opposition, the opposition between two orientations of the self as rooted in two orientations of the will. His aim is not to endorse the emotionless self but rather to commend the self whose emotions are rightly directed. The story that he tells is no more the story of the opposition of the passions to the will than it is the story of the opposition of the body to the mind. It is the story of two loves, love for self and love for God.

---

22. On this point, see James Wetzel, *Augustine and the Limits of Virtue* (Cambridge: Cambridge University Press, 1992) 98-111.

What the primordial fall represents, then, is the beginning of the misdirected will, grounded in a misdirected love, in the first created pair of human beings. In part, the story can be told as a sequence of overt events. In paradise, Adam and Eve lived in a setting in which nothing was lacking that a good will might desire and nothing present that might do harm to either the body or the mind. Their love for God was undisturbed, and it was a source of undiluted gladness since the object of their love was always present. Even their obedience to the divine command not to eat of the tree of the knowledge of good and evil was motivated not by any fear of punishment but rather by love of righteousness. And if they had continued in this way, all humanity — their posterity — would have enjoyed the same undiminished joy and would have gained the further happiness of having this happiness fully secured against any possibility of either sin or death. In this paradisiacal setting there appears the devil, the chief of the fallen angels, consumed by vicious envy of the as yet unfallen couple. Using the serpent as his instrument, he deceives the woman — the weaker sex in Augustine's view and so more susceptible to deception — into violating the divine command. As for Adam, even though he is not deceived by the serpent's guile and knows that the violation is a sin, he is unwilling to be separated from his only companion, and so he joins her in the evil act. The overt act, however, is rooted in the hidden inner reaches of the will. As Augustine presents the matter, the woman would not have believed that the serpent spoke the truth and the man would not have given priority to her wish over the divine command unless they were already evil in the will. The deep dimension of the human fall, then, lies not in the overt sequence of action and event but rather in the secret inner workings of the will where the first human pair had already turned away from God.[23] And it is here that the true seriousness of the fall is exposed to view. It was not simply what might appear a relatively trivial act of minor disobedience. It was rather a fundamental movement of self-assertion in which humanity, abandoning its true foundation, tried instead to make itself its own foundation. In doing so, it turned away from the light that enabled it to see truly and from the fire that enabled it to love rightly, and so it was plunged into murky darkness on the one hand and reduced to the pursuit of its own pleasure on the other.

Thus their self-assertion did not lead humanity into a any new realm of unimpaired liberty and freedom unconstrained by God. Instead it plunged human beings into a dire existence of subjection to death and of the agonizing inner conflict within the self. And it is at this point, in Book XIV,28, that Augustine concludes his account of the origins of the two cities with his statement that "two loves have made two cities. Love of self, even to the point of contempt for God, made the

---

23. For further discussion of Augustine's approach to both the angelic and the human fall, with special reference to the view of moral agency it entails, see William S. Babcock, "The Human and the Angelic Fall: Will and Moral Agency in Augustine's *City of God*" in *Augustine: From Rhetor to Theologian*, ed. Joanne McWilliam (Waterloo, Ont.: Wilfrid Laurier University Press, 1992) 133-149; idem, "Augustine on Sin and Moral Agency" in *The Ethics of St. Augustine* 87-113.

earthly city; and love of God, even to the point of contempt for self, made the heavenly city. Thus the former glories in itself, and the latter glories in the Lord. The former seeks its glory from men, but the latter finds its highest glory in God.... In the former, the lust for domination dominates both its princes and the nations that it subjugates; in the latter, both leaders and followers serve one another in love, the leaders by their counsel, the followers by their obedience. The former loves its own strength, displayed in its men of power; the latter says to its God, *I love you, O Lord, my strength* (Ps 18:1)." It is no accident, of course, that this passage echoes Augustine's earlier description of Rome with its longing for glory and its lust for domination. In his account of the origins of the two cities, Augustine has set a new context for understanding the workings of human society and, more specifically, for understanding the human forces at work in Rome's own history as an exemplification of the pattern of the earthly city.

Augustine's tracking of the two cities through human history largely consists of charting the sequence of biblical generations in which the heavenly and earthly city are respectively represented, coupled with drawing a pattern of correlations between biblical history and the various kingdoms that rose into and fell from prominence through the course of time, culminating in the rise of Rome itself to the status of world domination. For the purposes of this introduction, there is no need to trace his account in detail. It is important, however, to see how Augustine characterizes the two cities and the interactions between them in their earthly histories. He begins with the first children of Adam and Eve — Cain, who was born first and belonged to the earthly city, and Abel, who was born later and belonged to the city of God. The sequence of their births exemplifies a truth which also holds good for each human individual. All are born of a "condemned stock" — that is, all are born of fallen humanity, subject to death and enslaved to sin[24] — and therefore all are of necessity evil and carnal due to Adam's fall. In the words of Paul, *It is not the spiritual that comes first, but the animal, and then the spiritual* (1 Cor 15:46). For it is only if a person is reborn by grace that love of self will begin to lose its hold on him and a new love for God will emerge, and he will afterwards become good and spiritual when love for God becomes the prime and ultimately the sole shaping force in his life. And the same pattern obtains with regard to the human race as a whole. That Cain, the first to be born, was a citizen of this world is signified by the fact that he founded a city. His aim, then, was to make himself at home in this life and to invest himself in a society of this world. But Abel, who was born later, founded no city. Instead, he was by grace a pilgrim in this world

---

24. Augustine does not suppose that all humanity is born of a condemned stock, enslaved to sin and subject to death as the result of someone else's (Adam's) sin, the guilt and punishment for which has been imposed on Adam's posterity from the outside, so to speak. His view is rather that all were present in Adam when he sinned, and were in fact co-agents with him of his sin. Whether this notion of co-agency in an ancestor's sin can stand up to close examination is, of course, a question. But at least it shows what Augustine's idea was. For a study of Augustine on original sin, see A. A. Sage, "Le Péché originel dans le pensé de saint Augustin, de 412-430," *Revue des etudes augustiniennes* 15 (1969) 75-112.

and a citizen of the city above, the heavenly city. Thus the status of the heavenly city — or, at least, of that part of the heavenly city that is here on earth — is the status of a pilgrim who is not yet at home but is rather on the way toward a destination that he has not yet reached.

Augustine uses the births of Abraham's two sons, Ishmael and Isaac, to reinforce and further interpret this pattern. Ishmael was born of Hagar, as Augustine puts it, in the normal course of human sexuality and procreation. But Isaac was born of Sarah; and, because Sarah was then too old to bear children and, in any case, had been barren all her life, his birth represents something utterly beyond the course of nature. Although both were born of Abraham's seed, then, Ishmael's birth displays the ordinary workings of human nature, while Isaac's signifies the intervention of divine grace. And once again Augustine interprets the two births in terms of two mutually opposed orientations of the will. Ishmael stands for the children of nature, that is, of fallen human nature focused on the self. In contrast, Isaac belongs to the children of grace who are citizens of the heavenly city and who are not dominated by love for their own "personal and private will." They are characterized rather by a love that "rejoices in the common and immutable good and joins many hearts into one — a love, that is, which is perfectly at one in the obedience of charity" (XV,3).

Here, then, are the factors that will be in play in Augustine's characterizations of the two cities and of the interactions between them. The earthly city, pursuing its own personal and private good, will look for its good here on earth, and its joy, Augustine says, will come from sharing in this good. But Augustine also makes it clear that, because such goods as can be found in this earthly life are limited goods that cannot be shared without being diminished, they inevitably give rise to anxieties (about gaining or losing them) and conflicts (between those who seek to gain or keep them for themselves). As a prime example, Augustine cites the case of Romulus and Remus, the twin brothers of Roman legend, each of whom wanted for himself the glory of founding the Roman republic. To have a living co-ruler, however, would have meant having less power, less dominion, and therefore less glory for oneself. Consequently, to secure total dominion and power for himself, Romulus murdered Remus and made himself the sole founder of Rome. The murder, in Augustine's view, exemplifies the way in which the earthly city is divided against itself "by lawsuits, wars, and conflicts" in which each side seeks victory over the other in a constant struggle to gain position and power. In contrast, the heavenly city finds its joy "in the common and immutable good" — God himself — which is not diminished when it is shared and thus does not generate the anxieties and conflicts that stem from competition for a limited good that one person or group can acquire only at the expense of another. Instead, its good is of such a kind that the more it is shared, the greater each person's possession of it becomes. The heavenly city, then, is characterized not only by love for the supreme and immutable good, but also by its citizens' love for each other, which brings them into unity and harmony rather than conflict and competition.

In addition to the antagonisms within the earthly city that mark its course through time, then, there is also an antagonism between the two cities which sets them at odds with each other in their historical existence; and this antagonism is also exemplified by a brother's murder of his brother. According to the biblical account, Cain and Abel each offered a sacrifice to God. Abel's was accepted, but Cain's was not; and, out of envy, Cain killed Abel. Why was Cain's sacrifice rejected? As Scripture tells the story, God told Cain that his sacrifice was *rightly offered* but not *rightly divided* (Gn 4:7 LXX).[25] Augustine considers various ways of interpreting this rather enigmatic text. He finds, however, that its most basic meaning is that Cain's sacrifice was wrongly divided in the sense that, although he offered something from his own possessions to God, he kept himself for himself; and this, Augustine says, is precisely what people do who "who follow their own will rather than God's...and yet still offer gifts to God" (XV,7). They imagine that, with their gifts, they will buy God's help not in healing their own misguided and misdirected desires but rather in fulfilling them. And there is a political as well as a personal dimension to this kind of attempt to make the divine serve human purposes. The earthly city worships a god or gods "with whose help it might reign in victory and in earthly peace, not from love of caring for others, but from lust to exercise dominion over others" (XV,7). In either case, however, whether at the personal or at the political level, the aim is to bring the divine into the service of one's own aims and ambitions rather than to delight in the divine in its own right. "For," as Augustine puts it, "the good make use of the world in order to enjoy God; but the evil, in contrast, want to make use of God in order to enjoy the world" (XV,7).[26] What turns the earthly city against the heavenly, then, is the very fact that the city of God does not support or join its attempts to gain its own ends; and just as the enmity between Cain and Abel was rooted in Cain's hatred for Abel, so the antagonism between the earthly and the heavenly cities is rooted in this hatred of the evil for the good.

It underscores the depth of Augustine's feeling that the primordial fall tore the human social fabric into shreds and broke the bonds of kinship which ought to have united human beings in harmony that he placed cases of fratricide, of brother killing brother, both at the point of the emergence of the two cities on the plane of human history and at the point of founding of the Roman empire, the great exemplification of the earthly city in his time. Even so, however, he refuses to reduce his charting of the interactions within and between the two cities to a stark record of the antagonisms between and within the two cities. If the earthly city is characterized by conflict and war in its competition for earthly goods, that

---

25. Augustine's Latin text of Genesis was based on a Greek translation of the Hebrew which is known as the Septuagint and is signified by the abbreviation LXX.
26. "Use" and "enjoyment" are central concepts in Augustine's thinking on ethics and values; for an excellent account of the way the concepts function in his thought, see Oliver O'Donovan, "*Usus* and *Fruitio* in Augustine, *De Doctrina Christiana* I," *Journal of Theological Studies*, N. S. 33 (1982) 361-397.

does not mean that the goods it seeks are not goods or that human society is not often better when it attains them. When one side triumphs over the other, Augustine argues, there will be a sort of earthly peace; and if the victory goes to the side that was fighting for the more just cause, "who can doubt that the victory deserves to be celebrated or that the resulting peace is very much to be desired? These are goods, and they are undoubtedly gifts from God" (XV,4). We need, then, to recognize a more complex pattern of conflict and to allow that, even within the pattern of conflict, there can be instances of social good.

Thus, when Augustine lists the forms of conflict that obtain in our present social interactions, his list is surprisingly nuanced. As the case of Romulus and Remus shows, there is conflict of the evil against the evil; and there is also, as Cain's murder of Abel indicates, the conflict of the evil against the good. But, while it is true that, when the good have attained perfection, there will be no conflict between them, it is still true that in the present, when they have not yet attained perfection, they can certainly be at odds with each other due to the fact that the self is still internally at odds with itself. In each individual, so long as love of self still has not been entirely eradicated by love of God, *what the flesh desires is opposed to the spirit, and what the spirit desires is opposed to the flesh* (Gal 5:17).[27] Consequently, the spiritual desires of one good person can be in conflict with the carnal desires of another, and the carnal desires of two good people can be opposed to each other (in the same way that the evil are opposed to each other), until the good are finally healed of all internal conflict in the ultimate restoration of the self to God. Augustine simply does not allow us the option of painting all human conflict in the harsh colors of the stark oppositions of evil against evil and evil against good. If the earthly city is marked by war and conflict, that does not mean that it has entirely cut itself off from all earthly good or from the possibility of attaining an earthly peace that comes from God; and if the heavenly city is characterized by love for God and love for others, that does not mean that its pilgrimage on earth is immune to the bitter struggles of the self against itself or of the self against others. Neither society can be reduced to a simple, monochromatic coloration. Neither city follows a course through time that can be characterized as unrelievedly evil or as unrelievedly good.

The Eternal Destinies of the Two Cities (Books XIX-XXII)

In Books XIX-XXII, which conclude *The City of God,* Augustine considers the final destinies of the two cities. But, working momentarily on the basis of reason rather than of divine authority, he starts by setting out the various arguments by which, as he says, human beings "have tried to contrive happiness for

---

27. For an attempt to convey something of the way in which Augustine understood this conflict of opposing desires in those who had, by grace, been turned toward love of God, see William S. Babcock, "Augustine and the Spirituality of Desire," *Augustinian Studies* 25 (1994) 179-199.

themselves in the midst of all the unhappiness of this life" (XIX,1). In short, he now turns his attention to an explicit discussion of a theme that has been in play, although never fully elaborated, throughout the work — namely, what constitutes the supreme good for human beings, the good that makes a person happy.[28] A formal definition of the supreme good would be that it is the good which is to be desired for its own sake, while other things are to be desired for the sake of attaining it (and, correlatively, the supreme evil is that which is to be avoided for its own sake, while other things are to be avoided for the sake of avoiding it). The issue, then, is to determine what the supreme good is for human beings, for it is the attainment of their supreme good that will bring them true happiness. In a rather artificial exercise, Augustine adopts from Varro an enumeration of the possible positions one might take on the supreme good. Varro first distinguishes four goods that all people seek naturally, that is, without the need for any prior instruction, without the need for any conscious deliberation, and without having to acquire virtue as a prerequisite to seeking them. These four are pleasure, "by which bodily sense is moved with delight," repose, "the state in which a person feels no bodily distress," the combination of both pleasure and repose, and finally "the primary goods of nature" (XIX,1), which include the first three as well as others that have to do with the wellbeing of the body (e.g., good health) and of the mind (e.g., mental acuity). Now these four goods can be related to virtue, which is "the art of living well" (XIX,1) in any one of three different ways: virtue can be sought for the sake of obtaining them; they can be sought for the sake of obtaining virtue; or both these goods and virtue can be sought, each for its own sake. By multiplying the four goods by the three possible relations to virtue, one comes up with twelve basic positions on the human good and what makes for human happiness.

But these twelve positions can be further multiplied by considering them in relation to a sequence of additional factors. For instance, there is a social factor. A person may hold any one of these twelve positions only for his own sake, or he may hold it also for the sake of others, seeking to promote their good as well as his own. Thus the social factor serves to double the number of positions, bringing the total up from twelve to twenty-four. Similarly, an epistemological factor — whether the view is held as certain and conclusive or as uncertain and open to doubt — again doubles the number of possible positions, bringing the total to forty-eight. By elaborating factors in this way, Augustine brings the grand total up to two hundred and eighty-eight possible positions on the supreme good for human beings. Again following Varro, however, he immediately narrows the number back down to twelve. For the list of differentiating factors does not really yield distinct positions on the human good but only different ways of holding the original twelve (either for oneself alone or for both oneself and others, either as known with certainty

---

28. On Augustine and the issues of the supreme good and human happiness, and on the background to his thought in ancient philosophy, see Ragnar Holte, *Béatitude et sagesse. Saint Augustin et le problem de la fin de l'homme dans la philosophie ancienne* (Paris: Etudes augustiniennes, 1962).

or as subject to doubt, and so forth). Varro then argues that he can reduce the list of the goods that people naturally seek from four to one by noting that the fourth on the list — the primary goods of nature — includes the other three and thus makes it unnecessary to count them separately. As a consequence, in Varro's calculation, we are left with three basic positions on the issue of the human good and human happiness, and the question is: which of these is true?

Since the point at issue, Varro argues, is the ultimate good not of a tree or of an animal or of any other thing but specifically of a human being, we must start by asking what a human being is. Now human nature includes two elements, the body and the soul, and, of these two, the soul is by far the better and more excellent. But a human being cannot be reduced to a body by itself, without a soul, or to a soul by itself, no matter how excellent, without a body. A human being consists, then, of both body and soul; and so, Varro concludes, the ultimate human good, the good that makes man happy, must include the good of both the body and the soul. On this ground, he holds that the primary goods of nature are to be sought for their own sake and that virtue is also to be sought for its own sake. At the same time, however, there is a kind of ranking of these goods in Varro's view. It is virtue that makes right use both of itself and of the other goods that make for human happiness; and so, although the other goods are to be sought in their own right and not for the sake of something else, they are not to be sought apart from virtue. Apart from virtue, they will not be used rightly, and in that case they should not really be called human goods at all. Thus, as Augustine summarizes Varro, the human life that is properly to be called happy is the life that enjoys both virtue and the other goods of soul and body without which virtue cannot exist.

Augustine does not rehearse Varro's argument, however, in order to endorse it. Instead, he uses it to provide the framework and the concepts that he will employ in mounting the counter-argument that will serve to define the way in which the city of God understands the human good and the realization of human happiness. In the first place, he simply asserts — on the basis not of reason, but of scriptural authority — that for the city of God the ultimate good is eternal life and the ultimate evil eternal death. He does not develop these themes here, however, because they are the topics that he will present in Books XXI (on eternal death as the realization of eternal punishment for the evil) and XXII (on eternal life as the realization of eternal happiness for the good). His concern, rather, is to show that the ultimate good and evil cannot be attained in this life, no matter which of Varro's goods, whether singly or in combination, is taken as the supreme good and the source of happiness. In this life, none of these goods can be made secure, and all of them are subject to impairment or to loss. It is sheer folly, then, to think that they can be the ground or the source of true and undiluted human happiness, untouched by anxiety or grief. The wellbeing of the body, for instance, is at risk of injury and disease, which may end the body's grace and beauty at a stroke. Likewise the goods of the mind are vulnerable to all sorts of disruption and of loss. Deafness and blindness may rob the mind of its perceptions. Mental disease may drive it mad, leaving it trapped in insane delusions that override and cancel out all its intelligence and reason. And in this life, virtue itself, the highest-ranked of Varro's goods, is engaged in a perpetual battle against the vices, a battle that indicates as clearly as can be that this is not the attainment of happiness but rather an unending engagement in struggle. The virtue of temperance, for instance, must constantly be on guard against the ways in which the desires of the flesh exercise their pull upon the mind, trying to entice its consent to all sorts of immoral and degrading acts. Similarly, the virtue of prudence must always be alert to distinguish the good from the evil so that we do not go wrong in our attempts to achieve the one and avoid the other. Again, the task of justice is to assign to each his due, establishing in the self a just order in which the soul is rightly subordinated to God and the flesh to the soul so that the whole person is properly set under God. But as long as the desires of the flesh are at odds with the desires of the spirit, we cannot say that justice has been achieved, and so we cannot claim that we have attained true and ultimate happiness. And finally there is the virtue of fortitude, the virtue that gives us the strength to endure evils with patience and with courage. But the very meaning of this virtue — as the patient endurance of evil — shows that, when we have it, far from attaining happiness, we are still confronted by evils on all sides. All this demonstrates as clearly as can be, Augustine argues, that it is nonsense to think that the supreme good can be found in this life or that human beings can attain happiness by their own efforts and without the help of God. True happiness is not something that human beings can contrive for themselves, and even the city of God, so long as it is on pilgrimage on earth, can claim to have its happiness only in hope, not in full reality — and its hope is itself a gift from God.

Given Augustine's stress on the way in which the primordial fall tore apart the human social fabric, it should come as no surprise that he puts special emphasis on the impossibility of attaining happiness in this life in the social realm. Human affairs are everywhere characterized by "injuries, suspicions, hostilities and war" (XIX,5). Peace is never more than an uncertain good, for we do not know the hearts of those with whom we wish to be at peace and, even if we could know their inmost feelings today, we would not know what twists and turns they might take tomorrow. There is always the possibility that secret treacheries lie hidden beneath a pretense of friendliness and good will. Augustine pursues these themes at every level of society, from the immediate household out into the wider context of the city, the world at large, and ultimately {to} the universe as a whole. He never draws the conclusion that the members of the city of God should seek to withdraw from the forms of human society, but he always underscores the ways in which human social interactions are fraught with antagonisms, hostilities, and betrayals that keep them from being a setting in which true happiness can be achieved in this life. A particularly poignant example, which Augustine cites at the level of the city, is the case of a judge who must reach decisions about guilt and innocence but can never know with certainty whether the accused is guilty or innocent or whether the witnesses are lying or telling the truth. Even the use of torture, which is designed to force a person to tell the truth, may lead him to lie in order to escape the pain. There is an unavoidable element of ignorance built into the process that makes certainty a harsh impossibility in reaching a verdict, imposing a sentence, and assigning punishment. But Augustine does not use the terrible uncertainties of the legal process to justify a Christian refusal to serve as judge. Rather he insists that the wise man will not ignore the claim of society's need for a legal system and will accept the "unavoidable necessity of judging" legal cases (XIX,6). The wise judge will not presume, however, that there is any happiness to be attained in his role; rather he will lament the misery that makes it necessary. And even at the level of the universe, where humans can have friendship with the holy angels who will never betray or turn against them, there is always the danger that demons, posing as angels of light, may deceive us into taking our enemies as friends.

Thus, if the peace which people can attain on earth counts as a good, it still cannot be construed as a good which represents the ultimate good for human beings and brings them true happiness. That form of peace can only be achieved in the life to come, and this point leads Augustine to a new characterization of the supreme good in which the ideas of peace and eternal life are intertwined. By itself — because earthly peace can never deliver true happiness — the word "peace" cannot serve to designate the supreme good. For that purpose, we need a phrase like "peace in life eternal" or "eternal life in peace," which introduces the notion of social peace into our understanding of eternal life as the ultimate good for human beings and indicates how that ultimate good repairs the damage done to the social fabric at man's primordial fall. Here Augustine undertakes an extended reflection on peace as an end that all human beings — and ultimately, all things, even inanimate things — seek and desire. Even war, the very antithesis of peace, is waged for the sake of attaining peace,[29] and even the most savage individuals and groups at least desire to be at peace within themselves. In its own way, too, the earthly city seeks a kind of peace, that is, an earthly peace which is realized through a pattern of authority and obedience among its citizens which, if not enough to establish complete concord, will at least bring about an accommodation among competing human wills with regard to the things of this life. In contrast, the heavenly city — on pilgrimage, not at home, while it is here on earth — is not captivated by earthly things, and it does not allow them to deflect it from its ultimate destination. But it, too, must make use of temporal things to sustain itself during its earthly existence, and, for precisely this reason, it too has a stake in earthly peace. During its earthly pilgrimage, then, it will not hesitate to obey the laws of the earthly city, the laws by which the things necessary for sustaining this mortal life are regulated and administered.

Once again, then, it is clear that Augustine will not allow us to reduce the interaction between the two cities to patterns of simplistic opposition. The notion

---

29. For studies of Augustine's views on war, see John Langan, "The Elements of Augustine's Just War Theory," *Journal of Religious Ethics* 12 (1984) 19-38; David A. Lenihan, "The Just War Theory in the Works of Saint Augustine," *Augustinian Studies* 19 (1988) 37-70.

of earthly peace provides a point of convergence between the two in which they make common use of the things of this temporal existence. The heavenly city, so long as it is on pilgrimage, calls forth citizens from all peoples and gathers together a pilgrim society of all languages without regard to any differences in the manners, laws and institutions by which earthly peace is achieved and sustained. It does not reject or abolish these but follows and preserves them, provided only that they do not impinge on or interfere with the practice of the religion that directs all worship to the one true God. Thus the heavenly city also makes use of earthly peace, and it too seeks an accommodation of competing wills with regard to the things of this life. If the fall has torn the social fabric, then, it has not made social existence impossible, whether within the earthly city or between the earthly and the heavenly cities. Unlike the earthly city, however, the heavenly city directs its use of earthly peace toward the ultimate peace which is, in the strict sense, the only true peace and the only peace that provides true happiness for human beings. It has not yet attained this peace; but it possesses it in faith and hope, if not yet in full reality, and it anticipates it by shaping all its actions in love of God and neighbor.

In this context, Augustine returns to a topic that, far back in Book II, he had said he would discuss further. There he had promised to show that, according to the definition that Cicero had given in *The Republic*, Rome was never a republic. According to Cicero's definition, a republic is "the common good of a people," and a people is "a multitude joined together by a common sense for what is right and a community of interest." But a common sense for what is right is and must be a function of justice; and where there is no true justice there can be no right. "Thus unjust human institutions," Augustine argues, "should neither be called nor be considered right." (XIX,21) But justice itself is a function of proper service to the God. For it is when the soul serves God that it rules the body rightly; and, in the soul itself, the reason that is subject to God rightly rules sensual desire and the other vices. There is no justice, then, in a person whose self is not rightly oriented to God, and neither can there be any justice in a human society that is made up of such persons. But the Romans, as Augustine had earlier argued at length and as he now reiterates in a reprise of that argument, served unclean spirits, the demons, rather than the true God. Consequently they lacked justice and did not qualify as a social grouping joined by a common sense for what is right and a community of interest. They did not fit the definition of a people, and where there is no people, there can be no "common good of a people" and thus no republic. For justice is only found where the true God rules an obedient city that sacrifices only to him and not to any imposter gods.

There is, however, an alternate way of conceiving of a people. According to this alternate view, a people might be defined as "a multitude of rational beings joined together by a common agreement on the objects of their love" (XIX,24). According to this definition, obviously enough, the character of a people, whether for better or for worse, will be determined by what it loves. No matter what it loves, however, so long as it is in agreement on what it loves, it will count as a people. And here Augustine wants to make it clear that what he has said about Rome applies equally to the polities of the Greeks or the Egyptians or the Assyrians, all of whom counted as peoples in this sense, and thus as republics, when exercising their imperial rule over the smaller or larger areas that they controlled. It remains true, however, that, because they did not serve the true God and worship only him, they lacked justice. For the mind cannot rule either the body or the vices properly, "if it does not know the true God and, instead of being subject to his rule, is prostituted to the corrupting influence of the most vicious demons" (XIX,25). In fact, without knowledge of the true God, the very virtues that the mind imagines that it has in ruling the body and the vices for the sake of gaining the objects of its desire are actually vices, and not virtues at all, if the mind does not direct them to God. And even if the virtues are pursued for their own sake, and not for the sake of anything other than themselves, they still count as vices rather than as virtues because they represent an exercise in human pride. The basis for living virtuously does not lie within the self but beyond the self, and so reliance on the self alone in pursuing virtue is an expression of self-assertion rather than of the genuine virtue that is rooted in love for God.

But even a people that is alienated from God, a people that is rooted in pride and united only by agreement on the objects of its love, loves a "kind of peace of its own" (XIX,26), an earthly peace which is not to be despised. Because it does not make good use of this peace, it will not have it in the end; but, in the meantime, as long as the two cities are intermingled here on earth, that peace is also beneficial to the heavenly city, even though its members are "no more than pilgrims" (XIX,26) in the midst of earthly society. In contrast, however, there is a peace that is proper to the heavenly city and to it alone. It now has that peace with God through faith, and it will ultimately have that peace for all eternity with God through sight. For the present, however, because true human happiness cannot be attained in this life, both the earthly peace that the two cities share and the peace that is proper to the city of God alone count more as a solace and consolation in the midst of human wretchedness than as the joy of final blessedness. For, even though the justice of the city of God is true justice, it is not yet the perfect justice that will be realized in the life to come. Although reason does rightly rule the vices in the citizens of that city, it does not rule them without struggle and resistance on their part, and something invariably "creeps in" that leads the self into sin (XIX,27), even if only of a minor sort. Thus, as long as it is necessary to rule the vices, there is no full and complete peace. The battle against the vices is full of peril, and triumph over them is far from secure and effortless. It is only in the ultimate peace with God that there will be nothing at all, whether in the self or in the self's interactions with others, that fights against us. That is when both the self and the social fabric will be completely healed.

In contrast to the supreme peace that is the ultimate destiny of the city of God, there is the unending warfare that is the final end and punishment of the earthly city. Augustine does not picture a warfare consisting of great military battles between opposing armies. What he has in mind is rather perpetual conflict between opposing forces in which neither side ever gains the victory and so there is no cease from the resulting pain. On the one hand, this conflict takes the shape of a constant battle between the will and the passions in which the will seeks to govern the passions and the passions forever resist its attempts to establish control. In this sense, the final punishment of the ungodly takes the form of a deep and irresolvable division of the self against itself in which there is no hope of attaining resolution or achieving a peaceful coalescence of will and desire. On the other hand, the conflict involves a perpetual assault of the force of pain against the nature of the body in which, again, there is no possibility of resolution. In this life, when pain assails the body, either pain comes out victorious and death brings the struggle to an end or the body recovers and is restored to good health without pain. In either case, there is an end to torment. But the final destiny of the earthly city is torment without end from which there is no escape and for which there is no relief.

At this point, having provided an initial sketch of the destinies of the two cities, Augustine presents the last judgment, the point at which the two cities, intermingled during their histories in time, are at last fully separated and stand out in unmistakable opposition to each other. It is important to note, once again, that Augustine assigns the separation entirely to God and to the divine judgment. It is not for human beings, who cannot discern each other's hearts, to attempt to anticipate God by drawing their own lines of division between the two cities. Only God can read the human heart, and therefore only God can truly tell who is a member of which city and can rightly assign persons to the city to which they properly belong. Augustine's chief concern here is to demonstrate that there is a final judgment; and, since this is a matter that lies beyond human reason, he reverts once again to divine authority as the basis for his argument, citing verses from Scripture to indicate both that there will be a final judgment and what character it will have. At the same time, he wants to make it clear that God has not reserved his exercise of judgment for the end time, leaving it quiescent in the interim. Instead God is judging at all times, from the moment of his separation of the evil and the good angels at the beginning of creation and throughout the entire course of the world's history. It is due to his judgment that the life of both demons and of humans is now one of misery, ensnared in error and choked with suffering. And his judgment is also at work, at a less global level, in the events of history and in relation to the actions of both individuals and societies. Given the limitations and distortions of our fallen human understanding, however, we cannot see how God's judgment is at work in these cases or why it takes the form it does. We do not know, for instance, why one person, to all appearances innocent and good, should live in misery, while another, apparently evil in everything he does, should lead a life of joy. Such instances at least teach us not to put much weight on either the evils or the goods that are common to the evil and the good alike in this temporal life. Otherwise, however, God's *judgments are inscrutable, and his ways past finding out* (Rom 11:33); and in this life, although faith can be absolutely certain that God's judgments are always just, even faith cannot discern the patterns of justice that govern God's providential direction of the world. The last judgment represents, then, God's manifest judgment, as opposed to the hidden judgment that is operative prior to the end; and, in this sense, it is not only the great moment of separation between the evil and the good but also the great moment of clarification at which the ways of God are made plain.

The same texts which prove that there will be a final judgment also demonstrate that, with it, there will be a bodily resurrection in which all will be raised from the dead, the evil to eternal punishment and the good to eternal life. Augustine's interpretations of these texts involve a complex account of the end times in which he elaborates a non-millenarian view of the binding and loosing of the devil, the coming of Antichrist, and the thousand-year reign of the saints. He is determined to rule out any attempt at calculating a chronology either of the last judgment itself or of the events that will lead up to it in a final era of persecution of the Church when the devil is unleashed. But his main concern is simply to insist that there will be a point of manifest divine judgment and that it will be accompanied by a bodily resurrection of the dead. It is not disembodied souls that will face divine judgment but human beings who consist, as Augustine has already made clear, of souls and bodies together. For neither the soul nor the body, taken separately, can be construed as a human being apart from the other. And it is precisely human beings, in their full embodied reality, that will be judged when Christ returns as judge.

The last judgment, however, is not the climax of Augustine's work. It serves rather to set the stage for his presentation of the respective destinies of the two cities, eternal punishment for the earthly city and eternal happiness for the heavenly city. In a way, there is something strange about the manner in which Augustine treats the eternal punishment of the earthly city. In effect, the earthly city's punishment seems to eliminate everything that made it what it was. Earlier Augustine had said that, in its final destiny, the earthly city would no longer be a city; and, in fact, all the features that Augustine had used to define and characterize this city now disappear from view. There is no mention of its love of self, of its pride and self-assertion, of its desire for earthly goods, of its common agreement in the objects of its love, or of the love of earthly peace that it pursues for its own ends but still shares with the heavenly city. There is not even any mention of the contempt of God and the search for human glory that marked its whole approach to life and to its own version of virtue. All of these themes vanish, and the city itself seems to have been dissolved in the eternal torments of its own punishment. Its social character no longer has any role to play, and its psychological qualities have all been reduced to the sheer experience of pain. The one theme that does persist through the transition from judgment to punishment is Augustine's emphasis on the embodied self. He says that he will treat eternal punishment before turning to the eternal happiness of the saved precisely because it is harder to believe that the body can endure in unending pain than that they can exist in eternal blessedness. Consequently it will be easier to win acceptance for the eternal embodied happiness of the saints if he has first demonstrated that the body can survive without dissolution in the unending agonies of hell.

Augustine's treatment of the punishment of the condemned, then, does not take the form of a continuation of the themes that marked his earlier characterizations of the earthly city. Instead it focuses on two quite different points. One, as already indicated, is an argument for the claim that the body can survive in unending torment. In support of this claim Augustine cites examples from nature of material entities that survive in fire without being destroyed (such as the magma in a volcano) and denies that the presence of pain must also imply the possibility of death. After all, the soul is immortal but still feels pain, whether from injury to the body or from its own psychological agonies; and, in fact, without the soul to give it life, the body would be completely without feeling and thus incapable of pain. Augustine's point, then, is that in the eternal torment which is the destiny of the earthly city, the body will be so bound to the soul and the soul to the body that there is no longer any possibility of their separation. Death in that sense, the death of the whole person, no longer comes into play and no longer offers the prospect of relief from pain. In that death, which strikes all people in this life, the soul is compelled against its will to depart the body. But in the "second death" of eternal punishment, in antithetical contrast, the soul will be compelled against its will to remain forever in its body as the seat and center of the terrible agonies that both soul and body will suffer without end. And even the demons will suffer bodily as well as psychic pain, either because they too have bodies, which consist of a murky kind of air, or, if they are actually immaterial, because they will be joined to the material fires of hell in much the same way that the immaterial soul is joined to the material body in this life and is racked by its pain.

From this pain there is no release or relief. Augustine is not sympathetic to the claim that temporal sin does not deserve eternal punishment. In the case of criminal acts, it is not the time it takes to commit the crime that the determines the length of its punishment but rather the gravity of the act itself; and, similarly, to argue that the temporal sin of human beings is not enough to justify eternal punishment is to fail to appreciate the sheer enormity of the sin itself. Neither is Augustine sympathetic to the suggestion that participation in the sacraments or holding to the doctrines of the Church are enough, by themselves, to compensate for sin and reduce the time of its punishment. To have Christ as one's foundation means to love Christ above all else and to shape one's life in accord with that love.[30] Merely to take the sacraments or to hold certain beliefs without directing one's love and shaping one's life in this way is not to have Christ as one's foundation at all. Augustine is more sympathetic to the notions that the intercession of the saints can have real effects and that punishment can take a purgatorial and remedial form. He insists, however, that the intercessory prayers of the saints are

---

30. To have Christ as one's foundation is, obviously enough, the antithesis of trying to make oneself one's own foundation, as both angels and human beings did when they fell away from God.

aimed at the repentance of those for whom they intercede. But when repentance is no longer possible, as it is not in the pains of eternal punishment, they no longer apply. And while he grants that there is such a thing as purgatorial fire, whose purpose is certainly remedial,[31] he is adamant that it is not to be equated with the eternal fires of hell's unending torments. Furthermore, behind these issues, there lie, in Augustine's eyes, two broader and deeper points. One is the truthfulness of God, who has announced an eternal punishment and will be found to have been untruthful if the punishment turns out to be less than everlasting, and the other is the eternality of eternal happiness itself. If eternal pain is not actually eternal, then eternal happiness may also be less than eternal; and, if so, it will not be true and ultimate happiness because it will be a happiness that can be lost. For Augustine, then, the story of the earthly city and of its love is ultimately and finally dissolved in pain, an agony from which there is no release and no relief, and in which the city's social fabric is finally torn to shreds. It does not culminate in some supreme and climactic triumph of self-love but rather in the endless agony that is, for Augustine, the true upshot of love for self carried even to the point of contempt for God.

In contrast, the story of the heavenly city and its love has a very different ending. In this case, the defining characteristics of the city do not dissolve and disappear. Instead they reach their climax and culmination in a happiness that comes from the realization of its love, in the achievement of true peace, and in the attainment of unhindered fellowship among its citizens, both angelic and human, in which heart is open to heart and there is no lingering fear of hidden enmities or lurking treacheries. Here too, however, Augustine is especially concerned about the body, and he begins his presentation of eternal happiness with an additional extended argument for the resurrection of the body and for its elevation, precisely in its physical character, to heavenly status. If the resurrection seems incredible, he asserts, it is confirmed by two other "incredible things," both of which have actually occurred and therefore cannot be denied. One is that, just as God foretold, the whole world — contrary to all expectation — has come to believe in the resurrection; and the other is that the world's belief is the result of the preaching of a small group of insignificant and uneducated men (the apostles) whose persuasive power can therefore only be explained by the fact that it had the backing of God himself. The divine backing was evident in the miracles performed by the apostles themselves, and it is still evident in the miracles of the present, performed at the shrines and through the relics of the martyrs, whose own faith bears continued witness to the resurrection. Augustine also argues strongly that the resurrected body will have the form that the human body has at the "peak of youth," when people are at the prime of their physical fitness and development. It will be, then, a body without defect; and, since being female is not a defect, women will be raised not

---

31. In this regard, Augustine has a small role to play in the development of what would later become the doctrine of purgatory. On the origins of the idea of purgatory, see Jacques Le Goff, *The Birth of Purgatory*, trans. Arthur Goldhammer (Chicago: University of Chicago Press, 1984).

with male but with female bodies. Eternal happiness neither requires nor entails that women be transformed into men. Beyond this, Augustine maintains that the body will have its own role to play in the culminating vision of God which is the source and basis of the heavenly city's eternal happiness. The saved will see God not only with the eyes of the mind but also, and specifically, with the eyes of the body. Augustine is not sure whether this means that the material body, in its resurrected state, will have acquired the power to perceive immaterial things (for God is most certainly not a material object) or whether it means that the eyes of the resurrected body will be able to discern God in material beings in much the same way that we now discern the life in living beings even though we cannot see life itself apart from its physical manifestations. In either case, however, the body is included in, not excluded from, the realization of ultimate human happiness. It is not the disembodied self, fleeing from all bodies, but rather the embodied self — with its body now restored to it and fully in harmony with it — that will enjoy the unending happiness of the final vision of God.

What, then, will the saints be doing in their immortal and spiritual bodies? That is the question with which Augustine opens his discussion of the final and ultimate happiness of the city of God. The answer, he suggests, lies beyond all human understanding and experience; and so it can only be intimated by citing a sequence of scriptural passages. These passages, although Augustine rarely tries to explicate them at length, serve to bring to their climax the themes that he has used throughout *The City of God* to delineate the heavenly city and to evoke the hope in which it lives. There will be peace, *the peace of God which surpasses all understanding* (Phil 4:7); and so, because the saints will be made partakers in God's peace, they will know supreme peace in themselves, among themselves, and with God. The ultimate happiness will be a happiness undiminished by conflict, whether within the self or between selves, or with God's will and purposes. Again, if now we see only in part, then we will see *face to face* (1 Cor 13:12), no longer believing what we cannot see but rather seeing the one in whom we have believed. This is how the holy angels already see God. And the holy angels, Augustine notes, are also called "our angels" because they have already begun to have us as their fellow-citizens; and when the saints ultimately come to see as the angels see, this fellow-citizenship will be fully realized in the one company of the heavenly city. Then, too, "our thoughts will... lie open to each other" (XXII,29). For God *will make manifest the thoughts of the heart* (1 Cor 4:5), and there will no longer be any veil over the heart separating self from self in the community of the saints in eternal happiness.

What will the saints be doing in that happiness? *Blessed are those who dwell in your house, they will praise you for ever and ever* (Ps 84:4). Because this praise, as praise of God, is rightly directed, there will be true glory and true honor — unlike the false glory and honor sought by the Romans in their republic — in the eternal society of the saints. No one will be praised "in error or in flattery" (XXII,30). No one who is unworthy will be given honor, and no one who is worthy will be denied honor. Augustine does not, however, imagine a heavenly society in which there is no distinction of rank or grades of honor. Rather he conceives a community that is no longer racked by the envy of some for the status of others. In the heavenly city, "no inferior will envy any superior, any more than the other angels envy the archangels" (XXII,30). No one will wish to be something other than he is, and all will be linked by a bond of the utmost peace and concord to each other. For everyone, God will be *all in all* (1 Cor 15:28). He will be their God, and they will be his people — which means, Augustine says, that he will be their fulfillment, the sum of all that people rightly desire. It is in this sense that God will be "the end of our desires" (XXII,30), not because we will no longer have any desire but because we will have nothing else to desire. Our desire will have attained its end and will be wholly focused and concentrated on him. He is the end of our desires, then, in the sense that "he will be seen without end, loved without satiation, and praised without weariness" (XXII,30). God is inexhaustible. There is no danger that seeing, loving, and praising him will ever go stale or sink into boredom.

Like Dante at the end of the *Paradiso*,[32] Augustine makes no attempt to describe what the vision of God might be like. One of the Psalms says, *Be still, and see that I am God* (Ps 46:10), and Augustine ends *The City of God* by playing his own brief variations on this verse. In the ultimate happiness of the heavenly city, a happiness totally immune to any danger of damage or of loss, "we shall be still for all eternity, and shall see that he is God; and by him we shall be filled when he is all in all.…There we shall be still and see, see and love, love and praise. Behold what will be in the end without end! For what else is our end but to reach the kingdom that has no end" (XXII,30). Beyond this, he can only resort to silence, and it is in that silence that he brings the story of the love that made the heavenly city to its end and climax.

---

32. Dante ends the last canto of the *Paradiso* with a vivid image in which he joins the sun and the other stars in circling round a barely intimated vision of the triune God. But he attempts no real description of the content of that vision, and neither does Augustine at the end of *The City of God*.

THE TRANSLATION

There is a couplet in T. S. Eliot's "The Love Song of J. Alfred Prufrock" that reads:

In a minute there is time
For decisions and revisions which a minute will reverse.[1]

And in this brief couplet, it seems to me, Eliot has inadvertently captured something central to the nature of translation. It is a process in which every minute involves a multitude of decisions and revisions which the next minute will reverse — or will at least alter with new decisions and revisions: decisions about which words best render the words of the original text, about which phrasings best capture the tone and force of the original, about which sentence structures best convey the sometimes unreproducible sentence structures of the original, about which ways of framing arguments best replicate the ways in which the original frames its arguments, about trying to find a style that will best represent the style of the original, and so on and so on. Rarely are these decisions simple or obvious. Even the most basic and common verbal elements — an "and" or a "but" or a "for" — can, on occasion, pose problems that may require an alternate rendering if the point of the original is to be preserved.

Obviously it would be impossible to discuss all of the decisions and revisions that go into the translation of a text as long and as complex as *The City of God*. Some of the choices I have made, however, require at least some comment. In particular, I should explain the ways in which I have rendered certain of the key terms in Augustine's terminology. One example is *peregrinus* and its cognate *peregrinatio*. I have tried to be as consistent as I could in translating these terms respectively as "pilgrim" and "pilgrimage." But there are strong arguments for adopting other translations. A pilgrim, it might be said, is simply passing through on her way somewhere else and therefore has no investment in the place where she happens to find herself at any given moment. In speaking of the Christian as a pilgrim, however, or in characterizing the city of God as on pilgrimage in this world, Augustine clearly does not mean that either the Christian or the city of God has no stake at all in this life or in this world.[2] His point is rather that, whatever stake they may have in their present situation, they are never ultimately at home here in this world. Their homeland lies elsewhere; and so, at the deepest level, they are oriented toward that "elsewhere" — the eternal city of God — rather than to this present world, its values, and its social structures. Thus, it is argued, it would

---

1. T. S. Eliot, *The Complete Poems and Plays* (New York: Harcourt, Brace and Company, 1930) 5.
2. See, for example, **The** *City of God* XIX,17, where Augustine argues that both the heavenly and the earthly city, although in different ways, have a stake in earthly peace and desire an ordered human society.

be better to translate *pereginus* as "sojourner" or "resident alien" or "stranger" or with some similar form of words.[3] For Augustine, however, the terms *peregrinus* and *peregrinatio* always involve the sense that a pilgrim is on a path that leads toward a destination;[4] and to translate them in a way that leaves out the "destination" dimension of their meaning is to misrepresent what Augustine has in mind. Because "pilgrim" and "pilgrimage" do imply a destination, then, I have made the decision to use these terms, even though I hope it will be clear to readers of *The City of God* that Augustine does not presume that either the individual pilgrim or the pilgrim city of God has no interest, investment, or involvement in the sociopolitical patterns of life in this world.

Another, less controversial, term in Augustine's vocabulary is the verb *significare*, "to signify," with its cognate noun *signum*, "sign." It is fairly common, however, for translators of Augustine to render these terms into English as "to symbolize" and "symbol"; and these English terms, given the elaboration of theories of symbolism in our own times, may evoke a range of meanings that Augustine never had in mind or that lead in directions he would never have imagined. In fact, Augustine himself elaborated a theory of signs and signification in his earlier work *Teaching Christianity*,[5] and, so far as I can tell, his use of the terms in *The City of God* always exemplifies his own theory of how signs function to point beyond themselves to the specific things that, in one way or another, they signify. Thus I have tried to be as consistent as I could in using "signify" and "sign" for *significare* and *signum*. Given Augustine's theory of signification, these are more or less technical terms in his vocabulary, and I believe that they should be treated

---

3. See, e.g., the extended discussion in Eugene TeSelle, *Living in Two Cities: Augustinian Trajectories in Political Thought* (Scranton: University of Scranton Press, 1998) 45-71. See also Peter Brown's brief comments in *Augustine of Hippo: A Biography*, New Edition (Berkeley and Los Angeles: University of California Press, 2000) 323, although Brown does allow a sense in which *peregrinus* can be translated as "pilgrim."

4. See, in particular, *Teaching Christianity (De doctrina christiana)* I,4,8: "Suppose we were travellers (*peregrini*) who could live happily (*beate*) only in our homeland, and because our absence made us unhappy we wished to put an end to our misery and return to our homeland: we would need transport by land or sea which we could use to travel to our homeland, the object of our enjoyment. But if we were fascinated by the delights of the journey and the actual travelling, we would be perversely enjoying things that we should be using; and we would be reluctant to finish our journey quickly, being ensnared in the wrong kind of pleasure and estranged from the homeland whose pleasures would make us happy (*beatos*)." The translation, slightly modified, is from *Augustine: De Doctrina Christiana*, ed. and trans. by R. P. H. Green (Oxford: Oxford University Press, 1995). For Augustine, as this passage makes particularly clear, the *peregrinus* is traveling toward a destination and is not to become so entranced by the journey as to forget or postpone the destination toward which he or she is moving.

5. On Augustine's theory of signs, see especially R. A. Markus, "St. Augustine on Signs," *Phronesis* 2 (1957) 60-83; B. Darrell Jackson, "The Theory of Signs in St. Augustine's *De doctrina christiana*," *Revue d'Etudes Augustiniennes* 15 (1969) 9-49. Both articles are reprinted in *Augustine: A Collection of Critical Essays*, ed. R. A. Markus (Garden City: Doubleday, N.Y., 1972). See also William S. Babcock, "*Caritas* and Signification in *De doctrina christiana* 1-3," in *De doctrina christiana: A Classic of Western Culture*, ed. Duane W. H. Arnold and Pamela Bright (Notre Dame: University of Notre Dame Press, Ind., 1995), 145-163.

as such rather than allowed to suggest modes of symbolic meaning that may fall far outside his own definition of signs and how they signify.

The translation of the Latin term *beatitudo*, with its cognate adjective *beatus*, also deserves discussion. It is very common, if not quite standard, practice to translate the noun as "happiness" or "blessedness" and the adjective as "happy" or "blessed," depending on the context, and I have almost always done the same. It is important, however, to indicate that Augustine has a rather complex notion of happiness which cannot be reduced to a mere feeling of pleasure or flutter of euphoria. For Augustine, the desire for happiness is basic and common to all human beings, and happiness is always a matter of having what one wants. But here the complications begin. Not everything a person might want will actually bring happiness (think, for instance, of a child who wants to hold fire in his hands). Thus happiness will be achieved only when one has what one wants *and* when what one wants is the sort of thing that will actually bring happiness. In Augustine's view, however, temporal and transitory things — whether as simple as a piece of candy or as complex as possessing great wealth or exercising great power — cannot actually bring happiness. These are things that a person might never acquire, no matter how much she wants them; and, if acquired, they are always in danger of being lost through some adverse turn of events. Thus, both the wanting and the having of such things is always tinged with anxiety, with a fear that we might never get them or with a fear that we might lose them; and, for Augustine, happiness and fear or anxiety are mutually incompatible. There is a kind of "false happiness" or "misguided joy" that we can take in such things. But it is not to be equated with true happiness, which only comes when the things we want and have are invulnerable to loss. To be genuinely happy, then, a person must want and have something that is secure and enduring and that cannot be taken from her against her will. And, for Augustine, the only such object of desire and possession is the immutable and eternal object who is God. But there is more at issue here. Happiness is not only a matter of wanting and having something that cannot be lost against one's will, but is also a matter of wanting and having something that is genuinely fulfilling of the kind of being one is. Since human beings are rational creatures, they cannot find fulfillment in anything that does not engage them at the core of their being and bring them to the full realization of their rational selves. And again, for Augustine, it is God — and, specifically, the love of God above all else (although not to the exclusion of all else) — that does engage human beings at the core of their being and bring them to the full realization of themselves. Putting all this together, then, the best translation of *beatitudo* might be something like "fulfillment" or "ultimate fulfillment." These terms, however, cannot be made to fit the contexts in which Augustine uses *beatitudo* and *beatus*. That is why I have kept the more usual translations of "happiness" and "blessedness." But I did not want simply to employ these translations without at least attempting to convey something of the richness and complexity of the meaning of Augustine's notion of happiness.[6]

---

6. For further discussion of Augustine on happiness or human fulfillment, see Babcock, "*Cupiditas*

It is something of a problem, too, to find an apt and adequate translation of the Latin *res publica* as the term functions in Augustine's vocabulary. The English cognate is simply "republic." It is more common, however, to translate *res publica* as "commonwealth." "Commonwealth," however, does not have the resonances that *res publica* would have had for Augustine and for the culture in which he wrote *The City of God*. It does not call to mind either the history of the Roman republic or Cicero's treatise, *The Republic*, both of which were clearly at the forefront of Augustine's mind when he spoke of a republic. Nor does "commonwealth" serve as well as it might to highlight a fundamental contrast that always lurks just behind Augustine's usage in this case. A literal, if inelegant, translation of *res publica* would simply be the "public thing"; and the contrast between the public and the private is deeply embedded in Augustine's thought. For him, both the angelic and the human fall were a turn toward the self and, in that sense, a turn toward the private. It was a turn away from God, who is the common or public good for both angels and humans, in an attempt to construct a private good centered on the self and no longer meant to be held in common with others but rather to exclude or to diminish others. For any good that is less than God is a limited good, and, because it is limited, it is lessened when it is shared. (Augustine makes this point with special clarity when he says that Romulus killed his brother Remus precisely because his glory as the founder of Rome would be diminished if he had to share it with his twin).[7] Inevitably, then, any attempt to grasp a limited good becomes an assertion of the self against others and thus of the private against the public. Furthermore, it is important to note that *res* does not actually carry the neutral meaning of a "thing" in the phrase *res publica*. Instead it has a positive valence, representing a social good or benefit for the populace involved. Consequently, in the cases where Augustine discusses Cicero's definition of a *res publica* as the *res* of a people (specifically in *The City of God* II,21 and XIX,21), I have rendered it as "the common good of a people," trying in this way to capture the positive value that *res* has in this context. And one further comment on the term *res publica* is in order. It does not, whether in Augustine's usage or in Cicero's, refer to a specific form of government. It refers rather to something that might be expressed, quite abstractly, as an organized social body within which human beings give an ordered pattern to their lives and to their interactions with each other. When Augustine speaks of a "republic," therefore, he must not be taken as speaking of a particular form of government but rather to what might be called, in a modern phrase, "the body politic," whatever form of government it may happen to have.[8]

---

and *Caritas*: The Early Augustine on Love and Human Fulfillment."

7. See ***The** City of God* XV,5.
8. On this point, see the brief discussion in Robert Dodaro, *Christ and the Just Society in the Thought of Augustine* (Cambridge: Cambridge University Press, 2004) 8, n. 10, which gives further references. Unlike Dodaro, however, I have thought it better to run the risk of potential misunderstanding and translate *res publica* with "republic" rather than with "commonwealth," which has become the more usual way of rendering the term. "Commonwealth" seems to me to lose the resonances of "republic" with the Roman republic and with Cicero's *Republic* and to mute the important

Finally, on the subject of Augustine's terminology, I should make at least some brief comments on his vocabulary of love and desire and on the gendered character of his language. Augustine has a variety of terms that he uses for love: *dilectio*, *amor*, and *caritas*; and it has sometimes been supposed that each carries a distinct shade or range of meaning. In fact, however, he can and does use these terms interchangeably; and even *caritas*, despite its biblical resonances, does not have either any denotation or any connotation that fully, consistently, or schematically distinguishes it from the others.[9] Consequently, I have generally translated all of these terms with the word "love," except when it seemed desirable, from a stylistic point of view, to replicate a variation in Augustine's wording. Similarly, Augustine uses a variety of terms for desire: *libido*, *cupiditas*, and *concupiscentia* — as well as, of course, *desiderium* itself. In this case, it is tempting to translate each of the first three of these terms, since they often have a negative valence in Augustine's usage, with the word "lust," and I have not hesitated to follow suit when "lust" seems appropriate to the context. It should be noted, however, that all three of these words basically mean "desire" in Augustine's vocabulary and that they take on a negative or positive force in his usage according to the nature of the object of desire rather than according to any innate character of the desire itself. When, for instance, Augustine is playing off the wording of Gal 5:17, *Caro enim concupiscit adversus spiritum, spiritus autem adversus carnem*, he does not choose one word for the desire of the flesh that is opposed to the spirit and another for the desire of the spirit that is opposed to the flesh. In both cases, he retains the verbal form of *concupiscentia*. In this light, therefore, I have more generally used the one word "desire" for all of these terms, especially because the English nouns "libido" (with the Freudian overtones that it now has), "cupidity," and "concupiscence" can often evoke an extraneous sense of sexual titillation that is not actually present in Augustine's Latin. For him, the object of *libido* can be domination (and many other things) quite as much as sex, and *cupiditas* and *concupiscentia* are certainly not restricted to or even especially associated with the specifically sexual realm. If the English "desire" does not capture the rich variety of Augustine's vocabulary of desire, then, it at least avoids some potential misconceptions and misunderstandings.[10]

---

contrast between the public and the private that *res publica* always carries for Augustine.

9. It is true that *caritas*, in Augustine, is reserved for love of God and/or neighbor; but this does not mean that he will not equally speak of *amor* or even *dilectio* of God and neighbor. For a brief discussion of Augustine's vocabulary of love, see O'Donovan, *The Problem of Self-Love in St. Augustine* 11.

10. For further discussions of various aspects of Augustine's vocabulary of desire, see Gerald Bonner, "*Libido* and *Concupiscentia* in St. Augustine," *Studia Patristica* 6 (1962) 303-314 and François-Joseph Thonnard, "La notion de concupiscence en philosophie augustinienne," *Recherches augustiniennes* 3 (1965) 59-105. For the background to my own approach to the matter, see my article cited in note 5 on page xlviii and "Augustine and the Spirituality of Desire." For examples of Augustine's interpretation of Gal 5:17 in *The City of God*, see XV,5; XIX,4; XXII,23. See also the relevant section of his commentary on Galatians (46) and, for the wider context of his interpretation of both Gal 5:17 and *concupiscentia* in general, his treatise *Continence*.

On the issue of gendered language, there are two points I want to make. First, on the level of the divine, it should be noted that Augustine's God, being neither male nor female, is not gendered. But the Latin word for God — *Deus* — is masculine, and, correspondingly, all of Augustine's pronominal and adjectival references to God are also masculine. I have not tried to alter this fact but rather have retained it in this translation. To do otherwise would be, I think, to misrepresent the character — for better or worse — of Augustine's own work. On the level of the human, however, the situation is somewhat different. The Latin word for "man" in the generic sense is *homo*; and, although *homo* is a masculine noun, Augustine knows very well that it does not exclude but rather includes women. In fact, he makes this point quite explicitly at the end of *The City of God* XXII,18, where he says that even the Latin *vir*, which usually means "man" as opposed to "woman," can be taken in the generic sense of *homo* and can thus include women as well as men. In this case, then, without attempting systematically to eliminate all instances of "man" or "men" in the generic sense from the text, I have tried significantly to reduce them by using "human beings" or (more rarely) "humans" or "people" to render *homines* in English. This does not seem to me to represent a distortion of Augustine's usage but rather a more adequate way to reflect it in a time when we have become particularly sensitive to the issue of gendered language and to the ill-effects it can have.

Over and above my approach to these individual features of Augustine's vocabulary, I have made one innovation and taken one decision, both of which require comment. The innovation is that I have eliminated the subheadings that are usually inserted prior to the numbered subsections in the books of *The City of God*. These subheadings, or *capitula*, do not go back to Augustine himself, and they appear in only one of the oldest surviving manuscripts of the work, where they occur at the beginning of the work rather than interspersed throughout and, in fact, often differ from those found in later manuscripts. What is more, the *capitula* in the printed editions of *The City of God*, now inserted into the text itself, often have the confusing effect of interrupting rather than interpreting the flow of the argument or even diverting attention away from the actual point or points that Augustine is making. In their place, then, I have inserted subheadings of my own devising, not for each numbered section of the books of *The City of God* but rather at points that, in my judgment, mark important shifts of topic or stages of development in the argument of each book. In addition, in what I hope will be a further aid to the reader, I have provided initial summaries of the content and argument of the books prior to the translations of the books themselves. These summaries are, of course, entirely my own attempts to capture the import of each book, and they should not be taken as if Augustine himself had produced them. My hope, however, is that the combination of the initial summaries and the newly devised subheadings will serve to facilitate the reading and interpretation of *The City of God* more helpfully and more usefully than the traditional *capitula* ever did.[11]

---

11. For further detail on the history of the *capitula*, see O'Daly, *Augustine's City of God: A Reader's*

The decision that I have taken is to preserve what seems to be Augustine's own title for the work, *The City of God*, rather than the longer *The City of God against the Pagans*, which appears in the printed editions of the Latin text and in many (although not all) English translations of the work. There are several places in Augustine's own writings where he refers to *The City of God* by title, but always by the shorter and never by the longer version.[12] Therefore, even though the phrase "against the pagans" (*contra paganos*) is deeply embedded in the manuscript tradition and in the history of the printed editions and translations of *The City of God*, it seemed more apt to retain the title that Augustine himself used for his work.

Finally, it is important to acknowledge that this translation belongs to and fits within a history of English translations of *The City of God*. Of these, I have found three, in particular, to be helpful for my own work: the translation by George McCracken and several others that appeared in the Loeb Classical Library, with the Latin text on facing pages, from 1957 to 1972; the translation by Henry Bettenson, published in 1972; and the translation by F. W. Dyson, published in 1998.[13] All of these, in my judgment, have drawbacks of one sort or another. But that is true of any translation (including, no doubt, my own); and it would be a good deal less than gracious if I did not pay tribute to the help I have received from each in trying to puzzle out difficult passages in Augustine's work. I have also consulted other translations, both in English and in other languages, but these three regularly proved useful in addressing difficult points, even — and sometimes especially — when I disagreed with them on the sense or tone of passages in *The City of God*.

Last, but by no means least, I want to acknowledge the help I have received from Boniface Ramsey, the current editor of *The Works of Saint Augustine: A Translation for the 21st Century*, who both edited this translation and provided its annotation. I am most grateful to him for supplementing my own efforts in bringing this new translation to fruition.

The Latin text from which this translation was made is what remains the standard critical edition: *Sancti Aurelii Augustini Episcopi De Civitate Dei Libri XXII*, ed. B. Dombart and A. Kalb, 4th edition (Leipzig, 1928-29; repr. Stuttgart, 1981). Despite its age (it was first published by Dombart in 1853 and revised by Kalb for the 4th edition), it is still the best edition available. It is reprinted in the *Corpus Christianorum Latinorum* (2 vols., Turnhout, 1955).

Guide 277-278.

12. See, e.g., ***Revisions*** II,43; *The Trinity* XIII,12. For a brief discussion of the title, with additional citations of Augustine's own practice, see O'Daly, 273.

13. George E. McCracken, William M. Green, David S. Wiesen, et al., trans., *Saint Augustine: The City of God against the Pagans*, 7 vols., Loeb Classical Library (Cambridge, Mass. and London, 1957-72); Henry Bettenson, trans., *St Augustine: Concerning the City of God against the Pagans*, intro. by David Knowles (Harmondsworth: Penguin, 1972; reissued with an introduction by John O'Meara in 1984); R. W. Dyson, ed. and trans., *Augustine: The City of God against the Pagans*, Cambridge Texts in the History of Political Thought (Cambridge: Cambridge University Press, 1998).

A SELECT BIBLIOGRAPHY

Cochrane, Charles Norris. *Christianity and Classical Culture: A Study of Thought and Action from Augustus to Augustine.* Rev. ed. London: Oxford University Press, 1944.

Deane, Herbert A. *The Political and Social Ideas of St. Augustine.* New York: Columbia University Press, 1963.

Dodaro, Robert. *Christ and the Just Society in the Thought of St. Augustine.* Cambridge: Cambridge University Press, 2004.

Markus, R. A., ed. *Augustine: A Collection of Critical Essays.* Garden City: Doubleday & Company, Inc., 1972.

Markus, R. A. *Saeculum: History and Society in the Theology of St. Augustine.* 2nd ed. Cambridge: Cambridge University Press, 1989.

O'Daly, Gerard. *Augustine's City of God: A Reader's Guide.* Oxford: Oxford University Press, 1999.

TeSelle, Eugene. *Living in Two Cities: Augustinian Trajectories in Political Thought.* Scranton: University of Scranton Press, 1998.

van Oort, Johannes. *Jerusalem and Babylon: A Study into Augustine's City of God and the Sources of His Doctrine of the Two Cities.* Leiden: E. J. Brill, 1991.

Vessey, Mark et al., eds. *History, Apocalypse, and the Secular Imagination: New Essays on Augustine's City of God.* Bowling Green: Philosophy Documentation Center, 1999.

Williams, Rowan. "Politics and the Soul: A Reading of the *City of God*." *Milltown Studies* 19/20 (1987) 55-72.

REVISIONS II,43 (70)

1. In the meantime Rome was devastated by an assault on the part of the Goths acting under King Alaric and by a most destructive invasion. Worshipers of the many false gods, whom we usually call pagans, attempted to impute the devastation to the Christian religion and began to blaspheme against the true God with more harshness and bitterness than usual. Hence, burning with zeal for the house of God,[1] I started to write the books on *The City of God* in answer to their blasphemies and errors. This work occupied me for a number of years, because many other matters interfered that it would not have been right to put off, and I had to use my time to address them **first**. But **finally** this vast work on *The City of God*, in twenty-two books, was finished.

Of these, the first five refute those who want human affairs to prosper and who therefore think it necessary for this to worship the many gods that the pagans are accustomed to worship, and who contend that these evils arise and abound because this is forbidden.

The following five respond to those who acknowledge that these evils have never been wanting, nor ever will be, as far as human beings are concerned, and who say that they are sometimes great and sometimes small, depending on places, times and persons, but who argue that the worship of many gods, which involves sacrificing to them, is useful in view of the life that will exist after death.

With these ten books, then, those two vain opinions that are inimical to the

Christian religion are refuted.

2. But lest anyone blame us for having only disproved what other people say and for not having explained our [teachings], there is another part to this work which is devoted to that purpose and which is comprised of twelve books, although when necessary we also explain what is ours in the ten earlier [books] and disprove what is opposed to that in the twelve later ones.

Of the next twelve books, then, the first four deal with the origin of the two cities, of which one is God's and the other is this world's; the second four with their development or trajectory; and the third four, which are the last, with their merited ends.

And so, although all twenty-two books were written about both cities, they nonetheless took their title from the better one, so that it is called *The City of God*.

---

1. See Ps 69:9; Jn 2:17.

In the tenth of these books, the **flame** produced from heaven that ran between the divided victims in Abraham's sacrifice[2] ought not to have been characterized as a miracle,[3] because this was shown to him in a vision.

In the seventeenth, what was said of Samuel, "He was not from the sons of Aaron,"[4] should instead have been "He was not the son of a priest." It was a more legitimate custom, in fact, for the sons of priests to succeed the dead priests. For Samuel's father is numbered among the sons of Aaron,[5] but he was not a priest, nor is he [listed] among Aaron's sons as though he himself had begotten him, but he was like all of that people, who are called sons of Israel.

This work begins in this way: "[In this work, my dearest son Marcellus, I have taken up the task of defending] the most glorious city of God."

---

2. See Gn 15:17.
3. X,8.
4. XVII,5.
5. There is no reference to this in Scripture. See also *Revisions* II,55,2.

BOOK I

After the Preface, which announces the purpose of The City of God as a whole, Book I consists of a reply to the Roman critics of Christianity who blamed the sack of the city of Rome by Alaric and his Goths in 410 on Rome's abandonment of its traditional gods and its adoption of Christianity as its dominant and state-supported religion. It starts by reminding the Romans that many of them survived precisely because the Goths, contrary to all previous practice of war, respected Christ's churches as places of sanctuary and that Rome's own gods, as described by Virgil in the Aeneid, were themselves "conquered gods" who could not even protect Troy from defeat. It then considers at length the question of why divine providence extended mercy even to the evil and allowed even the good to suffer, suggesting that some of the evil may repent as a result of their experience and that the temporal sufferings of the good are a form of punishment for their failings but do not affect their true good and serve to test or to train them in the life of faith. Thus none of the various forms of Christian suffering in the sack of Rome — loss of wealth, torture, death, captivity, or rape — separated Christians from Christ; and not even rape can justify suicide, either to avoid rape or out of shame after rape, because rape cannot defile a person's true moral purity. Finally, the book upbraids the Romans for their moral laxity as expressed in their self-indulgent extravagance once they were no longer constrained by their fear of Carthage and in their crazed devotion to the immoralities portrayed in the theaters. It closes with a brief sketch of points to be discussed in the subsequent books.

Preface. In this work, my dearest son Marcellinus, I have taken up the task of defending the most glorious city of God, whether in the course of these present times when it is on pilgrimage among the ungodly, living by faith,[1] or in the stability of its eternal home which it now awaits in patience,[2] *until justice returns in judgment* (Ps 94:15), but will finally attain, by virtue of its surpassing excellence, in ultimate victory and perfect peace. I have undertaken to defend it against those who prefer their own gods to its founder; and, in doing so, I will keep my promise and pay my debt to you.[3] It is a massive work, and arduous, but *God is our helper* (Ps 62:8).

---

1. See Hab 2:4.
2. See Rom 8:25.
3. Marcellinus, an imperial official who had been sent to Africa to end the Donatist schism, had written to Augustine in 411 or 412 and asked him to respond to the opinion of Volusian, the proconsul of Africa, who believed that the practice of Christianity was incompatible with the requirements of Roman citizenship. Marcellinus's letter is listed in Augustine's correspondence and numbered 136. *The City of God* is Augustine's response to that request. The work was commenced while Marcellinus was still alive; he was falsely accused and executed as a traitor in 413.

For I know very well what efforts are needed to persuade the proud how great the power of humility is. But by humility we reach a height — a height not grasped by human arrogance but granted by divine grace — which transcends all these earthly pinnacles that totter with the shifts of time. For the king and founder of the city of which we are going to speak has made known, in the Scripture of his people, a provision of divine law which asserts, *God resists the proud but gives grace to the humble* (Jas 4:6). This belongs to God alone, but the inflated spirit of human pride strives to claim it for itself and loves to have the same thing said in its own praise, "To spare the conquered and subdue the proud."[4] That is why, when the plan of this work requires it and as the opportunity arises, I must also speak of the earthly city — the city which, when it seeks dominion, even though whole peoples are its slaves, is itself under the dominion of its very lust for domination.

Barbarian Respect for Christ's Churches as Places of Sanctuary

1. It is from this earthly city that there emerge the enemies against whom the city of God must be defended. Many of these, once the error of their impiety has been corrected, do become quite worthy citizens of God's city, but many others burn against it with the fires of fierce hatred. They are so ungrateful for the obvious benefits of its redeemer that they forget that they would not be wagging their tongues against it today if they had not, in fleeing the enemy's sword, found in the refuge of its sacred places the life in which they take such pride. Are not the Romans who assail Christ's name the very ones whom the barbarians spared for Christ's sake? The shrines of the martyrs and the basilicas of the apostles bear witness to the fact. During the devastation of the city they gave refuge to those who fled to them, both to their own people and to strangers as well. The bloodthirsty enemy raged just this far but no further. Here the frenzied slaughter came to a halt; here the merciful among the enemy brought those whom they had spared — and had even spared far away from these sacred sites — to save them from the assaults of others who showed no such mercy. Elsewhere these marauders raged and slaughtered as enemies do, but when they reached these places, where a ban had been imposed on acts that were otherwise permitted by the laws of war, all their murderous cruelty was reined in and their fierce desire for prisoners was shattered.

As a result, many escaped who now deride these Christian times and make Christ responsible for the evils that Rome endured. But they do not make Christ responsible for the good that happened to them — the fact that they themselves are still alive due to the honor in which Christ was held. This they ascribe rather to their fate. If they were sensible about it, however, they ought instead to attribute the harsh and bitter blows they suffered at the enemy's hands to the divine providence which often uses wars to correct and destroy the corrupt ways of human beings — or, again, uses such afflictions to put the righteous and the praiseworthy to the

---

4. Virgil, *Aeneid* VI,853.

test and, once they have been proved, either to convey them to a better world or to keep them here on earth for further service.

And they certainly ought to ascribe it to these Christian times that, contrary to the usages of war, the cruel barbarians spared them anywhere at all for the sake of Christ's name or spared them, more specifically, in the places specially dedicated to Christ's name — vast places, chosen to hold huge throngs, so that mercy might be spread more widely.[5] For this they ought to give thanks to God; for this they ought truly to flee to his name in order to escape the punishment of eternal fire, seeing that so many of them falsely assumed his name in order to escape the punishment of present destruction. For, among those whom you now see insolently and impudently insulting Christ's servants, there are many who would not have eluded that ruin and disaster if they had not pretended to be Christ's servants themselves. And now, in ungrateful pride and the most ungodly folly, they oppose his name with perverse hearts, incurring the punishment of eternal darkness — the very name to which they fled with lying lips, in order to enjoy this mere temporal light.

2. So many wars have been recorded, whether waged before Rome was founded or after her rise to power. Let them read the records and produce a single instance of a city captured by invading troops where the enemies who took it spared the people whom they found taking refuge in the temples of their gods, or where some barbarian commander ordered that, once a town was stormed, no one should be killed who was found in this or that temple. Did not Aeneas see Priam before the altars, "staining with his blood the fires he himself had consecrated"?[6] Did not Diomedes and Ulysses "slay the keepers of the topmost citadel, seize the sacred image, and with bloody hands dare to touch the fillets of the virgin goddess"?[7] Nor is there any truth to the words that come next: "The Greeks' hopes thereafter ebbed, slipped back, and failed."[8] Afterward, in fact, the Greeks conquered; they destroyed Troy with sword and flames; and they cut Priam down as he fled to the altars.[9]

Rome's "Conquered Gods"

Nor is it true that Troy perished because it lost Minerva. For what had Minerva herself lost first, with the result that Troy perished? Perhaps it was her guards? That was it, of course. Once her guards were killed, it was possible to take her away. The image was not protecting human beings; human beings were protecting the image.

---

5. Among these was certainly the old Basilica of Saint Peter, which was more than 340 feet long and designed to hold large crowds of pilgrims visiting the tomb of Saint Peter. Paulinus of Nola, Letter 13,11-14, written about fifteen years before *The City of God*, describes an agape sponsored by a wealthy Roman that attracted a throng of poor people to the basilica.
6. Virgil, *Aeneid* II,501-502.
7. Ibid. II,166-168.
8. Ibid. II,169-170.
9. See ibid. II,663.

What was the point, then, of worshiping her for the sake of having her guard the country and its people? She could not even guard her own guardians![10]

3. To think that the Romans used to rejoice that they had entrusted the protection of their city to gods such as these! What a miserable mistake! They are angry with us when we say such things about their gods, and yet they are not angry with their own authors. In fact, they paid a fee to be taught these authors in school, and considered their teachers to be fully worthy of a public stipend and high honors. Their small children read Virgil precisely so that — once their tender minds have soaked up the great poet, the best and most famous of them all — he cannot easily be forgotten or fade into oblivion (as Horace says, "New vessels will long preserve the scent of what they first contained"[11]). But in this Virgil's work, Juno is introduced as hostile to the Trojans, and as she stirs up Aeolus, king of the winds, against them, she is made to say, "A people I hate now sails the Tyrrhenian sea, carrying Troy and her conquered gods to Italy."[12] How wise was it, then, for them to entrust Rome — in order to keep it from being conquered — to these very "conquered gods"? But perhaps Juno was simply speaking like an angry woman here, without knowing what she said. Then what about Aeneas himself, so often called "the pious"?[13] Doesn't he tell us that "Panthus, Othrys' son, priest of the citadel and of Phoebus, snatching up the conquered gods and his small grandson, comes running in a frenzy to my door"?[14] And does he not portray these gods — which he does not hesitate to call conquered gods — as entrusted to his care, not he to theirs, when he is told, "To you Troy entrusts her sacred things and her native gods"?[15] Thus, if Virgil says both that these gods were conquered and that, in order somehow to escape despite the fact that they were conquered, they were entrusted to a man, what sort of madness is it to suppose that it was wise to entrust Rome to such guardians as these or to imagine that, if only she had not lost them, she could not possibly have been brought down! To worship conquered gods as protectors and defenders, what is that but to hold fast not to good divinities but to bad defaulters? Far wiser to believe not that Rome would not have met disaster if these gods had not perished, but rather that they would have perished long before if Rome had not preserved them as long as it could! A moment's thought is enough to show how silly it is to presume that Rome could not be conquered while under the protection of conquered defenders, and thus that she perished because she lost her guardian gods. In fact, the only cause there could be for her perishing is that

---

10. The image of Minerva, otherwise known as Pallas, goddess of war and wisdom, had been stolen from Troy by the Greeks. See ibid. II,223-267.
11. Letter I,2,69-70.
12. Virgil, *Aeneid* I,71-72.
13. Virgil frequently refers to his hero Aeneas as pious, intending to mean that he was devoted to, among others, the gods. Augustine is sarcastically suggesting that, if Aeneas were so pious, he should not have had to admit that he had protected the gods, rather than they him. See also below at III,14.
14. Virgil, *Aeneid* II,319-321.
15. Ibid. II,293.

she chose to have guardians who were themselves going to perish. Thus, when the poets wrote and sang about conquered gods, it is not that they simply took pleasure in lying; it is rather that the truth compelled them, as men of sense, to make this admission.

But these are matters which it will be more appropriate to treat fully and in detail in another place. Here, rather, I shall briefly set out, as best I can, what I had begun to say about those ungrateful people who blasphemously blame Christ for the evils they deservedly suffer for their own moral perversity. The fact that even such people as these were spared for Christ's sake is something they do not care to acknowledge, and in the madness of their sacrilegious perversity they wag their tongues against his name, the very tongues with which they falsely took on his name in order to save their lives, or at least the very tongues which they silenced in terror in the places consecrated to Christ so that, kept safe and protected where — thanks to him — they were unharmed by their enemies, they might then rush out against him, cursing him as their enemy.

[Chapters 4 — 6 recount how neither the Greeks nor the Romans respected the temples of the gods as places of sanctuary.]

7. Any devastation, slaughter, looting, burning, and affliction committed in that most recent calamity at Rome was done, then, according to the customary practice of war. What was quite new, however, and put a whole new face on things, was that barbarian brutality appeared in a guise so gentle that the very largest basilicas were selected and set apart to be filled with people who were spared. Here no one was to be slain; no one was to be dragged out; but many were led in by their merciful enemies to be set free, and none were led away into captivity by cruel foes. Anyone who does not see that this is to be attributed to Christ's name and to these Christian times is blind. Anyone who sees it and does not praise it is ungrateful. Anyone who opposes such praise is insane. Nor will anyone with any sense at all impute this simply to the barbarians' savagery. The one who overawed, reined in, and miraculously softened their utterly ferocious and brutal minds was the one who, long ago, said through the prophet, *I will punish their iniquities with the rod and their sins with scourges; but I will not take my mercy from them* (Ps 89:32-33).

Divine Providence, Human Suffering, and Temporal Goods and Evils

8. "But why," someone will ask, "was this divine mercy extended even to the ungodly and the ungrateful?"[16] What explanation can there be except that the one

---

16. What follows is a typical argument used by Augustine to explain the apparent arbitrariness of God's dealings with the good and the bad. See also *Exposition of Psalm 66*,3; *Sermon 50*,5. The argument recurs below at V,21.26 with respect to the distribution of earthly kingdoms to

who showed mercy was the one who daily *makes his sun rise on the good and on the evil and sends rain on the just and the unjust* (Mt 5:45)? For some of them, reflecting on this point, repent of their ungodliness and reform themselves. But others, as the Apostle says, *despise the riches of God's goodness and forbearance and by their hardness of heart and their impenitent heart are storing up wrath for themselves on the day of wrath and of the revelation of the righteous judgment of God, who will repay each according to his deeds* (Rom 2:4-6). It is still true, however, that God's patience invites the evil to repentance, just as God's scourge trains the good for patience; and so too, God's mercy embraces the good, to cherish them, just as God's severity takes hold of the evil, to punish them. It has pleased divine providence to prepare future goods for the righteous that will not be enjoyed by the unrighteous and future evils for the ungodly that will not torment the good. But God willed the temporal goods and evils of this life to be common to both, so that we would neither avidly desire goods which we see that the evil also possess nor shamefully avoid evils by which the good are also very often afflicted.

The most important point, however, is what sort of use we make of the things that are reckoned either as prosperity or as adversity. For the good are neither lifted up by temporal goods nor beaten down by temporal evils; but the evil, just because they are corrupted by temporal good fortune, feel temporal misfortune as punishment. Yet, even in distributing prosperity and adversity, God often shows his manner of working quite plainly. For if every sin received obvious punishment in the present, people would think that nothing was reserved for the last judgment; but if God's power never openly punished any sin in the present, people would think that there was no such thing as divine providence. In the same way, with regard to prosperity, if God did not grant it with the most open and obvious generosity to some who pray for it, we would claim that it was not his to give. And, on the other hand, if he granted it to all who asked, we would conclude that God was only to be served for the sake of this kind of reward — and that sort of service would make us not godly but grasping and avaricious.

This does not mean, however, that when the good and the evil suffer alike, there is no distinction between them simply because there is no distinction in what they suffer. Even when the sufferings are alike, the sufferers remain unlike; and even when virtue and vice undergo the same torment, they are not themselves the same.... Thus, under the same affliction, the evil detest and blaspheme God, but the good praise and pray to him. What is really important, then, is not the character of the suffering but rather the character of the sufferer. Stirred by the same motion, filth gives out a foul stench, but perfume a sweet fragrance.[17]

---

both good and bad rulers, and analogously below at XVIII,51 regarding the troubles that heretics cause orthodox Christians. Augustine uses basically the same argument below at II,23 — but this time to illustrate from the lives of four prominent figures from Roman history (Regulus, Marius, Metellus and Catiline) that the favors of the pagan gods were capricious.

17. Augustine is citing a commonplace proverb.

Why the Good also Suffered in the Sack of Rome: Failure to Correct the Evil

9. When all this is considered from the point of view of faith, then, what did Christians suffer in that time of devastation that would not work rather for their advancement? First, when they humbly reflect on the very sins for which God in his anger has filled the world with such terrible calamities, even though they themselves are far from being disgraceful and ungodly criminals, they still do not reckon themselves so entirely free from fault as to judge that they do not deserve to suffer even temporal evils for their failings. Leave aside the fact that each person, no matter how praiseworthy his life may be, sometimes gives in to carnal desire. Even if he does not fall into the atrocity of crime and the depths of shame and the abomination of ungodliness, he still commits some sins either rarely or all the more often the less serious the sins are. But leaving this aside, it is hard to find anyone who treats as they ought to be treated the very people on account of whose horrendous pride, lasciviousness, greed, and detestable wickedness and impiety God now smites the earth, just as he forewarned that he would.[18] It is hard to find anyone who lives among them as life ought to be lived among such people.

For all too often we wrongly shy away from our obligation to teach and admonish them, and sometimes even to rebuke and correct them. We shy away either because we are unwilling to make the effort or because we hesitate to offend their dignity or because we want to avoid enmities that might impede and harm us with respect to some temporal things which our desire still longs to acquire or which our weakness still fears to lose....

If anyone refrains from rebuking and correcting evildoers because he is waiting for a more propitious moment or because he is afraid that, by doing so, he might make them even worse or because he fears that, if he does so, they might start obstructing others who are weak and need guidance to a good and godly life, putting pressure on them and turning them away from the faith, this does not appear to be a pretense of desire but rather the counsel of love. What is blameworthy is that people who live quite differently from the wicked, and abhor their deeds, are nonetheless indulgent towards the sins of others when they ought to teach them otherwise and rebuke them. It is blameworthy, that is, when they do this for fear of offending people who might do them harm with regard to things which the good may certainly use, permissibly and innocently, but which they are pursuing more avidly than is proper for people who are only on pilgrimage in this world, bearing with them the hope of a heavenly homeland....

In this matter, however, there are some who have not an equal but a far more serious responsibility. They are the ones to whom it is said through the prophet, *He will certainly die in his sin, but his blood I will require at the hand of the watchman* (Ezk 33:6). For the reason why watchmen — that is, those who are set

---

18. See Is 24:1-23.

over the people — were established in the churches is precisely so that they would not be lenient in rebuking sins.... [19]

Then again, there is another reason why the good are afflicted with temporal evils, as in the case of Job — so that the human spirit may be tested and may learn for itself how strong its devotion really is, how strongly it loves God even without reward.

Forms of Christian Suffering: Loss of Riches

10. Now that we have properly weighed and examined these points, consider next whether any evil has happened to the faithful and godly that was not turned to their good. (Or are we to suppose that the Apostle's pronouncement was empty, when he said, *We know that all things work together for good for those who love God* [Rom 8:28]!). But they lost everything they had! Did they lose their faith? Their godliness? The goods of the inner man who is rich before God? These are the riches of Christians, to whom the Apostle, rich with these riches, said, *Godliness along with enough to suffice is great gain. For we brought nothing into this world, nor can we take anything out. And if we have food and clothing, we are content with these. For those who want to be rich fall into temptation and a snare and many foolish and harmful desires that plunge people into ruin and destruction. For the love of money is the root of all evils, and, in their longing for it, some have strayed away from the faith and entangled themselves in many pains.* (1 Tm 6:6-10) If those who lost all their earthly riches in Rome's devastation had possessed them in this way, as they had heard from one who was himself outwardly poor but inwardly rich — that is, if they had used the world as though not using it [20] — they would have been able to say, echoing one who was grievously tempted but never overcome, *Naked I came from my mother's womb, and naked I shall return to the earth. The Lord gave, and the Lord has taken away; as it pleased the Lord, so it has taken place; blessed be the name of the Lord.* (Jb 1:21) As a good servant, Job held the will of his Lord to be great treasure in itself, by attending on which he would grow rich in mind, and he did not grieve at losing in life the very things he would soon have lost in death. But those weaker Christians who clung to their earthly goods with some measure of desire, even though they did not prefer them to Christ, discovered in losing them how much they had sinned in loving them. The extent to which they grieved at their loss showed the extent to which they had, in the words of the Apostle cited above, *entangled themselves in many pains.* For it was appropriate that those who had long neglected the training of words should finally receive in addition the training of experience....

---

19. Augustine understands the watchman of whom Ezekiel speaks as the bishop, and he is undoubtedly making a reference here not only to bishops in general but to himself in particular. The Latin word for "watchman" is *speculator*; this translates the Greek *episkopos*, which also carries the meaning of "bishop."

20. See 1 Cor 7:31.

For if many rejoiced that they had put their riches in a place which the enemy happened not to reach, how much more certainly and securely were those able to rejoice who, at the urging of their God, had migrated to a place that it was completely impossible for the enemy to reach!

Our friend Paulinus, bishop of Nola, voluntarily went from the greatest riches to the most extreme poverty, and to the most abundant holiness. I learned from him afterwards that, when the barbarians sacked Nola itself and held him captive, he used to pray in his heart, "Lord, let me not be tortured for the sake of gold and silver, for you know where everything I own is." For he kept everything he owned where he had been told to store and treasure it up by the one who had foretold that these evils would happen in this world.... [21]

Forms of Christian Suffering: Torture and Famine

It is true that some good people, even some Christians, were tortured to make them hand over their goods to the enemy. But these people could neither hand over nor lose the good by which they were themselves good. In fact, if they preferred to be tortured rather than to hand over the mammon of unrighteousness, they were not actually good. Those who suffered as much for gold as they ought to have endured for Christ should have been prompted by this to learn, instead, to love him who enriches those who suffer for his sake with eternal felicity, and not to love gold and silver. For it is the height of wretchedness to suffer for gold and silver, regardless of whether they kept their wealth hidden by lying or gave it up by telling the truth. For under torture, no one lost Christ by confessing him, and no one kept his gold except by denying it. It may well be, then, that the tortures which taught that the good to be loved is the incorruptible good were more useful than the very goods for love of which their owners were tortured without any useful outcome at all.

But there were also some who had no goods to hand over but were tortured anyway, simply because they were not believed. It is possible, however, that these people desired riches and were not poor due to any holy will on their part. To these, then, it had to be shown that it is not wealth but the very desire for wealth that is worthy of such tortures....

They also say that many people, including Christians, were devastated by the prolonged famine. This also, however, the good and faithful turned to their advantage by enduring it with godliness. Those whom the famine killed, it snatched away — like bodily disease — from the evils of this life; and those whom it did not kill it taught to live more sparingly and to fast at greater length.

---

21. Paulinus, bishop of Nola, near Naples, from c. 410 until his death in 431, was a friend of Augustine exclusively by way of correspondence; they never met in person. His abnegation of great riches in favor of a life of simplicity, which he practiced with his wife Therasia, was considered remarkable and is mentioned by several early Christian writers in addition to Augustine — among them Ambrose, Letter 58,3; Jerome, Letter 118,5.

Forms of Christian Suffering:
Dreadful Types of Death and Death without Burial

11. But many Christians were killed, and many were consumed by various dreadful forms of death. If this is hard to bear, it is at any rate the common lot of all who are born into this life. I know this: that no one has died who was not going to die at some point. What is more, the end of life makes a long life the same as a short one; for the one is not better and the other worse, the one is not greater and the other less, once they are the same in no longer existing at all.[22] What does it matter what kind of death puts an end to this life, since the one whose life ends is not compelled to die a second time? In the daily chances of this life, every mortal is threatened in one way or another by innumerable deaths; and since it is always uncertain which of these will actually come upon him, I ask whether it is better to suffer one of them and die or to stay alive and fear all of them. I am well aware how quickly we would choose to live longer in fear of all these deaths rather than to die once with no other deaths to fear. But what the weak and frightened sense of the flesh shrinks away from is one thing, and what the carefully considered reasoning of the mind finds convincing is another.

Death should not be thought an evil when a good life precedes it. For nothing makes death an evil except what follows death. Consequently, those who are inevitably going to die have little reason to worry about how they are going to die, and much reason to worry about where they will be brought by dying. And since Christians know very well how much better was the death of the devout poor man with dogs licking his sores than was that of the impious rich man clad in purple and fine linen,[23] what harm did those terrible kinds of death do to the dead who had lived well?

12. But there was such a welter of corpses that they could not even be buried![24] Devout faith, however, does not find even this so very dreadful, but rather holds fast to the prediction that not even devouring beasts will keep our bodies from rising again, bodies of which not a hair of the head will perish.[25] If anything the enemy wished to do with the bodies of the slain could in any way obstruct the future life, the Truth would certainly not have said, *Do not fear those who kill the body but cannot kill the soul* (Mt 10:28)....

There were, then, many Christian bodies that earth did not cover, but no one has separated even one of them from heaven, or from earth, which is wholly filled with the presence of him who knows from where he will raise that which he created.... Therefore the care taken for the funeral, the arrangement for burial,

---

22. Much the same thought is expressed at greater length below at XIII, 10.
23. See Lk 16:19-31.
24. This and the following chapter are repeated verbatim in *The Care To Be Taken of the Dead* 4-5
25. See Lk 21:18.

the procession of mourners[26] — all these are more a comfort for the living than a help for the dead. If a costly burial were of any benefit for the ungodly, then a cheap one, or none at all, would actually do harm to the godly. In fact, however, a crowd of servants gave that rich man clad in purple a funeral that was magnificent in the sight of men, but far more splendid in the sight of the Lord was the funeral given to that poor man with his sores by the ministry of angels who carried him not to a marble tomb but to the bosom of Abraham.[27]

The people against whom I have undertaken to defend the city of God laugh at these things, but even their own philosophers have heaped scorn on concern about burial.[28] And often whole armies, when dying for their earthly homeland, showed no concern about where they would lie afterwards or for what beasts they would become food, and in this regard it was perfectly permissible for their poets to say, to general applause, "He who has no urn is covered by the sky."[29] They have no good reason, then, to taunt Christians about unburied bodies. For Christians, after all, have the promise that their flesh and all its members will be formed anew not only from the earth but even from the most hidden recesses of the other elements into which their disintegrated corpses have slipped away — to be restored to them and made whole in an instant of time.

13. This does not mean, however, that the bodies of the dead are to be despised and cast aside, and especially not those of the righteous and faithful, of which the Spirit has made holy use as instruments and vessels for all good works. For if a father's garment or ring, or anything of this kind, is the more precious to his children the more deeply they loved their parents, then the bodies themselves, which we wear far more intimately and closely than any garment, are by no means to be scorned. They are no mere adornment or external aid but belong to human nature itself.[30] It is for this reason that, in antiquity, funeral offices for the righteous were carried out with pious care, with last rites celebrated and provisions made for burial; and they themselves, while still alive, gave directions to their sons concerning the burial or even the transporting of their bodies.[31]...

The point which these authorities make, however, is not that there is any feeling in dead bodies. Rather, for the sake of reinforcing our faith in the resurrection, they indicate that even the bodies of the dead fall under the providence of God, to

---

26. On the rituals surrounding early Christian death and burial, of which the funeral procession formed an important part, see Alfred C. Rush, *Death and Burial in Christian Antiquity* (Washington: The Catholic University of America Press, 1941) 89-273.
27. See Lk 16:19-31. The rich man's funeral is not described in the parable; Augustine's imagination is at work here.
28. See Cicero, *Tusculan Disputations* I,102-104.
29. Lucan, *Pharsalia* VII,819.
30. This lapidary and unqualified defense of the body as intrinsic to the nature of the human being continues to be impressive even sixteen hundred years after it was written.
31. See Gn 47:29-30; 50:24.

whom such pious offices are pleasing. Here also we learn, to our benefit, how great the reward can be for the alms we give to those who are alive and have feeling, since even the attention and care we extend to lifeless human limbs are not lost with God....

And for this reason, when these rites were not available for Christian corpses in the devastation of that great city — or of any other cities — no blame fell to the living, who could not provide them, and no pain to the dead, who could not feel them in any case.

Forms of Christian Suffering: Captivity

14. But many Christians, they say, were also led into captivity. This is, of course, a great misery (if they could have been led anywhere where they did not find their God!). But there are in Holy Scripture great consolations for this calamity too. The three young men were in captivity;[32] so was Daniel;[33] so were other prophets.[34] But God, the comforter, did not fail them. So also, God did not abandon his faithful under the domination of a nation which, although barbarian, is still human, just as he did not abandon his prophet in the belly of the sea-monster....[35]

Captivity: the Example of Regulus and His Loyalty to His Gods

15. But they have, among their own famous men, a supreme example of captivity willingly endured for the sake of religion. Marcus Regulus, a general of the Roman people, was a captive of the Carthaginians. But the Carthaginians preferred an exchange of prisoners to get their own men back rather than to keep their Roman captives; and so, to obtain this end, they sent Regulus back to Rome with their own ambassadors, having first bound him by oath to return to Carthage if he did not accomplish what they wanted. Regulus went, and in the senate he persuaded them to take the opposite course, because he did not judge an exchange of prisoners to be to the advantage of the Roman republic. After persuading them, he was not compelled by his own people to return to the enemy. But because he had taken an oath, he voluntarily fulfilled it, and the Carthaginians put him to death with ingenious and terrible tortures. They shut him in a narrow box in which he was forced to stand upright. The box was studded on all sides with the sharpest nails so that he could not lean in any direction without horrible pain; and so they killed him by keeping him awake....[36]

---

32. See Dn 3.
33. See Dn 1:6.
34. See Ezk 1:1; Est 2:5-7.
35. See Jon 2.
36. Marcus Attilius Regulus (before 307-c. 250 B.C.) was often cited by the Romans as an example of honor and fidelity. The account of his death that Augustine gives is recorded in Horace, *Odes*

Regulus plainly worshiped the gods so conscientiously that, to keep his oath, he would not remain in his own country or go anywhere else but without a moment's hesitation went straight back to his bitterest enemies. If he thought that this would be to his benefit in this life, he was very much mistaken, for it earned him a horrible end. In fact, what he taught by his example was that the gods are of no use to their worshipers so far as temporal happiness is concerned. For, even though he was devoted to their worship, he was defeated and taken captive; and, because he was not willing to do anything but what he had sworn by the gods to do, he was tortured and put to death by a new, unprecedented, and horrible form of punishment. But if, on the other hand, worship of the gods brings happiness as its reward only after this life, why do people slander these Christian times? Why do they say that this disaster came upon the city of Rome because she stopped worshiping her gods when, no matter how diligently she worshiped them, she could still have been just as unfortunate as Regulus was?...

What are we to make, then, of people who glory in having such a citizen but fear to have such a city? And if they do not fear this, let them admit that the sort of thing that happened to Regulus could also happen to a city that worships the gods just as conscientiously as he did, and let them stop slandering these Christian times. And since the whole point at issue began with those Christians who were also taken captive, let those who impudently and foolishly mock our most wholesome religion keep the example of Regulus in mind and hold their tongues. He worshiped the gods most attentively and kept the oath he had sworn by them; but he was deprived of his homeland, the only homeland he had, and, held captive among his enemies, was put to a lingering death by a torture of unprecedented cruelty. If this was no disgrace to their gods, far less should the Christian name be accused for the captivity of its devoted followers who, awaiting a heavenly homeland with true faith, know that they are pilgrims even in their own homes.

Forms of Christian Suffering: Rape; Moral Purity and the Issue of Suicide

16. They certainly think they have a great charge to hurl against Christians when, to dramatize their sufferings in captivity, they add also the rape not only of married women and maidens intending to marry but even of certain women consecrated to the religious life. Here, however, it is not faith, not godliness, not even the virtue that is called chastity, which faces any problem, but rather our argument, which must find a way to negotiate the narrow line between the claims of modesty and the claims of reason.

Here we are not so much concerned to respond to outsiders as we are to comfort our own. In the first place, then, let it be stated and established that virtue, by which we live rightly, governs the members of the body from its seat in the mind

---

III,5, but is of doubtful authenticity.

and that the body becomes holy through its use by a holy will; and, so long as the will remains steadfast and unshaken, nothing that anyone else does with the body or to the body — and that cannot be avoided by the person who suffers it without some sin on his own part — brings any blame to the one who undergoes it.[37] Not only acts inflicting pain, however, but also acts gratifying lust can be perpetrated on the body of another; and when something like that happens — even when it does not shatter the chastity to which the supremely constant mind holds fast — it still brings on a sense of shame, for fear that people might think that an act which could not have occurred, perhaps, without some pleasure of the flesh must also have taken place with the consent of the mind.

17. And if, for this reason, some of these women took their own lives rather than suffer anything of this kind, who with any human feeling would refuse to forgive them? And if some were not willing to kill themselves, because they did not want to escape another's shameful act by committing a crime of their own, anyone who makes that a charge against them will lay himself open to the charge of being a fool. For if it is not lawful to kill even a guilty person on one's private authority — and no law grants the license to do that — then anyone who kills himself is certainly a murderer; and the more innocent he is with regard to whatever led him to think he ought to kill himself, the more guilty he is for killing himself.... Why, then, should a person who has done no evil do evil to himself? Why should he, in killing himself, kill an innocent person in order not to suffer the crime of another? Why should he perpetrate on himself a sin of his own to keep another's sin from being perpetrated on him?

18. But there remains the fear that even someone else's lust may bring defilement. It will not defile if it is another's; and if it does defile, it is not another's. Purity is a virtue of the mind, and it has fortitude as its companion, by which it determines to endure any evils rather than consent to evil.[38] No one, no matter how noble-minded and pure, has it in his power to determine what happens to his flesh, but only what his mind will accept or reject. Who of sound mind, then, will suppose that his purity is lost if it happens that his flesh is seized and held down and someone else's lust exercised and satisfied on it?... In fact, when the good of holy continence does not yield to the impurity of carnal desires, the body itself is sanctified as well; and, therefore, when this continence persists in its unshaken resolve not to yield, the holiness of the body itself is not destroyed, because the will to use the body in a holy manner remains and, so far as in it lies, so also does the capacity....

Let us rather learn from this that the body's holiness is not lost as long as the mind's holiness remains, even when the body itself is overpowered, just as, in

---

37. A similar thought is graphically expressed in *Lying* 15-17.
38. On the connection between fortitude and virginity, or chastity, see Philo, *On the Virtues* 1,34-8,50; Gregory of Nyssa, On Virginity 18,3.

contrast, the body's holiness is lost as soon as the mind's holiness is violated, even if the body itself is still intact.

For this reason, a woman who has been overpowered by force and violated by another's sin without any consent on her part has nothing which she ought to punish in herself by voluntary death. And all the less before it happens! Let no one incur the certain guilt of murder while the shameful act itself — and another's act at that — is still uncertain.

Rape and Suicide: the Example of Lucretia

19. We assert, then, that when the body is overpowered but the resolve to remain chaste stands firm, unaltered by any consent to evil, the crime belongs only to the man who took the woman by force and not at all to the woman who was taken by force, without her consent and against her will. Will those against whom we are defending as holy not only the minds but also the bodies of the Christian women who were raped in captivity dare to contradict this clear reasoning? They certainly extol with high praise the purity of Lucretia, that noble woman of ancient Rome.[39] When the son of Tarquin the king took her body by force and lustfully used it, she made that most villainous young man's crime known to her husband Collatinus and her kinsman Brutus, men of great distinction and courage, and bound them to take revenge. Then, sick at the vileness of what had been done to her and unable to bear it, she killed herself. What shall we say? Should she be judged adulterous or chaste? Who can think it worth laboring over the issue? In a declamation on the subject, someone put the matter admirably and truthfully: "Wonderful to relate, there were two, but only one committed adultery."[40] Splendidly put, and very true! He saw in this union of two bodies the utterly depraved desire of the one and the wholly pure will of the other, and he directed attention not to the conjunction of the bodies but to the diversity of the minds: "There were two," he said, "but only one committed adultery."

How is it, then, that the one who did not commit adultery was the one more severely punished? He was banished from his fatherland with his father; she suffered the supreme penalty....

We are concerned with the example of this noble woman, however, simply for the sake of refuting those who, with no understanding of holiness, jeer at the Christian women who were raped in captivity; and it is enough for our purposes that it was admirably said in her praise, "There were two, but only one committed adultery." For they preferred to believe that Lucretia was not one who could have

---

39. The story of Lucretia is told in Livy, *History of Rome* I,57-59 and seems to have had a historical basis. Lucretia's death can be dated to c. 508 B.C. The amount of space that Augustine devotes to her is a measure of the power of her example, which was considerable in the ancient Roman world. She is mentioned again below at II,17.
40. The source of the quotation is unknown.

stained herself with even a hint of consent to adultery. As a consequence, when she killed herself because she had endured an adulterer (even though she was not herself an adulteress), it was not out of the love of purity but out of the weakness of shame. What made her feel shame was the debased act of another committed on her but not with her; and, as a Roman woman too avid for praise, she was afraid that, if she continued to live, she would be thought to have suffered with pleasure what she actually suffered by violence when she was still alive. For this reason she thought that she must present her self-punishment to men's eyes in witness to her state of mind, since she could not show them her conscience itself. She blushed at the very thought that, if she were to bear patiently the foul act that another had done to her, she might be considered an accomplice in it.

This is not what those Christian women did who suffered similar things and yet are still alive. They did not avenge another's crime on themselves, not wanting to add crimes of their own to the crimes of others. For that is what they would have done if, when enemies committed rape on them out of lust, they had committed murder on themselves out of shame. They have the glory of chastity within them, the witness of conscience. They have this in the eyes of God, and they need nothing more. In fact, there is nothing more that they can rightly do, for they have no intention of straying from the authority of divine law by doing wrong to avoid the scandal of human suspicion.

[Chapters 20 — 22 expound the divine law against suicide and murder. Examples of divinely ordered exceptions to killing are cited from the Bible, as in the case of Abraham and Isaac, and in just war situations. Suicide is never divinely sanctioned.]

Suicide: the Example of Cato

23. But apart from Lucretia (and I have already said enough about my view of her), it is not easy for them to find an authoritative example to support their teaching, unless it is the famous Cato who killed himself at Utica.[41] It is not, of course, that Cato was the only one who did this. It is rather that he was held to be a man of learning and probity, and so one might have reason to think that what he did could have been done rightly and can still be done rightly.

What can I say about his act that is more telling than this — that his friends, who were also learned men, but more sensible, tried to dissuade him from it? They considered suicide the misdeed of a weak mind, not a strong one, an act showing weakness unable to bear adversity rather than honor on guard against disgrace. And Cato himself thought the same with regard to his dearly beloved son. For if it

---

41. Marcus Porcius Cato, the Younger (95-46 B.C.), was an unwavering political opponent of Julius Caesar and, when it was clear that Caesar would rule Rome, committed suicide rather than submit.

BOOK I 17

was shameful to live under Caesar's triumph, why was he the author of this shame for his son, whom he instructed to put all his hope in Caesar's generosity?[42] Why did he not compel his son to die with him? If it was praiseworthy for Torquatus to kill his son for engaging the enemy against orders, even though he came out the victor,[43] why did the vanquished Cato spare his vanquished son when he did not spare himself? Or was it more shameful to be the victor against orders than endure the victor against honor? Actually, then, Cato did not really judge it shameful to live under the victorious Caesar; otherwise he would have freed his son from this shame with a father's sword. What can we say, therefore, except that, as Caesar himself is reported to have said, Cato loved his son, whom he hoped and wished for Caesar to spare, just as much as he hated — or, to say it more gently, was ashamed — to let Caesar have the glory of sparing himself?[44]

24. Our opponents are unwilling to let us give preference over Cato to the holy man Job, who chose to endure horrendous evils in his flesh rather than to rid himself of all these torments by putting himself to death, or to give preference to other saints from our writings — writings raised to the heights by their supreme authority and wholly worthy of belief — who chose to bear captivity and enemy domination rather than to kill themselves. On the basis of their own writings, then, I shall prefer to Marcus Cato the same Marcus Regulus whom we have already mentioned. For Cato had never defeated Caesar, and, when he was defeated by Caesar, he disdained to submit and, rather than submit, chose to kill himself. Regulus, in contrast, had already defeated the Carthaginians, and, as a Roman commander holding a Roman command, he had brought back not a lamentable victory over fellow citizens but a laudable victory over the enemy. And afterwards, when he was defeated by the Carthaginians, he chose to endure them in servitude rather than to escape from them by dying. Accordingly, he preserved both his patience under Carthaginian domination and his constancy in love for the Romans, taking neither his vanquished body from his enemies nor his unvanquished spirit from his fellow citizens. Nor was it out of love for this life that he refused to kill himself. He proved this when, to keep his promise and his oath, he returned without hesitation to those same enemies whom he had offended more gravely by his words in the senate than by his arms in battle. Thus, even as one who set no store on this life, he obviously judged it a great crime to kill himself, since he chose to end this life among savage enemies by terrible tortures rather than to do away with himself.

Among all their praiseworthy men, renowned for their outstanding virtue, the Romans offer none better than Regulus. Good fortune did not corrupt him, for he remained a very poor man even in his great victory;[45] and bad fortune did not break

---

42. See Livy, *Periochae* 114.
43. Titus Manlius Torquatus, a fourth-century B.C. Roman general and political figure, had his son put to death for disobeying orders after a victorious battle. See Livy, *History of Rome* VIII,7.
44. See Appian, *Civil War* II,99.
45. See Valerius Maximus, *Memorable Deeds and Sayings* IV,4,1-6.

him, for he went back undaunted to his terrible end. But if the bravest and most distinguished men, defenders of an earthly homeland and of the gods — false gods, to be sure, but they were not false worshipers, being utterly faithful in keeping their oaths — if these men could by the law and custom of war strike down defeated enemies but refused, when defeated by their enemies, to strike themselves down and, though they had no fear of death, preferred to endure the victors as overlords rather than to inflict death on themselves, how much the more will Christians, who worship the true God and aspire to a supernal homeland, refrain from this crime if ever divine providence subjects them to their enemies for a time, either to test or to correct them! They are not abandoned in this humiliation by the Most High, who came in such humility for their sake, and, above all, they are bound by no military authority or oath of military service to strike down even a defeated enemy. What a terrible error sneaks in, then, when it is thought that a person may kill himself either because an enemy has sinned against him or to keep an enemy from sinning against him, even though he may not dare to kill the very enemy who has sinned or who is going to sin against him!...

Is Suicide Permissible to Avoid Sin?

26. But, they say, in a time of persecution, certain holy women, in order to escape those who were attacking their chastity, threw themselves into a river that would carry them away and drown them.[46] They died in that way, and yet in the Catholic Church they are venerated as martyrs, and great crowds frequent their shrines. I do not presume to make any rash judgment on these women. I do not know whether divine authority convinced the Church, by some trustworthy testimonies, to honor their memories in this way, and it may be that this is so. For what if the women did this not in human delusion but under divine command, not in error but in obedience — as in the case of Samson, which it would be utterly wrong for us not to believe?[47] For when God gives a command and makes it unambiguously clear that he gives the command, who will charge obedience with crime? Who will bring an accusation against piety's compliance?

---

46. Augustine is referring to Ambrose's treatise *On Virgins* III,7,32-36, written four decades before *The City of God*, in which Ambrose approvingly recounts the suicide of a certain Pelagia, along with her mother and sisters, who threw themselves into a river during the early-fourth-century persecution of Diocletian, in order to escape violation. The author may have conflated two stories here — that of Pelagia herself and that of three other women (Domnina, Berenice and Prosdocia) who were supposed to have killed themselves in the same way and for the same reason. Although he never mentions Ambrose by name, probably out of respect for the great bishop of Milan with whom he is disagreeing, Augustine's extensive treatment of suicide as a response to possible violation is almost certainly an attempt to offer a reasoned alternative to Ambrose's enthusiastic embrace of suicide (he compares the death of the women to baptism ibid. III,7,34) in the circumstances. But Ambrose was not the first to speak approvingly of suicide in such circumstances. See Eusebius, *Ecclesiastical History* VIII,14,17.
47. See Jgs 16:28-30.

BOOK I 19

But this does not mean that, if someone decides to sacrifice his son to God, his act is not wicked simply because Abraham was praised for doing the same. For when a soldier kills a man in obedience to the authority under which he is legitimately serving, he is not guilty of murder according to any laws of his city; in fact, he is guilty of dereliction of duty and insubordination if he refuses. But if he had done this of his own accord and on his own authority, he would have been liable to the charge of shedding human blood. Thus the act for which he is punished if he does it without orders is the very act for which he will be punished if he refuses to do it under orders. And if this is true when the command is given by a general, how much more is it true when the command is given by the creator! Anyone who knows that it is not lawful to kill oneself may still do so, then, as long as he is commanded to do so by the one whose commands it is not lawful to despise. Let him make very sure, however, that there is no room for doubt about the divine command.

It is through the ear that we become aware of a person's conscience; we do not presume to judge things hidden from us. *No one knows what goes on in a person except the spirit of the person that is in him* (1 Cor 2:11). But what we say, what we assert, what we approve in every way is this: no one ought to inflict voluntary death on himself on the pretext of escaping temporal troubles, lest he fall into eternal troubles; no one ought to do this because of another's sins, lest by doing so he incur a most serious sin of his own when he would not have been at all defiled by the other's sin; no one ought to do this because of his own past sins, for he has all the more need of this life so that they can be healed by repentance; and no one ought to do this out of desire for a better life that is hoped for after death, for those who are guilty of their own death are not received into the better life that follows death.

27. There remains one reason, of which I had already begun to speak, for thinking it an advantage to kill oneself, namely, to avoid falling into sin either through the lure of pleasure or through the ferocity of pain. If we decide to admit this reason, however, it will carry us along to the point of thinking that people should be urged to kill themselves as soon as they have been washed in the font of holy regeneration and received the forgiveness of all sins.[48] For the moment to avoid all future sins is obviously the moment at which all past sins have been blotted out. And if it is right to avoid sin by voluntary death, why not do it at that moment above all? Once baptized, why spare oneself? Once set free, why thrust one's head back into the dangers of this life, when nothing could be easier than to avoid them all by killing oneself? After all, Scripture says, *Whoever loves danger will fall into it* (Sir 3:26). Why, then, are so many and such grave dangers

---

48. This should be read in the context of the frequent early Christian practice of holding off baptism until later in life, or even until one's deathbed, because baptism provided the forgiveness of sins at a time in the Church's history when only one other opportunity, besides baptism, for sacramental forgiveness (involving an often arduous and humiliating process) was offered.

loved — or, if not loved, at least accepted — by remaining in this life when one may legitimately abandon it? Does foolish perversity go so far in overturning the heart and diverting it from attention to the truth as to lead it to think that, if a person ought to kill himself to avoid falling into sin under the domination of a single captor, he should still go on living when he must endure this world itself, which is full of trials at every moment — not only trials like the one he fears under a single master but countless others which there is no escaping in this life? Why, then, do we waste time on exhorting the baptized, striving to enflame them for virginal chastity, or for the continence of widowhood, or for the fidelity of the marriage bed? Why do this, when we have a better way, a shortcut removed from all risk of sinning? Let us just persuade everyone that we can to grasp death and inflict it on themselves immediately after the remission of their sins, and so send them to the Lord fully healed and wholly pure!...

28. Therefore, Christ's faithful, do not let your lives become a burden to you, even if your enemies have made a plaything of your chastity. You have a great and true consolation if you remain sure in your conscience that you did not consent to the sins of those who were permitted to sin against you. And if you should ask why they were permitted to do so: deep is the providence of the creator and ruler of the world, *and his judgments are inscrutable, and his ways past finding out* (Rom 11:33).

But even so, question your souls honestly. Perhaps you took too much pride in your virginity and continence or purity.[49] Perhaps you took delight in human praise and even envied others in this regard. I make no accusations where I have no knowledge, and I do not hear what your hearts say in reply to your questioning. If they respond that this is so, however, do not be surprised that you have lost that for which you longed to win human approval but have kept that which cannot be displayed to human eyes. If you did not consent to the sinners, divine aid was added to divine grace so that you would not lose the grace, and human glory was followed by human reproach so that you would not love the glory. Take comfort from both, you faint of heart: being proved *and* being chastised, being justified *and* being corrected....

29. The whole family of the supreme and true God, then, has its own consolation, a consolation which does not deceive and which is not based on hope in anything faltering or unreliable. And even the temporal life that the faithful have in this world is not to be regretted. In this life they are schooled for eternity and, like pilgrims, make use of earthly goods without being taken captive by them, while they are either proved or corrected by evils. Some jeer at their uprightness and, when they happen to fall into temporal evils, say to them, *Where is your God?* (Ps 42:3) But let such scoffers say where their own gods are when such things happen

---

49. The danger of being proud of one's virginity was frequently stressed in Christian antiquity from the very beginning (see Clement, 1 *Corinthians* 38; Ignatius, *Polycarp* 5,2) and is a major theme in *Holy Virginity* 31-52.

to them. It is, after all, precisely to avoid such evils that they worship their gods, or claim that they ought to be worshiped.

For the family of God responds: Our God is present everywhere, wholly present everywhere, nowhere confined. He can be present without being seen, absent without moving away. When he afflicts me with adversity, he is either testing my merits or chastising my sins, and he is holding an eternal reward for my faithful endurance of temporal evils....

The Perils of Unfettered Prosperity:
Scipio Nasica against Roman Extravagance

30. If the renowned Scipio Nasica, who was once your pontiff, were still alive, he would put a stop to your impudence. During the terror of the Punic War, when a man of the highest qualities was sought, the senate unanimously selected him to bring the sacred objects from Phrygia.[50] But you, perhaps, would hardly dare to look him in the face. For why, when afflicted by adversities, do you complain about these Christian times? Is it not simply because you want to remain secure in your extravagance and to wallow in the most abandoned self-indulgence, exempt from all austerity and hardship? You desire to have peace and all kinds of wealth in abundance, but not so that you may use them honorably — that is, modestly, soberly, moderately, and with godliness. Rather you want them in order to procure an infinite variety of pleasures for your mad excesses, giving rise, in times of prosperity, to moral evils worse than any raging enemies.

It was because he feared just this calamity that Scipio, your chief pontiff, the best of men in the judgment of the whole senate, opposed the destruction of Carthage, then Rome's rival for empire, and spoke against Cato who demanded its destruction.[51] He was afraid that security would be the undoing of frivolous minds, and he saw that terror was needed for the citizens, like a tutor for schoolchildren. Nor was he deceived in his opinion. The event itself proved how truly he had spoken. Once Carthage was destroyed, that is, once the great terror of the Roman republic was repulsed and eliminated, all the evils arising from prosperity immediately followed. First, harmony was corrupted and destroyed by fierce and bloody insurrections. Then, by a chain of evil causes, came the civil wars which brought such great slaughter, so much bloodshed, and such a savage frenzy of desire for proscriptions and plunder,

---

50. P. Cornelius Scipio Nasica (227-c. 171 B.C.) was a Roman politician renowned for his probity and wisdom. The "sacred objects from Phrygia" were in fact a sacred stone attached to the worship of the Phrygian goddess Cybele, sometimes known as the Great Mother (*Magna Mater*). See also below at II,4. Scipio Nasica's having been entrusted with this mission was an indication of the esteem in which he was held. See Livy, *History of Rome* XXIX,14,8.
51. Marcus Porcius Cato, the Elder (234-149 B.C.), opposed Scipio Nasica Corculum, the son of the previous Scipio Nasica (Augustine has confused the two), regarding the treatment of Carthage and was famous for repeating in his speeches in the Roman senate, "Carthage must be destroyed" (*Carthago delenda est*). See Plutarch, *Cato* 27.

that the Romans themselves — who used to fear evils from their enemies when their lives had greater moral integrity — now, with their integrity in ruins, suffered worse cruelties from their fellow citizens. And the lust for domination — which, of all the human vices, is found in its most undiluted form in the whole Roman people — after winning the day in a few of the more powerful, oppressed the rest, worn out and exhausted, under the yoke of servitude.

31. For, once it is embedded in arrogant minds, where can the lust for domination come to rest until, by passing from office to office, it has reached despotic power? In fact, there would be no provision for a sequence of offices if ambition were not so prevalent. But ambition would not be so prevalent except in a people corrupted by avarice and extravagance. And what makes a people avaricious and extravagant is prosperity — the very thing that Nasica, with great foresight, voted to guard against when he opposed destroying the enemy's largest, strongest, and wealthiest city. His aim was to keep lust under the restraint of fear so that lust, thus restrained, would not indulge itself in extravagance. And so, with extravagance under control, avarice would not make mischief; and, with these vices barred, virtue would grow and flourish to the city's benefit, and the liberty consistent with such virtue would endure....

The Theaters and the Gods

How eagerly a man such as this would also have banished theatrical performances themselves from the city of Rome, if only he had dared to resist the authority of those he imagined to be gods![52] He did not understand that these gods are actually pernicious demons;[53] or, if he did, he held that they should be appeased rather than scorned. For the divine teaching which purifies the heart by faith[54] had not yet been revealed to the peoples, the teaching which moves human affections in humble piety to the pursuit of heavenly — or more than heavenly — things and frees them from the domination of prideful demons.

32. Know, then, you who are ignorant of the fact, and you who pretend to be ignorant, and take note, you who mutter complaints against the deliverer who has set you free from such overlords:[55] the theatrical performances, those spectacles of shame and licentious folly, were instituted at Rome not by human vice but at the command of your gods. It would be more tolerable for you to confer divine honors on this Scipio than to worship gods of that sort, for those gods were defi-

---

52. The polemic against theatrical performances that begins here had a long history in early Christian writing. Tertullian's treatise *On the Spectacles* is an early and powerful example.
53. On the commonly accepted notion that the pagan gods were really demons, see Tertullian, *Apology* 22; Marcus Minucius Felix, *Octavius* 27. This idea recurs throughout *The City of God* and forms one of the bases for Augustine's argument against the worship of the pagan gods.
54. See Acts 15:9.
55. I.e., Christ.

nitely not as worthy as their priest. Listen here, then, if your minds, drunk from swilling error for so long, will allow you to think sensibly: the gods commanded theatrical performances to be put on for them in order to end a pestilence of the body; their priest, in contrast, prohibited the building of a theater in order to prevent a pestilence of the soul. If by any light of reason you value the soul more than the body, choose whom to worship! For that bodily pestilence did not abate just because a warlike people, previously accustomed only to the games of the circus, suddenly got caught up in a prissy craze for theatrical shows. Rather, the profane spirits in their guile, seeing that the pestilence was already about to reach its appointed end, took the opportunity to introduce another, far graver pestilence, which is their greatest delight — a pestilence not of bodies but of morals.[56] This blinded the minds of the miserable victims with such darkness and sullied them with such decadence that even now, with Rome just sacked, the people infected by this pestilence who were able to reach Carthage in their flight from Rome are in the theaters every day, raving for their favorite actors. Those who come after us, if they hear of this, may well find it hard to believe!

33. What insanity! What is this error — or rather not error but madness? As we have heard, the peoples of the East and the greatest cities of the uttermost parts of the earth were bewailing your downfall with public grief and mourning. But you were looking for theaters! You entered them, filled them, and behaved even more insanely than you had before. It was just this ruin and bane of souls, just this subversion of probity and integrity, that Scipio feared for you when he prohibited the building of the theater, when he discerned that you could easily be corrupted and subverted by prosperity, when he did not want you to be secure against the terror of an enemy. For he did not consider a republic happy when its walls were standing but its morals were in ruins. You gave more credit, however, to the seductions of impious demons than to the precautions of farsighted men. This is why you do not want to be blamed for the evils you do; this is why you blame the evils you suffer on Christian times. For, in your security, you are seeking not a republic at peace but unpunished extravagance; you were depraved by prosperity, but you could not be corrected by adversity. Scipio wanted you to live in terror of the enemy, so that you would not sink into extravagant living; but, even when crushed by the enemy, you have not suppressed your extravagance. You have lost the chance of gaining from calamity; you have become utterly wretched while, at the same time, you remained utterly foul....

The Intermingling of the Two Cities in this World

35. Let these be the answers — and others, if more fruitful and suitable ones can be found — that the redeemed family of the Lord Christ and the pilgrim city of

---

56. See Livy, *History of Rome* VII,2-3.

Christ the king make to their enemies. Remember, however, that among those very enemies are hidden some who will become citizens, and do not think it fruitless to bear their enmity until they come to confess the faith. By the same token, so long as it is on pilgrimage in this world, the city of God has with it, joined to it by participation in the sacraments,[57] some from the number of its enemies who will not be with it in the eternal destiny of the saints. Some of these are hidden, some out in the open, and, along with its enemies, they do not hesitate to murmur against God, whose sacrament they bear.[58] At one moment, they fill the theaters along with our enemies; at the next, they fill the churches along with us. But we have no reason to despair of the correction of at least some of these, for even among our most open adversaries there lie hidden, still unknown even to themselves, some who are predestined to be friends. In this world, in fact, these two cities remain intermixed and intermingled with each other until they are finally separated at the last judgment.[59] With God's help, I will set out what I think should be said about the origin, the course, and the appointed end of the two cities.[60] This will highlight the glory of the city of God, which will stand out the more clearly when set in contrast to the other city.

[Chapter 36, the final chapter of Book I, provides a brief preview of Book II.]

---

57. "Joined to it by participation in the sacraments": *connexos communione sacramentorum.* Although Augustine is certainly referring here primarily to baptism and the eucharist, he is probably not excluding other practices characteristic of Christianity, which he also understood as sacraments. See Fitzgerald 741-747.
58. "Whose sacrament they bear": *cuius sacramentum gerunt.* The reference is to baptism, whose spiritual effect is borne for life.
59. On the notion of the intermingling of the righteous and the unrighteous until the last judgment see also *On Baptism against the Donatists* IV,3,5; V,27,38; VI,1,1. The idea appears earlier as well in Origen, *Homily on Leviticus* 14,3.
60. This is a summary of Books XI XXII in a single phrase.

Study Questions for Book I

Political and social sanctuary is sought even today around the world in religious buildings or at sacred sites. Oppressed individuals or groups may find respite and relief from prosecution or persecution, at least temporarily. Can you think of recent situations where specific groups have sought and gained sanctuary from legal, political or armed conflict?

The "Gospel of prosperity" is a belief among some Christians today that financial success, along with physical, familial and social wellbeing are God-given rewards inherent in their practice of faithful discipleship. What problems might Augustine have with such a theology?

Rape is still used around the world as a weapon of war. Sexual violence and slavery remain endemic and even tolerated in many societies. Sexual harassment and assault persist in the workplace. What in Augustine's response to the sexual violence he addresses in Book I might inform a contemporary Christian response to such violations of human rights?

BOOK II

Book II briefly summarizes Book I and then turns to its own main argument, namely, that long before the Christian era, Rome's traditional gods had failed to protect it from disaster and calamity; and since these misfortunes predated Christ's human appearance, they cannot be blamed on Christianity or on the prohibition of sacrifices to the gods. The book focuses, in particular, on the failure of the gods to provide any moral guidance or precepts to direct human conduct. Instead they demanded the performance of immoral theatrical productions in their honor which appeared to give the stamp of divine authority and approval to depraved behavior, thus showing that they are not gods at all but rather malignant demons. Within this framework, the book exposes the inconsistencies between the Greek and the Roman attitudes to poets and actors in order to show that the Romans, in prohibiting actors from civic honors, demonstrate a higher moral standard than their own gods and, taking cues from the Roman historian Sallust, chronicles the moral decline of the Roman republic into social disorder and civil war in order to make it clear both that the gods did nothing to discourage or prevent this decline and that, in fact, lacking justice, the republic was not truly a republic at all since it did not represent a people cohering around a "common sense for what is right and a community of interest." The book ends by noting that if the gods provided any secret moral teaching reserved for the initiated few — which is doubtful at best — that secrecy stands in sharp contrast to the open and public moral teaching which Christianity provides for all in its churches. It concludes with an exhortation to the Romans to abandon their false gods and embrace the true God and the heavenly city.

[Chapters 1 – 2 summarize Book I, decry the obstinacy of unreasonable opponents of Augustine's arguments, and introduce Book II.]

2. ... Next I intend to speak about the evils which Rome has endured from its very beginnings, whether in the city itself or in the provinces now subject to it. All of these evils they would blame on the Christian religion, if only the Gospel's teaching had already, at that early point, rung out in its unrestrained witness against their false and fallacious gods.

The Disasters that Afflicted Rome Prior to the Coming of Christ

3. Keep it in mind, however, that in rehearsing these things I am still arguing against the ignorant, against the people whose ignorance has given rise to the popular proverb, "No rain? Blame the Christians!"[1] The well-educated among them, in contrast, love history and readily recognize the facts of the matter. In order to rouse the illiterate mobs to the full pitch of belligerence against us, however, they pretend not to know, and they make every effort to encourage the vulgar notion that the calamities which inevitably afflict humanity at given intervals of time and place occur because of the Christian name which is spreading everywhere, with great renown and unparalleled celebrity, in opposition to their gods.[2]

Let them recall with us, then, all the varied disasters that crushed the Roman state before Christ had come in the flesh and before his name became known among the peoples with all the glory that now sparks their fruitless envy. And if they can, let them defend their gods in this regard, assuming it is true that the whole point of worshiping these gods is precisely to keep their worshipers from suffering such evils as these. If they suffer catastrophes now, they claim that we are to blame. Why is it, then, that the gods allowed the disasters I am about to mention to happen to their worshipers long before the proclamation of Christ's name had caused them to take offence or had put an end to their sacrifices?

The Failure of the Gods to Provide Moral Guidance: the Rites of the Mother of the Gods

4. In the first place, why were their gods unwilling to take any pains to see that they did not fall into the very worst moral practices? The true God had reason to neglect those who did not worship him. But why did those gods — from whose worship these ungrateful people complain that they have been prohibited — provide no laws to help their worshipers to live rightly? Surely it would have been fitting that, just as the worshipers took pains over the rites of their gods, the gods would have taken pains over the conduct of their worshipers.

But, goes the reply, it is by his own will that a person is evil. Who denies that? But it was still incumbent on the gods as advisers not to conceal the precepts of a good life from the people who worshiped them but rather to see that these precepts were clearly set forth. Through prophets they should have addressed and rebuked sinners, openly threatening punishments to evildoers and openly promising rewards to those who lived rightly. But when did anything of this sort, spoken publicly and prominently, ever sound forth in the temples of these gods?

---

1. Tertullian recounts, partly humorously, a similar charge made at the end of the second century in his *Apology* 40: "If the Tiber rises as high as the city walls, if the Nile does not spread its waters over the fields, if the skies give no rain, if there is an earthquake, if there is famine or plague, at once the cry is, 'The Christians to the lion!'"
2. The idea that well-educated persons, who should know better, stir up less-well-educated people to hate Christianity occurs below at IV, 1. The theme hints at Augustine's suspicion of classical education.

As young men we too used to go to sacrilegious shows and entertainments. We watched madmen raving. We listened to singing boys. We took delight in the most degrading shows, presented to gods and goddesses, to the virgin Caelestis and to Berecynthia,[3] mother of them all. At the yearly festival of Berecynthia's purification,[4] in front of her litter, the vilest actors sang songs unfit for the ears I will not say of the mother of the gods but of the mother of any senator or of any decent citizen — unfit, in fact, for the ears of the mothers of the very actors themselves to hear. For there is something, after all, in our human veneration for our parents that not even the very worst vileness can erase. Thus the actors themselves would have been ashamed to rehearse before their mothers at home the obscenities of word and deed that they performed in public before the mother of the gods, with a vast throng of both sexes watching and listening. If enticing curiosity was able to bring the throng together in profusion, offended decency ought at least to have sent it away in confusion!...

6. What this shows is that those divinities took no care for the moral life of the cities and peoples who worshiped them. They allowed them to fall into terrible and detestable evils — not of field and vine, not of household and property, not even of the body which is subject to the mind, but of the very mind itself, which rules the flesh. They allowed them to fall into the moral depths, and they issued no dread prohibition to prevent this....

Did the Gods Sponsor any Public Teaching of Virtue?

7. Or will they perhaps remind us of the schools and disputations of the philosophers? In the first place these are not Roman but Greek; or if they are now to be considered Roman, since Greece too has become a Roman province, they are not precepts from the gods but rather the findings of human beings who, endowed with the keenest intelligence, tried by reasoning to discover what lay at the hidden roots of the natural world, what we should aspire to and what we should spurn in the moral life, as well as what follows, according to the very rules of reasoning, by valid inference and what does not follow or even leads to contradiction. Some of

---

3. Augustine may be treating Caelestis and Berecynthia as two separate goddesses here, as they had been in previous centuries, although by his time they were probably a single goddess under two names. Caelestis in particular was highly esteemed in North Africa and especially so in Carthage. She was adopted by the Romans, where she was usually identified with Juno and also known as Dea Caelestis ("the heavenly goddess") and Virgo Caelestis ("the heavenly virgin") See the following note and further references to Caelestis below at II,26.
4. Berecynthia was also known as Cybele, the Great Mother and "the mother of the gods," as she is called in the next few lines. The solemn reception of sacred objects associated with her at Rome under the aegis of Scipio Nasica is mentioned above at I,30. On each anniversary of this reception the sacred image was purified, or washed, with great pomp in a tributary of the Tiber River. For Varro's relatively detailed description of the Great Mother and aspects of her cult see below at VII,24, where she is identified with the goddess Tellus (Earth).

these philosophers, insofar as they were divinely assisted, did in fact make great discoveries. Insofar as they were held back by human infirmity, however, they went astray, especially when divine providence rightly resisted their pride in order to show, by contrast, that it is from humility that the way of godliness mounts on high.

But if the philosophers really did discover anything that could serve the purpose of living the good life and attaining the blessed life, how much more just it would have been to award divine honors to people such as them! How much better and more honorable it would have been for Plato's works to be read in a temple of Plato than for Galli to be castrated,[5] or the effeminate to be consecrated, or madmen to gash themselves in the temples of demons — or whatever other kind of cruelty and perversion, perversely cruel and cruelly perverse, was customarily celebrated in the rites of such gods! How much more satisfactory it would have been for training the young in justice to have the laws of the gods recited in public rather than wasting empty praise on the laws and regulations of the ancients. For the worshipers of such gods — once "desire tinctured with burning poison," as Persius says,[6] starts driving them on — would all rather fix their attention on Jupiter's deeds than on Plato's teaching or Cato's views. Thus, in Terence's play, the wanton youth gazes at a certain picture painted on the wall, "where was depicted how Jove is said once to have sent a golden shower down on Danae's lap";[7] and from such a great authority as this he draws a precedent for his own disgraceful conduct, boasting that in his act he is imitating a god. "And what a god," he says, "who from the heights of heaven shakes the temples with his thunder! Should I, a mere man, not do the same? Indeed, I did it, and with pleasure."[8]...

The Fables of the Poets and the Shows in the Theaters

8. ...There are also more acceptable theatrical shows, namely, comedies and tragedies — that is, poets' fables designed to be performed in public performances with much immorality of action but at least written, unlike many others, with no obscenity of language. These are even included in the studies of what is called an admirable and liberal education, and the older generation compels youngsters to read and to learn them.[9]

---

5. The Galli were the castrated priests of Cybele, who were mocked by both pagan and Christian writers. See Apuleius, *Golden Ass* 8; Juvenal, *Satires* 2; Justin Martyr, 1 *Apology* 27; Marcus Minucius Felix, *Octavius* 24.
6. *Satires* III,37.
7. *Eunuch* 584-585. Jupiter, in love with Danae, the daughter of Acrisius of Argos, transformed himself into a shower of gold that fell upon her lap and impregnated her.
8. Ibid. 590-591. For similar indignation over these few lines of Terence see also *Confessions* I, 16,26.
9. This is one of many places in his writings in which Augustine deplores the effects of a liberal education — as it was practiced at the time — on children. See especially *Confessions* I,13,20-18,31.

The Greeks and the Romans on Poets and Actors

9. What the earlier Romans thought on this score is made plain by Cicero in *The Republic*, where Scipio argues that "the comedies could never have won acceptance for their depravities in the theater, if the customs of daily life had not already paved the way for them."[10] And the even earlier Greeks at least maintained a kind of consistency in their flawed view. Among them, it was secured by law that comedy might say anything it liked, about anyone it liked, and do so by name. Thus, as Africanus[11] says in the same work, "Was there anyone comedy did not lay its hands on, or rather anyone it did not abuse? Was anyone spared? Certainly it ridiculed unprincipled demagogues who were stirring up discord in the state, men like Cleon, Cleophon, and Hyperbolus. Let us accept that, even though it is better for such citizens to be reprimanded by a censor than by a poet. But for Pericles[12] to be defiled in verse — and this produced on the stage — when he had led his city with the greatest authority for so many years, both in war and in peace, was no more appropriate than if our own Plautus or Naevius had decided to malign Publius and Gnaeus Scipio, or Caecilius to malign Marcus Cato." Then, a little later, he says, "Our Twelve Tables,[13] in contrast, although they prescribed the death penalty in only a very few cases, determined that among those few should be included the writing or reciting of a poem which defamed or disgraced another person. An admirable point! For our lives should be open to the judgment of magistrates and to legal adjudication, not exposed to the ingenuity of poets, nor should we give a hearing to the vilification of others without making legal provision for them to reply and to defend themselves in court."[14] I considered it best to take these excerpts word for word from the fourth book of Cicero's *Republic* (apart from omitting or transposing a few phrases for ease of understanding), for they are most relevant to the point I am trying hard to explain if I can. After making some further comments, Cicero concludes this topic by showing that it displeased the ancient Romans for any living person to be either praised or disparaged on the stage.

But the Greeks, as I noted, were more consistent, if more shameless, in allowing the practice. They saw that to discredit not only human beings but even the gods themselves in fables for the stage was acceptable and pleasing to their gods, whether they were discredited for depravities invented by the poets or for their actual depravities as reported by their worshipers and enacted in the theaters. (Would that these had seemed worthy only of a laugh and not also of actually being

---

10. *Republic* IV,10.
11. I.e., Scipio, who was given the name Africanus after having defeated Hannibal in the battle of Zama in north Africa in 202 B.C., thus concluding the Second Punic War.
12. Pericles (c. 495-429 B.C.) was an Athenian statesman and orator who gave his name to the period of Athens's greatest flourishing, the so-called "Age of Pericles."
13. The Twelve Tables, adopted and published in the middle of the fifth century B.C. in Rome, were a series of laws touching on different aspects of civil and private life. Very little of them has survived.
14. *Republic* IV,10.

imitated!) For it would have smacked too much of pride to spare the reputation of the city's leaders and citizens when the divinities themselves had no wish to have their own reputations spared....

[Chapters 10 – 13 argue that the Greek and Roman gods and goddesses are actually masquerading demons who trick humans into sacrilegious worship and incite them to destructive behaviors that imitate the immoral exploits of divinities portrayed on stage.]

13. ...Furthermore, although the Romans were driven by noxious superstition to worship the very gods who, as they saw, wanted theatrical obscenities to be consecrated in their honor, they still had enough concern for their own dignity and decency that they never honored the actors of these fables the way the Greeks did. In fact, as Scipio says in Cicero's work, "Since they held the dramatic arts and the theater generally in complete contempt, they decided not only to bar actors from the honors of civic life open to others but even to remove them from their tribe by notation of the censor."[15] This shows eminent good sense, and it is to be reckoned to the Romans' credit. But I could wish that their good sense had taken its own cue and had followed its own example. How right they were! Any Roman citizen who chose a theatrical career was not only denied any place of civic honor but was also barred by the censor's notation from keeping his place in his own tribe. Here was the genuinely Roman spirit, the spirit of a city eager to uphold its honor. But let someone tell me this: How can it be consistent, on the one hand, to exclude theatrical performers from all civic honor and, on the other, to include theatrical performances among the honors of the gods? For a long time Roman virtue knew nothing of the theatrical arts. If these arts had been sought out simply for the gratification of human pleasure, it would only have been through a flaw in human morality that they crept in. In fact, however, it was the gods who demanded that the shows be put on for them. How then can the actor be rejected when he is the very one through whom a god is worshiped? How can anyone have the gall to put a censor's notation on the actors of these theatrical obscenities and still adore the gods who exact these same obscenities?

Let the Greeks and the Romans fight it out in this dispute. The Greeks think they are right to honor actors because they worship the gods who demand the theatrical shows; the Romans do not allow actors to demean even a plebeian tribe, let alone the senate house. In this debate the following syllogism resolves the chief point at issue. The Greeks state the major premise: if such gods are to be worshiped, then surely such men are to be honored. The Romans add the minor premise: but such men are by no means to be honored. The Christians draw the conclusion: therefore such gods are by no means to be worshiped.

---

15. Ibid. IV,10.

Plato on the Poets

14. I want to ask next why the poets themselves, the authors of these fables, are not considered just as disreputable as the actors. They are prohibited by the law of the Twelve Tables from injuring the reputation of citizens, and yet they hurl scurrilous abuse against the gods. On what conceivable grounds is it right for the actors of poetic fictions that degrade the gods to be held in disgrace while the authors are held in honor? Perhaps the palm of victory should go rather to Plato, the Greek. When he reasoned out what the civic community should be like, he held that the poets should be banished from the city as enemies of the truth.[16] He was outraged at their abuse of the gods, and he had no wish for the minds of the citizens to be tainted and corrupted by the poet's fictions.

Now compare the humanity of Plato, banning the poets from the city to prevent them from deceiving the citizens, with the divinity of the gods, demanding theatrical shows in their own honor. Plato urged the frivolous and licentious Greeks[17] to keep such shows from even being written (although his argument did not persuade them). The gods in contrast, by their command, compelled the grave and conscientious Romans to have such shows not only written but also performed. And they wanted the shows not just to be performed but to be dedicated to themselves, to be consecrated to themselves, to be presented to themselves in solemn rites. To which, then, would it be more honorable for a city to award divine honors? To Plato, who prohibited these shameful and detestable shows, or to the demons, who delighted in deceiving the very people whom Plato could not persuade of the truth? Labeo held that Plato should be commemorated among the demigods, like Hercules and Romulus, and he ranks the demigods above the heroes, though he counts both among the divinities.[18] All the same, I have no doubt that the one he designates a demigod should be ranked not only above the heroes but above the very gods themselves....

16. Moreover, if the Romans had been able to receive laws for right living from their gods, they would not have needed to borrow the laws of Solon from the Athenians some years after Rome was founded.[19] (They did not simply keep those laws as they received them, however, but tried to improve and perfect them.) Note, too, that, even though Lycurgus put it out that he had established laws for the

---

16. See ibid. III,398a.
17. "Frivolous and licentious Greeks": *levitati lasciviaeque Graecorum*. As frivolous and licentious as they may have been, they compare favorably with the grave and conscientious Romans (*gravitati et modestiae Romanorum*) of the following sentence. See also above at I,4.
18. Cornelius Labeo was an important pagan theologian who flourished probably in the third century A.D. His distinction between good and bad gods was a significant one, although he may not have been the first to make it. Nothing is left of his writings except fragments.
19. See Livy, *History of Rome* III,31,8. Solon (c. 638-558 B.C.) was an Athenian statesman and legislator of whom very little has survived; his legislative wisdom was legendary.

Lacedaemonians on Apollo's authority,[20] the Romans sensibly refused to believe this, and, as a consequence, they took nothing from that source.[21] Numa Pompilius, who succeeded Romulus on the throne, is reported to have instituted certain laws (which, however, were by no means sufficient for governing the city),[22] and among these he established many sacred rites. But he is not said to have received any of these laws from divinities. Thus the Romans' gods took no care at all to safeguard their worshipers from evils of mind, evils of life, evils of moral conduct — evils which are so devastating that the Romans' own most learned men affirm that, through them, a republic is brought down to ruin even when its cities are still standing. Their gods' whole care was rather, as asserted above, to see that these evils would increase.

The Natural "Justice and Goodness" of the Romans

17. Perhaps the reason why the divinities established no laws for the Roman people is that, as Sallust says, "justice and goodness prevailed among them not so much by laws as by nature"?[23] It was from this "justice and goodness," I suppose, that the rape of the Sabine women came about.[24] For what is more just and good than to use the pretence of a show to lure in another people's daughters and then, instead of receiving them from their parents in marriage, to carry them off by force, each man as he could? For if the Sabines were wrong in refusing the request for their daughters, it was still far more wrong to seize them when they had not been given. And it would have been more just to wage war on a people who had refused a request for their daughters in marriage from a neighboring people, who shared the same country, than on a people who were requesting the return of their abducted daughters. That is how it should have happened, and in that case Mars might have helped his son in his struggle to avenge with arms the wrong done to him by the refusal of marriage and to attain in this way the women he wanted.[25] For some law of war, perhaps, might have justified a victor in carrying off women who had been unjustly refused. No law of peace, however, justified him in snatching away women who had not been given and then waging an unjust war on their parents who were justly enraged. The upshot, however, was more beneficial and fortunate: even though the circus games continued to be held as a memorial of the deception, the precedent of the crime itself found no favor in Rome's city and

---

20. See Cicero, *On Divination* I,43.
21. Lycurgus was a Spartan lawgiver. Some historians argue that he never existed, while those who say that he did place him in the years from c. 800 to c. 730 B.C.
22. See Cicero, *On Laws* II,10.
23. *Catiline Conspiracy* 9.
24. The so-called rape of the Sabine women is recorded in Livy, *History of Rome* I,9 and, according to legend, occurred soon after the founding of Rome. It is referred to again below at III,13.
25. According to legend, Romulus, who helped precipitate the abduction of the Sabine women, was the son of Mars, the god of war, and Ilia, a daughter of the King of Alba.

empire. It proved easier for the Romans to go wrong in consecrating Romulus as a god, even after his injustice, than to go wrong by permitting, in any law or custom, the imitation of his action in abducting women.

From this same "justice and goodness," after the expulsion of King Tarquin and his children — Tarquin's son had violently raped Lucretia — the consul Junius Brutus forced Lucius Tarquinius Collatinus, Lucretia's husband and his own fellow consul, a good and innocent man, to go into exile for no more reason than that he was related to the Tarquins and carried the Tarquin name.[26] Brutus carried out this crime with the support and favor of the people, the very people from whom that same Collatinus had received the consulship, as had Brutus himself.

From this same "justice and goodness," Marcus Camillus, an outstanding man of his era, was put on trial due to the envy of those who disparaged his virtue and the insolence of the tribunes of the people. After ten years of war, during which the Roman army fought poorly and was so gravely afflicted that Rome itself was cast into fear and doubt about its own safety, Camillus easily vanquished the Veians, the most dire of the enemies of the Roman people, and took their city captive with all its wealth. Then, sensing the ingratitude of the city he had liberated and convinced that he would be found guilty, he voluntarily went into exile and, in his absence, was fined 10,000 asses, despite the fact that he was soon to deliver his ungrateful country once again, this time from the Gauls.[27]

But it would be burdensome to recall all the foul and unjust actions by which Rome was convulsed during the time when the powerful were trying to subjugate the common people and the people were resisting subjugation. The leaders of both parties, in their zeal, acted far more from love of victory than from any thought for what might be equitable and good.

Roman Morality, the Constraint of Fear, and the Destruction of Carthage

18. I shall hold myself back, therefore, and shall instead simply cite the witness of Sallust. It was his praise of the Romans that gave my discussion its point of departure: "Justice and goodness prevailed among them not so much by laws as by nature." He was speaking of the period just after the expulsion of the kings when, in an unbelievably short space of time, the city experienced enormous growth. Yet he also admits, at the very start of the first book of his history, that even then, when government had passed from kings to consuls, oppressive actions by the powerful soon led to the alienation of the common people from the patricians, as well as to other discords in the city. He notes that it was during the period between the second and the last wars against Carthage that the Roman people conducted

---

26. See Livy, *History of Rome* I,58; II,2. See also above at I,19.
27. See ibid. V,21.32.46.49-50. Marcus Furius Camillus (c. 446-365 B.C.) was hailed as the second founder of Rome for his military deeds.

themselves with the highest morality and the greatest harmony, and he states that the reason for this moral goodness was not love of justice but rather sheer fear that no peace could be trusted so long as Carthage was still standing, which is why Nasica, seeking to restrain wickedness and to preserve that high moral conduct, opposed the destruction of Carthage with the aim of keeping vice in check through fear.[28] Sallust himself immediately adds, "But after the destruction of Carthage, discord, greed, ambition, and the other evils that ordinarily spring from prosperity increased all the more"[29] — and by saying "all the more" he gives us to understand that these evils used to arise and increase even before this. Then he goes on to give the reason why he said this: "For oppression by the more powerful, leading to the alienation of the people from the patricians and to other discords in the city, was present right from the beginning, and rule by equitable and moderate law, after the expulsion of the kings, lasted only so long as the fear of Tarquin and the draining war with Etruria continued."[30] You see how he states that, even during this brief period, it was due to fear that equitable and moderate law ruled for the most part after the kings were expelled, that is, were banished. And what the Romans feared was the war that King Tarquin was waging against them, in alliance with the Etruscans, after he was driven from his throne and from the city. And notice how Sallust goes on: "From then on, the patricians ordered the common people about like slaves, devalued their lives and their persons in the manner of the kings, drove them from their land, and, with the rest excluded, exercised power strictly on their own. Crushed by this savage treatment and especially by extortionate interest rates, and at the same time bearing the double burden of taxation and military service in ceaseless wars, the people finally armed themselves and took up a position on the Mons Sacer and the Aventine. And so they gained the tribunes of the people and other rights for themselves. The discord and strife only came to an end with the second Punic War."[31] You see, then, what the Romans were like after that time, that is, after the brief interval following the expulsion of the kings. And these are the people of whom Sallust claims that "justice and goodness prevailed among them not so much by laws as by nature"!

And if this is what the times were like when the Roman republic is said to have been at its finest and best, what are we to say or to think now of the following era when "little by little" — to use the words of the same historian — the republic "changed from the finest and best to become the worst and most depraved,"[32] that is, as Sallust records, during the period after the destruction of Carthage. How Sallust himself briefly recalls and describes this era can be read in his history. He shows how the moral evils which arose from prosperity led finally to civil wars. "From that time on," as he says, "the decline of traditional morality no longer took place

---

28. See above at I,30.
29. *History* I, fragment 10.
30. Ibid.
31. Ibid.
32. *Catiline Conspiracy* 5.

little by little, as before, but like a rushing torrent. The young were so corrupted by luxury and greed that it would be right to say that this was a generation which could neither preserve their own family property nor bear to have others preserve theirs."[33] Sallust then dwells on the vices of Sulla and other disgraces to the republic,[34] and other writers agree on this point, although they write far less eloquently.

So you see, I take it (and anyone who pays the slightest attention can hardly fail to notice) that Rome had sunk into the dregs of the worst immorality well before the coming of our heavenly king. For this all happened not only before Christ, present in the flesh, had begun to teach, but even before he was born of a virgin. The Romans do not dare to blame their gods for all the terrible moral evils of those times, whether the less serious evils of the earlier period or the more serious and horrible evils that followed the destruction of Carthage, even though it was precisely these gods who, with malignant cunning, sowed in human minds the outlook that produced such a wild tangle of vices. Why, then, do they blame Christ for the evils of the present, when Christ by his saving doctrine forbids the worship of false and deceiving gods? When Christ by divine authority denounces and condemns humanity's pernicious and shameful desires? When Christ everywhere withdraws his family by slow degrees from a world wasting and decaying with these evils in order to found with them an eternal and most glorious city — most glorious not as measured by vanity's applause but as measured by truth's own verdict?

19. There you have it: "little by little" the Roman republic "changed from the finest and best to become the worst and most depraved." (I am not the first to say this; their own authors, from whom we learned these things for a fee,[35] said it long ago, long before the coming of Christ.) There you have it: before the coming of Christ, after the destruction of Carthage, "the decline of traditional morality no longer took place little by little as before but like a rushing torrent. The young were so corrupted by luxury and greed."…

20. But the worshipers and lovers of the Roman gods, whom they delight to imitate even in the gods' most wicked and disgraceful acts, have no concern at all that the republic not be the worst and most depraved. "As long as it stands," they say, "as long as it flourishes, rich in its resources and glorious in its victories, or — better yet — secure in its peace, what has any of this to do with us? Our concern is rather for each of us to get richer all the time. It is wealth that sustains daily extravagance. It is through wealth that the powerful subject the weak to themselves. Let the poor fawn on the rich for the sake of filling their bellies and

---

33. *History* I, fragment 13.
34. See ibid. Lucius Cornelius Sulla (c. 138-78 B.C.) was a distinguished Roman statesman and general whose legacy was mixed, but who was generally esteemed for his achievements. Augustine finds much to admire in him, while regretting his eventual descent into violent injustice.
35. The mention of a fee suggests a certain contempt for the teachers, although their accepting a fee was completely justified. See *Confessions* I,13,22.

in order to enjoy a life of laziness under their patronage. Let the rich make ill use of the poor to gain clients for themselves and to feed their own arrogance. Let the people applaud not those who look out for their benefit but those who provide for their pleasure. Let nothing harsh be commanded and nothing shameful be prohibited. Let kings care only that their subjects are docile, not that they are good. Let provinces be subject to kings not as directors of conduct but as lords over their fate and providers of their pleasures, and let them honor their rulers not in sincere regard but in servile fear. Let the laws address harm done to another's vineyard rather than harm done to one's own moral character. Let no one be brought to court unless he threatens or actually does harm to another's property, house, or security against that person's will. Otherwise let everyone do whatever he wishes with what belongs to him, whether with his own people or with anyone else who is willing. Let there be plenty of public prostitutes for the sake of all who like to enjoy them and especially for the sake of those who cannot afford private mistresses. Let vast and lavishly furnished houses be built and sumptuous banquets be held where, day and night, anyone who wants can play, drink, vomit, and abandon himself. Let the din of dancing resound on all sides, and let the theaters boil over with cries of indecent delight and with every kind of cruel and shameful pleasure carried to the highest pitch. If anyone disapproves of this kind of happiness, let him be branded a public enemy. If anyone tries to change it or do away with it, let the uninhibited mob stop his mouth, toss him out, kill him off. Let those be considered the true gods who see to it that the people get this sort of happiness and who preserve it for them once they have it. Let these gods be worshiped as they wish; let them demand any shows they want, whatever they can afford with their worshipers — or from them. Just let them make sure that such happiness has nothing to fear from any enemy, any plague, or any kind of calamity at all."...

The Issue of Justice and Scipio's Definition of a Republic

21. But perhaps they scoff at the one who claimed that the Roman republic was "the worst and most depraved." Perhaps they do not care that it overflows with the shame and infamy of the worst and most depraved immorality, just so long as it continues to exist and endure. In that case, let them hear not Sallust's tale of how it became "the worst and most depraved" but Cicero's argument that in his day it had entirely perished and no republic at all remained. Cicero introduces Scipio — the very one who had destroyed Carthage[36] — and presents him as discussing the republic at a time when people were already beginning to sense that it was about to perish due to the corruption that Sallust describes. In fact, the discussion is set at the point when one of the Gracchi had already been put to death (and it was

---

36. This is the same Scipio who appears above at I,30, who is also referred to as Africanus. There is a question as to whether this is the same Scipio or whether Augustine is confusing two of the same name.

with the Gracchi, as Sallust writes, that the serious seditions began), for his death is recorded in that same work.[37]

At the end of Cicero's second book, Scipio says, "In music for strings or flutes and in song and vocal music, a certain harmony must be maintained among the different sounds, and if this is altered or discordant, the trained ear cannot bear to hear it. This harmony in concord and agreement is achieved by means of the modulation of highly dissimilar voices. And in the same way, from the high, the low, and between them the middle orders of society, as from sounds, a city comes together in agreement by means of a consensus, modulated by reason, of its very different parts. Now what the musicians call harmony in singing corresponds to concord in a city, which is the best and closest bond of well-being in a republic; and, without justice, it cannot exist at all."[38]

After Scipio had gone on to discuss more broadly and fully the great advantage of justice to the city and the great disadvantage of its absence, Philus, another of the participants in the discussion, intervened to ask that this very issue be considered in more detail and that more be said, in particular, on the topic of justice, inasmuch as it was then a commonplace to claim that a republic cannot be governed without injustice. Scipio accordingly agreed that this point should be pursued and explained. He replied that, in his view, nothing they had said so far about a republic provided any basis for continuing unless they first established not only that it is false that a republic cannot be governed without injustice but also that it is true beyond any doubt that a republic cannot be governed without the most supreme justice.[39]...

Scipio's Definition of a Republic

Once this point was treated satisfactorily, Scipio returns to the interrupted theme and recalls and recommends his own brief definition of a republic which, he had said, is the common good of a people.[40] He stipulates, however, that a people is not just any assembly of a multitude but rather an assembly joined together by a common sense for what is right and a community of interest. He then explains the great advantage of definition in debate, and he goes on to conclude from these definitions of his that a republic — that is, the common good of a people — only exists when it is well and justly governed, whether by a single king or by a few of the most prominent men or by the people as a whole.[41] But when the king is unjust (in this case, following the Greeks, he called the king a tyrant), or the most

---

37. The brothers Tiberius and Gaius Gracchus were second-century B.C. figures who attempted to reform the Roman polity; each suffered a violent death. Augustine mentions them again in III,24 and seems to view them at once cautiously and sympathetically.
38. *Republic* II,42-43.
39. See ibid. II,44.
40. See ibid. I,25. On translating Cicero's Latin for "republic" (*res publica*), see above at p. xiii.
41. See ibid. I,26.

prominent men are unjust (he termed the consensus of such men a faction), or the people itself is unjust (for this case he found no term in common use, although he might also have called the people itself a tyrant), the republic is not simply flawed, as had been argued the day before. Rather, as logical deduction from his definitions would show, it does not exist at all. For there is no common good of a people when a tyrant or a faction has taken it over, nor is the people itself any longer a people if it is unjust, since it is no longer a multitude joined together by a common sense for what is right and a community of interest — which was the very definition of a people. Thus, when the Roman republic was in the sorry state Sallust described, it was not simply "the worst and most depraved," as he claimed. In fact, according to the reasoning set out in this discussion of the republic by its great leaders of the time, it did not exist at all.

Cicero: the Republic Has Perished

Again, at the beginning of his fifth book, where he is speaking in his own right, not in the person of Scipio or anyone else, Cicero first quotes a line from the poet Ennius: "The mores and the men of old sustain the Roman state."[42] "This line," he goes on to say, "by virtue of both its brevity and its truth seems to me like something uttered by an oracle. For neither the men, if the mores had not been what they were, nor the mores, if these men had not been in charge, would have been able either to found such a great republic or to preserve it for so long, holding sway over such a vast and broad domain. Thus, long before any time we can remember, our ancestral way of life brought forth outstanding men, and these excellent men maintained the ancient ways and institutions of their elders. But our era received the republic like a magnificent painting that was fading with age, and it not only neglected to renew its original colors but did not even care enough to preserve at least its faint outline and the last remnants of its design. For what is left of the ancient mores which, as Ennius said, sustained the Roman state? We see them so fallen into oblivion that they are not only not cultivated but are scarcely even known. And what about the men? The ancient mores were lost for lack of such men, and we must not only be held accountable for so great an evil but must even somehow plead our case as if we were facing a capital charge. For it is due to our own vices, not to any mere chance or accident, that we now retain the republic in name only, having long ago lost it in reality."[43]

Cicero made this admission long after the death of Africanus, whom he took as one of the participants in the discussion in his work on *The Republic*, but still well before the coming of Christ.[44] If anyone had thought or said such things after the Christian religion had spread and was gaining strength, what Roman would not

---

42. The line is taken from *Annals*, fragments, XVIII.
43. Ibid. V,1.
44. Cicero lived from 106 to 43 B.C., and hence died four decades before the birth of Christ.

have claimed that the Christians were the ones to blame for this state of affairs? Why is it, then, that their own gods took no care to prevent the ruin and loss of the republic, whose loss Cicero so lugubriously laments long before Christ came in the flesh? Those who praise the republic should take a second look at its character in the time of "the mores and men of old," asking themselves whether true justice prevailed or whether even then, perhaps, it was not really alive in human conduct but was actually no more than a picture painted in as yet unfaded colors. For Cicero himself unwittingly suggested as much in the way he spoke of it.

God willing, however, we will look into this matter elsewhere.[45] For, in the appropriate place, I will try to show that, according to Cicero's own definitions of a republic and of a people, as briefly expressed through the mouth of Scipio (and as attested by many other statements in the discussion, statements made both by Cicero himself and by the characters he portrays as taking part in the debate), that republic never actually existed, because there was no true justice in it. According to more plausible definitions, of course, it was a republic in a way, and it was better administered by the earlier Romans than by their descendants. True justice, however, exists only in the republic whose founder and ruler is Christ — if indeed we want to call this too a republic, since we cannot deny that it is the common good of a people. But if this use of the term, which is ordinarily employed in other contexts with other meanings, is too remote from our usual way of speaking, true justice certainly exists in the city of which Holy Scripture says, *Glorious things are spoken of you, O city of God* (Ps 87:3)....

Had the Gods Withdrawn?

22. ... Faced with the immorality of such citizens as these, perhaps the Romans will dare to cite in defense of their gods, as they usually do, the well-known lines from Virgil, "They have all withdrawn, deserting shrine and altar, the gods by whom this realm once stood firm."[46] If so, then, first, they have no reason to complain that the gods deserted them because they took offense at the Christian religion. For their own ancestors, by their immoral conduct, had already driven that throng of tiny gods away from the city's altars like flies. But then, where was this crowd of divinities when, long before the decay of the ancient morality set in, Rome was taken and burned by the Gauls? Perhaps they were present but asleep? On that occasion, the whole city fell into the hands of the enemy. Only the Capitoline Hill remained, and it too would have been taken except that the geese, at least, stayed alert while the gods slept.[47] As a result, Rome very nearly fell into

---

45. See below at XIX,21.24.
46. *Aeneid* II,351-352.
47. The story of Rome saved from the Gauls by the honking of geese that were sacred to the goddess Juno is a famous one; the siege of the Gauls occurred c. 390 B.C. See Livy, *History of Rome* V,47.

the superstition of the Egyptians, who worship animals and birds, for they celebrated an annual festival of the goose.[48]

At the moment, however, my concern is not external evils such as these, evils of the body rather than the mind, whether brought about by enemy action or by some other disaster. At this point, I am dealing rather with the decay of morality which at first faded out little by little and then fell headlong like a torrent until — even though the walls and buildings remained intact — the republic was so ruined that even its preeminent authors do not hesitate to say that it was lost. Of course, the gods would have been right to withdraw, deserting shrine and altar, so that all was lost, if it were true that the city had despised the precepts they gave on justice and right living. But what kind of gods were they, I ask, if they were unwilling to live with a people that worshiped them, a people that lived evilly only because they themselves had done nothing to teach the people to live rightly?

The Gods and the Civil Wars: Marius

23. And what about the fact that these gods seem quite ready to assist people in gratifying their desires but clearly have no interest in helping people to restrain desire? They helped Marius, for example, who was an upstart of ignoble birth and ruthless in starting and waging civil wars, to become consul seven times and to die an old man during his seventh consulship so that he would not fall into the hands of Sulla, who would shortly be victorious.[49] And if it is not true that they helped Marius in these achievements, then it is no small thing to have it granted that so much of the temporal felicity they love so much can come to a person even without the favor of the gods. It is no small thing to have it granted that men like Marius can accumulate and enjoy health and strength, riches and honors, esteem and long life, in spite of the anger of the gods, while men like Regulus can be tormented by captivity, servitude, want, sleeplessness, and pain, and finally be put to death,[50] even though they have the gods as their friends. If they concede this point, they acknowledge at a stroke that the gods bring no benefits and that their worship is a waste of time. For if the gods made it a point that people should learn the very opposite of the virtues of soul and the proper ways of life whose rewards are to be hoped for after death, and if, with regard to the transient and temporal goods of

---

48. The Egyptian cult of animals is frequently mentioned in both pagan and Christian literature, often mockingly. See Cicero, *On the Nature of the Gods* I,36,101; *Tusculan Disputations* V,27; Clement of Alexandria, *Protreptikos* II,39; Origen, *Against Celsus* I,20. On the annual Roman celebration in honor of the goose, no longer observed by Augustine's time, see Plutarch, *On Roman Fortune* 12.
49. Marius and Sulla were engaged in violent civil strife on opposite sides, and each suffered defeat from the other. The victory had been Marius's when he died shortly after having become consul for a seventh unprecedented time. See Livy, *Periochae* 67-68. In Augustine's view, Sulla's faction was the more just of the two.
50. See above at I,15.

this life, they neither harm those whom they hate nor help those whom they love, what conceivable reason is there to worship them? What reason is there to demand their worship with such zeal? What reason is there to murmur in times of hardship as if the gods had taken offence and withdrawn? What reason is there to defame and revile the Christian religion with unworthy complaints on their account? On the other hand, if the gods do have the power of doing good or evil in these matters, why did they help Marius, the worst of men, and abandon Regulus, the best? Or should we suppose, on this basis, that the gods themselves are utterly wicked and unjust? And if people think that the gods should be feared and worshiped all the more for precisely this reason, let them give up that idea as well. For we find that Regulus worshiped them no less than Marius did. Nor should anyone think that, because the gods are presumed to have favored Marius more than Regulus, the life to be chosen is the one that is morally the worst. For Metellus, most excellent of Romans, had five sons who became consuls and enjoyed good fortune in temporal affairs as well,[51] while Cataline, the worst of the worst, met ill fortune, being weighed down by poverty and destroyed in a war brought on by his own crime.[52] And in any case, the truest and most certain happiness actually falls to the good, the worshipers of God, by whom alone it can be bestowed.

Thus, when the republic was perishing due to its moral failure, their gods in fact did nothing either to direct or to correct its ways so as to keep it from perishing. Instead, they added to its moral perversion and corruption so as to make sure that it would perish. And let not the gods pretend that they were good on the pretext that they withdrew, as if offended by the citizens' iniquity. They were most certainly present. They are unmasked; they are convicted: they could not help by giving precepts, nor could they hide by remaining silent....

[Chapter 24 reviews the devastation brought upon the Roman Republic by civil wars and the cruelty of the despot Sulla.]

25. ...I have been prompted to say these things because their own writers have not hesitated to say and write that the Roman republic had already perished due to its citizens' utter immorality and that it had wholly ceased to exist long before the coming of our Lord Jesus Christ. They do not blame their own gods for this ruin, but they blame our Christ for those transitory evils by which the good cannot be destroyed, regardless of whether they live or die. And they do this even though our Christ repeatedly delivered precepts supporting the highest morality and opposing moral corruption, while their own gods provided no such precepts for

---

51. Caecilius Metellus Macedonicus (c. 210-c. 116 B.C.) was considered the model of Roman good fortune and wellbeing. He had four sons, not five, all of whom became consuls.
52. Lucius Sergius Catalina, or Cataline (108-62 B.C.), engineered an attempt to overthrow the Roman republic in 63 B.C.

the people that worshiped them in order to keep the republic from perishing. In fact, by corrupting the republic's morality through the baneful authority of their own example, they worked rather to ensure that it would perish.

No one, I think, will now dare to claim that the republic perished at that point because the gods had "all withdrawn, deserting shrine and altar," as if they were friends of virtue offended at human vice. They are proved to have been present by all the signs — in entrails, in auguries, in prophecies — through which they were so eager to vaunt and commend themselves as foreseers of future events and as helpers in battle. If they had really withdrawn, the Romans would have been kindled far less fiercely to civil war, moved only by their own dark desires and not by the prodding of the gods....

[Chapters 26 – 27 show that the gods provided no moral teaching, either secret, hidden, or otherwise.]

Christianity's Public Teaching

28. Through Christ's name, humanity is rescued from the hellish yoke and penal society of those unclean powers and is brought over from the dark night of destructive impiety to the bright light of saving piety. The wicked and the ungrateful, held deep and tight in the grasp of that abominable spirit, mutter and complain about this. They resent the streams of people who flow to church in chaste celebration and with a decent separation of the sexes. There the people hear how they should live rightly here on earth for a time so that, after this life, they may live in blessedness forever. There the Sacred Scriptures and the teaching of righteousness sound out from an elevated place in the sight of all;[53] those who follow the teaching hear it to their gain, and those who do not, hear it to their condemnation. There, even if some come to scoff at these precepts, they either renounce all their insolence in a sudden change of heart or suppress it out of fear or shame. Where the precepts of the true God are commended or his miracles narrated or his gifts praised or his benefits implored, there is nothing shameful or disgraceful presented for them to watch or to imitate.

An Exhortation to the Romans to Abandon their False Gods

29. Desire these things, then, O admirable Roman character, O offspring of the Reguli, the Scaevolae, the Scipios and the Fabricii.[54] Desire these things. See how

---

53. This marks a relatively rare liturgical reference in Augustine's writings. He alludes not only to the Scripture reading and homily at the eucharist but also to the raised platform, or bema, where these occurred.
54. These were noble Roman families.

different they are from the shameful self-promotion and deceitful malignity of the demons. If by nature anything genuinely admirable shines out in you, it can be purified and perfected only by true godliness. By ungodliness it is ruined and marked out for punishment. Choose now which course to follow, then, so that you may be praised without any error — praised not in yourself but in the true God....

Do not pursue false and deceitful gods. Abandon them, rather, and despise them. Break out into true liberty! They are not gods; they are malignant spirits for whom your eternal happiness is punishment. Juno does not seem to have begrudged the Trojans (from whom you trace your origin according to the flesh[55]) possession of the Roman citadels as much as these demons begrudge the whole human race an eternal dwelling place. Yet you still hold them to be gods! In no small part, however, you yourself passed judgment on such spirits when you propitiated them with plays but determined that the actors who performed these same plays should be held in disgrace. Allow your liberty to be asserted against the unclean spirits who imposed on your necks the yoke of dedicating to them and celebrating for them their own shame and ignominy. You excluded from civic honor the actors who perform the divine crimes; now entreat the true God to exclude from among you the gods who take delight in their own crimes, whether true (which is utterly shameful) or false (which is utterly malicious). In refusing, of your own accord, to open civic society to actors and players, you did well. But be more fully alert. The divine majesty is by no means propitiated by arts which defile human dignity. How, then, can you imagine that gods who take delight in such observances are to be numbered among the holy powers of heaven, when you do not for one moment imagine that the men by whom these observances are performed are to be numbered among Roman citizens at any level whatsoever? The heavenly city is incomparably brighter. There victory is truth, dignity is holiness, peace is felicity, and life is eternity. Much less does it have such gods in its company, if you were ashamed to have such men in yours! If you desire to attain the blessed city, then, shun the company of demons. Gods who are propitiated by the disgraceful are not worthy to be worshiped by the honorable. So let these gods be removed from your religion by a Christian cleansing, just as those men were removed from your civic honors by the censor's ban.

As for carnal goods, which are all that the evil want to enjoy, and carnal evils, which are all that they want to avoid, the demons do not have the power over these things that people think they do (and, even if they did, we ought rather to despise these things than to worship demons for the sake of them, for, by worshiping them, we make it impossible for us to attain the things they begrudge us). Still, even in these matters, they do not have the power ascribed to them by those who claim we should worship them for the sake of these material goods and evils. This we shall see in what follows, and so the present book may end here.

---

55. See Virgil, *Aeneid* IV,234.

Study Questions for Book II

Among many religious adherents today there is an assumption that fidelity to prayer or religious ritual can exert an influence on divine providence for the benefit of the pious practitioner. Augustine builds his critique of Roman piety by prioritizing an ethic of justice. How is this Augustinian tension between piety and ethics operative in Christianity today? How is it operative in other religions?

Theater today is much more artistically complex, socially conscious, and intellectually sophisticated than the popular Roman shows that Augustine criticized so roundly. However, while visual and performing arts can challenge the values of contemporary society, they can also enshrine those values. What Augustinian cautions remain operative in a 21st-century critique of theater, film, and social media?

Augustine exposes tensions between the arts and politics in ancient Greece and Rome. How are the legal and social tensions between artists and politicians today in various countries similar to yet different from what existed in Greece and Rome?

BOOK III

Book III continues the argument of Book II, namely, that Rome's gods failed to protect it from many disasters which occurred prior to the coming of Christ and which, therefore, cannot be blamed on Christianity or on the discontinuation of sacrifices to the gods. Book III, however, focuses not on the moral evils that corrupted Rome's character but rather on such natural and political disasters as famine, plague, civic strife, and war, and on the dreadful human suffering that they caused in the history of the Roman republic from the era of the kings down to the triumph of Augustus. The overall point, once again, is that it is senseless to worship the gods either to avoid the evils or to obtain the goods of this temporal life. Throughout, Augustine emphasizes not only the failure of the gods to safeguard Rome but also the moral flaws and inconsistencies of their reputed behavior. For example, they were supposedly offended by the adultery of Paris and abandoned Troy but took no offense at Romulus's murder of his brother and protected Rome; or, again, they did nothing to save the city of Saguntum from destruction in the Second Punic War, even though the city kept faith with Rome instead of deserting to Hannibal, and so on. An underlying aim, then, is not only to show that the traditional gods did not and could not protect Rome from disaster but also to intimate that they are in fact malicious demons seeking to do harm.

1. ... At various times and in diverse places before the coming of our redeemer, the human race was ground down by innumerable and sometimes even incredible disasters. But what other gods did the world worship back then (with the exception, of course, of the one Hebrew people and a few other persons, here and there, who were found worthy of divine grace by the most hidden and most just judgment of God)? To keep from going on too long, however, I shall say nothing of the terrible evils that struck other peoples all over the world. I shall speak only of what pertains to Rome and the Roman empire, that is, the city proper and any lands which were either joined to it by alliance or subjected to it by conquest, and specifically of what they suffered before Christ's coming, when they already pertained, so to speak, to the body of the republic.

The Fall of Troy: the Gods and Laomedon's Perjury

2. To begin with — for I must not omit or neglect what I also mentioned in the first book[1] — why is it that even Troy, or Ilium,[2] from which the Roman people take their origin, was conquered, captured and destroyed by the Greeks, even though it had these same gods and worshiped them? Priam, they say, paid the penalty for the perjury of his father Laomedon.[3] Is it true, then, that Apollo and Neptune served Laomedon as hired hands? For it is said that Laomedon promised them their pay and then broke his oath.[4] It surprises me that Apollo, who was called the Foreknower, should have taken on the labor of so massive a job without being aware that Laomedon was going to break his promise. And, for that matter, it hardly seems right that Neptune, the king of the sea, Apollo's uncle and Jupiter's brother, should himself have been ignorant of what was going to happen....

The Fall of Troy: the Gods and Paris's Adultery

3. There is, then, no reason why anyone should imagine that the gods — by whom, they say, that realm once stood firm[5] — were angered by the Trojans' perjury when, in reality, they are proved to have been vanquished by the greater strength of the Greeks. Nor were they so outraged at the adultery of Paris (as, again, some say in their defense) that they abandoned Troy. For their customary practice is to promote and teach sins, not to avenge them. "The city of Rome, as I have been given to understand," says Sallust, "was first founded and inhabited by Trojans who were wandering as refugees under Aeneas's leadership with no fixed home."[6]

Clearly, then, if the divinities decided that Paris's adultery ought to be avenged, the Romans ought to have been punished even more, or certainly just as much, since Aeneas's mother did just this. How is it that the gods detested this shameful act in Paris's case but not in the case of Venus, one of their own, when she committed adultery with Anchises and gave birth to Aeneas?[7] Is it that Menelaus took offense in the one case but Vulcan consented in the other?[8] For the gods,

---

1. See above at I,3-4.
2. Ilium, a fortress within the city of Troy that was named after Ilus, a king of Troy, was often used to designate Troy as a whole.
3. See Virgil, *Aeneid* IV,542. Apollo and Neptune had helped Laomedon in building the walls of Troy, but he then refused to reward them for their efforts, despite his promise to do so. Laomedon's son Priam ruled during the Trojan War and was the last king of Troy.
4. See Homer, *Iliad* XXI,441-457.
5. See Virgil, *Aeneid* II,352.
6. *Catiline Conspiracy* 6.
7. In Greek mythology, Anchises was a prince of Dardania, a territory near Troy, whose beauty drew Venus to fall in love with him.
8. Menelaus, the king of Sparta, was the husband of Helen, whom Paris, the son of the king of Troy, abducted, which precipitated the Trojan War. The god Vulcan was the husband of Venus, who did not punish her for her adultery with Anchises.

I suppose, feel so little jealousy of their wives that they even stoop to share them with men!

Perhaps you think I am mocking these fables and that I am not treating such a weighty matter with the proper seriousness. If you like, then, we will presume that Aeneas was not Venus's son. I grant this — on the condition, however, that it is also true that Romulus was not the son of Mars. If the one, why not the other? Or is it permitted for gods to have intercourse with women but not for men to have intercourse with goddesses? It would be a harsh, or rather an incredible, stipulation that allowed Mars a sexual license under the law of Venus that it denied to Venus herself under her own law. But, in fact, both cases are confirmed by Roman authority. For Caesar believed no less strongly in recent times that Venus was his grandmother[9] than Romulus did in ancient times that Mars was his father.

4. Someone will ask, "Do you really believe such things?" I most certainly do not. Even Varro, the most learned of the Romans,[10] comes close to admitting that they are false, although he does not say this boldly and with confidence. But he does state that it is advantageous for civil societies to have brave men believe, even if it is false, that they are descended from the gods. For in that case the human mind, confident of its divine lineage, will enter more boldly into undertaking great deeds, will carry them out more eagerly, and therefore, due to their confidence, will complete them more successfully. You see how much room Varro's view (which I have expressed, as best I could, in my own words) opens up for falsehood. In this light, when even lies about the very gods themselves are thought to be of benefit for citizens, we may imagine how many things now held sacred and counted as religious could actually have been nothing more than mere human inventions....

Troy and Adultery, Rome and Fratricide

6. Here is another point: if human sins displeased those divinities so much that they abandoned Troy and gave it over to fire and sword because they took offense at Paris's act, then surely Romulus's murder of his brother ought to have stirred them up far more against the Romans than any trifling with a Greek husband did against the Trojans. Fratricide in a city just coming to birth should have sparked more anger than adultery in one already well-established in its reign.[11] Nor does it make any difference in the present case whether Romulus merely ordered the deed to be done or actually did it himself (a possibility which many brazenly

---

9. See Suetonius, *Lives of the Twelve Caesars*, Julius Caesar 6.
10. Marcus Terentius Varro (116-27 B.C.), a renowned Roman scholar of wide interests, is frequently referenced as an authority in *The City of God*, especially below at VI,2-12 (beginning with a lengthy encomium) and XIX,1-3. *The City of God* is frequently the sole source for many of the citations attributed to him, in which case there is no notation in this text.
11. Rome was just coming to birth, while Troy was well-established.

deny, many doubt in shame, and many hide away in sorrow). There is no need for us to take the time to inquire into this more fully, weighing the testimony of so many writers. Everyone agrees that Romulus's brother was murdered, and not by enemies or strangers. Regardless of whether Romulus committed the crime or merely ordered it, he was far more the head of the Romans than Paris was of the Trojans. Why is it, then, that the abductor of another man's wife provoked the gods' wrath on the Trojans, while the murderer of his own brother attracted the same gods' protection to the Romans?

On the other hand, even if Romulus played no role either in committing or in ordering the crime, the crime itself should still certainly have been avenged. In this sense, the city as a whole committed the crime since the city as a whole simply ignored it. And this is no longer fratricide but parricide, which is worse. For each of the two brothers was a founder of the city where one of the two was eliminated by the crime and not allowed to be a ruler. In my judgment, then, there is nothing that might explain what evil Troy deserved that would result in the gods' abandoning it so that it could be destroyed. Nor is there anything to explain what good Rome deserved that would result in the gods' dwelling in it so that it might prosper, unless it is simply that, being vanquished, the gods fled Troy and joined up with the Romans in order to deceive them as well. Most likely, however, they *both* stayed there in Troy to deceive, in their usual manner, the people who would once again inhabit those lands *and* gloried in yet greater honors here in Rome by virtue of practicing those same arts of deception all the more....

[Chapters 7 – 8 recount the brutal sack of hapless Troy by the Roman Gaius Flavius Fimbria.]

The Peace of Numa's Reign

9. The gods are also believed to have helped Numa Pompilius,[12] Romulus's successor, to have peace for the whole period of his reign and to shut the gates of Janus which, by custom, are kept open in times of war.[13] He earned this help, no doubt, because he instituted many religious rites among the Romans. It would certainly have been in order to congratulate this man for such a period of quiet, if only he had known enough to use it for salutary purposes and, giving up his

---

12. Numa Pompilius was king of Rome from 715 to 673 B.C. He is referenced again below at VII, 34-35.
13. According to legend, Janus was a king who reigned in ancient Italy and was numbered among the gods after his death. The doors of his temple in Rome were customarily shut in time of peace and open in time of war.

exceedingly dangerous curiosity,[14] to seek the true God with true piety. In reality, however, it is not that the gods gave him that time of quiet; it is rather that they might have deceived him less if they had found him less at leisure. For the less they found him occupied, the more they themselves occupied his time. Varro tells us what Numa undertook to do and by what arts he was able to ally such gods as these with himself and with his city. God willing, I shall discuss all this more fully in its proper place.[15] Here, however, the question has to do with the benefits brought by the gods.

Peace, of course, is a great benefit. But it is a benefit bestowed by the true God, and — like the sun, the rain,[16] and other supports of life — it is commonly bestowed even on the ungrateful and the scurrilous. But if it was the gods who brought this great good to Rome or to Pompilius, why is it that they never granted it to the Roman empire in later times, even in the periods when it was worthy of praise? Were the sacred rites more effective when they were first being instituted than when they were celebrated after they had been instituted? In Numa's time they did not yet exist but rather were added so that they would come to exist. Later, when they already existed, they were kept up so that they might bring benefits. How is it, then, that the forty-three years — or, as some would have it, the thirty-nine years — of Numa's reign passed in such prolonged peace, but afterwards, after the sacred rites had been established and the gods invoked by those rites had become the city's protectors and guardians, during all the long years from the founding of the city to the reign of Augustus, only one year is recorded (the year immediately following the First Punic War) when the Romans were able to close the gates of war.[17] And that year itself was reckoned a great marvel!...

[Chapters 10 – 11, and the beginning of 12 report the ebb and flow of wars, just and unjust, in Rome's history, and the importing of new gods and goddesses from conquered lands and peoples.]

12. ... Who, then, can count all the gods that were protecting Rome? Native and foreign gods, celestial and terrestrial gods, gods of the underworld, of the sea, of springs, of rivers, and, as Varro says, gods "certain and uncertain," and in every category, just as among the animals, male and female gods. Set under the protection

---

14. "Exceedingly dangerous curiosity": *perniciosissima curiositate*. "Curiosity" is generally a negative term for Augustine, denoting an overweening interest in something inconsequential or even bad. As well as below at IV,34 and X,9 see also *Confessions* II,6,13; III,3,5; X,35,54-57; Letter 118,1,1; *Demonic Divination* 3,7. In the case of Numa Pompilius the curiosity was clearly of a religious nature.
15. See below at VII,34.
16. See Mt 5:45.
17. I.e., in 235 B.C.

of all these gods, Rome surely should not have been assailed and afflicted by such massive and terrible disasters as the ones I shall mention, listing only a few out of many. For her protection, she had called together all too many gods, drawing them by a great cloud of her smoke as by a given sign; and by instituting and providing temples, altars, sacrifices, and priests for them, she offended the true and supreme God, to whom alone these services are rightly owed. In fact, Rome lived more happily when she had fewer gods, but the greater she became, the more gods she thought she should add, just as a larger ship needs more sailors. She despaired, I believe, of those fewer gods — under whom, in comparison with her worse life to come, she had lived better — thinking them insufficient to support her grandeur.

In the first place, even under the kings (with the exception of Numa Pompilius, of whom I have already spoken above[18]), there was the great evil of all that discord and rivalry, which spawned the murder of Romulus's brother.

The Seizing of the Sabine Women

13. And how is it that neither Juno, who with her husband Jupiter cherished "the Romans, lords of the world, the people of the toga,"[19] nor Venus herself could help the sons of Aeneas to win wives for themselves by good and just means? The result of their failure was sheer disaster: the Romans seized wives by trickery and so were soon compelled to do battle with their fathers-in-law; and the poor women, still not reconciled to their husbands after the wrong done to them, now received their fathers' blood as their dowry.[20] It is true that the Romans vanquished their neighbors in this conflict. But think of all the casualties on both sides and all the funerals of near neighbors and close relatives that were the cost of those victories. Think about the war between Caesar and Pompey. That involved only one father-in-law and only one son-in-law; but when Caesar's daughter, Pompey's wife, died, it was in deep and fully justified grief that Lucan cried out, "Battles on Emathia's plains, worse than civil war: our song is of crime passing itself off as just."[21]

Thus the Romans conquered, and so, with hands bloody from the slaughter of their fathers-in-law, they extorted misery-filled embraces from the daughters. And the daughters did not even dare to mourn for their murdered fathers, for fear of offending their victorious husbands. In fact, while the battle was still being waged, they did not even know which they should pray for. It was not Venus, then, but Bellona[22] who gave such marriages to the Roman people. Or perhaps that infernal Fury Alecto had more license to harm them, now that Juno was on their side, than

---

18. See above at III,9.
19. Virgil, *Aeneid* I,282.
20. This is the so-called rape of the Sabine women, also referred to above at II,17.
21. *Pharsalia* I,1.
22. I.e., the goddess of war.

she had earlier when Juno's prayers incited her against Aeneas.[23] Andromache was happier in her captivity than those Roman wives were in their weddings. She may have been Pyrrhus's slave, but at least he did not kill any Trojans after embracing her.[24] The Romans, in contrast, cut down in battle the fathers-in-law whose daughters they had embraced in the marriage-bed. Andromache, in her subjection to the victor, had only to mourn, not to fear, the death of her people.[25]

But the Roman wives, because linked with the combatants on both sides, feared their fathers' death when their husbands sallied forth and mourned it when they returned, yet they were not free to express either their fear or their grief. For either they loyally suffered torment at the slaying of their fellow-citizens, their relatives, their brothers, and their fathers, or they ruthlessly rejoiced at the victory of their husbands. And add to this the fact — such are the turns and twists of war — that some lost husbands to their parents' sword, and others lost both parent and husband to each other's swords.

The Romans, too, faced no small peril. There came a point at which their city was besieged and they were defending themselves behind closed gates; and when the gates were opened by deceit and the enemy admitted within the walls, an appalling and vicious battle was joined in the forum itself, a battle between sons-in-law and fathers-in-law. The ravishers were even getting the worst of it, and, repeatedly taking flight among the houses, they were badly besmirching their earlier victories, shameful and deplorable as they were. At this point Romulus, losing all hope in the valor of his followers, prayed to Jupiter that they might stand firm, and this was the occasion on which Jupiter took the title "Stayer."[26] There would have been no end to all this evil if the ravished women themselves had not dashed out, tearing their hair, and thrown themselves at their fathers' feet, calming their wholly just anger not by armed victory but by devout entreaty.[27] As a result, Romulus, who could not stand to have his own brother as co-ruler, was forced to put up with Titus Tatius, the Sabine king, as joint ruler. But how long could he endure him, when he could not bear even his own brother and twin? And so, when Tatius was also killed, Romulus obtained the sole rulership so that he might ultimately become a still greater god.[28]

What kind of marriage laws were these, what kind of incitements to war, what kind of ties of kinship, of affinity, of alliance, and of divinity? In short, what kind of life did the city have under the tutelage of all those gods! You see how many

---

23. See Virgil, *Aeneid* VII,325. Alecto was one of the three Furies, the other two being Tisiphone and Megaera; Alecto was known in particular for her anger.
24. Andromache was the wife of Hector, the Trojan hero. After his death she was allotted as spoils to Pyrrhus, also known as Neoptolemus, who had fought on the side of the Greeks.
25. See Virgil, *Aeneid* III,303-313.
26. *Jupiter Stator*. A temple in Rome was dedicated to Jupiter under this title. See Livy, *History of Rome* I,12.
27. See ibid. I,13.
28. See ibid. I,14.

weighty points might be made here, if I were not eager to deal with further issues and to move our discussion along to other items.

The War with Alba

14. After Numa, then, what happened under the other kings? What a monumental evil it was when the Albans were provoked into war, not only for the Albans but also for the Romans themselves; and this happened, no doubt, because Numa's long peace now seemed worth very little! What frequent massacres there were of the Roman and the Alban armies, and how diminished both cities were![29] Alba, the very Alba founded by Aeneas' own son Ascanius, the very city that was more properly Rome's mother than Troy itself, was provoked into conflict by King Tullus Hostilius, and in that conflict she both suffered and inflicted damage until everyone grew weary of so many battles with equal losses on both sides. They then decided to settle the war's outcome by combat between two sets of triplet brothers, one from each side. From the Romans came forth the three Horatii, and from the Albans, the three Curatii. Two of the Horatii were defeated and slain by the three Curatii; but the one remaining Horatius overcame and killed the three Curatii. Thus Rome emerged the victor, but at the cost of such slaughter, even in the final combat, that only one of the six returned home. And who suffered the loss on both sides? Who endured the grief? Who but the line of Aeneas, the posterity of Ascanius, the offspring of Venus, the grandsons of Jupiter? For when daughter city fought with mother city, this, too, was worse than civil war....

Then, as the fruit of victory, Alba was destroyed — the third dwelling place of those Trojan divinities after Ilium, which the Greeks overthrew, and Lavinium, where Aeneas had established his kingdom of wandering fugitives. But perhaps the gods, in their usual fashion, had already moved on from there as well, and that is why Alba was destroyed. Obviously "they had all withdrawn, deserting shrine and altar, the gods by whom that empire had once stood firm."[30]

They had withdrawn, no doubt, now for a third time, so that Rome might be the fourth city entrusted — most prudently, I am sure — to their care. For Alba, too, had lost their favor, where Amulius ruled after expelling his brother; and Rome had gained it, where Romulus ruled after killing his brother. But before Alba was destroyed, they claim, its people were transferred to Rome, so that from the two would come one city. Very well, grant that this happened. It is still true that Alba, Ascanius's kingdom and the third home of the Trojan gods, was overthrown by her daughter city; and it is still true that in order to make one people out of two from the survivors of the war — a pitiable coagulation — there first took place a vast outpouring of blood from both.

---

29. See ibid. I,23-26. The pretext for the war between Rome and Alba, which occurred in the seventh century B.C., was incursions by each side into the other's territory.
30. Virgil, *Aeneid* II,351-352.

But why should I list, one by one, the unending renewal of these same wars under the other kings — wars that seemed to have been ended by victories, wars which again and again came to a close in terrible slaughter, and which again and again, after treaties of peace, repeated themselves between fathers-in-law and sons-in-law, between their offspring and their descendants? It is no small indication of this calamitous state of affairs that none of these kings closed the gates of war.[31] None of them reigned in peace, despite the protection of so many gods.

The Deaths of the Kings

15. And what ends did the kings themselves meet? In the case of Romulus, the flattering fable of his reception into heaven sees to that. But so do certain Roman writers who say that he was actually torn to pieces by the senate because of his brutality. These writers claim that some fellow named Julius Proclus was suborned to say that Romulus had appeared to him and through him had commanded the Roman people to worship him among the divinities. By this means, so they say, the people, who had begun to swell up against the senate, were restrained and calmed.[32]

For an eclipse of the sun had also occurred, and the ignorant multitude, having no idea that this was the effect of the fixed pattern of the sun's regular course, attributed it to Romulus's merits. But surely, if this was really a mark of the sun's grief, they ought rather to have concluded that Romulus had been murdered and that the turning-away of the daylight was meant as an indication of the crime, which is just what happened in truth when the Lord was crucified due to the cruelty and impiety of the Jews.[33]...

In the same work, Cicero also speaks of Tullus Hostilius, the third king after Romulus, who was himself killed by lightning....

The other kings of the Roman people — with the exceptions of Numa Pompilius and Ancus Martius, who died of disease[34] — met appalling ends. Tullus Hostilius, the conqueror and destroyer of Alba, was, as I said, burned to a crisp by lightning with his entire household.[35] Tarquinius Priscus was murdered by his predecessor's sons.[36] Servius Tullius was killed by the terrible wickedness of his son-in-law, Tarquin the Proud, who succeeded him on the throne.[37] And yet the gods did not withdraw, "deserting shrine and altar," at this parricide committed against the best king of the Roman people, even though they say that these gods were so dismayed at Paris's mere adultery that they deserted poor Troy and

---

31. I.e., in the temple of Janus.
32. See Livy, *History of Rome* I,16.
33. See Lk 23:44-45.
34. See Eutropius, *Abridgement of Roman History* I,3.5.
35. See Livy, *History of Rome* I,31.
36. See ibid. I,40-41.
37. See ibid. I,48.

left it to be destroyed and burned by the Greeks. And Tarquin not only killed his father-in-law but succeeded him! No, the gods did not depart. They were there, and they stayed there to watch this abominable parricide who gained the throne by murdering his father-in-law and who went on to win glory in many wars and many victories and to build the Capitol from the spoils.[38]...

From the Expulsion of the Kings to the Second Punic War: the First Consuls

16. ... After the royal power was expelled, the first consuls were created. In fact, the consuls did not even complete their year in office. First, Junius Brutus banished his disgraced colleague, Lucius Tarquinius Collatinus, from the city.[39] Soon afterwards Brutus himself fell in battle, wounded by the enemy he had wounded — but not before he had killed both his own sons and his wife's brothers because he had learned that they were conspiring to restore Tarquin.[40]...

Lucretius also, who was chosen to replace Brutus, was carried off by illness before the end of the year. And so Publius Valerius, who had succeeded Collatinus, and Marcus Horatius, who was chosen in place of the deceased Lucretius, completed that terrible and death-filled year in which there were five consuls, the very year in which the Roman republic first put the new office and authority of the consulship itself in place.[41]...

From the Expulsion of the Kings to the Second Punic War: Conflict between Patricians and Plebeians

17. ... But why should I spend my own time in writing about all this, or my readers' time in reading about it? Sallust has briefly sketched the wretched state of the republic during that long period, lasting all the way down to the Second Punic War, when incessant wars abroad and all kinds of discord and civic strife at home kept it in constant turmoil. Its victories, therefore, were not the solid joys of the fortunate but rather the hollow consolations of the wretched, serving only to excite restless men and entice them to undergo one barren evil after another.

I hope that no good and prudent Romans will be angry at me for saying this.... And if any actually are angry, how would they ever put up with me if I were to say what Sallust says, "Any number of riots, insurrections, and, in the end, civil wars broke out, while a few powerful men, to whose influence most had given way, aimed at domination under the honorable pretext of defending either the patricians or the people. Citizens were not called good or bad on the basis of

---

38. See ibid. 53.55.
39. See Livy, *History of Rome* II,5.
40. See ibid.
41. See Livy, *History of Rome* II,8.

worthwhile service to the republic, for all were equally corrupt. Rather, whoever was the wealthiest and had the most power to do harm was counted as good, because he supported the existing state of affairs"?[42]...

From the Expulsion of the Kings to the Second Punic War: Famines, Plagues, and Wars

Where, then, were the gods when the Romans were beset with such great calamities? People suppose that these gods are to be worshiped for the sake of the trifling and deceptive happiness of this world, and by their cunning lies the gods sold the Romans on worshiping them. But where were they when the consul Valerius was killed while defending the Capitol when it was set on fire by exiles and slaves?[43] In fact, he was far more able to bring aid to Jupiter's temple than that whole swarm of divinities — along with their greatest and best king,[44] whose temple Valerius had saved — was able to come to his aid. Where were they when the city, worn out by the unending evils of sedition, was devastated by dire famine and plague during that brief interval of calm while she awaited the return of the legates sent to Athens to borrow its laws?[45] Where were they when the people, again suffering from famine, first created a prefect of public provisions and, as the famine grew more severe, Spurius Maelius, because he had distributed free grain to the hungry crowds, was accused of aspiring to be king and, at the insistence of that same prefect, was put to death by Quintus Servilius, master of the horse, on the authority of the aged dictator Lucius Quintius, throwing the whole city into dire and perilous turmoil?[46] Where were they when a terrible pestilence broke out and the people, in their utter exhaustion, decided to put on the novel rite of the lectisternia for their useless gods, something that had never been done before? Couches were spread out in honor of the gods, which is how this sacred, or rather sacrilegious, rite got its name.[47] Where were they when, for ten straight years, the Roman army fought poorly and suffered one disaster after another at the hands of the Veiians, until at last Furius Camillus stepped in, a man whom the ungrateful city afterwards condemned?[48] Where were they when the Gauls took Rome, sacked it, burned it, and filled it with corpses?[49] Where were they when that memorable plague inflicted such terrible suffering, including the death of Furius Camillus, who first defended his ungrateful republic from the Veiians

---

42. *History* I, fragment 12.
43. See Livy, *History of Rome* III,18.
44. "Along with their greatest and best king": *cum suo maximo atque optimo rege*. "Greatest and best," which Augustine uses sarcastically here, was one of the titles of Jupiter.
45. See Livy, *History of Rome* III,32.
46. See ibid. IV,13.
47. "Couches were spread out": *Lecti autem sternebantur*, hence lectisternia. See ibid. V,13.
48. See ibid. IV,58; V,10-25.
49. See ibid. V,38.

and later delivered it from the Gauls? It was during this plague that the Romans introduced the theatrical shows, another new pestilence — not of their bodies but, far more disastrously, of their moral character.[50]...

18. During the Punic Wars, when two powerful peoples were assaulting each other with all their strength and resources, and victory was long in doubt and hung in the balance between the two empires, how many smaller kingdoms were wiped out! How many large and celebrated towns were demolished, how many cities damaged or destroyed! How many regions and territories were laid waste, far and wide! How often defeat followed victory for both sides! How much life was lost, both among soldiers in battle and among unarmed civilian populations! What fleets of ships were destroyed in naval battles or sunk in various storms of one sort or another! If I tried to describe or even just to enumerate all these, I would be just one more writer of history....

The Second Punic War: Hannibal

19. As for the Second Punic War, it would take far too long to list all the disasters suffered by the two peoples who did battle with each other for such a long time over such a wide area. Even the writers whose aim is to praise Rome's empire rather than to narrate Rome's wars acknowledge that, in this case, the victor was more like one vanquished.[51] Starting from Spain, Hannibal crossed the Pyrenees, dashed across Gaul, and burst through the Alps.[52] In making this long circuit, he increased his strength by plundering and subduing everything in his path and then rushed through the alpine passes into Italy like a torrent in flood. What bloody battles were then fought! How often the Romans went down to defeat! How many towns went over to the enemy, how many were captured and crushed! How dire the battles were, and how often disaster for Rome meant glory for Hannibal! And what shall I say of the incredibly awful horror of Cannae, where even Hannibal, for all his ruthless cruelty, grew sated of slaughtering his bitterest enemies and, it is reported, gave orders to spare them? From Cannae, he sent a bushel basket of gold rings to Carthage in order to let his countrymen see that so many of Rome's elite had fallen in the battle that it was easier to grasp the loss by volume than by number....

The Second Punic War: the Destruction of Saguntum

20. But among all the evils of the Second Punic War, none was more heartbreaking, or more deserving of heartbroken lament, than the destruction of the

---

50. See ibid. VII,2-3. This is also referred to above at I,32 and II,8.
51. See Livy, *History of Rome* XXI,1.
52. Hannibal, the great Carthaginian general, lived from 247 to 183/182 B.C. His circuitous approach to Rome via the Alps was remarkable for its genius and daring.

Saguntines.[53] This Spanish city, a great friend of the Roman people, was overthrown for keeping faith with them. For when Hannibal broke his treaty with Rome, he looked for a means to provoke the Romans to war. Accordingly, he mounted a ferocious siege of Saguntum. When the news reached Rome, legates were sent to Hannibal to get him to lift the siege; and when they were scorned, they went on to Carthage, lodged their complaint about the broken treaty and returned to Rome without success. During these delays, that unfortunate city, overflowing with wealth, and precious both to its own region and to the Roman republic, was destroyed by the Carthaginians within eight or nine months. To read of its destruction, and even more to write of it, is a horror. I shall touch on it briefly, however, because it is highly pertinent to the point under discussion.

First the city was wasted by famine; and some even report that she fed on the corpses of her own inhabitants. Then, at the end of their rope, the Saguntines — to keep themselves, at least, from falling into Hannibal's hands as prisoners — built a huge public funeral pyre, ran everyone through with their swords, and threw themselves and their families into the flames. Here, surely, the gods could have taken some action, those gluttonous and worthless gods who gulp down the fat of sacrifices and deceive people with the fog of their false divinations. Here, surely, they could have done something to help a city that was a great friend of the Roman people; here they could have kept it from perishing when the reason it was perishing was precisely that it was keeping faith....

The Roman gods are worshiped, we are told, and are to be worshiped, in order to safeguard our happiness with regard to the fragile and transitory things of this life. What response, then, will the defenders and excusers of these gods give us on their behalf with respect to the destruction of Saguntum? What can they say, except what they said about the death of Regulus? There is, of course, this difference: Regulus was only one man, Saguntum an entire city, but the cause of destruction in both cases was the keeping of faith. It was to keep faith that Regulus chose to go back to the enemy, and it was to keep faith that Saguntum chose not to go over to the enemy's side.

Is it keeping faith, then, that provokes the wrath of the gods? Or is it rather that not only single individuals but also whole cities can perish despite the fact that they have the gods' favor? Let our opponents make the choice. If the gods are angered by the keeping of faith, let them seek out betrayers to be their worshipers. If both individuals and cities can perish in repeated and terrible torments, despite having the gods' favor, then worshiping the gods is simply fruitless so far as the happiness of this life is concerned. Therefore, as for those who imagine that they have been plunged into unhappiness just because the rites sacred to their gods

---

53. See Livy, *History of Rome* XXI,7-15.

have been abandoned, let them give up their anger. For, even if their gods were still present and were wholly favorable to them, it is still possible that they might not only have the complaints they do now but might even go to complete destruction, after the most horrible sufferings, as Regulus and the Saguntines did then.

From the Second to the Final Punic War: the Maltreatment of Scipio and the Cultivation of Luxury

21. It was during the period between the second and the final Carthaginian wars, according to Sallust, that the Romans held to the highest moral standards and lived in the greatest concord[54] (for, keeping the limits of my projected work in mind, I pass over many other points). But that very period of highest moral standards and greatest harmony also saw the accusation of Scipio and his departure from Rome. He was the liberator of Rome and of Italy. He enjoyed extraordinary fame and admiration for bringing the Second Punic War — with all its horror, ruin, and peril — to an end, for conquering Hannibal, and for subduing Carthage. His life is described, from his youth on, as dedicated to the gods and nurtured in their temples.[55] Yet, as the result of his enemies' accusations, he left Rome and — deprived of his native country, which by his valor he had restored to safety and freedom — spent the rest of his life in the town of Linternum, where he died. Even after his glorious triumph in Rome, in fact, he felt so little longing for that city that he is said to have given orders that not even after death should any funeral service be held in his ungrateful homeland.[56]

Not long after that, Asiatic luxury, worse than any armed enemy, crept into Rome for the first time through the agency of the proconsul Gnaeus Manlius, who triumphed over the Galatian.[57] It was then, we are told, that beds of bronze and expensive bed-coverings first made their appearance, and it was then that lute-girls were first introduced at banquets, along with other forms of licentious dissipation.[58] My purpose here, however, was not to speak of the evils which human beings gladly create for themselves, but rather of the evils which they cannot bear to suffer. Thus it is what I said about Scipio — that he submitted to his enemies and died outside the homeland he had saved — that is pertinent to the present discussion. For the Roman divinities whose temples he saved from Hannibal did nothing for him in return, even though it is only for the sake of just such temporal happiness that they are worshiped. But, because Sallust said that moral standards were at their highest during that period, I thought that I should also mention this point

---

54. See *History* I, fragment 11.
55. See Livy, *History of Rome* XXXVIII,51.
56. See ibid. XXXVIII,53.
57. Gnaeus Manlius Vulso was consul in 189 B.C., when he defeated the Galatian Gauls in present-day central Turkey.
58. See ibid. XXXIX,6.

about Asiatic luxury, so that people would understand that Sallust's claim is true only in comparison with other times when morals were undoubtedly worse in the midst of the most terrible civic discords.

In fact, it was during that period (that is, between the second and the final Carthaginian war) that the notorious Voconian Law was passed, forbidding anyone to name a woman as heir, not even an only daughter. If anything more unjust than this law could be said or thought, I have no idea what it could be.[59] Even so, during the entire interval between these two Punic Wars, only more tolerable forms of misfortune occurred. The army was wearied only in foreign wars and had the consolation of victories, and at home no savage conflicts raged as they did at other times. But in the last Punic War, Rome's rival for empire was completely destroyed in one assault by another Scipio, who gained the surname Africanus for his success, and, from that point on, Rome was ground down under such a mass of evils, arising from the prosperity and security of her affairs along with the resulting deep corruption of her morality, that it became obvious that Carthage's sudden overthrow did Rome far more harm than its previous long hostility had ever done.

From the Punic Wars to Augustus: the Massacre of the Romans under Mithridates

There follows the period down to Caesar Augustus, who appears to have wrested from the Romans a liberty which was no longer glorious, even in their own estimation, but rather contentious and destructive, and by this time plainly listless and feeble, and who brought everything back under arbitrary royal rule and did so as if he had restored and renewed the republic at a point when it had collapsed in disease-ridden old age. In this whole period, I pass over the military disasters which were suffered for one reason or another....

22. All this, as I say, I pass over, except that I simply cannot keep silent about the order of Mithridates, King of Asia, that all the Roman citizens dwelling anywhere in Asia — and there were a great number of them, all tending to their business affairs — should all be put to death in one day.[60] And that is exactly what happened. What a pathetic sight it was! Suddenly, wherever any Roman was found, in the field, on the road, in town, at home, in the street, in the forum, in the temple, in bed, at a banquet, he was cut down without warning and without the slightest religious feeling....

---

59. See Cicero, *Against Verres* II,1. Inasmuch as Augustine has a reputation for demeaning women, his strong sense of the injustice of the Voconian Law is worth noting. For a more benign interpretation of the Voconian Law see Suzanne Dixon, "Breaking the Law to Do the Right Thing: The Gradual Erosion of the Voconian Law in Ancient Rome," in *The Adelaide Law Review* 9 (1985) 519-534.
60. See Livy, *Periochae* 78.

Had all these victims disregarded the auguries? Did they have no household or public gods to consult before they set out on that journey without return? If not, then our opponents have no reason to complain about our own times in this regard, for the Romans turn out to have long held the auguries in contempt. On the other hand, if they did consult the gods, let someone say what good it did, even back when consulting them was perfectly legal, at least according to human law, and was forbidden by no one.[61]

Evils Internal to the Republic: Civil Strife and Civil War

23. But now let us at least mention, as briefly as possible, those evils which were all the more heartrending because they were internal to the republic: civil — or, rather, uncivil — discords, which were no longer mere riots but outright urban wars, in which so much blood was shed and factional strife now raged not by squabbles in the assemblies and voices raised against each other but by the open clash of steel and arms....

24. The civil disorders began with the disturbances sparked by the agrarian laws of the Gracchi.[62] For the Gracchi wanted to distribute among the people the lands wrongly held by the nobility. To dare to undo a long-standing injustice, however, was dangerous in the extreme; or rather, as the event showed, it was utterly ruinous. Think of all the mourning brought on when the elder Gracchus was killed, and again when the other Gracchus, his brother, was killed not long afterwards! High-born and low-born alike were put to death not by the due exercise of authority under law but in the raw conflict of armed mobs. After the younger Gracchus was slain, the consul Lucius Opimius — who had taken up arms against him in the city and, after defeating and killing him, along with his associates, had slaughtered untold numbers of citizens — held an investigation. He now used the mode of judicial inquiry to go after the younger Gracchus's remaining supporters, and he is reported to have had three thousand men put to death.[63] From the fact that what was supposedly a judicial inquiry produced so many deaths, we can begin to grasp what an enormous number of deaths must have come from the unrestrained clash of the armed mobs themselves. The man who killed Gracchus sold his victim's head to the consul for its weight in gold, in accord with an agreement made prior to the slaughter; and it was in this same slaughter that Marcus Fulvius, a man of consular rank, was killed along with his children....

26. ...What battles were fought, what blood was shed, for the sole purpose of bringing almost all the peoples of Italy into subjection like savage barbarians — and

---

61. Augustine is perhaps referring to the effective outlawing of pagan practices several centuries later, in 391, as the result of an edict of Valentinian II, Theodosius I, and Arcadius. See *Codex Theodosianus* XVI,10,10.
62. On the Gracchi see also above at II,21.
63. See Appian, *Civil War* I,26.

these the very peoples on whom Roman dominion most especially depended for its strength! The writers of history have hardly been able to find a satisfactory way of explaining how the Servile War, begun by a tiny band of gladiators (fewer than seventy, in fact), came to expand to such a vast number of such bitter and ferocious men who went on to defeat so many generals of the Roman people and to devastate so many cities and regions.[64] Nor was this the only Servile War.[65] Earlier, bands of slaves had depopulated the province of Macedonia, and then Sicily and the coast of Italy.[66] Who could find the words to match the magnitude of the events, the sheer horror of the pirates' initial acts of banditry and then the fierce wars they waged?...

Civil War: Marius and Sulla

27. ...In that war between Marius and Sulla — leaving aside those who fell in battle outside the walls — within the city itself the streets, squares, markets, theaters, and temples were so full of dead bodies that it was hard to tell at which point the victors did more killing, whether prior to the victory in order to achieve it or after the victory because they had achieved it. For as soon as Marius triumphed and gained his return from exile — leaving aside the general slaughter perpetrated on all sides — the head of the consul Octavius was put on display on the speakers' platform in the forum; the Caesars were murdered by Fimbria in their own homes; the two Crassi, father and son, were killed before each other's eyes; Baebius and Numitorius died when they were dragged on hooks and their entrails ripped out; Catulus evaded the hands of his enemies by drinking poison; and Merula, the flamen of Jupiter, slit his veins and so poured out an offering to Jupiter of his own blood. And, in addition, anyone whose greeting Marius refused to acknowledge by extending his right hand was immediately cut down before his very eyes.[67]

28. Then came Sulla's victory, which certainly avenged all this cruelty but was purchased at the price of terrible bloodshed among the citizenry. Even though the war was now over, its antagonisms lived on, and his victory was even more cruel in peace....

29. Is there any fury of foreign nations or any savagery on the part of barbarians that can be compared to this victory of citizens over fellow-citizens? Which was the more deadly, the more hideous, the more heart-rending for Rome to see: the incursion of the Gauls long ago and the more recent incursion of the Goths,[68] or the sheer ferocity of Marius and Sulla and other distinguished men in their

---

64. See Appian, *Civil War* I,116-120.
65. There was also the uprising of Spartacus during the years 73-71 B.C.
66. See Florus, *Epitome of Roman History* II,7 (III,19).
67. See Appian, *Civil War* I,95-96.
68. Augustine is referring here to the sack of Rome in 410 that led to the writing of *The City of God*.

factions? It was as if Rome's own bright eyes were on a rampage against her own limbs. The Gauls, it is true, murdered any senator they could find anywhere in the city outside of the stronghold of the Capitol, which was the only place that was defended anyway. But at least they sold life in exchange for gold to those who had dug themselves in on that hill — despite the fact that they could certainly have drained their life away by siege, even though they were unable to snatch it away at one blow of the sword. And the Goths, in fact, spared so many senators that the wonder is that they killed any at all.

In contrast, Sulla set himself up as victor, while Marius still lived, in the very Capitol that had remained safe from the Gauls. It was from there that he issued his murderous decrees; and when Marius escaped by fleeing (though he would shortly return even more ferocious and bloodthirsty), Sulla in the Capitol deprived many persons of life and property, even making use of senatorial decrees to do so. Then, in Sulla's absence, was there anything Marius's faction regarded as sacred or to be spared? They did not even spare Mucius, a citizen, senator, and pontiff, clinging piteously to the very altar where, so they say, the fate of Rome resides. And lastly, to say nothing of countless other deaths, Sulla's final list of proscriptions put more senators to death than the Goths were even able to plunder.

30. How can people be so shameless, then, so rash, so impudent, so foolish — or, rather, so utterly mad — that they do not blame their own gods for all these past evils, and yet do blame our Christ for any present evils? Those ruthless civil wars, as their own authors admit, were more bitter than all their foreign wars, and they are judged not merely to have distressed the republic but to have entirely destroyed it. But they began long before the coming of Christ, and, by a chain of criminal causes, they led from the wars of Marius and Sulla to the wars of Sertorius and Cataline (the former proscribed by Sulla, the latter nurtured by him), then to the war of Lepidus and Catulus (of whom the one desired to rescind, the other to defend the enactments of Sulla), and then to the wars of Pompey and Caesar (Pompey had been a partisan of Sulla and had equaled or even exceeded his power; Caesar could not bear Pompey's power, but only because he did not have it himself, and yet, after Pompey was defeated and killed, he surpassed it). And finally they led to another Caesar, afterwards called Augustus, during whose reign Christ was born.

Civil Wars in the Time of Augustus

For Augustus himself also waged civil wars with a number of enemies, and in those wars, too, many distinguished men perished, including Cicero, articulate and skilled as he was in the art of governing a republic. It is true that Gaius Caesar, the one who defeated Pompey, showed genuine clemency in exercising his victorious powers and granted both life and civic honors to his opponents. But a conspiracy made up of certain noble senators, claiming to act in defense of the liberty of the republic, murdered him in the very Senate House itself on the grounds that what he really wanted was to be king. Then Antony, a man of very different moral character, stained and corrupted by every vice, was seen to be striving for Caesar's power; and Cicero fiercely resisted him in the name of that same liberty of the homeland. At this point there emerged a young man of extraordinary qualities, that other Caesar, the adopted son of Gaius Caesar, who, as I said, was afterwards called Augustus. This young Caesar was favored by Cicero in order that his power might be nurtured against Antony. What Cicero hoped was that, once Antony's dominance had been repulsed and suppressed, this Caesar would restore the republic's liberty — which shows how blind and how incapable of foreseeing the future Cicero was! For that young man, the very one whose career and power Cicero had been promoting, permitted Cicero himself to be slain by Antony under the provisions of a kind of pact of alliance with the latter, and he brought firmly under his own rule the very liberty of the republic for which Cicero had spoken out so forcefully.

31. So then, let those who are ungrateful to Christ for his great benefits blame their own gods for these great evils. It is beyond doubt that, when these evils took place, the divinities' altars were "warm with Sabean incense and fragrant with fresh garlands,"[69] their priesthoods were honored, their shrines were resplendent, their sacrifices were made, their games were held, there were frenzies in their temples — and all this at a time when the blood of so many citizens was being shed everywhere by citizens, not just in other places but even in the midst of the very altars of the gods. Cicero did not choose to flee to a temple, because Mucius had already found that it did no good to make that choice. But those who, with much less reason, now hurl abuse at these Christian times either fled on their own to places most especially dedicated to Christ or were even led to those places by the barbarians themselves, in order to save their lives.

These Evils All Occurred Prior to Christianity, when the Gods Were Still Worshiped

Now — omitting the many other instances I have already cited, as well as the many more I decided it would take too long to relate — I am certain of one thing, and anyone who judges impartially will readily acknowledge the point: if the human race had received the teaching of Christ prior to the Punic Wars, and if a vast devastation had followed, such as that which afflicted Europe and Africa in those wars, there is not one of those who now berate us who would have blamed those evils on anything but the Christian religion. And their outcries would have been all the more intolerable if — speaking only of what pertains to the Romans — the reception and spread of the Christian religion had come before the invasion of the Gauls, or the flooding of the Tiber, or the fires that laid waste to Rome, or the worst evil of all, the Civil Wars.

---

69. Virgil, *Aeneid* I, 416-417.

There were other evils as well, evils so incredible when they occurred that they were counted as prodigies. And if these had happened in Christian times, who would have been blamed for them, as if they were crimes, but the Christian people?...

The kind of nonsense we are faced with, and to which we are forced to reply, would certainly blame all these evils, without exception, on the Christian religion, if it saw them in Christian times. And yet they do not blame such things on their own gods; rather they demand that their gods be worshiped for the sake of escaping the lesser evils of the present, despite the incontrovertible fact that those who used to worship them suffered these far greater evils in the past.

Study Questions for Book III

Natural disasters inflict disproportionate suffering on the world's poorest and most vulnerable peoples. These peoples are often the most religious. What role might religion play in contemporary political and economic debates about climate change and ecological justice?

The migration of peoples around the world has increased significantly in recent decades, due to political instability, economic inequality and growth in global population. One factor in Augustine's writing *The City of God* was the influx of refugees into Africa from Italy after the siege and sack of Rome in 410. What political and social parallels do you see between the 5th century instability of the Roman Empire and 21st-century issues of population growth and the movement of peoples?

Cinematic entertainers and media personalities hover in the popular imagination as if in an Olympian realm of utopian exceptionalism. Does such attention and adulation function in psychological and sociological roles similar to those of the popular, colorful divinities of antiquity?

BOOK IV

Book IV opens with a brief review of Books I-III and then turns to the question of why God aided the Romans in extending their empire. Instead of addressing this question directly (the direct response is reserved for Book V), it takes up two preliminary points. First it seeks to discredit the notion that empire is a great good, since empire comes at the expense of war and conquest and is an expression of political greed. Multiple small kingdoms, living at peace with themselves and their neighbors, would make for a better ordering of political society. Secondly, it seeks to disqualify the idea that any of Rome's traditional gods, whether major or minor, could possibly be responsible for the extent and duration of Rome's imperial sway. The minor gods are too restricted in their limited functions; and the major gods, although when interpreted with philosophical sophistication they may point in the direction of the one God who governs the destiny of kingdoms, do not function as the givers of the truly important divine gifts such as virtue and felicity. Even for the learned, then, it turns out to be impossible to escape the hold of traditional superstition that is cultivated and supported by the malignant demons who are the actual gods of Roman religion. Throughout the book, Augustine repeatedly emphasizes that it is only the grace of the true God which liberates from the hold of the demons and grants the gift of empire.

1. When I set out to speak of the city of God, I thought that I should first reply to its enemies. In their pursuit of earthly joys and their insatiable longing for fleeting goods, these people cry out against the Christian religion, the one true and saving religion, for any sorrows that they suffer on this score. Yet those sorrows come upon them not from God's severity, punishing them, but rather from God's mercy, admonishing them.

Among these enemies of ours, there is the great mass of the uneducated, who are all the more inflamed to hate us by what they suppose is the authority of the learned.[1] In their ignorance, they imagine that the happenings of their own times are quite extraordinary and never occurred before in other eras in the past, and they are encouraged in this view by those who know it to be false but keep their knowledge hidden in order to make it seem that they have good reason to complain about us. It was necessary, therefore, to demonstrate that the truth of the matter is very different from what they think, and to show this from the very books which their own authors wrote to present us with the history of times past. At the same

---

1. See also above at II,3.

time, it was necessary to make it clear that the false gods whom these people used to worship openly and still worship secretly[2] are nothing but unclean spirits, wholly malignant and utterly deceitful demons, so much so that they delight in crimes — crimes real or crimes imagined, but in either case their own crimes — which they wanted to have celebrated for them at their festivals. What they wanted was to make it impossible for human weakness to be restrained from committing abominable deeds due to the fact that imitating such acts has the support of a supposedly divine authority....

The Basis for Rome's Expansion

3. Let us now see, then, how it is that they dare to give the credit for the wide expanse and long duration of the Roman empire to those gods whom they claim to have worshiped with honor, despite the fact that their service consisted of the offering of abhorrent shows and the ministry of abhorrent men.

The Evaluation of Empire

First, however, I would like briefly to consider this question: What reason or sense is there in wanting to boast of the size and expanse of an empire when you cannot show that its people are happy? Or why boast of an empire if its people always dwell in the midst of the disasters of war and the spilling of blood — the blood of fellow-citizens or the blood of foreign enemies, but, in either case, human blood — and always live under the dark shadow of fear and in the lust for blood? Any joy they have may be compared to the fragile brilliance of glass: there is always the terrible fear that it will suddenly be shattered.

It will be easier to reach a decision on this point if we are not carried away by empty bombast and do not let the sharp edge of our inquiry be blunted by high-sounding terms when we hear of "peoples," "kingdoms," and "provinces." Instead, let us imagine two individuals, for single individuals, like single letters in a word, are the elements, so to speak, of which a city or a kingdom is made up, no matter how broad the territory it occupies. Let us suppose that one of these two individuals is poor, or rather of moderate means, and the other very rich. But the rich man is tortured by fears, wasted with griefs, aflame with greed, never free from care, always restless and uneasy, out of breath from unending struggles with his enemies. It is true enough that he increases his holdings beyond measure by going through these miseries; but at the same time, thanks to that very increase, he also multiplies his bitter cares. In contrast, the individual of moderate means is satisfied with his small and limited property; he is loved by family and friends; he enjoys sweet peace with his relations, neighbors, and friends; he is devout in his

---

2. The gods were being worshiped secretly presumably because paganism had been effectively outlawed by an imperial edict issued in 391. See *Codex Theodosianus* XVI,10,10.

piety, benevolent of mind, sound of body, moderate in his style of life, unblemished in character, and untroubled in conscience. I do not know whether anyone would be so foolish as to have any doubt about which of the two to prefer.[3] It is the same with two families, two peoples, or two kingdoms, as it is with the two individuals. The same rule of equanimity applies. If we are vigilant in using it and make it the rule for our inquiry, we shall have no difficulty in seeing where happiness lies, and where hollow show.

Therefore, if the true God is worshiped and is served with authentic rites and good morals, it is beneficial that good persons should rule far and wide and for a long time; and this is beneficial not so much for the good persons themselves as for those over whom they rule. For as far as they themselves are concerned, their piety and integrity, which are great gifts from God, are enough to bring them the true happiness by which this life is lived well and, thereafter, eternal life is attained. On this earth, then, the reign of the good is not so much of profit to themselves as it is to human society at large. In contrast, the reign of the wicked does harm rather to those who are the rulers. They devastate their own souls due to the wider scope they have for their wickedness, while those placed under them in servitude are not harmed at all, except by their own iniquity.[4] Thus the good person is free, even if a slave, and the evil person is enslaved, even if a ruler — enslaved not to one master but, what is far worse, to as many masters as he has vices. It is in reference to these vices that Scripture says, *For people are slaves to whatever masters them* (2 Pt 2:19).

4. Remove justice, then, and what are kingdoms but large gangs of robbers? And what are gangs of robbers but small kingdoms? The gang, too, is a group of men ruled by a leader's command. It is bound together by a pact of association, and its loot is divided according to an agreed law. If, by constantly adding desperate men, this scourge grows to such an extent that it acquires territory, establishes a home base, occupies cities, and subjugates peoples, it more openly assumes the name of kingdom, a name now publicly conferred on it due not to any reduction in greed but rather to the addition of impunity. For it was a witty and true response that a certain captured pirate made to the famous Alexander the Great. When the king asked the man what he meant by infesting the sea, he defiantly replied, "Just what you mean when you infest the whole world! But because I do it with one tiny ship, I am called a robber; and because you do it with a great fleet, you are called an emperor."[5] ...

---

3. Citing the advantages of poverty vis-à-vis wealth is a romantic notion not uncommon in ancient thought, both pagan and Christian. See, e.g., Lucan, *Pharsalia* V,527-567; Ambrose, *Hexaemeron* VI,8,52. Augustine initially posits a poor individual but, more reasonably, immediately changes his mind in favor of one of moderate means.
4. That the good are not hurt by the actions of the wicked is the argument presented at length above at I,10-29.
5. See Cicero, *Republic* III,24. Alexander the Great lived from 356 to 323 B.C.; he is referred to as Alexander of Macedon, where he was born, below at IV,7.

The Gods and the Rise and Fall of Assyrian Rule

6. Justinus, who followed Trogus Pompeius[6] in writing Greek or rather foreign history not only in Latin, as Trogus did, but also in abbreviated form, begins his work in this way: "At the beginning of the history of tribes and nations, power was in the hands of kings, who rose to this peak of authority not by courting popular support but because their moderation was recognized among good men. The peoples were not kept in check by any laws; it was the custom to defend rather than to extend the boundaries of one's rule; and kingdoms were confined each within the limits of its own homeland. Ninus,[7] king of the Assyrians, was the first to change the ancient and, as it were, ancestral custom of the peoples due to his novel lust for empire. He was the first to make war on his neighbors; and, subduing peoples still untrained to resist, he extended his rule all the way to the borders of Libya."[8] And a little later Justinus says, "Ninus secured the vast dominions he had won by constantly adding to them. Thus, strengthened by the new forces he gained from subjugating his neighbors, he went on to attack others, and each new victory became the instrument of the next until he subdued all the peoples of the east."[9]

Now, whether or not Justinus or Trogus wrote reliable accounts (for other more trustworthy accounts show that they lied about some matters), it is agreed among other writers that Ninus extended the kingdom of the Assyrians far and wide.[10] And the Assyrian kingdom lasted so long that the Roman empire has not yet reached the same age. For those who have studied the chronology of history write that, starting from the first year of Ninus's reign, it endured for 1240 years until it passed to the Medes. But to make war on one's neighbors, to go on from there to further attacks, to crush and subjugate peoples without provocation, all out of mere lust for dominion — what else are we to call this but armed robbery on a grand scale?

7. And if this Assyrian kingdom became so large and lasted so long without the help of the gods, why is it that the wide extent and lengthy duration of Rome's rule are ascribed to the Roman gods? Whatever caused the one is surely also the cause of the other. But if people claim that the Assyrian success is, in fact, to be ascribed to the gods' help, then I ask, which gods? For the other nations that Ninus subdued and subjugated did not then worship other gods. Or if the Assyrians did have special gods of their own — who were more highly skilled, as it were, in building and maintaining an empire — had these gods died when the Assyrians lost their empire? Or did they prefer to go over to the Medes because their back

---

6. Marcus Junianus Justinus was a third-century A.D. historian, while Pompeius Trogus wrote in the early first century A.D. Trogus's history has not survived except in the abbreviated form produced by Justinus.
7. Ninus is a largely mythical figure credited with the founding of Nineveh.
8. Justinus, *Epitome of the Philippic History of Pompeius Trogus* I,1.
9. Ibid.
10. See Diodorus Siculus, *Library of History* II,1-2.

wages had not been paid, or because they had the promise of higher pay? And then on to the Persians, when Cyrus enticed them with the promise of a still better deal?[11] The Persians, after all, ever since the very large but very brief kingdom of Alexander of Macedon, have maintained their rule right down to the present over no inconsiderable territory in the east.

If this is true, either the gods are faithless, abandoning their own people and going over to the enemy, something that even the man Camillus did not do when, after storming and taking a city which was a bitter enemy, he felt the sting of Rome's ingratitude, the very Rome for which he had won the victory; instead he later forgot the wrong done to him and, with only his homeland in mind, saved it a second time from the Gauls. Or else the gods are not as strong as gods ought to be, if they can be defeated by mere human plans or mere human strength. Or if, perhaps, when the gods wage war against each other, they are defeated not by human beings but by other gods who are the special gods of specific cities, then they obviously have enmities among themselves, which each takes up on behalf of his own faction. And it follows that no city should worship its own gods more than others, from whom its own gods might receive aid and support.

Finally, whatever may or may not be true about this transfer or flight or migration or desertion in battle on the part of the gods, it is certainly true that the name of Christ had not yet been preached in those eras or in those regions of the earth when those kingdoms were lost through incalculable military disasters and passed into other hands. For if, when their kingdom was taken from the Assyrians after more than twelve hundred years, the Christian religion had already been proclaiming another eternal kingdom and had already put an end to the sacrilegious worship of false gods, what would the foolish people of that nation have said? What else but that a kingdom which had endured so long could only have perished for one reason: because it had abandoned its own cults and embraced Christianity! Our opponents should see themselves mirrored in that foolish claim (which, after all, might well have been made), and, if there is any shame in them, they should be too embarrassed to make similar complaints of their own.

The Roman empire, however, is simply afflicted, not changed into something else. The same thing has happened to it in other eras, before Christ's name was proclaimed, and it has recovered from such affliction. There is no need, then, to despair of recovery now. For who knows God's will in this regard?

Which of the Gods Aided the Expansion of Rome?

8. Next let us ask, if you like, which god or which gods, from the whole throng that the Romans worshiped, they believe did the most to extend and preserve their

---

11. Cyrus the Great ruled Persia for about thirty years and died in 530 B.C.

empire.[12] For they obviously do not dare to ascribe any part in a work of such grandeur and so replete with nobility to Cloacina, or to Volupia, who gets her name from pleasure, or to Lubentina, whose name comes from lust, or to Vaticanus, who presides over the wails of infants, or to Cunina, who looks after their cradles.[13] But how can I possibly list the names of all their gods and goddesses in just one passage of this book? They themselves were hardly able to include them all in the huge volumes in which they marked out the specific responsibilities and individual areas of all their divinities....

I do not mention them all, for the whole business bores me, despite the fact that it does not make the Romans ashamed. The very few instances I have listed, however, should make it clear that they certainly do not venture to claim that these were the divinities that established, increased, and preserved the Roman empire. Each of these deities was so involved with his particular duties that nothing was assigned as a whole to any one of them....

The Greater Gods: Jupiter and the Elements of the Universe

9. Omitting this throng of godlings, then, or at least setting them aside for the time being, we ought to ask about the role of the more important gods, by which Rome became so great as to rule for such a long time over so many peoples. This, no doubt, was Jupiter's work. For he is the one they make the king of all the gods and goddesses. That is what his scepter indicates, as well as the Capitol on its high hill. It is of this god that they most aptly declare (even if it was said by a poet), "All things are full of Jupiter."[14] And he is the one whom Varro believes is worshiped, although called by another name, by those who worship only one god, without an image.[15] But if this is true, why was he so badly treated in Rome — and, in fact, among other peoples as well — that an image was made for him? Varro found this so offensive that, even though he was held down by the perverse custom of such a great city, he still did not hesitate to say and write that those who had set up images for the people had both reduced reverence and increased error.[16]

10. Again, why is Juno joined to him as his wife, who is called "sister and spouse"?[17] Because, they say, we locate Jupiter in the aether and Juno in the air; and these two elements are conjoined, the one above, the other below. He is not

---

12. The following chapters are reminiscent of Tertullian, *Apology* 25 and, much more extensively, of Arnobius, *Against the Nations* IV.
13. Cloacina, from *cloaca*, meaning "sewer"; Volupia, from *voluptas*, meaning "pleasure"; Lubentina, from *libido*, meaning "lust"; Vaticanus, from *vagitus*, meaning "wailing"; Cunina, from *cuna*, meaning "cradle."
14. Virgil, *Eclogues* III,60.
15. See *On the Latin Language* V,66.
16. Cited in Arnobius, *Against the Nations* VII,1.
17. Virgil, *Aeneid* I,47.

the one, then, of whom it was said, "All things are full of Jupiter" — assuming that Juno also fills some part of the whole. Or is it rather that both fill both, and both spouses are in both of these elements and in each of these elements at one and the same time? In that case, why is the aether allotted to Jupiter and the air to Juno? At any rate, these two would seem to be enough. Why is it that the sea is assigned to Neptune and the earth to Pluto? And to keep these also from going without wives, Salacia is added to Neptune and Proserpina to Pluto. For, they say, just as Juno occupies the lower part of the heavens — that is, the air[18] — so Salacia occupies the lower part of the sea and Proserpina the lower part of the earth.

They are looking for ways to patch up their fables, but without finding any. For, if things were as they say, their ancient teachers would have come up with three elements of the universe, not four.[19] so that these three married pairs could each be assigned as a pair to its own element. As it is, however, their teachers have clearly affirmed that the aether is one thing, the air another. But water, whether higher or lower, is still water. Or suppose that there is a difference: is the difference great enough that one part ceases to be water? And what else can the lower part of the earth be except earth, no matter how great the difference that distinguishes it from the higher part?...

Jupiter as the One God in All

11. Let them make whatever claims they want, then, in their naturalistic interpretations and arguments. Let Jupiter, on one view, be the soul of this material universe, who fills and moves the whole mass, which is constructed from and composed of the four elements — or from as many elements as they please. On another, let him yield their own parts of it to his sisters and brothers. On another, let him be the aether, so that from above he can embrace Juno, the air spread out below. On another, let him be the entire heaven, including the air, and let him impregnate with his fertile showers and seeds the earth which is at once his wife and his mother (since there is nothing shameful about this in the case of the gods!). And on still another — not that we need to review every possibility — let him be the one god of whom, as many think, the most outstanding poet said, "For God ranges through all lands, all tracts of sea, and heaven's depth."[20] Let him be Jupiter in the aether, Juno in the air, Neptune in the sea, Salacia in the lower part of the sea, Pluto in the earth, Proserpina in the lower part of the earth, Vesta in the domestic hearth, Vulcan in the craftsman's forge. Let him be the sun, the moon, and the stars among the heavenly bodies, Apollo among seers, Mercury in commerce, in

---

18. See Cicero, *On the Nature of the Gods* II,66.
19. I.e., air, earth and water, rather than air, earth, water and fire. Empedocles (c. 495-c. 435 B.C.) was apparently the first to speak of four elements as constitutive of the universe. See Diogenes Laertius, *Lives of Eminent Philosophers* VIII,76.
20. Virgil, *Georgics* IV,221-222.

Janus the initiator, in Terminus the ender, Saturn in time, Mars and Bellona in war, Liber in the vineyards, Ceres in the cornfields, Diana in the woods, and Minerva in intellectual insights.[21]

Finally, let him be in that throng of plebeian gods, as they might be called. Under the name of Liber, let him preside over the seed of men, and under the name of Libera over the seeds of women. Let him be Diespater, who brings the newborn into the light of day.[22] Let him be the goddess Mena, whom they put in charge of women's menstrual periods; and Lucina, who is invoked by women giving birth.[23] Let him bring help to the newborn by receiving them on the lap of earth and be called Opis.[24] Let him open babies' mouths to wail and be called the god Vaticanus; let him lift them up from the earth and be called the goddess Levana;[25] let him guard their cradles and be called Cunina. Let him, and no other, be the one present in the goddesses who sing the fates of newborn infants and are called Carmentes.[26] Let him preside over chance happenings and be called Fortuna.[27] In the goddess Rumina, let him bring milk from the breast for the infant (since the ancients called the breast *ruma*); in the goddess Potina, let him provide drink; and in the goddess Educa, let him offer food.[28] From the fear of infants, let him be called Paventia; from the hope which comes, Venilia; from pleasure, Volupia; from action, Agenoria.[29] From the spurs by which a person is driven to overdo, let him be named Stimula.[30] Let him be the goddess Strenia from making a person vigorous.[31] Let him be Numeria, who teaches people to count, and Camena, who teaches people to sing.[32] Let him also be the god Consus, from giving counsel, and the goddess Sentia, from inspiring thoughts.[33] Let him be the goddess Iuventas, who oversees the beginnings of young manhood after the boyhood toga is put aside; and let him also be Fortuna Barbata, who gives adult men their beards.[34] (For some reason, the Romans refused to honor these men by giving this divinity — who,

---

21. See Diogenes Laertius, *Lives of Eminent Philosophers* VII,147, for the Stoic notion that the one deity is called by different names in keeping with the different functions that he exercises.
22. Diespater, from *dies*, meaning "day," and *pater*, meaning "father."
23. Mena, from *menstrua*, meaning "monthly periods"; Lucina, meaning "bringing into the light," a metaphor for childbirth.
24. Opis, from *ops*, meaning "help."
25. Levana, from *levare*, meaning "to lift."
26. Carmentes, from *carmen*, meaning "song."
27. Fortuna, related to *fortuitus*, meaning "fortuitous."
28. Potina, from *potio*, meaning "drink"; Educo seems to be related to *educare*, meaning "to educate," or to *educere*, meaning "to lead forth," rather than to *esca*, meaning "food."
29. Paventia, from *pavor*, meaning "fear"; Venilia, from *venire*, meaning "to come"; Agenoria, from *agere*, meaning "to act."
30. Stimula, from *stimulus*, meaning "spur" or "goad."
31. Strenia, from *strenuus*, meaning "vigorous."
32. Numeria, from *numerare*, meaning "to count"; Camena, from *canere*, meaning "to sing."
33. Consus, from *concilium*, meaning "counsel"; Sentia, from *sententia*, meaning "thought."
34. Iuventas, from *iuventus*, meaning "youth" or "young manhood"; Fortuna Barbata, meaning "Bearded Fortune," from *barbata*, meaning "bearded."

whatever else he may be, is at least a male god — the masculine name Barbatus from *barba*, like Nodutus from *nodus*; and they could certainly have given him not the feminine name Fortuna but, in light of his beard, the masculine Fortunius.) In the god Iugatinus, let him join couples in marriage; and when the virgin bride's girdle is unloosed, let him be invoked with the name of the goddess Virginensis.[35] Let him be Mutunus or Tutunus, whom the Greeks call Priapus.[36]

If it does not make the Romans ashamed, let the one god Jupiter be everything I have named and anything I have not (for I did not suppose that I had to name everything). Let him be all these gods and goddesses; or, as some would have it, let all these be parts of him or powers of his. This is how things look to those who like to think that he is the soul of the world, a view held by their supposedly great and learned men.[37]

Why not Worship the One God Alone?

But if all this is true — and, for the moment, I do not ask whether it is or notn — what would they lose if, more prudently, they took a shorter way and simply worshiped the one god alone? What aspect of him would be slighted, so long as he himself were worshiped? But if they had good reason to fear that parts of him might get angry if overlooked or neglected, then it is not true that his whole life is, as they want to maintain, the life of a single living being which contains all the gods as powers or members or parts of itself. Rather, since one part can be angered more than another, and one part can be soothed while another is enraged, it turns out that each part has a life of its own, distinct from the others. But if it is claimed that all of them together — that is, the whole of Jupiter himself — might take offense if each part were not worshiped individually and given its due, this is utter nonsense. It is obvious that no part would be overlooked when the one who is worshiped is the very one who contains them all. For when they say (to leave aside all the other claims they make, which are beyond number) that all the stars are parts of Jupiter, and that they are alive and have rational souls, and therefore are incontestably gods, they do not notice how many of these stars they do not worship, how many they do not build temples to or erect altars for. In fact, they have held that altars should be erected and individual sacrifices made only to the tiniest handful of stars. If those that are not individually worshiped are all angry, then, are not the Romans afraid to live with only a few placated and all of heaven angry? Or if they do worship all the stars because all the stars are in Jupiter, and they worship Jupiter, they could just as well, by taking this shorter way, offer sup-

---

35. Iugatinus, from *iungere*, meaning "to join"; Virginensis, from *virgo*, meaning "virgin."
36. Mutunus and Tutunus were usually understood to be a single priapic divinity and were called Mutunus Tutunus, although here Augustine separates the two, as does Arnobius, *Against the Pagans* IV,11.
37. See Plato, *Philebus* 30a-d.

plications to all the gods in that one god alone. In that case none would be angered, because none would be slighted in the one god alone. And surely that would be better than worshiping only a few and thus giving good reason for anger to the many more who are neglected, especially when even Priapus, swelled up in his shameful nakedness,[38] is preferred to these stars shining down from their celestial abode.

God as the Soul of the World, the World as the Body of God

12. What? This is surely something that ought to trouble intelligent people. In fact, it ought to trouble people of all kinds, for no special ability is required here. With all zeal for debate and dispute set aside, let them consider this point: if God is the soul of the world and the world is to him what the body is to the soul, so that they make one living being, consisting of body and soul; and if this God is in some way the bosom of nature, containing all things in himself, so that from his soul, from which the whole mass of the world draws its life, the lives and souls of all living things are derived, each according to its lot at birth; then there is nothing left that is not a part of God. And if this is so, who can fail to see what irreverent and irreligious consequences follow? When anyone tramples on anything, he tramples on a part of God! When any living thing is killed, a part of God is slaughtered! And I simply refuse to mention all the possibilities that might come to mind but cannot be named without shame.[39]

13. But if their argument is that only rational animals, such as human beings, are parts of God, I simply do not see how, if the whole world is God, they can fail to include the beasts among his parts. There is no need, however, to argue the point. Confining ourselves to rational animals alone, that is, to human beings, what could be more misguided than to believe that, when a child is spanked, a part of God is spanked? Could anyone in his right mind bear to believe that parts of God become lustful, wicked, irreligious, and wholly worthy of condemnation? And finally, why is God angry with people who do not worship him when it is his own parts that are not worshiping him?

The only possibility left open to them, therefore, is to say that all the gods have their own lives, that each one lives for himself, that no one of them is a part of any other, and that all the gods who can be known and worshiped ought to be worshiped (although there are so many that not all can be known). And because Jupiter presides over all these gods as king, I presume that they consider him to be the one who established and expanded the Roman empire. For, if Jupiter himself did not do this, what other god do they believe could have undertaken such a

---

38. "Swelled up in his shameful nakedness" because Priapus was always depicted with a large erection.
39. The notion that the world has a soul, here understood as God, is a Stoic one. See Cicero, *On the Nature of the Gods* II,11. See also below at IV,31.

massive task? All the others, after all, would be occupied with their own specific tasks and responsibilities, and none of them would invade the sphere of any other. It is only by the king of the gods, therefore, that a human kingdom could be made to grow and expand.

Victory, Just War, and Foreign Iniquity

14. In this regard, I first ask why the empire itself is not one of the gods. Why should empire not be a god, if Victory is a goddess? For that matter, what need is there for Jupiter to be involved, if Victory is favorable and propitious and always goes to those whom she wishes to be the victors? So long as this goddess was favorable and propitious, even if Jupiter was on vacation or busy doing something else,[40] what nations would remain unconquered? What kingdoms would not submit?

But perhaps good men get no pleasure from waging wholly wicked and unrighteous war or from provoking, by deliberate aggression, peaceful neighbors who are doing them no harm, for the sole purpose of extending their dominion. If this is their view, I certainly approve and applaud.

15. Let them consider, then, whether it is really appropriate for good men to rejoice at the extent of their rule. For it was the iniquity of those against whom they waged just wars that helped the empire to grow. In fact, the empire would undoubtedly have remained small if its neighbors had been peaceful and just, never provoking them into war by doing them any injury. And, in that case, human affairs would have been happier. All kingdoms would have been small, rejoicing in concord with their neighbors, and so there would have been fully as many kingdoms among the peoples in the world as there are now houses among the citizens in a city. Thus, making war and extending their rule by subjugating other peoples may look like happiness to the wicked, but to the good it only looks like a necessary evil. But since it would be still worse for the unjust to rule over those who are relatively more just, even this necessity is not inappropriately called a kind of happiness. There is no doubt, however, that it is a greater happiness to live in concord with a good neighbor than to subjugate a bad neighbor who makes war. It is a bad prayer, then, to want to have someone to hate or to fear in order to have someone to conquer.

If, therefore, it was by waging just rather than irreligious and unjust wars that the Romans were able to acquire such a vast empire, perhaps they should even worship foreign iniquity as a goddess. For we see how much she has helped in giving the empire its great extent by making others unjust so that there would be peoples against whom just wars might be waged and the empire be enlarged. And why should not iniquity — or, at least, the iniquity of foreign peoples — be a

---

40. See Elijah's mockery of the priests of Baal in 1 K 18:27.

goddess, if fear and terror and fever all deserved to be Roman gods? It was due, then, to these two — that is, to foreign iniquity and the goddess Victory — that the empire grew, even when Jupiter was on holiday. Iniquity stirred up causes for wars, and Victory brought those wars to a happy conclusion. As for Jupiter, what part would he have to play? Any benefits that might be supposed to come from him were themselves held to be gods, themselves named as gods, and themselves invoked for the sake of the parts they played on their own. Of course, Jupiter might have had some part to play here, if he were called Empire in the same way that the goddess is called Victory. Or, if empire is, in fact, a gift of Jupiter, then why should not victory also be considered his gift? And it certainly would be considered a gift if it were not some stone on the Capitol[41] but rather the true *king of kings and lord of lords* (Rev 19:16) that people knew and worshiped....

The Goddesses Felicity and Fortune

18. And what about the point that Felicity is also a goddess?[42] She received a temple; she was worthy of an altar; appropriate rites were performed for her. She is the only one, then, who should have been worshiped. For where she is present, is any good absent? But what sense does it make that Fortune is also considered a goddess and is also worshiped? Or is felicity one thing and fortune another? Yes, because there can be bad fortune as well as good, but if happiness were bad, it would not be happiness at all. But surely we ought to regard all the gods of both sexes (if the gods, too, have sexes) as only good. This is what Plato says,[43] what other philosophers say, what outstanding rulers of the republic and of peoples say. How is it, then, that the goddess Fortune is sometimes good, sometimes bad? Perhaps, when she is bad, she is no longer a goddess but is suddenly changed into a malignant demon? In that case, how many goddesses are there of this kind? As many, surely, as there are fortunate men, that is, men of good fortune. But since there are simultaneously — that is, at exactly the same time — a great many others who have bad fortune, would Fortune (if she is the same goddess) be simultaneously both good and bad, good for some and bad for others? Or is she, as a goddess, always good? In that case she is the same as Felicity. So why are different names used?

There is nothing wrong with that; one thing is often called by two names. But why the different temples, the different altars, the different rites? The reason, they say, is that happiness is what the good have on the basis of their prior merits, while

---

41. A stone known as the *Iupiter lapis*, or stone of Jupiter, was kept in the temple of Jupiter on the Capitoline Hill in Rome and was used as an object on which to swear when oaths were taken.
42. The mention of Felicity, as one among many gods and goddesses, is an occasion for Augustine not only to expatiate on the goddess herself and her relatively insignificant place in the Roman pantheon but also to analyze briefly the nature of the felicity, or happiness, of which she was the tutelary deity.
43. See *Republic* II,378b.

what we call good fortune comes by chance[44] to the good and the bad alike, without any consideration of merits, and that is why she is called Fortune.[45] How, then, is she good, if she comes both to the good and to the bad without distinguishing between them? And why bother to worship her at all if she is so blind — striking people utterly at random — that she often passes over those who worship her and clings to those who despise her...?

Virtue and the Virtues: not Goddesses but Gifts of God

20. The Romans also made Virtue a goddess, and if she really were a goddess, she certainly ought to have taken precedence over many others. In fact, however, since virtue is not a goddess but rather a gift of God, let it be obtained from the One by whom alone it can be given. Then, that whole throng of false gods will simply vanish. But why was Faith also held to be a goddess? Why did she also receive a temple and an altar? Anyone who has the good sense to acknowledge her makes himself her dwelling place. Besides, how do they know what faith is, when her first and most important role is to bring people to believe in the true God? And why was Virtue not enough for them? Is not faith included in virtue? After all, they saw that virtue is to be classified under four headings — prudence, justice, fortitude, and temperance — and, since each of these has its own subdivisions, faith is one of the subdivisions of justice.[46] And for those of us who know what it means that the just shall live by faith (Rom 1:17), faith holds the highest place.

What astonishes me about these people who are so eager for a multitude of gods is this: if Faith is a goddess, why have they wronged so many other goddesses by leaving them aside, when they could have dedicated temples and altars to these as well? Why did temperance not deserve to be a goddess? After all, many Roman leaders gained no small glory in her name. Why is fortitude not a goddess? She was with Mucius when he put his right hand in the flames;[47] with Curtius when he threw himself headlong into the gaping earth for his country's sake;[48] and with

---

44. "By chance": *fortuito*.
45. See Seneca, Letter 91,4-7.
46. Prudence, justice, fortitude and temperance are the four so-called cardinal virtues first outlined by Plato (see *Republic* IV,427e-434c) and accepted into Christian usage, mostly notably by Ambrose, *On the Duties of the Clergy* I. On the relation of faith to justice see ibid. I,29,142, where faith is described as the foundation of justice.
47. Gaius Mucius Scaevola was said to have demonstrated his bravery to the Etruscans, with whom Rome was at war in 508 B.C., by thrusting his hand into an Etruscan campfire after he had been captured by the enemy. See Livy, *History of Rome* II,12.
48. According to legend, after having heard that Rome was threatened by a catastrophe unless it sacrificed what was dearest to it, Marcus Curtius, understanding that bravery was what Rome most esteemed, is said to have ridden on horseback into a chasm in the Roman Forum, which swallowed him alive. See ibid. VII,6.

the Decii, father and son, when by vow they devoted themselves to death to save the army[49] (she was with them, that is, if true fortitude was actually exemplified in each case, a point not now at issue). Why did prudence and why did wisdom not deserve a place among the divinities? Is it because all these are worshiped under the one general name of Virtue herself? In that case, it would also have been possible for one god to be worshiped, with other gods reckoned as parts of that one. But Faith and Modesty are both included in this one Virtue, and yet they still deserved to have separate altars in separate temples of their own.

Virtue and Felicity

21. It was not truth but folly that made these goddesses. For these virtues are gifts of the true God, not goddesses themselves. Still, where there is virtue and felicity, why look for anything else? What *would* satisfy a person for whom virtue and felicity are not enough? Virtue includes everything we should do, and felicity everything we should desire. If Jupiter was worshiped in the hope that he might grant these — for, if extent and duration of rule are a good thing, they belong to this same felicity — why is it not understood that they are gifts of God and not goddesses at all?...

[Chapters 22 – 23 review Varro's reports on the functions of the gods and goddesses.]

23. ... But if felicity is not a goddess, because — which is true — it is a gift of God, then let people seek the God who can actually give happiness. Let them abandon the noxious multitude of false gods which the empty-headed multitude of fools chases after. These fools make the gifts of God into gods for themselves and offend God himself, the giver of these gifts, by their proud and obstinate self-will. Thus no one can escape unhappiness who worships happiness as a goddess and forsakes God, the giver of happiness, just as no one can escape hunger who licks at a picture of bread and does not ask for real bread from a person who has it.

The Naming of Gods for Their Gifts and the God Who Gives Happiness

24. But I want to consider what the Romans have to say about this. Are we to believe, they ask, that our ancestors were such fools that they did not know that these things are divine gifts and not gods? They knew that such gifts are only

---

49. Publius Decius Mus was the name of both a father and his son who purposely exposed themselves to death in battle respectively in 340 and 295 B.C. See ibid. VIII,9 and X,28.

granted by the generosity of one god or another, but when they could not discover the names of some of these gods, they called them by the names of the gifts which they believed they gave. Sometimes they modified the words: from war, for instance, they derived the name Bellona rather than Bellum; from cradles, the name Cunina rather than Cuna; from crops, the name Segetia rather than Seges; from fruits, the name Pomona rather than Pomum; and from oxen, the name Bubona rather than Bos.[50] In other cases, without any change in the word, they simply used the name of the thing itself. Thus, the goddess who gives money was called Pecunia — which certainly does not mean that money itself was considered a goddess. And the same is true in the cases of Virtue, who gives virtue, Honor, who gives honor, Concord, who gives concord, and Victory, who gives victory. So also, they say, when Felicity is called a goddess, the reference is not to the gift that is given but rather to the divinity by whom happiness is given.

25. Now that we have this explanation before us, it will be much easier, perhaps, to make our case to those whose hearts are not already too hardened. Human weakness, then, has already recognized that happiness cannot be given except by some god; and this was recognized by people who were worshiping a great many gods, including Jupiter himself, their king. But because they did not know the name of the god by whom happiness is given, they chose to call him by the name of the gift they believed was given by him. And this clearly shows that they did not think that happiness could be given by Jupiter himself, whom they already worshiped, but only by the deity whom they thought they should worship under the name of felicity itself. I assert, then, that they themselves believed happiness was given by a god whom they did not know. Let that God be sought, then; let that God be worshiped; and he is enough. Let the din of innumerable demons be renounced. And let this God be less than enough for the person for whom his gift is less than enough. Let this God, the giver of happiness, I say, be less than enough to worship for the person for whom happiness itself is less than enough to receive. But as for the person for whom happiness is enough, since there is nothing more that a person ought to desire, let him serve the one God who is the giver of happiness. This God is not the one they call Jupiter. For if they had recognized in Jupiter the giver of happiness, they clearly would not have looked for some other god or goddess, under the name of felicity itself, by whom felicity might be given. Nor would they have supposed that Jupiter himself was to be worshiped with such awful insults, for he is said to be a seducer of other men's wives and the lover and ravisher of a beautiful boy.[51]...

---

50. "War": *bellum*; "cradle": *cuna*; "crop": *seges*; "fruit": *pomum*; "ox": *bos*.
51. Ganymede was the beautiful boy. See Ovid, *Metamorphoses* X,155-156.

[Chapter 26 repeats the theme from Books I and II that state sponsored theatrical shows and games celebrate "divine crimes" of false gods and goddesses.]

Three Views of the Gods

27. It is recorded that the pontiff Scaevola, whose literary knowledge was immense, argued that three views of the gods are passed down to us: one by the poets, another by the philosophers, and a third by political leaders.[52] The first, he says, is mere nonsense, because many disgraceful tales have been made up about the gods, and the second is not suitable for civic society, because some things it contains are superfluous and some are even harmful for the people to know. The superfluous matters are no great issue, for, as the commonplace among jurists goes, "superfluous things do no harm."[53] But what are the points that actually do harm when they are made known to the multitude? They are, he says, such statements as these: "That Hercules, Aesculapius, Castor, and Pollux are not gods, for the learned claim that these were men who passed beyond our human condition." What else? "That cities do not have true images of the gods, for the true god has neither sex nor age nor defined bodily parts." The pontiff does not want the people to know these things because, in fact, he does not consider them to be false. Clearly, then, his view is that it is expedient for cities to be deceived in matters of religion, and Varro himself has no hesitation about saying the same in his books on things divine. What a splendid religion! The weak may flee to it in order to be set free, and when they ask for the truth that will set them free,[54] it is considered expedient for them to be deceived!

As for the gods of the poets, the records are not silent about why Scaevola rejected them — because the poets distort the gods so much that their gods do not even stand up to comparison with good men. They make this god a thief; they make that god an adulterer; over and over again they make the gods say something or do something that is shameful or absurd. They say that three goddesses battled for the prize of beauty, and that the two who were defeated by Venus overthrew Troy.[55] They say that Jupiter himself was changed into a bull or, again, into a swan

---

52. This analysis was made by Varro. See below at VI,5. Quintus Mucius Scaevola was an authority on Roman law who died violently in 82 B.C.
53. The origin of the commonplace is unknown, but it is enshrined in the *Codex Justinianus* VI,23,17, where it is applied to wills.
54. See Jn 8:32.
55. The three goddesses were Aphrodite/Venus, Hera/Juno and Athena/Minerva. Augustine is referring to the so-called Judgment of Paris, in which Paris, the son of King Priam of Troy, chose Aphrodite as the most beautiful of the goddesses and as a result won Helen of Sparta for himself, who had been promised to him if he selected Aphrodite. Since she was already married to Menelaus of Sparta, war broke out between Greece and Troy, and Troy was ultimately defeated.

in order to have sex with some woman;[56] that a goddess married a man; and that Saturn devoured his children.[57] In short, no marvels or vices, no matter how far removed from the nature of the gods, can be imagined that are not found here.

Come, Scaevola, Pontifex Maximus, do away with the games if you can! Forbid the people to offer such honors to the immortal gods — shows where people like to admire the misbehavior of the gods and take delight in imitating them as far as they can. And if the people answer you by saying, "You pontiffs are the ones who introduced all this to us," then ask the gods themselves to lift the command that such shows be put on in their honor. It was at their instigation, after all, that you ordered the shows in the first place. And if the deeds they present are evil, and therefore in no way to be believed of the majesty of the gods, so much the greater is the injury done to the gods, about whom these tales are invented with impunity.

But the gods do not listen to you. They are demons; they teach depravity; they delight in acts of shame. Far from counting it an injury if such fictions are told of them, they cannot bear the injury of not having these fictions acted out at their festivals. Nor does it make any sense to appeal to Jupiter against them, especially in view of the fact that most of the crimes acted out in the theatrical shows are his. And even if you ascribe the name Jupiter to the god by whom this whole world is governed and administered, are you not doing him the greatest injury of all if you suppose that he is to be worshiped as one among these gods, and if you make him their king?

Rome's Gods Incapable of Extending or Preserving Rome's Empire

28. By no means were gods such as these able to enlarge and preserve the Roman empire — gods who are appeased, or rather accused, by having honors of such a sort paid to them that it is a greater crime that they delighted in these false tales than it would be if the tales about them were true. And if they did have the power to confer such a great gift, they would undoubtedly have given it to the Greeks, who worshiped them more honorably and more aptly in divine things of this sort, that is, in theatrical shows. For the Greeks did not exempt themselves from the biting attacks of the poets, by whom they saw the gods lacerated; rather, they gave the poets license to abuse anyone they wanted and, far from condemning actors as indecent, they held them worthy of even the highest honors....

---

56. According to legend, Jupiter changed himself into a bull to have sex with Europa (see Ovid, *Metamorphoses* II,833-875) and into a swan to have sex with Leda (see ibid. VI,108-109).
57. See Hesiod, *Theogony* 453-491.

Cicero and Varro on Superstition, Images of the Gods, and the Religion of the Populace

30. Cicero, himself an augur, mocks augury and mocks people who regulate their life-plans by the cries of the raven and the crow.[58] But an Academic philosopher like Cicero, who claims that everything is uncertain, does not deserve to be taken as an authority on such matters. In the second book of his *On the Nature of the Gods*, he introduces Quintus Lucilius Balbus as a participant in the discussion;[59] and, even though Balbus himself brings in superstitions as if they were grounded in science or philosophy, he is still indignant at the setting up of images and at opinions based on fables. This is what he says: "Do you not see, therefore, that reason is diverted from the good and useful investigation of nature to imaginary and fictitious gods? This has given rise to false opinions, to confused errors, and to superstitious old wives' tales. The forms of the gods are known to us, as are their ages, their garments and adornments, as well as their genealogies, marriages, and kinships. Everything about them has been made to look like human weakness. They are even represented to us with minds subject to the passions, for we have been told of the desires, the griefs and the angers of the gods. Nor are the gods, as the fables present them, exempt from wars and battles. Not only, as in Homer, do they intervene on behalf of opposing armies, some on one side, some on the other, but they also wage wars in their own right, as in the case of the Titans or the Giants. It is utterly absurd to say or to believe these things. They are empty and completely frivolous tales."[60] Notice here what is granted even by the defenders of the pagan gods!

Then Balbus declares that, while all this belongs to superstition, the things which he himself seems to teach, in accord with the Stoics, belong to religion. "For it was not only the philosophers," he says, "who distinguished superstition from religion; our ancestors did so as well. For people who spent whole days in prayer and in offering sacrifices so that their children might outlive them were called superstitious."[61] As anyone can see, he is trying hard, out of respect for the city's established customs, to praise the religion of his ancestors and wants desperately to separate it out from superstition, but he can find no way to do this. For if his ancestors called the people superstitious who spent whole days praying and sacrificing, what about the people who set up images of gods of different ages and distinct garments, with their various genealogies, marriages, and kinships — the very things that Balbus himself deplores? When he condemns all this as superstitious, he implicates his ancestors themselves in the blame: they are the very ones who set up and worshiped such images. And he implicates himself as

---

58. See *On Divination* II,3,8-72,150.
59. Quintus Lucilius Balbus was a Spanish Stoic philosopher and also the first foreign-born Roman consul (40 B.C.), whom Cicero appears to have esteemed.
60. *On the Nature of the Gods* II,28.
61. Ibid. "...so that their children might outlive them were called superstitious": *Ut sibi sui liberi superstites essent, superstitiosi sunt appellati*. The etymology is popular rather than accurate.

well. For, no matter how eloquently he tries to extricate and free himself from their hold, he still feels it necessary to worship such images, and in the popular assembly he would not even dare to whisper what he so eloquently declares in this philosophical discussion.

Let us Christians, therefore, give thanks to the Lord our God — not to heaven and earth, as Cicero argues, but to the One who made heaven and earth. For He, through the supreme humility of Christ, through the preaching of the apostles, and through the faith of the martyrs who died for the truth and now live with the truth, has overthrown the superstitions which Balbus, as if stammering,[62] barely begins to denounce. He has overthrown these superstitions by the free service of his people, overthrowing them not only in the hearts of the religious but also in the very temples of the superstitious.

31. What about Varro himself? We regret that he placed the theatrical shows among things divine, even though this does not represent his own judgment. For, although as a religious man he often urges people to worship the gods, does he not also admit that it is not on the basis of his own judgment that he follows what was established by the city of Rome? For he does not hesitate to admit that, if he were founding that city anew, he would instead consecrate the gods and their names according to the rule of nature. But as it is, he says that he feels bound, as one who belongs to an ancient people, to uphold the traditional account of the names and surnames of the gods as it came down from antiquity, and to make it the aim of his writing and research to encourage the common people to worship the gods rather than to despise them. By putting it this way, this singularly subtle man intimates clearly enough that he is holding some things back, things which were not only contemptible in his own view but would seem despicable even to the common people if not kept under wraps.

It might seem that I am only guessing here, except for the fact that Varro himself states quite openly in another place, where he is speaking of religious rites, that there are many things that are true which it is not useful for the common people to know, and many also which, even if false, it is expedient for the populace to think true; and this, he says, is the reason why the Greeks veiled their initiations and mysteries[63] in silence and kept them behind closed doors. Here Varro undoubtedly reveals the whole policy of the supposedly wise men by whom cities and peoples are ruled. But the malignant demons take great delight in this deception, for it means that they have both the deceivers and the deceived in their possession, and there is nothing that sets us free from their dominion except the grace of God through our Lord Jesus Christ.[64]

---

62. "Balbus...stammering": *Balbus...balbutiens*: a pun that Augustine could hardly resist.
63. "Initiations and mysteries": *teletas ac mysteria*. *Teleta* comes from the Greek *telete*, meaning "a making perfect"; the word, to which Augustine is one of the few witnesses in Latin literature, reappears below at X,9.23.
64. See Rom 7:24-25.

The same extremely shrewd and learned author also says that, in his view, the only people who have rightly discerned what God is are those who believed that he is the soul that governs the world by movement and reason. In this regard, Varro had not yet attained the real truth, for the true God is not a soul but the author and maker even of the soul itself. All the same, however, it seems clear that, if Varro could have been free to withstand the prejudice of custom, he would have acknowledged and argued that one God is to be worshiped, the one God who governs the world by movement and reason. And so the only question remaining at issue with him in this connection would be his claim that God is a soul and not rather the creator of the soul.[65]

Varro also says that for more than one hundred and seventy years the ancient Romans worshiped the gods without any image at all. "If this practice had persisted right down to the present," he says, "our worship of the gods would be more pure." In support of this claim, he cites, among other things, the witness of the Jewish people,[66] and he does not hesitate to end this passage by asserting that those who first set up images of the gods for the people both reduced reverence and increased error in their cities. For he rightly judged that gods represented in unfeeling images could easily be held in contempt. And when he says that they "increased error," not that they "passed along error," he obviously wants it to be understood that error was already present even before there were images. Thus, when he says that the only ones who rightly discerned what God is were those who believed that he is the soul governing the world, and when he judges that religion is observed more purely without images, who can fail to see how close he comes to the truth? For if he had just been able to stand up against such ancient and established error, he would undoubtedly have held that only one God should be worshiped, the one by whom he believed the world is governed, and that this God should be worshiped without images. And perhaps, being found so near the truth, he might easily have been prompted by the soul's mutability to recognize that the true God is an immutable nature which also created the soul itself.[67]

Since all this is so, it follows that when men such as Varro included in their writings any points that make a mockery of the many gods, they did this because they were compelled by the hidden will of God to acknowledge those points, and not because they were trying to persuade others of their truth. When we produce testimonies from their works, therefore, we produce them for the sake of refuting those who refuse to see how vast and how malign the power of the demons is — the power from which we are set free by the unique sacrifice of the holy blood shed for us and the gift of the Spirit bestowed on us.[68]

---

65. See above at IV,12.
66. See Ex 20:4-6.
67. One of God's most characteristic attributes, in Augustine's view, is his immutability, which stands in contrast to creation's mutability. See *Teaching Christianity* I,8,8-9,9; *Confessions* I,4,4; IX,10,24.
68. Augustine is referring either to the historical events of Calvary and Pentecost or to the sacramental

32. Varro also states that people are more inclined to follow the poets than the natural philosophers with regard to the genealogies of the gods; and that, he says, is why his ancestors, the ancient Romans, believed in the sex and the generations of the gods and charted their marriages. This certainly seems to have happened for no other reason than that supposedly wise and sensible men made it their business to deceive the people in matters of religion, and, in doing this, they made it their business not only to worship but also to imitate the demons, whose greatest pleasure is to deceive. For just as the demons can only keep their hold on those they have deluded and deceived, so also human rulers — not just rulers, certainly, but men like the demons — in the name of religion urged on the people as true what they knew to be mere illusion. In this way they tightened the bonds of civil society, as it were, so that they might likewise tighten their hold on their subjects. For what chance did any weak and uninstructed person have of escaping at one and the same time from the deceptions of both the civil rulers and the demons?[69]

The One True God Is the God Who Gives Earthly Kingdoms

33. God, therefore, the author and giver of happiness, because he is the one true God, himself gives earthly kingdoms to the good and to the evil alike. He does not do this rashly or, as it were, by chance, for he is God, not Fortune.[70] Rather he does this in accord with a temporal order of things which is hidden from us but fully known to him. Nor does he submit to this temporal order, as though its slave; rather he rules over it as its Lord and directs it as its Master. As for happiness, he gives this only to the good. Slaves can have or not have happiness, and rulers can have or not have happiness, although full happiness will come only in the life where no one will be a slave any longer. And the reason why God gives earthly kingdoms to the good and the evil alike is this: to keep his worshipers, who are still no more advanced in mind than little children, from yearning for this gift from him as if it were some great thing.

And this is the mystery of the Old Testament, where the New Testament was hidden[71] — that, in the Old Testament, the promises and gifts are of earthly things, although even then spiritual men understood (but did not yet openly proclaim) both the eternity signified by those temporal things and which of God's gifts are the ones that bring true happiness.

---

eucharist and the baptismal conferral of the Spirit (now known as confirmation) — or to both.
69. It is notable that Augustine understands that the cult of the gods was used as a tool by secular rulers to strengthen their hold on their people.
70. "By chance...Fortune": *fortuito...fortuna*.
71. See *Instructing Beginners in the Faith* 4,8 for a similar formulation.

34. Accordingly, to make it known that even those earthly goods, the only goods people yearn for who can imagine nothing better, are in the power of the one God himself, and not in the power of the many false gods whom the Romans used to believe they should worship, God multiplied his people in Egypt from a very few[72] and delivered them from Egypt by miraculous signs.[73] Nor did their women invoke Lucina when, in the face of the Egyptian persecutors who had resolved to kill all their infants, God himself saved their newborn children so that they might be multiplied by these marvelous means and the people be increased beyond belief.[74] The children nursed at the breast without the goddess Rumina, lay in their cradles without Cunina, took food and drink without Educa or Potina, were brought up without all those gods of childhood, married without the gods of marriage, and joined in marital intercourse without worshiping Priapus. Without any invocation of Neptune, the divided sea opened for them to cross and then overwhelmed their pursuing enemies in the returning waves.[75] When they received manna from heaven,[76] they did not consecrate any goddess Mannia;[77] nor did they worship Nymphs and Lymphs when the rock was struck and poured out water for their thirst.[78] They waged war without the mad rites of Mars and Bellona, and while they obviously did not conquer without victory, they still regarded victory not as a goddess but as a gift of their God. They had crops without Segetia, oxen without Bubona, honey without Mellona, fruits without Pomona. In short, all the things for which the Romans thought they had to pray to that throng of false gods, they received far more happily from the one true God.

And if they had not sinned against him, seduced by unholy curiosity as if by magic arts,[79] turning aside to strange gods and idols, and finally putting Christ to death, they would have continued in the same kingdom — a kingdom which, even if less extensive, would still have been more happy. That they are now dispersed through virtually all lands and peoples is due to the providence of the one true God. This is to the end that, wherever the images, altars, sacred groves, and temples of the false gods are overthrown and their sacrifices banned, it may be shown from the Jewish Scriptures how all this was prophesied very long ago. And so there will be no reason to suppose, when these prophecies are read in our Scriptures, that we made them up ourselves.

But what comes next is to be found in the following book, for we must here set a limit to the undue length of this one.

---

72. See Ex 1:7.
73. See Ex 7:8-12:29.
74. See Ex 1:17-19.
75. See Ex 14:21-29.
76. See Ex 16:4-35.
77. Although all the other gods whom Augustine mentions here enjoyed a cult in Rome, Mannia was fabricated by him to correspond with manna.
78. See Ex 17:1-6.
79. See above at III,9 for a similar view of curiosity.

Study Questions for Book IV

What aspects of Augustine's critique of empire readily apply to the imperial ambitions of the United States, China, Russia, the Islamic Caliphate or other partisan movements today?

Regarding political power, Augustine seems to favor subsidiarity, that is, the organizing principle that matters ought to be handled by the smallest, lowest or least centralized competent authority. How might Augustinian thought enrich subsidiarity as a tenet of Catholic social teaching? How might the Augustinian critique of empire enrich the even more basic principle of the common good?

Augustine's deconstruction of Greco-Roman religion extends to elements of superstition he discerned even among the most astute Greek philosophers. How might this type of Augustinian scrutiny of motivation benefit a contemporary psychology of religious experience?

BOOK V

Book V continues Augustine's answer to the question: Why did God grant imperial greatness to Rome? It starts by rejecting the notion that Rome's greatness is due either to chance or to fate, any more than it is due to the aid of Rome's traditional gods, and it presents an extended argument against both astrological fatalism and the Stoic conception of fate as an unbroken deterministic chain of causes. In relation to the latter, however, the book also rejects Cicero's attempt to safeguard freedom of will by denying the divine foreknowledge of future events, since a god without foreknowledge of the future is no god at all, and asserts instead that the free choices of the will themselves belong to the chain of causes foreknown by God and thus retain their freedom. The book then turns to the main question and asserts that the gift of empire, which comes only from the true God, was given on the basis of the Romans' virtues. These virtues were rooted in the Romans' love of praise and desire for glory, which prevailed so long as they sought empire by following the path of virtue, i.e., so long as the Romans suppressed their more base desires for the sake of empire instead of pursuing a deceptive honor for the sake of achieving domination over others rather than the genuine civic glory of service to the republic. The Roman virtues are not true virtue (which is rooted in true religion, the worship of the true God), but they are better to have than not to have in the earthly context, and they may even serve as examples for Christians that will counteract any impulse to Christian pride. Rome's empire, then, is its earthly reward for its earthly virtue. At the same time, however, Book V insists that empire, like other earthly gifts of God, is given to the good and to the evil alike and therefore is not to be valued on the same plane as the higher goods that are given to the good alone, and that there may be other reasons, hidden from human sight, for the divine gift of enduring empire to Rome. The book concludes with a kind of verbal portrait of the good Christian emperor (with the implication that not all Christian emperors are good), and with a presentation of Theodosius as a model Christian emperor.

Preface. It is clear, then, that happiness is the fulfillment of all that we ought to desire. It is not a goddess[1] but a gift of God, and therefore no god should be worshiped by men except one who can make them happy. Thus, if happiness itself were a goddess, there would be good reason to say that she alone should be worshiped. But God can also bestow the goods which even those who are not good — and therefore are not happy — can possess. Let us now see, then, why God willed the Roman empire to become so large and to last so long. For we have already stated at length that the throng of false gods whom the Romans worshiped

---

1. I.e., the goddess Felicity, referred to above at IV,18ff.

were not the ones who did this, and we shall make the same point again wherever it seems appropriate.

Neither Chance nor Fate Caused Rome's Greatness

1. The cause of the Roman empire's greatness, then, was neither chance nor fate. Such a view might accord with the judgment or opinion of people who say that things happen by chance when they have no cause at all, or no cause that arises from an intelligible order, and that things happen by fate when they occur not by divine will or by human will but by virtue of some order governed by necessity.[2] It is beyond doubt, however, that human kingdoms are established by divine providence. If anyone ascribes them to fate because he uses the term "fate" to mean the will and power of God, let him hold to his meaning but correct his terminology. Why not say at the outset what he will say later on, when someone asks him what he means by fate? For, when people hear this word as it is ordinarily used, they understand it to mean nothing other than the influence of the position of the stars at the time when a person is born or conceived. Some consider this to be quite separate from the will of God;[3] others insist that it depends on the will of God.[4]

Against Astrological Fatalism: the Case of Twins

But those who hold the opinion that, quite apart from the will of God, the stars determine what we shall do, what goods we shall have, or what evils we shall suffer, should be refused a hearing by everyone — not only by those who hold the true religion but also by those who worship gods of any kind, no matter how false. For what can this opinion mean except that there is no reason to worship or pray to any god at all? Our present argument is directed not against people who take this view but rather against those who oppose the Christian religion for the sake of defending what they think are gods.

As for those who make the position of the stars depend on God's will but hold that the stars somehow determine what sort of person each will be and what good or evil will come his way, they do heaven a grave injustice if they suppose that the supreme power of God has handed over to the stars the power to decide these things any way they want. They imagine, in effect, that heaven's luminous senate, meeting in its lustrous senate house, so to speak, decrees that crimes are to be committed, crimes so horrible that, if any earthly city had decreed them, the whole human race would decree that it should be destroyed. And further, what place is left for God's judgment on human actions — and God is himself, after all, the Lord

---

2. See Pseudo-Plutarch, *On Fate* 8-9.
3. See Diogenes Laertius, *Lives of Eminent Philosophers* VIII,27.
4. See Plato, *Timaeus* 41d-e.

of both stars and men — if celestial necessity is applied to the acts human beings do? Alternatively, if they claim that the stars received from the supreme God not the power to decree these crimes on their own but only to fulfill his commands in imposing such necessities on human beings, are we then to take a view of God himself that it seemed utterly unworthy to hold of the will of the stars?

On the other hand, it might be said that the stars only signify these things but do not cause them, so that their position merely functions as a kind of announcement which predicts future events but does not bring them about, and people of no ordinary learning have held exactly this view.[5] But this simply is not the way that astrologers usually speak. They do not say, for instance, "Mars in this position signifies murder" but rather "causes murder."[6] Let us concede, however, that the astrologers do not speak as precisely as they should, and that they ought to take from the philosophers the accurate form of words for declaring what they think they find in the position of the stars. Even granting this, however, how is it that the astrologers have never been able to explain why the lives of twins — their actions, their histories, their professions, their trades, their honors, their involvement with all the other circumstances of human life, and even their deaths — often show such differences that, in these respects, many complete strangers resemble them far more closely than they resemble each other? And this holds true despite the fact that only the smallest interval of time separated the birth of the one twin from the birth of the other, and despite the fact that they were conceived at the very same moment in a single act of intercourse.[7]

2. According to Cicero, the eminent physician Hippocrates left a record of two brothers who fell ill at the same time.[8] Their disease grew worse at the same time and then got better at the same time, and on this basis Hippocrates suspected that they were twins. The Stoic philosopher Posidonius,[9] who was much given to astrology, used to claim that this sort of thing happened because the two were born and were conceived under the same configuration of the stars. Thus what the physician believed was due to a similar physical constitution, the philosopher and astrologer ascribed to the influence and configuration of the stars at the time when they were conceived and born. In this case, the medical conjecture is far more acceptable and clearly more credible. For the bodily condition of the parents at the time of intercourse might well have affected the earliest beginnings of the children in such a way that, after their initial growth in their mother's body, they were born

---

5. See Plotinus, *Enneads* II,3,7.
6. See ibid. II,3,6.
7. The supposed effect of the stars on twins, as well as on persons born at exactly the same time from different mothers, is also discussed in *Confessions* VII,6,8-10. See likewise *Teaching Christianity* II,22,33-34.
8. Hippocrates (c. 460-c. 370 B.C.) was the famous Greek physician to whom the Hippocratic Oath has been attributed.
9. Posidonius (c. 135-51 B.C.) was an important Stoic philosopher and polymath who taught and corresponded with Cicero.

with like constitutions. From then on, they would have been nourished on the same foods in the same home, where, as medicine teaches, the air, the location, and the quality of the water all have a great influence on the body's condition, for good or for ill; they would also have been accustomed to the same kinds of exercise. And hence they would have been so similar in bodily condition that, in the same way, they might well have been struck by the same diseases at the same time from the same causes. But to want to link their parallel illnesses to the configuration of the heavens or the stars at the time of conception or birth, especially when so many individuals of the most diverse races, and with the most diverse upshots and outcomes, can have been conceived and born at the same time, in the same region of the earth, and under the same sky — what sort of impudence is that?

Furthermore, we know that twins do differ not only in what they do and where their ways take them but also in the illnesses they suffer. For this, as far as I can see, Hippocrates would provide the most obvious explanation: it may happen that they have different states of health due to differences in food and exercise, factors which come not from the body's constitution but from the mind's deliberate choice....

4. In the ancient era of our forefathers — to speak of a notable instance — twin brothers were born so close together that the second was holding the heel of the first.[10] But there was such a difference in their lives and characters, such a disparity in their actions, such a dissimilarity in their parents' love for them, that the very divergence between them made them enemies to each other. Does this mean that when one was walking the other was sitting, or that when one was sleeping the other was awake, or that when one was talking the other was silent? These are things that belong to those minute details which cannot be discerned by the people who record the position of the stars under which each person is born for the sake of consulting the astrologers. In this case, however, one twin lived the life of a hired servant, the other did not; one was loved by his mother, the other was not; one lost the honor then held in high regard among his people, the other gained it. And what about their wives, their children, their possessions? What a difference there was! If such matters as these depend on the brief moments of time that separate the birth of twins and are not ascribed to the constellations, why is it that the astrologers talk about such things when they interpret the constellations of others?...

6. And even in the very conception of twins, where it is certain that both are conceived at the same moment of time, how does it happen that, under the very same fate-determining constellation, one may be conceived as male, the other as female? I know twins of different sexes, both of whom are still alive and both still vigorous for their age. Although they are as alike in bodily appearance as people of different sexes can be, they are utterly unlike in mode and manner of life.

---

10. The reference is to Jacob and Esau. See Gn 25:2-36:43 for the account of their conception, birth and subsequent history. Their example is cited elsewhere by Augustine in the context of refuting astrology. See *Teaching Christianity* II,22,33.

Quite apart from their activities, which necessarily differ for men and women (he serves on the staff of a count and is almost always away from home, she does not leave her native soil and her rural estate), there is something more (which is far more incredible if you believe in fates fixed by the stars, but not at all surprising if you take human choices and divine gifts into account): he is married, she is a consecrated virgin; he has fathered a number of children, she has never married.

What extraordinary power the horoscope has! I have already shown well enough that it has no power at all. Whatever the truth may be, however, they claim that it wields its power at the point of birth. Does it wield no power, then, at the point of conception? In the case of twins, obviously enough, there is a single act of intercourse, and the force of nature is so great that, once a woman has conceived, it is completely impossible for her to conceive another child. From this it necessarily follows that twins must be conceived at the same moment. Or do they mean to claim, perhaps, that, because they were born under different horoscopes, one of the twins was changed into a male or the other into a female in the very process of being born?

It is not totally absurd to say that the stars do exercise a certain influence, although only with regard to physical differences. We see, for example, that the seasons of the year vary with the approach and receding of the sun and that certain kinds of things grow and diminish with the waxing and waning of the moon, such as sea-urchins and oysters and the wondrous tides of the ocean. What the mind wills, however, is not subject to the positions of the stars....

Against Astrological Fatalism: "Auspicious" Days

7. And who could possibly accept the notion that, by choosing certain days to act, people can contrive new fates for themselves by their own actions?... What singular nonsense! You choose a day for taking a wife. The reason, I suppose, is that unless the day is carefully chosen you might hit on an unlucky day and make an unhappy marriage. But where, then, is the fate decreed for you by the stars at your birth? Can a person change what has already been fixed for him by his choice of a day? And in that case, could not another power change the fate that he fixed for himself by choosing that day?

Again, if it is only human beings that are subject to the constellations and not everything beneath the heavens, why is it that people choose certain days as auspicious for the planting of vines or trees or grain, and others for domesticating cattle or for mating mares with a stallion or cows with a bull, and for other such things? But if what makes the choice of days so important in these matters is that the position of the stars, as it varies from moment to moment, governs all earthly bodies and every living thing on earth, people should give some thought to the sheer number of things which are born or originate or begin at any one point in time and yet come to such different ends that even a child must be convinced that these astrological observations are completely ridiculous....

Taking all this into account, it is not unreasonable to hold that, since by some miracle the astrologers actually do give a great number of true answers, this happens due to the hidden prompting of spirits (but not good spirits!), whose concern is to implant and fix in human minds these false and destructive beliefs about fates being written in the stars. It most certainly is not due to any art of observing and examining horoscopes, for there is no such art.

Fate as the Chain of Causes

8. There are some, however, who use the word "fate" not for the position of the stars at the moment of a thing's conception or birth or beginning but rather for the chain and sequence of all causes, due to which everything that happens happens. There is no need to go into heavy battle with these people over what is, after all, a merely verbal controversy. For they ascribe this order and chain of causes to the will and power of the supreme God, who is most rightly and properly believed both to know all things before they happen and to leave nothing unordered.[11] All powers are from him, although not the wills of all. Thus what they call fate is most especially the will of the supreme God, whose power extends invincibly through all things — as is shown by these verses, written, unless I am mistaken, by Annaeus Seneca: "Supreme father, ruler of high heaven, lead where you will. Ready and eager, I submit without delay. But if unwilling, I follow all the same. My evil will must suffer what it might have done as good. The fates lead the willing but drag the unwilling in their wake."[12] Surely it is obvious that, in this final line, what he calls "the fates" is simply what he previously spoke of as the will of the supreme father. This, he says, he is ready to obey, so that he might be led willingly rather than dragged unwillingly, since "the fates lead the willing but drag the unwilling in their wake."…

Cicero's Argument on Foreknowledge and Free Will

9. Cicero, in striving to refute the Stoics, concludes that he can get nowhere against them unless he does away with divination. He tries to do this by denying that there is any knowledge of the future, and with all his might he contends that there is no such thing, either on man's part or on God's, and thus no way of foretelling events. Hence he both denies God's foreknowledge and, using spurious arguments, tries to overthrow all prophecy, even when it is clearer than day. He takes as his targets certain oracles which can easily be refuted, although he does

---

11. On the divinely established good order of created things see below at XI,22 and XII,4-5.
12. Lucius Annaeus Seneca (c. 4 B.C.-65 A.D.) was a Stoic philosopher esteemed not only by pagans but also by Christians. Here Seneca is quoting the Greek philosopher Cleanthes (c. 330-c.230 B.C.), fragment 91 (A. C. Pearson, ed., *The Fragments of Zeno and Cleanthes* [London: C. J. Clay, 1891] 313-314). The final line, which Augustine cites again, is a famous one.

not make his case even against them. When it comes to refuting the conjectures of the astrologers, however, his argument is victorious, since their conjectures really are such that they destroy and refute themselves. Nevertheless, we are far more ready to put up with those who make the stars determine our fates than anyone who eliminates the foreknowledge of future events. For it is sheer madness both to acknowledge that God exists and, at the same time, to deny that he foreknows the future. Since Cicero himself also recognized this point, he even made an attempt at saying what is written in Scripture, *The fool has said in his heart, there is no God* (Ps 14:1). But he did not do this in his own person, for he saw how offensive it would be and how much trouble it would stir up. That is why, in his books *On the Nature of the Gods*, he had Cotta argue the case against the Stoics on this point and preferred to give his own verdict in favor of Lucilius Balbus, to whom he gave the assignment of defending the Stoic position, rather than to Cotta, who argued that there is no divine nature at all.[13] In his books *On Divination*, however, Cicero speaks in his own right and openly opposes foreknowledge of future events.[14] His whole purpose, it seems, is to avoid admitting the existence of fate and so to avoid the loss of free will. For he presumes that, if he concedes knowledge of the future, it will be utterly impossible to deny that fate follows as a necessary consequence.

But for our part, whatever twists and turns the philosophers' debates and disputes may take, we confess the supreme and true God, and so we also confess his will, his supreme power, and his foreknowledge. Nor are we afraid that, because the one whose foreknowledge cannot fail foreknows what we are going to do, it follows that we do not actually do of our own will what we do of our own will. This is what Cicero feared, and so he opposed foreknowledge. The Stoics had the same fear, and so they denied that everything happens by necessity, even though they asserted that everything does happen by fate.

What is it, then, that Cicero feared so much in the foreknowledge of future events that he tried to demolish it with his detestable argument? Plainly it is this: if all future events are foreknown, they will occur in the order in which it was foreknown that they were going to occur; and if they are going to occur in this order, then the order of events is fixed for the God who foreknows them; and if the order of events is fixed, then the order of causes is also fixed, for nothing can happen which is not preceded by some efficient cause.[15] But if there is a fixed order of causes by which everything that happens happens, then, Cicero claims, everything that happens happens by fate. And if this is so, nothing is in our power, and there is no such thing as the free choice of the will. If we grant this, Cicero states, the whole of human life is undermined. It is pointless to make laws, pointless to

---

13. See *On the Nature of the Gods* III passim.
14. See *On Divination* II,48-54.
15. Aristotle, *Metaphysics* V,1013a is the classic text on the four causes, among them the efficient. For a slightly more extended discussion of efficient causality see idem, *On the Generation of Animals* II,1. A little later in this section (9) Augustine names three other causes — fortuitous, natural and voluntary — that may all be identified with the efficient cause.

make use of reprimand or praise, of denunciation or exhortation,[16] and there is no justice in establishing rewards for the good and punishments for the evil. It is, then, to avoid these disgraceful, absurd, and dangerous consequences in human affairs that Cicero wants to eliminate the foreknowledge of future events. He forces the religious mind into the narrow straits of a dilemma; it must take one of two alternatives: either something does depend on our will or there is foreknowledge of future events. He considers it impossible for both to be true. Rather, to affirm the one is to deny the other. If we take foreknowledge of future events, the will's choice is eliminated; if we take the will's choice, foreknowledge of future events is eliminated. Accordingly, as a great and learned man, far-seeing and sharp-eyed in his concern for human life, Cicero himself took free choice of the will from these two alternatives, and, to uphold this, he denied foreknowledge of future events. As a result, although he wanted to make us free, he actually made us sacrilegious.

For, in fact, the religious mind chooses both, confesses both, and confirms both in its religious faith. How so? asks Cicero. If there is foreknowledge of future events, that whole chain of consequences must follow, until we come to the conclusion that nothing depends on our will. On the other hand, if something does depend on our will, then — taking the steps of the same argument in reverse — we come to the conclusion that there is no foreknowledge of future events. For this is how all those consequences are traced in reverse: if the will really does have the power to choose, then it is not true that everything happens by fate; if everything does not happen by fate, then it is not true that the order of all causes is fixed; if the order of causes is not fixed, then it is not true that the order of events is fixed for the God who foreknows them, for things cannot happen without efficient causes that precede them; if the order of events is not fixed for the God who foreknows them, then it is not true that all things occur as he foreknew that they would occur; and, if all things do not occur as he foreknew that they would occur, Cicero claims, then it is not true that in God there is foreknowledge of all future events.

Divine Foreknowledge and Human Freedom

Over against these audacious, sacrilegious, and ungodly assertions, we say both that God knows all things before they happen and that it is by our own will that we do whatever we feel and know we would not do unless we willed to do it.[17] We do not, however, say that all things happen by fate; rather we deny that anything happens by fate. For we have shown that the word "fate," as it is commonly used, that is, in reference to the position of the stars when a person is conceived

---

16. Augustine's presentation of Cicero's argument at this point looks forward to the objections to rebuking sinful monks which were made by the monks of Hadrumetum in the mid-420s and answered by Augustine in *Rebuke and Grace* 1,1-9,25.
17. Augustine advances the same argument that appears here regarding divine foreknowledge and human willing in *Free Will* III, 3, 6-4, 10.

or born, means nothing, since there is nothing there for it to assert. As to an order of causes, where the will of God mostly prevails, we neither deny it nor do we call it by the name "fate," unless, perhaps, we should understand "fate" to come from *fari*, that is, "to speak."[18] For we cannot deny that it is written in Scripture, *God has spoken once; these two things have I heard: that power belongs to God, and that mercy belongs to you, Lord, who render to each according to his works* (Ps 62:11-12). For we understand the words *God has spoken once* to mean "God has spoken immovably," that is, immutably, just as he knows immutably everything that will happen and everything that he himself is going to do. On these grounds, then, we might use "fate" as a term derived from speaking, if only the word were not already generally understood in another sense, toward which we have no desire for human hearts to be turned. Moreover, even if there is a fixed order of all causes for God, it does not follow that, as a consequence, nothing depends on the choice of our will. In fact, our wills are themselves included in the order of causes that is fixed for God and contained in his foreknowledge. For human wills are causes of human actions, and so the one who foreknew all the causes of things certainly could not have been ignorant of our wills, among those causes, since he foreknew them to be precisely the causes of our actions.

In fact, Cicero's own concession that nothing happens unless preceded by an efficient cause is enough to refute him on this point.[19] How does it help him to say that nothing happens without a cause, but that — since there is also a fortuitous cause, a natural cause, and a voluntary cause — not every cause is a matter of fate? It is enough that he allows that nothing happens without a preceding cause. For our part, we do not deny the existence of what are called fortuitous causes (from which "fortune" also takes its name),[20] but we assert that they are hidden, and we ascribe them to the will either of the true God or of some spirit or other. In addition, we do not by any means separate even natural causes from the will of the one who is the author and maker of all nature. And finally, voluntary causes stem either from God or from angels or from human beings or from animals (if, that is, the motions of non-rational animals by which they act according to their nature in seeking or shunning something can really be called actions of will). In speaking of the wills of angels, furthermore, I mean the wills of both good angels, whom we call angels of God, and evil angels, whom we call angels of the devil or also demons; and similarly by the wills of human beings I mean the wills of both good and evil men.

From this we conclude that there are no efficient causes of all that happens except voluntary causes, namely, causes stemming from that nature which is the breath of life. Ordinary air or wind, of course, can also be called "breath," but,

---

18. The etymology is in Varro, *On the Latin Language* VI,7.
19. See *On Divination* I,125.
20. "Fortuitous…fortune": *fortuitae…fortuna*. See above at IV,33.

because it is corporeal, it is not the breath of life. The breath of life, then, which gives life to all things and is the creator of every body and every created spirit, is God himself, the absolutely uncreated spirit. In his will lies the supreme power that aids the good wills of created spirits, judges their evil wills, and places all wills within his order. To some he grants empowerment, to some he does not. For just as he is the creator of all natures, so is he the giver of all empowerment. But he is not the giver of all wills. Evil wills most certainly are not from him, for they are contrary to nature, which does come from him. Thus bodies, rather, are subject to wills, some to our wills (that is, to the wills of all living mortal beings, but more to the wills of men than to the wills of beasts), and some to the wills of angels. But, more than anything, all bodies are subject to the will of God, to whom all wills are also subject, since they have no power except what he has granted. The cause of things, therefore, the cause which acts and is not acted on, is God. Other causes both act and are acted on, as is true of all created spirits and, in particular, of rational spirits. Material causes, however, which are acted on instead of acting themselves, are not to be counted among efficient causes, for they can only do what the wills of spirits do through them.

How can it be, then, that an order of causes which is fixed in God's foreknowledge entails that nothing depends on our will, when in fact our wills play such a large role in that very order of causes? So let Cicero argue his case with those who claim that this order of causes is determined by fate, or rather who call this very order itself fate. This is a view that we abhor, especially because of the word "fate," which is ordinarily understood in a sense that is completely untrue. As for Cicero's denial that the order of all causes is fully fixed and wholly known to God's foreknowledge, we detest his view even more than the Stoics do. Either he is denying that God exists (which, in fact, he tried to do, although in the person of another, in his books *On the Nature of the Gods*), or, if he allows that God exists but denies that God foreknows the future, he is still saying nothing different from what *the fool has said in his heart, There is no God* (Ps 14:1). For one who does not foreknow all future events most certainly is not God. Our wills, therefore, also have just as much power as God willed and foreknew that they would have. Whatever power they have, then, they have most assuredly, and, whatever they are going to do, they themselves will do most assuredly, for he whose foreknowledge cannot fail foreknew that they would have the power to do it and would do it. That is why, if I wanted to apply the term "fate" to anything at all, I would prefer to say that the fate of the weaker is the will of the stronger, who has him in his power, rather than that the order of causes (which the Stoics call fate, not in the usual sense but in a sense of their own) does away with the choice of our will.

10. There is no need, then, for us to fear that necessity for fear of which the Stoics labored to distinguish between the causes of things. Some they took out from under necessity, some they subjected to it. And, among those that they did not want to be under necessity, they placed our wills — obviously wishing to avoid the consequence that our wills would not be free if they were made subject to necessity. For if "necessity," in our case, is to be used of that which is not in our power but rather does what it can even when we do not will it — such as, for example, the necessity of death — then it is obvious that our wills, by which we live rightly or wrongly, are not subject to any such necessity as that. For we do many things which, if we did not will to do them, we certainly would not do. And chief among them is willing itself. If we will, it exists; if we do not will, it does not. For we would not will if we did not will to.

On the other hand, if necessity is defined in the sense according to which we say that it is necessary for something to be as it is or to happen as it does, I see no reason to fear that it will eliminate our freedom of will. We certainly do not make the life of God and the foreknowledge of God subject to necessity if we say that it is necessary for God to live eternally and to foreknow all things, just as his power is not diminished when we say that he cannot die or that he cannot be deceived. And this is not possible because, if it were possible, he would actually have less power. In fact, the one rightly called omnipotent is precisely the one who, even so, is not able to die or to be mistaken. For he is called omnipotent in virtue of doing what he wills, not in virtue of having to suffer what he does not will. If anything like that should happen to him, he most certainly would not be omnipotent. But it is precisely because he is omnipotent that some things are not possible for him. And the same applies when we say it is necessary that, when we will, we will by free choice: what we say is most certainly true, and yet the fact that it is true does not mean that we place free choice itself under a necessity that takes away its freedom.

Our wills, therefore, exist, and themselves do whatever we do by willing, which would not be done if we did not will to do it. And, even when a person suffers something imposed on him against his will by the will of others, still it is will that prevails, even if another's rather than his own. The power, however, comes from God. For if there were only the will, but a will unable to do what it willed, that will would be held in check by a still more powerful will. Even in that case, however, the will would still be the will, and it would be the will not of someone else but of precisely the person doing the willing, even though he was unable to carry out what he willed to do. Thus, what a person suffers against his will ought to be ascribed not to the wills of men, or angels, or any created spirit, but rather to the will of him who gives the power to those who do the willing.

The fact that God foreknew what would depend upon the power of our will does not mean, therefore, that nothing depends on our will. For the one who foreknew this did not foreknow nothing at all. On the contrary, if the one who foreknew what would depend upon our will actually knew something rather than nothing, it is obvious that there is something that depends on our will even for the one who foreknows it. By no means, therefore, are we compelled either to eliminate the will's choice in retaining God's foreknowledge or — which is blasphemous — to deny God's foreknowledge of future events in retaining the will's choice. Rather, we embrace both. With faith and with truth we confess both, the one so that we may believe rightly and the other so that we may live rightly. For there is no living rightly without believing rightly in God. Far be it from us, then, to deny God's foreknowledge for the sake of our wish to be free, for it is only by his help that we ever are or will be free.

Nor is it true that laws, reprimands, exhortations, praise, and blame are pointless, just because God foreknew that these would be brought into play. In fact, they are fully effective precisely to the extent that God foreknew that they would be effective. Prayers, too, are effective precisely in obtaining what God foreknew that he would grant to those who pray, and it is with justice that rewards are established for good deeds and punishments for sins. For the fact that God foreknew that a person was going to sin does not mean that, as a consequence, the person sins. On the contrary, there can be no doubt that it is the person himself who sins when he sins, and this is so because the one whose foreknowledge cannot fail foreknew that neither fate nor fortune nor anything else was going to sin, but precisely the person himself. If a person does not will to sin, of course, he obviously does not sin; but if he does not will to sin, this, too, was foreknown by God.

The Giver of Empire is the True God

11. The supreme and true God, therefore, with his Word and his Spirit, which three are one, is the one almighty God, the creator and maker of every soul and every body. It is by participation in him that all are happy who are happy in truth and not in empty illusion. He made man a rational animal, consisting of soul and body, and, when man sinned, he neither allowed him to go unpunished nor simply abandoned him without mercy. To the good and the evil alike he gave the being they share with stones, the reproductive life they share with plants, the life of the senses they share with animals, and the life of the intellect they share only with the angels. From him comes all mode, all form, and all order,[21] from him comes measure, number, and weight;[22] from him comes all that exists in nature, whatever its kind and whatever its rank in value. From him come the seeds of forms, the forms of seeds, and the motion of both seeds and forms. He gave also to flesh its origin, its beauty, its health, its fruitfulness in propagation, the disposition of its limbs, and their apt and harmonious arrangement. He also gave memory, sensation, and appetite to the irrational soul; and to the rational soul, in addition, he gave mind, intelligence, and will. Neither heaven nor earth, neither angel nor human being, not even the inner organs of the smallest and lowliest animal, not even a bird's feather or a tiny flower in the grass or a leaf on a tree, has he left without a harmony and,

---

21. The triad of mode, form and order begins a series of trinities here, which also includes measure, number and weight; the seeds of forms, the forms of seeds, and their motion; origin, beauty and health; propagation, disposition and arrangement; memory, sensation and appetite; and mind, intelligence and will. Although these natural trinities cannot help but hint at the divine Trinity, Augustine's chief purpose in listing them here seems to be to demonstrate the underlying orderly structure of creation on all its levels, on which point he concludes the chapter.

22. See Wis 11:20.

as it were, a kind of peace in the disposition of its parts.[23] And it is utterly beyond belief that he would have wished the kingdoms of men, their dominions and their enslavements, to fall outside the laws of his providence.

Roman Love of Glory and Roman Virtue

12. Let us consider, then, the moral qualities of the Romans and see why the true God, in whose power earthly kingdoms are also included, deigned to help them to extend their empire. It was to set the stage for a fuller discussion of this matter that I wrote the preceding book, showing that their gods, whom they thought should be worshiped even in trifling matters, have no power at all in this regard. For the same reason I wrote the preceding part of the present book, up to this point, in order to dispose of the question of fate. I certainly did not want anyone who is now persuaded that the Roman empire was not extended and preserved by the worship of those gods to attribute this instead to some sort of fate rather than to the all-powerful will of the supreme God.

The ancient and earliest Romans — like all the other nations, with the one exception of the Hebrew people — worshiped false gods and sacrificed victims not to God but to demons, but even so, as their own history teaches and stamps with approval, "they were eager for praise, generous with their money, and longed for boundless glory and riches with honor."[24] This glory they loved with a passion. It was for its sake that they wanted to live and for its sake that they did not hesitate to die. Their boundless desire for this one thing kept all their other desires in check. In short, since they considered it shameful for their country to serve, but glorious for it to dominate and rule, what they desired with all their hearts was first for it to be free and then for it to be dominant. It was for this reason that, unable to bear the rule of kings, "they limited command to a year and appointed two commanders for themselves,"[25] who were called consuls (from serving as counselors) rather than kings or lords (from reigning or lording over others).[26]...

Thus, when King Tarquin had been expelled and the consuls established,[27] there followed a period which this same author ranks among the glories of the Romans. "Once the city gained its liberty," he says, "it is incredible to relate how much and how quickly it grew, so great was the longing for glory that had taken hold."[28] It was, therefore, this eagerness for praise and longing for glory that accomplished so many wondrous things — things which were, beyond doubt, praiseworthy and glorious in human estimation....

---

23. On the order, and hence peace, of each part of the created world see below at XIX,13.
24. Sallust, *Catiline Conspiracy* 7.
25. Ibid. 6.
26. See Varro, *On the Latin Language* V,14.
27. See above at III,15-16.
28. Sallust, *Catiline Conspiracy* 7.

But, once liberty was won, such a longing for glory took hold of them that liberty alone was not enough unless they were also seeking domination, and what Virgil says, as if the words came from the mouth of Jupiter himself, was taken as a great thing: "Even savage Juno, who now torments sea and land and sky with terror, will be of better mind and, with me, will favor the Romans, the people of the toga, the masters of all the earth. That is my will. In time an age will come when the house of Assaracus will bring Phthia and famed Mycenae to servitude, and have dominion over vanquished Argos."[29] Virgil, of course, represented Jupiter as predicting the future; but, in fact, this is Virgil himself recalling the past and picturing the present state of things. My purpose in quoting these lines, however, is to show that, after liberty, the Romans valued dominion so highly that they ranked it among their greatest glories. Thus, in the following lines, the same poet ranks above the arts of other nations the specifically Roman arts of ruling and commanding peoples, of subjugating and subduing them: "Others may forge the bronze more delicately to breathing life, and may, I grant, carve living faces out from stone. They may plead cases at law with greater skill, and with compass chart the sky or tell the rising of the stars. But remember, Roman, that these will be your arts: to rule peoples by your command, to impose the ways of peace, to spare the conquered and subdue the proud."[30] The Romans practiced these arts with the greater skill when they were the less devoted to pleasure and to the enervation of mind and body that comes from pursuing and amassing wealth. Through wealth, however, they corrupted their morals by plundering their miserable citizens and lavishing gifts on degenerate actors.

But, at the time when Sallust was writing his prose and Virgil composing his verse, people of this sort had already come to prevail and abound, due to Rome's moral decline, and it was no longer by these Roman arts that men sought honor and glory but rather by guile and deceit. That is why Sallust says, "At first it was ambition rather than avarice that stirred men's minds, a vice that, even so, comes close to being a virtue. For the good and the worthless alike seek glory, honor, and power for themselves, but the former strive on the true path, while the latter, lacking any good arts, compete by guile and deceit."[31]...

Cato is given higher praise. Of him, in fact, Sallust says, "The less he sought glory, the more it followed him."[32] Glory, which the Romans burned with desire to have, is simply the judgment of men holding other men in high regard, and therefore virtue is better, since it is not content with mere human testimony apart from the witness of its own conscience. That is why the Apostle says, *For this is our glory, the testimony of our own conscience* (2 Cor 1:12); and in another passage, *But*

---

29. Virgil, *Aeneid* I,279-285. Assaracus was a mythical king of Dardania whose descendents included the founders of Rome. Hence "the house of Assaracus" represents Rome itself.
30. Ibid. VI,847-853.
31. *Catiline Conspiracy* 11.
32. *Catiline Conspiracy* 54.

let each test his own work, and then he will have glory in himself alone, and not in another (Gal 6:4). Therefore virtue should not follow on the glory, honor, and power which the Romans desired for themselves and which the good among them strove to attain by "good arts." Instead, glory, honor, and power should follow on virtue. For there is no true virtue except the virtue that is directed toward the end where man's good is actually found, the good than which there is no better. In truth, then, Cato ought not to have sought even the honors that he did seek. Rather, the city ought to have bestowed them on him, unsought, in recognition of his virtue.

But even though there were two Romans of great virtue at that time, Caesar and Cato, it seems that Cato's virtue came much closer to true virtue than did Caesar's. For let us see what the state's condition was at that time, and what it had been earlier, according to Cato's own judgment. "Do not imagine," he says, "that it was by force of arms that our ancestors made the republic great from its small beginnings. If that were true, we would have a far more excellent republic now than they did then. Indeed, we are far better supplied with allies and citizens, and with arms and horses, than they were. But it was other qualities that made them great, qualities which are wholly lacking in us: diligence at home, just rule abroad, and an independent spirit in counsel, addicted neither to crime nor to lust. Instead of these, what we have is self-indulgence and greed, public impoverishment and private wealth. We praise riches, we live for idleness, we make no distinction between good people and bad, and raw ambition usurps all the rewards that virtue ought to have. And it is no wonder — when each of you takes thought only for himself, when you are slaves to pleasure at home and to money and favor here in public — that any assault would come on a republic that has no defenses."[33]...

"But conversely," he adds, "once the state had been corrupted by luxury and idleness, the republic by its very size gave free rein to the vices of its generals and magistrates."[34] It was, therefore, the virtue of only a few — the few who strove for glory, honor, and power by the true way, that is, by virtue itself — that Cato praised. From their virtue came the diligence at home that Cato speaks of, the diligence that worked to enrich the public treasury and keep private fortunes slim. And so, in contrast, he sets it down as a vice that, when morals have been corrupted, we find public impoverishment and private wealth.

The Divine Gift of Empire to Rome: an Earthly Reward for Earthly Virtue

13. Thus, at a point when illustrious kingdoms had long existed in the east, God willed that there should arise in the west an empire which, although later in time, would be even more illustrious in its extent and grandeur. And in order to counteract the terrible evils of many other peoples, he granted it to the kind of men

---

33. Ibid. 52.
34. Ibid. 52.

who, for the sake of honor, praise, and glory, served the good of the country in which they sought their own glory and did not hesitate to put its well-being above their own. For the sake of this one vice — that is, the love of praise — these men suppressed the love of riches and many other vices.[35] For the most reasonable view is to admit that even the love of praise is, in fact, a vice. This is a point which did not escape the poet Horace, who says, "Do you swell with love of praise? There are certain rites of expiation which can restore you to health if, in purity, you read the little book three times."[36] And in a lyric poem, seeking to curb the lust for domination, the same author sings, "You will rule more widely by taming ardent greed than if you join Libya to distant Gades and thus make the two Punic peoples serve one master."[37] Nevertheless, it is for the better that people who do not restrain their baser lusts by the pious faith and the love of intelligible beauty that are given by the Holy Spirit at least do so by their desire for human praise and glory. They certainly are not saints, but at least they are less vile. Cicero, too, was unable to conceal this point. In the books he wrote *On the Republic*, where he speaks of the training of the civic leader — who, he says, ought to be nourished on glory — he goes on to add that his own ancestors did many marvelous and illustrious things due to their desire for glory.[38] Thus not only did they not resist this vice; they even supposed that it should be aroused and kindled precisely because they considered it to be beneficial for the republic. Not even in his philosophical works does Cicero conceal this pestilential view. Instead, he admits it there as plain as day. For, in speaking of the endeavors which should be pursued for the sake of the true good rather than for the sake of the winds of human praise, he introduced this universal generalization: "Honor nourishes the arts. Everyone is fired in his efforts by the thought of glory, but things that people hold in low esteem always lie neglected."[39]

14. Beyond doubt, therefore, it is better to resist this desire for praise than to yield to it. For each person is more like God the more pure he is of this impurity. And even if it is never fully eradicated from the heart in this life, since it never ceases to tempt the minds even of those who are making good progress, the desire for glory may at least be surpassed by the love of righteousness. In that case, if things that people hold in low esteem lie neglected at any point — presuming that those things are good, presuming that they are right — even the love of human praise itself will feel embarrassed and will yield to the love of truth. For when desire for glory holds a greater place in the heart than fear or love of God, this vice is so opposed to godly faith that the Lord said, *How can you believe when you look for glory from each other and do not seek the glory which comes from God alone* (Jn 5:44)? And again, with regard to certain persons who had believed

---

35. That vainglory keeps other vices at bay is also expressed in Cassian, *Conferences* V,12.
36. Letter I,1,36-37.
37. *Odes* II,2,9-12.
38. This reference to Cicero's *Republic* is found only here.
39. *Tusculan Disputations* I,4.

in him but were afraid to confess it openly, the evangelist says, *They loved human glory more than they loved the glory that comes from God* (Jn 12:43).

The holy apostles were not like this. They preached the name of Christ not only in places where it was held in low esteem (as Cicero says, "Things that people hold in low esteem always lie neglected") but even where it was held in the deepest loathing. They held fast to what they had heard from the good teacher[40] who is also the physician of minds,[41] *If anyone denies me before men, I will deny him before my Father who is in heaven* (Mt 10:33), or *before the angels of God* (Lk 12:9). In the midst of curses and reviling, in the midst of terrible persecutions and cruel punishments, they were not deterred from preaching human salvation, no matter how great the frenzy of human hatred. By their godly deeds and words, and by the godly lives they lived, they somehow conquered hard hearts and instilled the peace of righteousness in them, so that great glory followed them in the Church of Christ. But they did not rest content with that glory as if it were the end and goal of their virtue. Rather they referred that glory to the glory of God, by whose grace they were the kind of people they were, and with that same spark they kindled those in their care to love for the one by whom they also might become the same kind of people....

The apostles were followed by the martyrs, who surpassed men like Scaevola and Curtius and the Decii not by inflicting pain on themselves but by enduring the pain inflicted on them by others, as well as by their true virtue — true virtue because rooted in true piety — and also by their vast numbers. But since these Romans belonged to an earthly city, and since the goal set before them in all their services on its behalf was to secure its safety and to gain a kingdom not in heaven but on earth, not in eternal life but in a life where the dying pass away and are succeeded by those who are going to die in turn, what else was there for them to love but glory? And what glory but the glory by which they yearned to find a life after death, as it were, on the lips of those who praised them?...

The Roman Example: an Antidote to Christian Pride

17. ... Even in this respect, however, we may profit from the kindness of the Lord our God. Let us keep in mind how much those Romans disdained, what sufferings they endured, what passions they suppressed, all for the sake of human glory. They deserved to receive human glory as their reward for virtues of this sort. And let this thought take such hold on us that it stifles any pride on our part: the city in which it is promised that we shall reign is as far removed from this Rome as

---

40. See Lk 18:18.
41. "Physician of minds": *medico mentium*. The theme of Christ as physician or healer is an important one in Augustine. See Rudolph Arbesmann, "The Concept of 'Christus Medicus' in St. Augustine," in *Traditio* 10 (1954) 1-28.

heaven is from earth, as eternal life is from temporal joy, as solid glory is from empty praise, as the society of angels is from the society of mortals, as the light of the one who made the sun and moon is from the light of the sun and moon themselves. The citizens of such a marvelous homeland should not think that they have done anything remarkable if, for the sake of attaining it, they performed some good work or endured some few evils, given that the Romans did so much and suffered so much for the sake of an earthly country which they possessed already. And this point is especially noteworthy because the remission of sins, which gathers citizens for the eternal homeland, has a kind of likeness, a sort of shadow, in the asylum established by Romulus, where impunity for every sort of crime brought together the multitude that was to found the city of Rome....

[Chapter 18 gives examples of Romans who endured great difficulties and suffering, even sacrificing their sons out of lust for human praise and earthly glory.]

18. ...How would these feats, and any others of the same kind that may be found in their writings, ever have become so widely known or have been proclaimed with such renown if the Roman empire had not spread far and wide and grown large through its magnificent successes? It is thanks to that empire — so widespread, so long-lasting, so famous and glorious for the virtues of men such as those I have named — that those men received the reward that they sought in their efforts; and it is thanks to that empire that we have their examples set before us as a necessary admonition. If, for the sake of the most glorious city of God, we do not hold fast to the virtues of which they held to a kind of likeness for the sake of no more than the glory of the earthly city, we should be pierced with shame. And if we do hold fast to them, of course, we should not swell up with pride, for, as the Apostle says, *The sufferings of this present time are unworthy of the future glory which will be revealed in us* (Rom 8:18). In contrast, the lives of those Romans were judged worthy enough of human glory in this present age....

The Difference between the Desire for Glory and the Desire for Domination

19. There is, of course, a difference between the desire for human glory and the desire for domination. For, even though it is all too easy for anyone who takes excessive delight in human glory to slip over into an ardent pursuit of domination, it remains true that those who desire true glory, even if only the glory of human praise, will take care not to displease people of sound judgment. For there are many good qualities of character, and there are many who judge those qualities well, even though not many actually have them. And it is by means of these good qualities of character that the men strive for glory and power and domination of whom Sallust says, "But he strives by the true path."[42] In contrast, anyone who wants domination and power, but lacks the desire for glory that makes a person afraid to displease people of sound judgment, will generally seek to obtain what he loves by even the most blatantly criminal acts. The person who yearns for glory, therefore, will either strive by the true path or "compete by guile and deceit,"[43] wishing to seem good when he is not.

To one who possesses the virtues, then, it is a great virtue to despise glory, for his contempt for glory is seen by God, even if it is not apparent to human judgment. For no matter what he may do before human eyes to show that he holds glory in contempt, if people think that he is only trying to gain greater praise (that is, greater glory), there is no way that he can prove to the senses of those who suspect him that their suspicions have no basis. But the person who despises the judgment of those who praise him will also despise the temerity of those who suspect him....

In contrast, the person who despises glory but is avid for domination outdoes even the beasts in the vices of cruelty and of self-indulgence. Some Romans were like this. They had lost any concern for their good name but suffered no lack of desire for dominance. History tells us that there were many like this, but it was Nero Caesar who first reached the summit and, so to speak, the citadel of this vice. He went so far in self-indulgence that one might have thought there was nothing hard-fisted to fear from him, and yet he went so far in cruelty that one might have believed, if one did not know better, there was nothing flabby about him.[44] But even in the case of men such as this, the power to dominate is given only by the providence of the supreme God, when he judges that the state of human affairs deserves such overlords....

As best I could, then, I have explained why the one true and just God aided the Romans in attaining the glory of such a great empire, for they were good men within the context of the earthly city. It is possible, of course, that there is another more hidden reason, better known to God than to us, which has to do with the diverse merits of humankind. But even so, let it be agreed among all who are truly godly that no one can possibly have true virtue without true godliness — that is, without true worship of the true God — and that virtue is not true virtue when it is put to the service of human glory. But let it also be agreed that those who are not citizens of the eternal city (which is called the city of God in our Sacred Scriptures[45]) are more useful to the earthly city when they at least have the kind of virtue that serves human glory than when they do not.

---

42. *Catiline Conspiracy* 11.
43. Ibid.
44. See Tacitus, *Annals* XV,37; Suetonius, *Lives of the Twelve Caesars*, Nero.
45. See Pss 46:4; 48:1.8.

As for those who are endowed with true godliness and who lead good lives, if they also have the skill of governing peoples, there is no happier state of human affairs than when, by God's mercy, they hold power. Such men attribute their virtues, so far as they are able to have virtue in this life, only to the grace of God, for it is God who has given them these virtues in response to their willing, their believing, and their entreating. At the same time, they understand how far they fall short of perfect righteousness as it is found in the company of the holy angels, for which they are striving to prepare themselves. And so, no matter how much we may praise and proclaim the virtue which, lacking true godliness, serves the end of human glory, it is in no way to be compared with even the tiniest first steps of the saints, who have put their hope in the grace and mercy of the true God....

God Is the One Who Grants Power both to Kingdoms and to Individuals

21. All this being so, we should not ascribe the power of granting kingdoms and empires to any but the true God. It is he who gives happiness in the kingdom of heaven to the godly alone, and it is he who gives earthly kingdoms to the godly and the ungodly alike according to his pleasure, which never takes pleasure in anything unjust. For although we have discussed such things as God willed to make clear to us, it is a task too great for us, and, indeed, it far surpasses our powers to sort out the secrets of the human heart and by clear investigation to weigh up the merits of kingdoms. It was, therefore, the one true God, who never abandons the human race either in judgment or in aid, who gave a kingdom to the Romans when he wished and just so far as he wished. He was the one who gave a kingdom to the Assyrians, and then also to the Persians, who, as their writings indicate, worshiped only two gods, one good and one evil[46] — to say nothing of the Hebrew people (about whom I have already said as much as seemed necessary), who worshiped only the one God even when they had a kingdom....

The same is true of individual men. The same God who gave power to Marius also gave it to Gaius Caesar; the same God who gave power to Augustus also gave it to Nero; the same God who gave it to the Vespasians, father and son, the most temperate emperors, also gave it to Domitian, the cruelest; and — there is no need to mention each emperor individually — the same God who gave power to Constantine the Christian also gave it to Julian the Apostate.[47] Julian was a man of outstanding abilities, but a sacrilegious and detestable superstition deceived him through his love for domination. Devoted as he was to this superstition's vain

---

46. Augustine is referring here to the Zoroastrian religion, practiced in ancient Persia, which had a supreme and beneficent god, Ahura Mazda, and a spirit of evil, Angra Mainyu.
47. As is clear, Augustine arranges these political figures, mostly emperors, antithetically. Constantine (306-337) and Julian the Apostate (361-363) form the most poignant set of antitheses from the Christian standpoint: the former granted toleration to Christians, thus initiating the Christian era, while the latter attempted to undo Constantine's polity.

oracles, and relying on their assurance of victory, he burned the ships carrying his essential provisions. Then, pressing on feverishly with unrestrained daring, he was soon killed as the due price for his rashness. He left his army unsupplied in enemy territory, with the result that there was no way they could possibly have escaped from their plight if the boundaries of the Roman empire had not been changed, contrary to the omen of the god Terminus that I mentioned in the previous book.[48] For the god Terminus, who had not given way to Jupiter, did give way to necessity. Clearly the one true God rules and governs all these things as he pleases. And, if his reasons are hidden, does that mean that they are unjust?

22. So also the duration of wars is determined by his will and just judgment and mercy, either to chasten or to comfort humankind. That is why some wars come to an end more quickly and others more slowly....

The Good Christian Emperor

24. As for us, if we call certain Christian emperors happy, the reason is not that they had longer reigns or that they died peacefully and left sons ruling after them; it is not that they subdued the republic's enemies or that they were able to guard against and suppress insurgencies against them by hostile citizens. After all, even some worshipers of demons, who do not belong to the kingdom of God to which these emperors belong, have deserved to receive these and other gifts and consolations of this troubled life. And this happened by the mercy of God, to keep those who believe in him from desiring to receive such things from him as if they were the highest goods.

Rather,[49] we call Christian emperors happy if they rule justly; if they do not swell with pride among the voices of those who honor them too highly and the obsequiousness of those who acclaim them too humbly, but remember that they are only human beings; if they make their power the servant of God's majesty, using it to spread the worship of God as much as possible; if they fear, love, and worship God; if, more than their own kingdom, they love the one where they do not fear to have co-rulers; if they are slow to punish and quick to pardon; if they enforce punishment only as necessary for governing and defending the republic, not to satisfy their personal animosities; if they grant pardon not to let wrongdoing go unpunished but in the hope of its being corrected; if they compensate for the harsh decisions they are often compelled to make with the leniency of mercy

---

48. "Boundaries...Terminus": *termini...Terminus*.
49. The section that begins here is a so-called "mirror for princes" and, albeit brief, is the first Christian example of that genre, unless, with less justification, one were also to include Eusebius of Caesarea's writings on Constantine (see note 51 below) in that category. The purpose of a "mirror for princes" was to provide instruction to rulers to help them rule wisely, although wise rule was not always understood as virtuous rule, as exemplified in Niccolo Machiavelli's *Prince*, the most famous work of its type.

and the generosity of beneficence; if the more they are in a position to give free rein to self-indulgence the more they hold it in check; if they prefer to govern their own base desires more than to govern any peoples; if they do all this not out of a craving for empty glory but rather out of love for eternal happiness; and if, for their sins, they do not neglect to offer their true God the sacrifice of humility and compassion and prayer. It is Christian emperors such as this that we say are happy. For the present, they are happy in hope; hereafter, they will be happy in reality, when that to which we now look forward has actually arrived.

25. For God, in his goodness, did not want people who believe that he should be worshiped for the sake of eternal life to imagine that no one, thinking that spirits have great power in such matters, could attain earthly kingdoms and the heights of power without offering worship to demons. And so he heaped worldly gifts, beyond anyone's most audacious wishes, on the emperor Constantine, who offered no worship to demons but worshiped the true God alone. God even granted him the founding of a city to share in Roman rule — the daughter, so to speak, of Rome itself, but wholly without any temple or image of the demons.[50] He had a long reign, and, as sole Augustus, he held and defended the whole Roman world. He was supremely victorious in the wars that he directed and waged, and in every case was successful in crushing tyrants. He died of sickness and old age after a long life, and he left sons to rule after him.[51]

But on the other hand, to keep any emperor from becoming Christian simply to gain Constantine's happy success — since no one should be Christian except for the sake of eternal life — God removed Jovian far more quickly than he did Julian.[52] and he allowed Gratian to be killed by a usurper's sword.[53] In a sense, however, Gratian's death was far less harsh than that of Pompey the Great, who did worship the supposed gods of Rome. For Pompey could not be avenged by Cato, whom he had left, in a manner of speaking, as his heir in the civil war, but Gratian — although godly souls require no such consolations — was avenged by Theodosius, whom he had made his co-ruler despite the fact that he had a little brother of his own. For Gratian was more eager to have a faithful colleague than to pile up an excess of power.

---

50. I.e., the city of Constantinople, founded in 330.
51. In composing this section on Constantine, Augustine must have been influenced, at least indirectly, by Eusebius of Caesarea's fulsome encomiums of the emperor — namely, his *Life of Constantine* and *Praises of Constantine* 1-10. Augustine could not have known, for example, that Constantine had his wife Fausta and his son Crispus murdered in 326, that he was generally cruel to his enemies, or that he was baptized only on his deathbed by Eusebius of Nicomedia, an Arian sympathizer.
52. Jovian, a committed Christian, ruled from 363 to 364.
53. Gratian co-ruled the empire from 367 to 383. The usurper was the Roman general Magnus Maximus, who ruled from 383 to 388 and who was not directly responsible for the emperor's death. A few lines later Augustine refers to Gratian as one of the "godly souls" (*piae animae*) — undoubtedly because of his support of orthodox Christianity and his close relationship with Ambrose of Milan.

The Emperor Theodosius

26. Thus Theodosius kept faith with Gratian not only while he was alive but also after his death. For when Gratian's little brother Valentinian was banished by Maximus, Gratian's murderer, Theodosius, as a Christian, took him under his protection in his part of the empire and watched over him with fatherly affection.[54] Because Valentinian was destitute of all resources, Theodosius could easily have removed him, if he had been fired more by the desire to extend his rule than by the love of doing good. Instead he took Valentinian under his wing, preserved his imperial dignity, and consoled him with kindness and graciousness. Then, even though Maximus' success had made him a terror, Theodosius, despite all his anxious cares, did not lapse into sacrilegious and illicit superstitions. Instead he sent to John, a hermit established in the Egyptian desert.[55] For Theodosius had learned, due to John's growing fame, that this servant of God was gifted with the spirit of prophecy. From John he received a most certain assurance of victory. He soon destroyed the tyrant Maximus and, with the greatest mercy and veneration, restored the boy Valentinian to the part of the empire from which he had been forced to flee. When Valentinian was killed soon afterwards, whether by treachery or by some other plot or by accident, another tyrant, Eugenius, was illegally intruded as emperor in his place.[56] Once again Theodosius received a prophetic response and, made confident by his faith in it, crushed the tyrant. It was more by prayer than by sword that he fought against Eugenius's formidable army. Soldiers who were there have told me that the javelins they were throwing were ripped from their hands by a fierce wind blowing from Theodosius's position toward the enemy, and not only did this wind hurl their weapons toward the enemy at amazing speed but it also twisted the enemy's javelins back around toward their own bodies.[57] Thus even the poet Claudian, although a stranger to Christ's name, still says in praise of Theodosius, "O dearly beloved of God, for whom the very air does battle, and the winds, your sworn allies, come at the trumpet's call!"[58]

Being now the victor, as he had believed and predicted he would be, Theodosius threw down the statues of Jupiter which had been consecrated against him by rites of some kind and set up in the Alps. Those statues held thunderbolts made of

---

54. Theodosius I ("the Great") was co-emperor or emperor from 379 to 395. His friendship with Ambrose and his establishment of orthodox Christianity as the state religion were surely what won Augustine's high approval. Valentinian II was born c. 371 and became co-emperor in 375; he was either murdered or committed suicide in 392.
55. This was John of Lycopolis, one of the most famous of the Desert Fathers. His correspondence with Theodosius is mentioned in Palladius, *Lausiac History* 35,2; Cassian, *Institutes* IV,23; idem, *Conferences* XXIV,26,17.
56. Eugenius was proclaimed emperor by the pagan Frank Arbogast after the death of Valentinian II and reigned from 392 to 394.
57. See Paulus Orosius, *Against the Pagans* VII,35.
58. *Panegyric on the Third Consulate of Honorius Augustus* 96-98.

gold; and when the emperor's couriers (as the joy of the occasion allowed) made a joke about them, saying that they would not mind being struck by that kind of thunderbolt, Theodosius kindly gave the thunderbolts to them with a laugh. The sons of his enemies, whose fathers had been killed — not by his command — in the violence of war, took refuge in a church, even though they were not yet Christians.[59] Seizing the occasion, Theodosius wished them to become Christians; and he loved them with Christian charity, not depriving them of their property but rather adding to their honors. Following the victory, he gave no opening for private animosities against anyone. He was not like Cinna and Marius and Sulla and other such men,[60] who did not want to end the civil wars even after those wars had ended. Instead, rather than wishing the war's end to bring harm to anyone, Theodosius grieved that the war had ever begun.

In the midst of all these happenings, Theodosius did not cease, from the very beginning of his reign, to help the Church in her struggles against the ungodly by issuing the most just and merciful legislation. The heretic Valens had favored the Arians and had grievously afflicted the Church.[61] But Theodosius took more joy in being a member of the Church than in ruling the world. He ordered the destruction of pagan statues everywhere, for he knew full well that even earthly rewards do not lie in the power of demons but rather in the power of the true God. And what was more admirable than his devout humility when he punished the people of Thessalonica for their terrible crime? At the intercession of the bishops, he had at first promised that he would be lenient, but the uproar of certain persons close to him forced him to take vengeance on the people. But then, corrected by the discipline of the Church, he did penance with such deep humility that the people, as they prayed for him, felt more grief at seeing the imperial majesty lying prostrate than they felt fear of the imperial wrath against sin.[62]

These deeds, and others like them, which it would take too long to tell, are the good works that Theodosius took with him from the fog of this temporal life which, no matter how sublime and elevated, is still no more than fog. The reward for these works is eternal happiness, which God gives only to the truly devout. All the other things of this life, whether its high points or its bare necessities, God bestows on the good and the evil alike: such things as the world itself, light, air,

---

59. These were the sons of Eugenius and Arbogast.
60. See above at III,28.
61. Valens, the brother of Valentinian I, ruled as co-emperor from 364 to 378.
62. The "terrible crime" occurred in the summer of 390, when a mob of Thessalonians killed Botheric, the military commander of Thessalonica, in retaliation for the imprisonment of a popular but immoral charioteer. Theodosius was enraged and ordered the massacre of the population. Ambrose of Milan tried to prevent this exceedingly disproportionate punishment but was apparently overruled by the emperor's courtiers. Several thousand Thessalonians were killed, and Ambrose in response briefly excommunicated Theodosius and required that he perform public penance. See Ambrose, Letter 51; Paulinus of Milan, *Life of Saint Ambrose* 24. Augustine's sympathies clearly lie with the emperor and not with the Thessalonians; it is strange that he does not mention Ambrose by name but refers instead to unnamed bishops.

land, water, and the fruits of the earth, as well as the soul, body, senses, mind, and life of man himself. And included among these things is also the scope of empire, no matter how great or how small, which God dispenses in accord with his governance of the ages.

I see, however, that we must also respond to those people who, although they have been shown by the most obvious proofs that the throng of false gods is of no help whatsoever in obtaining the temporal goods which are the only goods that foolish people desire to have, still try to claim — even after they have been disproved and refuted on this score — that the gods are to be worshiped not for any benefit in this present life but rather for the sake of the life which is to come after death. For I judge that I have already given an adequate reply in these five books to the people who, as friends of this world, want to worship mere vanities and complain that they are not allowed to follow their childish notions in this regard.

When I had published the first three books and they had begun to circulate widely, I heard that certain persons were preparing some sort of written response to them.[63] Then I was told that they had already written the response but were waiting for a time when they could publish it without risk. My advice to these persons is that they not wish for what is not in their interest. It is easy for anyone who will not keep quiet to seem to have given a response. What, after all, is more talkative than sheer folly? But the fact that folly, if it wishes, can shout louder than truth does not mean that it is able to do what truth does. Let them consider the whole matter with care. Perhaps, if they can judge without partisan prejudice, they will see that there are some arguments which can be scoffed at, but cannot be overthrown, by impudent babble and the frivolity of satire and mime. If so, let them keep their nonsense in check and choose rather to be corrected by the prudent than to be praised by the impudent....

---

63. The written response to the three books seems not to have survived. Augustine is unusually harsh in describing his critics, but his apparently willing publication of an unfinished work put him in a somewhat compromised position.

Study Questions for Book V

Social scientists continue to study relationships between human behavior and political, social and economic change, looking for correlations or even possible causality. Nobel prizes in economics have been awarded for discerning such connections. How might Augustine's insistence on free will serve as a philosophical corrective or caveat for social science methodology or conclusions?

Fame remains a powerful personal stimulus and a strong social currency. Notice, admiration, flattery and approval satisfy the narcissistic longings we all have at some level. So we often behave and interact to impress others and win their acceptance. In this we are like the ancient Romans whose motivation to virtuous deeds was mixed with prideful desire for praise and glory. How can Augustine's counsel of humility, aided by divine grace, serve to elucidate our motivation and purify our dedication to God and service to society?

Utopia, as Thomas More's neologism reminds us, does not exist. There is no perfect government or ideal society on this earth, as Augustine indicates throughout *The City of God*. With good and selfless leadership we can sometimes arrive at a "good enough" society — though such achievements are constantly under threat from the forces of selfishness. Is Augustine's portrait of a "good emperor" relevant to "good enough" political leadership in contemporary societies and political systems? For Augustine what is the most reliable source of virtue for the good leader?

BOOK VI

In Book VI Augustine turns from the question of whether the gods should be worshiped for the sake of benefits in this life to the question of whether they should be worshiped for the sake of the life to come after death; and, from the outset, he makes it clear that Rome's traditional gods do not have the power to bestow eternal life. He shapes his argument in response to Varro, the Roman scholar and antiquarian, and specifically in response to Varro's account of Roman religion. The argument has two main elements. First, Augustine suggests that Varro's organization of his (now lost) Antiquities, which treats "human matters" before "divine matters" on the ground that the painter comes before the painting, tacitly acknowledges that Rome's gods were merely human inventions, not real beings. Second, taking off from Varro's distinction among three types of theology — the mythical theology of the poets, the natural theology of the philosophers (which is largely reserved for later discussion), and the civic theology of the cities — he points to the fact that Varro condemns the first and approves the third but presents the gods of the city in such a way that they are virtually indistinguishable from the gods of the poets. On this basis he contends that Varro must actually have disapproved of the civic gods as well but lacked the boldness to stand out against the force of Rome's religious traditions and customs. In contrast, Augustine notes, Seneca openly denounced Rome's traditional gods, but he felt that the gods should be worshiped all the same, as a matter of law and custom rather than of truth. Augustine's conclusion, then, is that neither the gods of the poets nor the gods of the city can possibly be understood as givers of eternal life; instead they are to be understood as malignant demons who have deceived humans into treating them as gods. Hence they are not to be worshiped for the sake of the life to come after death.

Preface. In the five preceding books I believe that I have provided an adequate argument against those who suppose that many false gods are to be venerated and worshiped for the sake of benefits in this mortal life and in earthly matters. They worship their gods with the rites and service that the Greeks call *latreia,* which in fact is due only to the one true God. But Christian truth shows that these gods are either useless images or unclean spirits and baneful demons or, at any rate, mere created beings and not the creator....

The Issue: Are the Gods to Be Worshiped for the Sake of Eternal Life?

1. Now, therefore, as the promised order requires, I must also refute and instruct those who contend that the gods of the nations — whom the Christian religion is overthrowing — are to be worshiped not for the sake of this life but for the sake of the life which is to come after death. It is appropriate, then, to take the beginning of my discussion from the truthful oracle of a holy Psalm: *Blessed is the man whose hope is the Lord God, and who has not turned his eye to vanities and to lying delusions* (Ps 40:4). In the midst of all these vanities and lying delusions, however, we ought to listen with far less impatience to those philosophers who disapprove of the opinions and errors of the peoples — the peoples who set up images for the divinities, who made up many false and unworthy stories about those they called immortal gods, or who believed the stories that had been made up before, and who, having believed these stories, wove them into their worship and sacred rites. These philosophers have not freely proclaimed their disapproval of such things, but they have at least murmured it in their own discussions, and so it is not wholly inappropriate to discuss with them this question as to whether, for the sake of the life which is to come after death, we should worship not the one God who made every spiritual and corporeal creature but the many gods who were made by that one God and set on high by him. For this is the view held by some of those same philosophers, the ones more excellent and noble than the rest.[1]

But as for those gods (some of whom I mentioned in the fourth book[2]) to whom responsibilities for petty little matters are assigned, one to each, who could possibly bear to have it claimed or argued that such gods offer eternal life to anyone? There are most learned and acute men who pride themselves on the great benefit they confer in writing books to teach people to know why they should pray to each god and what they should ask for from each. Their aim is to keep people from falling into the disgraceful absurdity, which is a common jest in the mimes, of asking for water from Liber or for wine from the Lymphs.[3] But suppose that a person who prays to the immortal gods does ask the Lymphs for wine, and they reply, "We only have water. Ask Liber for wine." Will these authorities tell him that he can rightly say, "If you have no wine, at least give me eternal life"? What could be more outlandish than this absurdity? Assuming that the Lymphs do not try to deceive the person, like the demons they are, they would probably burst out laughing (for they are usually ready to laugh at the drop of a hat[4]). Their answer would probably be: "O man, do you think we have it in our power to give life, when you have been told that we do not even have wine in our power?"

---

1. See Plato, *Timaeus* 40-41.
2. See above at IV,8.11.15.18-24.28.34.
3. Liber was the god of wine, and a Lymph was a water goddess.
4. See Virgil, *Eclogues* III,9.

It is, therefore, the most shameless folly to ask or hope for eternal life from such gods. They are each said to watch over only a single small bit of this brief and care-filled life, or of anything relevant to sustaining this life and propping it up. The result is that if anyone asks from one god what is under the protection and power of another, this is so inappropriate and so absurd that it looks exactly like the buffoonery of the mimes. When this is done intentionally by mimes, it rightly gets a laugh in the theater, but when it is done unintentionally by fools, it even more rightly gets mocked in the world at large. That is why learned men have ingeniously worked out and committed to writing which god or goddess should be asked for what, at least so far as the gods established by cities are concerned — what should be asked from Liber, for example, what from the Lymphs, what from Vulcan, and so forth for all the rest of them. Some of these gods I mentioned in the fourth book, some of them I simply decided to omit. But if it is a mistake to ask for wine from Ceres, or bread from Liber, or water from Vulcan, or fire from the Lymphs, how much the more ridiculous it should be considered to ask any of these gods for eternal life!

When we were asking which gods or goddesses should be considered capable of bestowing earthly rule on men, it was shown, after all aspects of the matter had been discussed, that it is far from the truth to suppose that even earthly kingdoms are established by any of those many false divinities. Is it not utterly insane impiety, then, to believe that any of them is able to give eternal life, which is beyond any doubt or comparison to be preferred above all earthly kingdoms?... And so, if (as the argument of the last two books has taught us) not one god from that throng of the plebeian or even of the noble gods is worthy to grant mortal kingdoms to mortals, how much less is any one of them able to make mortals into immortals!...

Varro and His Work on Roman Religion

2. Who has taken greater pains in investigating these matters than Marcus Varro?[5] Who has made more learned discoveries? Who has weighed the issues more attentively? Who has written more carefully or more fully on the subject? And, even though his style is less polished, he is so full of knowledge and ideas that, in all the forms of learning which we call secular and others call liberal, he is as instructive for the student of history as Cicero is delightful for the student of eloquence....

3. Varro wrote forty-one books of *Antiquities*, and he divided them into "Human Matters" and "Divine Matters," assigning twenty-five books to human matters and sixteen to divine matters.[6]...

---

5. On Varro see above at III,4.
6. Varro's monumental *Antiquities* does not survive apart from fragments gathered from other

4. ...Varro himself states that he wrote first about human matters and only then about divine matters, because cities came into existence first, and then these rites were instituted by them. The true religion, however, was not instituted by any earthly city; instead, clearly, the true religion itself instituted the heavenly city. And it is the true God, the giver of eternal life, who inspires and teaches true religion to his true worshipers.

When Varro confesses, then, that he wrote first about human matters and then about divine matters because divine things were instituted by men, he gives this as his reason: "Just as the painter is prior to the painting, and the builder prior to the building, so cities are prior to the things they institute."... Here, then, he openly admits that even these divine things were, like a painting or a structure, instituted by men....

Thus it is not that Varro wanted to put human matters ahead of divine matters; it is rather that he did not want to put false matters ahead of true matters. For, in the books that he wrote on human matters, he followed the history of actual events. But in those that he wrote on the matters that he calls divine, what is there but mere opinion and empty fantasies? And this, no doubt, is exactly what he wanted to indicate by means of subtle hints, not only by writing about divine matters after human matters but also by giving his reason for doing so. If he had not given his reason, some people might have defended his procedure on other grounds. In giving the precise reason that he gave, however, he left no room for others to make guesses of their own, and he gave proof enough that what he had done was to give men priority over what men instituted, not the nature of men priority over the nature of the gods. Thus he admitted that, when he wrote his books on divine matters, he was not writing about the truth that belongs to nature but about the falsehood that belongs to error. As I mentioned in the fourth book,[7] he stated this more clearly elsewhere. For he said that, if he were himself founding a new city, he would have written in accord with the rule of nature, but since he found himself situated in an already–established city, he could do nothing but follow its customs.

Varro's Three Types of Theology

5. Again, what does Varro have in mind when he says that there are three kinds of theology, that is, three kinds of explanatory accounts of the gods? Of these, one is called mythical, another physical, and the third civic....

Varro then goes on to say, "They call 'mythical' the theology used chiefly by the poets, 'physical' that used by the philosophers, and 'civic' that used by

---

sources, in particular *The City of God*. Thanks to Augustine's description here, we know of the parts into which the work was divided. Varro's treatise is also referred to and analyzed at length in Tertullian, *To the Nations* II,1-8.

7. See above at IV,31.

the people in general. In the first kind I named," he continues, "there are many fictions that are contrary to the dignity and nature of the immortals. For it is here that one god is born from the head, another from the thigh, and yet another from drops of blood; it is here that gods steal, commit adultery, and are enslaved to human beings; it is here, in short, that everything is attributed to the gods that can happen to a man, even to the lowest and most contemptible of men." In this case — where he could, where he dared, where he thought he could get away with it — Varro clearly stated, without even the least shadow of ambiguity, what a great injury is done to the nature of the gods by these lying fables. For he was speaking not of natural theology, nor of civic theology, but of mythical theology, which he thought that he could and should freely denounce.

Let us see what he says about the second kind. "The second kind I pointed to is the one on which the philosophers have left us many books in which they discuss who the gods are, where they are, of what kind they are, and of what quality, whether they exist from some point in time or from all eternity, whether they consist of fire, as Heraclitus believes, or of numbers, as Pythagoras holds, or of atoms, as Epicurus says.[8] And so on with other points, which the ears can more easily bear to hear inside the walls of a school than outside in the forum." He found nothing to condemn in this kind of theology, which they call physical and which pertains to the philosophers; he simply notes their controversies with each other, which resulted in a multitude of quarreling sects. But he did remove this kind of theology from the forum, that is, from the people, and shut it up within the walls of the school. On the other hand, he did not remove that first mendacious and disgraceful kind of theology from the cities. How discriminating are the religious ears of the populace, and among them the ears of the Romans! They cannot bear to hear the debates of the philosophers on the immortal gods, but they are not only able to bear but are even delighted to hear what poets sing and actors perform, despite the fact that these are fictions contrary to the dignity and nature of the immortals, since they can happen to a man, even to the lowest and most contemptible of men. And not only that, but they have decided that these tales are pleasing to the gods and that they should be used to placate the gods....

Let us also examine the civic theology. "The third kind," he says, "is that which citizens in their cities, and especially the priests, ought to know and administer. In this we are told which gods are to receive public worship and what rites and sacrifices are appropriate to each." And let us also note what comes next: "The first theology is especially suited to the theater, the second to the world, and the third to the city." Who does not see to which he awards the prize? Obviously it is the second, which he had earlier said was the concern of the philosophers. For this, he affirms, has to do with the world, and the philosophers hold the view

---

8. Heraclitus (c. 535-c. 475 B.C.) held that fire was the source of the other elements. Pythagoras (c.570-c.495 B.C.) believed that the universe was arranged according to mathematical principles. Epicurus (341-270 B.C.) posited that the movement of atoms — i.e., minute indivisible objects — was the determining factor in the fate of the world.

that nothing is superior to the world. As for the two other theologies, the first and the third, the one suited to the theater and the other to the city — has he really separated them, or has he actually united them? For, although we see that cities are in the world, we also see that it is quite possible that something belonging to the city does not belong to the world. Due to false opinions, it can happen that in the city things are worshiped and things are believed which simply do not exist at all, whether in the world or out of it. But where is the theater, if not in the city? Who established the theater, if not the city? Why was it established, if not for theatrical performances? And where do theatrical performances fit, if not among the divine matters which Varro's books describe with such skill?

6. O Marcus Varro, you are the most acute and undoubtedly the most learned man of all. But you are still only a man, not a god, and you have not been lifted up by the Spirit of God into truth and freedom[9] so as to see and proclaim divine things. You clearly perceive that divine matters should be set apart from human follies and falsehoods. But you are afraid to take a stand against the utterly vicious opinions and customs of the people in their public superstitions, which are completely opposed to the nature of the gods, even to the nature of such gods as the feeble human mind thinks it finds in the elements of this world. You see this yourself, when you consider the matter from all sides, and all your writings echo your view. But in your situation, what good is human ingenuity, no matter how outstanding it is? In such straits, what support can you find in human learning, no matter how vast and varied it is? You desire to worship the natural gods; you are compelled to worship the civic. You have discovered other gods — the mythical gods — on whom you feel free to vomit out what you think, but in so doing you also splatter the civic gods, whether you want to or not. You say, true enough, that the mythical gods are suited to the theater, the natural gods to the world, and the civic gods to the city. But the world is a divine work, while cities and theaters are mere human works, and the gods ridiculed in the theaters are none other than the gods adored in the temples, and the gods for whom you put on the games are none other than the gods to whom you sacrifice victims. How much more candid and perceptive your scheme of division would be if you simply said that some gods are natural and some are instituted by men. And, with reference to the gods instituted by men, how much better it would be if you simply admitted that, while the writings of the poets give one account and the writings of the priests another, the two are on such friendly terms with each other, linked together in a fellowship of falsehood, that they both give delight to the demons, to whom the teaching of the truth is hateful.

---

9. See Jn 8:32.

The Intertwining of the Mythical and Civic Theologies

Therefore, leaving aside for a moment the theology that they call natural, which is to be discussed later, does anyone actually find it acceptable to ask or hope for eternal life from the gods of poets and theaters, of games and plays? God forbid! Rather, may the true God protect us from such wild and sacrilegious madness! What? Are we to ask for eternal life from gods who are pleased and appeased by these shows, as long as their criminal acts are celebrated in them? No one, I think, is quite so demented as to leap over this precipice of raging impiety. No one, therefore, obtains eternal life by either the mythical or the civic theology. The former sows the seeds by inventing disgraceful tales about the gods; the latter reaps the harvest by stamping them with its favor. The former scatters lies; the latter gathers them in. The one tars divine matters with false crimes; the other counts the plays portraying these crimes as divine matters. The one recites unspeakable fictions about the gods in the poems of men; the other consecrates those fictions in the festivals of the gods themselves. The one sings of the crimes and shameless deeds of the divinities; the other loves to dote on them. The one publishes or invents these deeds; the other either attests to their truth or delights in them even though they are false. Both are vile, and both are damnable; but one, that of the theater, declares its foulness in public, while the other, that of the city, takes that foulness as its chief ornament. Will anyone hope for eternal life from something that pollutes even this brief and temporal life?...

7. Thus the mythical theology — the theology of the theater and the stage, full of degradation and shame — reverts back to the civic theology, and the whole of the mythical theology, which is rightly considered worthy of condemnation and scorn, turns out to be a part of the civic theology, which is held worthy of veneration and observance! And, as I have tried to show, it is no incongruous part, foreign to the body as a whole, ineptly joined and fastened to it. Quite the opposite! It is wholly consonant with it, united with it in a perfect fit, like a limb of the same body. For what do the cult statues show if not exactly the same forms, ages, sexes, and dress of the gods? The poets have a bearded Jupiter and a beardless Mercury; do not the pontiffs have exactly the same? The mimes represent Priapus with enormous genitals; do not the priests do exactly the same? Does the Priapus set up to be adored in the sacred precincts look any different from the Priapus who comes out to be ridiculed in the theaters? Saturn is represented as old and Apollo as young by the actors; do not their statues in the shrines show them exactly the same? Why are Forculus, who presides at the doors, and Limentinus, who guards the threshold, male gods, while Cardea, who keeps the hinge, is female? Are not precisely the same things found in the books on divine matters (things which serious poets considered unworthy to appear in their poems)? The Diana of the theater bears arms; is the Diana of the city a mere girl? The Apollo of the stage plays the lyre; does the Apollo of Delphi lack this art?

But these examples are positively respectable compared to others that are more disgraceful. What conception of Jupiter was in the minds of those who put his nurse on the Capitol? Did they not confirm the view of Euhemerus, who wrote — not as a babbling story-teller but as a careful historian — that all such gods were originally human beings and mortal?[10] And what about the people who put the "banqueting gods" at Jupiter's table as his parasites?[11] What else did they want but to correlate the sacred rites with scenes from the mimes? If a mime had said that these were parasites of Jupiter, invited to dine with him, it would seem obvious that he was looking for a laugh. But it was Varro who said it! And he said it not when he was mocking the gods but when he was commending them. And the proof that he wrote this comes not from his books on human matters but precisely from his books on divine matters, and it comes not where he was describing the stage plays but precisely where he was expounding the regulations of the Capitoline temple. In short, Varro is defeated by this kind of evidence and is forced to confess that, just as men made the gods in human form, so they believed that the gods delighted in human pleasures....

The Implied Aim of Varro's Account of Civic Theology

8. ... How, then, can the power to give eternal life be attributed to any of those gods, when their cult statues and sacred rites show that in form, age, sex, dress, marriage partners, genealogies, and ceremonies they are virtually identical to the mythical gods, the gods that are openly condemned? In all this, it is clear either that they were originally human beings, for whom sacred rites and ceremonies were instituted to honor the life or death of each, and that it was the demons who implanted and confirmed this error, or that they are themselves foul spirits who seized any opportunity to sneak into people's minds and deceive them....

9. ... And what are we to make of Varro's distinction between the religious person and the superstitious person? He says that the superstitious person fears the gods, while the religious person, in contrast, does not fear the gods as enemies but rather reveres them as parents. In addition, he says that all the gods are so good that they are more ready to spare the guilty than to harm the innocent. At the same time, however, he mentions that three gods are employed to guard a woman after childbirth in order to keep the god Silvanus from slipping in by

---

10. Euhemerus was a Greek thinker who lived during the late fourth and early third centuries B.C. Only fragments exist of his writings. His chief contribution to Western thought, although he was not the first to express it, was the idea that the gods were originally humans and that divine myths can be traced to historical events; hence the term "euhemerism," which refers to this approach to pagan religion. Augustine often invokes euhemeristic arguments to explain the gods.
11. See Bibliothèque Augustinienne 34, 566-567, note 11, which suggests that Augustine may have misunderstood the rare custom of offering a banquet to a single god — in this case Jupiter — by assuming that other gods were also in attendance.

night and distressing her. To represent these three guardians, three men go about the thresholds of the house at night; first they strike the threshold with an axe, then they strike it with a pestle, and, third, they sweep it with brooms. Due to the display of these three signs of agriculture, Silvanus is prevented from entering. For trees are not cut down and pruned without iron tools, nor is grain ground without a pestle, nor is the harvested grain piled up without brooms. From these three activities, three gods get their names — Intercidona from cutting down with an axe, Pilumnus from the pestle, and Deverra from brooms; and these three gods were the guardians who preserved the new mother from attack by the god Silvanus.[12] Thus the protection of the good gods would not have been effective against the fury of a harmful god, unless they were many against one. Nor would it have been effective unless they fought against the dire, horrifying, uncultivated, forest-dwelling god with the signs of agriculture as his contraries. Is this, then, the innocence of the gods? Is this their concord and harmony? Are these the divinities who watch over the safety of cities, divinities more ridiculous than any farce enacted in the theater?

When a man and a woman are yoked in marriage, the god Iugatinus is brought in.[13] That we can put up with. But the bride has to be escorted home, so the god Domiducus is summoned.[14] To install her in the house, the god Domitius is invoked.[15] To see that she remains with her husband, the goddess Manturna is added on as well.[16] What more do people want? Show a little consideration for human decency. Let the desire of flesh and blood do the rest, once modesty has gained its privacy. Why fill the bridal chamber with a throng of divinities after even the bridal party has taken its leave?[17] The purpose of having the throng there is not to heighten the concern for modesty due to the thought that the gods are present; it is rather to make sure that, with their cooperation, there will be no difficulty in taking the virginity of the bride, a member of the weaker sex, and fearful of her new situation....

Let them still go on. Let them try, with all the subtlety that they can muster, to distinguish the civic theology from the mythical theology, the cities from the theaters, the temples from the stage, the sacred rites of the pontiffs from the songs of the poets, as if they were distinguishing the decent from the disgraceful, the weighty from the frivolous, the serious from the ludicrous, things to be sought from things to be scorned. We see what they are doing. They know that the theatrical and mythical theology derives from the civic theology and reflects

---

12. "Intercidona...cutting down": *Intercidonam...intercisione*; "Pilumnus...pestle": *Pilumnum... pilo*; "Deverra...brooms": *Deverra...scopis* (the verb *deverrere*, meaning "to sweep," is understood). Silvanus is taken from *silva*, meaning "woods," or, by extension, "crops" or "growth."
13. "Yoked...Iugatinus": *coniunguntur...Iugatinus*.
14. "Escorted home...Domiducus": *domum...ducenda...Domiducus*.
15. "House...Domitius": *domo...Domitius*.
16. "Remains...Manturna": *maneat...Manturna*.
17. The same sentiments are expressed in Tertullian, *To the Nations* II,11.

it back in the songs of the poets like an image in a mirror. Thus, after expounding the theology that they do not dare to condemn, they attack and denounce its image without restraint, and their aim is that all who realize what they have in mind will despise not just the image but the very face it reflects. The gods themselves, however, when they see themselves in that same mirror, so to speak, love what they see, because who and what they are is seen all the better when seen in both the image and the original. That is why, by their terrifying commands, they compelled their worshipers to dedicate the indecencies of the mythical theology to them, to include these indecencies in their solemn festivals, and to count them as divine matters. In doing this, they have taught us all the more clearly that they are themselves utterly unclean spirits, and, at the same time, they have made the theology of the theater, which is rejected and condemned, an integral part of the theology of the city, which is regarded as chosen and approved. Thus, even though the whole of their theology is disgraceful and false and contains only imaginary gods, one part of it is found in the writings of the priests and another in the songs of the poets. Whether it has other parts as well is another question. For now, given Varro's classification, I think that I have shown well enough that the theology of the city and the theology of the theater both belong to the one civic theology. And so, because they are both alike in being disgraceful, absurd, unworthy, and false, far be it from anyone who is truly religious to hope for eternal life from either one of them.

Finally, it is Varro himself who begins the listing and enumeration of the gods from the point at which a person is conceived. He starts with Janus, carries the sequence down to the point of death in decrepit old age, and closes the list of gods related to the stages of a person's life with the goddess Nenia, who is invoked in song at the funerals of the very old.[18] Then he begins to point out other gods who pertain not to the person himself but to the things which are of concern to human beings, such as food and clothing and any other necessities of this life. In all instances, he shows what the role of each god is and what should be sought from each. But nowhere in his meticulous review of the gods does he ever point out or name any gods from whom we should ask for eternal life — which is the one most central reason why we are Christians.

Who, then, is so slow-witted that he does not see Varro's aim in laying out and explaining the civic theology so carefully, in showing how similar it is to the unworthy and debased mythical theology, and in teaching clearly enough that the mythical theology is itself a part of the civic theology? It is quite obvious that his purpose is to ready a place in human minds for the natural philosophy which, he says, belongs to the philosophers. His approach is subtle: he denounces the mythical theology; and, even though he clearly does not dare to denounce the civic theology, simply by presenting it in the way he does he shows that it ought to be denounced. And so, once both have been rejected by the verdict of people who

---

18. Janus was the god of beginnings, Nenia the goddess of funeral songs (*nenia* means "funeral song").

understand the matter rightly, the only choice left is the natural theology. And this I will discuss more fully, with the help of the true God, in its proper place.

Seneca's Boldness and Varro's Timidity

10. Varro lacked the boldness to dare to condemn openly the theology of the city in the same way that he condemned the theology of the theater, despite the fact that they are so very much alike. Annaeus Seneca — who flourished, as we learn from various indications, in the time of our apostles — had that boldness, if not fully, at least to some degree.[19] It was present in his writings but not in his life. For, in the book that he composed against superstitions, he condemned the civic and urban theology much more fully and strongly than Varro did the theatrical and mythical theology. In dealing with cult images, he says, "To beings who are holy, immortal, and inviolate they dedicate images made of the vilest inert material. They make those beings look like men, or beasts, or fish; and some even make them bisexual, with discordant bodies. And they call them divinities even though, if they were suddenly to come to life and meet us in the street, they would be considered monsters." Then, a little further on, when he was commending the natural theology and had summarized the views of certain philosophers, he puts a question to himself: "At this point, someone says, 'Am I to believe that heaven and earth are gods, and that some gods are above the moon and others below it? Am I to put up with either Plato or Strato the Peripatetic, the one claiming that God has no body, the other that God has no soul?"[20] And to this, Seneca replies, "What then? Do the dreams of Titus Tatius or Romulus or Tullus Hostilius strike you as any closer to the truth?[21] Cloacina was consecrated as a goddess by Tatius; Picus and Tiberinus were consecrated by Romulus; and Hostilius made gods of Panic and Pallor, the most debased emotional states of mankind. One of these is simply the convulsion of a terrified mind, and the other is not even a disease of the body but only a color that it takes on. Would you prefer to believe that these are divinities and to grant them a place in heaven?"...

Varro did not have this kind of boldness. He only dared to condemn the poetic theology, not the civic theology that Seneca cut to ribbons. But, if we want the truth of the matter, the temples where these things are actually done in reality are far worse than the theaters where they are only acted out in make-believe. And so, with regard to the rites of the civic theology, the role that Seneca

---

19. On Seneca see above V,8 footnote 12. The work that Augustine cites in the succeeding lines, *On Superstition*, is lost; this is the sole remaining fragment apart from a doubtful citation in Tertullian, *Apology* 12.
20. Plato's views are well known. Strato the Peripatetic (c.335-c.269 B.C.) was a Greek philosopher with a materialistic and even atheistic view of nature. Rather than believing that God had no soul, he seems not to have believed in God at all.
21. For Titus Tatius, the Sabine king who supposedly ruled at the same time as Romulus, see above at III,13. For Tullus Hostilius see above at III,14-15.

chooses for the wise man is to exclude them from the religion of his soul but to pretend to go along with them in his actions. For he says, "The wise man will observe all these rites not because they are pleasing to the gods but because they are enjoined by law." And a little later he says, "What about the way we unite the gods in marriage! We do not do even this with any true regard for piety, but unite brothers and sisters. We marry Bellona to Mars, Venus to Vulcan, and Salacia to Neptune. At the same time, we leave some unwed, as if no suitable match could be arranged, especially since some are widows, such as Populonia, Fulgora, and the goddess Rumina.[22] But I am not at all surprised that there has been no suitor for these. And as for all that ignoble throng of gods assembled through the ages by ancient superstition, we will adore them, but only with the reminder that their worship has far more to do with custom than with truth."

In Seneca's view, then, neither law nor custom established anything in the civic theology which either pleased the gods or pertained to truth. But because he was a distinguished senator of the Roman people, Seneca himself, whom the philosophers had in a sense made free, still worshiped what he condemned, did what he denounced, and adored what he accused. Philosophy, clearly, had taught him something important — not to be superstitious in the world, but still, for the sake of the laws of the city and the customs of men, to imitate in the temple the part of an actor on the stage. This was all the more reprehensible in that he acted out the lie in such a way that the people presumed him to be acting out the truth. An actor, in contrast, seeks to delight by amusing people rather than to deceive by deluding them.

Seneca on the Jews

11. Among the other superstitions of the civic theology, Seneca also censures the rites of the Jews. He asserts, in particular, that it is no benefit for them to keep the sabbath because, by imposing one day of rest in every seven, they lose almost a seventh of their life in inactivity and often suffer harm due to not acting in times of urgency. He ventures to mention the Christians, who even then were already very hostile to the Jews, but only in neutral terms, for fear of praising them against the ancient custom of his homeland, or perhaps for fear of condemning them against his own convictions. When speaking of the Jews, however, he says, "In the meantime, the customs of this degraded people have become so prevalent that they are now accepted throughout the world; the conquered have given their laws to the conquerors." He showed surprise in saying this, and, without knowing what God was working out, he openly adds a remark that signifies what he thought himself of the character of their rites: "At least

---

22. Populonia was a goddess venerated by the Oscans and Sabellians, peoples of southern and central Italy. Fulgora was the goddess of lightening. Rumina was the goddess of suckling animals.

they know the reasons for their rites. The greater part of our people have no idea why they do what they do."

But as to why, and to what extent, the Jewish rites were established by divine authority and later, at the proper time, and by that same authority, were taken over by the people of God, to whom the mystery of eternal life has been revealed — these are questions that I have discussed elsewhere, especially when arguing against the Manicheans.[23] In this work, I shall have to discuss them at a more appropriate point.[24]

Neither the Mythical nor the Civic Theology Holds the Promise of Eternal Life

12. Here, then, are three theologies, which the Greeks call mythical, physical, and political, and which, in Latin, may be called fabulous, natural, and civic. It is now clear that no one should hope for eternal life from either the mythical or the civic theology. The worshipers of the many false gods have themselves openly condemned the mythical theology, and the civic theology has now been shown to be a part of the mythical and has been found to be exactly like it, or even worse....

Not only are these gods not to be worshiped for the sake of earthly and temporal things, as we showed in the preceding five books, but far less are they to be worshiped for the sake of eternal life, the life to come after death, as we have argued in the present book, with the help of the earlier ones. But since the force of inveterate custom has very deep roots, if it seems to anyone that I have not said enough to make the case that the civic theology should be rejected and scorned, let him turn his attention to the next book, which, with God's help, I must add to this one.

---

23. See *Answer to Faustus, a Manichean.*
24. See below at XVII passim.

Study Questions for Book VI

Death confirms the hard reality of human limitation. Yet the denial of death remains a basic human instinct. For Augustine the transformation of human life beyond death lies in our divinization, that is, in the divine welcome to participate in the eternal communion of love that is the Trinity. How might Christian belief in God's promise of eternal life through Jesus Christ transform our daily experience of the limits of our own power to effect change and make progress? How does Christian hope in eternal life with God help us to be more effective in resolving challenges within our families, at work, in our civic or religious communities, or amidst seemingly intractable global problems?

Christian faith must sometimes confront the assumptions, practices and mores of the culture in which the Church lives. Biblical narratives together with Christian symbols and sacraments offer believers alternative interpretations of the meaning of life. The Church's moral teachings present the challenge of making life choices in light of divine revelation. Augustine challenged the pagan mythology of Rome and its civic enshrinement, because he found in Christian faith and teaching — rooted in the mystery of Christ, the Word Made Flesh — a nobler understanding of humanity's meaning and purpose. What cultural, social and political critiques might today's Christians advance in the service of a new Christian humanism?

Augustine admired Seneca for his censure of the Roman pantheon, but did not approve his compromise to allow civic religion for the sake of Roman custom. The Church today lives amidst many different societies and cultures where it must have a voice in the public square for the sake of the Gospel and the common good. How should it negotiate the art of compromise amidst partisan politics, ethnic diversity and legal systems? What should be the Church's public role in countries where it is only a tolerated minority?

BOOK VII

Book VII continues Augustine's response to Varro, turning now to Varro's account of the select gods, i.e., the major gods of the Roman religious tradition. Although Varro discusses the select gods in the context of his treatment of civic theology, he appears to have interpreted them primarily in naturalistic or philosophical terms by correlating them with various natural processes and the forces underlying those processes; and he correlates Jupiter, in particular, with the world-soul, the force underlying and directing the world as a whole. Augustine's reply has several dimensions: (1) He points out that Varro associates the select gods with lesser deities in ways that compromise their dignity, reduce their status, and suggest that they are not competent to carry out their functions without help from others. (2) He argues that Varro's naturalistic interpretations of the gods generate all sorts of inconsistencies and absurdities which cannot be resolved. (3) He insists that the naturalistic interpretation of the civic gods does nothing to vindicate, compensate for, or overcome the moral atrocities contained in the stories about the gods and most especially in the rites enacted in Rome's worship of them. (4) He claims that, in any case, worship of the world, of the world-soul, or of forces operative in the world does not count as worship of the one true God, who is the one actually responsible for all the forces and functions that Varro has assigned to the select gods, and from whom alone human beings can attain the happiness of eternal life. (5) Finally, he suggests that the lost books of Numa on the religious rites that he instituted as Rome's second king contained the true explanations of the civic gods and their rites. These explanations must, however, have exposed the demonic origins of the rites, for Numa buried the books rather than allowing them to see the light of day, and, when they were rediscovered, the senate ordered that they be burned. In Augustine's view, then, the best explanation of Rome's civic gods is that they were originally human beings and that their elevation to divine standing was the result of demonic deception.

Preface. I am trying, with great care, to uproot and eradicate the perverse and ancient views that long-standing error has fixed deeply and tenaciously in humanity's darkened minds, for these views are hostile to true religion. And I am cooperating, in my small measure, with the grace of the true God, who alone can accomplish this, and I rely on his help.[1] Those of livelier mind and superior ability, for whom the preceding books are enough, and more than enough, for this purpose, must be patient and wait calmly at this point. For the sake of others, they must not regard as superfluous what they no longer consider necessary for themselves. We are dealing with a matter of supreme importance when we declare that the true and truly holy Divinity, despite the fact that he provides us with the helps necessary for the fragile life we now live, should not be sought or worshiped for the sake of the mere passing smoke of this life but rather for the sake of the life of blessedness, which can only be eternal life.

1. This Divinity or, as I may say, this Deity (for our writers do not hesitate to use this word as a more express translation of what the Greeks call *theotes*) — this Divinity or Deity, then, is not to be found in the civic theology that Marcus Varro set forth in sixteen books. In short, there is no way to reach the happiness of eternal life by worshiping the sort of gods established by the cities, or by the sort of worship offered to them. If anyone has not yet been persuaded of this point by the sixth book, just completed, perhaps he will find, when he has read this one, that he has nothing further to desire in order to settle the issue.

The Select Gods and Their Functions

It is possible that someone might think that at least the select and principal gods, whom Varro included in his final book and about whom I have said very little up to this point, should be worshiped for the sake of the life of happiness, which can only be eternal life. Here I am not going to repeat what Tertullian said, perhaps with more wit than truth: "If some gods are selected like onions, then surely all the rest are rejected as no good."[2] I do not say this, for I see that, even from among the select, some are selected for a greater and more preeminent role. In the military, for instance, when recruits have been chosen, some of them are again chosen for a greater task at arms; and in the Church, when some are elected as leaders, it certainly is not true that the rest are rejected, since all the good and faithful are rightly called elect.[3] Again, cornerstones are selected for a building, but the rest are not rejected;[4] they are simply assigned to other parts of the structure. Some grapes are selected for eating, but the others are not rejected; we simply leave them for drinking. But there is no need to multiply examples. The point is obvious. Consequently, the mere fact that some gods were selected from many does not mean that there is any reason to vilify either the one who wrote about them, or the ones who worship them, or the gods themselves. Rather

---

1. Note the theology of grace that marks this sentence, penned not long after Augustine's first written encounter with Pelagianism in 411-412 (*On the Punishment and Remission of Sins and the Baptism of Infants*).
2. See *To the Nations* II,9.
3. See 1 Pt 2:9.
4. See Ps 118:22.

we should take note of who these select gods are and for what purpose they seem to have been selected.

2. At any rate, these are the gods that Varro commends as select in the course of his one book on the topic: Janus, Jupiter, Saturn, Genius, Mercury, Apollo, Mars, Vulcan, Neptune, Sol, Orcus, Liber Pater, Tellus, Ceres, Juno, Luna, Diana, Minerva, Venus, Vesta. There are twenty in all, twelve male and eight female.

Are these divinities called select because of their greater functions in the world or because they are better known to the people and receive a greater form of worship? If it is because they are responsible for greater tasks in the world, we should not find them included among that plebeian throng of divinities who are assigned to trifling little jobs. Yet right at the start, at the moment of conception — which is when all those tasks begin that are distributed, bit by bit, among the divinities — it is Janus himself who opens the way for the receiving of the seed. Saturn is also there, on account of the seed itself. Liber is there, who delivers the male of the seed that he ejaculates. Libera is there, whom they want to identify with Venus and who confers the same benefit on the woman, so that she also is delivered of the seed she emits. All of these are among the gods who are called select. But also there is the goddess Mena, who presides over the menstrual flow,[5] and she is a nonentity, even if she is a daughter of Jupiter. In fact, however, in his book on the select gods, Varro assigns the province of the menstrual flow to Juno herself, who is actually the queen of the select gods; but here, as Juno Lucina, she presides over the menstrual blood along with Mena, her step-daughter. Also present are two exceedingly obscure gods, Vitumnus and Sentinus, one of whom bestows life and the other sensation on the fetus;[6] and, even though they are complete nonentities, they clearly provide far more than do all those noble and select gods. For, without life and sensation, all that the woman carries in her womb amounts to no more than a worthless who-knows-what, comparable to mire and dust.

The Absurdities and Inconsistencies in Varro's Account of the Select Gods

3. What was it, then, that drove so many select gods to such very minor tasks, where they are surpassed in the munificence of their gifts by Vitumnus and Sentinus, "whom an obscure fame has hidden from view"?[7] For the select Janus confers access — a door,[8] as it were — for the seed; the select Saturn confers the seed itself; the select Liber confers the emission of the seed on men; and Libera, who is also Ceres or Venus, confers the same on women; the select Juno (not by

---

5. "Mena...menstrual": *Mena...menstruis*.
6. "Vitumnus...Sentinus...life...sensation": *Vitumnus...Sentinus...vitam...sensus*.
7. Virgil, *Aeneid* V,302.
8. "Janus...door": *Ianus...ianuam*.

herself, but along with Mena, Jupiter's daughter) confers the menstrual flow so that what has been conceived may grow. But it is the obscure nonentity Vitumnus who confers life, and the obscure nonentity Sentinus who confers sensation, and these two things are as far superior to the others as they are themselves inferior to intellect and reason. For just as beings that have reason and intellect are plainly better than those that live and feel like cattle, without reason or intellect, so also those that are endowed with life and sensation are rightly ranked ahead of those that have neither life nor sensation. And so Vitumnus, the giver of life, and Sentinus, the giver of sensation, ought to have a higher claim to be counted as select gods than Janus, the admitter of seed, and Saturn, the giver or sower of seed, and Liber and Libera, the dischargers or emitters of seed. For the seed is not worth a thought unless it attains life and sensation — select gifts which are given not by select gods but by a pair of unknown gods who are totally neglected in comparison with the dignity of the others....

Thus we see that in these tiny little tasks, which are distributed bit by bit among so many gods, even the select gods do their work, like the senate, along with the plebeian classes, and we find that some gods who were not considered the least bit worthy of being selected perform much greater and better tasks than do those who are called select. And so we are left to conclude that it was not because of their more eminent functions in the world, but simply because they happened to become better known to the people, that some gods were designated select and principal. Thus even Varro himself says that some father-gods and some mothergods have fallen into obscurity, just as some human beings do....

The Indecent Acts Attributed to the Select Gods

4. But anyone who seeks distinction and renown might well congratulate these select gods and call them fortunate if he did not notice that they were selected more for insults than for honors. For, by its very obscurity, that throng of lower gods was protected from having scandals heaped upon it. We smile, of course, when we see them distributed, in the fictions of human opinion, to the various tasks shared out among them, like so many minor tax collectors, or so many workmen in the silversmiths' quarter, where one little piece passes through the hands of many artisans before it comes out finished, even though it could have been finished by a single perfect artisan. But it was thought that the only way to take full advantage of having a multitude of workers was for each to learn, quickly and easily, a single part of the craft, so that none would be compelled to master, slowly and with difficulty, the craft as a whole.[9] All the same, it would be hard to find even one of the non-select gods who gained ill-famed fame through any crime, and it would be just as hard to find even one of the select gods who

---

9. Augustine seems to be referring to a particular street in Carthage where the silversmiths worked, which he also refers to in *Confessions* VI,9,14. This is an early description of mass production using an assembly line. See Bibliothèque Augustinienne 34, 577, note 29.

does not bear the mark of some notorious outrage. The select gods have descended to the menial tasks of the non-select, but the non-select gods have not moved up to the criminal heights of the select....

Varro's Naturalistic Interpretations of the Select Gods

5. But let us listen, rather, to the naturalistic interpretations by means of which they try to color over the disgrace of their wretched error and give it the appearance of profound doctrine. In the first place, in commending these interpretations, Varro says that the ancients devised the images, attributes, and adornments of the gods such that, when those who had approached the mysteries of doctrine perceived them with their eyes, they might also see with their mind the soul of the world and its parts, that is, the true gods. He claims that those who made the images of the gods in human form seem to have been following the idea that the mind of mortals, which is in the human body, is very like the immortal mind. It is as if vessels were set up to represent the gods. A wine jar, for example, might be set up in the temple of Liber to signify wine, the container standing for what it contains.[10] Similarly, the rational soul was signified by an image in human form, because the human form is, so to speak, the vessel which ordinarily contains the nature of which they want God, or the gods, to consist.

Such are the mysteries of doctrine which that most learned man had penetrated in order to bring them out into the light of day. But, O most acute of men, while you were deep among those mysteries of doctrine, did you lose the wisdom by which you once soberly concluded that those who first set up images for the people reduced reverence and increased error among their fellow-citizens, and that the ancient Romans honored the gods more purely when they had no images? Those ancients were the authorities that gave you the courage to speak out against the later Romans. For, if the earliest Romans had also worshiped images, you might well have suppressed in timid silence your whole sense that images should not have been set up at all, even though your sense was right; and, in that case, you might well have proclaimed all the more expansively and loftily the mysteries of doctrine that you found in this kind of vicious and vacuous fiction. But your soul, for all its learning and ingenuity (which is why we feel so sorry for you), could never have reached its God through those mysteries of doctrine — the God, that is, not *with* whom it was made but *by* whom it was made; the God of whom it is not a part but a creation; the God who is not the soul of all things but the maker of every soul; the God in whose light alone the soul attains happiness, so long as it is not ungrateful for his grace.

The upcoming discussion will show what these mysteries of doctrine amount to and how much weight they should be given. For the moment, note only that this most learned man declares that the soul of the world and its parts

---

10. Liber was the god of wine.

are the true gods. It is evident, then, that his full theology — that is, the natural theology to which he ascribes so much — could reach no further than the nature of the rational soul. He speaks very briefly about natural theology at the start of his last book, the book on the select gods, and, in reviewing this book, we shall see whether he is able to bring civic theology into accord with natural theology by means of his naturalistic interpretations. If so, then the whole of theology is natural theology, and, in that case, what need was there to take such pains to distinguish the civic from the natural theology? But if there was good reason to make the distinction, then, since not even the natural theology that he favors is true (for it reaches only as far as the soul, not as far as the true God who made the soul), how much more abject and false is the civic theology, which is mainly concerned with the nature of bodies! Varro's own interpretations, which he worked out and expounded with such care, will prove the point. Of necessity, then, I will have to cite some of them.

6. In his preliminary remarks about natural theology, then, Varro states that, in his judgment, God is the soul of the world (which the Greeks call the *cosmos*), and that this world is itself God. But just as a wise man, even though he consists of both body and mind, is called wise by virtue of his mind, so the world is called God by virtue of its mind, even though it consists of both mind and body. Here Varro seems, in a sense, to acknowledge that there is one God. In order to bring in many more, however, he goes on to say that the world is divided into two parts, heaven and earth; that the heaven is twofold, divided into aether and air; that the earth is divided into water and land; and that, of these, aether is the highest, air second, water third, and earth the lowest.[11] All these four parts, he claims, are full of souls, with immortal souls in the aether and air, and mortal souls in the water and earth. From the highest circle of heaven down to the circle of the moon, there are aetherial souls, the stars and planets, and these are not only understood to be, but are actually seen to be, heavenly gods. Then, between the orbit of the moon and the highest region of clouds and winds, there are aerial souls, but these are seen only with the mind, not with the eyes, and are called heroes and lares and genii.[12] This is, in brief, the natural theology that Varro sets out in his preliminary remarks, and it is the theology favored not only by Varro but by many philosophers as well. We will need to discuss it in more detail when, with the help of the true God, I have completed what remains to be said about the civic theology, insofar as it has to do with the select gods....

---

11. Aether was thought to exist above the terrestrial sphere and to be the habitation of the gods. See above at IV,11.
12. Heroes were demigods, while lars and genii were minor tutelary deities associated with particular places.

[Chapters 7 – 27 elaborate in detail Varro's naturalistic interpretations of the "select" divinities, that is, the twelve greater gods and eight greater goddesses in Roman civic and mythical theologies.]

To Worship the World or the World's Soul Is not to Worship the True God

27. ...When I consider the naturalistic interpretations by which learned and acute men try to turn these human matters into divine matters, I see nothing that cannot be referred to temporal and earthly operations and to a material nature; and, even if that nature is invisible, it is still mutable. Such a nature is by no means the true God. If it were simply a matter of giving these select gods interpretations that are at least compatible with religion and reverence, it would be deeply regrettable that these interpretations do nothing to announce or proclaim the true God. But we might still be able to put up with them, in one way or another, if only such foul and disgraceful deeds were not done or commanded. As it is, however, since it is bad enough to worship a body or a soul in place of the true God, by whose indwelling alone the soul is made happy, how much worse it is to worship them in such a way that neither the body nor the soul of the worshiper gains either salvation or even human decency! As a consequence, if people worship some element of the world or some created spirit, even if that spirit is not evil and unclean, with the kind of temple, priesthood, and sacrifice that are due to the true God, the worship is evil. It is not evil because these means of worship are evil but because they should only be used in the worship of the one to whom alone such worship and service are due.

But if anyone claims that he is worshiping the one true God — that is, the creator of every soul and body — by means of lifeless and monstrous images, homicidal sacrifices, the crowning of male organs, commerce in prostitutes, the slashing of limbs, the cutting-off of genitals, the consecration of effeminates, and festivals of impure and obscene shows, his worship is a sin. What makes it a sin is not that he is worshiping one who should not be worshiped but rather that he is worshiping the one who should be worshiped in a way in which he should not be worshiped. If, however, anyone uses such means — that is, disgraceful and wicked means — to worship not the true God, the maker of soul and body, but a creature (even if not an evil creature), whether that creature is a soul or a body or a soul together with a body, he sins twice against God: first, because he worships in place of God what is not God; and, second, because he uses means of worship that should not be used either in worshiping God or even in worshiping what is not God.

But how the Romans worship — that is, how disgracefully and abominably they worship — is common knowledge. What or whom they worship, however, might have remained obscure, if their own historians had not attested that the very rites which they themselves admit are foul and shameful were instituted in response to divinities who demanded them with terrible threats. As it is, however, all ambiguity is removed. Clearly it is evil demons and unclean spirits who have been invited by all this civic theology to take up residence in lifeless statues and, by means of those statues, to take possession of foolish hearts....

The One True God and His Works

29. For everything in the theology of these gods which they refer back to the world by means of their naturalistic explanations may instead be ascribed, without any fear of sacrilege, to the true God, the God who made the world and who is the creator of every soul and every body.[13] We may put it this way: we worship God, not heaven and earth, which are the two parts of which the world consists. Nor do we worship any soul or souls diffused throughout all living things. Rather, we worship God, who made heaven and earth and all things in them, and who made every soul, whether it has only life but lacks sensation and reason, or also has sensation, or also has intelligence as well.

30. And I shall now begin to enumerate those works of the one and true God on the basis of which the Romans, in an effort to give an ostensibly respectable interpretation of their disgraceful and wicked rites, fashioned a host of false gods for themselves. We worship the God who assigned to all the natures he created both the beginnings and the endings of their existing and their moving; who holds, knows, and regulates the causes of things; who established the power of seeds; who bestowed the rational soul, which is called the mind,[14] on the living beings whom he willed to have it; who gave the faculty and the use of speech; who imparted the gift of foretelling the future to the spirits he pleased, and who himself foretells the future through those whom he pleases, and who takes away illness through those whom he pleases; who also governs the beginning, the course, and the end of wars, when humanity needs to be corrected and chastised in this way; who created and rules the fire of this world, with all its power and violence, governing it to ensure the equilibrium of nature's vastness;[15] who is the creator and governor of all waters; who made the sun to be the brightest of all corporeal lights and gave it its appropriate power and motion; who has not withdrawn his dominion and power from the very underworld itself; who supplies

---

13. Augustine now counters Varro's naturalistic understanding of the gods with a brief though relatively comprehensive account of Christian belief, beginning with God as creator and sustainer, proceeding on to the redemption effected by Christ, and concluding, in section 32, with an appeal to the prophetic witness of Scripture.
14. "Rational soul...mind": *rationalem animam...animus*.
15. "The fire of this world": *mundi huius ignem*. As described, this is something on an entirely different level than the more domestic fire mentioned later in this section. Perhaps Augustine has in mind the cosmic fire that appears in Stoic philosophy.

seeds and foods, whether dry or liquid, to mortals, assigning to each what suits its nature; who established the earth and made it fertile; who bestows its fruits on animals and men; who knows and ordains not only primary but also secondary causes; who set the course of the moon; who provides pathways in heaven and on earth for movements from place to place; who granted to the human intellect, which he created, knowledge of the various arts to enhance life and nature; who instituted the union of male and female to serve the propagation of offspring; who conferred the gift of earthly fire on human gatherings for ready use as a source of heat and light.

These are precisely the points which the acute and learned Varro has worked so hard to distribute among the select gods by means of his naturalistic interpretations, whether borrowed from some other source or conjectures of his own. In fact, however, it is the one true God who makes and does all these things. He does so, however, as God: that is, he is wholly present in all places and contained in no place; he is not restricted by any bonds; he is not divisible into parts; nor is he changeable in any part; he fills heaven and earth by virtue of his present power, not because his nature is in need of anything beyond itself. Thus he directs all the things he has created in such a way that he allows each to initiate and enact its own proper motions. For, although they cannot be anything without him, they are not what he is. He also does many things through angels, but it is only through himself that he makes the angels blessed. Similarly, although he sends angels to men for various purposes, he only makes men blessed — as he does the angels — through himself, and not through the angels. And it is from this one and true God that we hope for eternal life.

31. For, over and above benefits of this sort, which he bestows on the good and the evil alike in accord with his governance of nature (about which I have said a good deal), we have received from him a great proof of his great love, a proof proper to the good alone. It is certainly true that we can never thank him enough for the fact that we exist, that we have life, that we behold heaven and earth, and that we have mind and reason by which to seek him, the very one who created all these things. But beyond this, when we were burdened and weighed down by sins, turned away from the contemplation of his light, and blinded by our love of darkness (that is, of wickedness) he did not utterly abandon us. Rather he sent us his Word, who is his only Son, so that — from the fact that he assumed flesh, was born, and suffered for our sake — we might learn how very much God valued human beings and might be purified of all our sins by that one sacrifice, and, with love of him spread abroad in our hearts by his Spirit[16] and all our difficulties now overcome, might come into eternal rest and the ineffable sweetness of contemplating him. What hearts, what tongues, could ever claim to be adequate to thank him for this?

---

16. See Rom 5:5.

32. From the very beginning of the human race, this mystery of eternal life was proclaimed by angels, through certain signs and symbols appropriate to the times, to those to whom it was right that it should be known. Later the Hebrew people were gathered into one republic, as it were, to enact this mystery; to them the course of events from the coming of Christ up to the present, and even beyond, was foretold, sometimes by people who spoke with knowledge, sometimes by those who spoke in ignorance. Still later, this same people was scattered among the nations to bear witness to the Scriptures in which the eternal salvation that was to come in Christ was foretold. For not only all the prophecies set down in words, and not only the precepts of life which shape morality and piety and are contained in these writings, but also the rites, the priesthood, the tabernacle or temple, the altars, the sacrifices, the ceremonies, the festal days, and everything else that pertains to the service due to God — which is properly called *latreia* in Greek — all signified and foretold the things that we believe have already been fulfilled, or that we see are now being fulfilled, or that we are confident will be fulfilled for the sake of the eternal life of the faithful in Christ.

33. It was through this one and true religion, therefore, that the gods of the nations could be exposed as foul and unclean demons who, in the guise of souls of the dead or under the appearance of creatures of this world, desire to be thought gods. Arrogant in their impurity, they rejoice in wicked and disgraceful things as if these were divine honors, and they resent any conversion to the true God on the part of human souls. From their vicious and unholy dominion man is set free when he believes in him who, to raise man up, offered an example of humility as great as the pride by which the demons fell.

Included among the demons are not only the gods of whom we have already spoken at some length, and other Roman gods, as well as the similar gods of other lands and peoples, but also the select gods we are now discussing, who were selected to form a kind of senate of the gods. But they were selected, it is clear, for the notoriety of their crimes, not for the preeminence of their virtues. Seeking to make the disgraceful decent, Varro tries to refer the rites of these gods back to his supposedly naturalistic explanations. But he can find no way to reconcile and harmonize the two, for, in fact, the reasons for those rites are not what he thinks, or rather are not what he wants them to be thought. If his explanations, or any similar interpretations, actually held good, then — even though they have nothing to do with the true God or with eternal life, which is what we should seek in religion — they would at least serve to mitigate to some small degree the offense caused by any indecent or absurd features of the rites, when people have no sense for what they mean. They would at least reduce the indecency or absurdity by providing some sort of explanation for it drawn from the nature of things. This is exactly what Varro tried to do with regard to certain of the fables of the theaters and the mysteries enacted in the temples; but far from exonerating the theaters by showing their resemblance to the temples, he only succeeded in condemning the temples by showing their resemblance to the theaters. Still, he tried as best he could to give an explanation in terms of natural causes that would soothe the feelings offended by the horrors of the rites.

Numa's Explanations of the Rites that He Instituted

34. In contrast, as the learned Varro himself reports, the explanations of the sacred rites given in the books of Numa Pompilius could not be tolerated at all. They were judged unworthy not only of being read and known by religious people but even of being preserved in writing, no matter how dark the hiding place. For I will now tell what, in the third book of this work, I promised to tell at the appropriate point.[17] Here is what we read in Varro's book *On the Worship of the Gods*: "A certain Terentius had a field on the Janiculum, and, when his plowman was plowing near the tomb of Numa Pompilius, the plow turned up from the ground the books in which Numa had written down the reasons for his religious institutions. Terentius took them to the praetor[18] in the city, and the praetor, after reading the opening sections, referred such an important matter to the senate. But when the leading senators had read some of the reasons why this or that practice had been instituted in the sacred rites, the senate declared itself in agreement with the dead Numa, and, as pious conscript fathers,[19] the senators decreed that the praetor should burn the books."[20]

Each person may believe what he likes, or, rather, each distinguished defender of such impiety may say whatever his contentious ravings suggest to him. So far as I am concerned, however, it is enough to point out that the reasons for the sacred rites written out by King Pompilius, himself the founder of the rites, were not fit to be made known to the people, or to the senate, or even to the priests themselves. Numa Pompilius had penetrated to these secrets of the demons by an illicit curiosity, and had written them down in order to have something he could read to refresh his memory. But even though he was a king, with no one to fear, he still did not dare to teach them to anyone or even to destroy them by obliterating them or disposing of them in some other way. He did not want anyone to know what they said, for fear of teaching men abhorrent things, but he was afraid to harm them, for fear of making the demons angry. So he buried them where he thought it would be safe, never imagining that a plow could come so close to his tomb. But the senate, even though they feared to condemn the religion of their ancestors, and so felt compelled to approve Numa's action, judged his books to be so pernicious that they did not even order them to be buried again, for fear that human curiosity would be all the more eager to search out

---

17. See above at III,9.
18. The praetor was a magistrate or judge; in this instance he was a certain Quintus Petilius.
19. "Conscript fathers": *patres conscripti*, i.e., "chosen" or "enrolled fathers." This was a common designation for the members of the senate.
20. For the whole account see Livy, *History of Rome* XL,29.

something that had once seen the light of day. Instead they ordered the accursed records to be destroyed by fire. Because they felt that it was now necessary to keep on performing those sacred rites, they thought it better for people to remain in error, not knowing the reasons for their rites, than for the city to be thrown into turmoil by knowing what those reasons were.

35. For even Numa himself, to whom no prophet of God or holy angel was sent, was forced to practice hydromancy. He saw in water the images of gods, or rather the conjuring tricks of demons, from whom he heard what rites he should institute and observe. Varro reports that this kind of divination was imported from the Persians, and he notes that it was used by Numa himself and later by the philosopher Pythagoras. He reports that blood was also used to consult the dwellers in the underworld, and he tells us that this practice was called *nekromantia* in Greek.[21] But whether called hydromancy or necromancy, it amounts to the same thing: the dead seem to give divinations. As for the arts by which this was achieved, that is their business. I have no wish to observe that, even before the coming of our Savior, these arts were generally prohibited by law in the cities of the gentiles and punished with the harshest penalties. I have no wish to make this observation because it may, perhaps, be true that such arts were permitted back in Numa's time. At any rate, it was by these arts that Pompilius learned about those sacred rites, the practice of which he made known but the reasons for which he buried in the ground (which indicates just how much he himself feared what he had learned); and when the books containing those reasons were unearthed, the senate burned them. What is it to me, then, that Varro offers other, supposedly naturalistic, explanations for those rites? If Numa's books had contained explanations of this sort, they clearly would not have been burned. For, if they had, the conscript fathers would also have burned the books that Varro wrote and published, despite the fact that his books were dedicated to the pontiff Caesar.

According to the explanation given in the book by Varro that I cited above, the reason why Numa Pompilius is said to have had the nymph Egeria as his wife is that he drew,[22] that is, took away, water to use for hydromancy.[23] It is in this way that actual events are turned into fables by sprinkling them with lies. It was by hydromancy, then, that this most inquisitive Roman king learned about both the rites themselves, which the pontiffs were to include in their books, and the reasons for those rites, which he was not willing for anyone but himself to know. Accordingly, he wrote out the reasons separately, and he made sure that they died with him, so to speak, by taking pains to keep them from people's knowledge and to entomb them in the ground. Numa's books, then, either described the sordid and noxious lusts of the demons in such a way as to make the whole

---

21. See *Logistoricus*, fragment 43.
22. "Egeria...drew": *egesserit...Egeriam*.
23. See *Logistoricus*, fragment 43.

civic theology seem despicable, even to people who had incorporated so many disgusting practices into their sacred rites; or else they showed that all the gods, whom almost all peoples of the gentiles had for such a long time believed to be immortal, were nothing more than dead men. But the same demons delighted in rites of this sort, and they intruded themselves to be worshiped in place of the dead men whom they had, by providing the evidence of false miracles, caused to be regarded as gods.

It was by the hidden providence of God, however, that the demons — won over by their friend Pompilius through the arts of hydromancy — were permitted to confess all these things to him. But they were not allowed to warn him that he should burn his books before he died rather than burying them. Nor were they able to keep Numa's books from becoming known either by blocking the plow that unearthed them or by obstructing Varro's pen, due to which the history of these events has come down to our time. For the demons cannot do what they are not permitted to do, and permission is only granted by the deep and just judgment of the supreme God, who acts according to the merits of those whom it is just for the demons either merely to afflict or even to dominate and deceive. But we can see how dangerous those writings were considered to be, and how alien to the worship of true divinity, from the fact that the senate preferred to burn what Pompilius had only hidden rather than to fear what he feared when he did not dare to burn them himself.

Thus, the person who does not even wish to live a godly life in the present may go ahead and seek eternal life through such rites as these. But the person who does not wish to keep company with malignant demons need have no fear of the noxious superstition by which they are worshiped. Instead, let him acknowledge the true religion, by which the demons are unmasked and sent down to defeat.

Study Questions for Book VII

Psychology addresses our tendency to idealize others. We place certain persons on pedestals because of their achievements, their intelligence, their ethics, their looks, or for any number of other reasons. They may be people we know personally at some level, or they may be distant political or pop culture figures whom we know only through the filters of media. In either case, to idealize is to relegate someone to a superhuman status, to "divinize" a person, so to speak. Augustine's critique of Roman divinities deconstructs them by locating their origins in the idealization of past heroes and heroines of Roman history. What might be the usefulness of Augustine's deconstructive approach for a critique of contemporary idealizations of political or cultural heroic figures?

Contemporary atheism rests largely on the 19th-century German philosopher Ludwig Feuerbach's claim that monotheism is simply an extrapolation of human knowledge, power and love to infinity. We project these basic human attributes onto an imagined divinity and thereby diminish or surrender our human dignity. How might Augustinian realism, based on a theology of sin, serve as a corrective to contemporary atheism and its idealizations of humanity?

Augustine mentions the "conspiracy theory" that the early Roman King Numa discovered the spurious and diabolic origins of Roman divinities and rituals, and so he buried the evidence. When the Church enters the public square for dialogue and debate on matters pertinent to the common good, it will encounter the inevitable human tendencies to deceive, to prevaricate, to demonize. How should it conduct itself amidst such challenging conversations, often so difficult, but always so essential?

BOOK VIII

Having responded to the mythical and the civic theologies, as interpreted by Varro, in Books VI and VII, Augustine now turns to theology understood as that aspect of philosophy which centers on reasoning or speaking about the divine. After defining philosophy as the love of wisdom, which properly means the love of God who is wisdom, and after giving a brief summary of the pre-Platonic and Platonic philosophical tradition, Augustine explains why he has selected the Platonists as his conversation partners in this arena — namely, because the Platonists enjoy a higher reputation than do the other philosophical schools; they are superior to the other philosophers in their views on the first principle of the world, on the criterion of truth, and on the supreme good for human beings (i.e., in the areas of physics, logic, and ethics); and they stand closer to Christianity than the others. Since the Platonists affirm one supreme and transcendent God, the issue between them and the Christians can be brought into sharp focus: Is worship to be given only to the one God or to many other gods as well? Augustine first takes up the views of the Platonist Apuleius, who maintains that the demons are superior to human beings because they have lighter bodies and inhabit the air, and who represents the demons as intermediaries between the gods and men, carrying men's prayers to the gods and bringing the gods' responses back to men. In reply, Augustine argues that it is neither quality of body nor location in the hierarchy of the universe but rather capacity for moral goodness which determines superiority among rational creatures, and that it is absurd to think that the morally evil demons could or should serve as intermediaries between the good gods and human beings, who have a higher capacity for goodness than do the demons themselves. Finally, Augustine responds to the views of Hermes Trismegistus, whose work — in the selective use that Augustine makes of it — suggests that human beings create gods by using magical arts to induce demons to inhabit statues of the gods, giving the statues the power to respond to human requests, and that the gods were originally human beings. Using quotations from Hermes's own work against him, Augustine points out, on Hermes's own account of the matter, that the art of making gods rests on error, unbelief, and irreligion, and that the worship of the gods is the worship of dead men (which is to be distinguished from the honor that Christians pay to the martyrs, because Christians do not worship the martyrs or offer sacrifices to them). Overall, then, the claim of Book VIII is that there is no reason to honor or worship the demons as gods and still less to worship them for the sake of eternal life after death; it leaves open, however, the question as to whether there might possibly be good demons as well as evil demons.

1. We now stand in need of far greater mental concentration than was required for solving and explaining the questions at issue in our earlier books. For, when it comes to the theology which the Romans call natural theology, it is not with just ordinary people that we must carry on our discussion. Natural theology is neither the fabulous nor the civic theology; that is, it is neither the theology of the theater nor the theology of the city, of which the one parades the crimes of the gods and the other displays their still more criminal desires (and so indicates that they are actually malignant demons rather than gods). And so in this case we must discuss the issues with the philosophers, whose very name, if translated into Latin, declares their love of wisdom.[1]

And if God, who made all things, is wisdom, as divine authority and truth have shown, then the true philosopher is a lover of God. But since the thing itself, to which we give this name, is not found in all who boast of the name — for it is not necessarily the case that those who are called philosophers are lovers of true wisdom — we obviously have to make a selection from all the philosophers whose views we have been able to ascertain from their writings. From these we need to choose the ones with whom the question may be treated at the level it deserves. For I have not set out in this work to refute all the empty opinions of all philosophers but only those views which have to do with theology (a Greek word which we understand to signify reasoning or speaking about the divine[2]). Nor have I set out to refute the views on theology of all philosophers. Rather, I address only the views of those philosophers who agree that the divine exists and that it cares about human affairs, but who still do not consider the worship of one immutable God sufficient to attain a life of blessedness, even after death. Instead, these philosophers hold that to achieve this end we must also worship many gods who were created and established by that one God.

These philosophers come closer to the truth than even Varro did. He was able to extend the whole reach of natural theology only as far as this world and its soul, but they acknowledge a God above the whole realm of soul, a God who made not only this visible world, which is often called heaven and earth, but also every soul whatsoever. They acknowledge, too, that it is this God who makes the rational and intellectual soul — and the human soul is of this kind — blessed by participation in his immutable and incorporeal light. Anyone with even the slightest grasp of these matters knows that these philosophers are called Platonists, a term derived from the name of their teacher Plato. With reference to Plato, then, I shall touch briefly on the points I consider necessary for the present issue, starting with the thinkers who preceded him in this field of learning.

---

1. The word "philosophy" is composed of two Greek words meaning "love" and "wisdom," hence "love of wisdom."
2. The word "theology" is composed of two Greek words meaning "God" and "reasoning" or "speech," hence "reasoning about God" or "speech about God."

Plato's Predecessors

2. In the literature of the Greeks, whose language is held in higher esteem than that of any other people,[3] two types of philosophy are handed down to us.[4] One, the Italian, comes from the part of Italy which was formerly called Magna Graecia;[5] and the other, the Ionian, comes from the lands which are still called Greece today. The Italian school had as its founder Pythagoras of Samos, from whom, they also say, the word "philosophy" itself took its origin.[6] Before his time, those who seemed somehow to stand out from others in living a praiseworthy life were called "wise." But when Pythagoras was asked what his profession was, he replied that he was a philosopher, that is, a student or a lover of wisdom, for it seemed to him the height of arrogance to claim to be wise.[7]

The originator of the Ionian school, on the other hand, was Thales of Miletus, one of those who were called the Seven Sages.[8] The other six were distinguished for their mode of life and for certain precepts appropriate to living the good life. Thales, in contrast, stood out because he investigated the nature of things and committed his inquiries to writing in order to insure that he would have successors. He was especially remarkable for his ability to predict solar and lunar eclipses due to his grasp of astronomical calculations. At the same time, he held that water is the first principle of things and that from it originate all the elements of the world, the world itself, and all that comes into being in the world. But he set no divine intelligence over this work, which seems so marvelous to us when we contemplate the universe.

His student Anaximander succeeded him,[9] and he had a different view on the nature of things. He did not think that everything is engendered from one thing, as Thales held that all is engendered from moisture; rather he held that each thing

---

3. This is an idea occasionally expressed in Augustine. See below at VIII,10 and XVIII,37; *Questions on the Heptateuch* VII,37. See also Cicero, *On the Nature of the Gods* I,8.
4. What follows is a rather remarkable series of thumbnail sketches of the great Greek philosophers, culminating with Plato. How deep Augustine's knowledge was of any of them, including Plato himself, is a matter of speculation.
5. Magna Graecia, or Great Greece, was located on the coast of the Tarentine Gulf in southern Italy and had been colonized by Greeks since the eighth century.
6. On Pythagoras see also above at VI,5.
7. See Cicero, *Tusculan Disputations* V,8-9.
8. Thales flourished c. 585 B.C. See Diogenes Laertius, *Lives of Eminent Philosophers* I,22-40. The others most commonly included among the Seven Sages are Cleobulus of Lindos, Solon of Athens, Chilon of Sparta, Bias of Priene, Pittacus of Mytilene and Periander of Corinth. The first such list appears in Plato, *Protagoras* 343a, where Myson of Chenae takes the place of Periander of Corinth. As Augustine notes, apart from Thales, who was also interested in the world of nature, the Sages were mainly known for their ethical bent, expressed in pithy moral sayings. Thales himself, however, is probably most renowned for the maxim "Know thyself" (see Diogenes Laertius, *Lives of Eminent Philosophers* I,40).
9. Anaximander (c. 610-c. 546 B.C.) was also from Miletus. See Diogenes Laertius, *Lives of Eminent Philosophers* II,1-2.

is engendered from its own proper principle. He believed that these principles of individual things are infinite in number and held that they engender innumerable worlds, as well as all that arises in those worlds. In his judgment, these worlds alternately dissolve and are reborn over whatever periods of duration each is able to sustain. Like Thales, he did not attribute anything in the working of these things to a divine intelligence. He left his pupil Anaximenes as his successor,[10] who ascribed all the causes of things to the infinite air. Anaximenes did not deny the gods, nor did he keep silent about them. He did not believe, however, that they created the air but rather that they themselves originated from air.

In contrast, Anaximenes' pupil Anaxagoras[11] held and taught that there is a divine mind that produces everything we see from infinite matter, which consists of particles of all things, each similar to the others. Each individual thing is made up of its own specific particles but has the divine mind as its maker. Diogenes,[12] another pupil of Anaximenes, also affirmed that air is in fact the material from which all things are made, but he maintained that it partakes of divine reason, without which nothing could be made from it. Anaxagoras was succeeded by his pupil Archelaus.[13] He too held that each individual thing is composed of particles, each similar to the others; but he also claimed that there is an indwelling mind which brings everything to pass by conjoining and dispersing eternal bodies, that is, by conjoining and dispersing those particles. Socrates is reported to have been the student of Archelaus, and it is Socrates who was the teacher of Plato, on whose account I have briefly rehearsed all these details.

Socrates

3. Socrates is remembered, then, as the first to have turned the whole of philosophy to the correction and regulation of morals.[14] All his predecessors had devoted their chief efforts to the investigation of the physical, that is, the natural order. In my view, however, it is impossible to reach any clear decision as to whether Socrates did this because he grew weary of obscure and inconclusive matters and so put his mind to discovering something clear and certain that was essential to the life of happiness, which appears to have been the one goal of all the tireless and laborious efforts of the philosophers, or whether, as some more generously suppose, he did this because he did not like to see minds sullied by earthly desires attempting to reach out toward the divine. He saw that they were inquiring into the causes of things, but he believed that the first and highest causes are

---

10. Anaximenes (c. 585-528 B.C.) was from Miletus as well. See ibid. II,3-5.
11. Anaxagoras (c. 500-428 B.C.) flourished in Athens. See ibid. II,6-15.
12. Diogenes of Apollonia flourished c. 425 in Athens. *Pace* Augustine, he could not have been a student of Anaximenes, who died in 528 B.C.
13. Archelaus flourished in Athens in the fifth century. See Diogenes Laertius, *Lives of Eminent Philosophers* II,16-17.
14. Socrates lived from c. 469 to 399 B.C.

only to be found in the will of the one supreme God. As a consequence, he held that these causes can only be understood by a mind that has been purified, and therefore he considered it essential to strive to purify one's life by good morals, so that the mind, once freed from the burden of its down-weighing desires, might raise itself by its natural vigor to eternal things and, in purity of understanding, contemplate the nature of the incorporeal and unchanging light in which the causes of all created natures have their stable dwelling.[15]

All agree, however, that, with wonderful charm of discourse and sharpness of wit, he would hunt out and chase down the folly of ignorant people who thought they knew something about even those moral issues to which it was apparent that he had devoted his whole mind (although it was his practice either to confess his ignorance or to conceal his knowledge in these matters). As a consequence, he stirred up a great deal of hostility, was condemned on a false charge, and was sentenced to death. Later, however, the very city of Athens which had publicly condemned him went into public mourning for him, and popular indignation turned so strongly against his two accusers that one of them was seized and killed by the violence of the mob and the other escaped a similar fate only by going voluntarily into permanent exile.

Thanks to the renown of both his life and his death, then, Socrates left behind numerous followers of his philosophy, who vied with each other in their eagerness to debate the moral questions where the point at issue is the supreme good by which a person is made happy. But since Socrates's own discussions did not make clear what the supreme good is (for he would entertain, assert, and demolish every proposal), each of his followers took whatever pleased him from those discussions, and each defined the final good however it seemed best to him. Now the term "final good" means that due to which each person, when he attains it, is happy. But Socrates's followers maintained such a diversity of opinions among themselves that — hard as it is to believe of followers of one and the same teacher — some, like Aristippus, claimed that pleasure is the supreme good,[16] while others, like Antisthenes, held that it is virtue.[17] Thus some held one opinion, others held another, and it would take far too long to list them all.

Plato and the Platonic Division of Philosophy

4. Among the disciples of Socrates, however, it was Plato — and certainly not without reason — who shone with the brightest reputation and completely

---

15. See Plato, *Phaedo* 65a-66a.
16. Aristippus of Cyrene (c. 435-c.356 B.C.) had a more nuanced view of pleasure than Augustine has the inclination (and perhaps the knowledge) to discuss here. See Diogenes Laertius, *Lives of Eminent Philosophers* II,65-102.
17. Antisthenes (c. 445-c. 365 B.C.) is credited with being the founder of Cynic philosophy. See ibid. VI,1-19.

overshadowed all the rest.[18] He was an Athenian by birth, of high standing in the community, and he far outdistanced his fellow-students in his remarkable ability. Even so, he did not believe that his own ability and his Socratic training were enough to bring his philosophy to its full realization. Consequently, he traveled as far and as wide as he could, wherever the report of any higher knowledge to be acquired might take him. Thus in Egypt he learned the teachings that were highly prized there, and from Egypt he came to the part of Italy where the Pythagoreans' fame was celebrated. There he studied under the most eminent teachers and readily grasped whatever in the Italian philosophy was then flourishing.[19] And due to his singular devotion to his master Socrates, he made him the chief speaker in almost all his dialogues. In this way, he blended what he had learned from others or had seen for himself, pushing his own intelligence as far as he could, with Socrates's charm and moral arguments.

Now, since the pursuit of wisdom has to do both with action and with contemplation, its one part may be called active and its other contemplative. The active part is concerned with the conduct of life, that is, with the shaping of morals, and the contemplative part is concerned with the investigation of natural causes and the purest form of truth. Socrates is reported to have excelled in the former, and Pythagoras is said to have concentrated the force of his intelligence as far as possible on the latter. And Plato is praised for having brought philosophy to its perfection by joining the two. He then divided philosophy into three parts — the moral, which has chiefly to do with action; the natural, which is given over to contemplation; and the logical, which distinguishes the true from the false.[20] This last is certainly necessary to both the others, that is, to both action and contemplation, but it is still contemplation that most especially claims the discernment of truth for itself. Plato's threefold division, therefore, is not opposed to the distinction according to which the whole pursuit of wisdom is understood to consist in action and contemplation.

In my judgment, however, it would take too long to discuss in detail what Plato believed with regard to each of these parts, that is, what he knew or believed to be the end of all actions, the cause of all natures, and the light of all reasonings, nor do I think that we should make any rash affirmations on this score. For Plato makes a point of continuing the well-known practice of his master

---

18. Plato (c. 424-c. 348 B.C.), the founder of the Academy of Athens and the author of numerous writings that have survived, was the most respected of the Greek philosophers — revered, albeit not uncritically, not only by Augustine but by a substantial portion of the Church Fathers. Nonetheless, when Augustine speaks of Plato, the Platonists and Platonism, he seems to be referring less to the doctrines of Plato himself and more to those that were derived from his thought over the centuries and that we now place under the umbrella of Neoplatonism. For a brief summary of Plato's influence on Augustine see Allan D. Fitzgerald, ed., *Augustine through the Ages: An Encyclopedia* (Grand Rapids: Eerdmans 1999) 651-654.
19. On Plato's travels see Diogenes Laertius, *Lives of Eminent Philosophers* III,6.
20. See Apuleius, *On the Teaching of Plato* I,3. This was also common Stoic teaching. See Diogenes Laertius, *Lives of Eminent Philosophers* VII,39-40.

Socrates, whom he portrays in his works as one of the participants in the discussion, of conceal-ing his own knowledge and opinions. He himself approved of this practice, and, as a result, it is no easy matter to discern Plato's own views on important issues.

All the same, however, there are certain things that we read in Plato — whether things he said himself or things which he relates and records as said by others, but which he seems to endorse — that I ought to mention and include in this work. These are views which either support the true religion that our faith receives and defends or which seem to oppose it, as in the question of whether there is one god or many and how this matter bears on the truly blessed life that comes after death. For those who are most highly praised for rightly ranking Plato far above the other philosophers of the nations, and for having understood him more acutely and followed him more accurately, hold, it seems, a view of God such that they find in him the cause of existence, the ground of understanding, and the pattern for leading one's life. Of these three, the first is understood to pertain to the natural, the second to the rational, and the third to the moral part of philosophy. For if man was created in such a way that, through what is most excellent in him, he may attain to that which is most excellent of all — that is, to the one true and best God, without whom no nature exists, no teaching instructs, and no practice brings benefit — then what we should seek is the one in whom all things are held together for us; what we should learn to know is the one in whom all things are certain for us; and what we should love is the one in whom all things are right for us.[21]

The Superiority of the Platonists

5. Thus, if Plato has stated that the wise man is one who imitates, knows, and loves this God, and who is blessed by participation in him, what need is there to investigate other philosophers? No one has come closer to us than the Platonists. Let the mythical theology, then, which delights the minds of the ungodly with the crimes of the gods give way to the Platonists; so too, the civic theology in which impure demons, under the name of gods, have seduced people devoted to earthly delights and have wanted to take human errors as divine honors. These demons excite their worshipers with the most depraved zeal for watching their own crimes in stage shows, as if this were an act of worship, and the spectators themselves present an even more delightful show for the demons. In this civic theology, any ostensibly respectable rites performed in the temples are defiled by their association with the obscenities of the theaters, and any shameful acts

---

21. It is tempting to conclude that in the natural, rational and moral parts of classical Greek philosophy, as Augustine explains them here, he finds a hint of the Trinity, which in the Father causes or creates, in the Son provides understanding or teaches, and in the Spirit offers a pattern of life or of righteousness. See below.

performed in the theaters are praiseworthy in comparison with the foulness of the temples. Let the explanations of Varro also give way to the Platonists, those interpretations in which he accounts for these rites in terms of heaven and earth and the seeds and operations of mortal things. The rites do not signify what he tries to suggest that they do, and so truth does not follow his efforts, and even if they did, the rational soul should not worship as its god things which are placed beneath it in the order of nature, nor should it rank above itself, as gods, things which the true God has ranked it above.

And let those writings which certainly pertained to the sacred rites also give way to the Platonists — the writings that Numa Pompilius took such pains to conceal by having them buried with him and that the senate ordered to be burned when they were later turned up by the plow....

6. As we see, therefore, it is not without reason that the Platonist philosophers are ranked above the rest in fame and glory. They saw that no material body is God, and therefore they went beyond all bodies in their search for God. They saw that nothing mutable is the supreme God, and therefore they went beyond every soul and all mutable spirits in their search for the supreme God.[22] They also saw that, in every mutable thing, the form that makes it what it is, in whatever measure and of whatever nature it is, can only have its existence from him who truly *is* because he exists immutably. It follows, then, that the whole material world, with its shapes, its qualities, its ordered motion, with the elements arrayed from heaven down to earth, and with whatever bodies exist in them, and that all life, whether life which only nourishes and sustains existence, like the life in trees, or life which also has feeling and sensation, like the life in animals, or life which has all this and has intelligence as well, like the life in human beings, or life which has no need to take nourishment but still sustains existence and has sensation and intelligence, like the life in angels — it follows, then, that all these can only have existence from him who simply *is*. For, to him, it is not one thing to exist and another to live, as if he could exist without being alive; nor is it one thing to live and another to have intelligence, as if he could live without having intelligence; nor is it one thing to have intelligence and another to be happy, as if he could have intelligence without being happy. To him, rather, to exist simply is to live, to have intelligence, and to be happy.[23]

In view of this immutability and simplicity, the Platonists understood that he made all these things and could not himself have been made by anything. For they noted that whatever exists is either body or life, that life is something better than body, and that the form of a body is perceived by the senses, while

---

22. See Plato, *Timaeus* 28b-29a; Plotinus, *Enneads* I,6,7.
23. "To live, to have intelligence and to be happy" is a trinity that hints at the divine Trinity. On the lack of distinction between existing (*esse*) and living (*vivere*) in God see *The Trinity* VI,10,11 and XV,5,7.

that of life is perceived by the intelligence. As a consequence, they ranked the intelligible form higher than the sensible form. We call "sensible" those things which can be perceived by the body's sight and touch, and we call "intelligible" those which can be understood by the perception of the mind. For there is no corporeal beauty, whether in the state of a body (its shape, for example) or in its motion (a melody, for instance), which is not judged by the mind. And this would certainly not be possible unless there were a higher form of this sort in the mind, a form with no bulk of mass, with no sound of voice, with no extension in space or duration in time. But even here, if this mental form were not mutable, one person would not be better than another in making judgments about the sensible form. The more able would not be better than the slower-witted; the more skilled would not be better than the less skilled; the more practiced would not be better than the less practiced; and even the same person, in becoming more advanced, would in fact be no better than he was before. And it is beyond doubt that anything which is capable of being better or worse is mutable.

Thus men of ability and learning, well-practiced in these matters, easily came to the conclusion that the primary form is not found in things where form is proved to be subject to change.[24] In their view, then, both body and mind may be endowed with form to a greater or a lesser extent, and, if they could lack all form, they would not exist at all. As a consequence, they saw that there must be something in which the primary form is unchangeable and therefore not subject to comparative degree, and they were completely right to believe that that is where the first principle of things exists, which was not itself created and by which all things were created. Thus God himself showed them what is known of him, when the invisible things of God, as well as his eternal power and divinity, were understood and seen by them through the things that he made.[25] For he is the one by whom all visible and temporal things were made.

But I have now said enough with regard to the part of philosophy which the Platonists call physical, that is, natural philosophy.

7. As for their teaching with regard to the second part of philosophy, which they call logic or rational philosophy, I would not even think of comparing the Platonists with those who located the criterion of truth in the bodily senses and concluded that everything we learn is to be measured by such unreliable and deceptive standards! Such are the Epicureans, and various others like them,[26] and even the Stoics themselves, who, though much enamoured of the skill in debating which they call dialectic, still imagine that this is to be derived from the bodily senses. It is from the senses, they assert, that the mind conceives the ideas (which they call *ennoiai*) of those things which they explain by means of

---

24. See Plato, *Timaeus* 27e-28a; Plotinus, *Enneads* III,6,11-12.
25. See Rom 1:19-20.
26. See Diogenes Laertius, *Lives of Eminent Philosophers* X,31-32.

definition;[27] and it is from the senses, they claim, that their whole account of learning and teaching is derived and deduced. In this connection, however, when the Stoics say that only the wise are beautiful, I cannot help but wonder what bodily senses they use to discern this kind of beauty, what fleshly eyes they use to catch sight of the form and the splendor of wisdom.

In contrast, the philosophers whom we deservedly rank above all the rest have distinguished the things discerned by the mind from those perceived by the senses, neither depriving the senses of what they are able to do nor ascribing more to them than they are able to do. And they have stated that the light of the mind which is at work in all human learning is the very same God by whom all things were made.[28]

8. There remains, then, the moral part of philosophy, which is called ethics in Greek. Here the object of inquiry is the supreme good which, if we direct all our actions to it, and if we desire it not for the sake of anything else but for its own sake alone, will, when attained, leave us nothing further to seek for our happiness. For this reason it is also called the final good, since we want other things for the sake of it but want it only for its own sake.

Some have claimed that this good which confers happiness stems from the body,[29] others that it stems from the soul,[30] and still others that it stems from both.[31] They saw, obviously enough, that man consists of soul and body, and therefore they believed that human well-being could come from one or the other of these, or from both together, as a kind of final good by which they might be happy and to which they might refer all their actions without seeking anything further to which it should itself be referred. Accordingly, those who are said to have introduced a third sort of goods, called extrinsic goods, such as honor, glory, money, and the like, did not introduce them as final goods, that is, as goods to be sought for their own sake, but rather as goods to be sought for the sake of something else; and this sort of good, they maintained, is good for good men, but evil for evil men.[32] Thus, whether they looked for the human good from the soul or from the body or from both together, they still presumed that it should only be looked for from man himself. Those who sought it from the body sought it from the lower part of man; those who sought it from the soul, from the higher part of man; and those who sought it from both, from the whole man. No matter, then, whether they sought it from a part or from the whole, they still sought it only

---

27. See ibid. VII,42.51.54.
28. See Plato, *Republic* VI,509d-511e.
29. See Diogenes Laertius, *Lives of Eminent Philosophers* II,88-90, citing the teaching of Aristippus.
30. See Plato, *Republic* VII,532a-535a.
31. See Diogenes Laertius, *Lives of Eminent Philosophers* VII,85-89, citing various Stoics.
32. See Plato, *Republic* IX,580d-583b; Diogenes Laertius, *Lives of Eminent Philosophers* VII,102-107, citing Stoic teaching.

from man. But these three different views did not produce only three different sects of philosophers; rather they produced a great many, because different philosophers held all sorts of divergent opinions as to the good of the body, the good of the soul, and the good of both together.[33]

Let them all, therefore, give way to the philosophers who asserted that human beings are happy not in the enjoyment of the body, nor in the enjoyment of the soul, but in the enjoyment of God, enjoying him not as the soul enjoys the body or as the soul enjoys itself or as a friend enjoys a friend but rather as the eye enjoys the light[34] — if, that is, we can draw any likeness at all between the one thing and the other. What sort of likeness that might be we shall make clear in another place, so far as we can, if God himself provides his help. For the moment, it is enough to note that Plato determined that the final good is to live in accord with virtue, that this is possible only for the person who knows and imitates God, and that there is no other cause of happiness. For this reason, he does not doubt that what it means to do philosophy is to love God, whose nature is incorporeal. And from this it certainly follows that the person who pursues wisdom — that is, the philosopher — will be happy when he begins to enjoy God.... This true and supreme good, Plato says, is God, and that is why he wants the philosopher to be a lover of God, so that, since the aim of philosophy is precisely the happy life, the person who loves God may attain happiness in the enjoyment of God.

The Closeness of the Platonists to Christianity

9. Any philosophers, then, who held these views concerning the supreme and true God — namely, that he is the author of created things, the light by which things are known, and the good for the sake of which things are done; and that it is from him that we receive the principle of nature, the truth of doctrine, and the happiness of life — we rank above the rest, and we acknowledge that they stand closest to us. This is true whether these philosophers are most properly called Platonists or whether they apply some other name to their school, whether it was only the chief figures of the Ionian school (Plato himself, for example, and those who rightly understood him) who held these views or whether members of the Italian school held them as well (due to Pythagoras and the Pythagoreans and any others from that region who were of the same opinion), or whether some per-

---

33. At XIX,2 below, Augustine observes that Varro discovered as many as 288 possible philosophies based on these divisions.
34. In *Teaching Christianity* I,22,20-21 Augustine famously restricts enjoyment (*frui*) to the enjoyment of God and permits only use (*uti*) of everything else. Here, as there, enjoyment is of God, and the eye-light relationship is illustrative of the human-God relationship. In what follows Augustine elaborates on the proper understanding of enjoyment. For further discussion of enjoyment (and use) see below at XV,7; XIX,13; and also Oliver O'Donovan, "*Usus* and *Fruitio* in Augustine, *De Doctrina Christiana* I," in *Journal of Theological Studies* n.s. 33 (1982) 361-397; Fitzgerald 859-861.

sons from other nations who were considered wise men or philosophers are also found to have seen and taught these points (Atlantic Libyans, perhaps, or Egyptians, or Indians, or Persians, Chaldeans, Scythians, Gauls, or Spaniards).[35] We rank all these above the other philosophers, and we acknowledge that they are the ones whose views come closest to ours.

10. It is quite true, of course, that a Christian trained only in the literature of the Church may be unfamiliar with the name "Platonists" and may have no idea whether or not there were two schools of philosophy in the Greek tradition, the Ionian and the Italian. He will not be so far removed from human affairs, however, that he does not know that philosophers profess either the pursuit of wisdom or wisdom itself. Nevertheless, he will be on guard against those who shape their philosophy in accord with the elements of this world and not in accord with God, by whom the world itself was made. For he is put on guard by the Apostle's precept, and he listens faithfully to what the Apostle said: *See to it that no one deceives you through philosophy and empty deceit, according to the elements of the world* (Col 2:8). At the same time, however, he does not conclude that all philosophers are of this sort. For he also listens to what the same Apostle says of some of them: *For what is known of God is manifest among them, for God has shown it to them. For, from the creation of the world, the invisible things of God have been understood and seen through the things that are made, as well as his eternal power and divinity.* (Rom 1:19-20) And again, in speaking to the Athenians, after declaring a great truth about God which few can understand, that *in him we live and move and have our being*, the Apostle adds, *as some of your own have also said* (Acts 17:28). The Christian knows perfectly well, of course, that he must be on guard against even these philosophers when they go astray. For, in the same passage where the Apostle said that God made his invisible things manifest to them through the things that are made, so that they might be seen by the understanding, he also said that they did not rightly worship God himself, because they paid the divine honors due to God alone to other things to which they should not be given: *For, although they knew God, they did not glorify him as God or give thanks to him but became futile in their thinking, and their senseless heart was darkened. Claiming to be wise, they became fools and changed the glory of the incorruptible God into the likeness of an image of a corruptible man, and of birds, and of four-footed animals, and of reptiles.* (Rom 1:21-23)...

Here, then, is the reason why we rank the Platonists ahead of the others: although other philosophers have spent their talents and their energies in investigating the causes of things and the right way to learn and to live, the Platonists, with their knowledge of God, are the ones who have discovered where to locate

---

35. Augustine displays here an impressive openness to the possibility that a grasp of the truth need not be restricted to the most classical sources. Yet the idea is not original to Augustine, since a similar list appears in Diogenes Laertius, *Lives of Eminent Philosophers* I, 1.

the cause by which the universe was constituted, the light by which truth is perceived, and the fount at which happiness is imbibed.[36] Thus the philosophers who hold this view of God, whether these Platonists or any others from any nation, are in agreement with us. But I prefer to deal with the Platonists in particular because their writings are better known. The Greeks, whose language has the highest standing among the nations, have celebrated their works with great acclaim; and the Latins, impressed by their excellence or by their fame, have been all the more eager to study them and have made them even more famous and prominent by translating them into our language.

11. Some people who share in the grace of Christ with us are astonished when they hear or read that Plato held a view of God which, they see, comes very close to the truth of our religion. For this reason, a good many have presumed that, when Plato went to Egypt, he must have heard the prophet Jeremiah or have read, during that same journey, the writings of the prophets, and I have cited their opinion in some of my works. But a careful calculation of the dates contained in historical chronicles indicates that Plato was born about one hundred years after the time when Jeremiah prophesied; and, since Plato lived to be eighty-one, we find that there were some sixty years between the year of his death and the time when Ptolemy, the king of Egypt, sent for the prophetic writings of the Hebrew people from Judea and had them translated and preserved by seventy Hebrews who also knew the Greek language.[37] During his journey, then, Plato could neither have encountered Jeremiah, who had died many years before, nor have read those writings, which had not yet been translated into the Greek language in which he was so adept.[38]

Since he was an eager student, it is perhaps possible that he studied them with the help of an interpreter, as he did the works of the Egyptians — not, of course, in order to produce a written translation (for we are told that even Ptolemy, who could certainly inspire fear by virtue of his royal power, only gained this privilege in return for granting a great favor), but rather to learn as much as he could take in by discussing their content. Certain indications seem to support this possibility. For instance, the Book of Genesis begins in this way: *In the beginning God created heaven and earth. And the earth was invisible and unformed, and there was darkness over the abyss, and the spirit of God swept over*

---

36. Cause, light and fount suggest yet another trinitarian allusion.
37. Augustine is referring to the legendary (but to him and others real) account of the translation of the Hebrew Bible into a Greek version known as the Septuagint. See Josephus, *Antiquities* XII,2.
38. Augustine, perhaps following Ambrose in particular (see Ambrose, *Exposition of Psalm 118*, sermon 18,4), had originally believed that Plato met Jeremiah in Egypt and drawn some of his ideas from him (see *Teaching Christianity* II,28,43). Here he rejects this notion, and he formally corrects himself in *Revisions* II,4 (31), 2. Among others who believed that Plato had been exposed to Jewish prophecy is Justin Martyr, 1 *Apology* 59. Lactantius, *Divine Institutes* IV,2, however, asserts that Plato, when visiting Egypt, was providentially kept from such exposure.

the water. (Gn 1:1-2)[39] And in the *Timaeus*, the book he wrote on the formation of the world, Plato says that, in accomplishing that work, God first united earth and fire.[40] It is clear, however, that Plato assigns fire to the region of heaven, and so his claim bears a certain resemblance to the statement that *in the beginning God created heaven and earth.* Again, Plato speaks of water and air as the two intermediaries that were interposed between the extremes of earth and fire and linked them together,[41] and one might suppose that this is how he understood the scriptural passage, *the spirit of God swept over the water.* For, because "spirit" can also be used as a word for air, it might seem that Plato, not paying close enough attention to Scripture's usual way of designating the Spirit of God, presumed that the four elements were mentioned in this passage. Then, too, there is the fact that Plato says that the philosopher is a lover of God,[42] and nothing in those Sacred Scriptures is expressed more ardently than this. But most of all — and this, more than anything, almost leads me to agree that Plato was not unacquainted with the books of Scripture — there is this fact: when God's words were brought to the saintly Moses by an angel, and Moses asked for the name of the one who had charged him to go and deliver the Hebrew people from Egypt, the answer was *I am who I am, and you shall say to the children of Israel, He who is sent me to you* (Ex 3:14). It is as if, in comparison with the one who truly is, because he is immutable, the things which were created mutable have no real existence at all. This is precisely the view that Plato strongly maintained and rigorously urged,[43] and, as far as I know, it can nowhere be found in the works of those who preceded Plato, except where it is said, *I am who I am, and you shall say to them, He who is sent me to you.*

12. But no matter where Plato learned these things — whether from the books of ancient writers who preceded him or, rather, as the Apostle says, *Because what is known of God is manifest among them, for God has shown it to them. For, from the creation of the world, the invisible things of God have been understood and seen through the things that are made, as well as his eternal power and divinity* — I think I have made it clear enough that it was not without good reason that I chose the Platonic philosophers as the ones with whom to pursue the issue in natural theology that we are now addressing — that is, whether, for the sake of the happiness which is to come after death, it is right to worship one God or many. I chose them, in particular, because, just as their view of the one God who made heaven and earth is superior to the others', so too they are held in higher esteem and more preeminent regard than the others. And they have been ranked far above other philosophers by the judgment of posterity. Aristotle, a student

---

39. Justin Martyr, 1 *Apology* 59, cites Gn 1:1-2 as a part of Scripture that Plato must have known.
40. See *Timaeus* 31 b-c.
41. See ibid. 32 b-c.
42. See ibid. 90 b-c.
43. See ibid. 52 a-d.

of Plato, a man of outstanding ability, and, although certainly not equal to Plato in eloquence, easily superior to many others, founded the Peripatetic school (which got its name from his habit of walking up and down while he lectured), and, due to his brilliant reputation, he attracted a large number of students to his school even while his teacher was still alive.[44] Again after Plato's death, he was succeeded by his sister's son Speusippus and by his beloved student Xenocrates as the leaders of his school,[45] which was called the Academy, and, on this account, both they and their successors were called Academics. In spite of all this, however, the most distinguished philosophers of more recent times, who chose to follow Plato, did not want to be called either Peripatetics or Academics but simply Platonists. Of these, the most notable are the Greeks Plotinus, Iamblichus, and Porphyry,[46] but the African Apuleius also stands out as a noteworthy Platonist in both languages, that is, in both Greek and Latin.[47] All these, however, and others of their like, as well as Plato himself, thought that worship should be given to many gods.

The Issue: the Worship of Many Gods

13. Therefore, although the Platonists also differ from us in many other important respects, the first question I put to them concerns the point I have just mentioned, for this is no small matter and it is now the point at issue. The question is this: to which gods do they think that worship should be offered — to the good gods, to the evil gods, or to both the good gods and the evil? But we have Plato's own opinion on this matter, for he says that all gods are good and that there are no evil gods.[48]

It follows, then, that we should understand that worship is to be offered to the good gods. For, in that case, it will actually be offered to gods, since, if they are not good, they are not gods at all. If this is so — and what else is it fitting to believe of gods? — it immediately eliminates the view of many people who hold that the evil gods must be placated with sacrifices to keep them from doing us

---

44. Aristotle (384-322 B.C.) is far less cited than Plato in early Christian literature, and often negatively.
45. Speusippus (c. 408-c. 339 B.C.) was succeeded by Xenocrates (c. 396-c. 314 B.C.).
46. All these philosophers are classified as Neoplatonists. Plotinus (c. 204-c. 270 A.D.), the author of the *Enneads*, was an important influence on Augustine, particularly in the years after his conversion. Porphyry (234-c. 305) was a student of Plotinus, the publisher of some of his works, and his biographer. Iamblichus (245-325) was a student of Porphyry until he fell out with him.
47. Apuleius of Madaura (c. 125-c. 180), although best known as the author of *The Metamorphoses*, was also a student of Neoplatonism. His work *On the God of Socrates* is discussed by Augustine in the following pages.
48. See *Timaeus* 40d-41d.

harm, and that the good gods must be invoked to give us their aid. For there are no evil gods, and so it is to the good that the due honor of worship, as they say, is to be paid.[49]...

The Platonists on the Demons: Apuleius

14. There is, they say, a threefold division of all living beings that have a rational soul: gods, human beings, and demons. The gods occupy the most exalted place, human beings the lowest, and demons a place in between. The seat of the gods is in heaven, that of human beings is on earth, and that of the demons in the air. And just as the dignity of their locations differs among them, so does the dignity of their natures. The gods are superior to human beings and to demons, and human beings have been placed below the gods and the demons with respect to both the order of the elements and to the difference in their merits. The demons, then, stand midway between the two, and, just as they are to be ranked lower than the gods, below whom they dwell, so they are to be ranked higher than human beings, above whom they dwell. For, in common with the gods, they have immortality of the body, and, in common with human beings, they have the passions of the soul. And so, say the Platonists, it is no wonder if they also take delight in the obscenities of the stage and in the fictions of the poets, for they are subject to human emotions, which are wholly absent in the gods and completely alien to them.[50] From this we conclude that Plato, in detesting and banning poetic fictions, deprived not the gods — all of whom are good and exalted — but rather the demons of their pleasure in stage plays....

But if this is so, how is it that Plato dared, in banishing the poets from the city, to take away the pleasures of the theater — not from the gods, whom he kept far removed from all human contamination, but certainly from the demons themselves? How is it that he dared to do this, unless his aim was, by this means, to admonish the human mind, even while still confined in these dying members, to despise the demons' impure commands and, for the sake of the splendor of moral integrity, to detest their uncleanness? For, if it was a mark of the highest integrity for Plato to condemn and prohibit these pleasures, then it was certainly a mark of the lowest debasement for the demons to demand and require them....

[*Chapters 16 – 21 elaborate Apuleius's definition of the demons and the claim that demons are intermediaries between human beings and the gods. The beginning of chapter 16 is included here.*]

---

49. See Plotinus, *Enneads* II,9,16.
50. See Plato, *Symposium* 202d-203a.

16. When this same Platonist [Apuleius] discussed the morals of the demons, then, he said that they are subject to the same disturbances of mind as are human beings. They resent injuries, they are placated by flattery and gifts, they rejoice in honors, they take delight in various sacred rites and become irate when any of these are neglected.[51] Among other things, he also says that they underlie the divinations of augury, soothsaying, prophecies and dreams, and that the wonder-working of magicians comes from them as well.[52] But when he briefly defines them, he says that the demons are animal in genus, liable to the passions in soul, rational in mind, aerial in body, and eternal in life span. Of these five characteristics, he notes, the first three are common to them and to us, the fourth is unique to them, and the fifth they have in common with the gods.[53]...

22. ...What remains, therefore, is to conclude that we must simply reject the view that Apuleius tries to persuade us to accept (as do certain other philosophers who hold the same opinion); that is, we must simply reject the view that the demons are placed between the gods and human beings as intermediaries and interpreters who carry our petitions to the gods and bring back the gods' assistance to us. On the contrary, they are spirits rabid to do harm, wholly alien to justice, swollen with pride, livid with envy, and crafty in deceit. It is true that they dwell in the air, but that is because they were cast down from the sublime heights of the higher heaven for their irrevocable transgression and were justly condemned to live in the air as in a prison fit for them. Nor does the fact that the air is located above the earth and above the waters mean that, because they inhabit the air, the demons are superior in merit to human beings. For human beings easily surpass them not by virtue of their earthly body but rather — for those who have chosen the true God as their help — by virtue of their devoutness of mind....

Hermes Trismegistus on the Demons: the Art of Making Gods and the Coming Abolition of the Gods

23. The Egyptian Hermes, whom they call Trismegistus, thought and wrote quite differently on the subject of the demons.[54] Apuleius, it is true, denies that

---

51. See *On the God of Socrates* 12-14.
52. See ibid. 6.
53. See ibid. 7-8.
54. Hermes Trismegistus, or Thrice-great Hermes, was the putative descendent of the god Hermes/Mercury and the supposed Egyptian author of a collection of writings known as the *Hermetica*, or *Corpus Hermeticum*, containing spells, incantations and the like, as well as philosophical texts, all composed in Greek. The collection enjoyed a certain influence, even among Christians, until the Renaissance; the pagan author was thought to have prophesied the coming of Christianity. Recent scholarship suggests that it dates from the second or third century A.D., rather than from a more remote antiquity, as was originally believed, and was not the product of a single author. In what follows Augustine quotes from a section of the corpus known as *Asclepius*, so called after Hermes's interlocutor in an imaginary dialogue, who was understood to be the grand-

the demons are gods, but when he says that they occupy a kind of intermediate position between the gods and men, making it look as though they are necessary to men in their relations with the gods, he does nothing to separate their worship from the religion of the gods on high. This Egyptian, however, asserts that some gods were made by the supreme God, and others made by men.

Anyone who hears this, stated as I have stated it, might think that Hermes is speaking of images, since these are made by human hands. But he asserts that visible and tangible images are only, as it were, the bodies of the gods; and in them, he claims, there dwell certain spirits, specially summoned, who have the power either to do harm or to fulfill many of the desires of those who accord them divine honors and offer them the service of worship. According to Hermes, then, to make gods is to unite these invisible spirits by means of a certain art to visible objects made of corporeal material with the result that the images dedicated and subjected to them become, as it were, animated bodies; and human beings, he says, have received this great and marvelous power of making gods.

Here, as translated into our language, are the actual words of this Egyptian: "Since the subject of our discussion is the kinship and fellowship of men and gods, take note, O Asclepius, of the power and might of man. Just as the Lord and Father — or, what is highest of all, God — is the maker of the celestial gods, so man is the fashioner of the gods who are content to dwell in temples in proximity to human beings."[55] And a little later he says, "Thus humanity, always mindful of its nature and origin, perseveres in this imitation of divinity, so that, just as the Lord and Father made the eternal gods to be like himself, so humanity fashioned its own gods after the likeness of its own countenance."[56]

At this point, Asclepius, to whom Hermes's words were chiefly addressed, responded and asked, "Are you speaking of statues, O Trismegistus?" He replied, "I am speaking of statues. But you see, Asclepius, how far even you lack faith. For I am speaking of statues imbued with life, statues filled with sensation and spirit, statues that do great and wonderful works, statues that foreknow future events and predict them by casting lots, by prophecy, by dreams, and by many other means, statues that make people ill and cure them, bestowing sadness or joy on them according to their merits. Do you not know, Asclepius, that Egypt is an image of heaven or, more precisely, that it is a translation here below of all that is legislated and enacted in heaven? In fact, if truth be told, our land is the temple of the whole world. And yet, since it is fitting for a wise man to have foreknowledge of all things, it is not right for you to remain ignorant of this: a time will come when it will become clear that it is in vain that the Egyptians have served the gods with pious mind and earnest devotion."[57]

---

son of the god Aesculapius.
55. *Corpus Hermeticum* II,9,23.
56. Ibid.
57. Ibid. II,9,24.

Hermes then goes on at great length to expand on what he says in this passage, in which he seems to predict the present time, when the Christian religion, with a force and freedom flowing from its higher truth and greater holiness, is overthrowing all these false images, so that the grace of the most true Savior may set men free from the gods that man makes and subdue them to the God by whom man was made....

Hermes in fact says many things about the one true God, the maker of the world, that are in keeping with what the truth holds; and yet, somehow or other, by that darkening of his heart, he is brought down to the level of wanting human beings always to be subject to gods who, as he himself acknowledges, are made by men. And he laments the coming abolition of those gods. As if anything could be more wretched for a person than to be under the dominion of a figment of his own imagination! It is easier for a man to stop being human by virtue of worshiping things of his own making, as if they were gods, than it is for things of his making to start being gods by virtue of his worshiping them. For it is more likely that a man who *is set in honor, but does not understand*, will become *like the beasts* (Ps 49:20) than it is that a work made by a man will be raised above a work made by God, and made in his own image[58] — that is, man himself. Thus, when a person ranks something he made higher than he ranks himself, he deservedly falls away from the one who made him....

Hermes Trismegistus: the Art of Making Gods Is Rooted in Error and Unbelief

24. After treating many other matters, Hermes comes back to this topic and again discusses the gods that human beings have made. Here is what he says: "But now let what I have said on those matters be enough. Let us return once again to man and to reason, the divine gift due to which man is called a rational animal. For the things which have been said about man, even if marvelous, are not the most marvelous. For all the other marvels are put into the shade by the fact that man was able to discover the divine nature and to make it. Therefore, because our ancestors erred greatly in their conception of the gods, due to their unbelief and their neglect of worship and divine religion, they invented the art of making gods. To this invention they added a corresponding power derived from the nature of the world, mixing it in; and, because they could not make souls, they summoned the souls of demons or angels and installed them in the holy images and divine mysteries so that, through them, the idols might have the power of doing both good and evil."[59]...

---

58. See Gn 1:26.
59. *Corpus Hermeticum* II,13,37.

But when Hermes himself, who admires above everything else in man the power of this art by which he is enabled to make gods, and who mourns because the time is coming when all the figments of gods instituted by men will be abolished by order of the law itself, still admits and expressly states the causes for the discovery of this art, declaring that his forefathers invented the art of making gods as a result of great error, and unbelief, and not turning their mind to worship and divine religion, what should we say? Or, rather, what should we do except give all possible thanks to the Lord our God, who has abolished these things by causes that are the very opposite of the ones by which they were established? For what was established by a vast error was abolished by the way of truth; what was established by unbelief was abolished by faith; and what was established by turning from the worship of divine religion was abolished by turning to the one, true, and holy God.

Nor is this true only in Egypt, for which alone the spirit of the demons expressed grief through Hermes. It is also true in all the earth, which sings a new song to the Lord, just as the truly sacred and truly prophetic Scriptures foretold, where it is written, *Sing to the Lord a new song; sing to the Lord, all the earth* (Ps 96:1). In fact, the title of this Psalm is *When the house was being built after the captivity*. And, in truth, a house is now being built for the Lord in all the earth — namely, the city of God, which is the holy Church[60] — following the captivity in which demonic forces held captive the people, now believers in God, from whom the house is being built as from living stones.[61] For the fact that man made these gods does not mean that he was not held captive by the very gods he had made, once he was drawn into their company by worshiping them — into the company, I want to make clear, not of insensate idols but of cunning demons. What, after all, are idols except what the same Scriptures describe, *They have eyes, but do not see* (Ps 115:5), and any other description that can be given of material objects which, no matter how skillfully carved into images, still lack life and sensation? Unclean spirits, however, bound to these images by that nefarious art, had miserably enslaved the souls of their worshipers by gathering them into company with themselves. That is why the Apostle says, *We know that an idol is nothing, but what pagans sacrifice, they sacrifice to demons and not to God; I do not want you to keep company with demons* (1 Cor 10:19-20). It is after this

---

60. Here Augustine identifies the city of God with the Church, as, e.g., below at XIII,16. Yet elsewhere he implies that the city of God and the Church are not necessarily identical, and that the former must be understood rather in a mystical sense and that its inhabitants are defined by their love of God and contempt for self, just as the inhabitants of the city of man, its contrary, are defined by their hatred of God and their love of self. See below at XIV,28-XV,1. When an identification of the city of God and the Church occurs in Augustine's writings, then, the Church too must be understood mystically rather than merely institutionally — as the body of those who not only share in the visible sacraments but also, less visibly, love God and disdain themselves. On Augustine's ecclesiology see, as a brief summary, Allan D. Fitzgerald, ed., *Augustine through the Ages: An Encyclopedia* (Grand Rapids: Eerdmans, 1999) 169-176.

61. See 1 Pt 2:5.

captivity, therefore, in which human beings have been held captive by malign demons, that the house of God is being built in all the earth. And that is the reason for the title of the Psalm that says, *Sing to the Lord a new song; sing to the Lord all the earth. Sing to the Lord, bless his name; tell of his salvation from day to day. Declare his glory among the nations, his marvelous works among all peoples. For great is the Lord, and greatly to be praised; he is to be feared above all gods. For all the gods of the nations are demons, but the Lord made the heavens.* (Ps 96:1-5)

Thus, when Hermes grieved that the time was coming when the worship of idols would be abolished, as would the demons' domination over people who worshiped idols, it was at the prompting of an evil spirit that he longed for that captivity to last forever — the captivity at the end of which, as the psalmist sings, the house of the Lord is now being built in all the earth. Hermes foretold these happenings with sorrow; the prophets foretold them with rejoicing....

The gods whom Hermes called gods made by men, then, are gods such as these; they are worshiped by men such as these; and they were made by the art of men such as these. In short, they are demons bound to idols, through some strange art, by the chains of their own desires. But at least Hermes did not give them the role assigned to the demons by the Platonist Apuleius (about whose views we have already said enough, and have shown them to be inconsistent and absurd): he did not make them interpreters and intercessors between the gods, whom God made, and men, whom God also made, carrying prayers to the gods and bringing back gifts to men. For it is too foolish for words to believe that gods made by men carry more weight with gods made by God than do men themselves, who were made by the very same God....

For it is utterly impossible for these demons to be friends of the good gods, whom we call holy angels and rational creatures,[62] who have their dwelling in the holy habitation of heaven, *whether thrones or dominions or rulers or powers* (Col 1:16). The demons are as far removed from these in their cast of mind as vice is from virtue and malice from benevolence.

25. By no means, therefore, should we imagine that the path to the benevolence and beneficence of the gods — or, rather, of the good angels — leads through any supposed mediation on the part of demons. It leads rather through likeness to them in good will. By this means we come to be with them, to live with them, and to worship with them the God whom they worship, even though we cannot see them with our bodily eyes. To the extent, however, that we are in misery due to the unlikeness of our will to theirs, and due to the fragility of our frail existence, to that extent we are distant from them not in bodily location but rather in merit of life. For it is not because we dwell on earth under the conditions of the

---

62. Augustine is willing to identify the good gods of the Neoplatonic system with the angels of the Christian system. See below at IX,23.

flesh that we are not united with them; it is only if, in impurity of heart, we set our mind on earthly things. In the meantime, however, while we are being healed so that we may be as they are, we draw near to them by faith if, with their support, we believe that we are made blessed by the one by whom they themselves were made.

Hermes's Lament and the Memorial Shrines of Christian Martyrs

26. But we should certainly take note of something else that this Egyptian says. In lamenting the time to come when those things would be abolished from Egypt which were, as he admits, instituted by men who were gravely in error, and unbelieving, and had turned away from the worship of divine religion, he says, among other things, "Then this land, the most holy seat of shrines and temples, will be completely full of tombs and the dead."[63]...

What Hermes seems to be lamenting is that the memorials of our martyrs are taking the place of their temples and shrines, and anyone who reads his words with a perverse spirit or in hostility to us might well suppose that the pagans worshiped the gods in temples but that we worship the dead in tombs.[64]...

Christians Do not Worship the Martyrs

27. We, however, do not establish temples, or priesthoods, or rites and sacrifices for the martyrs. For it is not they themselves but rather their God who is our God. Of course, we honor their memorials as the memorials of holy men of God who have fought for the truth even to the death of their bodies, so that the true religion might be made known and false and fictitious religion be defeated. For, if there were any people in earlier times who believed as they did, they suppressed their beliefs due to fear. But has any of the faithful ever heard a priest standing at an altar, even if it was built over the holy body of a martyr for the honor and worship of God, say in his prayers, "I offer sacrifice to you, Peter, or Paul, or Cyprian"[65] For it is to God that sacrifice is offered at their memorials, the God who made them both men and martyrs and who joined them with his holy angels in heavenly honor, and the aim of this celebration is both that we may give thanks to the true God for the victories of the martyrs and that, in renewing our memory of them, we may encourage each other to imitate them in winning the crowns and

---

63. *Corpus Hermeticum* II,9,24.
64. This reproach was directed against Christians as early as the mid-second century; it was answered for the first time in *Martyrdom of Polycarp* 17.
65. It is noteworthy that, in giving his example, Augustine mentions Cyprian along with the two great apostles; it not only serves as a reference to a saint widely known to his congregation but is also an indication of the esteem in which he held the martyred bishop of Carthage, who died in 258.

palms of victory, calling on the same God to help us. Thus any forms of homage presented by religious believers at the places of the martyrs serve only as adornments of their memorials; they are not rites or sacrifices offered to the dead as gods. It is true that some people even bring feasts there, but this is not done by better Christians, and in most parts of the world there is no such custom.[66] And any who do bring feasts do it because they want the food to be sanctified to them through the merits of the martyrs and in the name of the Lord of the martyrs. Thus, when they have placed the food at the shrine, they say a prayer and then take it away either to eat it or to distribute some of it to the poor. But anyone who knows anything about the one sacrifice offered by Christians, which is also offered there, knows that this food is not a sacrifice to the martyrs.

In fact, we do not worship our martyrs at all, either with divine honors or with human crimes (as the pagans worship their gods); nor do we offer sacrifices to them; nor do we turn their disgraceful acts into sacred rites dedicated to them....

What more is there to say? No one of even middling intelligence has any doubt that these spirits are not to be worshiped for the sake of the life of happiness that comes after death. But perhaps some people will say that all of the gods are good and that, while some of the demons are evil, others are good; and perhaps they will claim that the ones we ought to worship are the ones whom they consider good, since they are the ones through whom we may attain the life of happiness for all eternity. It is in the next book, however, that we must see whether this idea holds up.

---

66. This was known as the *refrigerium* — a meal in honor of the dead that was held near their tombs. The custom was suppressed in Africa and elsewhere, as being both pagan and an occasion for excessive eating and drinking, but the suppression met with particular resistance in Africa. The next few lines describe a modification of the practice that was acceptable to Church authorities. See Johannes Quasten, "*Vetus superstitio et nova religio*: The Problem of Refrigerium in the Ancient Church of North Africa," in *Harvard Theological Review* 33 (1940) 253-266.

Study Questions for Book VIII

Augustine found in the Platonists serious conversation partners in his search for truth and understanding. Eight hundred years later Thomas Aquinas found a suitable partner in Aristotle. Under the influence of Martin Luther, reformation theology has emphasized the uniqueness of the Gospel and its superiority to all human wisdom. Yet, contemporary Christian theologians continue their inquiry in dialogue with all manner of philosophical schools and thinkers. The American theologian David Tracy insists that honest, consistent, challenging conversation amidst religious diversity and across philosophical difference is essential in a pluralistic world. How might conversation as method both critique and be critiqued by an Augustinian search for truth?

In his criticism of the hierarchical superiority of demons given them by Apuleius, Augustine emphasizes the capacity for moral goodness — absent among the demons, but the very vocation of human beings. Augustine's argument assumes a universality of moral principles, crossing religious and cultural boundaries. In today's growing encounter among world religions, Augustine's universality of moral principles serves as a helpful reminder of our commonalities amidst religious difference. How might Augustine's emphasis on will, enlightened and strengthened by divine grace, contribute to interreligious dialogue?

Religious symbols remain powerful today. Many indigenous religions retain a fear of the demonic powers invested in certain magical rites and arts. Islam, especially Sunni Islam, as well as Judaism prohibit the making of images, fearful of their idolatrous power to compromise worship of the one God. On the other hand, Christian sacramental symbols and rituals can be considered vacuous and feeble in a secular culture that scorns the hidden power of all religious symbols and rituals. Although it seems somewhat curious and alien to readers today, what might Augustine's concern about the power of Roman religious rites contribute to a contemporary Christian appreciation of sacraments and symbols?

BOOK IX

Taking up the question posed at the end of Book VIII, Book IX argues that there is no basis for a distinction between good and evil demons and that therefore there can be no good demons. The starting point is Apuleius's account of the demons which, Augustine insists, applies to all demons and defines them not only as subject to the passions but as subject to the passions in the highest and best part of the soul, the mind. Thus the demons lack the wisdom and virtue by which the mind might control and govern the passions, and so they cannot be classified as good. Furthermore, given that the demons are intermediate between the gods and human beings, they must share some characteristics with the gods and some with human beings. But what they share with the gods is an immortal body, and what they share with human beings is misery of soul; and, since they are in misery, they lack goodness and blessedness and so cannot be good. Nor can they serve as intermediaries. Themselves in misery, they cannot lead human beings out of misery; and, in their misery, they begrudge humans eternal blessedness, impeding them rather than helping them to attain it. The mediator whom human beings really need, therefore, is not one who is immortal in body and miserable in soul but rather one who is (temporarily) mortal in body and blessed in soul, that is, the Word of God, God himself, present in human form. Unlike the Platonists' gods, who are liable to contamination by contact with human beings, God remains completely uncontaminated by human contact and, on this ground too, is the mediator who truly offers human beings a path to blessedness. Finally, the good angels cannot be identified as good demons. They may be considered equivalent to the Platonists' gods, so long as these gods are understood to be immortal beings who were created by God and who are blessed not in their own right but only by adhering to their creator. These beings, however, cannot be mediators between God and men because, being immortal and blessed, they share no relevant characteristic with men (and, in any case, the angels do not want worship for themselves, but only for the one God). And since the demons also cannot be mediators, it is clear that neither demons nor angels /gods should be worshiped for the sake of happiness in the life to come after death.

[Chapters 1 – 2 introduce Book IX's continuing discussion about the differences among demons.]

Apuleius on the Demons and the Passions

3. What, then, is the difference between good and evil demons? The Platonist Apuleius discussed the demons in general, and he spoke at great length about their aerial bodies, but he said nothing at all about the virtues of soul with which they would be furnished if they were good. Thus he was silent about any basis for their happiness. But he was unable to remain silent about the mark of their misery. For he admits that their minds, due to which he classified them as rational, are not imbued and fortified with enough virtue to avoid yielding to the irrational passions of the soul. Rather, they are tossed about by stormy disturbances, as is usually the case with foolish minds. Here are Apuleius's own words on the topic: "It is from the number of the demons," he says, "that the poets — and in this case they do not veer too far from the truth — usually fashion their tales of the gods as haters or lovers of particular human beings, giving prosperity and success to some and, in contrast, opposing and afflicting others. Thus the demons feel pity and indignation, anguish and joy, and every facet of human emotion. They are tossed about by movements of the heart and turmoils of the mind like ours through all the wave-tossed seething of their thoughts, and all these tumults and tempests banish them far from the tranquility of the celestial gods."[1]

Is there any doubt that, in these words, Apuleius says not that some lower part of the demons' souls but that their very minds themselves (due to which they count as rational animals) are stirred up, like a stormy sea, by the tempest of the passions? Thus the demons are not to be compared, even for a moment, to wise men. Even under the conditions of this life, when the wise suffer such disturbances of the soul — and human infirmity is not immune to them — they resist them with untroubled mind. They do not yield to them so far as to approve or to do anything that might deviate from the path of wisdom and the law of justice. The demons, on the other hand, are like foolish and unjust mortals, not in body but in moral character (and I might well have said that they are worse, since they have been this way longer and cannot be cured by due punishment). They, too, are tossed about by turmoils of the mind itself, to use Apuleius's own word, and they do not have in any part of their soul a firm footing in truth and virtue from which to fight off the turbulent and depraved passions.

---

1. *On the God of Socrates* 12.

Philosophic Views of the Passions

4. There are two views held by the philosophers with respect to these motions of the mind, which the Greeks call *pathe*.[2] Some of our writers, such as Cicero,[3] call them "disturbances"; others call them "affections" or "affects";[4] and still others, like Apuleius, call them "passions,"[5] a more direct rendering of the Greek. At any rate, some philosophers say that these disturbances or affections or passions occur even in the wise man, although they are controlled and governed by reason, in that his mind, by its mastery, imposes laws on them, so to speak, which hold them to an unavoidable minimum. Those who take this view are either Platonists or Aristotelians (since Aristotle, who founded the Peripatetic school,[6] was a pupil of Plato). Others, however, like the Stoics, insist that no such passions ever occur in the wise man. But Cicero, in his work *On the Ends of the Good and the Evil*, argues convincingly that the quarrel between the latter (that is, the Stoics) and the Platonists and Peripatetics is actually a matter of words, not of substance.[7] The Stoics are unwilling to call bodily and external things "goods." Instead they call them "advantages,"[8] because they hold that there is no good for human beings except virtue, understood as the art of living rightly, which exists only in the mind. The other philosophers, in keeping with ordinary usage, simply call these things "goods" but insist that they are goods of little or no value in comparison with the virtue by which we live rightly. The result is that, whatever these things are called, whether goods or advantages, they are given the same value by both sides. On this issue, then, the Stoics are doing nothing more than indulging in a novel terminology. And it seems to me that here also, where the point at issue is whether the passions of the mind occur in the wise man, or whether he is instead completely immune to them, the controversy is again a matter of words, not of substance. For in my judgment, so far as the heart of the matter is concerned, rather than the mere sound of words, the view the Stoics hold on this point is no different from that of the Platonists and Peripatetics.

To keep from going on too long, I will omit other things which I might cite to prove the point, but I will mention one instance that makes the matter crystal clear. In the work entitled *Attic Nights*,[9] Aulus Gellius, a man of pol-

---

2. See Aristotle, *On the Soul* 402-403; Diogenes Laertius, *Lives of Eminent Philosophers* VII,110.
3. See *Tusculan Disputations* III,7; IV,10.
4. See Quintilian, *Oratorical Instruction* VI,2,20.
5. See *On the God of Socrates* 12.
6. So called after the Greek word *peripatetikos*, meaning "walking around," since Aristotle supposedly taught while walking around.
7. See *On the Ends of the Good and the Evil* IV,12,30.
8. "'goods'...'advantages'": *bona...commoda*.
9. See *Attic Nights* XIX,1. A potpourri of notes and citations on various topics, *Attic Nights* is the only surviving work of the Roman grammarian Aulus Gellius (c. 125-c. 180 A.D.).

ished eloquence and broad learning, writes that he once made a sea voyage with an eminent Stoic philosopher. When the ship began to pitch dangerously on a raging sea under a threatening sky, this philosopher — as Aulus Gellius relates at length and in detail, but I will touch on only briefly — turned pale with fear. This was noticed by the others on board, and, even though death was close at hand, they watched with great interest to see whether or not the philosopher's mind would be disturbed. When the storm was finally over, and people felt safe to talk and even gossip with each other, one of the passengers, a rich and self-indulgent Asiatic, jokingly mocked the philosopher for showing fear and turning pale, while he himself had remained quite unmoved at the approach of death. But the philosopher retorted with the answer Aristippus, the Socratic, gave to a man of like character who said the same thing to him under similar circumstances: "You had no reason to feel anxious about the life of a depraved scoundrel, but I was duty-bound to fear for the life of Aristippus."[10] This reply disposed of the rich man, but Aulus Gellius later asked the philosopher — not to ridicule him, but to learn from him — what the reason was for his panic. The Stoic was quite ready to instruct a person genuinely fired by zeal for knowledge; and he immediately pulled from his luggage a book by the Stoic Epictetus,[11] which contained teachings in accord with the doctrines of Zeno and Chrysippus, who were, as we know, the founders of Stoicism.[12]

In this book, Aulus Gellius tells us, he read that the Stoics believed that there are certain mental images, which they call phantasies, and that it is not in our power to control whether or when they strike the mind. When these images arise from threatening and terrifying circumstances, it is unavoidable that they affect even the mind of a wise man so that, for a moment, he feels a shudder of fear or the clutch of grief. It is as if these passions were simply too quick for the functioning of mind and reason. This does not mean, however, that the mind takes what the image shows as an evil, or that the mind agrees with it and consents to it. For consent, the Stoics insist, is in our power; and they maintain that the difference between the mind of a wise man and the mind of a fool is precisely that the fool's mind yields to these passions and gives them its mental assent, whereas the wise man, although he cannot help but experience them, retains with unshaken mind a true and stable view of what he ought rationally to seek or to avoid....

And perhaps the reason why the Stoics assert that the passions do not occur in the wise man is that the passions never cloud his wisdom — the wisdom by

---

10. On Aristippus see above at VIII,3. The same story is told less elaborately in Diogenes Laertius, *Lives of Eminent Philosophers* II,71.
11. Epictetus (c. 55-c. 135 A.D.) was among the most influential proponents of Stoicism. The book in question was either the *Discourses* or the *Enchiridion*, both of which were compiled from Epictetus's teachings by his disciple Arrian. Augustine himself had some exposure to the *Enchiridion*. See *Questions on the Heptateuch* I,30.
12. On Zeno of Citium (c. 334-c. 262 B.C.) see Diogenes Laertius, *Lives of Eminent Philosophers* VII,1-160. On Chrysippus (c. 279-c. 206 B.C.) see ibid. VII,179-202.

virtue of which he is wise — with any error or subvert it by any downfall. It remains true, however, that the passions do afflict the mind of the wise man, due to the things which the Stoics call advantages or disadvantages (although they are unwilling to call them goods or evils). For, clearly enough, if the philosopher in the story set no value at all on the things he thought he was about to lose in a shipwreck, such as his life and his bodily well-being, he would not have been in such dread of the danger as to betray his fear by turning pale. Nevertheless, he was able to undergo that distress and still hold to the firm conviction that life and bodily well-being, both of which were put at risk by the raging of the storm, are not goods which make the persons who possess them good in the way that justice does....

Thus the mind in which this conviction is firmly fixed permits no disturbances to prevail in it contrary to reason, even if they do occur in the lower parts of the soul. On the contrary, it is master over them, and, by resisting rather than consenting to them, it exercises the reign of virtue. Virgil describes Aeneas as just such a person when he says, "His mind remains unmoved; the tears flow to no effect."[13]

Scripture on the Passions

5. There is no need at present to set out at length and in detail what Divine Scripture, in which Christian learning is contained, teaches on the subject of these passions. Scripture, in fact, subordinates the mind itself to God, to be ruled and supported by him, and subordinates the passions to the mind, to be so moderated and restrained by it that they are converted into instruments of justice. In our practice, then, the question is not whether the godly mind is angered, but why; not whether it is saddened, but why; not whether it is afraid, but what it is afraid of. To be angry with sinners in order to correct them, to be saddened for the afflicted in order to relieve them, to be afraid for those in peril in order to save them from perishing — surely no one of sound judgment would fault these passions. It is the Stoic practice, true enough, to condemn compassion,[14] but how much more honorable it would have been if the Stoic in Aulus Gellius's story had been disturbed by compassion for a person in need of being saved rather than by fear of being shipwrecked himself. Far better, more humane, and more in keeping with the sensibilities of the godly, were Cicero's words in praise of Caesar: "Of all your virtues, none is more admirable or more appealing than your compassion."[15] For what is compassion but a kind of fellow-feeling in our hearts for the misery of another that compels us to come to his aid if we can? And this emotion is in full accord with reason when we show compassion in ways that

---

13. *Aeneid* IV,449.
14. See Epictetus, *Enchiridion* 16.
15. *On Behalf of Ligarius* 12,37.

keep justice unimpaired, as when we give to the poor or forgive the penitent. Cicero, an outstanding master of words, did not hesitate to call compassion a virtue, even though the Stoics feel no shame at listing it among the vices. But even the Stoics — as we are taught by the book of that preeminent Stoic Epictetus, which is based on the teachings of Zeno and Chrysippus, who were the founders of the school — admit passions of this sort into the mind of the wise man, who is, they insist, free of all vice. It follows, then, that they do not really consider these passions to be vices when they occur in the wise man, just so long as they carry no force contrary to reason or to the virtue of the mind. And it also follows that the position of the Peripatetics, as well as of the Platonists, is exactly the same as that of the Stoics themselves. As Cicero says, however, "disputes over words have long tormented the little Greeks,[16] who are far more eager for controversy than for truth."[17]

But it can still be asked, and with good reason, whether the fact that we are subject to passions of this kind, even when we are performing good works, is not actually a function of the infirmity of this present life. For, in contrast, the holy angels punish without anger those whom they receive for punishment under the eternal law of God; and they come to the aid of the miserable without any fellowfeeling of misery; and when those they love are in danger, they help them without any sense of fear. It is quite true, of course, that in ordinary human discourse the words for the passions are also applied to the angels, but that is due to a certain similarity between their actions and ours, not to any vulnerability to the passions on their part. In the same way, according to Scripture, God himself is angered, but he is not disturbed by any passion.[18] For this word is used to indicate the effect of his vengeance, not any emotive turbulence of his own.

The Demons' Mind, the Highest Part of the Soul, Is Subject to the Passions

6. Postponing the question of the holy angels for the time being, let us see what is involved when the Platonists say that the demons, appointed to serve as mediators between the gods and human beings, are tossed about by the storms of these passions....

7. ... For the poets were speaking of beings who are tossed about, as Apuleius attests, by movements of the heart and turmoils of the mind like ours, through all the wave-tossed seething of their thoughts. And due to these fluctuations, these

---

16. "Little Greeks": *homines graeculos*. The words are Cicero's but the sentiment is Augustine's as well.
17. *On the Orator* I,11,47.
18. See *Confessions* I,4,4: "You are angered and you are tranquil." God's anger, as described in the Old Testament, was a significant theological issue in the first three or four centuries of Christianity. See Ermin F. Micka, *The Problem of Divine Anger in Arnobius and Lactantius* = Studies in Christian Antiquity 4 (Washington: The Catholic University of America Press, 1943) 1-35.

beings can pursue their loves and hatreds not in the interests of justice but rather in the same way that a mob, which resembles them, expresses its partisan zeal for one side or the other in relation to wild beast fighters and charioteers.[19] It seems, then, that this Platonist philosopher took considerable pains to make sure that, when these tales were sung by the poets, we would not believe that they were told about the gods themselves, whose names the poets inserted into their fictions, but rather about the intermediary demons.[20]...

The Demons: Immortal Body, Vice-Ridden Soul

9. What sort of mediators between men and the gods are these demons, then, through whom men may solicit the friendship of the gods? In common with men, they are inferior with respect to the superior part of a living being, that is, the soul; and, in common with the gods, they are superior with respect to the inferior part of a living being, that is, the body. For a living being — that is, an animal — consists of soul and body, and, of these two, the soul is certainly superior to the body. Even when it is vice-ridden and weak, it is still undoubtedly superior to even the most strong and healthy body. For its nature is more excellent, and, even when stained with vice, it is not ranked lower than the body, just as gold, even when impure, is valued more highly than the purest silver or lead. But these mediators between the gods and men, through whose intermediation the human realm is joined to the divine, have an eternal body in common with the gods, but a vice-ridden soul in common with men — as if religion, by which the Platonists want human beings to be united with the gods through the agency of demons, were a matter of the body, not of the soul!...

10. Plotinus is praised for having understood Plato better than anyone else, at least in recent times.[21] And, in discussing human souls, he had this to say: "The Father, in his mercy, made mortal fetters for them."[22] In his judgment, then, the fact that humans have mortal bodies is due to the mercy of the divine Father. But the wickedness of the demons was not judged worthy of this mercy, and, along with the misery of a soul subject to the passions, they received not a mortal body, like man's, but an eternal body. If they had had a mortal body in common with men and a blessed soul in common with the gods, there is no doubt that they would have been happier than men. And if, along with a miserable soul, they had deserved to have a mortal body, they would at least have been on a par with human beings — provided that they also acquired some measure of piety, so that they might at least have found rest from their sufferings in death. As it is, how-

---

19. For similar imagery see *Expositions of Psalms* 39,8-9; 53,10.
20. See *On the God of Socrates* 12.
21. See Porphyry, *Life of Plotinus* 15. This is also Augustine's own view. See *Answer to the Academics* III,18,41.
22. *Enneads* IV,3,12.

ever, not only are they no happier than men because of their misery of soul, but they are more miserable than men because of the unending prison of their bodies. For Apuleius did not want us to think that the demons might make progress by means of some discipline of piety and wisdom, and so become gods; rather, he explicitly stated that the demons are demons for all eternity....

[Chapters 12 – 14 analyze demons as intermediate between gods and humans and argue that "good demons" are a logical impossibility.]

Evil Mediators and the Good Mediator

15. But if... all men, so long as they are mortal, are necessarily miserable as well, then we must seek an intermediary who is not only man but is also God, so that the blessed mortality of this intermediary may, by his intervention, lead men from their mortal misery to blessed immortality. It was necessary both that this mediator not fail to become mortal and that he not remain mortal. And he did, in fact, become mortal — not by any weakening of the divinity of the Word but rather by assuming the weakness of the flesh. But he did not remain mortal in that flesh, for he raised it from the dead. And the fruit of his mediation is this — that those for the sake of whose deliverance he was made mediator would themselves not remain in perpetual death, even of the flesh. It was necessary, therefore, for the mediator between us and God to have both transient mortality and permanent blessedness so that, by virtue of his transient state, he might put himself at one with those who are going to die and, from the realm of the dead, might bring them into his permanent state.

It is not possible, then, for good angels to be mediators between miserable mortals and blessed immortals, because they too are both blessed and immortal. It is possible for evil angels to be mediators, because they share immortality with the immortals and misery with the mortals. At the opposite pole from them, however, is the good mediator who, in contrast to their immortality and misery, both chose to become mortal for a time and had the power to remain blessed for all eternity. Proud in their immortality and hurtful in their misery, the evil angels sought to seduce men into misery by flaunting their immortality. To put a stop to them, the good mediator, by the humility of his death and the kindness of his blessedness, destroyed their hold on those whose hearts he purifies by faith[23] and has delivered from their foul dominion....

It is not because he is the Word, however, that he is the mediator. For the Word, of course, is supremely immortal and supremely blessed and so is far

---

23. See Acts 15:9.

removed from miserable mortals. He is the mediator, rather, due to the fact that he is man.[24] And by this very fact he shows us that, in order to attain the good which is not only blessed in itself but also makes us blessed, we have no need to look for other mediators by whose aid, we might think, we must strive to reach it step by step. It is God who is blessed in himself and also makes us blessed, and, because he became a participant in our humanity, he provided a shortcut to participation in his divinity. For, in delivering us from mortality and misery, he does not lead us to the immortal and blessed angels in order that, by participating in them, we too may become immortal and blessed. Rather, he leads us directly to the Trinity, by participation in whom the angels themselves are blessed. That is why, when he willed to be lower than the angels,[25] in the form of a servant,[26] in order to be the mediator, he still remained higher than the angels in the form of God.[27] At one and the same time he was both the way of life here below and life itself in heaven above.[28]

God, the Gods, the Demons and the Issue of Contamination by Human Contact

16. Thus the statement which Apuleius ascribes to Plato, that "no god has dealings with men,"[29] is not true. Apuleius also claims that the chief mark of the gods' sublime status is precisely the fact that they are not contaminated by any contact with humans.[30] To say this, however, is to admit that the demons are contaminated by human contact, and it follows that they are unable to purify those by whom they are themselves contaminated. Thus both are equally unclean, the demons due to their contact with men, and men due to their worship of the demons. On the other hand, if the demons are able to have contact and dealings with men without being contaminated, then they are clearly better than the gods. For if the gods were to have dealings with men, they would be contaminated. For it is said to be the chief mark of the gods that they are set apart on high, where contact with human beings cannot possibly contaminate them.

Apuleius asserts that, according to Plato's teaching, the supreme God, the creator of all things, whom we call the true God, is the one being who cannot even remotely be captured in words, due to the poverty of human speech. Even the wise, when they have withdrawn themselves as fully as possible from the body by sheer strength of mind, can scarcely attain knowledge of this God, and then only occasionally, like a sudden flash of dazzling light in the deepest dark-

---

24. See 1 Tm 2:5.
25. See Heb 2:7.9.
26. See Phil 2:7.
27. See Phil 2:6.
28. See Jn 14:6.
29. *On the God of Socrates* 4.
30. See ibid.

ness.[31] But if the truly supreme God, who is above all things, really does become present, by some intelligible and ineffable presence, to the minds of the wise, when they have withdrawn themselves as fully as possible from the body — even if only occasionally, even if only like a sudden flash of dazzling light — and yet is not contaminated by them, why is it that those gods of theirs are placed far away in their lofty location in order to keep them from being contaminated by human contact?...

17. It is astonishing to me that such learned men, who hold that all corporeal and sensible things are to be regarded as inferior to incorporeal and intelligible things, should even mention bodily contact when the point at issue is the life of happiness. What has become of that saying of Plotinus, "We must flee, therefore, to our beloved homeland. Our Father is there; all is there. What ship are we to use, then, what means of flight? We must become like God"?[32] If it is true that the more a person is like God, the closer he is to God, then the only way to be distant from God is to be unlike him. And the more the human soul sets its heart on temporal and mutable things, the more it is unlike that incorporeal, eternal, and immutable being.

To heal this condition, since it is impossible for the mortal and impure things here below to approach the immortal purity on high, a mediator is obviously needed. What is needed, however, is not the kind of mediator who comes close to the highest in having an immortal body but is like the lowest in having a diseased soul. For, due to that disease, such a mediator would be more inclined to begrudge us our healing than to aid us in being healed. What we need, instead, is a mediator who is joined to us here below by the mortality of his body but who also — due to the immortal righteousness of his spirit, through which he remains on high, not in spatial distance but in his supreme likeness to God — can truly provide divine aid in purifying and delivering us. For the God who is utterly beyond contamination would never fear contamination from the man with whom he clothed himself or from the men among whom he lived as man. And meanwhile there are two matters of no small importance that he showed us, for our salvation, by his incarnation — that true divinity cannot be contaminated by the flesh, and that we should not think that the demons are superior to us just because they do not have flesh. As Holy Scripture proclaims him, then, this is the *mediator between God and man, the man Jesus Christ* (1 Tim 2:5). But this is not the place to discuss, as fully as we could, either his divinity, by which he is forever equal to the Father, or his humanity, by which he became like us....

18. ...What the Platonists actually believe, then, is not that human beings are purified by the demons but rather that the demons are contaminated by human beings and that the gods themselves would also be contaminated if they were not

---

31. See ibid. 3.
32. *Enneads* I,6,8; II,3. Augustine has conflated Plotinus's words and changed them slightly.

protected by their location far above.[33] Who is so misguided as to imagine that he can be purified on such a path as this — a path where, we are told, human beings contaminate, the demons are contaminated, and the gods are liable to contamination? Who would not rather choose the path on which human beings elude the contaminating demons, the path on which humans are cleansed from contamination by a God who cannot be contaminated, so that they may enter into fellowship with the uncontaminated angels?

Good Angels Are not Good Demons

19. But I do not want it to appear that we, too, are merely arguing about words; and, since many of these demon-worshipers (to coin a term)[34] — Labeo among them[35] — claim that the beings whom they call demons are called angels by others, I see that I must say something here about the good angels. The Platonists do not deny that there are good angels, but they prefer to call them good demons rather than angels.

For our part, we follow the lead of Scripture, which is what makes us Christians. In Scripture we sometimes read of good angels, sometimes of evil angels, but never of good demons. In fact, wherever that term is found in Scripture, whether in the form *daemones* or in the form *daemonia*, it only signifies malignant spirits....

The Pride of the Demons, the Humility of Christ, and the Good Angels

20. Nevertheless, the very origin of the term "demon" suggests a point well worth knowing, especially in relation to the sacred books. The demons (the word is Greek) get their name from knowledge.[36] But the Apostle, speaking by the Holy Spirit, says, *Knowledge puffs up, but love builds up* (1 Cor 8:1), and the only right way to understand this is that knowledge is of no benefit without love. Without love, it puffs up; that is, it swells people up with a pride which is nothing but empty windiness. What the demons have, then, is knowledge without love, and, as a result, they are so puffed up, so proud, that they have made every effort to get for themselves the divine honors and religious service that they know full well is due only to the true God. And they are still doing this now, as much as they can and with whomever they can. Over against the pride of the demons, by

---

33. See Apuleius, *On the God of Socrates* 6.
34. "Demon-worshipers": *daemonicolarum*. The same neologism appears without comment in *Confessions* VIII,2,4 and elsewhere.
35. See above at II,14.
36. *Daemon* means "knowing" or "wise." See Plato, *Cratylus* 398b. This seems to be the correct etymology.

which mankind has deservedly been held captive, there stands, in contrast, the humility of God, made known in Christ. But human souls, puffed up with the uncleanness of pride, know nothing of the power of his humility. They are like the demons in pride but not in knowledge.

21. The demons themselves, however, know the power of his humility so well that, even when the Lord was clothed in the weakness of the flesh, they said to him, *What have you to do with us, Jesus of Nazareth? Have you come to destroy us?* (Mk 1:24) Their words make it clear both that they had great knowledge and that they had no love. They clearly feared punishment from him, but they did not love the righteousness in him. But he let himself be known to them only as far as he chose, and he chose to be known only as far as was fitting. He did not let himself be known to them as he is known to the holy angels, who, thanks to their participation in eternity, enjoy him as the Word of God.[37] Rather he made himself known to them as he had to be known in order to terrify those from whose tyrannical power he was about to deliver those predestined for his kingdom and for a glory that is eternally true and truly eternal....

22. The good angels, then, put no stock in the knowledge of corporeal and temporal things that puffs the demons up with pride. It is not that they are ignorant of such things. But what is dear to them is the love of God by which they are sanctified. They burn with a holy love for this love's beauty, which is not only incorporeal but also immutable and ineffable, and, in comparison with it, they hold in contempt all that is beneath it and all that is not what it is, including themselves, so that they may enjoy with all their goodness the good that makes them good. And they know temporal and mutable things with all the more certainty precisely because they see their principal causes in the Word of God, by whom the world was made. For it is by these causes that some things are approved, some things are condemned, and all things are ordered.

The demons, in contrast, do not contemplate the eternal and, so to speak, cardinal causes of temporal things in the Wisdom of God.[38] They do, however, foresee many more future events than human beings do because of their wider experience of certain indicators that are hidden from us; sometimes, too, they announce in advance things that they themselves have arranged. Accordingly, the demons are often mistaken, the angels absolutely never. For it is one thing to make guesses about temporal and mutable affairs on the basis of temporal and mutable indicators, and to insert into these affairs temporal and mutable measures expressive of one's own will and capacity, which is permitted to the demons to a

---

37. On the knowledge of the angels here and in what follows see below at XI,29 and also *The Literal Meaning of Genesis* IV,32,49-50.
38. See 1 Cor 1:24. Since this Wisdom performs the same function as the Word of God who is referred to just previously, clearly the second person of the Trinity is meant here. The present paragraph places angelic knowledge in the trinitarian context of God, his Wisdom and his Spirit.

certain extent. But it is quite another thing to foresee temporal changes under the eternal and immutable laws of God, which dwell in his Wisdom,[39] and to know the will of God, which is the most certain and most powerful of all causes, by participation in his Spirit,[40] which is granted to the holy angels by a just differentiation. Therefore, the holy angels are not only eternal but also blessed, and the good by which they are made blessed is the God by whom they were created. For they enjoy unfailing participation in him and unfailing contemplation of him.

Good Angels and the Gods

23. If the Platonists prefer to call these angels gods rather than demons and to number them among the gods who their founder and teacher Plato writes were created by the supreme God,[41] let them say this if they like, for there is no need to trouble ourselves over a merely semantic issue. For if they say that these beings are immortal but created by the supreme God, and that they are blessed not in their own right but only by adhering to the one whom made them, then they say what we say, no matter what they call them. And the fact that this is the view of the Platonists, whether of all of them or at least of the better part of them, can be discovered in their writings. So far as the name itself is concerned — that is, their practice of calling immortal and blessed creatures of this sort gods — there is virtually no disagreement between us and them. We, too, read in our Sacred Scriptures, *The God of gods, the Lord, has spoken* (Ps 50:1), and in another passage, *Confess to the God of gods* (Ps 136:2), and in another, *The Lord is a great king above all gods* (Ps 95:3)....

There is no need, then, for extended debate about the name, since the thing itself is so clear that it leaves no room for doubt. But when we say that angels from the number of these blessed immortals were sent to announce the will of God to men, the Platonists disagree. They believe that this service is performed not by those whom they call gods, that is, by immortal and blessed beings, but rather by demons, whom they do not go so far as to call blessed but only immortal. Or, if they do call them both immortal and blessed, they still regard them, at most, only as good demons and not as gods dwelling on high, remote from all human contact. And although this may seem a mere dispute about a word, it is still the case that the name of demon is so detestable that we should not apply it in any way to the holy angels.

---

39. Angelic (and human) wisdom has to do with the immutable and eternal (see *Teaching Christianity* I,8,8) and hence requires some sort of participation in the divine Wisdom.
40. On the appropriateness of referring to the Spirit in terms of will see *The Trinity* XV,20,38; 21,41.
41. See *Timaeus* 40a.

Conclusion: neither Angels nor Demons Are Mediators to Be Worshiped for the Sake of Eternal Life

This book, then, may now close with the knowledge that these immortal and blessed beings, who — whatever we call them — were created and made, are not intermediaries serving to lead miserable mortals to immortal blessedness. For they are separated from mortals both by their immortality and by their blessedness. As for the beings who actually do occupy an intermediate position, having immortality in common with those above them and misery in common with those below them, since it is due to their malice that they deserve to be miserable, they can only begrudge us, not grant us, the blessedness which they do not have themselves. Thus the friends of the demons provide no good reason why we ought to worship the demons as helpers rather than shun them as deceivers. And as for the spirits who are good, and therefore are not only immortal but blessed as well, the Platonists are of the opinion that they should be worshiped with rites and sacrifices, under the name of gods, for the sake of attaining a blessed life after death. But these beings, however they should be characterized and whatever they should be called, want such religious worship to be offered to none but the one God, by whom they were created and by participation in whom they are blessed. With the help of that same God we shall discuss this point more fully in the following book.

Study Questions for Book IX

Augustine's critique of the demons defaults to an Apollonian affirmation of the superiority of reason and thought. The Dionysian nature of demons, as Augustine analyzes it, is inferior because their passions infect and compromise their intelligence. How might Augustine's emphasis on love, elaborated in Books XI to XXII in which he surveys the origin, history and future of the "two loves that made two cities," provide for a dynamic Augustinian integration of intellect and will, energized by passions that are continuously transformed and elevated by grace?

For Augustine only Christ is the true Mediator between divine and human. The incarnation of the Word of God in Jesus provides Augustine the source of human virtue, and a critique of all other religious claims. In contemporary interreligious dialogue, Christians must reckon with the truth claims of other faiths that frame the intersection of the divine and human differently. How might Christians' faith in the mystery of Christ, and their dependence on divine grace, inform their participation in interreligious conversations?

Modern and postmodern thought often relegates belief in angels to ancient or medieval superstition. However, remarkable advances in 21st-century astrophysics have reopened metaphysical questions and invite reconsideration of scientific models and philosophical systems that foreclose human imagination. Augustine used belief in angels to rethink the nature of the Greek and Roman divinities. How might angelology function today as a reminder of the limits of human categories and an encouragement to remain open to as yet undiscovered aspects of the universe?

BOOK X

Book X completes Augustine's consideration of whether the gods — specifically, in this case, the good angels — are to be worshiped for the sake of happiness in the life after death. It begins with a definition of happiness for the rational soul, whether angelic or human: participation in the one God by clinging to him in love. This definition provides common ground with the Platonists and a basis for setting out the true meaning of worship as devotion of the self to God in love. In this light, the sacrifices commanded in the Old Testament can be seen to have been instituted not from any need on God's part for sacrifice but rather as signs signifying the true sacrifice, which is realized in love for God and for others. That sacrifice is due to God alone is confirmed by the miracles of the Old Testament, and it is this sacrifice that the angels want not for themselves but only for God, in whom they find their happiness and in whom, in their love for us, they want us to find happiness as well. Over against this form of devotion to God, there is the Platonist Porphyry's discussion of theurgy, a manipulation of the gods which, according to Porphyry, can achieve a limited purification of the soul but cannot provide a way of return of the rational soul to God. Augustine holds, however, that the gods involved are actually demons working against the restoration of the soul to God rather than good gods or angels aiding the soul on the path to ultimate happiness. Genuine purification of the soul takes place, rather, through the true mediator, who is the one "principle" that purifies the rational soul and, in fact, the whole person. But Porphyry is offended by the humility of Christ's incarnation and thus, in his pride, is prevented from recognizing the truth of Christianity and its triune God. Porphyry himself has made several corrections of Plato and has thus brought Platonism closer to the Christian position. Even so, Porphyry has not been able to find the universal way of the soul's liberation in any of his own inquiries and investigations. Nevertheless, he believes that there is such a universal way, and, if he had not been blinded by pride, he would have seen that Christianity provides that universal way, which was realized in the coming of Christ and in the life of the Church, which has vanquished the demons not by manipulating the gods but by the witness of the martyrs. To find and follow this way, then, human beings in their weakness should rely on divine authority and on the aid of the angelic beings who do not want worship for themselves but rather direct our worship to the one supreme God, who is at once their God and ours and who is the true source of eternal happiness.

1. In the view of everyone who is at all capable of using reason, it is a certainty that all people want to be happy.[1] But when, in their mortal weakness, they ask who is happy or what makes them happy, they give rise to a whole host of major controversies on which the philosophers have exhausted their energies and consumed their leisure. To bring in those controversies and discuss them at this point would take too long, and, in any case, it is not necessary. We dealt with this matter in the eighth book, when we were selecting the philosophers with whom to discuss the issue of the life of happiness that comes after death.[2] There we asked whether this life is to be attained by directing our religion and sacred rites to the one true God, who is the maker of the gods, or to many gods; and, if the reader will recall what I said there, he will not expect me to repeat the same points here, especially because, if he has forgotten, he can read them again to refresh his memory. We chose the Platonists, who are deservedly the most renowned of all the philosophers, because they were able to see that the human soul, even though it is immortal and rational or intellectual, can only be happy by participation in the light of the God by whom both it and the world were made. Thus they deny that anyone will attain what all human beings desire — that is, the life of happiness — unless he clings with all the purity of a chaste love to the one supreme good which is the immutable God.

But even these philosophers — either because they gave in to popular error and folly or because, as the Apostle says, *they became futile in their thinking* (Rom 1:21) — thought, or wanted others to think, that we should worship many gods. As a result, some of them went so far as to hold that the divine honors of rites and sacrifices should even be offered to demons. To these we have already replied in no small measure. The present issue, however, concerns the immortal and blessed beings who are established in heavenly thrones, dominions, principalities, and powers,[3] the beings whom the Platonists call gods and to some of whom they give the name either of good demons or, with us, of angels.[4] And what we must now consider and discuss is how we ought to believe that these beings want us to observe religion and piety — that is, to speak more plainly, whether they wish us to offer worship and sacrifices, and to consecrate in religious rites some part of our possessions or our very selves, to themselves also or only to their God, who is also our God....

[The remaining paragraphs of chapter 1 review Latin and Greek words for religion and posit the worship due to God alone.]

---

1. See *The Happy Life* 2,10; *The Trinity* XIII,4,7.
2. See above at VIII,5.
3. See Col 1:16.
4. See Porphyry, *Letter to Anebo*, fragment 10.

The One Source of Happiness, both Human and Angelic

2. But there is no conflict between us and these more eminent philosophers on this issue. They saw, and in their writings they affirmed in many ways and at great length, that these beings gain their happiness from the same source that we do — a certain intelligible light shed over them, which is their God, and which is something other than themselves. By this they are illuminated so that they shine bright with light and, by participation in it, exist in a state of perfection and of blessedness.

In explaining Plato's views, Plotinus often stresses that not even the soul which they believe to be the soul of the universe gains its blessedness from any other source than our soul does. It too gains its blessedness from a light which is other than itself, by which it was created, and by whose intelligible illumination it gleams with intelligible light.[5] Plotinus also draws an analogy between these incorporeal beings and the splendid corporeal bodies that we see in the heavens, likening God to the sun and the soul to the moon; for the Platonists suppose, of course, that the moon is illuminated by the light of the sun shed over it.[6] This great Platonist affirms, then, that the rational soul (or the intellectual soul, as we ought rather to call it) — and he includes in this class the souls of the immortal and blessed beings who, he has no doubt, dwell in heavenly habitations — has no nature above it except the nature of God, who fashioned the world and by whom the rational soul itself was made. Nor, he says, are the life of blessedness and the light by which the truth is understood granted to these supernal beings from any other source than the source from which they are also granted to us.[7] Thus he agrees with the Gospel, where we read, *There was a man sent from God, whose name was John. He came as a witness, in order to bear witness to the light, so that all might believe through him. He was not himself the light, but he came to bear witness to the light. This was the true light that enlightens everyone who comes into this world.* (Jn 1:6-9) This distinction shows quite clearly that the rational or intellectual soul, such as John had, cannot be its own light but shines rather by participation in another light, the true light. And John himself acknowledges this when, in bearing witness to God, he says, *From his fullness we have all received* (Jn 1:16).

3. This being so, if the Platonists (or any others who shared their views), knowing God, had glorified him as God and given thanks to him — if they had not become futile in their thinking,[8] sometimes themselves instigating popular error and sometimes simply being too timid to resist it — they would certainly have confessed that the one God of gods, who is both our God and theirs, is the

---

5. See Plotinus, *Enneads* V,1,2-3.
6. See ibid. V,6,4.
7. See ibid. V,1,10.
8. See Rom 1:21.

God who should be worshiped both by those immortal and blessed beings and by us as well, in our mortality and misery, so that we too may be able to attain immortality and blessedness.

It is to this God that we owe the service which is called *latreia* in Greek, whether enacted in certain sacraments or in our very selves. For we are all collectively his temple and individually his temples,[9] since he deigns to dwell both in the concord of all and in each individual. And he is no greater in all than he is in each, for he is neither enlarged by addition nor diminished by division. Our heart, when lifted up to him, is his altar.[10] It is with his only-begotten Son as our priest that we propitiate him. To him we sacrifice bleeding victims when we fight for his truth to the point of shedding blood. We honor him with the sweetest incense when, in his sight, we burn with devout and holy love. To him we vow and return both his gifts in us and our very selves. To him we dedicate and consecrate the memory of his benefits in solemn feasts and on appointed days, lest ungrateful forgetfulness creep in as time goes by.[11] To him we offer, on the altar of the heart, the sacrifice of humility and praise, kindled by the fire of love. In order to see him, as he can be seen, and to cling to him, we are cleansed of every stain of sin and evil desire and are consecrated in his name. For he is the source of our happiness, and he is the end of all desire. In electing him — or rather in re-electing him, for we had lost him by neglecting him — in re-electing him, then (and the word "religion" is also said to be derived from "re-elect"[12]), we set our course toward him in love, so that, when we reach him, we may be at rest, blessed because made perfect by the one who is our ultimate end. For our good, the final good about which there is so much dispute among the philosophers, is nothing other than to cling to him by whose incorporeal embrace alone, if one can speak of such a thing, the intellectual soul is filled and made fertile with true virtues.

We are enjoined to love this good with all our heart, all our soul, and all our strength. To this good we ought to be led by those who love us, and to it we ought to lead those whom we love. In this way are fulfilled those two commandments on which all the law and the prophets hang, *You shall love the Lord your God with all your heart, and with all your soul, and with all your mind*, and *You shall love your neighbor as yourself* (Mt 22:37.39). For, in order that a person may know what it means to love himself, an end has been appointed for him to which he is to refer everything he does so that he may attain happiness, for he who loves himself wants nothing other than to be happy. And this end is precisely to cling to God.[13] Therefore, when a person who now knows what it means to love himself

---

9. See 1 Cor 3:16-17.
10. A similar spiritual approach to sacrifice, as expressed here, is found in Tertullian, *On Prayer* 28.
11. On the idea that external observances foster an interior awareness see Letter 130, 9, 18.
12. "'Religion'...'re-elect'": *religio...religentes*. For the etymology of "religion" as Augustine gives it here, see Cicero, *On the Nature of the Gods* II,28,72. In *Revisions* I,13,9 Augustine notes two different etymologies — the present one and another that relates it to the word *religare*, meaning "to bind" (to God).
13. See Ps 73:28.

is commanded to love his neighbor as himself, what else is he commanded to do but, so far as possible, to urge his neighbor to love God?[14] This is the worship of God, this is true religion, this is genuine godliness, this is the service due to God alone....

5. But who would be such a fool as to think that the things offered to God in sacrifice are necessary to him or that he needs them for any use of his own? Divine Scripture makes this clear in any number of passages; but, to avoid going on at length, let it suffice to cite this brief text from the Psalm: *I said to the Lord, You are my God, for you have no need of my goods* (Ps 16:2). We must believe, therefore, that God not only has no need of cattle or any other corruptible and earthly thing but does not even need a person's righteousness itself. Rather we must hold that everything done in rightly worshiping God is of benefit not to God but to man. For no one would say that he had served the interests of a fountain by drinking from it, or that he had served the interests of a light by using it to see.

The Significance of the Sacrifices Commanded under the Old Law: the Self Directed to God in Love

Nor are those other sacrifices offered by the patriarchs of old with animal victims,[15] which the people of God now only read about but do not perform, to be understood in any other way than this: their role was to signify what is now done among us for the purpose of clinging to God and helping our neighbor to the same end. Sacrifice, therefore, is the visible sacrament of an invisible sacrifice; that is, it is a sacred sign. That is why the penitent in the prophet, or perhaps the prophet himself, in seeking God's forgiveness for his sins, says, *If you had desired sacrifice, I would certainly have given it; you take no delight in burnt offerings. The sacrifice to God is a contrite spirit; a contrite and humbled heart God will not despise.* (Ps 51:16-17)

Note how, in the very place where he said that God does *not* desire sacrifice, he showed that God *does* desire sacrifice. The sacrifice that he does not want, then, is the sacrifice of a slaughtered animal, and the sacrifice that he does want is the sacrifice of a contrite heart. Thus, the sacrifice that the prophet said God does not want signifies the sacrifice that he went on to say that God does want....

Again, in another prophet, it says, *How shall I reach out to the Lord, and how shall I receive my God, the Most High? Shall I reach out to him with burnt offerings, with calves a year old? Will the Lord be pleased with thousands of rams or with tens of thousands of fatted goats? Shall I give my firstborn for my transgression, the fruit of my loins for the sin of my soul? Has he told you, O man, what is good? Or what does the Lord require of you but to do justice, and to love mercy,*

---

14. See *Teaching Christianity* I,22,21.
15. See, e.g., Gn 8:20.

and to be ready to walk with the Lord, your God? (Mic 6:6-8) In the words of this prophet, too, the two kinds of sacrifice are distinguished, and it is declared quite plainly that God does not require for their own sake the sacrifices which are meant to signify the sacrifices that God does require. In the epistle inscribed to the Hebrews[16] it says, *Do not forget to do good and to share what you have, for such sacrifices are pleasing to God* (Heb 13:16). Accordingly, where Scripture says, *I desire mercy rather than sacrifice* (Mt 9:13; 12:7), we must understand it simply to mean that one kind of sacrifice is preferred to another....

6. The true sacrifice, then, is every act done in order that we might cling to God in holy fellowship, that is, every act which is referred to the final good in which we can be truly blessed. Thus, even the mercy which we extend to human beings is not a sacrifice if it is not done for God's sake. For, even though sacrifice is made or offered by man, it is still a divine matter, and so the ancient Latins, too, called it by this very term. Thus a person who is consecrated in the name of God and is vowed to God, insofar as he dies to the world so that he may live to God, is himself a sacrifice. For this, too, pertains to mercy, the mercy which a person extends to himself. And so it is written, *Have mercy on your soul by pleasing God* (Sir 30:24 Vulg).

Our body also is a sacrifice when we discipline it by temperance, if we do this, as we ought, for God's sake, so as not to present our members to sin as weapons of wickedness but rather to God as weapons of righteousness.[17] It is in exhorting us to this end that the Apostle says, *I appeal to you therefore, brothers, by the mercy of God, to present your bodies as a living sacrifice, holy and pleasing to God, which is your reasonable service* (Rom 12:1). And so, if the body, which, because it is inferior, the soul uses as a servant or instrument, is a sacrifice when its good and right use is directed to God, how much more does the soul itself become a sacrifice when it directs itself to God so that, aflame with the fire of love for him, it loses the form of worldly desire and, now subject to him, is reformed to him as to an unchanging form, thus pleasing him by receiving its beauty from his beauty! It is precisely this point that the same Apostle goes on to make in the next part of the passage: *And do not be conformed to this world, but be reformed by a renewal of your mind, so that you may discern what is the will of God, what is good and genuinely pleasing and perfect* (Rom 12:2).

Therefore, since true sacrifices are works of mercy, whether shown to ourselves or shown to our neighbors, which are directed to God; and since works of mercy are performed with no other object than that we might be delivered from misery and so become blessed — which only happens by means of that good of which it is

---

16. Augustine seems to employ a circumlocution here in order to avoid mentioning the author of the Epistle to the Hebrews; he acknowledges below at XVI,22 that there is some dispute as to whether or not it was written by Paul.

17. See Rom 6:13.

said, *But for me the good is to cling to God* (Ps 73:28) — it obviously follows that the whole redeemed city, that is, the congregation and fellowship of the saints, is offered to God as a universal sacrifice through the great priest who, in his passion, offered himself for us in the form of a servant,[18] to the end that we might be the body of such a great head.[19] For it was this servant form that he offered, and it was in this form that he was offered, because it is according to this form that he is the mediator, in this form that he is the priest, and in this form that he is the sacrifice. Thus, after the Apostle had exhorted us to present our bodies as a living sacrifice, holy, pleasing to God, our reasonable service, and not to be conformed to this world, but to be reformed in a renewal of our mind so that we might discern what is the will of God, what is good and genuinely pleasing and perfect, the whole of which sacrifice is we ourselves, he went on to say, *For by the grace of God given to me, I say to everyone among you not to think more of yourself than you ought to think, but to think temperately, as God has assigned to each his measure of faith. For just as in one body we have many members, and not all members have the same functions, so we, although many, are one body in Christ, and individually members of one another, having diverse gifts according to the grace given to us.* (Rom 12:3-6) This is the sacrifice of Christians: *although many, one body in Christ.* And this is the sacrifice that the Church continually celebrates in the sacrament of the altar (which is well known to the faithful), where it is made plain to her that, in the offering she makes, she herself is offered.[20]

7. As for those immortal and blessed beings who dwell in heavenly habitations and together rejoice in participation in their creator, who are constant by virtue of his eternity, certain by virtue of his truth, and holy by virtue of his gift — because, in their mercy, they love us miserable mortals and wish us also to become immortal and blessed, they rightly do not want us to sacrifice to themselves but rather to God, for they know that, together with us, they are themselves his sacrifice. For, along with them, we are the one city of God, to which it is said in the Psalm, *Glorious things are spoken of you, O city of God* (Ps 87:3). Part of this city, our part, is on pilgrimage far from home; and part, their part, gives us its help. It is from that supernal city, where God's intelligible and immutable will is law, from that supernal court, so to speak (for it shows care[21] for us), that there descended to us through the ministry of the angels the holy Scripture which reads, *Whoever sacrifices to*

---

18. See Phil 2:7.
19. This is the city of God in its purest sense, as Augustine understands it in its earthly instantiation — namely, the whole body of the saved with Christ as its head. In the following section (7) he points out that the city in its entirety consists of both human beings and angels.
20. It seems from Augustine's phrasing that "the sacrament of the altar," which is the eucharist or the sacramental body of Christ, is secondary to the sacrifice that is "we ourselves." But it would be correct to say that the sacrifice of the eucharist subsumes or represents the sacrifice of the body of Christ that is the faithful, or "we ourselves." This theme, in any event, is now temporarily left aside, to be resumed below at X,20.
21. "Court...care": *curia...cura.* See Varro, *On the Latin Language* VI,6. There is, however, no etymological connection between these words.

any god but to the Lord alone will be destroyed (Ex 22:20). This Scripture, this law, and such commandments as this have been attested by such great miracles that it is perfectly clear to whom these immortal and blessed beings, who desire for us what they have themselves, want us to sacrifice.

[Chapter 8 recounts miracles from Genesis 15, 18, 19, Numbers 11, 16, 21, and 2 Kings 18, which confirm the command to sacrifice to God alone.]

Porphyry on Theurgy and the Purification of the Soul

9. These miracles, and many others of the same kind — it would take too long to mention them all — were performed to promote the worship of the one true God and to ban worship of the many false gods. What is more, they were performed through simple faith and pious trust, not by means of incantations and charms composed by the art of baneful curiosity, an art which they call either magic or by the more detestable name of witchcraft or by the more honorable one of theurgy. Those who use these terms are trying, as it were, to draw a distinction among the devotees of these illicit arts; they want to make it look as though some deserve to be condemned, the ones whom the common people call sorcerers — for these, they say, are dealing in witchcraft — while others deserve praise, the ones whom they credit with practicing theurgy. In truth, however, both groups are entangled in the false rites of demons going under the name of angels.

Even Porphyry promises a kind of purification of the soul through theurgy, although he does so hesitantly and with some embarrassment about his argument.[22] At the same time, however, he denies that this art provides anyone with a way of return to God. You can see, then, that he fluctuates back and forth between the vice of sacrilegious curiosity and the profession of philosophy, his views alternating from the one side to the other. At one moment, he warns us to be on guard against this art as delusory, dangerous in actual practice, and prohibited by law; but at the next, as if giving in to those who praise the art, he states that it is useful for purifying part of the soul — not, of course, the intellectual part, by which we perceive the truth of intelligible things that have no bodily likenesses, but rather the spiritual part, by which we apprehend the images of bodily things. He asserts that by means of certain theurgic consecrations, which they call mysteries, this part of the soul is made fit and apt for the reception of spirits and angels and for seeing the gods. But he admits that the intellectual soul gains nothing from these theurgic mysteries with regard to the purification that would make it fit to see its God or to perceive the things that truly exist. From this we can understand what

---

22. See his fragmentary *Philosophy from Oracles*, which is perhaps to be identified with his *On the Return of the Soul*.

kind of seeing, and of what kind of gods, he says is brought about by theurgic consecrations — a seeing in which the things that truly exist are not seen at all. In fact he claims that the rational soul — or, as he prefers to call it, the intellectual soul — can escape into its own realm even without any purification of its spiritual part by the theurgic art. And, what is more, he says that even the theurgist's purification of the spiritual part does not actually go so far as to allow it, on this basis, to attain to immortality and eternity....

[The rest of chapter 9 and chapters 10 and 11 elaborate Porphyry's cautions about the dangers of theurgy, with references to Chaldean and Egyptian practices.]

The Visible Miracles and Visible Appearances of the Invisible God

12. But since it is really true that any number of extraordinary things are done by means of these theurgic arts, things that exceed every limit of human power, only one sensible conclusion remains: we must recognize that these marvels, which appear to be divinely foretold or divinely performed, but which have no relation to the worship of the one God (and clinging to the one God, as the Platonists also attest in numerous cases, is the sole good that brings blessedness), are simply the malicious tricks and enticing traps of malign demons, and true piety must be on guard against them. On the other hand, we must hold that any miracles which are divinely performed, whether through angels or in any other way, to encourage the worship and religion of the one God, in whom alone the life of blessedness is found, are performed either by or through those who genuinely love us in truth and piety, with God himself working in them. We have no obligation to listen to those who deny that the invisible God works visible miracles. By their own account, God made the world, and they certainly cannot deny that the world is visible. Any miracle done in this world is obviously less than this world as a whole, that is, heaven and earth and everything in them, and God most certainly made the world as a whole. But just as the God who made it is hidden and incomprehensible to human beings, so also is the manner in which he made it. Thus, even though the miracles of nature's visible order have lost their wonder for us, due to the fact that we see them all the time, still, when we view them wisely, they are greater than even the rarest and most unusual of miracles. For man is a greater miracle than any miracle done by man.

Thus God, who made the visible heaven and earth, does not disdain to work visible miracles in heaven or on earth. By means of them he rouses the soul, previously given over to visible things, to worship him, the invisible God. But when and where he works them is determined by his own immutable plan, in whose design all future times have already taken place. For although he moves temporal things through time, he is not himself moved through time.[23] Nor does he know things yet to be done in any other way than he knows things already done. Nor does he listen to those now calling upon him in any other way than he sees those who are going to call upon him in the future. For even when it is his angels who hear us, he himself hears us in them, being in them as in his true temple not made with hands, in the same way that he is in his human saints. And his commands, although performed in time, are beheld all at once by his eternal law.

13. Nor should it trouble us that, even though God is invisible, we are told that he often appeared to the patriarchs in visible form.[24] For just as the sound by which we hear a thought which was first formulated in the silence of the mind is not the same thing as the thought itself, so the visible form in which God was seen, even though he is by nature invisible, was not the same thing as God himself. Nevertheless, it was God himself who was seen in that bodily form, just as it is the thought itself that is heard in the sound of the voice, and the patriarchs were not unaware that they were seeing the invisible God in a bodily form which was not itself God. For even though Moses spoke to God when God spoke to him, he still said, *If I have found favor with you, show yourself to me, that I may see you and know you* (Ex 33:13)....

Divine Providence, the Education of Humanity, and the Giving of the Law

14. The right education of humanity in general, so far as the people of God is concerned, like the right education of a single individual, advances through certain eras of time, as if by the stages of an individual's growth and development, mounting up from temporal things to a comprehension of eternal things and from visible things to invisible things.[25] Even during the era in which visible rewards were promised from God, however, the worship of the one God was enjoined. This was to keep the human mind from making itself subject to any but the soul's true creator and Lord, even for the sake of the earthly benefits of this transitory life....

It is best, then, for the human soul, when it is still weak due to its earthly desires, to become accustomed to look to none but God alone for even the lowly and earthly goods that it desires in this temporal life and that are necessary for this transitory existence, even though these goods should be despised in comparison with the eternal benefits of that other life. For then, even in its desire for goods of this sort, it does not withdraw from the worship of him whom it only attains by despising and turning away from such things.

---

23. See *Confessions* I,4,4.
24. See, e.g., Gn 3:8; Ex 3:6. On the issue of seeing God, see Letters 147-148.
25. See *A Miscellany of Eighty-three Questions* 58,2; 64,2; *On Genesis: A Refutation of the Manicheans* I,23,35-24,42.

15. It pleased divine providence, then, to order the succession of eras in such a way that, as I have said, and as we read in the Acts of the Apostles, the law enjoining the worship of the one true God was given by the edicts of angels,[26] in which the person of God himself appeared visibly — not, of course, in his own substance, which remains forever invisible to corruptible eyes, but by certain indications given by the creature in obedience to its creator. There he spoke in the words of human speech, syllable by syllable, through the transitory moments of time; in his own nature, however, he speaks not corporeally but spiritually, not perceptibly but intelligibly, not temporally but, so to speak, eternally, neither beginning to speak nor ceasing to speak.[27] His ministers and messengers, who are eternally blessed in the enjoyment of his immutable truth, hear what he says as one integral whole, not with the ear of the body but with the ear of the mind, and without difficulty or delay, they do what, in this inexpressible way, they hear that they must do and must bring down to the realm of the visible and the sensible.

Now this law was given according to a sequence of times. Thus, as was said, it first held out the promise of earthly things. These, however, signified eternal things, which many celebrated in their visible sacraments[28] but few understood. Nevertheless, the combined testimony of all the words and things contained in the law enjoins the worship of one God as plainly as can be — not one of a throng of gods but the one God who made heaven and earth and who made every soul and every spirit that is not what he himself is. He made them, they were made, and both to exist and to thrive they need him by whom they were made.

Angels, Miracles, and the Worship of God

16. Which set of angels, then, do you think that we ought to believe with regard to eternal and blessed life? Those who themselves want to be worshiped with religious rituals, insisting that mortals offer them rites and sacrifices? Or those who say that all this worship is due only to the one God, the creator of all things, and instruct us to direct it with true godliness to him in contemplation of whom they themselves are now blessed and promise that we also will be blessed in the future? That vision of God is a vision of such beauty and is worthy of such love that Plotinus has absolutely no doubt about saying that, without it, a person is utterly wretched, no matter how abundantly endowed with any other kinds of goods.[29] Since, therefore, some angels prompt us by miraculous signs to worship (in the sense of *latreia*) the one God and others prompt us to worship themselves, and since the former forbid us to worship the latter, but the latter do not dare to forbid the worship of the one God, which of the two should we believe? Let the Platonists answer, let the philosophers

---

26. See Acts 7:53.
27. See *Exposition of Psalm* 44,5.
28. I.e., the observances of the Old Testament.
29. See *Enneads* I,6,7.

in general answer, let the theurgists — or rather the meddlers in magic,[30] for that is what all these arts really deserve to be called — answer. In short, let people in general answer, if there still lives in them any sense that they were created rational in nature. Let them answer, I say, and let them tell us whether we ought to sacrifice to those beings, whether gods or angels, who enjoin us to sacrifice to themselves, or rather to the one God to whom we are enjoined to sacrifice by those who forbid us to sacrifice either to themselves or to the others.

Even if neither of these performed any miracles but only gave commands — the ones ordering us to sacrifice to themselves, the others forbidding this, but commanding sacrifice to the one God alone — piety itself should be enough to determine which of these commands comes from arrogant pride and which from true religion. I will go even further: even if only those beings who seek sacrifice for themselves used miracles to influence human souls, while those who forbid this and enjoin sacrifice only to the one God never stooped to perform any visible miracles at all, it would still be true that the authority of the latter should be preferred not on the basis of the body's senses but on the basis of the mind's rationality. In fact, however, God has acted to make the pronouncement of his truth all the more persuasive by performing, through those immortal messengers who proclaim not their own arrogance but his majesty, miracles that are greater, more certain, and more celebrated. His purpose was to prevent those who seek sacrifice for themselves from easily persuading the weak in faith to embrace false religion merely by showing them wonders that astound the senses....

[The first part of chapter 17 recalls the Ark of the Covenant and the miracles associated with it in Exodus 13, 20, 25, 40, Joshua 3, 6, and 1 Samuel 4, 6.]

17. ...Miracles such as these are minor matters to God, but they are of great import for their salutary ability to overawe and instruct mortals. The philosophers, and especially the Platonists, are praised for being wiser than others precisely because... they have taught that divine providence directs even lowly and earthly things, basing their teaching on the beauty of design which is present not just in the bodies of animals but even in plants and grasses. But how much more plainly do miracles attest to divinity when they take place in immediate association with the proclamation that commends to us the religion which forbids sacrifice to any being in heaven, on earth, or under the earth and enjoins sacrifice to the one God alone! He alone, in loving us and being loved by us, makes us blessed. And by setting a limit to the time when such sacrifices were required, and by foretelling

---

30. Augustine uses the neologism *periurgi*, which reflects the Greek word *perierga* ("curious arts") in Acts 19:19 and is translated here as "meddlers in magic."

that they were to be changed into something better by a better priest, he attests that he has no desire for such sacrifices himself but rather uses them to signify other and better things. His aim was not that he himself might be exalted by such honors but rather that we, kindled by the flame of love for him, might be stirred to worship and cling to him, which is the good not for him but for us.

18. Perhaps someone will claim that these miracles are false, that they never happened but are merely lies written down in books. Anyone who says this, if he means that no written works of any kind should be believed on these matters, can by the same token say that there are no gods who concern themselves with the affairs of mortals. For it was precisely by the performance of miraculous works that the gods induced men to worship them, and the histories of the gentiles bear witness to these miracles (although, by their miracles, the gods were able only to put their wonderworking powers on display, not to show that they themselves served any useful purpose). Accordingly, in this work of ours — and we now have its tenth book in hand — we have not undertaken to refute either those who deny that there is any divine power at all or those who claim that it cares nothing for human affairs. Our dispute is rather with those who prefer their own gods to our God, the founder of the holy and most glorious city. They do not know that he is himself the invisible and immutable creator of this visible and mutable world and the true giver of the blessed life, which has its basis not in the things he created but in himself....

Sacrifice, the Angels, and the Worship of God

19. Some people suppose that visible sacrifices are appropriate for other gods, but that God — since he is invisible, greater, and better — should be offered invisible, greater, and better sacrifices, sacrifices such as the service of a pure mind and a good will. These people, however, obviously do not understand that these visible sacrifices are signs of invisible sacrifices in the same way that spoken words are signs of things. Therefore, just as in the case of prayer and praise we direct to God words that signify and offer to him the things in our hearts that are signified by our words, so also we should understand that, in the case of sacrifice, visible sacrifice is to be offered only to God and that, in our hearts, we should present our very selves as an invisible sacrifice to him. That is when the angels, and all the higher powers whose strength is due to their very goodness and devotion, favor us, rejoice with us, and help us with all their might to do this very thing. But if we desire to offer these sacrifices to the angels themselves, they are not willing to receive them, and, when they are sent to men in a way that allows us to perceive their presence, they explicitly forbid it. There are examples in Holy Scripture.[31]

Some people have thought that, by adoration or by sacrifice, they should give to angels the honor that is due to God, but they were prohibited by the an-

---

31. See Jdg 13:16; Rv 19:10; 22:9.

gels' own admonition and commanded to offer it only to him to whom the angels know that it can be offered without blasphemy. And the example of the holy angels was followed by holy men of God. For, in Lycaonia, Paul and Barnabas were taken for gods when they performed a miracle of healing, and the Lycaonians wanted to sacrifice victims to them, but in humble piety they refused the honor and proclaimed to them the God in whom they should believe.[32]...

20. In the form of God, then, the true mediator — since, by taking the form of a servant,[33] he became the mediator between God and man, the man Jesus Christ[34] — receives sacrifice together with the Father, with whom he is one God. In the form of a servant, however, he chose to be a sacrifice rather than to receive sacrifice, and he did so in order to keep anyone from thinking that sacrifice should be offered, even in this case, to any creature at all. At the same time, he is also the priest, himself making the offering as well as himself being the offering. And he wanted the sacrifice offered by the Church to be a daily sacrament of his sacrifice,[35] in which the Church, since it is the body of which he is the head,[36] learns to offer its very self through him. The sacrifices of the saints of old were the manifold and varied signs of this true sacrifice, for this one sacrifice was prefigured by many, just as one thing may be expressed by a variety of words, in order to recommend it highly but not monotonously. To this supreme and true sacrifice all false sacrifices have now given way....

Porphyry on the Principles and the Purification of the Soul

23. Even Porphyry says that divine oracles have replied that we are not cleansed by the mysteries of the moon and the sun. The purpose of their reply was to let it be known that man cannot be cleansed by the mysteries of any god. For if the mysteries of the moon and sun, whom they count as foremost among the celestial gods, do not cleanse, whose mysteries do? Consequently, Porphyry says, what the oracle indicates is that it is the principles[37] that are able to cleanse. For he does not want people to think, when they hear that the oracle said the mysteries of the sun and moon do not cleanse, that the mysteries of some other god from the divine throng do have the power to cleanse.

But we know what Porphyry means when, as a Platonist, he speaks of principles. He is speaking of God the Father and God the Son, whom he calls in Greek

---

32. See Acts 14:6-15.
33. See Phil 2:6.
34. See 1 Tm 2:5.
35. Although Augustine refers here to the daily offering of the sacrifice — i.e., the eucharist — he acknowledges in Letter 54,2,2 that it is not offered each day in every place. It is not entirely clear from his own writings whether or not the eucharist was celebrated daily in Hippo.
36. See Eph 4:15; Col 1:18.
37. "Principles": *principia*. The Latin means "principles" in the sense of beginnings, origins, sources.

the intellect or mind of the Father. Of the Holy Spirit, however, he says nothing or, at least, says nothing clearly, for I do not understand whom else he could mean in speaking of a being that holds an intermediate position between these two. For if, like Plotinus in his discussion of the three principal substances, Porphyry had wanted this being to be understood as the nature of soul, he certainly would not have spoken of it as intermediate between these two, that is, between the Father and the Son. Plotinus clearly ranks the nature of soul below the intellect of the Father;[38] but Porphyry, in putting it in the middle, ranks it not below but between the other two. No doubt he was saying, so far as he was able or so far as he was willing, what we say of the Holy Spirit — that the Holy Spirit is not the Spirit of the Father alone or of the Son alone but rather of both.[39] For philosophers speak without constraint, and they do not worry about giving offence to religious ears, even in matters that are exceedingly difficult to understand. But we are obliged by the dictates of religion to speak according to a fixed rule[40] in order to make sure that loose words do not give rise to sacrilegious opinions concerning the matters which the words signify.

24. When speaking of God, therefore, we do not speak of two or three principles any more than we are allowed to speak of two or three gods. It is true that in speaking of any one, whether of the Father or of the Son or of the Holy Spirit, we confess that each individually is God; but, unlike the Sabellian heretics, we do not say that the Father is the same as the Son and that the Holy Spirit is the same as the Father and the Son.[41] Rather we say that the Father is the Father of the Son, and that the Son is the Son of the Father, and that the Holy Spirit is the Spirit of both the Father and the Son but is neither the Father nor the Son. It was true, then, to say that it is only by a principle that human beings are cleansed, despite the fact that these philosophers referred to principles in the plural.

---

38. See *Enneads* V,1 passim.
39. Although Augustine does not specifically say here that the Spirit proceeds from both Father and Son, that is what is implied. With Ambrose (see *On the Holy Spirit* I,11,120) Augustine is among the first to make this fateful assertion which, since it appeared in the Nicene-Constantinopolitan Creed in the West over the course of the Early Middle Ages, has been referred to as the Filioque. See *The Trinity* IV,20,29; XV,17,29; 26,47.
40. The "fixed rule" (*certa regula*) is the so-called "rule of faith" (*fidei regula*), referred to as such below at XI,32-33 and elsewhere and often appealed to in early Christian literature. Although Augustine calls it "fixed," it was undefined in the strictest sense of the term, although it certainly included the most basic tenets of Christian belief.
41. The Sabellians, so called after a certain Sabellius (fl. late second-early third centuries), were also known as Modalists (from their belief that one divine person assumed three different modes) and Patripassianists (because, if there was only one divine person, then the Father must have undergone the Passion). See Tertullian, *Against Praxeas,* passim. Sabellianism had probably ceased to be a theological threat by Augustine's time. The Sabellians are mentioned again below at XI,10, where Augustine refers to them in the past tense.

Christ: the True Mediator and the True Principle of Our Purification

But because Porphyry was in subjection to invidious powers — he was ashamed of them but too much in fear of them to speak openly against them — he was not willing to recognize that the Lord Christ is the principle by whose incarnation we are cleansed. In fact, he despised him on account of the flesh he assumed in order to become the sacrifice of our cleansing. It was due to his pride, then, that Porphyry did not recognize this great sacrament[42] — the very pride that the true and gracious mediator overthrew by his humility. Christ showed himself to mortals in the very mortality that malign and deceitful mediators proudly exulted that they did not have; and, speaking as immortals to mortals, those deceitful mediators promised their deceptive help to wretched human beings. But the good and true mediator showed that it is sin that is evil, not the substance or nature of the flesh, which, along with a human soul, could be assumed and maintained without sin, and could be laid aside at death and changed into something better by resurrection. He also showed that death itself, although it is the penalty of sin, a penalty that he himself paid for us without sin, is not something to be avoided by committing sin but rather something to be endured, if the occasion arises, for righteousness's sake. For he was able to pay for our sins by dying precisely because he died and, at the same time, did not die for any sin on his part.

This Platonist, then, did not recognize that Christ is the principle; if he had, he would have known that he is our purification. For it is not the flesh that is the principle, nor the human soul, but the Word *through whom all things were made* (Jn 1:3). Thus the flesh does not purify in its own right; rather it purifies through the Word by whom it was assumed when *the Word became flesh and dwelt among us* (Jn 1:14). For when Christ spoke in a mystic sense of eating his flesh,[43] and those who did not understand took offence and went away saying, *This is a hard saying, who can bear it?* (Jn 6:60), his response to those who remained was, *It is the Spirit that gives life; the flesh is of no use* (Jn 6:60).

The principle, then, having assumed soul and flesh, cleanses the soul and the flesh of those who believe. That is why, when the Jews asked who he was, he replied that he was the principle.[44] But we, carnal, weak, guilty of sin, and shrouded in the darkness of ignorance, would be utterly unable to grasp this unless we were cleansed and healed by him through what we were and what we were not. We were men, but we were not righteous; in his incarnation, however, there was human nature, but it was righteous, not sinful. This is the mediation by which a helping hand is stretched out to those who lie fallen and prostrate; this is the seed ordained

---

42. I.e., the incarnation of the second person of the Trinity.
43. See Jn 6:35-58.
44. See Jn 8:25 Vulg., which reads *principium quia et loquor vobis* ("the beginning, because I am also speaking to you"). See *Homilies on the Gospel of John* 38,11.

by the angels, in whose edicts was given the law by which both the worship of the one God was enjoined and the coming of this mediator was promised.[45]...

[Chapter 25 shows how Psalm 73 teaches about the True Good.]

Porphyry on the Angels and the Theurgic Arts

26. As far as I can tell, Porphyry was somewhat embarrassed about his friends the theurgists. He more or less knew all the points I have made, but he did not feel free to speak out against the worship of many gods.[46] In fact, he even said that there are some angels who come down here below and divulge divine things to theurgists but others who declare on earth what is true of the Father, his height and his depth. But are we to believe that the angels whose mission is to declare the will of the Father want us to be subject to any but him whose will they announce to us? Even this Platonist quite rightly admonishes us to imitate them rather than to invoke them.[47]...

27. ...In contrast, those theurgists — or, rather, the demons, feigning the appearance and figures of gods — defile the human spirit rather than purifying it with their false apparitions and the deceiving trickery of their empty forms. For how can they cleanse the human spirit when their own spirit is unclean? If they were not unclean, they certainly would not have been bound by the incantations of an envious man, nor would they have suppressed out of fear, or denied out of any similar envy, the empty benefit which it seemed they were about to bestow. It is enough, however, that you[48] grant that the intellectual soul (that is, our mind) cannot possibly be cleansed by theurgic purification and that you admit that the spiritual soul (that is, the part of the soul inferior to the mind), even though you claim that it can be cleansed by this sort of art, still cannot be made immortal and eternal by that art. Christ, on the other hand, promises eternal life, and that is why — to your distress, but also to your wonder and amazement — the world is flocking to him....

You cannot deny that the theurgic discipline leads people astray, or that vast numbers are deceived by its blind and nonsensical teaching, or that it is most certainly an error to have recourse in action or supplication to principalities and

---

45. See Gal 3:19-20.
46. See *On Abstinence from Eating Animals* II,60.
47. See ibid. II,34-35.
48. The "you" seems to be Porphyry.

angels. But what good is this, when, on the other hand, as if to avoid seeming to undermine all the work you put into learning these arts, you still send people to theurgists so that those who do not live according to the intellectual soul may at least have their spiritual souls purified through them?

Porphyry's Failure to Recognize the Truth: Pride and Humility

28. Thus you send people into certain error, and you feel no shame about this great evil, despite the fact that you profess to be a lover of virtue and wisdom. But if you had truly and genuinely loved these things, you would have recognized *Christ the power of God and the wisdom of God* (1 Cor 1:24),[49] and you would not have been so puffed up with pride in empty knowledge [50] that you recoiled from his saving humility.

You do admit, however, that even the spiritual soul can, without any of the theurgic arts or any of the mysteries that you wasted so much effort to learn, be purified by the virtue of continence. Sometimes you even say that these mysteries do not elevate the soul after death, and so it now appears that, even after the end of this life, they are not of any use to what you call the spiritual soul. And yet you discuss them over and over again, in a variety of ways and all to no purpose, so far as I can judge, except to make yourself look like an expert in such things and to pander to those who are curious about illicit arts, or else yourself to rouse people's curiosity about them. But you do well when you say that this art is to be feared, due to the dangers involved both in its illegality and in its very practice itself. If only those poor wretches would at least learn this much from you, and turn away from this art to keep from being consumed by it, or never come near it at all!...

29. You proclaim the Father and the Son, whom you call the intellect or mind of the Father, and a third intermediate between these two, by whom we presume that you mean the Holy Spirit,[51] and, as is your custom, you call these three gods. In this regard, even though you are using inaccurate terms, you Platonists have to some extent, as if through some faint and shadowy image, caught sight of what we should strive to attain. But you are not willing to acknowledge the incarnation of the immutable Son of God,[52] by which we are saved and through which we are enabled to arrive at the realities in which we believe and which, in some small measure, we understand. In a fashion, then, you see — if only from a great distance and with clouded vision — the country in which we should abide, but you do not keep to the path that leads to it.

---

49. The "lover of virtue" should have found in Christ, *the power* (virtus) *of God*, the object of his love.
50. See 1 Cor 8:1.
51. See above at X,23.
52. This is the objection raised against the Neoplatonists in *Confessions* VII,9,13-15.

You do, however, admit that there is such a thing as grace, for you say that it has been granted only to a few to attain to God by the power of intelligence. You do not say "It pleased only a few" or "Only a few desired" but "It has been granted only to a few." There is no doubt, then, that in saying this you are acknowledging the grace of God, not the sufficiency of man. You even use this term quite openly when, following Plato's opinion,[53] you state that, beyond doubt, man cannot by any means achieve the perfection of wisdom in this life, but that, for those who live according to intellect, everything they lack can be made up after this life by God's providence and grace.

If only you had recognized *the grace of God through Jesus Christ our Lord* (Rom 7:25)! If only you had been able to see that his very incarnation, by which he assumed a human soul and body, is the supreme example of grace! But what am I doing? I know that it is pointless to speak to a dead man, but that applies only to you. There are also people who hold you in high regard and feel real affection for you, either due to some sort of love of wisdom or due to their curiosity about those arts which you should never have studied; and, in rebuking you, I am speaking to them. And that, perhaps, is not so pointless after all! The grace of God could not have been more graciously commended to us than it was in that the only Son of God, while he remained immutably himself, put on humanity and, by the mediation of a man, bestowed upon men the spirit of his love. By this love a way was opened for men to come to him who was so distant from men — as distant as the immortal is from the mortal, as the immutable is from the mutable, as the righteous is from the ungodly, as the blessed is from the wretched. And because he had implanted in us by nature the desire for blessedness and immortality, he, remaining blessed while he assumed mortality in order to grant us what we love, taught us by his suffering to despise what we fear.

But it takes humility to accept this truth, and it is only with great diffculty that your stiff neck can be persuaded to submit. What is so incredible, however, about saying that God assumed a human soul and body, especially for philosophers like you who hold views that should prompt you to believe it? You yourselves hold such a high notion of the intellectual soul — which is, after all, the human soul — that you claim it can become consubstantial with the mind of the Father, which you acknowledge to be the Son of God. What is so incredible, then, about one intellectual soul being assumed, in some unique and inexpressible way, for the salvation of many? We know, on the evidence of our very nature itself, that the body is united with the soul to make a whole and complete human being. And if this were not so utterly commonplace, it would plainly be even more incredible. After all, it should be far easier to believe in the union of spirit with spirit or, to employ your own usual terms, of the incorporeal with the incorporeal — even if one is human and the other divine, even if one is mutable and the other immutable — than to believe in the union of a body with something incorporeal.

---

53. See *Phaedo* 67b-68b.

Or is what offends you, perhaps, the unprecedented birth of his body from a virgin? But this should not offend you at all. On the contrary, the fact that a miraculous person was born in a miraculous way should lead you to embrace godliness.

Or is it a difficulty that, after his body had been laid aside in death and changed for the better by resurrection, he carried it up on high, now incorruptible and no longer mortal? Perhaps you are unwilling to believe this because you note that Porphyry, in the books he wrote *On the Return of the Soul*, the very books from which I have cited so much, repeatedly teaches that the soul must flee from all bodies[54] if it is to attain enduring happiness with God.[55] In truth, however, it is Porphyry himself who needs to be corrected on this point, especially in light of the incredible notions you hold, along with him, about the soul of this visible world with its huge corporeal mass. Following Plato, you claim that the world is a living thing, and not only living but fully blessed, and you even want to assert that it is eternal. But if it is true that in order to attain happiness a soul must flee from all bodies, how can it be true that the world's soul is never released from its body and yet, at the same time, is never lacking for happiness? Again, you acknowledge in your books that the sun and the other stars are bodies, and everyone unhesitatingly agrees with you in seeing and saying that this is true. But you also claim, on the basis of what you take to be a higher knowledge, that they are living beings who are both supremely blessed and eternally joined to these bodies. Why, then, when the Christian faith is commended to you, do you completely forget, or at least pretend not to know, what you yourselves customarily discuss and teach? Why is it that you are unwilling to become Christians simply because you hold opinions which, in fact, you yourselves oppose? What reason is there, except that Christ came in humility and you are proud? It may be that those who are most learned in the Christian Scriptures are sometimes too detailed in their discussions of what the bodies of the saints will be like in the resurrection.[56] We have no doubt, however, that their bodies will be eternal and that they will be the sort of bodies Christ demonstrated in the example of his own resurrection. And whatever their bodies may be like, we proclaim that they will be wholly incorruptible and immortal and will in no way hinder the contemplation by which the soul is fixed on God. In any case, since you also claim that there are in the heavens the immortal bodies of beings who are immortally blessed, why do you persist in the opinion that, for us to be happy, we must flee from all bodies? Why do you persist in this opinion, trying to make it look as though you have rational grounds for fleeing from the Christian faith, unless it is because — to say it again — Christ is humble and you are proud?

---

54. A famous assertion of Porphyry, also cited below at XII,27 and XXII,12.26. See *Revisions* I,4,3, where Augustine refers regretfully to his use of the idea in *Soliloquies* I,14,24 and qualifies it as a false opinion.
55. Whereas previously Augustine seemed to have been addressing Porphyry himself, by this point he is certainly no longer doing so; instead he is speaking to anyone who embraces Porphyry's philosophy.
56. Augustine discusses the resurrection body at length below at XXII.

Perhaps you are ashamed to be corrected? This, too, is a fault found only in the proud. It is embarrassing, apparently, for learned men to turn from being disciples of Plato and to become disciples of Christ, who, by his spirit, taught a mere fisherman to understand and to say, *In the beginning was the Word, and the Word was with God, and the Word was God. He was in the beginning with God. All things were made through him, and nothing that was made was made without him. In him was life, and that life was the light of men; and the light shines in the darkness, and the darkness has not comprehended it.* (Jn 1:1-5) This is the beginning of the holy gospel, called *According to John*, and, as I was often told by Simplician, a saintly old man who later became bishop of Milan,[57] a certain Platonist used to say that these words should be inscribed in letters of gold and displayed in the most prominent place in every church. But there is a reason why God, the great teacher, seemed worthless to the eyes of the proud — because *the Word became flesh and dwelt among us* (Jn 1:14). It is not enough, then, that these wretched people are sick. They also have to exult in their illness and feel ashamed of the medicine by which they could be healed. But the result is not that they are raised up but rather that they are afflicted all the more grievously by their fall.

Corrections of Plato

30. If it is considered disrespectful to correct Plato on any point, why did Porphyry himself make a number of by no means insignificant corrections? There is no question, for instance, that Plato wrote that human souls return after death, even entering the bodies of beasts.[58] This was also the view held by Plotinus, Porphyry's teacher.[59] But Porphyry rightly found it unpalatable. Instead, he held that human souls return only to human bodies, although not to those they had previously discarded but rather to new and different bodies. He was ashamed, it seems, to hold Plato's view, for fear that a mother might return to the body of a mule and be ridden by her son. But apparently he was not ashamed to hold a belief in which a mother might return to the body of a girl and marry her own son! How much more honorable it is to believe what the holy and truthful angels taught; what the prophets, inspired by the Spirit of God, declared; what the very one whose coming as savior was foretold by messengers sent in advance also declared; and what the apostles, who were sent forth and who filled the whole world with the gospel, proclaimed! How much more honorable it is, I repeat, to believe that souls return once for all to their own bodies than it is to maintain that they return over and over again to a whole variety of bodies! As I said, however, Porphyry did make a significant correction in this view, at least to the extent that he held that human souls can be sent down only into human bodies and did not hesitate to deny that they are imprisoned in the bodies of beasts.

---

57. Simplician was bishop of Milan from 397 to 400 or 401.
58. See *Phaedo* 81e-82a.
59. See *Enneads* III,4,2.

Porphyry also says that God put the soul into the world so that, having come to recognize the evils of matter, it might return to the Father and never again be held down in the defiling pollution of such things. And here again, even if he has not got things quite right — for the soul was actually put into the body to do good, since it would not learn about evils if it did no evil — he corrects the opinion of other Platonists on a matter of no small importance: he acknowledges that the soul, once cleansed from all evils and established with the Father, is never again going to suffer the evils of this world. In taking this view, he does away with a claim considered especially characteristic of the Platonists — that just as the dead come from the living, so the living always come from the dead.[60]...

Porphyry was quite right to reject this, for, in all truth, it is absurd to believe that in that other life — which could not be completely blessed unless it was completely certain that it would last forever — souls come to desire the taint of corruptible bodies and so turn back from it to them. As if the result of perfect purification were a demand for new defilement! For, if perfect purification causes souls to forget all evils, and if forgetfulness of evils causes them to desire bodies, where they will again be entangled in evils, then supreme happiness will turn out to be the cause of unhappiness, and perfect wisdom the cause of foolishness, and supreme purity the cause of impurity. Nor will the soul truly be happy in a place where, no matter how long it stays, it must be deceived in order to be happy. For it will not be happy unless it feels secure, and in order to feel secure it must believe that it will always be happy. But this belief will be false, since at some point it is going to be miserable again. How, then, can a soul rejoice in truth, when the reason for its rejoicing is false? Porphyry saw this, and for this reason he said that the purified soul returns to the Father precisely so that it may never again be held down in the defiling pollution of evils.... And if that is so, then we have here a Platonist whose position is better than Plato's. We have here a Platonist who saw what Plato failed to see; and even though he came after such a great and distinguished teacher, he did not shrink from correcting him. He put the truth ahead of the man.

The Soul Has not Always Existed

31. With regard to matters which it is not possible for us to search out by human ingenuity, then, why do we not instead believe the divine, which tells us that the soul itself is not coeternal with God but was created and, before that, did not exist? The Platonists were convinced that they had good reason for refusing to believe this; they argued that nothing could exist eternally if it had not always existed. When Plato writes about the world, however, and about the gods whom God made in the world, he expressly states that they had a beginning, that they began to exist, and yet that they will have no end. They will endure for all eternity, he asserts, by the

---

60. See *Phaedo* 70c.

supremely powerful will of their creator.[61] The Platonists, however, have found a way to interpret this point; they claim that Plato did not mean a beginning in time but rather a beginning by way of the dependence of one thing on another....

But if the soul has always existed, are we therefore to say that its misery has also always existed? And if there is something in the soul which has not always existed but began to exist in time, why is it not perfectly possible that the soul itself began to exist in time and, before that, did not exist? Again, there is no doubt, as Porphyry himself admits, that the soul's blessedness — which, after its experience of evils, is more secure and will endure forever — also had a beginning in time; and yet it will exist forever, despite the fact that it once did not exist. Thus the Platonists' entire argument collapses. It presumed that nothing could exist without end in time except what had no beginning in time. But we have found that the soul's blessedness will have no end in time, despite the fact that it does have a beginning in time....

The Universal Way of the Soul's Liberation

32. This is the religion that contains the universal way of the soul's liberation, for no soul can be liberated by any other way.[62] For it is, as it were, the royal road[63] which alone leads to a kingdom that does not totter on a temporal summit but stands fast on an eternal foundation.

When, near the end of the first book of *On the Return of the Soul*, Porphyry says that no view containing a universal way of the soul's liberation has as yet been received into any specific philosophical school — not from any supremely true philosophy, not from the morals and practice of the Indians, not from the initiations of the Chaldeans, nor from any other way — and that no such way has as yet come to his knowledge from his historical inquiries, he acknowledges beyond any doubt that there is such a way, but it has not yet come to his knowledge. Nothing that he had learned from all his diligent study, nothing that he seemed — if not to himself, at least to others — to know and to comprehend, was enough to satisfy him. For he felt that there was still a need for some preeminent authority that it would be right to follow in a matter of this import....

---

61. See *Timaeus* 41a-b.
62. This concluding section appeals repeatedly to the notion of Christianity as the "universal way" (*universalis via*) of salvation. It is noteworthy that Augustine does not mention at some point that Christianity's claim to the catholicity was equivalent to its claim to universality — at least, in the sense that the term "catholic" had acquired by the fourth century, implying exclusive possession of all the means of salvation, as in Cyril of Jerusalem, *Catechesis* 18, 23.
63. In antiquity the royal road (*via regalis*) was generally the shortest and safest way between two locations. See Nm 20:17 and 21:22 for its use in Scripture. For its use as a spiritual term see Jean Leclercq, "La voie royale," in *Supplément de la Vie spirituelle* (Nov. 1948) 338-352.

What, then, does Porphyry want us to understand by this universal way of the soul's liberation? It has not yet been received either from any supremely true philosophy or from the teachings of the peoples held in high regard in the area of supposedly divine matters due to the fact that they were especially inquisitive about knowing and worshiping various types of angels, and it has not yet come to his knowledge from his own historical inquiries. But what is this universal way if not a way that was divinely imparted not as the exclusive property of any one people but as the common property of all peoples?

Porphyry, a man of no ordinary ability, has no doubt that there is such a way. He certainly does not believe that divine providence could have left humanity without such a universal way of the soul's liberation. For he does not tell us that there is no such way; he only says that this great good, this great aid, has not yet been received or has not yet come to his knowledge. And no wonder! For Porphyry lived at a point in human history when this universal way of the soul's liberation, which is nothing other than the Christian religion, was allowed to be attacked by worshipers of idols and demons and by earthly rulers. This was allowed in order to make up and consecrate the number of the martyrs — that is, the witnesses to the truth[64] — through whom we are shown that we should endure all bodily evils for the sake of loyalty to the faith and commending the truth. Porphyry saw what was happening, and he presumed that this way would soon perish due to persecution and, therefore, that it was not the universal way of the soul's liberation. He did not realize that the very persecutions which troubled him, and which he feared he would suffer himself if he chose this way, actually served rather to establish it all the more firmly and to commend it all the more strongly.

This, then, is the universal way of the soul's liberation, that is, the way granted by divine mercy to all peoples. And no people to whom knowledge of this way has come or will come ever had or ever will have good reason to ask, Why now? or Why so late? For the purposes of the one who sends it are impenetrable to human insight. Even Porphyry himself sensed this, when he said that this gift from God had not yet been received and had not yet come to his knowledge. For he did not conclude that, simply because it had not yet been received into his faith or simply because it had not yet come to his knowledge, it was not true.

This, I say, is the universal way of liberation for those who believe. It is the way about which the faithful Abraham received the oracle, *In your seed all peoples will be blessed* (Gen 22:18)....

This is the universal way, of which holy prophecy says, *May God have mercy on us and bless us; may he make his face shine upon us, that we may know your way upon earth, your salvation among all peoples* (Ps 67:1-2). That is why, when he long afterwards assumed flesh from Abraham's seed, the Savior said of himself, *I am the way, the truth, and the life* (Jn 14:6).

---

64. "Martyr" comes from a Greek word meaning "witness."

This is the universal way of which it was prophesied so long before, *In the last days, the mountain of the Lord shall be manifested, made ready on the summit of the mountains, and be raised above the hills; and all peoples shall come to it, and many nations shall enter and say, Come, let us go up to the mountain of the Lord and into the house of the God of Jacob; and he will announce his way to us, and we shall enter into it. For the law shall go forth from Zion, and the word of the Lord from Jerusalem.* (Is 2:2-3) This way, therefore, is not the way of one people but of all peoples universally, and the law and the word of the Lord did not remain in Zion and Jerusalem but went forth to spread itself through all the world. That is why the mediator himself, after his resurrection, said to his trembling disciples, *All that was written about me in the law and the prophets and the Psalms had to be fulfilled. Then he opened their minds to understand the Scriptures, and he said to them that it was necessary for Christ to suffer and to rise from the dead on the third day, and for repentance and forgiveness of sins to be proclaimed in his name to all peoples, beginning from Jerusalem.* (Lk 24:44-47)

This, then, is the universal way of the soul's liberation, which the holy angels and the holy prophets first foretold, where they could, among a few men who found God's grace, and especially among the Hebrew people, whose very republic was in a sense consecrated to serve as a prophecy and a foretelling of the city of God that was to be gathered together from all peoples....

This way cleanses the whole man and prepares mortal man for immortality in all his constituent parts. In fact, it was precisely so that there would be no need to seek out one purification for the part which Porphyry calls intellectual, another for the part which he calls spiritual, and yet another for the body itself, that the most true and powerful purifier and savior assumed the whole man. This way has never been lacking to mankind — for, on the one side, it was foretold that these things would happen and, on the other, it was announced that they had happened — and apart from this way, no one has been delivered, no one is being delivered, and no one will be delivered.

As for Porphyry's claim that the universal way of the soul's liberation had not yet come to his knowledge through his historical inquiries, what history can possibly be found that is more striking than this history, which has taken hold of the entire world by virtue of its towering authority? What history can possibly be found that is more trustworthy than this history, in which events of the past are narrated in such a way that events of the future are also foretold, many of which we already see fulfilled and the rest of which we confidently hope will be fulfilled?...

In these ten books, then, even if less fully than a few people expected of us, we have satisfied the desires of some, so far as the true God and Lord has deigned to give us his help, by refuting the objections of the ungodly, who prefer their own gods to the founder of the holy city which we have undertaken to discuss. Of these ten books, the first five were written against those who suppose that the gods are to be worshiped for the sake of the goods of this life, and the last five against those who hold that the worship of the gods should be maintained for the sake of the life to come after death. Next, as we promised in the first book,[65] I shall set forth, so far as I am aided by God, what I judge should be said about the origin, the course, and the due ends of the two cities, which are, as we have said, deeply interwoven and mixed together in this world.

---

65. See above at I, preface.

Study Questions for Book X

Augustine understands that true happiness is found only in God, who alone promises eternal life. The way to eternal happiness is through love of God and neighbor. Eternal happiness is not a reward or *quid pro quo* for ritual sacrifices made to God. Rather, true worship is devotion of the self to God in love, and true sacrifice is made in daily acts of love of God and neighbor. How might Augustine's understandings of happiness, worship and sacrifice inform a Christian understanding of prayer and sacrament?

The ethos of empire is control: the effective control of peoples through war, subjugation, taxation and law, and the presumed control of gods through civic religion and ritual. Augustine's corrective of empire advocates justice and humility: justice as the foundation for relations among peoples, humility as the only reasonable stance humans can assume before true divinity. How can Augustine's corrective of empire inform contemporary Christian participation in civic debate and political engagement?

Much of ancient religion emphasized human ascent to the divine. Such ascent was assumed in the political divinization of the emperor or practiced in the ascetic mysticism of the philosopher. The majority of humanity did not have access to either. The masses were left to scavenge for bits of divinity among civic rituals or magical arts. Porphyry searched for a universal way to God, open to all. Augustine found that universal way in the descent of God into creation and history through Christ. How does the essential Christian doctrine of the Incarnation continue to offend and scandalize? How are the two movements of ascent and descent felt and practiced among the religions of today?

BOOK XI

Book XI begins Augustine's extended discussion of the origins (Books XI-XIV), the course through time (Books XV-XVIII), and the merited ends (Books XIX-XXII) of the two cities, the heavenly and the earthly. Its specific topic is the initial formation of the two cities at the level of the angels. It deals, then, with the creation of the angels and their separation, due to the fall of some angels, into two groups or companies, the holy angels and the fallen or apostate angels. After brief introductory discussions of the need for the guidance of authoritative Scripture in areas beyond the reach of reason and the compatibility of the act of creation with the immutability of God (the fact that creation took place at a certain point does not involve any change in God), the book takes the form of a complex commentary on the account of creation in Genesis 1. It correlates the creation of the angels with God's creation of light and the separation of the good angels from the evil angels with God's separation of the light from the darkness, stressing the point that the evil angels, and in particular the devil himself, were not created evil and were not evil by nature but rather became evil due to their own self-willed turn away from God and toward themselves, which plunged them into darkness. The reason for creation, which echoes Plato, is that a good God might make good things, and therefore nothing in the created order is either evil by nature (against the Manicheans) or imposed as a form of punishment for sin (against Origen). Evil is rather a function of the will and, far from having any substantial reality in its own right, is simply a privation of good. Along the way, the book addresses a number of related issues — e.g., the form of the angels' knowledge, what constitutes the holy angels' happiness or blessedness, the meaning of the six days of creation and the seventh day, the day of God's rest, and the trinitarian imprint left on creation by the triune God — and, at the end, it considers some alternate interpretations of Genesis 1 in relation to the angels' creation and fall. It is to kindle and encourage inquiry that Scripture allows a variety of interpretations, just so long as none are at odds with the rule of faith.

1. We are speaking of the city of God that is attested by the Scriptures, which have subjected every kind of human genius to themselves, not by virtue of any chance impulse of the soul but by virtue of the disposition of supreme providence, for they surpass all writings of all peoples by their divine authority. In these Scriptures it is written, *Glorious things are spoken of you, city of God* (Ps 87:3). And in another Psalm we read, *Great is the Lord and greatly to be praised in the city* *of our God, in his holy mountain, increasing the rejoicings of all the earth* (Ps 48:1-2); and a little later in the same Psalm, *As we have heard, so also have we seen in the city of the Lord of hosts, in the city of our God; God has established it forever* (Ps 48:8). And again in another Psalm, *A river's flow makes glad the city of God, the Most High has sanctified his tabernacle; God is in the midst of it and shall not be moved* (Ps 46:4-5). From these testimonies and others like them — it would take too long to list them all — we have learned that there is a city of God, and we have longed to become citizens of that city by virtue of the love that its founder has inspired in us.

In contrast, the citizens of the earthly city prefer their own gods to the founder of this holy city. They do not know that he is the God of gods — not of false gods, that is, impious and arrogant gods, who, because they are deprived of his immutable light which is common to all and are therefore reduced to a kind of impoverished power, strive somehow to amass private powers for themselves and seek divine honors from their deluded subjects. He is rather the God of pious and holy gods, who delight in submitting themselves to one rather than having many submit to them and in worshiping God rather than being worshiped in place of God.

In the previous ten books, with the help of our Lord and king, we have responded to the enemies of this holy city as best we could. Now, knowing what is expected of me and not unmindful of my obligation, and relying always on the help of that same Lord and king, I shall begin to discuss, to the best of my ability, the origin, the course, and the merited ends of the two cities, the earthly and the heavenly, which, as we have said, are somehow interwoven and mixed together in the interim of this present age. And first I shall indicate how these two cities took their origins in a prior division among the angels.

2. It is a great and exceedingly rare thing for a person, after he has considered the whole corporeal and incorporeal creation and found it mutable, to go beyond it by sheer concentration of mind and arrive at the immutable substance of God, there to learn from God himself that all nature that is not what God himself is was, in fact, made by none other than God.[1] For in this case God does not speak with a person through any corporeal means, making sounds for bodily ears in such a way that there is a vibration in the airy spaces between the speaker and the hearer, nor does he speak through some spiritual means which is represented by bodily images, as happens in dreams or anything else of that sort (for even in this instance he speaks as though for the ears of the body, due to the fact that he speaks as though through a body and as though across an intervening interval of bodily space, for such visions are very like bodies). Rather he speaks by means of the truth itself, if anyone is capable of hearing him with the mind instead of the

---

1. What Augustine describes here in abstract terms he famously portrays as an actual experience in *Confessions* IX,10,23-25; see also ibid. VII,17,23.

body. For here he speaks to that part of man which is better than everything else of which a man consists and than which only God himself is better.[2]

Faith, the Mediator, and the Authority of Scripture

For, since man is most rightly understood — or, if this is not possible, at least most rightly believed — to be made in the image of God,[3] he undoubtedly stands nearer to God, above him, by virtue of that part of him by which he himself surpasses those lower parts which he has in common with the beasts. But because the mind itself, by nature the seat of reason and intelligence, is enfeebled by dark and inveterate faults and is unable not only to cling to and enjoy but even to endure God's immutable light, until it has been renewed from day to day, and healed, and made capable of such happiness, it had first to be trained and cleansed by faith. And in order that, by faith, the mind might walk more confidently toward the truth, the truth itself, God, the Son of God, having assumed humanity without ceasing to be God, established and founded this same faith, so that man might have a path to man's God through the man who was God. For this is *the mediator between God and man, the man Christ Jesus* (1 Tm 2:5). For it is as man that he is the mediator, and it is as man, too, that he is the way.[4] If there is a way between one who strives and that toward which he strives, there is hope of reaching the goal, but if there is no way, or if the way is not known, what use is it to know the goal?[5] And there is only one way that is fully proof against all errors, in that he is himself both God and man: the goal as God, the way as man.

3. This mediator spoke first through the prophets, then through himself, and later through the apostles, telling us as much as he judged sufficient. He also established the Scriptures which are called canonical. These Scriptures have preeminent authority, and we put our trust in them concerning those matters of which it is not expedient for us to be ignorant but which we are incapable of knowing on our own. For we are able to know, by witnessing them ourselves, things that are not remote from our senses, whether interior or exterior (which is why such things are called "present," since we say that they are "before our senses,"[6] as, for instance, things present to the eyes are "before our eyes"). But, in the case of things that are remote from our senses, since we cannot know them by witnessing them ourselves, we require other witnesses to tell us about them, and we put our faith in those from whose senses we believe that these things are not or were not remote. Thus, in the

---

2. I.e., the mind (*mens*) is better than anything but God himself.
3. See Gn 1:26.
4. See Jn 14:6.
5. Augustine is probably referring to the conclusion of the previous book (X,32), where he discusses Porphyry's failure to discover "the universal way of the soul's liberation," although he has a sense of the goal itself. See likewise *Confessions* VII,20,26-21,27, where the Platonists are said to be able to see the goal but not to know the way.
6. "Present...before our senses": *praesentia...prae sensibus*.

case of visible things that we have not seen ourselves, we put our faith in those who have seen them, and likewise with regard to the other things that pertain to the other bodily senses. And, in just the same way, in the case of things that are perceived by the intellect and the mind (and this is itself quite rightly called a matter of sense, which is why it is designated with the term *sententia*[7])— that is, in the case of invisible things which are remote from our interior sense — it is right for us to put our faith in those who have learned of these things as they are arrayed in that incorporeal light or who behold them as they unfailingly endure in that incorporeal light.

Creation, Time, and the Immutability of God

4. Of all visible things the greatest is the world; of all invisible things the greatest is God. But we *see* that the world exists, while we *believe* that God exists. We believe that God made the world, and we base our belief on no one more safely than on God himself. Where did we hear him say so? Nowhere better, as yet, than in the Holy Scriptures, where his prophet said, *In the beginning God made heaven and earth* (Gn 1:1). Was his prophet there when God made heaven and earth? Of course not, but the wisdom of God, through which all things were made, was there,[8] and this wisdom also transfers itself to holy souls, and makes them friends of God and prophets,[9] and tells them inwardly and soundlessly of God's works. The angels of God also speak to them, the angels *who always see the Father's face* (Mt 18:10) and who announce his will to those for whom it is fitting to know it. One of these was the prophet who said and wrote, *In the beginning God made heaven and earth*. And so worthy was he as a witness through whom we should put our faith in God that, by the same Spirit of God through whom he came to know what was revealed to him on this score, he also foretold, long beforehand, our future faith itself.

But why did the eternal God decide to make heaven and earth just then, when he had not made them before?[10] If the people who ask this question want to make it seem that the world is eternal, without any beginning, and therefore was not created by God, they have gone far astray from the truth and are raving with the deadly disease of impiety. Even if we leave the voices of the prophets entirely aside, the world itself, by its perfectly ordered change and movement and by the supremely beautiful appearance of all things visible, silently proclaims both that it was made and that it could only have been made by God, who is himself inexpressibly and invisibly great and inexpressibly and invisibly beautiful.

---

7. "Sense...*sententia*": *sensus*...thought.
8. See Prv 8:27-30.
9. See Wis 7:27.
10. See Cicero, *On the Nature of the Gods* I,9. The question arises also in *Confessions* XI,10,12.

There are some, in fact, who grant that the world was created by God but want to say that it has no beginning in time, only a beginning in the sense of creation, so that, in some scarcely intelligible way, it was always created.[11] They say this because it seems to them to defend God against the charge of acting on random impulse. They do not want anyone to imagine that it suddenly occurred to God to make the world, when it had never occurred to him before, or that he just happened to have a change of will, when in truth he is not mutable in any way at all....

Let them believe that it was possible for the world to be created in time, but that nevertheless, in making it, God did not in any way change his eternal will and design.

5. Next we must see what reply we should give to those who agree that God is the creator of the world but still ask about when it was created; and we must see, too, what reply they themselves might give to the question of where it was created. For, just as one can ask why it was created at that moment and not earlier, so one can ask why it was created here where it is and not elsewhere. For, if they consider the infinite expanses of time prior to the world, during which it seems to them that God could not possibly have been inactive, let them likewise consider the infinite expanses of space beyond the world. If anyone claims that the Omnipotent could not possibly have been at rest in those expanses of space, will it not follow that they are compelled to join Epicurus in his dream of innumerable worlds? The only difference will be that, while Epicurus asserts that these worlds come into and pass out of existence due to the random motion of atoms,[12] they will be saying that they are made by the work of God. For, if they are unwilling to allow that God is at rest in that interminable immensity of space stretching out in all directions beyond the world, and if they hold that nothing can cause those worlds to be destroyed (just as they hold that nothing can cause this world to be destroyed), the result can only be innumerable worlds.

For we are now dealing with those who agree with us that God is incorporeal and the creator of all natures which are not what he is himself. It would be altogether unworthy to admit others into this dispute about religion, especially because, among those who suppose that religious rites are to be offered to many gods, these philosophers are the ones who have surpassed all others in preeminence and authority, and they have done so precisely because, although certainly far from the truth, they are still closer to it than the rest. They hold a proper conception of God, neither enclosing the divine substance in any place, nor setting any limits to it, nor giving it any extension in space, but rather acknowledging that it is everywhere incorporeally present in its entirety. Are they then going to say that it is absent from the vast expanses of space beyond the world and occupies only the one place where the world is located, which is no more than a tiny place in

---

11. This is the view associated with Greek philosophy in general, and especially with Aristotle. See *Physics* I,7.
12. See Epicurus, *Letter to Herodotus*.

comparison with that infinite expanse of space? My own opinion is that they will not go so far as this kind of empty nonsense.

Since these philosophers claim, therefore, that there is only one world which, although huge in its corporeal mass, is still finite and set within the bounds of its own location, and since they also claim that it was created by the working of God, let them give the same answer to the question of God's resting from work in the infinite expanses of time prior to the world that they give to the question of God's resting from work in the infinite expanses of space beyond the world. And, just as it does not follow that God established the world in the place where it is, and not in some other, by mere chance rather than by divine reason, even though no human reason can possibly comprehend why the divine reason did so, and even though the place chosen had no special merit to set it apart from an infinite number of others that were equally available, neither does it follow that we should suppose that it was a mere matter of chance that God created the world when he did and not earlier, even though earlier times had similarly gone by in the infinite expanses of the past without any differentiation to make the choice of one preferable to the choice of another. But, if they assert that it is inane for human thought to imagine infinite expanses of space, since there is no space outside the world, our reply to them is that it is equally inane for people to conceive of past times when God was at rest, since there is no time prior to the world.

6. For, if eternity and time are rightly distinguished on the ground that time does not exist without some movement and change, while in eternity there is no change at all, who does not see that time would not exist if no creature had been made to bring about change by means of some motion?[13] And who does not see that time is a function of this motion and change, when things that cannot exist simultaneously succeed each other at shorter or longer intervals of delay? Therefore, since God, in whose eternity there is no change whatsoever, is the creator and governor of time, I do not see how it can be said that he created the world after expanses of time, unless it is claimed that, prior to the world, there was already some created being by virtue of whose motions time was able to pass.

Again, if the holy and utterly truthful Scriptures say that *in the beginning God made heaven and earth* precisely to make us understand that nothing whatsoever was made prior to this (for if God had made something prior to everything else that he made, that is what Scripture would have said that he made in the beginning), it is beyond doubt that the world was not made in time but with time. For what happens in time happens both after some time and before some time, after the time that has passed and before the time that is to come. But there could not

---

13. The discussion of time immediately precedes an exegesis of the opening chapters of Genesis, which Augustine had previously interpreted most notably and lengthily in *Confessions* XI-XIII; *On Genesis: A Refutation of the Manicheans*; *An Unfinished Literal Commentary on Genesis*; and *The Literal Meaning of Genesis*.

have been any time that had passed, because there was no created being to provide the change and motion of which time is a function. Thus, if change and movement were created when the world was made, the world was made with time, and this seems to hold good in the very order of the first six or seven days. For both the morning and the evening of these days are enumerated until, on the sixth day, all that God made during those days is completed, and, on the seventh day, God's rest is presented in a great mystery. But what kind of days these are it is extremely difficult, or even impossible to conceive let alone to put into words.

The Days of Creation and the Forms of Knowledge

7. We note, of course, that the days known to us have evenings and mornings only because of the setting and rising of the sun; but those first three days passed without the sun, which was made, we are told, on the fourth day.[14] Scripture narrates that, at the first, light was made by the Word of God, and that God separated the light from the darkness and called the light day and the darkness night.[15] But what kind of light it was, and by what alternating motion it made evening and morning, and what sort of evening and morning these were, are all things far removed from our senses. Nor is it possible for us to understand how it was so, but we must still believe it without the least hesitation. For either this was some corporeal light, whether in the upper parts of the world, far beyond our sight, or from which the sun was later set alight, or else the word *light* was used to signify the holy city, made up of holy angels and blessed spirits, of which the Apostle says, *the Jerusalem above, our eternal mother in heaven* (Gal 4:26), and says again in another place, *For you are all children of light and children of the day; we are not of the night or of darkness* (1 Thes 5:5). But for this latter view to hold good, we must be able to find a somehow appropriate meaning for both the evening and the morning of this day.

Now, in comparison with the creator's knowledge, a creature's knowledge is like the dusk of evening. But when that knowledge is directed to the praise and love of the creator, it becomes the full light of morning, and it never sinks into night as long as the creator is not abandoned out of love for a creature. Thus, when Scripture enumerated those first days in order, it never used the word "night." It nowhere says "night came" but rather *evening came and morning came, one day* (Gn 1:5). And so on for the second day and for the rest. In truth, knowledge of a creature, taken in itself, is more dim and drained of color, so to speak, than when it is known in the wisdom of God, in the art by which it was made....

---

14. See Gn 1:14-19.
15. See Gn 1:3-4.

8. But when God rests from all his works on the seventh day and sanctifies it,[16] we are not to understand this in a childish way, as if God had labored at his work.[17] For *he spoke and they were created* (Pss 33:9; 148:5) by a word which was not audible and temporal but intelligible and eternal. Instead God's rest signifies the rest of those who rest in God,[18] just as the joy of a house signifies the joy of those who are rejoicing in the house....

The Creation of the Angels

9. At present, however, I have undertaken to discuss the origin of the holy city; and I have concluded that I ought first to deal with the topic of the holy angels. They form the greater part of that city, and the more blessed part, since they have never been on pilgrimage in this world. With God's help, then, I shall take pains to explain, as far as seems sufficient, what the divine testimonies tell us on this score.

When Sacred Scripture speaks of the creation of the world, nothing explicit is said about whether, or in what order, the angels were created. But if they were not omitted altogether, they were signified either by the word *heaven*, where Scripture says, *In the beginning God made heaven and earth*, or more probably by the word *light*, the light of which I have been speaking. And I do not think that they were omitted altogether, for it is written that on the seventh day God rested from all the works that he had made, while the book itself opens with the words, *In the beginning God made heaven and earth*, so that God seems to have made nothing prior to heaven and earth. He began, then, with heaven and earth, and the earth itself, as Scripture goes on to say, was invisible and unformed.[19] And, since light had not yet been created, darkness was over the deep[20] — that is, it was over some sort of undifferentiated confusion of earth and water. For where there is no light, of necessity there is darkness. And if all things were then arranged in order by God's work of creation — which, we are told, was completed in six days — how could the angels have been omitted, as if they were not included among the works of God from which he rested on the seventh day?

But if it is not omitted here that the angels are a work of God, neither is it expressly stated. Elsewhere, however, Scripture testifies to this with the greatest clarity. In the hymn of the three men in the furnace, after saying, *Bless the Lord, all you works of the Lord* (Dn 3:57 LXX), they include the angels in their listing of those works. And in a Psalm there is sung, *Praise the Lord from the heavens; praise him in the heights. Praise him, all his angels; praise him, all his hosts.*

---

16. See Gn 2:2-3.
17. This would be the anthropomorphic position.
18. See below at XXII,30.
19. See Gn 1:2.
20. See ibid.

Praise him, sun and moon; praise him, all stars and light. Praise him, you highest heavens, and you waters above the heavens. Let them praise the name of the Lord, for he spoke and they were made, he commanded and they were created. (Ps 148:1-5) Here, too, it is most plainly stated by divine authority that the angels were created by God, for they are listed among the other things of heaven, and with reference to all of those things it says, *He spoke and they were made* (Ps 148:5)....

For when God said, *Let there be light* (Gn 1:3), and light was created, if the creation of the angels is rightly understood to be included in this light, then they were surely created as participants in the eternal light which is itself the immutable wisdom of God, by which all things were made, and which we call the only-begotten Son of God. Thus the angels, illumined by the light that created them, themselves became light and were called *day* by virtue of their participation in the immutable light and day which is the Word of God, by which both they and everything else were created. For *the true light that enlightens everyone coming into this world* (Jn 1:9) also enlightens every pure angel, so that he is light not in himself but in God. If an angel turns away from God, he becomes unclean, as are all those who are called unclean spirits. Deprived of their participation in the eternal light, they are no longer light in the Lord but rather darkness in themselves. For evil has no nature of its own; what we call evil is rather the loss of good.[21]

The Divine Simplicity

10. There is, then, a good which alone is simple and therefore alone is immutable, and this is God. All other goods were created by this good, but they are not simple, and therefore they are mutable. They are, I stress, created; that is, they are made, not begotten. For what is begotten of the simple good is itself equally simple, and it is what its begetter is. We call these two the Father and the Son; and both together, with their Spirit, are one God. And this Spirit, the Spirit of the Father and the Son, is called *holy* in Sacred Scripture in a distinctive meaning of the term.[22]

Now the Spirit is other than the Father and the Son, for it is neither the Father nor the Son. But I said "other," not "something other," because it is equally simple and is equally the immutable and co-eternal good. And this Trinity is one God, and the fact that it is a Trinity does not mean that it is not simple. For we do not call the nature of this good simple on the ground that there is in it only the Father, or only the Son, or only the Holy Spirit, nor do we call it simple on the ground that it is a Trinity in name only, without subsisting persons, as the Sabellian heretics

---

21. Arriving at this understanding of evil, as the deprivation of good, had been central to the lengthy process of Augustine's conversion to Catholic Christianity. See *Confessions* VII,11,17-16,22. Plotinus, *Enneads* III,2,5 was probably influential in establishing Augustine's position.
22. See, e.g., Mt 28:19; Eph 1:13; 1 Thes 4:8.

supposed.[23] It is called simple, rather, because it is what it has, with the exception of what is said of one person in relation to another. For the Father obviously has the Son and yet is not himself the Son, and the Son has the Father and yet is not himself the Father. He is what he has, therefore, with regard to what is said of him in himself, not what is said of him in relation to another. Thus it is in himself that he is said to be living, because he has life, and he himself is that very life.

The reason why a nature is called simple, then, is that it has nothing that it can lose. There is no difference between what it is and what it has, as there is between a vessel and the liquid it contains, or between a body and its color, or between the air and light or heat, or between the soul and its wisdom. None of these is what it has: the vessel is not the liquid, the body is not its color, the air is not the light or the heat, and the soul is not its wisdom. That is why they can be deprived of what they have and can be altered or changed in their characteristics and qualities....

Accordingly, then, it is the things that are originally and truly divine that are called simple, because in them there is no difference between quality and substance, nor are they divine or wise or blessed by virtue of their participation in something else. In Holy Scripture, it is true, the Spirit of wisdom is called manifold because it contains many things in itself,[24] but what it contains it also is, and all of these are one. For wisdom is not many things but one, in which there are infinite, and yet definite, stores of intelligible things, including the invisible and immutable exemplars of even the visible and mutable things created through it. For God made nothing unknowingly (which cannot rightly be said of any human craftsman), and if he made all things knowingly, he certainly made what he knew. From this there comes to mind a startling but nevertheless true observation: this world could not be known to us if it did not already exist, but it could not exist if it were not already known to God.

The Angelic Fall

11. Since all this is so, it is by no means the case that the spirits whom we call angels were at first darkness for any space of time; rather, at the very moment they were made, they were simultaneously made and made light. They were not created in this way, however, simply to exist and to live in any way at all. On the contrary, they were illuminated so that they would live wisely and blessedly. But certain angels turned away from this illumination and did not obtain the excellence of a wise and blessed life, for there is no such life unless it is eternal and is sure and certain of its eternity.[25] These angels do, however, have life with reason, although

---

23. The Sabellians, who believed that God was one person possessing three modes of presentation, are mentioned above at X,24.
24. See Wis 7:22.
25. I.e., inasmuch as true blessedness is eternal and known to be so, the angels who were going to fall could not have been truly blessed. See *The Literal Meaning of Genesis* XI,17,22.

reason without wisdom, and this they cannot lose even if they wish. But who can determine how far they participated in that wisdom before they sinned? And how shall we say that they participated equally in it with those who are truly and fully blessed precisely because they are not in the least mistaken about the eternity of their happiness? For, if they had participated equally in wisdom, they too would have continued in its eternity; they would have been equally blessed, because equally certain of their blessedness. For life, no matter how long it lasts, cannot truly be called eternal life if it is going to have an end; it is termed life simply from being alive, but it is termed eternal life only from having no end. Consequently, although a thing that is eternal is not necessarily blessed (for the penal fire is also said to be eternal[26]), nevertheless, if no life is truly and perfectly happy unless it is eternal, then these angels did not have a genuinely blessed life, for it was going to come to an end, and therefore it was not eternal, whether they knew this or, not knowing it, thought otherwise. If they knew it, it was fear, and if they did not know it, it was error, which kept them from being fully happy. And, even if their ignorance did not mean that they put their trust in falsities or uncertainties but simply that they could reach no firm decision as to whether their good was eternal or was going to come to an end, this very doubt about such a great happiness kept them from having the true fullness of the blessed life which we believe that the holy angels have....

12. Nor are the angels the only ones among rational or intellectual creatures who we think should be called blessed. For who would dare to deny that the first human beings in paradise were blessed before they sinned, even though they had no certainty about how long their blessedness would last or whether it would be eternal (and it would have been eternal if they had not sinned)? In our own day, after all, there is nothing brash about calling blessed those whom we see living this life righteously and piously, with the hope of future immortality, with no guilt weighing down their conscience, and readily obtaining divine mercy for the sins of our human frailty. Even though these people are certain of the reward for their perseverance, they are found to be uncertain of their perseverance itself. For who can know that he will persevere to the end in doing and advancing in righteousness unless he is made certain by some revelation from him who, in his just and hidden judgment, deceives no one but instructs only a few in this regard? So far as delight in present good is concerned, then, the first man in paradise was happier than any righteous man in this condition of mortal weakness. So far as hope for future good is concerned, however, anyone in the worst of bodily torments to whom it has been made clear — not as a matter of opinion but as certain truth — that he will join the company of the angels in participating without end in the supreme God, free from all distress, is happier than the first man who, for all his great happiness in paradise, was uncertain of his destiny.

13. As a consequence, anyone can now see without difficulty that the happiness which an intellectual nature desires when its purpose is rightly directed results

---

26. The eternity of hellfire is the burden of much of Book XXI.

from a conjunction of two factors, namely, that it enjoys the immutable good which is God, free from any distress, and that it is certain that it is going to continue in that good for all eternity without being plagued by any doubt or deceived by any error. With devout faith we believe that the angels of light have this happiness. And by force of reason we gather that the sinful angels, who were deprived of that light due to their own depravity, did not have this happiness even before they fell. But, if they lived for any time at all before they sinned, we must certainly believe that they had some form of happiness, even if without foreknowledge of their future....

The Case of the Devil

But perhaps someone will cite what the Lord said of the devil in the Gospel — *He was a murderer from the beginning and did not stand in the truth* (Jn 8:44)— and will claim that we should take this to mean not merely that he was a murderer from the beginning, that is, from the beginning of the human race, from the moment when man was created, whom he was able to kill by deceiving him, but also that he did not stand in the truth from the very moment of his own creation and therefore was never blessed with the holy angels. Instead, he refused to be subject to his creator, and, due to his pride, he rejoiced in his power as if it were his own private possession. As a result, he was both deceived and deceiving. For no one evades the power of the Almighty, and anyone who refuses to hold fast in devout submission to what truly is seeks, in his self-exalting pride, to simulate what is not. And the blessed apostle John can also be understood in this sense where he says, *The devil sins from the beginning* (1 Jn 3:8), that is, from the moment he was created he refused righteousness, which no will can have unless it is devout and subject to God.

To accept this view is not to agree with the Manichean heretics — or any other baneful sects that think as they do — that the devil has some sort of evil nature of his own, drawn, as it were, from some opposing principle. The Manicheans are so caught up in folly that they pay no attention to what the Lord actually said, even though, like us, they recognize the authority of the words of the Gospel. The Lord did not say, "The devil was alien to the truth," but rather, *He did not stand in the truth*. By this he wanted us to understand that the devil had fallen away from the truth. If he had continued to stand in the truth, he would have been made a participant in the truth and would have remained blessed with the holy angels....

15. ... He began, therefore, as the Lord's handiwork. For there is no nature, even among the least and the lowest of the smallest animals, that was not constituted by God, from whom comes all measure, all form, and all order, and nothing can be found or conceived that lacks these. How much more, then, is this true of the angelic creation, which surpasses all God's other works in the dignity of its nature!

16. For among the things which exist in some mode, and which are other than God, who made them, those that have life are ranked above those that do not have life — those which have the power of reproduction or even of appetition, for example, above those that lack this impulse.[27] And among living things, the sentient rank above those that lack sensation — animals, for example, above trees. And among the sentient, those with intelligence rank above those lacking intelligence — human beings, for example, above cattle. And among those with intelligence, the immortal are ranked above the mortal — angels, for example, above human beings. But these are rankings based on the order of nature. There are, however, other evaluations based on the use to which things are put; and on this basis it often happens that we rank some things that lack sensation above some that have sensation — so much so, in fact, that, if we had the power, we would gladly remove these sentient things entirely from the natural order, either because we are unaware of the place they hold in that order or because, even though we are aware of their place in nature, we still put our own convenience first. For who would not prefer to have food in his house rather than mice, or money rather than fleas? But there is nothing surprising about this. Even in evaluating human beings themselves, whose nature certainly ranks high for its dignity, a horse is often worth more than a slave, or a jewel more than a maidservant.

So far as judging freely is concerned, then, the reasoning of a thoughtful person is far different from the poverty of a needy person or the pleasure of a person animated by desire. Reason weighs things as they are in their own right, according to the grades of the natural order, while poverty considers only what will serve its own need. Reason looks for what appears true to the light of the mind, while pleasure looks only for what gratifies the senses of the body. In the case of rational natures, however, will and love carry so much weight that, even though angels rank above human beings according to the order of nature, good human beings rank above evil angels according to the law of righteousness.

17. Rightly understood, then, *This is the beginning of the Lord's handiwork* refers not to the devil's malice but to his nature. For there can be no doubt that, where the vice of malice occurs, there was first a nature without vice. Vice is so contrary to nature that it can only do harm to nature. To withdraw from God would not be a vice, then, unless being with God was what actually accorded with the nature whose vice this is. Even an evil will, therefore, is strong proof of a good nature. But just as God is supremely good in his creating of good natures, so he is supremely just in his regulating of evil wills. And so, while evil wills make evil use of good natures, God makes good use even of evil wills. Thus he caused the devil, who was good by God's institution but evil by his own will, to be relegated to the lower depths and to be mocked by his angels; that is, God caused the temptations of the

---

27. See *Teaching Christianity* I,8,8 for another instance of an ascending order from non-sentient to immortal beings.

devil to work to the benefit of his saints, even though the devil's own desire was to do them harm. When God created the devil, then, he was by no means unaware of the devil's future maliciousness, and he foresaw the good that he himself was going to bring out of the devil's evil. That is why the Psalm says, *Here is the dragon whom you made to be mocked in it.* The point is to let it be understood that from the very moment when God created the devil — even though, in his goodness, he created him good — he had already, in his foreknowledge, planned out how he would make use of the devil even as evil....

The Separation of the Holy Angels from the Fallen Angels

19. The obscurity of the divine discourse actually serves the useful purpose of giving birth to many views of the truth and bringing them into the light of knowledge, one person understanding the divine words in this way and another in that.[28] At the same time, however, any interpretation of an obscure passage should be confirmed either by the plain evidence of the facts or by other passages which are not open to doubt.[29] In this way, by examining many views, either we shall arrive at the meaning of the author himself or, if that remains hidden, the examination of a profoundly obscure passage will at least provide the occasion for voicing some other truths. Now, it does not seem to me to be absurdly out of keeping with the works of God to hold that, if we understand the angels to have been created when that first light was made, then the separation of the holy and the unclean angels took place where Scripture says, *And God separated the light from the darkness, and God called the light day, and the darkness he called night* (Gn 1:4-5). Only God, of course, could have made this separation, for only he could also foreknow, even before it happened, that some angels were going to fall and, deprived of the light of truth, were going to remain in the darkness of pride....

The Goodness of God and the Goodness of Creation

21. For how else are we to understand the statement that is repeated throughout — *And God saw that it was good* (Gen 1:4.10.12.18.21.25) — except as approval of a work made according to the design which is the Wisdom of God?[30] It is not that God only learned that his work was good after it was made. On the contrary, nothing he made would have been made if it had not first been known to him. Thus, when God "sees" that a thing is good — and, if he had not seen this before

---

28. On the possibility that a given passage of Scripture could legitimately be interpreted in various ways see *Confessions* XII,24,33-32,43. See also below at XI,32.
29. On explaining more obscure passages of Scripture by way of less obscure passages see *Teaching Christianity* II,9,14.
30. Christ is the Wisdom of God. See 1 Cor 1:24. Later in this section the design (*ars*) is more explicitly identified with Christ, the Word.

it was made, it would never have been made at all — he is plainly teaching us, not learning for himself, that it is good. Plato even dared to go so far as to say that, when the whole world was completed, God was elated with joy.[31] But Plato was by no means so foolish here as to suppose that God was made happier by the novelty of his work; he simply wanted to indicate that the work which had already pleased the artist in the design for making it also pleased him now that it was made. It is not that God's knowledge varies in any way. Future things do not bear on it in one way, present things in another, and past things in yet another. Unlike us, God does not look forward to the future, look straight at the present, and look back to the past. Rather he sees things in some other way, vastly and profoundly different from our customary manner of thought. He does not see by shifting his attention from one thing to another; rather, he immutably sees all things at once. Things which happen in time are either future (not yet in being), or present (now in being), or past (no longer in being), but God apprehends all of these in a stable and eternal present. Nor does he see in one way with the eyes and in another with the mind, for he does not consist of mind and body. Nor does he see in one way now, another way earlier, and another way later. For his knowledge is not like ours; it is not altered by the variation of the three tenses, namely, the past, the present, and the future. *With him*, instead, *there is no variation or shadow of movement* (Jas 1:17).

Nor does God's attention pass from thought to thought; rather, everything that he knows is simultaneously present to his incorporeal gaze. For, just as he moves temporal things without any temporal motions of his own, so he knows the sequence of times without any temporal notions of his own. Thus, the point at which he saw that what he had made was good was the same point at which he saw that it was good to make it. And the fact that he saw it after it was made did not double his knowledge or increase it in any way, as if his knowledge of it had been any less before he made it than it was when he saw it. In fact, he would not have made his works so perfectly if his knowledge had not been so perfect that nothing could be added to it from the works that he made....

There are three points that we especially ought to know about anything created, and it was proper for all three to be imparted to us: who made it, the means by which he made it, and why he made it. Thus Scripture says, *God said, Let there be light, and light was made. And God saw that it was good.* If, therefore, we ask who made it, the answer is "God." If we ask by what means he made it, the answer is that God said, "Let it be," and it was made. And if we ask why he made it, the answer is "Because it was good."

No maker is more excellent than God, no design is more efficacious than God's Word,[32] and no reason why is better than that something good should be created

---

31. See *Timaeus* 37d.
32. "No design is more efficacious than God's Word": *nec ars efficacior Dei Verbo*. One might have expected *nec ars efficacior illa Dei Verbi* ("No design is more efficacious than that of God's Word"), or *nec artifex efficacior Dei Verbo* ("No designer is more efficacious than God's Word").

by a good God. Plato also gives this as the most supremely just reason for creating the world — that good works might be made by a good God.[33] Plato may have read this passage of Scripture;[34] or he may have come to know of it from those who had read it; or, with his acute insight, he may have understood and seen the invisible things of God through the things that God made;[35] or he may himself have learned of them from those who had seen them.

22. When this reason, which is so very just and apt — namely, that the goodness of God should create good things — is carefully considered and devoutly weighed, it puts an end to all controversies on the part of those who inquire about the origin of the world. Certain heretics, however, have not been willing to accept this reason.[36] In their view, there are too many things — such as fire, cold, wild beasts, and the like — which are unsuited to the needy and frail mortality of this flesh (which itself stems from just punishment), and which actually do it harm. These heretics do not notice how flourishing such things are in their rightful places and in their own natures, or with what ordered beauty they are arranged, or how much they contribute, each according to its own share of beauty, to the whole scheme of things, as if to the common wellbeing of all, or how much they actually work to our own benefit, if only we make appropriate and intelligent use of them.[37] Even poisons, which are fatal when used wrongly, are turned into healing medicines when properly employed; and, on the other hand, even things that give us delight, such as food and drink and sunlight, are seen to be harmful when immoderately or improperly used. In this way, divine providence warns us not to blame things without thought but rather to inquire diligently into their usefulness. And when our insight or our weakness fails us, we should believe that their usefulness is simply obscure, as were various other things that we have barely been able to discover. The very fact that a thing's usefulness is hard to find, in fact, serves us either as an exercise in humility or as an antidote to pride. For there is no nature whatsoever that is evil; in fact, "evil" is nothing but a term for the privation of good.

Across the range from earthly things to heavenly ones, however, and from visible things to invisible ones, some good things are better than others, and it is precisely their inequality that makes it possible for them all to exist. Besides, God is a great artificer in great things; but this does not mean that he is any less so in small things. Such small things are not to be measured by their grandeur, for they have none, but rather by the wisdom of their maker. Think, for instance, of a person's visible appearance. If one eyebrow is shaved off, how very little it

---

33. See Timaeus 28a
34. On Plato's supposed familiarity with Scripture, or with its authors, see above at VIII,11.
35. See Rom 1:20.
36. These heretics are the Manicheans, who believed that evil had its own creator.
37. On the harmony of creation, which is not always evident to the observer because it includes what appears to be bad in addition to what is good, see below at XII,4 and XIX,12; *Order* I,1,2; *Free Will* III,9,25-28.

takes away from the body, and how very much it takes away from its beauty! For beauty is not a matter of size but of the symmetry and proportion of the parts.[38]...

23. It should come as far more of a surprise, however, that, even among those who believe with us that there is one first principle of all things and that no nature which is not what God is can exist unless it is created by him, there are some who were unwilling to accept with good and simple faith such a good and simple reason for creating the world — that the good God might create good things, and that there might be, below God, things that are not what God is but are still good, and are things that only a good God would create. Instead, they claim that souls — although certainly not parts of God but rather created by God — sinned by withdrawing from their creator and, having fallen in various degrees, according to their various sins, from heaven all the way down to earth, merited various bodies as their penal shackles. The result, they assert, is this world, and the reason for making this world was not that good things might be created but rather that evil things might be kept under constraint.

Origen is rightly faulted on this score. For this is precisely the view that he took and presented in the work which he calls *Peri Archon*, that is, *On First Principles*.[39] And I am more surprised than I can say that such a learned and practiced interpreter of the Church's writings failed to observe, first of all, how opposed this view is to the meaning of the highly authoritative scriptural account which, after each of God's works, adds, *And God saw that it was good*, and, after all of his works were complete, says, *And God saw everything that he had made, and indeed it was very good* (Gn 1:31). Here we are clearly meant to understand that there was no other reason for creating the world than that good things might be made by a good God. If no one in this world had sinned, the world would have been adorned and filled only with natures that are good. And the fact that sin did occur does not mean that, as a result, all things are full of sin, for by far the greater number of the good among the celestial beings preserve the order of their nature. And the evil will that refused to preserve the order of its nature did not, by its refusal, escape the laws of the just God who orders all things well. For, just like a painting, when it has dark colors in their proper places, so the entire universe — if anyone could see it whole — is beautiful even when it has sinners, despite the fact that, when sinners are considered in themselves, their ugliness is repulsive.

---

38. On the role of proportion (*dimensio*) in bodily beauty see also below at XXII,19 (where the relevant term is *congruentia*).
39. See *On First Principles* I,4,1. For a discussion of this problematic doctrine see Henri Crouzel *Origen*, trans. by A. S. Worrall (San Francisco: Harper and Row, 1989) 205-218. Origen (c.185-c.154) was one of the most seminal and influential theologians of the ancient Church and was known to Augustine both by reputation and by exposure to some of the writings of his that had been translated from Greek into Latin by Rufinus and Jerome. For Origen's impact on Augustine see Allan D. Fitzgerald, ed., *Augustine through the Ages: An Encyclopedia* (Grand Rapids: Eerdmans, 1999) 603-607. He is cited again at XXI,17.

Further, Origen and all who hold his views ought to have seen that, if their opinion were true and the world was in fact made so that souls would receive bodies, like prisons in which they are jailed as punishment, each according to the merits of its sin, with higher and lighter bodies for those who sinned less and lower and heavier bodies for those who sinned more, then it is the demons who ought to have earthly bodies rather than men, and least of all good men. For nothing is worse than the demons, and no bodies are lower and heavier than earthly bodies. As it is, however, so that we may recognize that the merits of souls are not to be measured by the qualities of their bodies, the worst demon was given an aerial body, while human beings — despite the fact that their evil, even now, is far less and far milder than the malice of the demons, and was certainly so before they sinned — were given bodies of clay.[40]...

Thus, when the three questions which I suggested above — Who made it? By what means did he make it? Why did he make it?[41] — are asked with regard to any creature, the answers are: God made it, by means of his Word, because it is good. Whether what we have here is a profound and mystic intimation to us of the Trinity itself, that is, of the Father, the Son, and the Holy Spirit, or whether some consideration might arise to prevent us from taking this passage of Scripture in this sense, is a question for extended discussion. But we should not be expected to explain everything in one volume.

Traces of the Trinity in Creation

24. [42] We believe, hold, and faithfully proclaim[43] that the Father begot the Word, that is, the Wisdom by which all things were made, his only-begotten Son, the one begetting the one, the eternal the coeternal, the supremely good the equally good; and that the Holy Spirit is at once the Spirit of the Father and of the Son, himself consubstantial and coeternal with both; and that this whole is both a Trinity due to the distinctive properties of the persons and one God due to their inseparable divinity, just as it is one omnipotent God due to their inseparable omnipotence. This is so, however, in such a way that, even when the question has to do with each individually, the answer must be that each of them is God and each of them is omnipotent, but, when the question has to do with all three at once, there are not three gods or three omnipotents but rather one God omnipotent.[44] That is how

---

40. See Gn 2:7.
41. See above at XI,21.
42. Chapters 24 and 26 correspond roughly to the division of *The Trinity*, which in its first half treats of the Trinity more from a doctrinal perspective and in its second half more from the perspective of discovering the image of the Trinity in the human person.
43. A solemn trinity of verbs precedes Augustine's brief exposition of the Trinity, which contains a number of triads (e.g., origin, enlightenment, felicity).
44. See *The Trinity* V,8,9.

great the inseparable unity is in the three, and that is how it wishes to have itself proclaimed....

Here, then, is the origin, the enlightenment, and the felicity of the holy city which is above, in the holy angels. For if we ask, How does it come to be? God founded it. If we ask, How does it come to be wise? it is illumined by God. If we ask, How does it come to be happy? it enjoys God. It is defined by subsisting in God; it is illumined by contemplating God; it is made joyful by clinging to God. It is, it sees, it loves. It finds its strength in God's eternity, its light in God's truth, its joy in God's goodness.

25. So far as it is given to me to understand the matter, it was on this account that the philosophers wanted their discipline to have three parts, or rather were able to discern that it has three parts, for they did not institute this division but simply discovered that it was already there. Of these, one part is called physical, another logical, and the third ethical. The Latin terms for these are now commonly used in the writings of many authors, so that they are called natural, rational, and moral philosophy respectively, and I touched briefly on these in the eighth book.[45] It does not follow, of course, that in making this three-part division these philosophers had any notion of a Trinity corresponding to God. It is true, however, that Plato is said to have been the first to discover and recommend this scheme, and to him it seemed that there is no other maker of all natures than God, no other giver of understanding, and no other inspirer of the love required for the good and happy life....

26. And, in fact, we even recognize in ourselves an image of God, that is, the supreme Trinity. It is not equal to God but rather falls far short of him. Nor is it coeternal with God; nor, to put the whole matter briefly, is it of the same substance as God. There is nothing else, however, among all the things made by God, that is closer to him by nature, even though it still needs to be reformed and perfected in order to be nearest to him in likeness as well. For we exist, and we know that we exist, and we love both this existence and this knowledge. Moreover, with respect to these three points, there is no need to worry about mistaking falsehood for truth. For our contact with these things does not come by means of any bodily sense, as it does in the case of external objects. We perceive colors, for instance, by seeing, sounds by hearing, odors by smelling, flavors by tasting, and hard and soft objects by touching. We also have images of all these sensible objects, images which are very similar to them except that they are not themselves corporeal, and it is these images that we consider in thought, that we retain in memory, and that stir our desire for the objects themselves. There is, however, no deceptive representation of images or phantasms involved in my complete certainty that I exist, and that I know I exist, and that I love my existence.

---

45. See above at VIII,4.

So far as these truths are concerned, I have no fear whatsoever of the arguments of the Academics when they ask, "What if you are mistaken?" For if I am mistaken, I exist.[46] For someone who does not exist certainly cannot be mistaken; and so, if I am mistaken, I exist. And since, if I am mistaken, it follows that I exist, how can I possibly be mistaken in supposing that I exist when it is certain that, if I am mistaken, I exist? Even if I were mistaken, therefore, I would have to exist in order to be mistaken; and so there is no doubt that I am not mistaken in knowing that I exist. And it follows that I also am not mistaken in knowing that I know. For just as I know that I exist, so also I know that I know it. And when I love these two things, I add this same love — as a third thing of no lesser value than the first two — to the things that I know. For, when I am not mistaken about the things that I love, I am not mistaken that I love; and, in fact, even if those things were false, it would still be true that I love false things....

27. In fact, by a kind of natural instinct, simply to exist is such a source of pleasure that, for this very reason, even those who are miserable do not want to die; and, when they perceive that they are miserable, it is not themselves but rather their misery that they want taken out of the world.[47]... For why do they fear to die and prefer to live in distress rather than end all distress by dying, except that this shows clearly enough how nature recoils from nonexistence? And this is also why, when they know they are going to die, they desire this mercy for themselves, as a great boon — to live a little longer in their misery and to die a little later. Beyond doubt, then, they show us just how gratefully they would accept even an immortality which put no end to their destitution.

What? Do not even the irrational animals, to whom it is not given to think about these things, from the largest dragons down to the tiniest worms, all show that they want to exist and, on this account, try to avoid death with every movement they can make? What? Do not the very trees and shrubs, which have no sensation to prompt them to avoid death by visible movements, sink roots deep into the ground to draw in nourishment so that they can put out healthy top-shoots into the air and thus, in their fashion, preserve their existence? Finally, even mere physical objects, which lack not only sensation but even any sort of reproductive life, still either spring up above or sink down below or remain balanced in between in order to maintain their being at the level where, according to their nature, they are able to exist....

28. But we have said enough — at least as far as the scheme of this work seemed to require — about these two things, namely, existence and knowledge, and about

---

46. See *Free Will* II,3,7; *The Trinity* XV,12,21.
47. Augustine's comments here and in what follows on the absolute desire to remain in existence rather than to end one's life, however miserable it may be, are somewhat balanced below at XIX,4, where he concedes the attractiveness of suicide in certain circumstances, although without condoning it.

how much they are loved in us, and how some likeness of them (even if different) is found even in the things that are below us. Nothing, however, has been said about the love with which they are loved, and specifically about whether this love is itself loved. But it is loved, and here is the proof: when persons are more rightly loved, that love is loved all the more. For it is not the person who merely *knows* the good that is justifiably called good; it is rather the person who *loves* the good. Why, then, do we not see that we also love in ourselves the very love by which we love whatever good we love? For there is also the love by which we love what ought not to be loved, and anyone who loves the love by which he loves what ought to be loved hates this other love in himself. Both loves can be present in the same person, and it is good for a person that the love by which we live evilly should lose strength, while the love by which we live well gains strength, until all of our life is perfectly healed and transformed into good....

We are, however, human beings, created in the image of our creator,[48] whose eternity is true, whose truth is eternal, whose love is eternal and true, and who is himself the eternal, true, and beloved Trinity,[49] in whom there is neither confusion nor separation. And the things that are below us would not exist at all, nor would they be shaped by any form, nor would they seek or hold to any order, if they had not been made by him who supremely is, who is supremely wise, and who is supremely good.[50] As we run through all the things that he made in such marvelous stability, then, let us gather up the traces of himself that he left more deeply impressed in some places, less deeply in others. And in contemplating his image in ourselves, let us, like the younger son in the Gospel, come to ourselves and get up and return to the one from whom we departed by sinning.[51] There our existence will have no death, there our knowledge will have no error, there our love will have no obstacle

The Holy Angels and Their Knowledge

29. The holy angels, of course, do not learn to know God through the sound of spoken words but through the very presence of immutable Truth itself, that is, his only-begotten Word. They know this Word himself, and the Father, and their Holy Spirit; and they know that this Trinity is inseparable and that each of the persons in it is a substantial being, yet that they are not three gods but one God; and they know all this in such a way that it is better known to them than we are to ourselves. They also know every creature better there — that is, in God's wisdom,

---

48. See Gn 1:26.
49. For the identical triad see below at XII,1. God is addressed as eternal truth, true love, and beloved eternity in *Confessions* VII,10,16.
50. Note the created trinity of existence, form and order that corresponds to the uncreated Trinity of existence, wisdom and goodness.
51. See Lk 15:17-20.

as in the very design by which it was made — than they know it in itself; and so they know even themselves better there than they do in themselves, although, of course, they also know themselves in themselves. For they were made, and they are other than the one who made them. In him, therefore, they have a kind of daylight knowledge, while in themselves they have a kind of twilight knowledge, as I said previously.[52]

For there is a great difference between knowing something in the exemplar according to which it was made and knowing it in itself. A straight line, for instance, or a geometrical figure is known in one way when we see it with the mind and in another when we draw it in the dust; and justice, too, is known in one way in the immutable truth and in another in the soul of a just person. And so it is with all other things, such as the firmament between the waters above and the waters below, which is called heaven; such as the gathering together of the waters below, and the baring of the earth, and the bringing forth of plants and trees; such as the establishing of the sun, the moon, and the stars; such as the bringing forth of the animals from the waters, the birds and the fish, and the monsters that swim; and the bringing forth of the animals, too, that walk or creep upon the earth, including man himself, who excels everything else on earth. All these are known by the angels in one way in the Word of God where they have their causes and their reasons, that is, the causes and reasons according to which they were made, enduring and unchanging, and in another way in themselves. In the former, their knowledge is more clear, in the latter more obscure, just as the knowledge of the design is more clear than knowledge of the works produced from the design. But, even so, when these works are referred to the praise and veneration of the creator himself, it is like the coming of full morning light in the minds of those who contemplate them....

31. ...The holy angels, for whose society and company we yearn during this most laborious pilgrimage, have complete facility of knowledge and felicity of rest, just as they have eternity of abiding with God. And it is without difficulty that they help us, for there is no labor involved in their free, pure, and spiritual movements.

Alternative Views of the Creation of the Angels

32. Perhaps, however, someone will dispute our view and claim that, in fact, there is no reference to the holy angels where Scripture says, *Let there be light, and light was made.* He may believe or teach that it was rather some corporeal light that was first made then but that the angels were created at some prior point not only before the firmament was created between the waters above and below and

---

52. See above at XI,7.

called heaven but even before the moment of which it is said, *In the beginning God made heaven and earth....*

Let each interpret this passage as he likes, for it is so profound that, to stimulate the reader's mind, it can give rise to many different opinions which are not in conflict with the rule of faith,[53] provided only that no one has any doubt that the holy angels in their sublime abodes, although by no means coeternal with God, are nevertheless fully assured and completely certain of their true and eternal happiness....

33. ... For this reason, even if some other light is to be understood in the passage of Genesis where we read, *God said, Let there be light, and light was made,* and even if some other darkness is signified in the passage where it is written, *And God separated the light from the darkness* (Gn 1:4), we still hold that these two companies of angels are represented here[54] — one enjoying God, the other swollen with pride; one to whom it is said, *Adore him, all his angels* (Ps 148:2), the other whose prince says, *All these I shall give you if you fall down and adore me* (Mt 4:9); one burning with holy love for God, the other smoldering with unclean love for its own exaltation....

Here, then, are the two disparate and opposed companies of angels, the one both good by nature and righteous by will, the other good by nature but perverse by will.

While the two are declared by other more explicit testimonies from Divine Scripture, I am convinced that they are also signified in this book, called Genesis, by the words *light* and *darkness*. And, even if the author actually had some other sense in mind in this passage, it has not been without use for us to consider the obscurities of this view. For, even if we have failed to discover the real intention of the author of this book, we still have said nothing inconsistent with the rule of faith, which is known quite well enough to the faithful from other sacred writings of the same authority....

Conclusion

34. ...But, if we were thoroughly to examine and discuss every detail given in this divine book on the creation of the world, we would not only have to say a great deal more but would also have to digress at length from the purpose for which I undertook this work. And, since I have now said enough, as it seems to me, about these two divergent and mutually opposed companies of angels — in which we also see, in a way, the beginnings of the two human cities that I intend to discuss next — let us at last bring this book to a close.

---

53. On "the rule of faith" (*regula fidei*), also referred to as "the fixed rule," see above at X,23.
54. The words that follow anticipate the more famous delineation of the two cities below at XIV,28.

Study Questions for Book XI

In Augustine's account, the mystery of will emerges at the very origin of creation, in the eternal divine decision to share infinite goodness. Will is also at the origin of the two cities as they emerge in the angelic response to that goodness: either loving acceptance or selfish rejection. No other ancient philosopher put as much emphasis on will as Augustine. How potent or important a category is will in contemporary political, psychological or philosophical analyses?

Augustine consistently affirms that faith and reason are the two reliable guides in the search for truth. Reason has built-in limits. Our scientific knowledge, for example, is limited by the paradigms and models that articulate our present laws and theories. Reason is even more fundamentally limited by language: words both express and foreclose meaning, and share the limitations of the culture, history and human perspective within which they arise. The volitional dimension of faith distinguishes it from reason. However, faith also is expressed in language. Hence, the importance of Sacred Scripture which gives us inspired language with which to express and exercise faith. How does Augustine negotiate the use of faith and reason in his interpretation of Sacred Scripture?

Scripture is our daily bread: it satisfies our spiritual hunger. To derive nourishment from Scripture, however, requires that we "chew" on it, turning it over in our minds, slowly digesting it, savoring its many and varied flavors, discerning layers of meaning and considering alternative interpretations. In Book XI and subsequent books of *The City of God*, and throughout his writings and preaching, Augustine models this approach to Scripture. Yet he also insists on the rule of faith for the interpretation of Sacred Scripture. What is that rule?

BOOK XII

Book XII first continues Augustine's discussion of the angels, locating the distinction between the good and the evil angels not in any difference in their natures but in the fault of the evil angels, namely, their evil will. More specifically, it insists that, while an evil will is the efficient cause of an evil act, there is no efficient cause of an evil will, for the evil will itself is not an effect but rather a defect, a defection from God on the part of the will itself. Thus, the first evil will cannot be explained by reference to any other force or factor, whether internal or external, but only in terms of its own turn away from God in pride. This turn is possible because the angels, as beings created out of nothing, are mutable and thus capable of change, but it is not explained or caused by their mutability. It is a function only of their own defection from God and toward a lesser form of good, as if this lesser good were the supreme good (which is not a fault on the part of the lesser good but rather on the part of the agent who accords it a higher value than it actually has). The book then turns to the origin of humankind, arguing for the biblical chronology over against alternate chronologies and especially against theories of repeated world cycles. The latter are not required in order to make the creation of man at a certain point of time compatible with the unchanging eternity of God. Nor are they required to reduce the immense sequence of temporal events and bring it within the scope of the divine knowledge, for God's knowledge encompasses the infinite (e.g., an infinite number series) and thus does not need a finite sequence of temporal events that is repeated over and over again through time. Instead, it can take in the full course of events from the world's beginning to its end, even if the course of events extends to infinity. Furthermore, and most decisively, the theory of repeated world cycles is refuted by the saints' attainment of ultimate and unending happiness, a new event that occurs in time and is never repeated. It is never repeated because, once attained, the saints' happiness is never lost. A muted but crucial theme of the book emerges in its final sections. This theme underscores the social character of humankind, rooted in God's creation of humanity from a single individual and expressed in the bond of kinship that ought to unite all human beings in concord.

1. Before I go on to talk about the creation of mankind, where the origin of the two cities will appear at the level of the race of rational mortals,[1] just as it

---

1. By "rational mortals" Augustine of course means human beings, as he also does in *Order*

was seen at the level of the angels in the previous book, I see that I must first say something more about the angels themselves in order to show, as best I can, that there is nothing inappropriate or incongruous in speaking of a society that includes both human beings and angels. My aim is to indicate that we are justified in speaking not of four cities or societies — that is, two of angels and two more of human beings — but rather of two, one consisting of the good, the other of the evil, and each including not only angels but also human beings.

The Difference between the Good and the Evil Angels: not Nature but Fault

It is illegitimate to doubt that the contrary urges of the good and bad angels arose not from any difference in nature or originating principle — for God, the good author and creator of all substances, created them both — but rather from a difference of will and desire. For some remained constant in the good that is common to all — which, for them, is God himself — and in his eternity, truth, and love.[2] Others, however, took delight in their own power, as if they were themselves their own good, and these fell away from the higher good that is common to all, the good which makes blessed, and turned instead to private ends of their own. They exchanged the heights of eternity for the self-exaltation of pride, the certainty of truth for the cunning of folly, and the oneness of love for the zeal of partisanship, and so they became arrogant, deceitful, and invidious.

The cause of happiness for the good angels, therefore, is clinging to God,[3] and so the cause of misery for the evil angels must be understood as the opposite, which is not clinging to God. Consequently, if the right answer to the question as to why the good angels are happy is that they cling to God, and if the right answer to the question as to why the evil angels are in misery is that they do not cling to God, it follows that there is no other good that brings happiness for a rational or intellectual creature but God. Thus, although not every creature is capable of being happy (for beasts, trees, stones, and the like do not attain or acquire this gift), those creatures which are capable of happiness cannot attain happiness on their own, since they were created out of nothing, but only from the one by whom they were created. For it is by attaining him that they are happy and by losing him that they are in misery. But he whose happiness comes not from another good, but from the goodness that he himself is, cannot be in misery, for he cannot lose what is his very self.

We assert, therefore, that there is no immutable good except for the one, true and blessed God. The things that he made are most certainly good, because they

---

II,11,31 and *The Magnitude of the Soul* 25,47. Aristotle, *Nicomachean Ethics* I,13, is the most apt source of the expression, although the text there does not include the notion of mortality.

2. The triad of eternity, truth and love (*aeternitate veritate caritate*) here repeats the same triad above at XI,28.
3. See Ps 73:28.

were made by him, but they are mutable, because they were made not out of him but out of nothing. Accordingly, although they are not the highest goods, since God is a greater good than they are, these mutable goods are still great goods which can, to be happy, cling to the immutable good; and the immutable good is so very much their good that, without it, they are necessarily in misery....

2. I make this point in order to keep anyone from thinking it possible, when we speak of apostate angels, that they received a different nature, as though from a different originating principle, or that God was not the author of their nature. There is no faster or easier way to avoid the great impiety of this error than to understand as fully as possible what God said through the angel when he sent Moses to the children of Israel, *I am who am* (Ex 3:14).

For, since God is the supreme being — that is, he supremely *is* and is therefore immutable — he gave being to the things he created out of nothing, but not supreme being such as he himself is. To some he gave being more fully, and to others he gave it less fully, and so he arranged created natures according to their degrees of being. (Just as the word "wisdom" comes from the verb "to be wise,"[4] so the word "being" comes from the verb "to be"; it is, of course, a new word which was not used by Latin authors of old but has come into use in our times to give our language a term for what the Greeks call *ousia*, for which it is a literal equivalent.[5]) Thus the only nature contrary to the nature which supremely is, and by which everything else that is was made, is a nature which has no being at all. For it is obvious that the contrary of that which has being is that which does not. And it follows that there is no being contrary to God, that is, to the supreme being, who is the author of all beings of any kind whatsoever.

3. Scripture does mention enemies of God,[6] but they oppose God's rule due not to their nature but to their own faults, and they have power to harm not him but only themselves. For they are his enemies not because of their ability to hurt him but rather because of their will to resist him. For God is immutable and wholly incorruptible. Therefore the fault by which those who are called God's enemies resist him holds no evil for God but only for themselves, and it is evil for them precisely because it corrupts the good of their nature. It is not their nature, therefore, that is contrary to God but their fault; and it is contrary to God because it is evil, the contrary of the good. And who will deny that God is supremely good? Their fault, then, is contrary to God, as evil is to the good.

Furthermore, the nature which it damages is also a good, and so the fault is contrary to this good as well. It is contrary to God, however, only as evil is to good,

---

4. "Wisdom...to be wise": *sapientia...sapere*.
5. "Being...to be": *essentia...esse*. Despite Augustine's claim that *essentia* was a new word, in fact its existence seems to be traceable back at least six centuries before his use of it. See Quintilian, who attributes it to Plautus (c. 254c. 184 B.C.) in *Institutes* II,14,2; III,6,23; VIII,3,33.
6. See Acts 5:39; Rom 5:10.

but it is contrary to the nature it damages not only as evil but also as harmful to it. No evils, of course, are harmful to God, but they are harmful to natures that are mutable and corruptible, even though, as the faults themselves attest, these natures are also good. If they were not good, the faults could not possibly do them harm. For how else do they harm them other than by depriving them of their integrity, beauty, wellbeing, virtue, and any other good of nature which is characteristically destroyed or diminished due to some fault? But, if there were no good there at all, the fault could not deprive the nature of any good, and so there would be no harm done, and thus there would be no fault. For there can be no fault where there is no harm done. Accordingly, we gather that, although a fault cannot do harm to the immutable good, it is still true that it can only do its harm to a good, for there is no fault involved except where it actually does harm. We may also put it this way: there can be no fault in the supreme good, but neither can there be any fault except in some good.

In some cases, then, there can be things that are solely good, but there can never be things that are solely evil. For even those natures which have been vitiated by the will's original turn to evil, although they are evil insofar as they are vitiated, are still good insofar as they are natures. And when a vitiated nature undergoes punishment, there is, over and above the good of its nature as nature, the further good that it does not go unpunished. For this is just, and everything just is undoubtedly good. For no one is punished for faults of nature but only for faults of will. Even a vice that has grown and hardened due to habit and has become almost natural took its origin from the will. Here we are speaking, of course, of that nature which possesses a mind capable of the intelligible light by which we distinguish the just from the unjust.

4. In contrast, it is absurd to think that the faults of beasts, trees, and other mutable and mortal things which entirely lack intellect or sensation or even life itself deserve to be condemned. These faults do corrupt their perishable nature, but such creatures, at the will of the creator, have received their own measure so that, by passing away and giving place to another, they might enact the lower beauty of the seasons which is, in its own way, appropriate to the parts of this world. For, while it is true that earthly things should not have been put on a par with heavenly things, neither ought they to have been excluded from the universe merely because heavenly things are better than they are. Accordingly, in the regions where such things have their proper place, some arise as others pass away, and the weaker succumb to the stronger, and those that are overcome are transformed into the attributes of those that overcome; and this is the order of transitory things. We human beings do not take delight in the beauty of this order. For, because we are ourselves parts of it, woven into it by virtue of our mortal condition, we are unable to discern the whole in which the items that offend us are quite fittingly and attractively embedded. That is why, in cases where we are less able to see it for ourselves, we are most rightly enjoined to accept the providence of the creator on faith. This keeps us from daring, in the foolishness of human temerity, to find fault at any point with the work of such a marvelous maker....

5. All natures, because they exist and therefore have a mode of their own, a form of their own, and a certain peace with themselves, are certainly good. And when they are where they ought to be according to the order of nature, they preserve their own being to the degree that they have received it. Those which have not received eternal being undergo change, for better or for worse, to serve the use and the movement of the things under which they have been placed by the creator's law, and they tend, by divine providence, to the end which is set for them in the scheme according to which the universe is governed. As a consequence, not even that degree of corruption which brings mutable and mortal natures to total annihilation causes what previously existed to cease existing in such a way as to keep what ought subsequently to exist from coming about. And, since this is so, God, who supremely is, and by whom, therefore, every being that does not supremely exist was made (for no being made out of nothing should count as equal to him, nor would it be able to exist at all if it had not been made by him), is not to be reviled when we take offense at any faults but is rather to be praised when we take all natures into consideration.

The Cause of the First Evil Will

6. Thus, the truest cause of the happiness of the good angels is that they cling to him who supremely is. And when we ask about the cause of the misery of the evil angels, what rightly comes to mind is that they turned away from him who supremely is and turned to themselves, who have no supreme existence. And what else are we to call this vice but pride? For in fact *the beginning of all sin is pride* (Sir 10:13). They did not will, then, to keep their strength for him.[7] They would have had greater being if they had clung to him who supremely is; but, in preferring themselves to him, they preferred what has lesser existence. This was the first defect, the first impoverishment, the first fault of that nature which was so created that, although not possessing supreme existence, it was still capable of enjoying him who supremely is and so of attaining happiness. In turning away from him, it plainly was not brought down to the point of having no existence at all, but it was brought down to the point of having a lesser existence and, on this account, became miserable.

But, if we look for the efficient cause of this evil will, we find none. For what is it that makes the will evil, when it is the will itself that makes the act evil? Accordingly, an evil will is the efficient cause of an evil act, but nothing is the efficient cause of an evil will....

For, when the will abandons what is superior and turns itself to what is inferior, it becomes evil — not because that to which it turns is evil, but because the turning itself is perverse. It is not, then, that the inferior thing made the will evil; it is rather that the will itself, because it became evil, had a depraved and inordinate desire for the inferior thing.

---

7. See Ps 59:9.

Suppose that two people who are of precisely the same disposition in mind and body both see the beauty of one and the same body. The sight stirs one of them to illicit enjoyment, while the other stands firm in his chastity of will. What do we suppose is the cause that gives rise to an evil will in the one but not in the other? What caused it in the one in whom it was caused? Not the beauty of the body, for that did not cause an evil will in both, even though both had exactly the same view of it. Was it the flesh of the beholder? Then why did not the other's flesh do the same? Or was it the mind? Then why not the mind of both? For we presumed that they both had the same disposition of mind and body. Are we to say that one of them was tempted by the hidden prompting of a malign spirit, as if it were not by his own will that he consented to this prompting or to any other kind of persuasion?

What we are trying to find, then, is what caused this consent, this evil will which he made open to the one who was persuading him to evil. But we can also eliminate this block to our inquiry: if both were exposed to the same temptation, and the one gave in and consented to it while the other remained just as he was, what can this mean except that the one did not will and the other did will to fall away from chastity? And what accounts for this except each one's own will, given that they were both the same in disposition of body and mind? The same beauty was equally seen by the eyes of both; the hidden temptation was equally present to both. And so, when people want to know what caused his own will to be evil in one of the two, if they examine the matter carefully, nothing comes to mind....

7. No one, therefore, should look for an efficient cause for an evil will. For it is not an efficient but rather a deficient cause, because the evil will itself is not an effect but rather a defect. For to defect from what has supreme existence to what has lesser existence is itself to begin to have an evil will. And since the causes of such defections, as I have said, are not efficient but rather deficient causes, to want to discover such causes is like wanting to see darkness or to hear silence. It is true, of course, that both of these are known to us, the one by no other means than the eyes and the other by no other means than the ears. This, however, is not due to perception but rather to lack of perception. Therefore, let no one seek to know from me what I know that I do not know — unless, perhaps, what he wants to learn is not to know what we ought to know cannot be known....

8. I do know this, that the nature of God cannot be deficient at any time, at any point, or in any way, but things that were created out of nothing can be deficient. Nevertheless, to the degree that such things have more existence and do good (for it is then that they really accomplish something), they have efficient causes. On the other hand, to the degree that they are deficient and thus do evil (for what do they accomplish then except sheer futility?), they have deficient causes. I also know that, when an evil will arises in anyone, what arises in him is something that would not arise if he did not will it, and, because these defections are not necessary but voluntary, the punishment that follows is just. For these are not defections toward things that are evil but are evil defections; that is, they are not defections toward evil natures but rather are evil precisely because, against the order of nature, they defect from that which has supreme existence and defect to that which has lesser existence.

For avarice is not a fault in gold; it is rather a fault in the person who loves gold perversely and so has abandoned righteousness, which ought to be ranked incomparably higher than gold. Nor is dissipation a fault in beautiful and enticing bodies; it is rather a fault in the soul that perversely loves bodily pleasures and so has neglected temperance, by which we are made fit for things that are spiritually more beautiful and incorruptibly more enticing. Nor is self-exaltation a fault in human praise; it is rather a fault in the soul that perversely loves people to praise it and so pays no attention to the witness of conscience. Nor is pride a fault in the one who bestows power or even in power itself; it is rather a fault in the soul which perversely loves its own power and so holds in contempt the more righteous power of a higher power. And, by the same token, anyone who perversely loves the good of any nature at all, even if he should happen to attain it, himself becomes evil in that very good, and wretched in that he is deprived of a greater good.

9. There is, then, no natural or, if it can be put this way, essential cause of an evil will. For the evil of mutable spirits, by which the good of their nature is diminished and depraved, originates with the evil will itself. And there is no cause of such a will except the defection by which God is abandoned, and even the cause of this defection is altogether lacking.

The Cause of the Good Will of the Good Angels

But, if we say that there is also no efficient cause of the good will, we need to be on guard against having it believed that the good will of the good angels was not made but is rather coeternal with God. But, since they were themselves created, how can it be claimed that their good will was not created? And, since it was created, was it created together with them? Or did they first exist without it? But, if it was created together with them, there is no doubt that it was created by the one by whom they were themselves created; and, as soon as they were created, they clung to their creator with the love with which they were created. And the reason why the evil angels were separated from their company is that, while the good angels continued in that same good will, the evil angels were changed by defecting from it — that is, by an evil will, a will that was evil due to the very fact that they defected from that good will. And they would not have defected from it if they had not willed to do so....

As for the angels who, although created good, are nevertheless evil, they are evil due to their own evil will, and their evil will was not caused by their good nature, except in that they willingly defected from the good. Thus, it is not good that causes evil but rather defection from the good. These angels, then, either received less grace of divine love than did those who continued in that same grace or, if both were created equally good, while the evil angels fell due to their evil will, the good angels, with fuller help from God, attained that complete happiness from which they were completely certain that they would never fall (as already discussed in the previous book[8]).

We must confess, then, with the praise due to the creator, that it is not only with reference to holy men but also with reference to the holy angels that it can be said that the love of God has been poured out on them through the Holy Spirit who was given to them.[9] Nor is it true only of men but first and foremost of the angels that their good is what is written in Scripture: *But for me the good is to cling to God* (Ps 73:28). Those who hold this good in common form a holy society both with him to whom they cling and with each other. They constitute the one city of God and are at the same time both his living sacrifice[10] and his living temple.[11]

One part of this city is gathered in from mortal human beings and is destined to be united with the immortal angels; but it is either now on pilgrimage here on earth, at the mercy of change and circumstance, or, in the case of those who have met death, is now at rest in the secret repositories and abiding places of souls. And I see that I must now speak, just as I did with regard to the angels, about how this part took its rise with the same God as its creator. In fact, it is from one man, whom God created first, that the human race took its origin, according to the faith of Sacred Scripture which has — and not without good reason — extraordinary authority throughout the world and among all nations. For, among other true things it said, it foretold with true divinity that all nations would believe in it.

The Origin of Humankind

10. Let us leave aside, then, the conjectures of people who have no idea what they are saying with regard to the nature and origin of the human race. For there are some who hold that human beings have always existed, just as they believed about the world itself. Thus Apuleius, in describing this class of living beings, says, "Individually, they are mortal; but collectively, as an entire species, they are everlasting."[12] If the human race always existed, however, how can their histories be true when they tell us who first discovered what, who first instituted the liberal studies and other arts, or who first settled this or that region or area of the world or this or that island? But, when this question is put to them, their response is that, at certain intervals of time, most but not all of the earth is so devastated by floods and conflagrations that human beings are reduced to a bare few, from whose off-

---

8. See above at XI,13.
9. See Rom 5:5.
10. See above at X,6.
11. See 2 Cor 6:16.
12. *On the God of Socrates* 4.

spring the original multitudes are again restored; and, as a result, everything that was cut short or eradicated by these vast devastations is discovered and instituted all over again, as if for the first time, when in fact it is only being renewed. And besides, they say, it is quite impossible for a human being to come into existence except from a human being who already exists. They are only saying what they think, however, not what they know.

11 (10). [13] These people are also led astray by certain wholly fallacious writings which cover, so they tell us, many thousands of years in their recording of history. On the basis of Sacred Scripture, however, we calculate that not even six thousand years have passed since the origin of humankind.[14] But, to avoid arguing at length over how the empty claims of the writings which refer to many more thousands of years are refuted and how they are found to carry no real authority on this subject, consider only the well-known letter that Alexander the Great wrote to his mother Olympias.[15] In that letter he incorporates the narrative of a certain Egyptian priest, which the latter had taken from writings held to be sacred among the Egyptians and which refers to kingdoms that are also known to Greek history.

Among these, according to Alexander's letter, the kingdom of the Assyrians lasted more than five thousand years. But in Greek history it only lasted some thirteen hundred years from the reign of Belus himself, whom the Egyptian priest also posits as the first king of that kingdom. Again, the Egyptian assigns more than eight thousand years to the empire of the Persians and the Macedonians down to the time of Alexander himself, to whom he was speaking. But among the Greeks, in contrast, only 485 years are allotted to the Macedonian empire down to the death of Alexander, and only 233 years are reckoned to the Persian empire until it was brought to an end by Alexander's own triumph over it.

Thus, the Greek figures are far smaller than the Egyptian, and, even if they were multiplied by three, they still would not equal the Egyptian numbers. For it is reported that the Egyptians once had such short years that they only lasted four months, and so the fuller and more accurate year, which is now common both to them and to us, would have included three of those old Egyptian years. But even so, as I said, the Greek history still does not coincide with the Egyptian chronology. And there is good reason to put our confidence in the Greek account, for it does not exceed the true number of years that is contained in our writings, which are truly sacred....

---

13. Some editions of *The City of God* do not begin a new chapter at this point and hence vary by one chapter for the rest of Book XII.
14. According to the calculations of Eusebius of Caesarea in *Chronicles* I,18,9, if one were to use information gleaned from the Septuagint, one would note that the period from the creation of Adam to the coming of Christ lasted 5528 years. Assuming that Augustine wrote Book XII around the year 420, this would be approximately fifty years short of 6000.
15. The letter was a fabrication.

12 (11). There are others who do not hold that this world is eternal. But, whether they think that this is only one of innumerable worlds[16] or suppose that this is the only world there is, they maintain that at fixed intervals it arises and perishes innumerable times through the ages. Of necessity, then, they must allow that the human race first came into existence without any other human beings to give it birth. For, unlike those who hold with floods and conflagrations on earth that, in their view, do not quite engulf the entire world and who can therefore claim that a few people always remain from whom the original multitudes are again restored, these people cannot presume that, when the whole world perishes, some human beings still survive. Rather, just as they claim that the world itself is reborn from its own matter, so they claim that the human race is reborn in the world from its elements and that only then do the offspring of mortals, like those of the other animals, come teeming forth from their parents.

The "Date" of Man's Creation

13 (12). When the question of the world's origin was under discussion, we answered those who are unwilling to accept not that the world always existed but rather that — as even Plato himself quite openly acknowledges (although many believe that what he said was not what he really thought)[17] — it had a beginning.[18] And I would want to give this same response with regard to the first creation of man for the sake of those who are similarly troubled as to why man was not created during the innumerable and infinite ages of the past but instead was created so recently that it turns out, according to Sacred Scripture, that he came into existence less than six thousand years ago. If this brief span of time disturbs them because the years since man's creation, as recorded in our authorities, seem so very short to them, they should take note that nothing which has any limit lasts all that long and that, compared to unending eternity, all the finite expanses of time must be reckoned not just as very little but as nothing at all. As a consequence, even if we said not that five thousand or six thousand but that sixty thousand or six hundred thousand years had passed since God created man — or sixty or six hundred or six hundred thousand times that number, or even if we multiplied this total by itself again and again until we no longer had a name for the number — it would still be possible to ask why he did not create man before that.

For God's eternal wait before creating man stretches back without beginning; and it is so great that, no matter how ineffably large the number of ages we compare to it, that number, so long as it is bounded by the defined limit of a fixed extent,

---

16. This opinion was that of Epicurus. See Diogenes Laertius, *Lives of Eminent Philosophers* X,45. But Augustine probably knew of the same view as attributed to Origen. See Origen, *On First Principles* II,3,1; Jerome, Letter 124,5.
17. See *Timaeus* 28a-b.
18. See above at XI,5-6.

should seem no more than the tiniest drop of water in comparison with the entire sea, as far as the ocean flows. For, of these two, one is as small as can be and the other incomparably large, but both are still finite. And, as for any expanse of time that starts from some beginning and comes to some end, no matter how far it may extend, if it is compared to what is utterly without beginning, I simply do not know whether it should be reckoned as infinitesimally small or rather as nothing at all....

Thus, the question we are asking now, after a mere five thousand years or so, our posterity could equally well ask, with the same curiosity, after six hundred thousand years, assuming that this mortal humanity of ours, in its ignorance and frailty, should endure that long as generations come and go. And those who came before us could also have raised the very same question back in the early days of man's creation. In fact, the first man himself, on the day after he was created, or even on the very day he was created, could have asked why he was not created earlier. And, no matter how much earlier he might have been created, the import of this controversy about the beginning of temporal things would have been no different then than it is now or than it would be at any subsequent time.

Against Theories of World Cycles

14 (13). The philosophers of this world have supposed that this controversy neither can nor should be resolved in any other way than by introducing cycles of time.[19] In these cycles, they have claimed, the same things have perpetually been renewed and repeated in the natural order, and in the same way there will continue to be, from now on, an unceasing sequence of ages coming and going in turn. These cycles, in their view, either took place in one enduring world, or, alternatively, the world, arising and declining at fixed intervals, always displays as if new the very same things that have happened and are going to happen again. And they can find no way to set the immortal soul free from this ridiculous game, even when the soul attains wisdom, as it makes its unending round between false happiness and true misery.

For how can happiness be true happiness when it has no assurance that it will continue for eternity, and when it is true either that the soul, in its utter ignorance of the truth, knows nothing of its coming misery or that, in the midst of its happiness, it is consumed with unhappiness at the thought of its coming misery? If, however, the soul passes to happiness and leaves behind miseries to which it is never going to return, then something genuinely new occurs in time that will have no end in time. Why, then, cannot the same also be true of the world? Why cannot it also be true of man, created in the world? And so, by holding to the straight

---

19. This was a common theme of the early Greek philosophers and is suggested in Plato, *Meno* 81bc; *Phaedo* 72a-c.

path of sound doctrine, we may avoid the false cycles invented by men of false and falsifying wisdom....

In their view, for example, just as the philosopher Plato taught his students during a certain age in the city of Athens in the school called the Academy, so during innumerable past ages, at exceedingly long but still fixed intervals, the same Plato and the same city and the same school and the same students were repeated again and again, and are going to be repeated again and again through innumerable ages to come. By no means, I say, should we believe such things. For Christ died once for our sins and, *rising from the dead, shall never die again, and death shall no longer have dominion over him* (Rom 6:9), and after the resurrection we ourselves shall always be with the Lord, to whom we now say, as the holy Psalm directs us, *You, O Lord, will preserve us, and will guard us from this generation and for all eternity* (Ps 12:7). And, in my judgment, what comes next applies quite well to these philosophers: *The ungodly shall walk in a circle* (Ps 12:9 LXX) — not because their life is going to recur in the circles that they imagine but rather because, in the present, the pathway of their error, that is, of their false doctrine, is itself a circle.

Eternity and Time

15 (14). Is it any wonder, then, that they find no way in or way out as they wander in circles? They know neither what start gave the human race and this mortal condition of ours their beginning nor what end will bring them to a close. For they are unable to penetrate the depth of God in which, although he himself is eternal and without beginning, he nevertheless gave time its beginning and created man in time, whom he had never created before — not by some new and sudden design but rather by his immutable and eternal purpose.

Who can search out this unsearchable depth of God?[20] Who can scrutinize the inscrutable depth by which God, without ever changing his will, created temporal man — before whom no human beings had ever existed — and multiplied the human race from just one man?...

16 (15). ... On the other hand, suppose that I say that the angels were not created in time but before all time, and that they were the ones over whom God was Lord, since he has never not been Lord. In that case, I shall be asked whether, if they were created before all time, it is possible for created beings to have always existed. Here, it might seem, the response should be, Why not say that they always existed? for it is certainly not inappropriate to say that something that exists for all time always exists. In fact, it is so true that they existed for all time that they were even created before all time. At least, this is so if time began with the heav-

---

20. See Rom 11:33.

ens and the angels already existed prior to the heavens. Let us presume, however, that time did not begin with the heavens but existed even before the heavens. Here I am not thinking of time in the sense of hours, days, months, and years, for these measures of periods of time, which we usually and quite properly call time, obviously did begin with the motion of the heavenly bodies — which is why God said, when he created those bodies, *And let them be for signs and for times and for days and for years* (Gn 1:14). Rather, I am thinking of time as a function of some changing motion in which one part comes earlier and another later, due to the fact that both parts cannot exist simultaneously. If, then, there was something of this sort in the angels' motions prior to the heavens, so that time already existed before the heavens and the angels were involved in temporal motion from the very moment of their creation, it is still true that they have existed for all time, since time itself came into being when they did. And who would say that what existed for all time did not always exist?

If I give this response, however, someone will say, How can it be that the angels are not coeternal with the creator, if both he and they have always existed? And, if the angels are understood to have always existed, how is it that we are also to say that they were created? How shall I answer this? Or should we say that they have, in fact, always existed, since they have existed for all time inasmuch as they were created with time or time created with them, but it is still true that they were created? For we certainly are not going to deny that time itself was created, even though no one doubts that time has existed for all time.

For if time did not exist for all time, then there was a time when time did not exist. And even a complete fool would not say that! We can rightly say that there was a time when Rome did not exist, that there was a time when Jerusalem did not exist, that there was a time when Abraham did not exist, that there was a time when man did not exist, and so forth. And finally, if the world was not created at the beginning of time but rather was created after some period of time, we can also say that there was a time when the world did not exist. But to say that there was a time when time did not exist is as inept as it is to say that man existed when man did not exist, or that this world existed when this world did not exist. If we have two different instances in mind, of course, then there is a sense in which we can say that one man existed when another man did not exist, and similarly, therefore, we can rightly say that one time existed when another time did not exist. But would even the greatest fool in the world say that there was a time when time did not exist?

Thus, we say that time was created, despite the fact that, because time has existed for all time, we also say that time has always existed. And, in the same way, it does not follow from the fact that the angels always existed that they were not created. They are said to have always existed because they existed for all time; and they existed for all time because, without them, time itself would not have existed. For, where there is no creature by whose changing motions time is enacted, there can be no time at all. And so, even if the angels always existed, it is still true that they were created, and it does not follow from the fact that they always existed that they are coeternal with the creator. For the creator has always existed in unchanging eternity, but they, in contrast, were created. And the reason we say that they have always existed is that they have existed for all time, since, without them, time itself could not have existed....

17(16). I confess that I do not know what ages passed before the human race was created, but I have no doubt that no creature is coeternal with the creator....

Time, Infinity, and the Divine Knowledge

18(17). I also have no doubt that, before the first human being was created, no human being whatsoever had ever existed — neither the same human being brought back time after time in imagined cycles nor anyone else of a like nature. Nor do the arguments of the philosophers shake me in this belief. The most acute of these arguments, supposedly, is the claim that no knowledge can comprehend anything infinite. For this reason, they assert, God's own conceptions of all the finite things that he makes are themselves finite in total. At the same time, however, we must not believe that God's goodness was ever inactive. Otherwise, they insist, it will seem that his activity began at some temporal point, after an eternity of previous inactivity. It will look as if he had come to regret his earlier inactivity, which had no beginning, and so gave a beginning to his work. And so, they claim, it is necessarily true that the same things are always repeated, and that the same things that occur are always going to be repeated, and thus either the world endures through change — noting that, although it never did not exist and although it had no beginning in time, it was still created — or else its coming and its going have always been repeated and are always going to be repeated in those recurring cycles. Otherwise, if we say that God first began his works at some point of time, people will believe that he somehow came to condemn his own earlier inactivity, which had no beginning, as lazy and slothful and therefore displeasing, and they will think that this is why he made a change....

These are the arguments by which the ungodly try to divert our simple piety from the straight path and to make us walk in circles with them; and, if reason could not refute them, faith should laugh in their face. In fact, however, with the help of our Lord God, clear reason shatters these revolving circles which mere opinion contrives. For what most especially leads these philosophers astray, so that they prefer to walk in their false circle rather than to take the true and straight path, is this: they measure the wholly immutable divine mind, which has the capacity to grasp all infinity and which numbers all innumerable things all at once, without shifting its thought from one to another, by their own narrow and mutable human mind. And what happens to them is what the Apostle describes: *Comparing themselves with themselves, they do not understand* (2 Cor 10:12). For, when it occurs to them to do something new, they do in fact act with a new purpose in mind (since the minds they have are most definitely mutable). And, because they are not conceiving of God, whom they are unable to conceive, but rather are conceiving of themselves in place of God, they are not comparing God with God but instead are comparing themselves with themselves.

As for us, however, we are forbidden to believe that God is affected in one way when he is at rest and in another when he is at work. In fact, it is wrong to speak of God as affected at all, as if something might take place in his nature that was not there before. For anything that is affected undergoes some shift, and everything that undergoes some shift is mutable. Thus we should not think that God's rest involves any laziness, sloth, or idleness, just as we should not think that his work involves any toil, effort, or industriousness. God knows how to be active while at rest and how to be at rest while active. He is able to bring to a new work a plan that is not new but eternal, and it is not out of regret for his prior inactivity that he begins to do what he had not done before....

19 (18). But there is also the other point that they make, that not even God's knowledge can comprehend things that are infinite.[21] It only remains, then, for them to dare to say that God does not know all numbers, and so to plunge into the deep abyss of impiety. For it is absolutely certain that numbers are infinite, inasmuch as, no matter what the number is at which you think to make an end, that very number — not to mention the fact that it can be increased simply by adding one — can not only be doubled, no matter how large it is or how great the quantity it expresses, but can also be multiplied at will in accord with the system and science of numbers. Furthermore, each number is defined by its own properties, and as a consequence no number can be equal to any other. They are, therefore, unequal to and different from each other, and, while each individually is finite, all together they are infinite. Does this mean, then, that God does not know all numbers due to their infinity? Does it mean that God's knowledge only extends to a certain total of numbers but remains ignorant of all the rest? Who would be so completely demented as to say such a thing?

Nor are these philosophers in any position to scoff at numbers or to claim that they have nothing to do with God's knowledge. For, on their side, Plato stresses with great authority that God fashioned the world on the basis of numbers.[22] And, on our side, we read these words addressed to God, *You have arranged all things by measure and number and weight* (Wis 11:20). And the prophet also says of God, *Who brings out the age by number* (Is 40:26 LXX). And in the Gospel the savior says, *And even your hairs are all numbered* (Mt 10:30). We must never doubt, therefore, that every number is known to him *whose understanding*, as the Psalm declares, *is unnumbered* (Ps 147:5). Thus, even though there is no number for the infinite number of numbers, this infinity of numbers is still not beyond the

---

21. This was Origen's position in *On First Principles* II,9,1; III,5,2; IV,4,8.
22. See *Timaeus* 34b-36d.

comprehension of him *whose understanding is unnumbered.* And so, if everything that is comprehended by knowledge is rendered finite by the comprehension of the knower, then, in some inexpressible way, all infinity is rendered finite to God because it is certainly not incomprehensible to his knowledge.

Consequently, if the infinity of numbers cannot be infinite to God's knowledge, which comprehends it, who are we mere humans to presume to set limits on his knowledge by saying that, unless the same temporal things are repeated over and over in the same cycles of time, God is unable either to foreknow all that he makes in order to make it or to know all that he makes after he has made it? For God's wisdom, which is simple in its multiplicity and uniform in its multiformity, comprehends all incomprehensible things with a comprehension which is so incomprehensible that, even if he willed always to make whatever came later completely new and unlike whatever came earlier, he still could have nothing unplanned or unforeseen. Nor would he foresee these things only at the last minute; rather, his eternal foreknowledge would include them all....

Ultimate Happiness: the Refutation of the Theory of World Cycles

21 (20). For devout ears it is unbearable to hear that, after passing through a life burdened with so many and such terrible calamities (if, in fact, it should be called life at all when it is rather a form of death, and a form of death so oppressive that we even fear the death that liberates us from it, because of our love for this form of death), and after its heavy and horrible evils have at last been expiated and ended through true religion and true wisdom, we finally achieve the vision of God and so gain blessedness in the contemplation of incorporeal light through participation in his immutable immortality, which we burn with love to attain, only to find that, of necessity, we must lose all this at some point, and that those who lose it are cast down from that eternity, that truth, that happiness,[23] and again entangled in hellish mortality, disgraceful folly, and detestable miseries, where God is lost, where truth is hated, and where happiness is sought in foul iniquities, and that this has happened and is going to happen over and over again, without any end, at certain fixed and measured intervals of ages past and ages to come. And, according to these philosophers, the reason for these fixed cycles, forever coming and going and coming again, bringing us false happiness and true misery in turn (which, however, are both eternal due to this unending round), is to make it possible for God to know his own works. For, in their view, it is impossible for God either to be at rest from his creating or to grasp an infinity of things by his knowing....

But these views are false. Piety cries out against them. Truth refutes them. For we are truly promised a true happiness, a happiness that will be secure and

---

23. The triad of eternity, truth and happiness (*aeternitate veritate felicitate*) suggests the divine Trinity.

certain, that will always be retained and will never be disrupted by any unhappiness. Let us follow, therefore, the straight path that we have in Christ,[24] and, with him as our leader and savior, let us turn our mind and the direction of our faith away from the inane and empty cycles of the ungodly. For if Porphyry, himself a Platonist, refused to follow the Platonic view with regard to these cycles and their ceaseless alternation of souls going and returning — regardless of whether he was distressed by the sheer absurdity of the thing or whether he was already in awe of the Christian era — and if he preferred to say (as I mentioned in the tenth book) that the soul is placed in this world to gain knowledge of evils so that, once freed and purged from them, it might suffer no further evil after its return to the Father,[25] then how much more ought we ourselves to detest and shun this falsehood which is so starkly hostile to the Christian faith!...

Therefore, since we have now exploded the whole notion of those cycles in which, so it was presumed, the soul is necessarily going to return to its same miseries, no possibility remains that is more in keeping with true piety than to believe that it is not impossible for God both to create new things that he has never created before and, by virtue of his ineffable foreknowledge, to do so without any change of will....

God's Creation of the Human Race from One Man

22 (21). As far as I could, then, I have explained the exceedingly difficult question regarding God's eternity and how he creates new things without any change of will. In this light, it is not hard to see that what took place — namely, that God multiplied the human race from one man whom he created first — was much better than if he had started it from several. For, while God created some animals that are solitary and, preferring solitude, keep to themselves, such as eagles, kites, lions, wolves, and the like, he created others that are gregarious and would rather gather together and live in flocks, such as doves, starlings, deer, fallow-deer, and so forth.[26] But he did not propagate either of these kinds from single individuals; rather, he ordered many of them into existence all at once. Man, however, whose nature was in a manner to be intermediate between the angels and the beasts, God created in such a way that, if he submitted to his creator as his true Lord, and, if he kept God's commandments in devout obedience, he would, without dying, obtain a blessed and unending immortality and pass over into the company of the angels; but, if he offended the Lord his God by using his free will proudly and disobediently, he would be given over to death and would live like the beasts, a slave to lust and destined for eternal punishment after death. And in this case he created one single individual, but not so that man would be left alone, bereft of

---

24. See Jn 14:6.
25. See above at X,30.
26. The same distinction between solitary and gregarious animals is made below at XIX,12.

human society. Rather, God's purpose was that the unity of human society and the bond of human intimacy would be all the more strongly commended to human beings if they were linked to one another not only by likeness of nature but also by the sense of kinship.[27] In fact, he did not even create the woman who was to be united with the man in the same way that he chose to create the man himself; instead he created her out of that man, so that the human race might be wholly derived from just one man.[28]

23 (22). God knew full well, however, that man was going to sin and that, having become subject to death, he would propagate men who were themselves going to die. He knew, too, that mortals would go to such savage lengths in sinning that even beasts lacking any rational will, the beasts that came in teeming numbers from the waters and the earth, would live together more securely and more peacefully with their own kind than would human beings, whose race was produced from a single individual precisely in order to encourage harmony among them. For not even lions or dragons have ever waged such wars among themselves as have human beings. But God also foresaw that, by his grace, a godly people would be called to adoption and that, justified by the Holy Spirit, with their sins forgiven, they would be united with the holy angels in eternal peace, when the last enemy, death, had been destroyed.[29] And he knew that this people would benefit from reflecting on the fact that God started the human race from a single individual for the express purpose of showing men how much he prizes unity among many.

24 (23). Thus, God created man in his own image.[30] Indeed, he created for him a soul such that, through reason and intelligence, he would outshine all the animals of land, sea, and sky, which do not have a mind of this sort. When God had fashioned man from the dust of the earth, he endowed him with a soul such as I have just indicated. Either he implanted in man, by breathing, a soul that he had already made; or, rather, he made the soul by breathing and wanted the very breath he made by breathing to be man's soul[31] (for what else is it "to breathe" than "to make breath"?). After this, he took a bone from the man's side and, from it, made him a wife to help in begetting children.[32] All this he did as God. For we are not to think of these things in our usual carnal way, as if God worked in the manner of craftsmen who, as we see all the time, use their bodily members to fashion from earthly material whatever they are able to make by exercising their skill.[33] God's

---

27. On the kinship of human beings through the first parents, a theme repeated below at XII,28, see also *The Catholic Way of Life* 30,63; *The Excellence of Marriage* 1,1. For this commonplace see as well Lactantius, *Divine Institutes* VI,10; John Chrysostom, Sermon on 1 Timothy 12,4.
28. See Gn 2:21-22.
29. See 1 Cor 15:26.
30. See Gn 1:26.
31. See Gn 2:21-24.
32. See Gn 2:21-24.
33. Augustine has the anthropomorphite error in mind here, as he does in several other places in

hand is God's power, which works invisibly even in producing visible results. But this is regarded not as true but as mere fable by those who use our ordinary and everyday works to measure the power and wisdom of God, thanks to which he has both the knowledge and the ability to make the very seeds themselves, even without seeds. Because they know nothing of the things that were first created, they find them incredible — as if the things which they know perfectly well about human conception and birth would not seem even more incredible if told to people who have no experience of them (although many assign even these phenomena to natural and physical causes rather than to the workings of the divine mind).

God the Sole Creator

25 (24). In these books, however, we are not concerned with those who do not believe that the divine mind makes or cares for these things. But there are others who follow their master Plato in believing that all mortal creatures — among whom man holds the preeminent place, like that of the gods themselves — were created not by the supreme God who fashioned the world but by other lesser gods, whom he himself created and who were acting by his permission or at his command.[34] If these people would only rid themselves of the superstition by which they seek to justify the rites and sacrifices they offer to such gods as if they were their creators, they would easily rid themselves, too, of the error of this view. For it is an abomination to believe or say — even before we can understand why — that any but God alone is the creator of any nature, no matter how minor or mortal. As for the angels, whom these philosophers prefer to call gods (even though they do have their own role to play, whether at God's command or by God's permission, in bringing forth the things of this world), we no more call them the creators of living beings than we call farmers the creators of crops and trees.

26 (25). For there is one kind of form that is applied *externally* to any sort of bodily matter, as is the case with the work done by potters, smiths, and artisans of this sort, who even paint and fashion forms that resemble the bodies of animals. But there is another kind of form which has efficient causes that work *internally* and stem from the secret and hidden choice of a living and intelligent nature which makes not only the natural forms of bodies but also the very souls of living creatures, although it is not itself made. The first kind of form can be ascribed to any craftsman at all, but the second can be ascribed only to one craftsman, creator, and maker, namely, to God, who made the world itself and the angels, when there was no world and there were no angels.

The City of God.
34. See *Timaeus* 41a-43b.

For it was by this divine and, if I may put it this way, effective power — which cannot be made but can only make — that the roundness of the heavens and the roundness of the sun received their form when the world came into being; and it was by the same divine and effective power — which cannot be made but can only make — that the roundness of the eye and the roundness of the apple received their form, as did the other natural shapes which we see imprinted on anything whatsoever as it comes into being, imprinted not externally but by the inward power of the creator, who said, *I fill heaven and earth* (Jer 23:24), and whose wisdom it is that *reaches mightily from one end to the other and orders all things sweetly* (Wis 8:1)....

It is his hidden power, which penetrates all things by that presence of its which cannot be defiled, that gives existence to anything that exists in any way at all and insofar as it exists at all; for, unless he made it, not only would it not exist in this way or that, but it could not exist at all....

27 (26). When Plato asserted that lesser gods, who were created by the supreme God, were the makers of the other living creatures, he doubtless meant that they took the immortal part from God himself and themselves did no more than to join the mortal part to it. He did not mean, then, that they are the creators of our souls but only of our bodies. But Porphyry states that, for the sake of purifying the soul, we must flee all bodies,[35] and he holds, along with Plato and the other Platonists, that as punishment for those who live unbridled and dishonorable lives they return to mortal bodies (even to the bodies of beasts in Plato's view, but only to the bodies of men in Porphyry's). It follows, then, that the very gods — as they call them — whom they want us to worship as our parents and creators are, in fact, nothing more than the makers of our shackles and prisons. They are not our creators but our jailers and warders, who incarcerate us in bitter prisons and bind us with heavy chains. The Platonists, therefore, should either stop threatening us with our bodies as the punishment for our souls or stop proclaiming that we ought to worship gods whose only contribution to our make-up they urge us to flee and to shun as far as we possibly can.

In fact, however, both of these opinions are utterly false. For it is not true that souls pay their penalty of punishment by returning again to this life; nor is there any other creator of any living thing, whether in heaven or on earth, but the one who made both heaven and earth. In fact, if the only reason for our life in this body is to undergo punishment, how is it that Plato himself says elsewhere that the world could only have become its best and most beautiful by being filled with all kinds of living creatures, both immortal and mortal?[36] And if our creation is a divine gift, even if we are created mortal, how can it be a punishment to return to

---

35. A famous assertion taken from *On the Return of the Soul* and cited also above at X,29 and below at XXII,12.26.
36. See *Timaeus* 29b.

these bodies — to return, that is, to benefits divinely bestowed on us? And if God, as Plato repeatedly states,[37] contained in his eternal intelligence not only the form of the whole world but also the forms of all living creatures, how could it not be true that he himself created them all? Or are we to think that he was unwilling to be the maker of some of them, even though his inexpressible — and inexpressibly praiseworthy — mind held the art of producing them all?

Humanity's Social Character

28 (27). It is with good reason, then, that true religion acknowledges and proclaims that the creator of the whole world is also the creator of all living beings, that is, of both souls and bodies. Preeminent among those on earth is man, whom God created in his own image,[38] and, for the reason I have mentioned (although some other and greater reason may lie hidden from us), he was created one, a single individual, but he was not left alone. For there is nothing more contentious by virtue of its fault than the human race, but also nothing more social by virtue of its nature. Nor is there anything more appropriate for human nature to do to counter the vice of contentiousness, whether to keep it from arising in the first place or to heal it after it has arisen, than to recall our first parent. For God chose to create him as one for the propagation of a multitude precisely for the purpose of admonishing us that we should maintain unity and concord even when we are many. And the fact that the woman was made for him from his own side[39] also signifies just how precious the union between husband and wife should be.

These works of God are extraordinary, of course, because they came first. And those who do not believe in them ought not to believe in any marvels at all, for not even these would be called marvels if they had occurred in the usual course of nature. But is there anything, under the supreme governance of divine providence, which occurs to no purpose, even if the reason for it remains hidden? One of the sacred Psalms declares, *Come and see the works of the Lord, what marvels he has placed upon the earth* (Ps 46:8). In another place, then, I shall discuss — so far as I have God's help — why the woman was made from the man's side and what this first marvel prefigured.[40]

For the present, however, since I must bring this book to a close, let us reckon that in this first man, who was created in the beginning, there arose — not yet in plain sight, of course, but already in the foreknowledge of God — two societies, like two cities, in the human race. For it was from him that all human beings were to come, some to be joined with the evil angels in their punishment, and others to

---

37. See *Republic* X,597b.
38. See Gn 1:26.
39. See Gn 2:21-22.
40. See below at XXII,17.

be joined with the good angels in their reward, according to the hidden but always just judgment of God. For, because Scripture says, *All the ways of the Lord are mercy and truth* (Ps 25:10), his grace cannot be unjust, nor can his justice be cruel.

Study Questions for Book XII

Augustine wrestled with the origin of evil. He locates the source of evil in the mystery of free will, that is, in a created being's prideful ability to choose as ultimate, infinite and supreme something which is not. Thus evil originates in angelic pride, before the creation of human beings. What do the defective choices of the angels and subsequently of Adam and Eve say about Augustine's anthropology, that is, his understanding of what it means to be human?

Cyclic understandings of the cosmos are found in ancient philosophy, as well as in contemporary Eastern religions. Science postulates an endless succession of cosmic expansions from and contractions to a singularity. Augustine's argument in this matter is complicated. The infinite knowledge of God is above both cyclic and linear models, even infinite linearity. Augustine locates the core of his argument for a finite linear universe and history in the importance of human happiness, that is, in the fulfillment of the purpose for which humans have been created: loving relationship with God. Does Augustine's anthropological argument for understanding the universe have something to contribute to contemporary debates on the nature of the cosmos?

The Qur'an affirms that the equality among all persons derives from our common parentage in Adam and Eve. Augustine sees the bond of kinship among all human beings to be rooted in the one divine act that created Adam. Augustine's emphasis is on the divine act, not necessarily on gender. What points of difference and commonality between Islam and Christianity regarding justice and equality might these two readings of Genesis involve?

BOOK XIII

Book XIII takes up two major issues: the meaning of death and the status of the body. It sets out four meanings of death: the death of the soul, when God abandons the soul; the death of the body, when the soul abandons the body; the death of the whole person, soul and body; and the second or final death of eternal punishment. All of these deaths count as punishment for sin. God created the first human beings in such a way that, if they had not sinned, they would not have died; and, since the whole human race was present in Adam and thus participated in his sin, the whole human race justly incurred the punishment of death. As a result, human nature was changed for the worse and came under the necessity of death. Thus death is always an evil, even though it may sometimes, as in the case of the martyrs, be turned to the service of righteousness. The death with which God threatened the first parents in paradise included all four forms of death. The death of the soul, abandoned by God because it had itself abandoned God, is marked by the stirrings of disobedient desires of the flesh and, unless grace intervenes, is followed by the whole disastrous sequence of deaths culminating in the second or final death of eternal punishment in which the body, although dead in a sense, still feels the torments of eternal pain. The body itself, however, is not a punishment; and, contrary to the Platonic view, it is not inimical to ultimate blessedness. In fact, Plato himself teaches that by divine will the celestial gods are forever joined to their celestial bodies and are thus both immortal and blessed precisely in their embodied state. It is not true, therefore, that eternal happiness can only be attained by flight from the body. Nor is it true that the body cannot exist in heaven. Just as human beings can make vessels that float on water even though they are manufactured from materials that ordinarily sink in water, so God can cause bodies to exist in heaven even though they are made of earth. It is not the body itself that weighs down and burdens the soul but rather the corruptible body, the body as it became in the wake of human sin. The body of the resurrected saints, however, will be perfectly attuned to the soul, not resisting but rather expressing and supporting its desires and purposes. It will no longer be subject to death and will no longer require food and drink to ward off the distress of hunger and thirst. In the words of St. Paul, it will be a spiritual body in the sense that, unlike the animal body of the first human beings, it will be totally unable to die. Ultimate human happiness, then, will consist in an embodied, not a disembodied, eternal existence, i.e., existence in a resurrected body that is spiritual in character but retains its physical nature. Finally, at its close, the book briefly points to the issue of pre-fallen human sexuality as a question for further discussion.

1. Now that we have addressed the very difficult questions of the origin of our world and the beginning of the human race, the right order of things requires that our line of discussion turn next to the fall of the first human being — or, rather, of the first human beings — and to the origin and propagation of human death. For God did not create men like the angels; that is, he did not make them completely incapable of dying, even if they sinned. Rather he made them in such a way that, if they fulfilled their duty of obedience, angelic immortality and a blessed eternity would follow without any intervening death, but, if they disobeyed, they would most justly be condemned to the punishment of death. But I have already made this point in the preceding book.[1]

The Meanings of Death

2. I see, however, that I need to discuss a little more fully the kind of death that is in question here. For, although the human soul is rightly said to be immortal, it does suffer a kind of death of its own. The soul is called immortal because it never wholly loses all life and feeling, and the body is called mortal because it can be wholly abandoned by life and cannot live at all on its own. The death of the soul occurs, then, when it is abandoned by God, just as the death of the body occurs when it is abandoned by the soul. And the death of the two together — that is, the death of the whole human being — happens when the soul, itself abandoned by God, abandons the body. For, in that case, neither does the soul draw life from God nor the body from the soul.

This death of the whole human being is followed by what the authority of Divine Scripture calls the second death.[2] This is the death to which the Savior referred when he said, *Fear him who has the power to destroy both body and soul in hell* (Mt 10:28). But, since this second death only occurs after the soul and body have been so tightly bound together that nothing can pull them apart, it may seem strange that the body is said to be destroyed by a death in which it is not abandoned by the soul but rather undergoes torment precisely because it retains both its soul and its feeling. For, in that final and eternal punishment (which I shall have to discuss more fully in its proper place[3]), we can rightly speak of the death of the soul, since it will draw no life from God. But how can we speak of the death of the body, since it will draw life from the soul? For without the soul it could not feel the bodily torments that will beset it after the resurrection. Perhaps it is because life of any sort is a good, while pain is an evil, that we ought not to say that the body is alive when its soul is present not for the sake of giving it life but only for the sake of giving it pain.

---

1. See above at XII,22.
2. See Rv 2:11; 21:8.
3. See Book XXI.

The soul, then, draws life from God when it lives rightly, for it can only live rightly when God works what is good in it. The body, on the other hand, draws life from the soul when the soul lives in the body, whether or not the soul itself draws life from God. For the life in the bodies of the ungodly is not the life of their souls but the life of their bodies, and even dead souls — that is, souls that have been abandoned by God — can confer such life on bodies, since their own life, by virtue of which they are immortal, no matter how slight it may be, does not end. In the final damnation, however, it is not without reason that life is called death rather than life. For at that point, although man continues to have feeling, his feeling is made neither delightful by pleasure nor beneficial by rest but, rather, punitive by pain. And this is called the second death because it comes after the first, in which there takes place a separation of conjoined natures, whether of God and the soul or of the soul and the body. Thus it can be said of the first death, the death of the body, that it is a good for those who are good and an evil for those who are evil. But the second death, since it happens to no one who is good, is obviously not a good for anyone at all.

Death as Punishment

3. But here a question arises that we must not gloss over — whether it is really true that the death by which soul and body are separated is a good for those who are good. If this is true, how can we maintain that this death is also the punishment for sin? If the first human beings had not sinned, they most certainly would not have suffered this death. How, then, can it be a good for those who are good, when it could only happen to those who are evil? And, if it could only happen to those who are evil, it ought not to be a good for those who are good but rather ought not to happen to them at all. For why should there be any punishment for those in whom there is nothing that deserves to be punished?

Consequently we must acknowledge that the first human beings were, in fact, so created that, if they had not sinned, they would not have experienced any kind of death. But we must also acknowledge that, as the first sinners, these same human beings were punished with death in such a way that whatever sprang from their stock would also be held liable to the same penalty. For what was born from them was no different than what they themselves were. In keeping with the sheer magnitude of their offense, their condemnation changed their nature for the worse, and, as a consequence, what first came about as punishment for the first human beings who sinned now occurs naturally in all people who are born.

For man does not come from man in the same way that man came from the dust.[4] Dust was the material for the making of man, but man is the parent for the begetting of man. Flesh is not the same as earth, even though flesh was made

---

4. See Gn 2:7.

from earth, but the human offspring is the same as the human parent. Thus the entire human race, which was going to pass through the woman and become its progeny, was present in the first man when that couple received the divine sentence of condemnation; and what man became — not when he was created but when he sinned and was punished — is what man begot, so far as the origin of sin and death is concerned.

The first man was not reduced by sin or its punishment to the infantile weakness and helplessness of mind and body that we see in little children....

The first man neither slid back nor was pushed back to the rudimentary stage of infancy as a result of his unlawful presumption and his just condemnation. Human nature was so vitiated and changed in him, however, that he suffered the rebellious disobedience of desire in his members and was bound over to the necessity of dying, and so he gave birth to what he himself had become as a result of his fault and his punishment, that is, to children subject to sin and death. But, if infants are released from the bonds of sin through the grace of Christ the mediator, they can suffer only the death that separates the soul from the body. Set free from the hold of sin, they do not pass on to the punishment of that second unending death.

4. If anyone is troubled as to why those whose guilt is removed by grace should suffer even the first death, since it too is a punishment for sin, this question has already been discussed and resolved in another of my works, *The Baptism of Little Ones*. There I state that the soul's experience of separation from the body remains, even after its link with guilt has already been removed, for this reason: if the sacrament of regeneration[5] were immediately followed by the immortality of the body, the very nerve of faith would be cut. For faith is only faith when we look forward in hope to what we do not yet see in reality.[6]

And it was by the strength of faith and the contest of faith, at least in earlier times, that even the fear of death had to be overcome, and this was especially clear in the case of the holy martyrs. There obviously would have been no victory and no glory in this contest — since there would have been no contest at all — if, after the washing of regeneration,[7] the saints were already incapable of suffering bodily death. In that case, who would not run to the grace of Christ, along with the children who were to be baptized, just to avoid being parted from the body? Thus, faith would not be tested by virtue of having an invisible prize. In fact, it would no longer be faith at all, if it immediately expected and received the reward for its work....

6. Thus, so far as the death of the body is concerned — that is, the separation of the soul from the body — it is not a good for anyone when it is suffered by those

---

5. I.e., baptism.
6. See *The Punishment and Forgiveness of Sins and the Baptism of Little Ones* II,31,50-51. Augustine is alluding to Heb 11:1. "Hope...reality": *spe...re* — a frequent wordplay in Augustine.
7. See Tit 3:5.

who we say are dying. For the very force that tears apart the two that were conjoined and intertwined in the living person produces an anguished feeling that is contrary to nature and that lasts until all feeling is gone, which was present precisely due to the joining of soul and flesh. Sometimes all this distress is cut short by a single blow to the body or a snatching away of the soul which, coming so suddenly, keeps it from being felt at all. But, whatever it is that with such a feeling of anguish deprives the dying of all feeling, it increases the merit of patience when it is endured with faith and piety. It does not, however, erase the term "punishment." For death is undoubtedly the punishment of all who are born in unbroken succession from the first man. But, if it is undergone for the sake of godliness and righteousness, it becomes the glory of those who are born again; and so, even though death is the retribution for sin, it sometimes ensures that there is no retribution for sin.

The Death of the Saints

7. For, when anyone dies for confessing Christ, even if he has not received the washing of regeneration, this counts just as fully for the remission of his sins as if he had been washed in the sacred font of baptism.[8] It is true that Christ said, *No one will enter the kingdom of heaven unless he is born again of water and the Spirit* (Jn 3:5), but in another saying he made an exception for this case, where he says in no less general terms, *Everyone who acknowledges me before men, him I also shall acknowledge before my Father who is in heaven* (Mt 10:32). And in another place he states, *Whoever loses his life for my sake will find it* (Mt 16:25).

It is for this reason that Scripture says, *Precious in the sight of the Lord is the death of his saints* (Ps 116:15). For what is more precious than a death by which all a person's sins are forgiven and his merits immensely increased? Even those who were baptized when they could no longer defer death, and so departed this life with all their sins wiped clean, are not equal in merit to those who did not defer death, even though they could have done so, because they preferred to end their life by confessing Christ rather than, by denying him, to live long enough to receive his baptism. Even if they had denied Christ due to their fear of death, however, this too would certainly have been forgiven them in the washing of baptism, in which even the monstrous crime of those who killed Christ was forgiven.[9] How, then, could the martyrs possibly have loved Christ so much that they were unable to deny him, despite the fact that they faced such mortal peril and despite the fact that they had such a sure hope of forgiveness, without the overflowing grace of that Spirit which *blows where it chooses* (Jn 3:8)?

Precious, therefore, is the death of the saints, for whom Christ's death had already paid the price in advance with such overwhelming grace that they did not

---

8. See Tit 3:5. Martyrdom was recognized as a substitute for water baptism as early as the end of the second century in Tertullian, *On Baptism* 16.
9. See Acts 2:23.36-41.

hesitate to pay the price of their own death in order to gain him. Their death showed that what had originally been established for the punishment of sin has been put to such use that from it was born the more abundant fruit of righteousness. But, even so, death should not be considered a good just because it has been turned to such advantage — not on its own strength but thanks to the divine bounty — that what was formerly set before us as a thing to be feared lest sin should be committed is now set before us as a thing to be endured, with the result that no sin is committed and, even if sin has been committed, it is blotted out, and in either case the palm of righteousness, which is owed for a great victory, is awarded.

8. For, if we consider the matter more carefully, we see that, even when a person dies a faithful and praiseworthy death, he is guarding against death. He accepts one aspect of death in order to avoid the whole of death and, beyond that, in order to escape the second death which has no end. He accepts the separation of the soul from the body in order to avoid having God separated from the soul when the soul is itself separated from the body and as a result — with the first death, the death of the whole person, complete — incurs the second, eternal death. Therefore, as I have said,[10] death is not a good for anyone when it is being suffered by the dying and is bringing about their death, but it is praiseworthy to endure death for the sake of maintaining or attaining the good....

"Before Death," "after Death," and "in Death"

9. As for the time at which souls are separated from the body, whether in the case of the good or in the case of the evil, should it be termed "after death" or "in death"? If we say that it is after death, then it is no longer death itself, which is finished and in the past, but is rather the present life of the soul following death, whether that life is good or evil. In that case, death was an evil for them when it was happening — that is, while they were actually suffering death as they were in the process of dying — since the harsh and anguished sensation of death was then present, and this evil is put to good use by the good. But, once death is over, how can it be either good or evil when it no longer exists at all?

But, if we take a still closer look, it will turn out that not even the harsh and anguished feeling that we said is present in dying really counts as death. For, as long as they have feeling, they are obviously still alive; and, if they are still alive, we should say that they are before death, not that they are in death. For, when death actually comes, it takes away all the feeling that anguishes the body while death is approaching. For this reason it is difficult to explain how it is that we describe people as "dying" who are not yet dead but who, as death draws near, are racked by their final and mortal agony. And this difficulty remains, even though it is quite

---

10. See above at XIII,6.

right to say that they are dying, because, once their impending death has actually arrived, we no longer say that they are dying but that they are dead.

No one is dying, then, unless he is living, for, even when a person is at the last extremity of life (as when we say that his soul is about to depart), anyone whose soul has not yet left is plainly still alive. One and the same person, therefore, is both dying and living at the same time. He is approaching death and leaving life. But he is still in life, because his soul is still present in his body, and he is not yet in death, because his soul has not yet left his body. But if, when the soul has left, he is not in death but rather after death, who can say when he is actually in death? In fact, if no one can be both dying and living at the same time, then no one will ever be dying, since, as long as the soul is in the body, we cannot deny that he is living. But if, instead, we should say that a person in whose body death is already at work is dying, and if it is true that no one can be both living and dying at the same time, then I have no idea when a person is ever living.

10. From the very moment when a person first comes into existence in this body that is doomed to die, there is never a time when death is not at work in him. For all the change that he undergoes during the whole span of this life (if it should be called life at all) culminates in bringing him to death. Certainly there is no one who is not closer to death a year later than he was a year earlier, or tomorrow than he is today, or today than he was yesterday, or a moment later than he is now, or now than he was a moment ago. Any time we live reduces our time to live, and the time we have left daily becomes less and less. The span of this life, then, is no more than a race toward death in which no one is allowed to pause for a bit or to slow down for a moment, but all are driven at the same rate and forced along the same route. For the person who lived a shorter life did not pass each day more quickly than the person who lived a longer life; rather, since equal moments were equally taken from both, the one was simply closer than the other to the goal toward which both were racing at the same speed. It is one thing to have completed more of the path and quite another to have moved at a slower pace. Thus, the person who takes more time on the way to death does not travel more slowly; he simply travels a longer distance.

Again, if a person begins to die — begins, that is, to be in death — from the moment at which death itself begins its work in him, it is clear that he is in death from the very moment at which he first comes into existence in this body.[11] For death is the taking away of life, and so, when his life is completely taken away, he will not be in death but after death. For what else is going on during each day, each hour, each moment, but death? And, when these are all used up, death, which was at work up to that point, is over, and the time which was "in death," while life was being taken away, now begins to be "after death."...

---

11. See Seneca, *Consolation Addressed to Marcia* 21,6.

The Threat of Death

12. If it is asked, then, which death God threatened to inflict on the first human beings if they should break the commandment they had received from him and should fail to continue in obedience — whether the death of the soul, the death of the body, the death of the whole man, or the death that is called the second death — the answer must be: all of these. For the first death consists of two of these, and total death consists of all of them....

13. For, immediately after the first human beings disobeyed the commandment, divine grace abandoned them, and they were made ashamed by the nakedness of their bodies. Thus they used fig leaves, which were perhaps the first things they found in their distress, to cover their shameful members,[12] which were, of course, the same members as before but previously were no source of shame. They felt, then, a new stirring of their disobedient flesh as a punishment in turn for their own disobedience.

For the soul, now rejoicing in its own freedom for perversity and disdaining to serve God, was itself stripped of the body's former service to it, and, because it had by its own will deserted its Lord above, it no longer controlled its servant below by its own will. Nor did it have the flesh fully submissive to it, as it could always have had if it had itself remained submissive to God. It was at that point, then, that the desires of the flesh began to oppose the spirit;[13] and we are now born with this conflict, drawing with us the origin of death and carrying in our members and in our vitiated nature, as a result of the first transgression, its combat against us or rather its victory over us.

14. For God created man righteous; he is the author of natures, not of vices. But man, willingly depraved and justly condemned, gave birth to depraved and condemned offspring. For we were all in that one man, since we all were that one man who fell into sin through the woman who was made from him prior to sin. The specific forms in which we were individually to live as particular individuals had not yet been created and distributed to us, but the seminal nature from which we would all be propagated was already present. And, once this nature was vitiated on account of sin, and bound by the chain of death, and justly condemned, man could not be born of man in any other condition. And so from the evil use of free will there arose a series of calamities which led the human race by a succession of miseries from its depraved origin, as from a corrupt root, right through to the final ruination of the second death, which has no end, and the only exceptions are those who are delivered through the grace of God.

---

12. See Gn 3:7.
13. See Gal 5:17.

15. But since God's threat said, *You shall die the death* (Gn 2:17), not "You shall die the deaths," let us take it to refer only to the death that occurs when the soul is abandoned by its own life, which is God. It is not, however, that the soul was first abandoned by God and then, as a result, abandoned him; rather, it first abandoned him and then, as a result, was abandoned by him. For the soul's will comes first with respect to its evil, but its creator's will comes first with respect to its good, whether in making it when it did not exist or in remaking it when it had fallen and perished. But, even if we take it that this was the death God threatened when he said, *On the day that you eat of it you shall die the death* (Gn 2:17)— as if he said, "On the day that you disobediently abandon me, I shall justly abandon you" — it is surely true that, in this death, there was also the threat of the other deaths that were undoubtedly going to follow it....

And with these two deaths, the first death, which is the death of the whole man, was complete, and, unless man is delivered by grace, it is followed in the end by the second death. For the body, which is from the earth, would not return to earth except for its own death, which occurs when it is abandoned by its own life, which is the soul. Thus Christians who truly hold the catholic faith are agreed that even the death of the body was not inflicted on us by any law of nature, for God did not create any death for man in this sense, but rather was justly inflicted on us for sin. For it was in punishing sin that God said to the first man, in whom we were all then present, *You are earth, and to earth you shall go.*

The Body and Ultimate Blessedness

16. But the philosophers against whose slanders we are defending the city of God — that is, his Church[14] — think themselves wise when they scoff at our claim that the soul's separation from the body is to be counted as one of its punishments. In their view, it is precisely when the soul is divested of all body and returns to God, simple and alone and naked, as it were, that it attains perfect blessedness.

If I found nothing in these philosophers' own writings to refute this view, I would have to undertake a rather laborious argument to show that it is not the body as such but rather the corruptible body that is a burden to the soul. That is the point of the passage from our Scripture.., *For the corruptible body weighs down the soul* (Wis 9:15). The insertion of the word *corruptible* plainly indicates that it is not the body in itself but rather the body as it became due to sin and sin's punishment that weighs down the soul. And, even if the word had not been inserted, we should not interpret the passage in any other way. In fact, however, Plato states quite openly that the gods who were made by the supreme god have immortal bodies, and he portrays the supreme god, the one who made them, as

---

14. On the identification of the city of God and the Church see above at VIII,24.

promising these gods — as a great benefit — that they will continue in their bodies for all eternity and will never be separated from them by any death. Why is it, then, that these philosophers, just to excoriate the Christian faith, pretend not to know what they know perfectly well and even prefer to speak against themselves, opposing their own position, just so long as they never stop contradicting us?

Here are Plato's own words (as Cicero translated them into Latin), where he portrays the supreme God as speaking to the gods he had made: "You who have sprung from the stock of the gods, listen. The works of which I am the parent and author cannot be dissolved against my will, even though everything that is joined together can be taken apart. But it is by no means good to wish to dissolve what is bound together by reason. Because you had a beginning, it is not possible for you to be immortal and indissoluble. Nevertheless, you will surely not be dissolved, nor will any fate of death destroy you or prove more powerful than my purpose, which secures your perpetuity more surely than do the bodies to which you were bound at birth."[15] Note that Plato says both that the gods are mortal by reason of the joining together of soul and body and yet that they are immortal by reason of the will and purpose of the god who made them.

If it is a punishment, then, for the soul to be joined together with any body whatsoever, why is it that god addresses these gods as if they were afraid of dying, that is, of being separated from the body? Why is it that he gives them an assurance of their immortality not on the basis of their nature, which is composite and not simple, but on the basis of his own invincible will, by which he has the power to guarantee that things that had a beginning do not perish and things that were joined together are not dissolved but rather will endure without corruption?

It is another question, however, whether what Plato says here about the stars is actually true. For we should not simply concede to him that those luminous globes or little orbs that shine upon the earth by day or night with their corporeal light are animated by some sort of souls of their own, and that these are intellectual and blessed souls.[16] Plato makes the same claim, and makes it insistently, about the world as a whole, as if it were one immense animate being, in which all other animate beings are contained.[17] But this, as I said, is another question, which I have not undertaken to discuss at this point.

Instead, I thought that I should raise just the one issue against those who make it a point of pride to be called or to be Platonists, and whose pride in this name

---

15. *Timaeus* 41b. Much of the same passage is quoted again, although not word for word, below at XXII,26 and also in Sermon 241,8. Cicero's translation of *Timaeus* was incomplete and has survived only in fragments.
16. As Augustine indicates here, whether the stars were ensouled and rational was a contested point even in Christian times. In addition to Plato, Augustine may have been thinking of Origen, who was the most famous Christian proponent of the notion that the stars were living beings, as in *On First Principles* I,7.
17. See *Timaeus* 38c-40d.

makes them ashamed to be Christians. They fear that sharing a name with the vulgar crowd will cheapen the elite status of those who wear the philosopher's cloak,[18] a status that is the more inflated the more it is restricted to the few. And so, looking for something to oppose in Christian teaching, they attack the eternity of the body, claiming that it is mutually contradictory for us both to seek the blessedness of the soul and to insist that it will forever be in the body, as though it were a bitter form of bondage for the soul to be joined to the body. And they make this claim despite the fact that it is their own founder and teacher, Plato, who says that it was a gift granted by the supreme god to the gods he created that they should never die, that is, should never be separated from the bodies to which he had joined them.

The Issue of the Eternity of the Body

17. These philosophers also argue that it is impossible for earthly bodies to be eternal, despite the fact that they themselves have no doubt that the whole earth is itself a central and eternal member of their god — not, that is, of the supreme god but of the great god who is the whole world. They hold, then, that the supreme god made for them another, whom they regard as a god — namely, this world — who is to be ranked above the other gods, who are below him; and they maintain that this god is animate, having, as they assert, a rational or intellectual soul enclosed in the great mass of his body.[19] In their view, too, the supreme god established the four elements as the members of this body, arranged and distributed in their proper places; and they insist that the conjunction of these elements is indissoluble and eternal, so that this great god of theirs will never die. But if the earth is eternal as the central member in the body of a greater animate being, why cannot the bodies of other earthly animate beings also be eternal, if God should so will it?

But earth, they claim, must return to earth, from which the earthly bodies of animals were taken; and this, they say, is why it turns out to be necessary for these earthly bodies to dissolve and perish and thus be restored to the stable and eternal earth from which they had been taken. But what if someone made a similar point about fire, claiming that the bodies taken from the universal fire to make the animate beings of the heavens must return to the fire from which they were taken? In that case, surely, the immortality that Plato — as if it were the supreme god himself who was speaking — promised to such gods will fall victim, so to speak, to the sheer force of this argument. Or does this never happen in the heavenly realm because God — whose will, as Plato says, no power can vanquish — does not will it? But then, what prevents God from being able to do the same thing in the case of earthly bodies, especially since Plato himself acknowledges that God can ensure that things which have a beginning do not perish, that things

---

18. "Those who wear the philosopher's cloak": *palliatorum* — i.e., those dressed in the pallium, a Greek garment traditionally worn by those professing to be philosophers.
19. See *Timaeus* 30b.

which have been joined together are not taken apart, that things taken from the elements do not return to them, and that souls, once established in their bodies, never abandon them but rather enjoy immortality and eternal blessedness with them? Why is it not possible, then, for God to keep earthly bodies from dying? Or is it that God's power goes only as far as Platonists want, not as far as Christians believe? Were the philosophers, then, capable of knowing God's purpose and power but the prophets were not? On the contrary, God's Spirit taught his prophets to declare his will so far as he thought fitting, but the philosophers, in trying to discover his will, were deceived by human conjecture....

Against the View that the Earthly Body Cannot Be in Heaven

18. But earthly bodies, these philosophers claim, are necessarily held down on earth or pulled down to earth by their natural weight and, as a consequence, cannot be in heaven. The first human beings were, in fact, on earth in a wooded and fruitful place that received the name "paradise."[20] But, since we must respond to their point — both to account for Christ's body, with which he ascended into heaven, and to account for the kind of body that the saints will have at the resurrection — let them consider the issue of earthly weights a little more closely.

For, if human art can somehow make it happen that vessels fashioned from metals that sink as soon as they are placed in water are actually able to float, how much more credibly and efficaciously can God's operation, working in some hidden way, achieve similar effects! Plato himself says that, due to God's all-powerful will, things that had a beginning cannot perish, and things that have been joined together cannot be taken apart, even though it is far more extraordinary for something incorporeal to be joined to a body than it is for one body to be joined to another, no matter how different the two bodies are. Surely, then, God can grant it to earthly masses that they are not pulled downwards by any weight, and can grant it to supremely happy souls themselves that they have earthly but now incorruptible bodies which they may place where they want and move as they want with perfect facility of location and movement....

But our faith in the resurrection of the dead and in their immortal bodies is a matter that must be discussed more fully, God willing, at the end of this work.[21]

Self-Contradictions in the Platonic View of the Body

19. Now, however, let us go on with the discussion that we had begun about the bodies of the first human beings. For, except as the merited consequence of

---

20. See Gn 2:8-9.
21. See below at XXII,11-21.30.

sin, they could not have incurred even that death which is said to be a good for the good, which is known not only to those who understand or believe but to everyone, in which the separation of the soul from the body takes place, and due to which the body of a living being that was plainly alive is now plainly dead. And, although it would be unforgivable to doubt that the souls of the righteous and godly dead are living in peace, it would be still better for them to be living with their own bodies in perfect health[22] — so much better, in fact, that even those who maintain that the supreme happiness is to be without any body at all contradict their own opinion by taking an opposing view. For none of them is bold enough to rank wise men, whether still alive or already dead — that is, whether already rid of the body or soon to relinquish it — above the immortal gods; and, according to Plato, the supreme god promises the immortal gods the unparalleled gift of indissoluble life, that is, life in eternal union with their own bodies.

But this very same Plato maintains that things are never better for human beings, assuming that they have lived this life piously and righteously, than when they are separated from their bodies and are received into the bosom of the very gods who never depart from their own bodies, "so that, forgetting everything, they may again behold the vault on high and begin once more to desire a return to bodies."[23] For that is how Virgil, in great admiration, expresses the Platonic teaching. It is clear, then, that Plato does not think that the souls of mortals can always remain in their bodies. He holds, rather, that they are severed from them by the necessity of death. But neither does he think that they can endure forever without bodies. Instead, he supposes that they move back and forth in unending alternation from death to life and from life to death. Consequently it appears that the only difference between the wise and other people is this: after death, the wise are carried up to the stars so that they may rest for a somewhat longer time, each on the star appropriate to him, and then, having forgotten their former misery and having been overcome by the yearning to possess bodies, may return from the stars to the labors and tribulations of mortals; but those, on the other hand, who have led foolish lives are returned almost at once to the bodies they severally deserve, whether of human beings or of mere beasts.[24] This is, then, the dire condition to which Plato consigned even good and wise souls. For they were not given bodies with which they could live eternally and immortally, and so they can neither remain in their bodies permanently nor persist without them in eternal purity.

In Christian times, as I have already indicated in the previous books,[25] Porphyry was embarrassed at this Platonic teaching, and he not only rejected animal bodies for human souls but also insisted that the souls of the wise are set free from all bodily ties and, fleeing from all bodies, are preserved with the Father in happiness

---

22. This assertion is explained in *The Literal Meaning of Genesis* XII,35,68.
23. *Aeneid* VI,750-751, summarizing Plato, *Phaedrus* 248ab.
24. See *Phaedrus* 248a-249e.
25. See above at X,30.

without end. Thus, in order to keep from seeming to be outdone by Christ, who promised everlasting life to the saints, Porphyry also established purified souls in eternal happiness without any return to their former miseries. But, in order to oppose Christ, he denied the resurrection of incorruptible bodies and asserted that these souls would live for all eternity, not only without earthly bodies but without any bodies at all.[26]

Despite holding this view, however, such as it is, Porphyry still did not teach that these souls should offer no religious service to the gods that do have bodies. Why not, unless it is because he believed that these souls, even when associated with no bodies, remain inferior to those gods? Therefore, if these philosophers are not willing — and I do not think they are — to rank human souls above gods who are supremely happy even though they are united to eternal bodies, why do they find it absurd when the Christian faith proclaims that the first human beings were created in such a way that, if they had not sinned, they would not have been parted from their bodies by death but rather would have been gifted with immortality as a reward for maintaining their obedience and would have lived with those bodies for all eternity? And why do they find it absurd that, at the resurrection, the saints are going to have the very bodies in which they labored here on earth, but with no possibility that any corruption or distress will affect their flesh or that any pain or sorrow will disturb their happiness?

20. Furthermore, even now the souls of the departed saints feel no distress about the death by which they were separated from their bodies, for their flesh rests in hope,[27] no matter what indignities it may seem to have suffered after all sensation was gone. For it is not due to forgetfulness, as Plato thought, that they desire bodies. Rather, it is because they remember what was promised to them by the one who deceives no one, and who assured them that even the very hairs of their heads would remain intact,[28] that they look forward with patience and longing to the resurrection of the bodies in which they have endured many hardships but in which they will never again experience any such thing.

For, if they did not hate their flesh when, in its weakness, it resisted their mind and they had to restrain it by the spiritual law, how much the more do they love it when it is itself to become spiritual. For, just as the spirit is not improperly called carnal when it serves the flesh, so the flesh will rightly be called spiritual when it serves the spirit. It is not that the flesh will be turned into spirit, as some people imagine in the light of what Scripture says, *It is sown an animal body, it is raised a spiritual body* (1 Cor 15:44). It is rather that the flesh will be subject to the spirit with a supreme and marvelous readiness to obey, even to the point of fulfilling the spirit's unwavering will for inseparable immortality without imposing any feeling of distress or any corruptibility or heaviness of its own.

---

26. See below at XXII,27.
27. See Ps 16:9.
28. See Lk 21:18.

The Body in Paradise

For not only will the body not be such as it is now, even when it is in the best of health; it will not even be such as it was in the first human beings prior to sin. For, even though they were not going to die unless they sinned, they still made use of food, as people do, because their bodies were not yet spiritual but still animal and earthly. Even though their bodies were not growing old and so were not approaching the necessity of death — a status bestowed on them by the marvelous grace of God from the tree of life which stood in the middle of paradise along with the forbidden tree[29]— they consumed other foods, except for the one tree that had been forbidden to them. That tree, however, was not forbidden because it was itself evil but rather to commend the good of pure and simple obedience, which is the great virtue of a rational creature set under its creator and Lord. For, where nothing evil was touched but only something forbidden, disobedience alone was the sin.

The purpose of the other foods they consumed, therefore, was to keep their animal bodies from experiencing any distress due to hunger or thirst. But they ate from the tree of life to keep death from stealing upon them from any side and to keep from being worn down by extreme old age when their lives had run their course. The other foods served as nourishment, we might say, but this food served as a sacrament.[30] And so, we can see, the tree of life was to the corporeal paradise what the wisdom of God is to the spiritual — that is, the intelligible — paradise. For Scripture says of that wisdom, *She is a tree of life to those who embrace her* (Prv 3:18).

Spiritual Interpretations of Paradise

21. It is for this reason that some people refer that whole paradise — the paradise where, as the truth of Scripture tells us, the first human beings, the parents of the human race, lived — to intelligible realities. They turn its trees and fruit-bearing plants into virtues and forms of life, as if they were not actually visible and corporeal objects but rather were only spoken of or written of in this guise in order to signify intelligible matters.[31]

But to say that there could not have been a corporeal paradise simply because it can also be understood as a spiritual paradise is like saying that Abraham did not

---

29. See Gn 2:9.16-17.
30. Note the use of the term "sacrament" to refer to the food of the tree of life.
31. See Basil the Great, *Hexaemeron* IX,1 for a similar complaint on the over-allegorization of paradise directed against Origen (although he is not mentioned by name). Augustine may also have Origen in mind. For Origen's exegetical approach to paradise see *On First Principles* IV,3,1. Augustine expresses the same concern with respect to the allegorization of paradise in particular in *The Literal Meaning of Genesis* VIII,1,1-2,5 and with respect to Scripture in general below at XV,27 and XVII,3.

have two wives, Hagar and Sarah, who gave him two sons, one by the slave and one by the free woman,[32] simply because the Apostle says that the two covenants were prefigured in them.[33] It is like saying that there was no rock from which water flowed when Moses struck it[34] simply because the rock can also be understood to signify Christ in a figurative sense, for the same Apostle says, *And the rock was Christ* (1 Cor 10:4).

Nothing prevents us, therefore, from understanding paradise as the life of the blessed, taking its four rivers as the four virtues (prudence, fortitude, temperance, and justice), its trees as all useful teachings, the fruits of the trees as the morals of the godly, the tree of life as wisdom, the very mother of all goods, and the tree of the knowledge of good and evil as the experience of disobeying a commandment.[35] For it was certainly a good thing — because it was just — that God established a punishment for sinners, but it is not a good thing for man to experience that punishment.

These things may also be understood to refer to the Church, so that, still better, we may take them as prior and prophetic indicators of things to come. Thus, paradise indicates the Church itself, as we read about it in the Song of Songs; the four rivers of paradise indicate the four Gospels; the fruit-bearing trees indicate the saints, and their fruit the works of the saints; the tree of life indicates the holy of holies, Christ himself; and the tree of the knowledge of good and evil indicates the will's choice of itself as its object.[36] For, if a person disdains the divine will, he can only do himself harm, and so he learns what a difference there is between clinging to the good that is common to all and delighting in his own private good. For he who loves himself is handed over to himself so that when, as a consequence, he is overwhelmed with fears and anxieties, he may — if he is still aware of his own miseries — sing the words of the Psalm, *My soul is troubled within me* (Ps 42:6), and, when set right, may then say, *I shall keep my strength for you* (Ps. 59:9).

Nothing prevents us, then, from offering these interpretations and any others that might be more appropriate with regard to the spiritual understanding of paradise — just so long as we also believe in the truth of the history as it is presented to us in a most faithful narrative of those events.

---

32. See Gn 16:3-4; 21:2.
33. See Gal 4:22-24.
34. See Ex 17:6.
35. This moral allegory of paradise can be found in Philo, *Allegorical Interpretation* I,14,43-33,105, which Augustine is unlikely to have read but which is resumed in large part in Ambrose, *On Paradise* 1,2-3,18, with which he was almost certainly familiar.
36. The ecclesiastical (or typological) interpretation of paradise is a commonplace. See Hippolytus, *Commentary on Daniel* I,17; Origen, *Commentary on the Song of Songs* III,8; Methodius of Olympus, *Symposium* 9,3.

The Resurrected Body

22. Thus, the bodies that the righteous will have in the resurrection will need no tree to protect them from dying of disease or of advanced old age, nor will they need any other bodily foods to ward off the distress of hunger and thirst. They will be endowed with the secure and wholly inviolable gift of immortality, and so they will not eat unless they wish to do so; that is, eating will be a possibility but not a necessity for them....

The Christian faith has no doubt at all with regard to the Savior himself: even after his resurrection, in his already spiritual but still real flesh, he took food and drink with his disciples.[37] For it is not the ability but rather the need to eat and drink that will be removed from such bodies. These bodies will be spiritual, therefore, not because they will cease to be bodies but because they will be sustained by a life-giving spirit.[38]

23. For, just as the ones that have a living soul but not yet a life-giving spirit are called animal bodies[39] but are still bodies and not souls, so the others are called spiritual bodies. By no means, however, should we imagine that they are going to be spirits. They will be bodies and will have the substance of flesh, but, because they have a life-giving spirit, will suffer none of the flesh's heaviness and corruption. At that point man will no longer be earthly but will be heavenly — not because his body, which was made from earth, will not be the same, but because by divine gift it will now be such that it is suited for dwelling in heaven, and this will come about due not to a loss in its nature but to a change in its quality.

The Animal Body and the Spiritual Body

But the first man — *from the earth, earthly* (1 Cor 15:47) — became a living soul, not a life-giving spirit,[40] for the latter was held in reserve for him as a reward for obedience. There is no doubt, then, that his body was not spiritual but animal. It needed food and drink to avoid the pangs of hunger and thirst, and it was protected from the necessity of death and held in the flower of youth not by absolute and indissoluble immortality but by the tree of life. Even so, he would surely not have died if he had not, by sinning, fallen under the sentence of God, who had given him fair warning in advance; and, although he certainly was not denied food outside of paradise, he was banned from the tree of life and was delivered over to time and old age to bring him to his end, at least with respect to the life which, if he had

---

37. See Lk 24:42-43.
38. See 1 Cor 15:45.
39. "Animal bodies": *animalia corpora* — i.e., bodies endowed with a soul (*anima*). In its original sense, an animal is an ensouled or animated being.
40. See 1 Cor 15:45.

not sinned, he could have lived forever in paradise — although still in an animal body until the point came at which it was made spiritual in reward for obedience.

Thus, even if we presume that what was signified when God said, *On the day that you eat of it you shall die the death* (Gn 2:17), also included that obvious death in which the soul is separated from the body, it still should not seem absurd that the first human beings were not instantly severed from their bodies on the very day that they ate the forbidden and death-dealing food. For on that very day, in fact, their nature was changed for the worse and vitiated; and, due to their wholly just separation from the tree of life, they were subjected to the necessity of bodily death, which characterizes us from birth....

[*The rest of chapter 23 and most of chapter 24 reflect on the differences between the "animal body" and the "spiritual body" of the just who have been resurrected, and on the words "spirit" and "breath" as used in Genesis (LXX).*]

24. ...Thus, the animal body, in which, as the Apostle says, the first man, Adam, was made, was not made in such a way that it was wholly impossible for it to die. Rather, it was made in such a way that it would not have died if man had not sinned. For it is the body that will be spiritual and immortal due to the life-giving spirit that will be wholly unable to die. In this respect it is like the soul, which was created immortal. For, although the soul may be called dead due to sin when it lacks a certain kind of life of its own, namely, the Spirit of God, by which it could also have lived wisely and happily, it nonetheless continues to live by virtue of a kind of life which, although miserable, is still properly its own, because it was created immortal. The same is true of the rebellious angels. By sinning they died in a sense, because they abandoned the fount of life,[41] which is God, by drinking from which they could have lived wisely and happily. But, because they were created immortal, they could not die in such a way that they wholly ceased to live and to feel. And, following the last judgment, they will be cast down into the second death, and even there they will not lack life. For they will certainly not lack feeling, since they are going to be in torment. But the people who belong to the grace of God and are fellow citizens of the holy angels who remained in the life of blessedness will be endowed with spiritual bodies in such a way that they will never again either sin or die. They will be clothed with an immortality like that of the angels, which cannot be taken away even by sin, and, although the nature of the flesh will stay the same, it will no longer be characterized by any fleshly corruptibility or heaviness.

---

41. See Jer 2:13.

The Question of Human Sexuality before the Fall

But now there arises an issue that, of necessity, has to be discussed and, with the help of the Lord God of truth, resolved: if the sexual desire of their disobedient members only arose in those first human beings due to their sin of disobedience, when divine grace had forsaken them, and if it was only then that they opened their eyes to their own nakedness — that is, really began to notice it — and only then that they covered their shameful members because the shameless stirrings of those parts could not be controlled by their will, then how would they have produced children if they had remained without sin, just as they were created? But, because this book must be brought to a close, and because such a major issue should not be squeezed into a brief discussion, it will be put off to the next book for more appropriate examination.

Study Questions for Book XIII

Today we speak of death in categories very different from those of Augustine. Clinical death occurs when all evident signs of life are gone, but a person may be resuscitated; brain death occurs with the irreversible cessation of brain and brain stem function; biological death is the irreversible disintegration of life at the cellular level and the collapse of the intricately interdependent systems of the body. Yet Augustine invites us to reflect on the meaning of our embodied existence beyond the categories of medical science. He makes room for a wider understanding of the personal disintegrations brought on by death. Can Augustine's scriptural understanding of death as punishment for sin be retrieved for fruitful theological dialogue today, perhaps through the category of disintegration?

Augustine's embrace of Neoplatonism shortly before his conversion to Christianity, together with his previous adherence to Manichean dualism, has sparked much debate on Augustine's openness to the goodness of physical creation and the body. However, one can trace a gradual "conversion" in Augustine's writings on the Book of Genesis regarding the biblical affirmation of the goodness of all creation. That affirmation is evident throughout *The City of God*. What significance lies in Augustine appeal to Plato's writings about Greek divinities to affirm the goodness and ultimate significance of embodied existence?

In Augustine's commentary, the resurrected body will be perfectly attuned to the soul, not antagonistic or rebellious towards it as it is in this life. Body and soul will be fully and totally integrated in a life of eternal happiness. Is there some continuity between the gradual transformation or divinization of the believer by grace during this life and the final redemption of the total person, body and soul, in heaven? Are the effects of grace on the relationship between body and soul in any way evident in this life, even before we die?

BOOK XIV

Book XIV falls into two main parts. The first opens with the assertion that, under the reign of death, there are — despite all variations in religion, language, and custom — only two types of human society, one that wishes to live according to the flesh and another that wishes to live according to the spirit. It then goes on to explain what it means to live according to the flesh. This cannot simply be equated with the pursuit of bodily or sensual pleasure but is rather rooted in a misdirection of the self. It is thus to be understood as living according to the self, or according to man, as opposed to living according to God. The source of this misdirection of the self is not the body, which is good. Even if, in this present life, the corruptible body weighs upon the soul, it is not the corruptible flesh that made the soul sinful but rather the sinful soul that made the body corruptible. Nor can the influence of the body be blamed for the emotions — the classical four passions of desire, joy, fear, and grief — that beset the self in this life. The passions are, in fact, modes of willing and therefore expressions of a person's love. They are good when a person's will and love are right and evil only when the person's will and love are directed to the wrong objects. The Stoic ideal of passionlessness or apatheia is thus to be rejected. To be without emotion in this life is inhuman, and even in their ultimate redemption the saints will feel love and gladness. Against this background, the second main part of the book pictures the life of the first human pair in paradise and then charts their fall into sin and its penal consequences. With no illness or death to fear, Adam and Eve were not afflicted by fear or grief. Their love for God and for each other was undisturbed, and, since what they loved was always present to be enjoyed, it brought them great gladness. But the devil, in his envy of still unfallen humanity, deceived the woman into eating from the forbidden tree, and the man, unwilling to be separated from his only companion, joined her in sin. This open act of disobedience to divine command was rooted, however, in a prior and hidden defection of the will from the uprightness in which God had created it. Thus the devil would not have ensnared man in the open sin of disobedience if man had not already begun to please himself in pride. As a result of the pair's sin, human nature was changed for the worse, becoming subject to corruption and death, and man was given over to himself — not in such a way that he became his own master but rather in such a way that he was set at odds with himself. Thus the retribution for disobedience to God was man's disobedience to himself. Human beings can no longer do what they will: the mind is often emotionally distressed against their will, and the flesh feels pain, grows old and dies against their will. This disobedience to self is especially evident in the fact that sexual desire and the sexual organs are no longer under the will's control: they may be aroused when arousal is not wanted and may refuse to be aroused when arousal is wanted. This lack of sexual self-control is the source of the shame that leads human beings to shroud their sexual activity in privacy, away from the public eye. It does not mean, however, that Adam and Eve in paradise, lacking this form of sexual desire, would not have had children. Instead, their sexual activity would have been directed by the will, not instigated by lust, for the bearing of children belongs to the good of marriage and is not a consequence of the punishment of sin. At the end, the book returns to the theme of the two societies, insisting that human sin cannot defeat the divine purpose and that, therefore, due to the intervention of divine grace, two loves have made two cities: love of God even to the point of contempt of self the heavenly city, and love of self even to the point of contempt of God the earthly city.

1. As we have already said in the preceding books,[1] God chose to give human beings their start from a single person. He did this, as we said, so that the human race would not only be joined in a society formed by likeness of nature but would also be bound together in unity and concord by the tie of kinship, mutually linked by the bond of peace. And the individual members of this race would not have been subject to death if the first two — of whom was created from nothing,[2] and the other from him[3] — had not merited death by their disobedience. So terrible was the sin of these two that, due to their sin, human nature was changed for the worse and was also transmitted to their posterity under the bondage of sin and the necessity of death.

The reign of death held such dominion over human beings that it would have pitched them all headlong into the second unending death, as the punishment they deserved, if the undeserved grace of God had not delivered some of them from its hold. And so it has happened that, even though there are a great many peoples spread across the world, living under various religious rites and moral customs and distinguished by a wide variety of languages, weaponry, and dress, there are actually only two types of human society; and, following our Scriptures, we may rightly speak of these as two cities.[4] One is the city of those who wish to live according to the flesh, the other of those who wish to live according to the spirit. Each desires its own kind of peace, and, when it finds what it seeks, each lives in its own kind of peace.

---

1. See above at XII,22.28.
2. See Gn 1:27.
3. See Gn 2:21-22.
4. On the variety to be found in the two cities, despite the fact that they remain only two, see below at XIX,17.

Living according to the Flesh and Living according to the Spirit

2. First, then, we need to see what it means to live according to the flesh and what it means to live according to the spirit. For anyone who takes only a superficial view of what I have said, without remembering or without paying attention to how Scripture expresses itself on this matter, could easily go wrong. He could think, for example, that the Epicurean philosophers clearly live according to the flesh, simply because they have taken bodily pleasure as man's highest good;[5] and he could think the same of any other philosophers who hold, in one way or another, that the good of the body is man's highest good. He could also think that this is true of the whole range of ordinary people who follow no philosophic teaching but show a propensity for lust and find delight only in the pleasures grasped by the bodily senses. And, on the other hand, he might suppose that the Stoics live according to the spirit, simply because they place the highest human good in the mind.[6] For what is the mind, if not spirit? In fact, however, it is clear that, as Scripture uses these expressions, all of these live according to the flesh....

Divine Scripture uses *flesh* in a variety of ways, and it would take too long to collect and examine them all. Therefore, to explore what it means to live according to the flesh — which is clearly evil, even though the nature of the flesh is not in itself evil — let us carefully examine the passage in the epistle which the apostle Paul wrote to the Galatians where he says, *Now the works of the flesh are obvious: fornication, impurity, licentiousness, idolatry, sorcery, enmity, strife, jealousy, anger, dissension, heresies, envy, drunkenness, carousing, and the like. I am warning you, as I warned you before, that those who do such things will not gain the kingdom of God.* (Gal 5:19-21)

This whole passage from the Apostle's epistle, when considered as fully as our present purpose seems to require, will be able to resolve the question of what it means to live according to the flesh. For, among the works of the flesh which he said were obvious and which he listed and condemned, we find not only those that have to do with the pleasures of the flesh (such as fornication, impurity, licentiousness, drunkenness, and carousing) but also those that represent vices of the mind and have nothing to do with fleshly pleasure. For who does not see that idolatry, sorcery, enmity, strife, jealousy, anger, dissension, heresies, and envy are all vices of the mind rather than of the flesh? It may actually happen that a person holds back from bodily pleasures for the sake of serving an idol or due to some heretical error; and yet even then, despite the fact that the person seems to restrain and repress the desires of the flesh, he is convicted, on the Apostle's authority, of living according to the flesh. By the very fact that he is abstaining from the pleasures of the flesh he is shown to be doing the works of the flesh!...

---

5. See Diogenes Laertius, *Lives of Eminent Philosophers* X,128-129.
6. See ibid. VII,87.

The Meaning of "Flesh"

3. Now, someone may claim that the flesh is the cause of every sort of vice in moral failure, since it is due to the influence of the flesh on the soul that the soul lives that kind of life. But anyone who says this obviously has not given careful consideration to the whole nature of man. It is true that *the corruptible body weighs down the soul* (Wis 9:15). But the same Apostle, in discussing this corruptible body, after saying, *Even though our outer man is undergoing corruption* (2 Cor 4:16), then went on to say a little later, *We know that if the earthly dwelling we inhabit is destroyed, we have a building from God, a dwelling not made with hands, eternal in the heavens. For in this dwelling we groan, longing to be clothed with our dwelling from heaven, if only we shall not be found naked once we have put it on. For we who are in this dwelling groan under its weight not because we want to be stripped of it but because we want to be clothed over, so that what is mortal may be swallowed up by life.* (2 Cor 5:1-4) We are, then, weighed down by the corruptible body; but, because we know that the cause of this weight is not the very nature and substance of the body but rather its corruption, we want not to be stripped of the body but instead to be clothed with its immortality. For at that point, too, the body will still be there; but, because it will no longer be corruptible, it will not weigh us down. Now, therefore, *the corruptible body weighs down the soul, and this earthly dwelling presses down the mind that thinks many thoughts* (Wis 9:15). Those who hold that all the evils of the soul stem from the body, however, are wrong.

It is true enough that Virgil seems to set forth the Platonic view in glorious verse when he says, "Heavenly is the origin of these seeds, and fiery their force, were they not held back by harmful bodies and slowed by earthly limbs and death-bound members."[7] And, because he wants us to recognize that the body is the source of all four of the well-known passions of the mind — desire, fear, joy, and grief[8] — as if these were the origins of all sins and vices, he goes on to add, "Hence they fear and they desire, they grieve and they rejoice. They do not look upward to the sky but are confined in darkness, held captive in a blind prison."[9] But our faith holds otherwise. For the corruption of the body, which weighs down the soul, is not the cause of the first sin but rather its punishment. It was not the corruptible flesh that made the soul sinful but the sinful soul that made the flesh corruptible.

Although some incitements to vice and even some vicious desires themselves may stem from this corruption of the flesh, it would still be quite wrong to ascribe all the vices of a wicked life to the flesh. To do so would be to absolve the devil, who has no flesh, from all these vices. For, even though we cannot say that the devil is guilty of fornication or drunkenness or any other sort of evil that has to do with the pleasures of the flesh (despite the fact that he is the one who secretly

---

7. *Aeneid* VI,730-732.
8. See Cicero, *Tusculan Disputations* III,10,22-11,25.
9. *Aeneid* VI,733-734.

persuades and incites us to such sins), he is still proud and envious in the highest degree. And these vices have taken such hold of him that, because of them, he is destined to eternal punishment in the prison of this murky air of ours....

For it is not by having flesh, which the devil does not have, that man has become like the devil; it is rather by living according to self, that is, according to man. For the devil chose to live according to self when he did not stand fast in the truth; and so the lie that he told came not from God but from himself. Thus the devil is not only a liar but the very father of lies.[10] He was, in fact, the first to lie; and falsehood, like sin, began with him.

Living according to Man, or Self, and Living according to God

4. It is, then, when man lives according to man and not according to God that he is like the devil. For even an angel should not have lived according to an angel but rather according to God, so as to stand fast in the truth and to speak God's truth rather than his own lie. For in another passage the Apostle says, *But if through my falsehood God's truth abounds* (Rom 3:7). Thus, in the case of man that falsehood is ours, but that truth is God's.

When man lives according to truth, then, he does not live according to self but according to God. For it is God who said, *I am the truth* (Jn 14:6). But when he lives according to himself — that is, when he lives according to man and not according to God — he most assuredly lives according to a lie. This is not because man himself is falsehood, for his author and creator is God, who is certainly not the author and creator of falsehood. It is rather because man was created upright, to live according to his creator and not according to himself — that is, to do God's will rather than his own. Not to live as he was created to live, then, is to live a lie.

Man obviously wills to be happy, even when he is not living in a way that makes it possible for him to attain happiness. And what could be more false than such a will? It is no mere empty words, then, to say that every sin is a falsehood. For sin only takes place due to our willing either that things should go well for us or that they should not go badly for us. Thus the falsehood is this: we sin so that things may go well for us, and instead the result is that they go badly; or we sin so that things may go better for us, and instead the result is that they get worse. What is the reason for this except that a man's wellbeing can only come from God, not from himself? But he forsakes God by sinning, and it is precisely by living according to himself that he sins.

Thus my assertion that two different and mutually opposed cities came into existence due to the fact that some people live according to the flesh and others according to the spirit can also be put in this way: it is due to the fact that some live according to man and others according to God. Paul shows this very clearly

---

10. See Jn 8:44.

when he says to the Corinthians, *For as long as there is jealousy and strife among you, are you not of the flesh and walking according to man?* (1 Cor 3:3) To walk according to man, then, is exactly the same as to be of the flesh, for the flesh — that is, a part of man — stands for man himself....

The Flesh, or the Body, Is not Evil

5. With regard to our sins and vices, then, there is no reason to insult the creator by putting the blame on the nature of the flesh, which in fact is good in its kind and in its order. But it is not good to forsake the good creator and live according to a created good, whether one chooses to live according to the flesh, or according to the soul, or according to the whole man, who consists of soul and flesh and can, as a consequence, be signified either by "soul" alone or by "flesh" alone. For anyone who praises the nature of the soul as the highest good and blames the nature of the flesh as something evil is undoubtedly fleshly in both his attraction to the soul and his flight from the flesh, since his view is based on human folly rather than divine truth.

The Platonists, of course, are not as foolish as the Manicheans. They do not detest earthly bodies as the very nature of evil.[11] Rather, they ascribe all the elements from which this visible and tangible world is put together, along with their properties, to God as their maker. But they still take the view that souls are so influenced by earthly limbs and death-bound members that these are the source of the soul's diseased desires and fears and joys and sorrows. And these four disturbances (as Cicero calls them[12]) or passions (the usual term, taken directly from the Greek[17]) include all the vices of human immorality....

The Will, the Passions, and Love

6. The important factor here is the quality of a person's will. If it is perverse, these emotions will be perverse; but, if it is right, they will be not only blameless but even praiseworthy. The will is involved in all of them; or, rather, they are all nothing more than modes of willing. For what are desire and joy but the will consenting to things that we want? And what are fear and grief but the will dissenting from things that we do not want? When the consent takes the form of seeking the things that we want, it is called desire; and when it takes the form of enjoying the things that we want, it is called joy. Similarly, when we dissent from something that we do not want to have happen, it is called fear; and when we dissent from something that actually does happen to us against our will, it is called grief. And in general, as a person's will is attracted or repelled in accord with the diversity

---

11. For the Manicheans, matter in general was evil.
12. See *Tusculan Disputations* IV,5,10.

of things that are pursued or avoided, so it is changed and turned into emotions of the one sort or the other.

Therefore, the person who lives according to God and not according to man must be a lover of the good, and it follows that he will hate the evil. And, since no one is evil by nature, but whoever is evil is evil due to some fault, the person who lives according to God owes a perfect hatred to those who are evil[13]— that is, he will neither hate the person because of the fault nor love the fault because of the person but will rather hate the fault and love the person. For, once the fault is cured, all that he should love will remain, and nothing will remain that he should hate.

7. When a person is resolved on loving God and on loving his neighbor as himself,[14] not according to man but according to God, it is undoubtedly on account of this love that he is called a person of good will. This disposition is more commonly called charity in Holy Scripture, but according to the same sacred writings it is also called love.[15] For the Apostle teaches that the person chosen to rule the people ought to be a lover of the good.[16] And the Lord himself, when questioning the apostle Peter, asked, *Do you cherish me more than these?* (Jn 21:15) And Peter answered, *Lord, you know that I love you* (Jn 21:15). And the Lord again asked not whether Peter loved him but whether he cherished him, and Peter again answered, *Lord, you know that I love you* (Jn 21:16). But when Jesus asked for a third time, he himself did not ask, "Do you cherish me," but rather, *Do you love me?* (Jn 21:17) At this point the evangelist observes, *Peter felt hurt because he said to him for the third time, Do you love me?* (Jn 21:17) In fact, however, it was not three times but only once that the Lord asked, *Do you love me?* The other two times he asked, *Do you cherish me?*[17] From this we can see, then, that even when the Lord asked, *Do you cherish me?* what he meant was no different from when he asked, *Do you love me?* Peter, however, did not change the word he used for the same thing but replied the third time, *Lord, you know everything; you know that I love you* (Jn 21:17).

I thought that I should mention this because some people suppose that cherishing and charity are different from love.[18] They claim that cherishing is to be taken in a good sense and love in a bad sense. It is quite certain, however, that not even the writers of secular literature spoke in this way. And so the philosophers

---

13. See Ps 139:21.
14. See Mt 22:37-39 par.
15. "Charity...love": *caritas...amor.*
16. "Lover": *amator.* See Tit 1:8.
17. "Love...cherish": forms of the verbs *amare* and *diligere* respectively.
18. "Cherishing...charity...love": *dilectionem...caritatem...amorem. Dilectio, caritas* and *amor* are the principle terms that Augustine uses for love. Sometimes he gives different weights to them, emphasizing either positive or negative possibilities. But at other times, as here, he treats them all as positive and as practically indistinguishable. See also below at XV,22, where *dilectio* is translated as "affection."

will have to see for themselves whether and on what grounds they can make such a distinction. Their books, at any rate, indicate clearly enough that they place a high value on love when it is concerned with good things and directed toward God himself. But the point I wanted to make is that the Scriptures of our religion, whose authority we rank above all other writings, make no distinction between love and cherishing or charity. For I have already shown that they speak of love in a good sense....

A right will, therefore, is a good love, and a perverse will is an evil love. Thus, love longing for what it loves is desire, and love actually possessing and enjoying what it loves is joy. Love seeking to escape what opposes it is fear, and love experiencing what opposes it, when it actually happens, is grief. These feelings are all bad, then, when the love is bad, and they are all good when the love is good.[19]...

8. In place of three of these passions the Stoics wanted to claim that there are in the mind of the wise man three dispositions which are called *eupatheiai* in Greek[20] and which Cicero calls "constant dispositions" in Latin[21] — will in place of desire, gladness in place of joy, and caution in place of fear. They denied, however, that there could be anything in the mind of the wise man that corresponds to distress or to pain, which, to avoid ambiguity, we have preferred to call "grief."

Will, they say, pursues the good, which is what the wise man does; gladness comes from attaining the good, which the wise man invariably attains; and caution avoids evil, which is what the wise man ought to avoid. But because grief arises from an evil that has already happened, and because the Stoics hold that no evil can happen to the wise man, they maintain that there can be nothing in his mind that corresponds to grief. In effect, then, they are saying that only the wise man can have will, gladness, and caution, while the foolish can feel only desire, joy, fear, and grief. The first three are constant dispositions, and the latter four are disturbances, as Cicero calls them, or passions, as most call them. As I have said, however, the first three are called *eupatheiai* in Greek, and the latter four *pathe*.[22]...

Will, caution, and gladness are common to both the good and the evil; and, to say the same thing in other words, desire, fear, and joy are also common to both the good and the evil. But the good have these emotions in a good way and the evil in a bad way, just as the human will is either rightly directed or wrongly directed. And even grief itself, despite the fact that the Stoics thought that they could find nothing corresponding to it in the mind of a wise man, is found in a good

---

19. This recalls Augustine's translation of the cardinal virtues into forms of love in *The Catholic Way of Life and the Manichean Way of Life* I,15,25.
20. Diogenes Laertius, *Lives of Eminent Philosophers* VII,116. *Eupatheiai* might be translated as "appropriate passions."
21. "Constant dispositions": *constantias*, or "constants." See *Tusculan Disputations* IV,6,11-14.
22. *Pathe* is usually translated simply as "passions."

sense, especially in our writers. For the Apostle praises the Corinthians for feeling grief in a godly way. Perhaps, however, someone will observe that the Apostle congratulates them for feeling the grief of repentance, the sort of grief that can only be felt by those who have sinned. For this is what he says: *I see that my letter grieved you, though only briefly. Now I rejoice, not because you were grieved but because your grief led to repentance. For you felt a godly grief, so that you suffered no damage from us in any way. For godly grief produces a repentance that leads to salvation and brings no regret, but worldly grief produces death. For see what earnestness this godly grief has produced in you.* (2 Cor 7:8-11)

This makes it possible for the Stoics, on their part, to respond that grief does seem to serve a useful purpose in leading to repentance for sin, but that there can be no grief in the mind of the wise man because, in his case, there is no sin for which he might grieve and repent, nor does he endure or experience any other evil that might lead him to grieve. For a story is told about Alcibiades (if my memory has not deceived me about the man's name). To himself he seemed to be happy, but when Socrates, by argument, proved to him how miserable he was because he was foolish, he burst into tears.[23] In his case, then, foolishness was the cause of this useful and desirable grief, the grief of a person who laments that he is what he ought not to be. But it is not the fool, the Stoics claim, but the wise man who cannot feel grief.

The Passions in the City of God

9. With regard to this question of the disturbances of the mind, however, I have already given my response to these philosophers in the ninth book of this work,[24] showing that they are more eager for controversy than for truth on this issue, which is far more a dispute over words than over reality. Among us Christians, in contrast, the citizens of the city of God, who live according to God during the pilgrimage of this life, feel fear and desire, pain and gladness, in accord with Holy Scripture and sound doctrine; and, because their love is right, they have all these emotions in the right way.

They fear eternal punishment, and they desire eternal life. They are pained in reality because they are still groaning inwardly while they wait for adoption, the redemption of their bodies,[25] and they are gladdened in hope because *the saying that is written shall be fulfilled: Death is swallowed up in victory* (1 Cor 15:54). Again, they fear to sin, and they desire to persevere. They are pained by their sins, and they are gladdened by their good works. That they may fear to sin, they are told, *Because iniquity will abound, the love of many shall grow cold* (Mt 24:12).

---

23. See Cicero, *Tusculan Disputations* III,32,77.
24. See above at IX,4-5.
25. See Rom 8:23.

That they may desire to persevere, Scripture tells them, *The one who perseveres to the end shall be saved* (Mt 10:22). That they may be pained by their sins, they are told, *If we say that we have no sin, we deceive ourselves, and the truth is not in us* (1 Jn 1:8). That they may be gladdened by good works, they are told, *God loves a cheerful giver* (2 Cor 9:7)....

Nor is it only on their own account that the citizens of the city of God are moved by these feelings. It is also on account of those whom they desire to see delivered and fear to see perish, and over whom they are pained if they do perish and gladdened if they are delivered. We who have come into Christ's Church from the gentile world should most especially keep in mind that best and strongest of men who glories in his own weaknesses,[26] the teacher of the gentiles in faith and truth, who worked harder than all his fellow apostles[27] and who taught the people of God in his many epistles, not only those whom he saw at the time but also those whom he foresaw in the future. He was an athlete of Christ, taught by him,[28] anointed by him, crucified with him,[29] glorying in him.[30] In the theater of this world, where he became a spectacle to both men and angels,[31] he fought a great fight according to the rules and pressed on toward the prize of his heavenly calling.[32] With the eyes of faith, the citizens of God's city gladly watch him rejoicing with those who rejoice, weeping with those who weep,[33] facing battles without and fears within,[34] desiring to depart and be with Christ,[35] longing to see the Romans in order to reap some harvest among them also, as he had among the rest of the gentiles.[36] They gladly watch him feeling jealousy for the Corinthians and, in this very jealousy, fearing that their minds might be led astray from the purity that is in Christ.[37] They gladly watch him feeling deep grief and unceasing anguish of heart for the Israelites[38] because, being ignorant of God's righteousness and willing to establish their own, they have not submitted to the righteousness of God;[39] and they gladly watch him declaring not only his pain but also his mourning for some who had previously sinned and had not repented of their impurity and fornication.[40]

---

26. See 2 Cor 12:19. The encomium of the apostle Paul that begins here attests to the high place that he occupied in the thought of Augustine, not only as a theological but also as a moral inspiration, and is typical of the early Church's attitude in his regard.
27. See 1 Cor 15:10.
28. See Gal 1:12.
29. See Gal 2:19.
30. See Rom 15:17.
31. See 1 Cor 4:9.
32. See Phil 3:14; 2 Tm 4:7-8.
33. See Rom 12:15.
34. See 2 Cor 7:5.
35. See Phil 1:23.
36. See Rom 1:11-13.
37. See 2 Cor 11:2-3.
38. See Rom 9:2.
39. See Rom 10:3.
40. See 2 Cor 12:21.

If these emotions and feelings, which spring from love of the good and holy charity, are to be called vices, then we might as well allow real vices to be called virtues. But, since these emotions are in accord with right reason when they occur where they ought properly to occur, who would dare to call them diseased or vice-ridden passions in this case? For this reason, even the Lord himself, when he condescended to live a human life in the form of a servant[41] (although wholly without sin[42]), showed these emotions where he judged that they ought to be shown. For there was nothing fake about the human emotion of one who had a true human body and a true human mind.[43] It is certainly not false, therefore, when the Gospel reports that he was grieved and angered at the Jews' hardness of heart,[44] or that he said, *For your sake I am glad so that you may believe* (Jn 11:15), or that he even shed tears when he was about to raise Lazarus,[45] or that he desired to eat the Passover with his disciples,[46] or that his soul was grieved when his passion drew near.[47] Rather, for the sake of his fixed purpose, he took on these emotions in his human mind when he willed, just as he became man when he willed.

The Emotions and the Future Life

Even when we have these emotions in the right way and according to God, however, we have to acknowledge that they belong to this life, not to the future life that is our hope, and that we often give way to them against our will. Sometimes, then, even though we are moved not by blameworthy desire but by praiseworthy charity, we still weep even when we do not want to.[48] In our case, then, it is due to the weakness of the human condition that we have these emotions. But that is not true of the Lord Jesus, for even his weakness was an expression of his power. So long as we bear the weakness of this life, however, we certainly would not be living rightly if we did not feel these emotions at all. For the Apostle berated and denounced certain people who were, he said, unfeeling.[49] And a holy Psalm blames those of whom it says, *I looked for someone to grieve with me, but there was none* (Ps 69:20). For, so long as we are in this place of misery, to live entirely without pain — as one of this world's men of letters saw and said — "comes only at the high price of an inhuman mind and an unfeeling body."[50]

---

41. See Phil 2:7.
42. See Heb 4:15.
43. This is perhaps said in view of Apollinarian doctrine, which held that the Word, or the *Logos*, took place of a human mind in Christ. Apollinaris of Laodicea (c. 310 – c. 390), from whom the doctrine takes its name, was responsible for promoting it.
44. See Mk 3:5.
45. See Jn 11:35.
46. See Lk 22:15.
47. See Mt 26:38.
48. As an example of Augustine's sensitivity on this issue, see *Confessions* IX,12,33.
49. See Rom 1:31.
50. Cicero, *Tusculan Disputations* III,6,12.

In this regard, let us consider what is called *apatheia* in Greek, which, if it could be put into Latin, would be called "impassibility."[51] If we are to understand this to mean living without those emotions which come upon us against reason and disturb the mind — for *apatheia* obviously refers to the mind, not to the body — then it is clearly a good and is much to be desired, but it does not belong to this life. For it is not in the voice of just any sort of people, but in the voice of those who are most godly and are most righteous and holy, that Scripture says, *If we say that we have no sin, we deceive ourselves, and the truth is not in us* (1 Jn 1:8). This *apatheia*, then, will come only when there is no sin in man. In this present life, however, we do well if we live without censure. And if anyone thinks that he lives without sin, he succeeds only in forfeiting forgiveness, not in avoiding sin.

But if *apatheia* means that no emotion at all can touch the mind, who would not regard this stupor as worse than all the vices? There is nothing absurd, then, about saying that perfect happiness will be free from the pangs of fear and from all forms of grief; but only a person wholly shut off from the truth would say that it will feel no love and gladness. Again, if *apatheia* means that no fear terrifies us and no pain hurts us, then we must certainly shun *apatheia* in this life if we want to live rightly, that is, if we want to live according to God. But, in the life of happiness which, it is promised, will be eternal, it is clearly something that we should hope for.

There is the kind of fear of which the apostle John says: *There is no fear in love, but perfect love casts out fear, for fear has to do with punishment, and whoever feels fear is not perfect in love* (1 Jn 4:18). But this is not the same kind of fear as Paul's fear that the Corinthians might be led astray by the serpent's cunning.[52] Paul's fear is the kind of fear that love feels; and, in fact, it is only love that feels this fear. But the other kind of fear, which love does not feel, is the fear of which the apostle Paul himself says, *You did not receive a spirit of slavery to fall back into fear* (Rom 8:15). On the other hand, the fear that is *pure, enduring forever* (Ps 19:9)— if it will be present in the world to come (and how else can it be understood to endure forever?)— is not the kind of fear that frightens a person away from an evil that might occur but rather the kind that holds him to a good that cannot be lost.[53]

---

51. In what follows Augustine briefly discusses the controversial topic of *apatheia*, which had already been addressed with less nuance by Jerome at about the same time in his Letter 133,1-3. Augustine may have this letter in mind (like Jerome, he translates *apatheia* as *impassibilitas*, or "impassivity"), as well as Jerome's *Answer to the Pelagians*, in which he argues that the Stoic notion of *apatheia* forms part of the basis of Pelagian doctrine, which allows for the possibility of sinlessness in this life. Augustine distinguishes between two kinds of *apatheia* — complete control of the emotions (*affectus*) that disturb the mind, which equates with sinlessness and which, though desirable in this life, is attainable only in eternal life; and the elimination of all the emotions, which may be possible in this life (as Augustine seems to allow theoretically) but neither desirable nor, when it comes to such emotions as love and gladness, possible or desirable in eternal life.
52. See 2 Cor 11:3.
53. On the two types of fear see also *Homilies on the First Epistle of John* 9,4-8; Cassian, *Conferences* XI,13.

For, where the love of a good already attained is immutable, there, surely, any fear of an evil to be avoided is a fear without anxiety (if we can say such a thing). For fear that is pure signifies the will whereby we shall necessarily will not to sin and shall necessarily will to guard against sin, not from any anxiety that in our weakness we might fall into sin but with the utter tranquility of love. Or, if no fear of any kind will be present in the total security of our unending and blissful joys, then to say *The fear of the Lord is pure, enduring forever* (Ps 19:9) is like saying *The patience of the poor shall not perish forever* (Ps 9:18). For it is not that patience itself will last forever, because there is no need for patience where there are no evils to be endured. It is rather that the goal reached through patience will endure for all eternity. And perhaps it is in this sense that this pure fear is said to endure forever, that is, in the sense that the goal to which it leads will endure forever.

All this being so, since we must lead a right life to reach a happy life, it follows that a right life will have all these emotions in the right way, and a perverse life will have them in a perverse way. But the life that is both happy and eternal will have a love and a gladness that are not only right but also assured, and it will have no fear or grief at all. And so it is now clear what qualities the citizens of the city of God ought to have during this pilgrimage here on earth in living according to the spirit and not according to the flesh, that is, in living according to God and not according to man; and it is clear, too, what qualities they will have in the immortality toward which they are traveling.

In contrast, the city, that is, the society, of the ungodly — who live not according to God but according to man, and, in their very worship of false divinity and contempt for true divinity, follow the teachings of men or of demons — is racked by perverse forms of these emotions as though by diseases and disruptions. And, if this city has any citizens who appear to control and in some way to temper these emotions, they are so proud and puffed up in their impiety that, for this very reason, the tumors of their pride expand as the pangs of their pain shrink. And, if some of these, with a vanity as monstrous as it is rare, are so enamored of their own self-restraint that they are not stirred or excited or swayed or influenced by any emotion at all, the truth is that they are losing all humanity rather than gaining real tranquility. For the fact that something is difficult does not make it right, nor does the fact that something has no feeling mean that it is in good health.

Emotion in the First Human Beings

10. But what of the first man — or rather of the first human beings, since there was a married pair?[54] It is not unreasonable to ask whether they felt in their animal bodies prior to sin the kinds of emotion that we shall not feel in our spiritual

---

54. That Adam and Eve were married is a noteworthy affirmation on the part of Augustine, inasmuch as this was not universally accepted in the early Church. See, e.g., Tertullian, *On Monogamy* 5; Gregory of Nyssa, *On Virginity* 12,4.

bodies when all sin has been purged and ended. If they did, how could it be true that they were genuinely happy in that memorable place of happiness, that is, in paradise? For who can truly be called happy if he is afflicted by fear or grief? But what possible reason could they have had for fear or for grief in the midst of such a marvelous abundance of such marvelous goods, where there was no death or any bodily illness to fear, and where nothing was absent that a good will might acquire and nothing was present that might do harm to either the flesh or the mind of a person living in happiness?

The pair lived in faithful and unalloyed fellowship, and their love for God and for each other was undisturbed. And from this love came great gladness, for what they loved was always present to be enjoyed. There was a tranquil avoidance of sin, and, as long as this lasted, no evil broke in from any side to bring them sorrow. Or did they, perhaps, desire to touch the forbidden tree and eat its fruit but were held back by fear of dying? In that case both desire and fear were already troubling them, even in that place. By no means, however, should we imagine that this was true where there was no sin whatsoever. For it plainly counts as sin to desire what the law of God prohibits and to abstain from it only from fear of punishment rather than from love of righteousness. By no means, I say, should we imagine that, prior to all sin, there was already present in paradise such sin that they felt with regard to a tree exactly what the Lord said with regard to a woman, *If anyone looks at a woman with lust for her, he has already committed adultery with her in his heart* (Mt 5:28).

How fortunate, then, were the first human beings! No disturbances of mind upset them; no distresses of body afflicted them. And all human society would have been just as fortunate if only the first pair had not committed the evil that would be transmitted to their posterity, and if only none of their stock had sown in iniquity what they would reap in damnation. This felicity would have continued until, through the blessing that said, *Be fruitful and multiply* (Gn 1:28), the number of the predestined saints was completed; and then another and greater felicity would have been granted, which was granted to the most blessed angels, where there would already have been the certain assurance that no one would sin and no one would die, and where the life of the saints, without any prior experience of toil, pain, or death, would already have been what it will be, after going through all these experiences, when incorruption is restored to the body at the resurrection of the dead.

The First Evil Will

11. But, because God foreknew all things and therefore could not have been unaware that man was going to sin, what we say about the city of God ought to correspond with his foreknowledge and design rather than with imaginings that could not actually have come to our knowledge because they were not actually in God's design. In fact, there was no way in which man could upset the divine purpose by his sin — as if he could have compelled God to change what he had determined! For God in his foreknowledge had anticipated both how evil man, whom he had created good, would become and what good, even so, he would himself bring forth from man. And, even if God is said to change his decrees (for we even read in Scripture, in a figurative expression, that God repented[55]), such statements are made from the point of view of human hopes and expectations or with respect to the orderly course of natural causes, not from the point of view of almighty God's foreknowledge of what he was going to do. As it is written, then, God *made man upright* (Qo 7:29) and therefore possessed of a good will. For man would not have been upright if he did not have a good will. A good will is, then, the work of God, since man was created with it by God.

In contrast, the first evil will, since it preceded all evil works in man, was a kind of defection from God's work to the will's own works rather than being any sort of work in its own right, and the will's own works were evil because they were willed according to self and not according to God. Thus the will itself — or rather man himself, insofar as his will was evil — was, so to speak, the evil tree that bore these works as its evil fruit.[56] Furthermore, although an evil will, because it is a fault, is contrary to nature rather than in accord with nature, it still belongs to the nature in which it is a fault, for a fault cannot exist except in a nature. But it can only exist in a nature which the creator created out of nothing, not in a nature which he begot out of himself in the way that he begot the Word through whom all things were made.[57] For, although God fashioned man from the dust of the earth,[58] the earth itself and all earthly matter come from nothing whatsoever, and the soul which God gave to the body when man was made was also created out of nothing.

Evil things, however, are overcome by good things. This is in fact so true that, although evil things are allowed to exist in order to show how the creator's all-foreseeing justice can use even these for the good, good things can exist without the evil, as can the true and supreme God himself, and as can all heavenly creatures, invisible and visible, above this murky air of ours. But evil things cannot exist without the good, for the natures in which they inhere, insofar as they are natures, are most certainly good. What is more, evil is eliminated not by removing the nature which it had entered or by removing any part of that nature but rather by healing and rectifying the nature that had become vitiated and depraved.

The will's choice, then, is only truly free when it is not enslaved to vices and sins. That is how it was given by God. But what it lost by its own fault can only be restored by the one who was able to give it in the first place. That is the reason why the Truth says, *If the Son sets you free, you will be free indeed* (Jn 8:36). And this

---

55. See Gn 6:6; 1 S 15:11.
56. See Mt 7:17-18.
57. See Jn 1:3.
58. See Gn 2:6.

is the same as if he said, "If the Son makes you saved, you will be saved indeed." For he is our liberator in precisely the same way that he is our savior.

The Human Fall

Thus, man lived according to God in a paradise both corporeal and spiritual. It was not a merely corporeal paradise providing good things for the body without also being spiritual to provide good things for the mind. Nor was it a merely spiritual paradise for man to enjoy through his inner senses without also being corporeal for him to enjoy through his outer senses. It was plainly both, and it plainly provided for both. But then came that proud and therefore envious angel who, through his pride, had turned away from God and had turned to himself. With a tyrant's disdain, so to speak, he chose to rejoice at having subjects rather than to be a subject himself; and so he fell from the spiritual paradise. As best I could, I have discussed his fall — and that of his companions who, from being angels of God, were turned into his angels — in the eleventh and twelfth books of this work.[59] After his fall, he sought to worm his way into the heart of man by cunning and false counsel, for, after his own fall, he was consumed with envy of the still unfallen human beings. To this end he chose as his mouthpiece a serpent in the corporeal paradise where, along with the two humans, the male and the female, there lived all the other terrestrial animals, tame and harmless. This slippery animal, which moves in twists and coils, was obviously suitable for his work. By his angelic presence and his superior nature, he made the serpent his subject in spiritual wickedness, and, misusing it as his instrument, he had deceitful conversation with the woman. He began, that is, with the lower lesser part of the human couple so that, by stages, he might reach them both, presuming that the man would not be so easy to dupe and could not be deceived into erring himself but would fall prey to another's error.

That is what happened in Aaron's case when the people went astray. He did not consent to make an idol because he was convinced; instead he gave in because he felt constrained.[60] Nor is it credible that Solomon made the error of thinking that he ought to serve idols; it was rather by the enticements of women that he was compelled into such a sacrilegious act.[61] And it was the same with that man and his wife. They were alone with each other, two human beings, a married couple; and we must believe that it was not because he thought she was speaking the truth that he was seduced into transgressing God's law but because he yielded to the tie that bound them together. It was not without reason, then, that the Apostle said, *Adam was not deceived, but the woman was deceived* (1 Tm 2:14). For she accepted what the serpent said to her as if it were true, while he was unwilling to be separated from his only companion, even when it came to sharing in sin. He was no less guilty on that account, however, if he sinned knowingly and deliberately.

---

59. See above at XI,13 and XII,6.9.
60. See Ex 32:1-5.
61. See 1 K 11:1-8.

That is why the Apostle does not say that Adam did not sin but that *Adam was not deceived*. For he is plainly referring to Adam when he says, *Through one man sin came into the world* (Rom 5:12), and again, more explicitly, when he says a little further on, *Like the transgression of Adam* (Rom 5:14).

The Apostle wanted us to understand that the "deceived" are those who do not think that what they are doing is sin. But Adam knew. Otherwise, how could it be true that *Adam was not deceived*? Since he was still unacquainted with God's severity, however, he could have been mistaken in believing that he had committed a pardonable offence. Thus, while he was not deceived in the same way that the woman was deceived, he was still mistaken about how his excuse would be judged when he said, *The woman whom you gave to be with me, she gave me fruit from the tree, and I ate* (Gn 3:12). What need, then, to say more? They were not both deceived by credulity, but they were both taken captive by sin and entangled in the devil's snares.

12. Someone may want to ask why human nature is not changed by other sins in the same way that it was changed by the transgression of the first two human beings. As a result of their sin it was made subject to all the corruption that we see and feel and, through this, to death as well. At the same time, it was disturbed and tossed about by a flood of powerful and conflicting emotions; and so it became very different from what it had been in paradise prior to sin, even though man then had an animal body just as he does now.

As I say, if anyone is concerned about this, he should not think that the sin committed was minor or trivial just because it only had to do with food, and a food that was not even evil or harmful, except that it was forbidden. For God certainly would not have created or planted anything evil in that place of preeminent felicity. What was at stake in God's precept, however, was obedience, and this virtue is in a way the mother and guardian of all virtues in a rational creature. For the rational creature was so made that it is beneficial for it to be subject to God but ruinous for it to follow its own will rather than the will of its creator. Furthermore, where there was such an abundance of other foods, a command prohibiting the eating of one kind of food was as easy to observe as it was simple to remember, especially when desire was not yet at odds with the will (which only came later, due to the punishment of the transgression). Thus the injustice of violating the command was all the greater precisely because it would have been so very easy to observe and keep it.

The Evil Will Precedes the Evil Act

13. It was actually in secret, however, that the first human beings began to be evil, and it was as a consequence of this that they subsequently slipped into open disobedience. For there would have been no evil act unless there had first been an evil will. And what could have been the beginning of their evil will except pride?

For *pride is the beginning of all sin* (Sir 10:13).[62] And what is pride but an appetite for perverse exaltation? For it is perverse exaltation to abandon the principle to which the mind ought to adhere and instead, as it were, to become and to be one's own principle. This happens when a person is overly pleased with himself, and he is overly pleased with himself when he defects from that immutable good which ought to please him far more than he pleases himself. And this defection is voluntary. For, if the will had remained steadfast in love for the higher and immutable good by which it was illumined with the light to see and kindled with the fire to love, it would not have turned away from that good in order to please itself; and it would not have been so darkened and chilled as to allow the woman to think that the serpent had spoken the truth or allow the man to put his wife's will ahead of God's command and to imagine that it was a pardonable transgression if he did not forsake his life-companion even when it came to sharing in sin.

Thus, the evil act — that is, the transgression of eating the forbidden food — was committed by people who were already evil, and it would not have been committed if they had not already been evil. For only an evil tree would have produced that evil fruit. Furthermore, it happened contrary to nature that the tree was evil, for it certainly would not have happened without a fault of will, which is contrary to nature. But only a nature created out of nothing could have been perverted by a fault. That it is a nature, therefore, is due to the fact that it was created by God, but that it fell away from what it was is due to the fact that it was created out of nothing.

But man did not fall away so completely as to lose all being and cease to exist; rather, in turning to himself, he became less than he was when he still clung to the one who supremely exists. Thus, to abandon God and to exist in oneself — that is, to be pleased with oneself — does not mean that one immediately loses all being but rather that one veers toward nothingness. That is why, according to Holy Scripture, the proud are also given another name and are called *self-pleasers* (2 Pt 2:10). For it is good to lift up your heart[63] — not to self, however, which is due to pride, but to the Lord, which is due to obedience. And obedience can belong only to the humble.

Humility and Pride

Surprisingly, then, there is in humility something that lifts up the heart, and there is in exaltation something that brings down the heart. It certainly seems

---

62. The best Hebrew and Greek manuscripts indicate that this verse should read *The beginning of pride is sin* rather than *Pride is the beginning of all sin*. See W. W. Green, "*Initium omnis peccati superbia*: Augustine on Pride as the First Sin," in *University of California Publications in Classical Philology* 13 (1949) 413. Augustine had before him a Latin version of the text that reversed the order; it is also reversed in both the Septuagint and the Vulgate.
63. Augustine is alluding here to a liturgical formula — "Lift up your hearts" — which is part of the dialogue which precedes the preface of the eucharistic liturgy and which dates to at least the early third century. See Hippolytus (?), *Apostolic Tradition* 4.

somewhat paradoxical that exaltation should bring down and humility should lift up. Devout humility, however, makes the heart subject to what is superior to it. But nothing is superior to God, and so the humility that makes the heart subject to God actually exalts it. In contrast, exaltation expresses a fault, and, for that very reason, it spurns subjection and falls away from him who has no superior. As a result, it brings the heart down, and what is written comes to pass: *You cast them down while they were being exalted* (Ps 73:18). It does not say "when they had been exalted," as if they were first exalted and then cast down. Rather, it says that they were cast down exactly while they were being exalted. In itself, then, to be exalted is already to be cast down.

For this reason humility is especially commended in the city of God and to the city of God in the present, while it is on pilgrimage in this world; and humility is especially proclaimed in its king, who is Christ. At the same time, Sacred Scripture teaches that the opposite of this virtue, the vice of exaltation, is especially dominant in his adversary, who is the devil. Here, certainly, is the great difference that distinguishes the two cities of which we are speaking, one a company of the godly, the other a company of the godless, each including the angels that belong to it: in one the love of God comes before all else and in the other love of self.

The devil, therefore, would not have ensnared man in the open and obvious sin of doing what God had forbidden if man had not already begun to be pleased with himself. For it is precisely because he had begun to be pleased with himself that he was also delighted to hear *You shall be like gods* (Gn 3:5). But they would have been better able to be like gods if they had clung to the true and supreme principle in obedience, instead of taking themselves as their own principle in pride.[64] For created gods are not gods by virtue of any truth of their own but by virtue of participation in the true God. By grasping for more, then, a person becomes less when, in choosing to be self-sufficient, he defects from the only one who is truly sufficient for him.

The first evil, then, is this: when man is pleased with himself, as if he were himself light, he turns away from the light which, if it pleased him, would have made him light himself. This evil came first, in secret, and its result was the evil that was committed in the open. For what Scripture says is true: *Before a fall the heart is exalted, and prior to honor it is humbled* (Prv 18:12). In short, the fall that takes place in secret precedes the fall that takes place in full view, even though the former is not counted as a fall.[65] For who thinks of exaltation as a fall, despite the fact that it already includes the defection by which a person turns away from the Most High? On the other hand, who fails to see that there is a fall when an obvious and unmistakable transgression of a commandment takes place?...

---

64. "Principle": *principium*. The Latin word usually means "beginning" or "source" — in this case the source of being.
65. The notion of a hidden fall in paradise that preceded the open fall is found also in Origen, *On Prayer* 29,18.

14. But still worse and more damnable is the pride that tries to take refuge in an excuse, even when the sins are perfectly obvious. That is what the first human beings did when the woman said, *The serpent deceived me, and I ate* (Gn 3:13), and the man said, *The woman whom you gave to be with me, she gave me fruit from the tree, and I ate.* No plea for pardon sounds here, no entreaty for healing. Although, unlike Cain,[66] they did not deny what they had done, their pride still tried to shift its own wrongful act onto another, the woman's pride blaming the serpent and the man's pride blaming the woman. But, where the transgression of the divine command is so obvious, their words serve more as an accusation than as an excuse. For the fact that the woman acted on the serpent's instigation and the man on the woman's invitation does not mean that they themselves were not the ones who acted — as if anything ought to take priority over God when it comes either to believing someone's words or yielding to someone's suggestion!

The Punishment of Sin

15. Thus, man scorned the command of God, who had created him[67] who had made him in his own image,[68] who had set him above the other animals,[69] who had established him in paradise,[70] who had provided him with an abundance of all things for his wellbeing,[71] and who had not burdened him with numerous oppressive and difficult commandments but had given him one very brief and easy command to guide him in wholesome obedience.[72] By this commandment God sought to impress on his creature, for whom free service is a benefit and an advantage, that he is Lord. And because man scorned this commandment, the condemnation that followed was just. The consequence of that condemnation was that man, who would have become spiritual even in his flesh by keeping the commandment, instead became fleshly even in his mind; and man, who had become pleased with himself due to his pride, was now given over to himself due to God's justice. He was not given over to himself, however, in such a way that he was fully his own master. Rather, he was at odds with himself, and, in place of the freedom he desired, he lived a life of harsh and bitter slavery under the one to whom he had given his consent by sinning.[73] By his own will he was dead in spirit, and against his own will he was going to die in body as well.[74] He had forsaken eternal life, and, unless delivered by grace, he was condemned to eternal death....

---

66. See Gn 4:9.
67. See Gn 1:27; 2:7.
68. See Gn 1:26-27.
69. See Gn 1:28; 2:19-20.
70. See Gn 2:8.
71. See Gn 1:29; 2:16.
72. See Gn 2:17.
73. See Gn 3:18-19.
74. See Gn 3:19.

To put it briefly, then, in the punishment of that sin the retribution for disobedience was simply disobedience itself. For what is man's misery if not his own disobedience to himself, with the result that, because he would not do what he could, he now cannot do what he would?[75]...

Lust, Human Sexuality, and the Sense of Shame

16. There are, then, lusts for many things; but when the word is used without reference to any specific object, the only thing that usually comes to mind is the lust that arouses the lewd parts of the body.[76] This lust not only takes over the whole body externally but also seizes the person inwardly. When it moves the whole man by combining and intermingling the emotion of the mind with the craving of the flesh, there follows a pleasure greater than any other bodily pleasure; and, at the moment this pleasure reaches its climax, almost all mental alertness and cognitive vigilance, so to speak, are obliterated. Any friend of wisdom and holy joys, living the married life but *knowing*, as the Apostle warns us, *how to possess his vessel in holiness and honor, not in diseased desire, like the gentiles who do not know God* (1 Thes 4:4-5), would surely prefer, if possible, to beget children without this kind of lust. For then, even in the role of procreation, the parts created for this work would serve his mind, just as his other members serve his mind in the various works to which they are assigned, not incited by the fire of lust but acting at the will's behest.

As it is, however, not even those who love this pleasure are roused either to marital intercourse or to impure and shameful acts strictly at their own will. Instead, the impulse sometimes intrudes when it is not wanted, and sometimes it deserts the eager lover, leaving the body cold while desire is blazing in the mind. And so, strangely enough, lust refuses its service not only to the will to procreate but even to the lust for wanton enjoyment; and, although it is in general wholly opposed to the mind's control, there are times when it is divided against itself, arousing the mind but refusing to follow its own lead by arousing the body as well.[77]

17. There is good reason, then, to be especially ashamed of this lust; and there is good reason, too, why the members that it stirs or fails to stir at its own whim, so to speak, and not at our choice, should be called our shameful parts. Prior to man's sin they were not shameful, for, as Scripture says, *They were naked and were not ashamed* (Gn 2:25). It is not that they were unaware of their nakedness. It is rather

---

75. See Rom 7:15-20; Terence, *Andria* II,1,305-306.
76. For a detailed discussion of Augustine's attitude toward sexuality, exemplified in what follows, see Peter Brown, *The Body and Society: Men, Women and Sexual Renunciation in Early Christianity* (New York: Columbia University Press, 1988) 387-427.
77. See *Marriage and Desire* I,6,7.

that their nakedness was not yet indecent because lust was not yet stirring those members without regard to their will, and the flesh was not yet bearing witness against man's disobedience, as it were, by its own disobedience....

18. ...And what about marital intercourse, which takes place, according to the terms of the marriage contract, for the sake of producing children?[78] Even though it is legal and honorable, it still seeks out a room removed from witnesses, does it not? The bridegroom, before he even begins to caress his bride, sends away all the servants and even his groomsmen and anyone else whom the ties of kinship had allowed to enter, does he not? And since, as a certain "supreme master of Roman eloquence"[79] declares, "all right actions want to be placed in the full light of day,"[80] that is, desire to be known, this right action also desires to be known; but it still blushes to be seen. For who does not know what married couples do between themselves to beget children, especially since it is precisely for this purpose that men take wives with so much ceremony? And yet, when the act from which children come is actually being performed, not even the children who have already been born are allowed to witness it. For this right action may desire to be known by the light of the mind, but it shrinks from the light of the eyes. Why is this, if not because something that is by nature decent is performed in such a way that it is accompanied by an element of shame, by way of punishment?

19. It is on this account, too, that the philosophers who have come closest to the truth acknowledged that anger and lust are vice-promoting parts of the soul, since they are turbulent and disorderly emotions which stir us to acts that wisdom forbids and therefore require mind and reason to keep them under control. This third part of the soul, they claim, is located in a kind of citadel from which to rule the other two, so that, when reason commands and anger and lust are at its service, justice may be preserved among all the parts of man's soul.[81]

These philosophers admit, then, that these two parts of the soul incite to vice even in the case of the wise and temperate man. That is why the mind reins them in by subduing and restraining them, calling them back from the things that they are unjustly moved to do and allowing them to do the things that are permitted by the law of wisdom, such as anger for the purpose of imposing just constraints or lust for the purpose of producing offspring. But in paradise, I say, prior to sin, these two parts of the soul did not incite to vice. For they were not then moved toward anything contrary to a right will, nor was there any need for the ruling reins of reason, so to speak, to hold them back.

---

78. According to Roman law, marriage was for the purpose of begetting children. See Suetonius, *Lives of the Twelve Caesars*, Julius Caesar 52,3; Aulus Gellius, *Attic Nights* IV,3,2.
79. Lucan, *Pharsalia* VII,62-63.
80. Cicero, *Tusculan Disputations* II,26,64.
81. The division of the soul into three parts, the irascible or spirited, yielding anger (*ira*), the appetitive or concupiscible, yielding lust (*libido*), and the rational, whose purpose is to govern the other two and thus preserve justice, can be traced to Plato, *Republic* IV,431a-444b; IX,580c-592b.

Now, however, they are moved contrary to the will, and those who live temperate, just, and godly lives only keep them under control, sometimes with ease and sometimes with difficulty, by restraining and resisting them. This is most definitely not a healthy state, due to nature, but rather a weakened state, due to guilt. And, if modesty does not hide the acts of anger and of the other emotions, as expressed in word and deed, in the same way that it hides the acts of lust performed by the sexual organs, that is only because, in the case of the other members of the body, it is not the emotions themselves that set them in motion. It is rather the will that sets them in motion, when it gives its consent to the emotions, for the will has complete control over the use of these other members. No one who speaks a word in anger, or even hits out at another, could possibly do so if his tongue or his hand were not in some way set in motion by the will's command; and, even when there is no anger, it is still the will that sets them in motion. In the case of the sexual organs, however, lust has somehow taken such complete control of them that they are incapable of being moved if lust is absent, and they do not move at all unless it arises either on its own or in response to stimulation. It is this that causes shame; it is this that, in embarrassment, shuns the eyes of onlookers. A man would rather put up with a crowd of spectators when he is unjustly venting his anger on another than have a single individual watching even when he is justly having intercourse with his wife....

20. ...There is no doubt, then, that human nature is ashamed of this lust, and rightly so. For the disobedience of this lust, which has made the sexual members of the body completely subject to its urges and has snatched them away from the will's control, shows quite clearly what the retribution was for man's first sin. And it was particularly apt that this retribution should appear in the part of the body that engenders the very nature that was changed for the worse by that first and terrible sin. No one can be rescued from the meshes of that sin — which was committed when all men existed in one man, to the common ruin of them all, and was punished by the justice of God — unless it is expiated in each man individually by the grace of God.

Human Procreation Prior to the Fall

21. By no means, then, should we believe that it was due to this lust, which led them to cover those organs in shame, that the couple established in paradise was going to fulfill the words of God's blessing, *Be fruitful and multiply, and fill the earth* (Gn 1:28). On the contrary, it was only after their sin that this lust arose. It was only after their sin that their nature — not without shame, since it had lost the power to have every part of the body serve it — felt, noticed, blushed at, and concealed this lust. But the nuptial blessing, bidding the married couple to be fruitful and multiply and fill the earth, even though it held good for them after they sinned, was originally given before they sinned; and it was given before they sinned precisely so that people would realize that the procreation of children belongs to the glory of marriage, not to the punishment of sin....

22. For our part we have no doubt that to be fruitful and multiply and fill the earth, in accord with God's blessing, is a gift of marriage and that God instituted marriage from the beginning, prior to man's sin, by creating male and female, each sex being plainly evident in the flesh. And the blessing itself was clearly linked to this work of God. For, after saying *Male and female he created them* (Gn 1:27), Scripture immediately goes on to say, *And God blessed them and said to them, Be fruitful and multiply, and fill the earth and rule over it* (Gn 1:28), and so on....

It is certain, then, that male and female were constituted at the first just as we now see and know them, two human beings of different sex, and that they are said to be *one* either because of their union or because of the woman's origin, due to her creation from the side of the man.[82] For it is to this first example, as a precedent instituted by God, that the Apostle also appeals when he admonishes each of us that husbands should love their wives.[83]

Sexuality before the Fall

23. If anyone says that there would have been no intercourse and no bearing of children if the first human beings had not sinned, that is tantamount to saying that man's sin was necessary in order to complete the number of the saints. For if, apart from their sin, they would have remained alone — due to the fact that, as some think, they could not have had children unless they sinned — then it is obvious that sin was necessary for there to be not just two righteous persons but many. But, if it is absurd to believe this, we must believe instead that, even if no one had sinned, the number of the saints would still have been large enough to fill up that most blessed city and, in fact, would have been just as large as the number now being gathered, by God's grace, from the multitude of sinners as long as the children of this age[84] beget and are begotten.

It follows that, even if there had been no sin, the marriage of the first human beings, which was worthy of the delight of paradise, would have produced children to love, but without any lust to be ashamed of. As it is, however, we have no example to show how this could have taken place. But that is no reason why it should seem incredible that this one member of the body could then have served the will without any stirring of lust, just as so many other members serve it now. We move our hands and feet to perform their tasks when and as we will, with no resistance on their part, and we do this with all the ease that we observe in ourselves and others.

---

82. See Gn 2:21-23.
83. See Eph 5:25; Col 3:19.
84. See Lk 20:34.

We see this most especially in the case of craftsmen engaged in their various tasks where active training develops skill in a weaker and slower nature. Why should we not believe, then, that the sexual members could have served people for the task of generating children in complete obedience to the will's command, just as the other members do, even if there had been no lust, which came in retribution for sin's disobedience?...

But, when restraint is imposed by the governing will on the other members, without which the organs that are excited by lust against the will cannot satisfy their appetite, modesty is preserved, not because delight in sin has been removed but because it is not permitted. In paradise, there is no doubt, marriage would not have experienced this resistance, this opposition, this conflict between lust and will — or, at least, it would not have felt any needs of lust at odds with the sufficiency of will — if the culpable disobedience of sin had not been punished with the penal disobedience of the sexual organs. Instead, those organs, like the body's other members, would have served the will, and so all the body's members would have served the will. Thus the instrument created for this purpose would have sown its seed upon "the field of generation"[85] in the same way that the hand now sows seed upon the ground, and there would have been no need for modesty to resist our wish to discuss this matter in greater detail or to compel us to apologize and ask for pardon from chaste ears. Instead, without any fear of obscenity, discussion would range freely over everything that might come to mind with regard to bodily members of this sort, and there would not even be any words that might be called obscene. Rather, whatever was said on this subject would be as fully respectable as what we say when speaking of other parts of the body....

24. Thus the man would have sown, and the woman would have received, the seed of offspring at the time and to the extent needed, and their genital organs would have been moved by the will rather than being excited by lust. For at our command we move not only those members which have bones and joints, such as the hands, feet, and fingers, but also those which are loosely made of soft tissue. When we will, we move these by shaking or extend them by stretching or bend them by flexing or harden them by contracting, such as those which the will moves, so far as it can, in the mouth and face. And even the lungs — which are the softest of all the internal organs except for the innermost parts, and for this reason are protected in the cavity of the chest — serve the will for the purpose of drawing in and exhaling breath, and for producing and modulating the voice; like the bellows of blacksmiths and organists, they serve the will of anyone who breathes out or breathes in, or speaks, or shouts, or sings....

Is there any reason, then, why we should not believe that, prior to the sin of disobedience and the punishment of corruptibility, the human members could have served the human will for the purpose of generating children without any lust

---

85. Virgil, *Georgics* III,136.

coming into play? Man was given over to himself, therefore, because he abandoned God by pleasing himself; and, because he did not obey God, he could not even obey himself. This is the root of the more obvious misery that man does not live as he wishes to live. For, if he lived as he wished, he would consider himself happy; but, even then, if he lived shamefully, he would not really be happy....

The Happiness of Paradise

26. In paradise, then, man lived as he wanted for as long as what he wanted was at one with God's command. He lived in the enjoyment of God, from whose goodness he himself was good. He lived without any lack, and he had it in his power to live this way forever. There was food to keep away hunger, drink to keep away thirst, and the tree of life to keep away the decay of old age. There was no corruption in the body, or arising from the body, to inflict distress on any of his senses. There was no fear of disease from within or of injury from without. He had supreme health in his flesh and complete tranquillity in his soul.

Just as in paradise there was no extreme of heat or cold, neither in the one who lived there was there any impulse of desire or fear to oppose his good will. There was no grief at all, nor was there any empty joy. Rather, true gladness flowed continually from God, for whom there burned *love from a pure heart, and a good conscience, and genuine faith* (1 Tm 1:5). Between husband and wife there was a faithful partnership of genuine love, an alertness of mind and body in true concord, and an effortless observance of the commandment. Weariness did not fatigue them in their leisure, and sleep did not press itself upon them against their will.

Far be it from us to imagine that, in the midst of such material ease and such human happiness, the seed of offspring could not have been sown without the disease of lust. Rather, the sexual members would have been moved at the will's command, as the other members are; and, without the enticing goad of sexual heat, the husband would have poured his seed into his wife's womb with tranquility of mind and with no corruption of her bodily integrity. For the mere fact that it cannot be proved by experience is no reason not to believe that, when those parts of the body were not activated by boiling heat but were rather brought into play by the will's power as the need arose, the male seed could have been discharged into the wife's womb without harm to the woman's genital integrity, just as the flow of menstrual blood can now be discharged from a virgin's womb without any such harm. For the seed could be injected through the same passage by which the menstrual flow is ejected. And, just as the woman's womb would have been opened for childbirth not with groans of pain but by the simple impulse of having reached full term, so the two sexes would have been conjoined for impregnation and conception not by lustful appetite but by an act of will.

We are speaking here about things that cause us to feel shame; and so, even though we are simply trying as best we can to imagine what they might have been like before they became a cause for shame, our discussion must be curbed by a modesty that holds us back instead of being carried further by what little eloquence we have. Even those who could have experienced what I am talking about never actually did experience it. Their sin occurred first, and they were exiled from paradise before they could come together in the work of propagation as an act of tranquil choice. As it is, then, when these things are mentioned, how can anything now occur to the human senses except the boiling lust of our actual experience rather than the placid will of my conjecture? That is why a sense of shame inhibits my speech, even though reason does not lack material for thought.

Man's Sin and God's Foreknowledge

It is certain, however, that almighty God, the supreme and supremely good creator, who helps and rewards good wills, who abandons and condemns evil wills, and who orders both alike, did not lack a plan for completing the fixed number of citizens that in his wisdom he had predestined for his city, even from the condemned human race. He does not now choose them for their merits, since the whole mass has been condemned,[86] so to speak, in its vitiated root. Rather, he chooses them by grace, and he shows his generosity to those he has delivered not only in his dealings with them but also in his dealings with those he has not delivered. For each person can recognize that he has been rescued from evils due not to any goodness on his own part but to a goodness freely given, when he is exempted from the common destiny of those whose just punishment he had shared. Is there any reason, then, why God should not have created people who, he foreknew, were going to sin? Especially since he would be able to demonstrate, in them and through them, both what their guilt deserved and what his grace would give, and since, under God's creating and directing power, the right order of things would not be perverted by the perverse order of wrongdoers.

27. Sinners, therefore, whether angels or humans, do nothing that impedes the *great works of the Lord, designed to match his every will* (Ps 111:2); for in his providence and omnipotence God distributes to each what is due to each and knows how to make good use not only of the good but also of the evil....

As it turned out, then, no future event was unknown to God, and yet God did not, by his foreknowledge, compel anyone to sin. By their subsequent experience, however, he did demonstrate to rational creatures, both angels and human beings, what a difference there is between the creature's personal presumption and his own divine protection. For who would dare to believe or to say that it was not in

---

86. "The whole mass has been condemned": *universa massa...damnata est. Massa* is a term frequently employed by Augustine to refer to humanity under the aspect of its unredeemed sinfulness; it is sometimes accompanied by the adjective *damnata*. See below at XV, 1.21 and XXI,12. For a summary of the use and meaning of *massa* see Allan D. Fitzgerald, ed., *Augustine through the Ages: An Encyclopedia* (Grand Rapids: Eerdmans, 1999) 545-547.

God's power to make sure that neither angel nor human being would fall? But God preferred to leave the issue in their power and thus demonstrate how greatly their pride avails for evil and how greatly his grace avails for good.

Two Loves Have Made Two Cities

28. Two loves, then, have made two cities.[87] Love of self, even to the point of contempt for God, made the earthly city, and love of God, even to the point of contempt for self, made the heavenly city. Thus the former glories in itself, and the latter glories in the Lord. The former seeks its glory from men, but the latter finds its highest glory in God, the witness of our conscience. The former lifts up its head in its own glory; the latter says to its God, *My glory, and the one who lifts up my head* (Ps 3:3). In the former the lust for domination dominates both its princes and the nations that it subjugates; in the latter both leaders and followers serve one another in love, the leaders by their counsel, the followers by their obedience. The former loves its own strength, displayed in its men of power; the latter says to its God, *I love you, O Lord, my strength* (Ps 18:1).

In the former, then, its wise men, who live according to man, have pursued the goods either of the body or of their own mind or of both together; or, at best, any who were able to know God *did not honor him as God or give thanks to him, but they became futile in their thinking, and their foolish heart was darkened. Claiming to be wise* — that is, exalting themselves in their own wisdom, under the domination of pride — *they became fools; and they changed the glory of the incorruptible God into the likeness of an image of a corruptible man or of birds or of four-footed beasts or of serpents* — for in adoring idols of this kind they were either leaders or followers of the people — *and worshiped and served the creature rather than the creator, who is blessed forever.* (Rom 1:21-23.25) In the latter, in contrast, there is no human wisdom except the piety which rightly worships the true God and which looks for its reward in the company of the saints, that is, in the company of both holy men and holy angels, in order *that God may be all in all* (1 Cor 15:28).

---

87. What follows is probably the best-known passage in *The City of God*, which serves as a concise summary of the entire work. There are similar passages in *The Literal Meaning of Genesis* XI,15,20 and *Exposition of Psalm* 64,2 (where the two cities are symbolized by Jerusalem and Babylon).

Study Questions for Book XIV

St. Paul's distinction in Rom 8:9 between living according to the spirit and living according to the flesh underlies Book XIV. Augustine interprets this Pauline passage carefully, emphasizing that Paul's spirit-flesh dichotomy is not the same as the Platonic soul-body distinction. To live according to the spirit is to live selflessly, loving God and neighbor. To live according to the flesh is to live selfishly, putting oneself ahead of God and neighbor. Do you think Augustine's careful reading of Paul is widespread among contemporary Christian preachers and believers?

Augustine would not have been a good Buddhist, patiently striving to move beyond the passions and desires that inflict so much suffering on human beings. Apatheia, the Stoic excising of passion from our daily experience, relegates fervor, ardor and emotion to the fringes of the philosophical or spiritual life. Rather, Augustine values human passions as full-blooded, robustly embodied expressions of will that can be ordered to love. What in the life narratives of Siddhartha Gautama and Augustine might illustrate the different role assigned to passion by these two religious geniuses?

"Pride goes before destruction, and a haughty spirit before a fall (Prv 16:18)." In Book XIV Augustine offers a psychological, existential interpretation of Gn 3. His commentary elucidates the scriptural story of the temptation and sin of Adam and Eve by suggesting that, long before Eve's encounter with the serpent, both she and Adam had grown prideful and haughty. Their pride, a corruption of their human will, had emerged slowly and secretly and had remained hidden. It was revealed and unmasked by the act of disobedience. What do chapters 13-14 show us about Augustine's scriptural hermeneutics?

Augustine's suggestion in chapters 23-26 that Adam and Eve had sexual relations in the Garden of Eden "not by a lustful appetite but by an act of will" and his detailed description of this tranquil intercourse is an interesting exercise of imagination. Did this prelapsarian sex, which Augustine read into the text, involve at least some measure of "ordered passion" (as opposed to lustful passion) that he writes about earlier in Book XIV. Or, was it *apathetic* sex? In any case, Augustine, in contrast to contemporaries of his like Jerome, affirms the goodness of sex and marriage as part of God's creation. Might his curious interpretations in this regard offer categories to understand the maturation of sexual intercourse through the intentional ordering of passion by loving partners?

BOOK XV

In Book XV Augustine begins his tracing of the two cities through historical time, covering the period from Adam to the flood. At the start he uses the story of Cain and Abel, which he interweaves with the story of Abraham's two sons, Ishmael and Isaac, together with the Pauline opposition between the flesh and the spirit, to indicate the character of the two cities and to map the complex pattern of contrasts and conflicts between them, the one formed by nature, the other by grace, the one oriented to this world and its limited goods, which inevitably generate conflict and competition, the other to the eternal good, which engenders undivided love. Within this pattern, Israel — the Jews, the earthly Jerusalem — occupies a special place: it belongs to the earthly city but at the same time serves as an image of the heavenly city. Thus it is in the line of descent that leads from Seth, the son of Adam who replaced the murdered Abel, through Noah to Abraham, the patriarch from whom the Israelite people emerged, that Augustine tracks the course of the heavenly city in the first age of its pilgrimage on earth. In contrast, the line of descent from Cain represents the separate course of the earthly city. In fact, however, neither city completely excludes the other in their respective earthly histories; and, by the time of the flood, the two cities have become so completely intermingled — the members of the heavenly city submerging themselves in the wickedness of the earthly city as a result of their attraction to the merely physical beauty of the daughters of men — that only Noah, his wife, and their sons and daughters-in-law deserve to be saved from the general destruction. Throughout, Augustine is concerned to preserve both the historical reliability of Scripture and its figurative meaning, refusing to sacrifice either one for the sake of the other. Thus, to support the credibility of the biblical narrative, he provides an extensive explanation for the longevity of the ancients who lived prior to the flood, while at the same time finding prophetic anticipations of the Church in the names of the men included in the line of descent leading from Seth to Noah; and again, at the end of the book, he insists that the prophetic meaning of the story of the flood and Noah's ark as a prefiguration of salvation through Christ does not cancel its actual historicity any more than its reality as a historical event cancels its prophetic significance.

1. Many opinions have been held, and much has been said and written, about the felicity of paradise, about paradise itself, about the life there of the first human beings, and about their sin and punishment. We too have spoken about these matters in the preceding books, following Holy Scripture and presenting either what we read directly in Scripture or what we could draw from Scripture in accord with its authority. To pursue these issues in more detail, however, would give rise to a great number and variety of discussions that would take more volumes to unravel than this work requires or our time permits. We do not have the leisure to linger over every puzzle that might be raised by people who have time on their hands and want to go into every detail, the kind of people who are more ready to pose questions than they are capable of understanding the answers.

All the same, I think that I have already dealt adequately with the great and difficult questions concerning the beginning of the world, of the soul, and of the human race itself. We have divided the human race into two groups, one consisting of those who live according to man and the other of those who live according to God.[1] Speaking allegorically, we also call these two groups two cities, that is, two human societies, one predestined to reign with God for all eternity, the other to undergo eternal punishment with the devil.[2] But this is their final end, which is to be discussed later.[3] At this point, since enough has been said about the rise of these two cities, whether in the angels, whose number is beyond our knowing, or in the two first human beings, it seems to me that I should now undertake to trace the course that each has followed from the point at which the first two human beings began to have children down to the point at which humans will cease to have children. For the course followed by the two cities that we are discussing runs through this whole period, or age, in which the dying pass away and the newborn take their place.

Cain and Abel, the Earthly City and the Heavenly City

Cain, then, was the first child born to those two parents of the human race,[4] and he belonged to the city of men. Abel was born later,[5] and he belonged to the city of God. Now, in the case of a single individual we find, in the words of the Apostle, that *it is not the spiritual that is first, but the animal, and then the spiritual* (1 Cor 15:46), and that is why each one of us, since he comes from a condemned

---

1. See above at XIV,28.
2. Although Augustine may be accused here, as well as below at XXII,24, of teaching double predestination (i.e., predestination from eternity not only to heaven but also to hell), it should be noted that there is an asymmetry to his teaching on this score. On the one hand, those condemned to eternal punishment are condemned on the basis of their own moral failing, both as participants in and as co-agents of Adam's sin and (except in the case of infants who die before achieving the status of moral agents) for their own personal sin. On the other hand, those elected to eternal salvation are chosen by the sheer grace of God, utterly without regard to any good or evil that they may previously have done.
3. See below at XXI-XXII.
4. See Gn 4:1.
5. See Gn 4:2.

stock, is of necessity first evil and carnal due to Adam, but, if he advances by being reborn in Christ, will afterwards be good and spiritual. And it is just the same in the case of the whole human race. When those two cities began to run their course of birth and death, the first to be born was the citizen of this world, and only after him was there born the pilgrim in this world, who belonged to the city of God, predestined by grace and chosen by grace — by grace a pilgrim below and by grace a citizen above. So far as he himself is concerned, he comes from the same lump that was wholly condemned[6] at the start; but, like a potter (and the Apostle uses this image not to be insolent but to be apt), God made *from the same lump one vessel for honor and another for dishonor* (Rom 9:21). The vessel for dishonor, however, was made first, and then the vessel for honor. For in the individual case also, as I have already said, the unworthy comes first. That is where we have to start, but that is not where we have to stay. Afterwards comes the worthy, which we may approach by advancing towards it and where we may remain once we have reached it. It is certainly not true, then, that every evil person will be good, but it is certainly true that no one will be good who was not previously evil. And the sooner a person changes for the better, the faster he will take on the name for what he has gained and cover over the earlier term with the later one.

Scripture states, then, that Cain founded a city;[7] but Abel, as a pilgrim, did not. For the city of the saints is on high, even though it brings forth citizens here below, in whom it is on pilgrimage until the time of its kingdom arrives. Then it will gather them all together as they rise again in their bodies, and the promised kingdom will be given to them, where, with their prince, the *king of the ages* (1 Tm 1:17), they will reign for time without end.

Israel: the Earthly Image of the Heavenly City

2. There was, to be sure, a kind of shadow and prophetic image of this city which served to signify it here on earth, although not to make it actually present, at the time when it needed to be made manifest. And this shadow was also called the holy city by virtue of the fact that it was an image signifying the truth, even though not presenting it as distinctly as it would come to be. The Apostle is speaking of this subservient city, and of the free city that it signifies, when he says to the Galatians, *Tell me, you who desire to be under the law, have you not heard the law? For it is written that Abraham had two sons, one by a slave woman and one by a free woman. But the one born of the slave was born according to the flesh, and the one born of the free woman was born through the promise. These things are an allegory. These women are two covenants. One woman, in fact, is from Mount Sinai, bearing children for servitude; this is Hagar. For Sinai is a mountain in*

---

6. "Lump... condemned": *massa... damnata*, See also above at XIV, 26 and below at XV, 21 and XXI, 12.
7. See Gn 4:17.

Arabia, and it corresponds to the present Jerusalem, which is in servitude with her children. But the Jerusalem above is free, and she is our mother. For it is written, Rejoice, you barren one who bears no children, exclaim and shout, you who are not in labor, for the children of the desolate woman outnumber those of the married woman. But we, brothers, are children of the promise, like Isaac. But, just as at that time the child who was born according to the flesh persecuted the child who was born according to the Spirit, so it is now. But what does Scripture say? Cast out the slave and her son, for the son of the slave shall not be heir with the son of the free woman. So then, brothers, we are children not of the slave but of the free woman, by virtue of the freedom with which Christ has set us free. (Gal 4:21-5:1) This mode of interpretation, which comes down to us by apostolic authority, shows us how we ought to understand the Scriptures of the two covenants, the old and the new. For one part of the earthly city, because it signifies not itself but another, was made an image of the heavenly city, and it is therefore in servitude. For it was not established for its own sake but for the sake of signifying another city; and, since it was itself preceded by a prior sign, the prefiguring image was itself prefigured. For Hagar, Sarah's slave, together with her son, was a kind of image of this image. But the shadows were to pass away when the light came, and that is why Sarah, who was free and who signified the free city — which the prior shadow, Hagar, served to signify in another way — said, *Cast out the slave and her son, for the son of the slave shall not be heir with my son Isaac* (Gn 21:10), or, as the Apostle puts it, *with the son of the free woman* (Gal 4:30).

The Earthly City and the Heavenly City, Born of Nature and Born of Grace

In the earthly city, then, we find two features, one pointing to its own presence, the other serving by its presence to signify the heavenly city. What gives birth to citizens of the earthly city, however, is a nature vitiated by sin, and what gives birth to citizens of the heavenly city is grace liberating that nature from sin. Consequently, the former are called *vessels of wrath* (Rom 9:22) and the latter are called *vessels of mercy* (Rom 9:23). This is also signified in Abraham's two sons. For one of them, Ishmael, was born of the slave named Hagar according to the flesh, and the other, Isaac, was born of Sarah, the free woman, according to the promise. Both sons, obviously enough, came from Abraham's seed, but the one was begotten in the ordinary way, showing how nature works, while the other was given by the promise, signifying divine grace. In the one case human practice is displayed; in the other divine beneficence is acclaimed.

3. Sarah, plainly, was barren, and, in her despair of having children, she wanted at least to have from her slave what she realized that she could not have from herself. So she gave her slave to be made pregnant by her husband, with whom she had wanted to have children herself but could not.[8] In this way, then, she exacted her

---

8. See Gn 16:1-3.

due from her husband, exercising her own right in another's womb.[9] Ishmael was born, therefore, in the ordinary human way, by sexual intercourse according to the regular course of nature. That is why it says that he was born *according to the flesh* (Gal 4:23). It is not that such things are not benefits that come from God, or that they are not the work of God, whose creative wisdom *reaches mightily*, as Scripture says, *from one end to the other, and arranges all things sweetly* (Wis 8:1). But, when it was a matter of signifying an unmerited gift of God, freely bestowed on humankind by divine grace, it was right for a son to be given in a manner that did not follow the usual course of nature. For nature denies children to the kind of sexual intercourse of husband and wife that was possible for Abraham and Sarah at their age; and, besides, because Sarah was barren, she was not even able to have children when the root of the problem was not that she had passed the age of fertility but that she lacked the fertility appropriate to her age.

The fact that no fruit of posterity was owed to a nature in this condition signifies, then, that human nature — vitiated by sin and therefore justly condemned — did not deserve any true happiness for the future. Thus Isaac, who was born through the promise, is rightly taken to signify the children of grace, who are citizens of the free city and who share in eternal peace, where there is no love for one's personal and, so to say, private will, but rather a love that rejoices in the common and immutable good and joins many hearts into one, namely, a love which is perfectly at one in the obedience of charity.

The Goods of the Earthly City and the Conflicts to Which They Give Rise

4. The earthly city, in contrast, will not be everlasting, for, when it is condemned to its final punishment, it will no longer be a city. It has its good here on earth, and its joy — such joy as can be had from things of this sort — comes from sharing in this good. And, since its good is not the sort of good that brings no anxieties to those who love it, the earthly city is often divided against itself by lawsuits, wars and conflicts, and by seeking victories that either bring death or are themselves doomed to be short-lived. For, if any part of it rises up in war against another part, it seeks to be the victor over nations when it is itself the prisoner of its vices; and if, when it triumphs, it is puffed up with pride, its victory brings death. But, if it takes the human condition and all its vicissitudes into account and is more distressed by the adversities that may occur than elated by its present prosperity, then its victory is at best short-lived. For it will not be able to rule for long over those whom it was able to subdue in the moment of victory.

It would be wrong, however, to say that the things which this city desires are not goods; for even this city, in its own human fashion, is better when it has them. For it desires a sort of earthly peace for the sake of the lowest goods, and it is that peace which it wants to achieve by waging war. For, if it triumphs and there is no

---

9. See Rom 7:3-4.

one left to resist it, there will be peace, which the opposing parties did not have so long as they were fighting each other, in their wretched need, over things that they could not both possess at the same time. It is for this peace that grueling wars are fought, and it is this peace that supposedly glorious victory obtains.

And, when the victory goes to those who were fighting for the more just cause, who can doubt that the victory deserves to be celebrated or that the resulting peace is very much to be desired? These are goods, and they are undoubtedly gifts from God. But, if the higher goods are neglected, which belong to the city on high, where victory will be secure in supreme and eternal peace, and if these lower goods are desired so much that people believe them to be the only goods or love them more than the goods that they believe to be higher, then misery will necessarily follow, and their previous misery will only be made worse.

5. So it is that the first founder of the earthly city was a fratricide; for, overcome by envy, he killed his own brother, who was a citizen of the eternal city on pilgrimage on this earth. It is no wonder, then, that this first example — or archetype, as the Greeks call it — was reflected by an image of the same kind at the founding, long afterwards, of the city that was to be the head of the earthly city of which we are speaking and which was to rule over so many peoples. There also, as one of the poets says in telling of the crime, "the first walls dripped with a brother's blood."[10] For this is how Rome was founded when, as Roman history attests, Remus was killed by his brother Romulus.[11] These two, however, were both citizens of the earthly city. Both wanted the glory of founding the Roman republic, but, as cofounders, they could not both have as much glory as only one would have as the single founder of Rome. For the rule of anyone wishing to glory in his own dominion would obviously be less if his power were diminished by the presence of a living co-ruler. Therefore, in order for one to have total domination, his colleague was removed, and what would have been kept smaller and better by innocence grew into something larger and worse by crime.

In contrast, the brothers Cain and Abel did not both have the same desire for earthly gains. Nor did the one who killed the other feel envious of his brother because his own dominion would be restricted if they both held rule at once, for Abel did not want to have dominion in the city founded by his brother. Cain's envy was rather the diabolical envy that the evil feel toward the good simply because they are good, while they themselves are evil. For a person's possession of the good is by no means diminished when another comes or continues to share in it. On the contrary, goodness is a possession that spreads out more and more widely insofar as those who share it are united in undivided love. In fact, anyone who is unwilling to share this possession will find that he does not possess it at all, but, the more he is able to love the one who shares it with him, the greater he will find that his own possession of it becomes.

---

10. Lucan, *Pharsalia* I,95.
11. See above at III,6; Livy, *History of Rome* I,7.

Conflict between the Two Cities: the Flesh and the Spirit

Thus, the conflict that arose between Remus and Romulus showed how the earthly city is divided against itself, and the conflict between Cain and Abel demonstrated the antagonism between the two cities themselves, the city of God and the city of men. The evil, then, fight against each other, and, likewise, the evil and the good fight against each other. But the good, if they have attained perfection, cannot fight against each other. While they are making progress, however, but have not yet attained perfection, they can fight against each other in that someone who is good may fight against another due to that part of him by which he also fights against himself. Even in the case of a single individual, *what the flesh desires is opposed to the spirit, and what the spirit desires is opposed to the flesh* (Gal 5:17). Thus, one person's spiritual desire can fight against another's carnal desire, and his carnal desire can fight against another's spiritual desire, in the same way that the good and the evil fight against each other. And the carnal desires of two good people who have not yet attained perfection can obviously fight against each other in just the same way that the evil fight against each other, at least until the health of those who are in the process of being healed is brought to its ultimate triumph....

The apostle John, in speaking of these brothers, says, *Do not be like Cain, who was from the evil one and murdered his brother. And why did he murder him? Because his own deeds were evil and his brother's righteous.* (1 Jn 3:12) We are given to understand, then, that the reason why God did not honor Cain's gift is that it was wrongly divided in the sense that, although he gave something of his own to God, he gave himself to himself. And this is precisely what is done by all those who follow their own will rather than God's — that is, who live in perversity of heart rather than righteousness of heart — and yet still offer gifts to God. They suppose that, by means of these gifts, they are buying God's help not in healing their debased desires but rather in fulfilling them. And this is characteristic of the earthly city: to worship a god or gods with whose help it might reign in victory and earthly peace, not from love of caring for others but rather from the lust to exercise dominion over others. For the good make use of the world in order to enjoy God, but the evil, in contrast, want to make use of God in order to enjoy the world.[12] This is true, at least, of those who still believe that there is a God and that he cares about human affairs, for those who do not believe even this are in a far worse state. Thus, when Cain saw that God had honored his brother's sacrifice but not his own, he ought surely to have changed his ways and imitated his good brother rather than standing on his pride and envying his brother. In fact, however, he went into a sulk, and his countenance fell. This sin — sulking over another's goodness, and a brother's goodness at that — is one that God most especially rebukes, and it was precisely to rebuke it that God questioned Cain, asking, *Why are you sulking, and why has your countenance fallen?* (Gn 4:6) For God saw that he envied his brother, and that is what he rebuked....

---

12. Augustine contrasts enjoying (*frui*) and using (*uti*) here as he does above at VIII,8 and elsewhere.

The Presentation of the Two Cities in the Lines of Descent from Cain and Seth

8. What I need to do now, it seems to me, is to defend the historical record so that Scripture will not seem incredible in saying that a city was built by one man at a time when it appears that there were no more than four males on earth — or rather three, after Cain killed his brother. These three were the first man, the father of all, Cain himself, and Cain's son Enoch, for whom the city was named.[13] But people who feel troubled about this point have paid too little attention to the fact that the writer of this sacred history had no need to name all the men who might have existed at that time. He needed to name only those required by the plan of the work he had undertaken. The aim of this writer, in whom the Holy Spirit was at work, was simply to arrive at Abraham through a succession of specified generations descended from one man and then to go on from Abraham's seed to the people of God, which was set apart from the other nations and in which was prefigured and foretold everything foreseen in the Spirit that was going to happen with regard to the city whose kingdom will be eternal and with regard to Christ, its king and founder. But he did not ignore that other human society which we call the earthly city. Rather, he said enough about it to let the city of God stand out in contrast to its opposite.

Thus Divine Scripture, when it records the number of years those early men lived, concludes by saying in each case, *And he had sons and daughters, and all the days* that this or that man lived *were* so many years, *and he died* (Gn 5:4-31). But the fact that it does not name these sons and daughters certainly does not keep us from presuming that, during all the years that men lived in that first age of this world, any number of people could have been born and any number of cities could have been founded as they joined together in groups. The intention of God, however, by whose inspiration these accounts were written, was to mark and distinguish these two societies from the start in their different generations. Thus, the generations of men — that is, of those living according to man — and the generations of the children of God — that is, of those living according to God — are interwoven in Scripture down to the time of the flood, where the differentiation and the combination of the two societies are narrated. Their differentiation is made clear by the fact that the generations of each are listed separately, the one deriving from the fratricide Cain and the other from the brother called Seth, who was also born to Adam, taking the place of the son who had been killed by his brother.[14] And their combination is made clear by the fact that, as the good became worse and worse, they all became so evil that they were all wiped out by the flood — with the exception of one just man, whose name was Noah, along with his wife, his three sons, and his three daughters-in-

---

13. See Gn 4:17.
14. See Gn 4:25.

BOOK XV

law. These eight were the only human beings who were worthy to escape in the ark from that destruction of all mortal life.[15]...

The Long Lives of the Ancients

9. Thus, no one who considers the matter with care can doubt that Cain could have founded not just a city of some sort but a city of considerable size at a time when the lives of mortals were so prolonged. But one of the unbelievers, perhaps, might take issue with us over the sheer number of years that people are reported to have lived, according to our authorities, in that period, claiming that this is incredible. Similarly, there are those who do not believe that human bodies were far larger then than they are now. But Virgil, the most distinguished of their poets,[16] speaks of an enormous stone set up as a boundary marker between fields that a mighty warrior of those times snatched up in battle, who ran with it, whirled it round, and hurled it. "A dozen hand-picked men could hardly have lifted that stone," Virgil says, "with bodies such as the earth produces now."[17] Plainly he is pointing out that in those days the earth regularly produced larger bodies than it does now. How much the more was that true, then, in the earlier ages of the world, prior to that famous and memorable flood.

With regard to the size of bodies, however, skeptics are generally convinced by the tombs that are uncovered by the passage of time or the force of rivers or by various other circumstances. Bones of incredible size have appeared in them or fallen out of them. On the shore at Utica, I myself — not alone, but with several others — saw a human molar so enormous that, if it had been cut up into pieces the size of our teeth, it would, we estimated, have made a hundred of them.[18] But that tooth, I imagine, belonged to some giant. For not only were bodies in general larger then than ours are now, but the giants towered far above the rest, just as in later times, including our own, there have nearly always been some bodies that far surpassed the size of others.[19] Pliny the Elder, a very learned man, testifies that as more and more time passes, the bodies produced by nature become smaller and smaller. He notes that even Homer often lamented this fact in his poetry; and he does not ridicule Homer's laments as mere poetic fictions but rather — as himself a recorder of nature's marvels — takes them as reliable history.[20] But, as I have

---

15. See Gn 6:5-8:19.
16. I.e., of the unbelievers' poets.
17. *Aeneid* XII,899-900.
18. Augustine's amazement at the huge human molar, which must in fact have been something else, is an instance of his occasional interest in the unusual
19. It is surprising that, although he mentions them below at XXII,8, Augustine says nothing here of the martyrs Gervasius and Protasius, whose bodies were claimed by Ambrose, their discoverer, to be exceptionally large. See Ambrose, Letter 22,2.
20. See Pliny, *Natural History* VII,16,73-74; Homer, *Iliad* V,304.

said, the frequent discovery of bones reveals the size of ancient bodies even to much later ages, simply because bones last for such a long time.

In contrast, no such tangible evidence can bring the longevity of the individuals who lived in those times into the realm of our current experience. That is no reason, however, to scoff at the reliability of our sacred history. In fact, the more certain it is that we are seeing its prophecies fulfilled before our very eyes, the more insolent it becomes to disbelieve what it tells us of the past. Furthermore, Pliny also reports that there still exists today a people whose members live to be two hundred years old.[21] Thus, if we believe that even today places unknown to us show a human longevity beyond our experience, why should we not believe the same of unknown times in the past? Or is it somehow credible that something is true at another place that is not true here, but somehow incredible that something was true at another time that is not true now?...

[Chapters 10 – 21 address the longevity of the patriarchs and other figures in Genesis, their remarkable fertility, the practice of polygamy and kinship relations in these early human societies, and display Augustine's conviction that as far as possible these narratives should be understood as history.]

21. ... Here, then, we have the two cities set before us, the one existing in the reality of this world, the other in the hope of God. They came forth, as it were, from the common door of mortality, which was opened in Adam, to pursue and complete their respective courses to their own distinct and destined ends. Then begins the chronological enumeration in which, after a recapitulation from Adam, the other generations are added, and from this condemned beginning in Adam, as from one lump consigned to a deserved condemnation,[22] God makes some vessels of wrath for dishonor and some vessels of mercy for honor.[23] To the former he renders what they deserve by way of punishment, and to the latter he grants what they do not deserve by way of grace.[24] And he does this so that, by this very comparison with the vessels of wrath, the heavenly city on pilgrimage here on earth may learn not to put its trust in its own freedom of will but rather may *hope to call upon the name of the Lord God.* For, although man's nature was made good by God, who is good, it was also made mutable by God, who is immutable, because it was made out of nothing, and so the will in that nature can both turn away from the good to do evil, which happens by free choice, and turn away from the evil to do good, which does not happen without God's help.

---

21. See Pliny, *Natural History* VII,48,154, citing Hellanicus of Mytilene.
22. "As from one lump consigned to a deserved condemnation": *veluti massa una meritae damnationi tradita.*
23. See Rom 9:22-23.
24. This is a highly succinct formulation of Augustine's doctrine of grace and predestination.

The Intermingling of the Two Cities: the Sons of God and the Daughters of Men

22. As the human race progressed and increased, then, it was by this free choice in willing that there took place a mixing and a kind of intermingling of the two cities due to their common participation in wickedness. This evil, once again, took its cause from the female sex, but not in the same way as did the evil at the beginning. In this case, the women were not seduced by anyone's deceit into persuading men into sin. Rather, women who had been morally depraved from the beginning in the earthly city — that is, in the society of the earthborn — were loved for the beauty of their bodies by the sons of God, that is, by the citizens of the other city which is on pilgrimage in this world.[25] Such beauty is certainly a good, a gift from God, but it is a gift that is also given to the evil in order to keep the good from considering it a good of any great consequence.

Thus, in departing from a great good and one that is reserved for the good alone, men fell into a minimal good, which is not reserved for the good alone but is common to the good and the evil alike. And so the sons of God were taken captive by love for the daughters of men; and, in order to enjoy them as wives, they deserted the godliness they had maintained in their holy society and sank down into the ways of the society of the earthborn. For bodily beauty is most certainly created by God. But it is a temporal, carnal, and lesser good, and it is loved wrongly when it is preferred to God, who is the eternal, inward, and everlasting good, just as gold is loved wrongly by misers when they desert justice for its sake, although the fault lies not with the gold but rather with the man. This is true of every created thing. For, although it is good, it can be loved both rightly and wrongly — rightly when the proper order is preserved, wrongly when the proper order is overturned. This is a point I made briefly in some verses in praise of the paschal candle: "These things are yours; they are good because you are good, and you made them. Nothing of ours is in them except for our sin, when we neglect right order and love the things you made in place of you yourself."[26]

But if the creator is truly loved — that is, if he himself is loved and not something else in place of him — then he cannot be loved wrongly. For we must observe right order even in our love for the very love by which we love rightly what we ought to love.[27] Otherwise, the virtue by which life is lived rightly will not be in us. Thus it seems to me that a brief and true definition of virtue is "rightly ordered love." That is why, in the holy Song of Songs, Christ's bride, the city of God, sings, *Set charity in order in me* (Song 2:4). It was, then, when they overturned the right

---

25. See Gn 6:1-2.
26. These verses are part of a longer poem written by Augustine and referred to as *On the Soul*. See Alexander Ries, ed., *Anthologia Latina* I,2 (Leipzig: Teubner, 1870) 38.
27. See above at XI,28; *Miscellany of Eighty-three Questions* 35,1.

order of this charity — that is, of this affection and love[28] — that the sons of men neglected God and gave their affection to the daughters of men.

These two names are enough in themselves to distinguish the two cities. For it is not that the sons of God were not sons of men by nature; it is rather that they had begun to have another name by grace. In fact, in the same passage of Scripture where the sons of God are said to have given their affection to the daughters of men, they are also called angels of God.[29] Thus many imagine that they were not men but angels....

23. ... But these sons of God were not angels of God — as some people suppose — in any sense that meant they were not human beings. Scripture itself unambiguously declares that they were undoubtedly human beings. For, after saying that *the angels of God saw that the daughters of men were good; and they took wives for themselves from all that they chose* (Gn 6:2), it immediately goes on to say, *And the Lord God said, My spirit shall not abide in these men forever, for they are flesh* (Gn 6:3). It was, in fact, through the Spirit of God that they were made angels of God and sons of God; but, because they turned away to lower things, they are called *men*, the name they have by nature, not by grace. They are also called *flesh*, since they deserted the spirit and, in deserting it, were themselves deserted....

The Flood, Noah, and the Ark

24. ...And it is with good reason that we believe that, when the flood occurred, there were no longer any people to be found on earth who did not deserve to die the kind of death that is imposed on the ungodly as punishment. Such a death, of course, could not inflict any harm on the good (who, in any case, are going to die at some point[30]) after they die. It is still true, however, that none of those whom Holy Scripture mentions as descended from the seed of Seth died in the flood. Here, then, is the cause of the flood as told by divine inspiration: *The Lord God saw that the wickedness of men had multiplied on the earth and that everyone was relentlessly plotting evil in his heart all his days. And God considered the fact that he had made man on the earth, and he reconsidered, and God said, I will blot out man, whom I made, from the face of the earth, man and beast, and creeping things, and the birds of the air, for I am angry that I have made them.* (Gn 6:5-7)

25. God's anger, however, is not any passionate upset of mind; rather, it is a judgment that imposes punishment on sin. And his consideration and reconsideration are simply his unchanging plan for things that are themselves subject to change. For, unlike human beings, God does not repent of any action he has taken, and

---

28. "Charity...affection...love": *caritatis...dilectionis...amoris.* See above at XIV,7.
29. See Gn 6:2 LXX.
30. See above at I,11 for a similar thought.

his purpose with regard to absolutely everything is as fixed as his foreknowledge of it is utterly certain. But, if Scripture did not make use of terms of this kind, it would not present itself in an idiom familiar to all kinds of people — all of whom it wants to take under its care — so as to terrify the proud, arouse the uncaring, prod the inquirer, and nourish the intelligent. For it would do none of these things if it did not first stoop down and, as it were, descend to the level of the fallen.[31] And, when it announces the destruction of all animals on the earth and in the air, it is showing us the sheer magnitude of the coming disaster; it is not threatening the destruction of creatures without reason, as if they too had sinned.

26. It was at this point, however, that God directed Noah to build an ark. Noah was a righteous man; and, as truthful Scripture truly says of him, he was perfect in his generation.[32] He was not perfect, of course, in the sense in which the citizens of the city of God will be perfect when they are perfected in that immortality by which they will be made equal to the angels,[33] but he was as perfect as they are able to be in this pilgrimage here on earth. In the ark, Noah and his family — that is, his wife, his sons, and his sons' wives — were to be rescued from the devastation of the flood, along with the animals that came to him in the ark at God's command.[34]

This is, beyond any doubt, a figure of the city of God on pilgrimage in this world, that is, a figure of the Church which is saved through the wood on which hung *the mediator between God and man, the man Christ Jesus* (1 Tm 2:5).[35]

For the very dimensions of the ark — its length, height, and breadth — signify the human body, in the reality of which it was foretold that Christ would come to humankind, and in the reality of which he did in fact come.[36] For the length of the human body from the top of the head to the bottom of the foot is six times its breadth from side to side, and ten times its depth as measured on the side from back to belly. Thus, if you measure a person lying either on his back or on his face, his length from head to foot is six times his breadth from right to left or left to right and ten times his height from the ground. That is why the ark was made three hundred cubits in length, fifty cubits in breadth, and thirty cubits in height.[37] And as for the door that was cut in its side, it is clearly the wound that was made when the Crucified's side was pierced by the spear. This is plainly the way of entrance

---

31. Gn 6:7, with its mention of God's anger (or regret), is a classic example in Augustine and elsewhere of Scripture's use of language that is accommodated to human understanding and that can therefore lead to anthropomorphism. See *Miscellany of Eighty-three Questions* 52; *The Trinity* I,1,2.
32. See Gn 6:9.
33. See Lk 20:36.
34. See Gn 6:18-20.
35. The wood of the ark foreshadows the wood of the cross. See Justin Martyr, *Dialogue with Trypho* 138.
36. A comparison between the dimensions of the ark and those of the human body, with christological implications, is also made in *Answer to Faustus, a Manichean* XII,14. The idea seems to have originated in Philo, *Questions on Genesis* II,5.
37. See Gn 6:15.

for those who come to him, for from that wound flowed the sacraments by which believers are initiated.[38] Again, the order that the ark be made of squared timbers signifies the life of the saints, which is stable on all sides; for, no matter which way you turn a squared object, it will be stable. And all the other details that are mentioned with regard to the construction of the ark are signs of aspects of the Church.

It would take too long, however, to run through all of them here. Besides, we have already done this in the work that we wrote against Faustus the Manichaean, who denied that there are any prophecies of Christ in the books of the Hebrews.[39] And in any case it is always possible that some other person may be able to explain these things more aptly than I or anyone else can. But, if the interpreter does not want to stray off from the sense intended by the author of this account, everything he says must refer in one way or another to the city of God of which we are speaking, which is on pilgrimage in the midst of this wicked world as though in the midst of a flood....

The Flood: History and Allegory

27. No one should suppose that the account of the flood was written without purpose; or that we should seek in it only historical truth without any allegorical meaning; or, conversely, that the events never actually took place and the words have only figurative meaning; or that, whatever else it may be, the account has no relation to prophecy about the Church. Only a twisted mind would claim that books preserved for thousands of years[40] with such religious care and with such concern for their well-regulated transmission were written for no reason, or that we should see in them no more than bare historical events. For, leaving everything else aside, if it was only the sheer number of the animals that required the ark to be so large, what was it that required the inclusion of two of each unclean species, but seven of each clean species,[41] when both could easily have been preserved in the same number? And besides, was not God — who ordered these animals to be preserved in order to restore their species — perfectly capable of re-establishing them in the same way that he had established them in the first place?

On the other hand, there are those who claim that there were no such actual events but that these are only figures meant to signify something else. Their view is, first, that there could not possibly have been a flood so vast that the water rose fifteen cubits above the highest mountains....

---

38. I.e., the sacraments of baptism (symbolized by water) and the eucharist (symbolized by blood). See Jn 19:34. This is the nearly unanimous understanding of the Johannine verse, and was certainly intended by the evangelist himself.
39. See *Answer to Faustus, a Manichean* XII,14.
40. This is an exaggeration: the books of the Old Testament had by Augustine's time been preserved only for hundreds and not for thousands of years.
41. See Gn 7:2. In fact the Hebrew text refers to seven pairs of clean animals, and not simply to seven (*septena...animalia*).

These people also insist that an ark of that size could not possibly have held so many kinds of animals of both sexes, two of each unclean and seven of each clean species....

All this being so, no one, no matter how stubborn, will be so defiant as to imagine that the account of the flood was written without purpose. Nor can it plausibly be claimed that the events took place but signify nothing beyond themselves; or that the events never actually took place and that the words have only figurative meaning; or that what the account is meant to signify bears no relation to the Church. Instead, we must believe that the account was committed to memory and to writing for a wise purpose, that the events actually took place, that they signify something beyond themselves, and that what they signify pertains to prefiguring the Church.[42]

Now that this book has reached this point, however, I must bring it to a close so that I can next examine the courses followed by the two cities — that is, the earthly city living according to man and the heavenly city living according to God — after the flood and in the following eras.

---

42. Augustine is insistent that the ark is not merely an optional image of the Church but a necessary one. The connection between the ark and the Church is ancient and is already hinted at in 1Pt 3:20-21. For numerous references to this connection see Jean Daniélou, *The Bible and the Liturgy* (Notre Dame: University of Notre Dame Press, 1956) 83-85, to which add the comment of Jerome in *Dialogue against Lucifer* 22: "The day would not be long enough for me to explain all the mysteries of the ark and compare them with the Church."

Study Questions for Book XV

Augustine's method for tracing the history of the two cities comprises two different tools. One is the binary distinction between flesh and spirit, nature and grace, this world and eternity, and selfishness and selfless love. This distinction is captured in the differences between biblical actors such as Cain and Abel, the human race in general and Noah's family in particular, and Ishmael and Isaac. Augustine's second tool functions as something of a converse of the first: it is his recognition of the complexity of the interaction and intermingling of the two cities from the very beginnings of humanity. Do you find theological antecedents in Augustine's method in *The City of God* to later distinctions found between Protestant and Catholic theologies?

The Jewish people are presented in Augustine's account as an image of the heavenly city, yet they belong to the earthly city, which serves as an illustration of his recognition of the complexity and intermingling of the two cities. He will later argue, against other bishops who were antagonistic to the Jews, for the preservation of Jewish communities, in recognition of their essential role in the history of salvation. What might be relevant in Augustine's approach for a theology of religions today?

Augustine affirms the historical reliability of Scripture, even of what today we call the pre-history of Gn 1-11, from Adam and Eve up to Noah and the flood. At the same time he allows for the figurative meanings of biblical characters and events. Might this creative tension between historicity and symbolic meaning have value for contemporary narrative criticism in biblical studies?

BOOK XVI

Book XVI tracks the two cities in the period from the flood to Abraham and then, with the dominant focus on the city of God and only rare and incidental references to the earthly city, in the period from Abraham to David. It highlights the prophetic significance of the historical events in both periods, emphasizing the way in which they anticipate and foreshadow later developments. The book opens onto the first period by indicating the prophetic import of the episode of Noah's drunkenness in his vineyard as an anticipation of Christ's passion and resurrection and then connects the heavenly city with the generations descending from Noah's son Shem and the earthly city with the generations descending from his son Ham, although noting that members of both cities are included in both lines of descent. It also stresses the episode of the tower of Babel as the moment when human pride was divinely punished by the division of the human race into separate languages with Hebrew, which was previously the universal language of all mankind, now remaining only in the line of descent from Heber, Shem's great-great-grandson, from whom the language took its name. It is at this point that Augustine establishes the link between the earthly city and the kingdom of Assyria. In the second period, the book focuses on the divine promises made respectively to Abraham, Isaac and Jacob, indicating how they apply in one respect to Abraham's seed "according to the flesh," that is, to the people of Israel, and in another to his seed "according to faith," that is, the heavenly city and the Church. It then provides a rather hurried survey of the sequence of events from Moses to David. Along the way it addresses certain moral issues — Abraham's and Isaac's passing off their wives as their sisters, Abraham's and Jacob's polygamy — in ways designed to protect the patriarchs' moral integrity against charges of lying and lust. And throughout the book Augustine seeks to establish a clear chronology that determines the number of years in each period and that removes any questions of inconsistency which might appear to arise from the biblical account.

The Prophetic Significance of Noah and His Sons

1. Did the path of the holy city run in one continuous course after the flood, or was it interrupted by intervening periods of ungodliness when there was no one alive who worshiped the true God? It is difficult to find a clear answer to this question in the words of Scripture. For after Noah, who with his wife and three sons and their wives deserved to be saved in the ark from the devastation of the flood, we find no one in the canonical books until Abraham whose piety is clearly proclaimed by the divine writings.[1] The one exception is that Noah commends his two sons Shem and Japheth in a prophetic blessing,[2] for he anticipated and foresaw what was going to happen in the distant future. This prophetic anticipation also explains why it was that Noah cursed his middle son — that is, the one younger than the firstborn and older than the last — who had sinned against his father. He did not curse him in his own right but rather in the person of his son, Noah's grandson, in these words: *Cursed be Canaan; he shall be a slave and a servant to his brothers* (Gn 9:25). Now Canaan was the son of Ham, who did not cover the nakedness of his sleeping father but rather revealed it.[3] This also explains why Noah went on to add a blessing on his two other sons, the oldest and the youngest, saying, *Blessed be the Lord God of Shem, and Canaan shall be his slave; may God enlarge Japheth, and may he dwell in the houses of Shem* (Gn 9:26-27). In the same way, Noah's planting of the vineyard, his getting drunk from its fruit, his nakedness while sleeping,[4] and all the other events recorded here, are heavy with prophetic meanings and screened by prophetic veils.

2. But, now that the outcome of all this has actually been realized in posterity, what was once hidden has been made sufficiently clear. For anyone who considers the matter with care and intelligence cannot help but recognize the fulfillment of these things in Christ. For the name of Shem, from whose seed Christ was born in the flesh, means "named."[5] And what name is more widely named than the name of Christ, which now spreads its fragrance everywhere — so much so that in the Song of Songs, in prophetic anticipation, his name is compared to *perfume poured out* (Song 1:3)? And does not the whole breadth of the peoples dwell in his houses, that is, in Christ's churches? For Japheth's name means "breadth."[6] Again, Noah's middle son, Ham, whose name means "hot,"[7] as if separating himself from the other two and remaining in between them, is reckoned neither in the firstfruits of Israel nor in the fullness of the gentiles, and what does he signify if not the hot race of the heretics, who burn not with the spirit of wisdom but rather with impatience? For it is generally their spirit of impatience that sets the heretics' hearts on fire and leads them to disturb the peace of the saints. But such things actually turn out to be of use for those who are making progress, just as the Apostle says, *There must also be heresies, so that those who are approved may become known among you* (1 Cor 11:19). Again, it is written, *The well-instructed son will be wise, and he will use the foolish as his servant* (Prv 10:4 LXX). For, when stirred up by the

---

1. For Noah see Gn 6:9; for Abraham see, e.g., Gn 15:6; 22:12.
2. See Gn 9:26-27.
3. See Gn 9:21-22.
4. See Gn 9:20-21.
5. See Jerome, *Interpretation of Hebrew Names*, Genesis, s.v. Sem.
6. See ibid. s.v. Japhet.
7. See ibid. s.v. Chan.

heated restlessness of the heretics, many things pertaining to the Catholic faith are studied more closely, understood more clearly, and proclaimed more insistently, so that they can be defended against heretical attack. Thus an issue raised by an opponent turns out to be an occasion for learning.[8] There is no absurdity, however, in taking Noah's middle son as a figure not only of those in open separation from the Church but also of those who glory in the Christian name but lead profligate lives. For these people both proclaim Christ's passion, which was signified by Noah's nakedness,[9] in what they say and defame it in the evil that they do. They are the ones, therefore, of whom it was said, *By their fruits you shall know them* (Mt 7:20).

It is for this reason that Ham was cursed in the person of his son (in his fruit, as it were), that is, in his actions. It is appropriate, then, that Canaan, the name of his son, means "their motion,"[10] for what is "their motion" but "their actions"? Shem and Japheth, on the other hand, represent the circumcision and the uncircumcision, or, as the Apostle also calls them, the Jews and the Greeks,[11] but only those Jews and Greeks who are called and justified. And, when they learned of their father's nakedness, which signified the Savior's passion, they took a garment, spread it over their backs, entered the tent with their backs turned, and covered their father's nakedness. They did not look at what they reverently covered.[12] For in a sense, with regard to the passion of Christ, we both honor what was done for us and turn our backs on the crime of the Jews. The garment signifies the mystery, and their backs signify our memory of things past. For in this present time, when Japheth dwells in the houses of Shem and the wicked brother remains in between them,[13] the Church celebrates the passion of Christ as an event in the past; it no longer looks forward to its coming in the future....

The wicked only preach this passion of Christ outwardly, with the sound of their voice, for they do not understand what they are preaching. The upright, in contrast, have this great mystery within, in the inner man,[14] and they honor the weakness and foolishness of God inwardly, in the heart, because it is stronger and wiser than men. It is a figure of this that Ham went out and announced his father's nakedness outside, but Shem and Japheth — in order to cover, that is, to honor, Noah's nakedness — went in. That is, they acted in a more inward way.

We search out these hidden meanings of Divine Scripture as best we can, sometimes more aptly and sometimes less so, but always holding faithfully to the certainty that these things were not done and recorded without some prefiguration of things to come and that they are to be referred to nothing other than Christ and

---

8. This is the classic argument for the existence of heresy.
9. On Noah as an image of Christ in his passion see Cyprian, Letter 63,3. The symbolism is explained later in this section.
10. See Jerome, *Interpretation of Hebrew Names*, Genesis, s.v. Chanaan.
11. See 1 Cor 1:22.
12. See Gn 9:23.
13. See Gn 9:27.
14. See Rom 7:22.

his Church,[15] which is the city of God.[16] From the very beginning of the human race there have been prophetic anticipations of that city, and we now see those prophecies being fulfilled in every respect.

Thus, from the blessing of Noah's two sons and the cursing of his middle son on down to Abraham, more than a thousand years later, there is no mention of any just men who worshiped God rightly. I cannot believe that there actually were none. If they were all listed, however, it would have taken too long and would have exemplified historical thoroughness rather than prophetic foresight. As a consequence, the writer of these Sacred Scriptures — or, rather, the Spirit of God through him[17] — takes up only those instances in which not only past events are narrated but also future events are foretold, although only the instances that have to do with the city of God. For whatever is said here about those who are not citizens of that city is said for one purpose — that the city of God may gain profit or prominence by comparison with its opposite. We should not imagine, of course, that every narrated event signifies something beyond itself,[18] but even those that do not signify anything beyond themselves are interwoven in the account for the sake of those that do. It is only the blade of the plough that cuts through the earth, but the other parts of the plough are necessary for this to happen. And it is only the strings of the lyre (and of other musical instruments of this kind) that are designed to make music; but, for them to be able to do what they are designed to do, there must also be the other parts that make up the structure of these instruments, the parts that are not plucked by the musician but to which the parts that resonate when plucked are connected. Similarly, in the prophetic history some things are said which signify nothing beyond themselves but to which those that *do* signify something more than themselves are attached and with which they are, so to speak, bound together....

[Chapter 3 reviews the generations of the sons of Noah recounted in Genesis 10.]

The Tower of Confusion and the Diversity of Human Languages

4. Despite the fact that each nation is said to have had its own language, the narrator here goes back to the time when everyone had the same language, and, taking

---

15. I.e., the Old Testament in its entirety is prophetic of Christ and the Church, the Church being understood in terms of both community and sacraments.
16. Note the identification here of the Church and the city of God. See above at VIII,24.
17. Augustine's understanding of biblical inspiration emphasized the role of the Holy Spirit at the expense of the contribution of the Bible's human authors. See *Teaching Christianity* III,27,38.
18. Augustine may have in mind the opinion of Origen, in *On First Principles* IV,3,5, that all Scripture has a spiritual meaning but not necessarily a literal one. For examples of things recorded in Scripture that are to be taken precisely as written, and with no spiritual meaning intended, see Sermon 89,5.

that as his starting point, he now explains how it happened that the present diversity of languages came about. *And the whole earth,* he says, *had one language, and there was one speech for all. And it happened that, as they moved out from the east, they came upon a plain in the land of Shinar, and they settled there. And they said to each other, Come, let us make bricks and bake them in fire. And they made bricks for stone, and they had bitumen for mortar; and they said, Come, let us build ourselves a city, and a tower whose top will reach the heavens, and let us make a name for ourselves before we are scattered across the face of all the earth. And the Lord came down to see the city and the tower which the sons of men had built. And the Lord God said, Look, they are one people, and they all have one language; and they have started to do this, and now they will not fail in anything that they try to do. Come, let us go down and confuse their language there, so that they may not understand each other's speech. And the Lord scattered them abroad from there over the face of all the earth, and they stopped building the city and the tower. For this reason, its name is called Confusion, because there the Lord confused the language of all the earth, and from there the Lord God dispersed them over the face of all the earth.* (Gn 11:1-9)

This city which was called Confusion is Babylon itself, whose marvelous construction is praised even by pagan historians (for in fact Babylon means "confusion"[19])....

But what could empty human presumption have achieved, no matter how vast or how high a building it erected up into the heavens in opposition to God, even if the building surpassed every mountain and even if it outstripped the whole region of this cloudy air? What harm, after all, could any act of spiritual or physical pride do to God, no matter how high it might aim? It is humility that builds a safe and true way to the heavens, lifting up the heart to God, not against God,...

6. ...From those three men, then, the sons of Noah, seventy-three nations — or, rather, seventy-two, as calculation is going to show — and the same number of languages came into being on the earth, and, as they increased, they filled even the islands. The number of nations, however, grew far more than the number of languages. For even in Africa alone we know of many barbarous peoples who share a single language.[20]...

Are Monstrous Races Descended from Noah and thus from Adam?

8. Another question is whether we should believe that certain monstrous races of men — people of whom pagan history tells — were descended from the sons of

---

19. See Jerome, *Interpretation of Hebrew Names,* Genesis, s.v. Babylon.
20. Since he would not have even known of the existence of sub-Saharan Africa, Augustine is referring here to North Africa, which was simply called "Africa" in the Roman world.

Noah or rather from that one man from whom they came themselves.[21] Some of these are reported to have only one eye, in the middle of their forehead; others to have the soles of their feet pointing backwards, behind their legs; and still others to have the nature of both sexes, with the right breast male and the left breast female, alternately begetting and conceiving when they mate with each other. There are some who are said to have no mouth and to live solely by breathing through their nostrils; others who grow only a cubit high, whom the Greeks call pygmies from their word for a cubit; and elsewhere we are told of females who conceive at the age of five and do not live beyond the age of eight. Again, they tell of a race of people who have only one leg leading to their feet, a leg that does not bend at the knee, and yet they move amazingly fast; they call these people skiopods or shadow-feet because, in hot weather, they lie on the ground on their backs and take shelter in the shade of their feet. There are some people with no necks, who have their eyes in their shoulders, and there are other kinds of humans, or quasi-humans, who are pictured in mosaic along the waterfront at Carthage, taken from books of historical curiosities.[22] And what am I to say of the cynocephali, those dog-headed men whose dogs' heads and whose very barking itself show that they are more beasts than men?[23]

There is no need, of course, to believe in all the kinds of human beings that are said to exist. But none of the faithful should have any doubt that anyone who is born anywhere as a human being, that is, as a rational and mortal being, derives from the original, first-created man — no matter how strange he may appear to our senses in his bodily form, his color, his mode of movement, his voice, or in any power, part, or quality of his nature whatsoever. Even so, however, the distinction remains clear between what obtains by nature in most cases and what counts as a marvel by virtue of its very rarity.

It is true, too, that the same kind of explanation that we give for monstrous births among us can also be used to account for some of these monstrous peoples. For God is the creator of all things; and he himself knows where and when it is right or was right for anything to be created. He knows how to weave together the beauty of the whole in the similarity and diversity of its parts. But the person who is unable to see the whole is offended at what appears to be the deformity of a part, for he does not know how it fits in or how it is connected with the whole. We know of people who were born with more than five fingers or more than five toes. This is too trivial an instance to count as any great aberration, but no one should be so foolish as to imagine that God made a mistake in these cases with regard to the number of human fingers, despite the fact that he has no idea why God did what he did. Thus, even if a greater variation should occur, God knows what he is doing, and no one has any right to condemn God's works....

---

21. Augustine consistently displays interest in the fabulous and freakish, as he does here. He may have obtained some of his information from Pliny, *Natural History* VIII,1,1-4,37.
22. Augustine mentions here an otherwise unknown detail about Carthage.
23. There was a minor deity called Cynocephalus, in the singular.

On this issue, then, I draw a tentative and cautious conclusion: either the things written about such races are sheer nonsense; or, if such things do exist, then those races are not human; or, if they are human, then they are descended from Adam.

9. As for the fable of the antipodes — that is, the fable that there are people who live on the opposite side of the earth, where the sun rises when it sets for us, whose footprints stand opposite ours — there is no reason to believe this.[24] No one claims to have learned this on the basis of any sound historical knowledge. Rather, they make a conjecture based on the reasoning that the earth is suspended in the sphere of the heavens and that the world is the same both above and below. On this ground, they form the opinion that the other half of the world, the half that lies below, cannot lack human inhabitants. But they fail to notice that — even if the world is held to be round and global in shape, or is shown to be so by some proof — it still does not follow that the land on the other side is not covered by a gathering of the waters.[25] What is more, even if the land is not covered by water, there is no reason to leap to the conclusion that there are human beings living there. For there is no falsehood of any sort in Scripture, which proves that it is reliable in its narration of past events by virtue of the fact that its predictions of future events have been fulfilled, and it is too absurd for words to suggest that some people might have sailed from this side of the world and arrived at the other, crossing the vast tract of Ocean,[26] just so that the human race, descended from that one first man, would be established there as well.

The Line of Descent from Shem

Let us search, then, among those peoples of mankind who were, we gather, divided at that time into seventy-two nations and as many languages, to see whether we can find among them the city of God in its pilgrimage on earth. We have followed its course down to the flood and the ark, and we have shown how it then continued in the sons of Noah through his blessings of them, and especially in the oldest of Noah's sons, who was called Shem, for Japheth's blessing was simply that he would dwell in his brother's houses.[27]

10. It is clear, then, that we must follow the line of descent from Shem himself in order to trace the city of God after the flood, just as we followed the line of

---

24. For a brief survey of ancient thought on the antipodes, both skeptical and credulous, see Bibliothèque Augustinienne 36,715-717.
25. See Gn 1:10.
26. According to a common opinion of the ancients, Ocean (usually rendered in English without the definite article) was a vast body of water surrounding all known land, and hence making it an island, which was small in comparison. Ocean was sometimes called "the Atlantic," and, inasmuch as it was located to the west of the Straits of Gibraltar, was roughly equivalent to the Atlantic Ocean. See Cicero, *Republic* VI,21.
27. See Gn 9:27.

descent from the man called Seth to trace it prior to the flood. It is for this reason that Divine Scripture, after showing us the earthly city in Babylon — that is, in confusion — reverts to the patriarch Shem by way of recapitulation and then gives the order of generations down to Abraham, recording also the number of years that passed before each fathered a son belonging to this line of descent and how long each lived....

Thus, omitting the other sons of Shem as irrelevant for the purpose, the account links in sequence the order of generations through which it is able to arrive at Abraham, just as, before the flood, it linked in sequence only those generations through which it arrived at Noah in the line of descent that stemmed from the son of Adam called Seth. Accordingly, the connected sequence of generations begins in this way: *These are the generations of Shem. Shem was a hundred years old when he fathered Arpachshad, two years after the flood; and Shem lived five hundred years after he fathered Arpachshad, and he fathered sons and daughters, and he died.* (Gn 11:10-11) The account continues in the same way, listing the others in the sequence, stating in what year of his life each fathered the son belonging to the line of descent leading to Abraham, and telling us how long he lived after that. It notes, too, that each also fathered other sons and daughters, and it does this so that we might understand how the human population was able to grow. Otherwise, thinking only of the few men who are mentioned by name, we might wonder, like children, how in the world such vast tracts of lands and kingdoms could possibly have been repopulated from the offspring of Shem. And this is especially true in relation to the kingdom of the Assyrians. For it was from there that Ninus, the renowned conqueror of all the peoples of the east, ruled with unparalleled prosperity and put together for his successors an immensely vast and stable empire that would last for a very long time.[28]...

The City of God among the Peoples of Earth

Thus, when we look for the city of God among those seventy-two peoples, we cannot definitely affirm that at the time when they all had one language — that is, one mode of speech — the human race had already been so estranged from the worship of the true God that true piety remained only in those generations descended from the seed of Shem through Arpachshad and leading to Abraham. But, in the sheer pride of building a tower up to the heavens, which signifies godless self-exaltation, there appeared the city, that is, the society, of the ungodly. Whether this city did not exist at all prior to that point, however, or whether it existed but lay hidden, or whether both cities existed all along — the godly city in the two sons of Noah whom he blessed and in their posterity, and the ungodly city in the son whom he cursed and in his progeny, which included that *mighty hunter against the Lord* (Gn 10:9) — is no easy matter to decide.

---

28. On Ninus see above at IV,6-7.

For it may be — and this is certainly the more credible idea — that, even before the building of Babylon began, there were already people among the descendants of the two sons whom Noah blessed who held God in contempt, and already people among the descendants of Ham who genuinely worshiped God. In any case, however, we must hold that there was never a time when the world lacked both kinds of people. In fact, even when Scripture says, *They have all fallen away, they are all alike of no worth; there is no one who does good, no, not one* (Pss 14:3; 53:3), we also read in the very same Psalms, *Have they no knowledge, all those evildoers, who eat up my people like bread?* (Pss 14:4; 53:4) Thus it is clear that even then there were people of God. And it is also clear that the verse which says, *There is no one who does good, no, not one*, was spoken of the sons of men, not of the sons of God. For the preceding verse says, *God looked down from heaven on the sons of men to see if there were any who understood, any who sought God* (Pss 14:2; 53:2), and it is in this light that the words are added which indicate that it is all the *sons of men* who are reprobate, that is, all who belong to the city that lives according to man, not according to God.

Heber and the Hebrew Language

11. Thus, just as there were sons of pestilence at the time when all peoples had one language (for there was also one language before the flood and yet, with the exception of the one household of the righteous Noah, all deserved to be wiped out by the flood), so also, when the peoples were rightly punished for their ungodly self-exaltation and were divided by diversity of language, and the city of the ungodly received the name Confusion (that is, when it was called Babylon), there remained the house of Heber in which the language was still spoken that was formerly the language of all. It is for this reason, as I noted above, that in the enumeration of Shem's sons, who were each the separate ancestors of separate peoples, Heber is listed first, despite the fact that he was actually Shem's great-great-grandson (that is, despite the fact that he is actually found to come in the fifth generation from Shem). And, because this language — which there is good reason to believe was at first the language common to the whole human race — remained in use in Heber's family even after the other peoples were divided by separate languages, it was called Hebrew from then on. For at that point it needed to be distinguished from the other languages by a name of its own, in the same way that the other languages were each given names of their own. In contrast, during the time when it was the only language, it was simply called the human language, or human speech, since it was the one language spoken by all mankind.[29] ...

---

29. Hebrew was widely believed by early Christian writers, as well as by their Jewish contemporaries, to have been the original language because, according to the Gn 1, God spoke in Hebrew when he created the world. See James Kugel, *Traditions of the Bible* (Cambridge, MA: Harvard University Press, 1998) 235-237.

Nor is it without significance that this is the language that Abraham used but could not transmit to all his descendants apart from those who were descended from him through Jacob and who, by coming together in prime and preeminent fashion to form the people of God, were able to keep God's covenants and maintain the lineage of Christ. Nor did Heber himself hand that language on to all his progeny but only to the line whose generations led down to Abraham. Therefore, even though it is not expressly stated that there was any godly race of men at the time when Babylon was being founded by the ungodly, the point of this obscurity is not to thwart the efforts of the inquirer but rather to stimulate them. For we read that there was originally one language common to all; and Heber is listed before all the sons of Shem, despite the fact that he is actually fifth in the line of descent from him; and Hebrew is the name of the language preserved by the authority of the patriarchs and prophets not only in their speech but also in their sacred writings. And in this light, when it is asked, with regard to the division of languages, where that language could have persisted which was previously the common language of all (for it is beyond doubt that, where this language survived, the punishment imposed by the change of languages did not apply), the only reply that comes to mind is that it persisted precisely among the people descended from the man from whom it took its own name. And it is no small indication of the righteousness of this people that, when other peoples were punished by having their language changed, no such punishment was imposed on them....

A Turning Point: Abraham

12. Let us now review the course of the city of God from the turning point which occurred with father Abraham. From that point on, our knowledge of this city begins to be more evident, and the divine promises, which we now see fulfilled in Christ, are represented more clearly. As we have learned from the indications in Holy Scripture, then, Abraham was born in the territory of the Chaldeans,[30] a land that belonged to the Assyrian kingdom. Even at that time, however, ungodly superstitions prevailed among the Chaldeans, as among the other peoples. Only in the household of Terah, to whom Abraham was born,[31] did the worship of the one true God continue; and, as we may believe, it was also only in that household that the Hebrew language survived (although, according to the account of Joshua, son of Nun, even Terah himself served alien gods in Mesopotamia,[32] just as those who were more evidently the people of God would do in Egypt). All the rest of Heber's descendants, however, had gradually merged into other languages and other peoples.

---

30. See Gn 11:28.
31. See Gn 11:26.
32. See Jos 24:2.

From then on, just as only the household of Noah had endured through the flood of waters to replenish the human race, so only the household of Terah, in the midst of the flood of superstitions then covering the whole world, endured as the one place in which the tender planting of the city of God was kept safe. In the former case, it is after the generations down to Noah have been enumerated, along with the numbers of their years, and after the cause of the flood has been explained, but before God began to speak to Noah about the building of the ark, that Scripture says, *These are the generations of Noah* (Gn 6:9). And again, in the present case, it is after the generations from the son of Noah called Shem down to Abraham have been enumerated that a key turning point is indicated in the same way when Scripture says, *These are the generations of Terah. Terah fathered Abram, Nahor, and Haran, and Haran fathered Lot. And Haran died before his father Terah in the land where he was born, in the territory of the Chaldeans. And Abram and Nahor took wives for themselves; the name of Abram's wife was Sarai, and the name of Nahor's wife was Milcah, the daughter of Haran.* (Gn 11:27-29) This Haran was the father of Milcah and Iscah,[33] and Iscah is believed to be identical with Sarai, Abraham's wife.[34]

[Chapters 13 – 15 comment on Abraham's life in Haran and his call from God to leave Haran for Canaan at age seventy-five.]

The First of God's Promises to Abraham

16. We must now take account of the promises that God made to Abraham. For in these promises the oracles of our God — that is, of the one true God — begin to appear more clearly, oracles that have to do with the godly people which prophetic authority foretold. The first of these promises reads as follows, *And the Lord said to Abram, Go from your country and your kindred and your father's house, and go to the land that I will show you, and I will make of you a great nation, and I will bless you and make your name great, and you shall be blessed, and I will bless those who bless you and curse those who curse you, and in you all the tribes of the earth shall be blessed* (Gn 12:1-3).

We should note, then, that two things were promised to Abraham. One is that his seed was going to possess the land of Canaan, and this is signified where it says, *Go to the land that I will show you, and I will make of you a great nation.* But the other is far more notable, for it has to do not with his bodily seed but with his spiritual seed, through which he is the father not just of the one people of the Israelites but of all the peoples that follow in the footsteps of his faith, and this is first promised in the words, *And in you all the tribes of the earth shall be blessed....*

---

33. See Gn 11:29.
34. See Jerome, *Hebrew Questions on Genesis*, ad loc.

17. At this same time, there were prominent kingdoms of the gentiles, in which the city of the earthborn — that is, the society of those living according to man — rose to extraordinary power under the dominance of the apostate angels, namely, the three kingdoms of the Sicyonians,[35] the Egyptians, and the Assyrians. But the Assyrian kingdom was by far the most powerful and the most exalted. For its famous king Ninus, the son of Bel,[36] had subjugated the peoples of all Asia except for India. And when I say "Asia" here I do not mean that part which is only one province of this greater Asia but rather what is called "all Asia." Some people have counted this as one of the two parts of the entire world, but most count it as one of the three parts of the entire world, namely, Asia, Europe, and Africa.[37] They do not, however, make this a division into three equal parts. For the part called Asia stretches from the south through the east to the north, but Europe extends from the north to the west, and then Africa extends from the west to the south. Thus Europe and Africa are seen to take up one half of the world, while Asia alone takes up the other half. Europe and Africa count as two distinct parts, however, because, between them, water flows in from Ocean, separating their landmasses, and this water forms our Great Sea.[38] Consequently, if you divide the world into two parts, the east and the west, Asia will be in one, and Europe and Africa will both be in the other. That is why, of the three kingdoms that were then prominent, the kingdom of the Sicyonians was not subject to the Assyrians, since it was in Europe. But how could the kingdom of the Egyptians not have been subject to those who held all Asia (with the single exception, we are told, of India)?

It was in Assyria, therefore, that the dominion of the ungodly city prevailed, and its head was Babylon, whose name, "Confusion," is supremely apt for the earthborn city. Ninus was ruling there at this time, following the death of his father Bel, who had reigned for sixty-five years as its first king. His son Ninus, who succeeded to the kingdom when his father died, reigned for fifty-two years, and he had held the throne for forty-three years when Abraham was born. This was about 1200 years before Rome was founded as a second Babylon, so to speak, in the west.

The Second Promise to Abraham

18. Thus Abraham left Haran at the age of seventy-five, when his father was 145 years old; and he went to the land of Canaan with Lot, his brother's son, and his wife Sarah and came at last to Shechem, where he again received a divine oracle,

---

35. Sicyon was a Greek city-state that flourished from the eighth to sixth centuries B.C. It was never as dominant as Augustine suggests that it was. Below at XVIII,2 Augustine describes it as very ancient (which it was not) and very small (which it was).
36. Bel is in fact the name of a Babylonian deity.
37. Augustine is relying on an ancient Greek concept of the threefold division of the world. He intends the term "Asia" to mean not simply the Roman province of that name, which covered all of what is now southwest Turkey in Asia, but an entire continent, such as he knew of it.
38. I.e., the Mediterranean.

of which Scripture says, *And the Lord appeared to Abram and said to him, To your seed I will give this land* (Gn 12:7). Nothing is said here about the seed by which he became the father of all peoples. The only seed mentioned is that by which he is the father of the one Israelite people, for this was the seed that would possess that land.

19. Then, when he had built an altar there and invoked the name of God, he left that place and lived in the desert, and from there he was compelled by the stress of famine to go to Egypt. In Egypt he called his wife his sister, and this was not a lie, for she was also that, since she was closely related to him by blood.[39] In the same way, Lot was called Abraham's brother since, as his brother's son, he was equally closely related to him.[40] Thus Abraham did not deny that Sarah was his wife but simply kept quiet about it. He committed the defense of his wife's chastity to God, and, as a man, he took precautions against human treachery. For, if he had not taken measures to guard against danger so far as possible, he would have been tempting God rather than putting his hope in God. I have already said enough about this, however, in my response to the false accusations of Faustus the Manichaean.[41] And in fact Abraham's trust in God was vindicated by the outcome. For Pharaoh, the king of Egypt, who had taken Sarah as his wife, was grievously afflicted and returned her to her husband.[42] And it would be utterly wrong to imagine that she had been defiled by intercourse with another man, for it is far more plausible to think that Pharaoh's terrible afflictions kept him from having intercourse with her.

20. After Abraham came back from Egypt, returning to the place from which he had come, his brother's son Lot parted from him and went to the land of Sodom, but not due to any break in their affection for each other. In truth, they had both become wealthy men and had begun to have many herders for their flocks. Because these herders were quarreling with each other, Abraham and Lot parted in order to avoid conflict and discord between their households. For such conflicts, as is the way with human beings, could even have given rise to quarrels between themselves. Here is what Abraham said to Lot in order to forestall this evil: *Let there be no quarrel between me and you, and between my herders and your herders, for we are brothers. See, is not the whole land before you? Part from me. If you go to the left, I will go to the right; or, if you go to the right, I will go to the left.* (Gn 13:8-9) Perhaps this was the start of the conciliatory custom among men that,

---

39. See Gn 12:10-16. Augustine's treatises *On Lying* and *Against Lying* testify to his horror of deception and help to explain his concern lest Abraham be thought a liar. Yet it is noteworthy that he does not refer here to Gn 20:12 — where Abraham claims that Sarah is his father's daughter but not his mother's, in other words that she was his half-sister, which would have exonerated him from lying.
40. The Septuagint and the Vulgate Latin text of Gn 13:8 translate the Hebrew "kinsfolk" — Abraham's word to describe his and Lot's relationship — as "brothers." Lot is referred to as Abraham's brother's son at Gn 12:5 and elsewhere.
41. See *Answer to Faustus, a Manichean* XXII,33-36
42. See Gn 12:17-20.

when any landed property is to be shared out, the elder makes the division and the younger makes the choice.[43]

The Third Promise to Abraham

21. Thus Abraham and Lot parted company and lived separately, not due to any dishonor of discord but due rather to the need to support their households, with Abraham living in the land of Canaan and Lot among the people of Sodom. And at this point the Lord said to Abraham in a third oracle, *Raise your eyes and look from the place where you now are to the north and to the south and to the east and to the sea; for all the land that you see I will give to you and to your seed forever, and I will make your seed like the sands of the earth. If anyone can number the sands of the earth, your seed will also be numbered. Rise up, walk through the land in its length and its breadth, for I will give it to you.* (Gn 13:14-17)

It is not entirely clear whether this promise includes the seed by which Abraham became the father of all peoples. For it might well seem that when the oracle says, *I will make your seed like the sands of the earth* (Gn 13:16), it is referring to this seed. This is an instance of the figure of speech that the Greeks call hyperbole, which is definitely figurative rather than literal.[44] And no one who has studied Scripture will have any doubt that it makes use of this figure, as it does of other tropes. This trope — that is, this figure of speech — occurs when what is said is far more sweeping than what the statement actually means. For who does not see that the number of the sands is incomparably greater than the number of all human beings could possibly be, even taken from Adam himself right down to the end of the world? How much more numerous they are, then, than Abraham's seed alone, even if we include not only those who specifically belong to the people of Israel but also those who are and will be his seed by their imitation of his faith over the whole world and among all peoples! That seed, in comparison with the multitude of the ungodly, is no more than a mere few.[45] But those few make a countless multitude of their own, and it is this multitude that was signified, in hyperbole, by the sands of the earth. The multitude promised to Abraham is innumerable, however, only to human beings, not to God, for to God not even the sands of the earth are beyond counting.

Thus, since it is not just the Israelite people but the whole seed of Abraham — to which the promise of many offspring is also given, not according to the flesh but according to the spirit — which is most appropriately compared to the multitude of the sands, we can presume that the promise given here refers to both....

---

43. See Seneca, *Controversies* VI,3: "Let the older brother divide the patrimony; let the younger one make the choice."
44. See Aristotle, *Rhetoric* 1413a. One of Aristotle's examples here is almost identical to the scriptural text cited by Augustine.
45. Augustine's consistent belief is that the lost will far outnumber the saved. See below at XXI,12.

No one doubts, however, that the one land referred to here is the land called Canaan. But the fact that the promise says *I will give it to you and to your seed forever* (Gn 13:15) can be disturbing to some people if they take *forever* to mean "for all eternity." But, if they interpret this expression here in accord with our confident belief that the beginning of the future age starts with the ending of the present age, this will not trouble them at all.[46] For, even though the Israelites have been expelled from Jerusalem, they still remain in other cities of the land of Canaan; and furthermore, since it is inhabited by Christians, that whole land is itself the seed of Abraham.

Abraham's Vision at Mamre

22. After receiving this promise, Abraham moved on and settled in Hebron, which is another place in the same land, near the oak of Mamre. Then, when five kings went to war against four and Lot was taken captive along with the defeated Sodomites, Abraham liberated him from the enemies who had attacked Sodom. Abraham brought 318 men with him into battle, men who had been born in his own household, and he won a victory for the kings of Sodom. But he refused to take any of the spoils when the king for whom he had won the victory offered them to him. At that time, however, he was openly given a blessing by Melchizedek, who was a priest of the most high God.[47] (Many great things are written of Melchizedek in the Epistle to the Hebrews, which most ascribe to the apostle Paul, although some deny this.[48]) It is here, beyond any doubt, that there first appeared the sacrifice which is now offered to God by Christians throughout the entire world and in which is fulfilled what was long afterwards said in prophecy to Christ, who was yet to come in the flesh, *You are a priest forever according to the order of Melchizedek* (Ps 110:4)— not, that is, according to the order of Aaron, for Aaron's order was to be abolished when the things augured by these shadows dawned like the coming of the day.[49]

---

46. The Latin for "forever" in the scriptural verse (Gn 13:15) is *in saeculum*, which is a common idiom. But *saeculum* can also have the meaning of "age" or "world."
47. See Gn 13:18-14:24.
48. See Heb 7:1-10. Jerome, *On Illustrious Men* 5, summarizes the different opinions on the authorship of the Epistle to the Hebrews, mentioning claims for Barnabas, Luke and Clement of Rome, although he himself opts for Paul. Origen, cited in Eusebius, *Ecclesiastical History* VI,25, argued with the greatest plausibility that the epistle was written not by Paul but by someone who was conversant with Paul's ideas. While quoting from the epistle above at X,5, Augustine refrains from mentioning its author, and here he seems careful not to take a firm stand, although he inclines toward Paul's authorship.
49. In keeping with a tradition that preceded him by several centuries, Augustine likens Melchizedek to Christ and his offering to the eucharist. The former analogy is the more ancient and dates from the New Testament (Heb 7:1-10), the latter from at least the late second century (Clement

23. It was at this time, also, that the word of the Lord was given to Abraham in a vision. For, when God promised him protection and a truly great reward, Abraham, anxious about his posterity, declared that a certain Eliezer, a slave born in his household, was to be his heir. And immediately an heir was promised to him, not that household slave but one who would come forth from Abraham himself, and again he was promised an innumerable seed, not like the sands of the earth but like the stars of the heavens.[50] Here, it seems to me, the promise is rather of a posterity exalted in heavenly bliss. For, on the score of quantity alone, what do the stars of the heavens amount to in comparison with the sands of the earth? On the other hand, however, one might argue that this comparison to the stars is similar to the comparison to the sands, in that the stars also cannot be numbered, since we must believe that not all of them can be seen. For, the more acute one's sight, the more stars one sees, and so there is good reason to suppose that some stars are hidden from even the keenest eyes, quite apart from the stars that are said to rise and set in another part of the world, far removed from us. And as for those who boast that they have grasped and recorded the whole number of the stars — such as Aratus or Eudoxus or any others there may be — the authority of this book holds them in contempt.[51]

It is also at this point that the statement occurs which the Apostle later cites in order to commend God's grace: *Abraham believed God, and it was reckoned to him as righteousness* (Gn 15:6; Rom 4:3; Gal 3:6). His aim was to keep the circumcised from boasting and to keep them from refusing to admit uncircumcised peoples to faith in Christ. For, at the time when Abraham's faith was reckoned to him as righteousness, he was still uncircumcised.

24. In the same vision, when God was speaking to Abraham, he also said this to him: *I am your God, who brought you out of the land of the Chaldeans in order to give you this land so that you might inherit it* (Gn 15:7). And, when Abraham asked by what he was to know that he would inherit it, God said to him, *Bring me a heifer three years old, a female goat three years old, a ram three years old, a turtledove, and a pigeon. He brought him all these, divided them in half, and set the pieces facing each other, but he did not divide the birds. And,* as it is written, *birds came down on the carcasses that had been divided in two, and Abram sat there with them. And toward sunset fear fell upon Abram, and a terrible dark dread came over him, and the Lord said to Abram, Know this for certain, that your seed shall be aliens in a land that is not their own, and they shall reduce them to slavery*

---

of Alexandria, *Stromata* IV,161).
50. See Gn 15:1-5.
51. Eudoxus of Cnidus (c. 410-355/347 B.C.) was a highly respected Greek astronomer and mathematician whose work entitled *Phaenomena* was put into verse by Aratus of Soli (c. 315-240 B.C.), which was in turn quoted by Paul in Acts 17:28b. Augustine's expression of contempt seems highhanded in the context. His suggestion that the number of the stars might verge on the infinite, however, is remarkably prescient.

and shall afflict them four hundred years, but I will bring judgment on the nation that they will serve, and afterward they shall go out with many goods. But, as for you, you shall go to your fathers in peace, nourished in a good old age. But in the fourth generation they shall come back here. For the sins of the Amorites are not yet complete, even now. And, as the sun was going down, a flame appeared, and behold, a smoking furnace and flaming torches that passed between those divided pieces. On that day the Lord God made a covenant with Abram, saying, To your seed I will give this land, from the river of Egypt to the great river, the river Euphrates, the land of the Kenites, the Kenizzites, the Kadmonites, the Hittites, the Perizzites, the Rephaim, the Amorites, the Canaanites, the Hivites, the Girgashites, and the Jebusites. (Gn 15:9-21)

All these things were done and said by God in a vision, but to discuss each point in detail would take too long and would go beyond the intent of this work. We ought, therefore, to cover only what we need to know. First, then, after it was said that Abraham believed God and it was reckoned to him as righteousness, it was no failure of faith on his part that he asked, *Lord God, by what shall I know that I shall inherit it?* (Gn 15:8) He was referring, of course, to the promised inheritance of the land. But he did not ask, "How shall I know?" as if he did not yet believe. Rather, he asked, *By what shall I know?* — that is, he asked for some likeness by which he might know how what he already believed would take place. In just the same way it was no lack of faith on the part of the virgin Mary that she asked, *How will this happen, since I know no man?* (Lk 1:34) She was certain that it would happen but was asking how it would happen; and, when she had asked, she heard. And here too a likeness was given — the likeness of the animals, the heifer, the female goat, the ram, and the two birds, the turtledove and the pigeon — so that Abraham might know that what he already had no doubt was going to happen would happen in the way that these indicated.

Thus the heifer may have signified the people set under the yoke of the law, and the female goat the same people in their future sinfulness,[52] and the ram the same people yet again, in the coming reign. These animals are said to be three years old because the key eras of time are those running from Adam to Noah, from Noah to Abraham, and from Abraham to David,[53] who, after Saul was rejected, was the first to be established as ruler of the Israelite people by the Lord's will. It was therefore in this third period, extending from Abraham to David, that this people reached adolescence in what was, as it were, the third era of its life. Or it may be that it is more fitting to take these animals to have some other signification.

---

52. The goat is a symbol of sinfulness. See Lv 16:20-22; Mt 25:32-33.
53. This division of ages, in which biblical eras correspond to periods of human life, is frequent in Augustine. See below at XVI,43; *Miscellany of Eighty-three Questions* 58,2; *On Genesis: A Refutation of the Manicheans* I,23,35-37; *Instructing Beginners in Faith* 22,39.

I have no doubt at all, however, that it is Abraham's spiritual seed that is prefigured by the addition of the turtledove and the pigeon. For the reason that Scripture said, *But he did not divide the birds* (Gn 15:10), is that the carnal are divided among themselves, but the spiritual are in no way divided, whether, like the turtledove, they withdraw from the business of human affairs or, like the pigeon, they live in the midst of them. Furthermore, both of these birds are simple and harmless,[54] which signifies that in the same Israelite people to whom that land was to be given there would be individual sons of the promise and heirs of the kingdom destined to dwell in eternal happiness. As for the birds who descended on the divided carcasses, however, they do not signify anything good but rather represent the spirits of this lower air,[55] seeking their own kind of food from the division of carnal creatures. Again, the fact that Abraham sat there with them signifies that even among these divisions of the carnal against the carnal the truly faithful will persevere to the end. And the fear and the terrible dark dread that came over Abraham toward sunset signify that, as the end of this world approaches, the faithful will face great distress and tribulation, about which the Lord says in the Gospel, *For at that time there shall be great tribulation, such as there has not been since the beginning* (Mt 24:21).

On the other hand, the words spoken to Abraham — *Know this for certain, that your seed shall be aliens in a land that is not their own, and they shall reduce them to slavery and shall afflict them four hundred years* (Gn 15:13)— were plainly a prophecy about the people of Israel, who were going to be slaves in Egypt....

The next statement — *And as the sun was going down, a flame appeared, and behold, a smoking furnace and flaming torches that passed between those divided pieces* (Gn 15:17)— signifies that, at the end of the world, the carnal are to be judged by fire. For, just as the dark dread that came over Abraham toward sunset — that is, as the end of the world was approaching — signifies the affliction of the city of God that is expected to come under Antichrist, such affliction as there never was before, so also this fire, appearing as the sun was actually setting — that is, at the actual end of the world — signifies the day of judgment, separating those of the carnal who are to be saved by fire from those of the carnal who are to be damned in fire.[56]

Lastly, the covenant made with Abraham specifically refers to the land of Canaan and names eleven peoples living there, from the river of Egypt to the great river Euphrates. This does not mean, however, the land from the great river of Egypt — that is, the Nile — but rather the land from the small river that divides Egypt from Palestine, where the city of Rhinocorura is located.[57]

---

54. See Mt 10:16.
55. I.e., demons.
56. See below at XXI,26, where Augustine cites 1 Cor 3:11-15 in distinguishing between purgatorial and eternal punishment by fire.
57. Rhinocorura, or Rhinocolura, was an Egyptian town in the southeast corner of the Mediterranean.

Abraham's Sons: the Birth of Ishmael and the Promise of Isaac

25. Then comes the period of Abraham's sons, one by the maidservant Hagar and one by the free woman Sarah; of these I have already spoken in the previous book.[58] In the circumstances, however, Abraham is by no means to be branded as a criminal with regard to this concubine.[59] In fact, it is clear that he made use of her only to have a child, not to gratify his lust. He was not demeaning his wife but rather obeying her. For she believed that it would be some consolation for her own childlessness if she made her maidservant's fertile womb her own, by her own choice, since she could not have children by nature. As a wife, she exercised the right of which the Apostle said, *So also the husband does not have authority over his own body, but the wife does* (1 Cor 7:4), and she exercised this right in order to bear a child from another woman, since she could not do so from herself. There is no lascivious desire here, no degrading dissipation. The maidservant is given by the wife to her husband for the sake of having a child and is accepted by her husband for the sake of having a child. It is not guilty sensuality but rather the fruit of nature that both are seeking. But, when the maidservant became pregnant, she held her barren mistress in contempt, and Sarah, with a woman's suspicion, put the blame on her husband. Even then, however, Abraham showed that he had been no servile lover but rather a free begetter, and he proved that he had guarded his wife's honor in his relations with Hagar, not satisfying his own pleasure but rather obeying his wife's will. He had accepted Hagar but had not sought her; he had come to her but had not doted on her; he had impregnated her but had not loved her. For he said to Sarah, *See, your maidservant is in your power; do to her as you please* (Gn 16:6). What a man, who treated women in a manly way — his wife with honor, his maidservant out of obedience, and no one immodestly![60]

26. After this, Ishmael was born of Hagar,[61] and Abraham might have presumed that in him was fulfilled the promise made to him when he had proposed to adopt his house-born slave as heir and God told him, *This man shall not be your heir; but he who shall issue from you, he shall be your heir* (Gn 15:4). Therefore, to keep him from thinking that this promise had been fulfilled in the maidservant's son, *when he was ninety-nine years old the Lord appeared to him and said to him, I am God; be pleasing in my sight and be beyond reproach, and I will make my covenant between me and you and will multiply you exceedingly. And Abraham fell on his face, and God said to him, As for me, this is my covenant with you. You shall be the father of many nations, and your name shall no longer be called Abram, but your name shall be Abraham, because I have made you the father of many nations.*

---

58. See above at XV,3.
59. On what follows see also *Answer to Faustus, a Manichean* XXII,30-32; *The Lord's Sermon on the Mount* I,16,49.
60. "With honor...out of obedience...immodestly": *temperanter...obtemperanter...intemperanter.*
61. See Gn 16:15.

I will cause you to increase very greatly and will make nations of you, and kings shall come forth from you. And I will establish my covenant between me and you, and with your seed after you throughout their generations, as an eternal covenant to be God to you and to your seed after you....

As for Sarai your wife, her name shall not be called Sarai, but Sarah shall be her name. I will bless her, and I will give you a son by her; and I will bless him, and he shall become nations, and kings of nations shall come forth from him. And Abraham fell on his face and laughed and said to himself, Will a child be born to me when I am a hundred years old? Will Sarah give birth when she is ninety years old? And Abraham said to God, O that Ishmael might live in your sight! But God said to Abraham, See, your wife Sarah shall bear you a son, and you shall name him Isaac, and I will establish my covenant with him as an eternal covenant to be God to him and to his seed after him. As for Ishmael, I have heard you; see, I have blessed him, and I will increase him and will multiply him greatly. He shall father twelve nations, and I will make him a great nation. But I will establish my covenant with Isaac, whom Sarah will bear to you at this time next year. (Gn 17:1-7.15-21)

Here we have more explicit promises regarding the calling of the peoples in Isaac, that is, in the son of the promise. In him grace is signified, not nature, in that he is promised as the son of an old man and a barren old woman. For, even though God is also at work in the natural course of procreation, it is when nature has failed and is at an end that God's work is clear, and in that case his grace is recognized the more clearly. And since this was to happen not by generation but by regeneration, circumcision was enjoined at the very point when a son was promised from Sarah. And the fact that God orders the circumcision not only of all sons but also of house-born and bought slaves testifies that this grace pertains to all. For what else does circumcision signify but the renewal of nature by the removal of old age? And what else does the eighth day signify but Christ, who rose again after the seven-day week was complete, that is, after the day of the sabbath?[62] Again, the names of the parents are changed; everything rings with newness; and the new covenant is veiled in the old. For what else is that which is called the Old Testament but the hidden form of the New? And what else is that which is called the New Testament but the revealed form of the Old?[63] Abraham's laughter is the exultation of one who gives thanks, not the derision of one who has doubts. And what Abraham said to himself— *Will a child be born to me when I am a hundred years old? Will Sarah give birth when she is ninety years old?* (Gn 17:17)— is no expression of doubt; it is rather an expression of wonder....

---

62. Although the eighth day is highly symbolic in Christian literature, it is rarely a symbol of Christ himself, as it is here.
63. See *Instructing Beginners in Faith* 4,8 for the classic expression of this formula.

God's Appearance to Abraham at Mamre

29. God appeared again to Abraham at the oak of Mamre as three men, and it is not to be doubted that these men were angels, despite the fact that some imagine that one of them was the Lord Christ, asserting that Christ was visible even before he took flesh.[64] It is, in fact, possible for the divine and invisible power, the incorporeal and immutable nature, to appear to mortal sight without any change on its own part, not through what it is in itself, but through something subject to it. And what is not subject to it? But if their reason for claiming that one of the three was Christ is that, even though Abraham saw three men, he still spoke to the Lord in the singular (for this is what Scripture says, *And see, three men were standing near him; and when he saw them, he ran from the door of his tent to meet them, and he bowed down to the ground and said, Lord, if I have found favor with you* [Gn 18:2-3]), and so forth, then why do they not also notice that two of the three had gone away to destroy the people of Sodom at the very point when Abraham was still speaking to one of them, calling him Lord and begging him not to destroy the righteous along with the ungodly in Sodom?[65]...

Scripture, however, attests that they were actually angels, not only here in the Book of Genesis where the events are related but also in the Epistle to the Hebrews where, in praising hospitality, it says, *In this some have even entertained angels without knowing it* (Heb 13:2).

Thus, when a son by Sarah — Isaac — was again promised to Abraham through these three men, it was at the same time a divine response that was given to him in these words: *Abraham shall become a great and numerous people, and in him all the peoples of the earth shall be blessed* (Gn 18:18). Here, then, two things are promised, in brief and in full: the people of Israel according to the flesh, and all peoples according to faith.

30. After this promise, when Lot had been delivered from Sodom, fire rained down from heaven, and the whole region of that ungodly city was turned to ashes.[66] It was a place where sex between men had become so customary that it enjoyed the same license that the laws ordinarily give to other practices. But their punishment was also a precursor of the divine judgement to come. For what does it mean that those who were being delivered by the angels were forbidden to look back[67] except that the mind must not turn back to the old life that it puts off when it is regenerated by grace, if we expect to escape the final judgment? Again, Lot's

---

64. The argument that Augustine uses in this section to show that the three visitors were angels and not divine persons, or two angels and one divine person (Christ), appears also in *The Trinity* II,11,20-12,22. For the view that the Son, and not angels, appeared at both Mamre and Sodom, as well as elsewhere, see Eusebius, *Ecclesiastical History* I,2,7-16.
65. See Gn 18:16-19:1.
66. See Gn 19:24-25.
67. See Gn 19:17.

wife, turned to salt, remained in the place where she had looked back,[68] providing the faithful with a seasoning of wisdom, so to speak, to put them on guard against her example....

The Birth and the Sacrifice of Isaac

31. After this, a son was born to Abraham by Sarah, just as God had promised, and he named him Isaac, which means "laughter."[69] For, when this son was promised to him, his father laughed in astonishment and joy.[70] And, when the promise was given again by the three men, his mother had also laughed, although in doubt as well as in joy. But, when the angel rebuked her because her laughter, even though it was an expression of joy, was not an expression of complete faith, she was afterwards made firm in her faith by that same angel.[71] This is, then, how the boy received his name. And, when Isaac was born and was given that name, Sarah proved that her laughter expressed no mocking derision but rather exulting joy, for she said, *The Lord has brought me laughter, for everyone who hears will rejoice with me* (Gn 21:6). A little later, however, the maidservant was cast out of the household with her son; and, according to the Apostle, the two covenants are signified here, the Old and the New, with Sarah as the figure of the Jerusalem above, that is, of the city of God.[72]

32. In the midst of these events (it would take too long to tell of them all) Abraham was tempted with regard to sacrificing his dearly beloved son Isaac, so that his devout obedience might be put to the test, making it known not to God but to the ages.[73] For we should not take every temptation as a matter of blame, since a temptation in which a person meets the test should be a cause of rejoicing. And it is generally true that the human soul can only come to real knowledge of itself by trying its strength in response to the questions that temptation raises, giving its response not just in word but in actual experience. For then, if it acknowledges God's gift, it is truly devout; it is established with the firmness of grace, not puffed up with empty boasting.

Abraham, of course, would never have believed that God takes delight in human victims — despite the fact that, when the divine command sounds, it is to be obeyed, not disputed. Even so, Abraham is to be praised for immediately believing that his son, when sacrificed, would rise again. For, when he was unwilling to comply with his wife's desire to expel the maidservant and her son, God had said

---

68. See Gn 19:26.
69. See Jerome, *Interpretation of Hebrew Names*, Genesis, s.v. Isaac.
70. See Gn 17:17.
71. See Gn 18:12-15.
72. See Gal 4:22-26.
73. See Gn 22:1-14.

to him, *In Isaac shall your seed be called* (Gn 21:12). It is true, of course, that God then goes on to say, *And I will also make a great nation of this maidservant's son, because he is your seed* (Gn 21:13). Why, then, does it say, *In Isaac shall your seed be called*, when God also calls Ishmael his seed? But the Apostle explains the meaning of *in Isaac shall your seed be called* in this way: *It is not*, he says, *the children of the flesh that are the children of God; it is rather the children of the promise that are counted as his seed* (Rom 9:8). Thus, it is the children of the promise that are called in Isaac to be the seed of Abraham; that is, they are gathered together in Christ at grace's call. And so, holding firmly to this promise — since it had to be fulfilled through the very one whom God was ordering him to kill — the devout father never doubted that a son who could be given to him after he had lost all hope for a son could also be restored to him after being sacrificed....

For this reason, just as the Lord carried his own cross, so Isaac himself carried to the place of sacrifice the wood on which he was to be placed. And in the end, after his father was forbidden to strike him (since it was not right for Isaac to be slain), who was that ram whose immolation completed the sacrifice with blood of symbolic significance? In fact, when Abraham noticed the ram, it was caught in a thicket by its horns. Of whom, then, was the ram a figure if not Jesus, who was crowned with Jewish thorns before he was sacrificed?[74]

But let us listen rather to the divine words spoken by the angel. For Scripture says, *And Abraham reached out his hand to pick up the knife in order to kill his son. And the angel of the Lord called out to him from heaven and said, Abraham! And he said, Here I am. And the angel said, Do not lay your hand on the boy or do anything to him, for now I know that you fear your God since, for my sake, you have not spared even your beloved son.* (Gn 22:10-12) In this case *now I know* meant "now I have made it known," for it is certainly not true that God did not know this before. Then, when the ram had been sacrificed in place of his son Isaac, we read that *Abraham called that place The Lord Saw, as they still say today, The Lord appeared on the mountain* (Gn 22:14). And just as *now I know* meant "now I have made it known," so here *The Lord Saw* meant "the Lord appeared," that is, "The Lord caused himself to be seen." *And the angel of the Lord called out to Abraham a second time from heaven and said, By myself I have sworn, says the Lord, because you have done this and for my sake have not spared your beloved son, I will bless you with my blessing, and I will multiply your seed as the stars of heaven and as the sand on the shore of the sea. And your seed shall possess the cities of their enemies as their inheritance, and in your seed all the peoples of earth shall be blessed, because you obeyed my voice.* (Gn 22:15-18) In this way, after the

---

74. In keeping with centuries-old tradition, Augustine proposes the following symbolism: God the Father is symbolized by Abraham, Christ by Isaac, the wood of the cross by the kindling wood that Isaac carried, and Christ crowned with thorns (see Mt 27:29 par.) by the ram caught in the thicket. See Irenaeus, *Against Heresies* IV,5,4; Origen, *Homily on Genesis* 8; Ambrose, *On Abraham* I,8,66-78.

burnt offering by which Christ was signified, the promise concerning the calling of the nations in the seed of Isaac was now confirmed by God's sworn oath. For he had often given his promise, but up to this point he had never sworn his oath. And what is the sworn oath of the true and truthful God but the confirmation of his promise and a kind of rebuke to those who do not believe him?

After this, Sarah died when she was 127 years old[75] and her husband was 137. For he was ten years older than she was, as he himself said when he was promised a son by her: *Will a child be born to me when I am a hundred years old? Will Sarah give birth when she is ninety years old?* (Gn 17:17) Then Abraham bought a field, in which he buried his wife. And, according to Stephen's account, it was at this point that Abraham became settled in that land, since that is when he first began to own property there, namely, after the death of his father, who is reckoned to have died two years before.[76]

33. Then, when Isaac was forty years old — that is, when his father was 140, three years after his mother's death — he married Rebecca, the granddaughter of his uncle Nahor.[77] But, when his father sent a servant to Mesopotamia to bring her back, Abraham said to this servant, *Put your hand under my thigh, and I shall make you swear by the Lord, the God of heaven and the Lord of earth, that you will not get a wife for my son Isaac from the daughters of the Canaanites* (Gn 24:2-3). And what does this show except that the Lord, the God of heaven and the Lord of earth, was going to come in flesh drawn from that thigh? And these are obviously no small indicators of the truth, announced ahead of time, that we now see fulfilled in Christ!

Abraham's Marriage to Keturah

34. But what does it mean that, after the death of Sarah, Abraham took Keturah as his wife? We should by no means suspect him of uncontrolled sexual desire, especially in light of his age and the sanctity of his faith. Was he still seeking to have children, then, even though God had already promised him with utter certainty that his children through Isaac would be multiplied as the stars of heaven and the sands of earth? But if Hagar and Ishmael, as the Apostle teaches, signify the carnal people of the old covenant,[78] why should not Keturah and her sons signify the carnal people who think they belong to the new covenant? Hagar and Keturah, in fact, were called Abraham's concubines as well as his wives; Sarah, in contrast, was never called his concubine....

---

75. See Gn 23:1.
76. See Acts 7:2-4.
77. See Gn 24:15.67.
78. See Gal 4:24-25.

Thus, the sons of his concubines did not go without gifts, but they do not come into the promised kingdom — neither the heretics nor the carnal Jews — because there is no heir but Isaac, and *it is not the children of the flesh that are the children of God; it is rather the children of the promise that are counted as his seed* (Rom 9:8), of whom it is said, *In Isaac shall your seed be called* (Gn 21:12; Rom 9:7). For I do not see any reason why Keturah, whom Abraham married after his wife's death, was called a concubine unless it was for the sake of indicating this mystery. But anyone who is not willing to grant this significance to these events should cast no blame on Abraham. For what if this was provided to refute future heretics who would oppose second marriages,[79] demonstrating in the very person of the father of many nations himself that a second marriage after the death of one's wife is no sin?

And Abraham died when he was 175 years old.[80] Thus he left behind his son Isaac, then aged seventy-five, whom he had fathered when he was himself a hundred years old.

The Twins Born to Isaac

35. Now, then, let us see how the times of the city of God unrolled through Abraham's descendants. From the first year of Isaac's life up to the sixtieth, when his sons were born, what is memorable is that, when he asked God that his wife, who was barren, might bear a child, God had already granted what he asked. For she had already conceived; and the twins, still shut in her womb, were struggling with each other.[81] In anguish she inquired of the Lord, and she received this reply: *Two nations are in your womb, and two peoples born of you shall be divided, and one people shall overcome the other, and the older shall serve the younger* (Gn 25:23). The apostle Paul wants us to see this as a great example of grace, because, before they were born or had done anything either good or evil, the younger was chosen without any merit on his part, and the older was rejected.[82] At this point, beyond any doubt, the two were on a par with regard to original sin; and, as far as personal sin was concerned, neither had committed any.

But the plan of the work I have undertaken does not permit me to say any more about this now, since I have already said a great deal about it elsewhere.[83] As for the statement that *the older shall serve the younger*, almost no one among us has

---

79. The most prominent of these, whom Augustine undoubtedly had in mind, was Tertullian, who is said to have inspired the heretical Cataphrygians and Novatianists. See *Heresies* 86; *The Excellence of Widowhood* 5,7. For Tertullian's position see his *On Monogamy*, passim.
80. See Gn 25:7-8.
81. See Gn 25:21-22.
82. See Rom 9:11-13.
83. See *Miscellany of Eighty-three Questions* LXVIII,6; *The Grace of Christ and Original Sin*.

understood it to mean anything other than that the older people, the Jews, would serve the younger people, the Christians.[84]...

God's Promise to Isaac

36. Isaac also received an oracle, like the oracles that his father had received at various times. Of this oracle it is written, *Now there was a famine in the land, besides the previous famine that took place in the time of Abraham. And Isaac went to Gerar, to King Abimelech of the Philistines. And the Lord appeared to him and said, Do not go down to Egypt; live in the land that I will tell you of, and dwell in this land, and I will be with you and I will bless you. For to you and to your seed I will give all this land, and I will uphold the oath that I swore to your father Abraham; and I will multiply your seed as the stars of heaven, and I will give your seed all this land, and all the peoples of earth shall be blessed in your seed, because your father Abraham obeyed my voice and kept my precepts, my commandments, my statutes, and my laws.* (Gn 26:1-5)

This patriarch had no other wife nor any concubine; he was content to have for his posterity the two twins he fathered in one act of intercourse. And when he was living among strangers he also feared the peril arising from his wife's beauty; and he did what his father had done, calling her his sister and not revealing that she was his wife, for she was in fact his kinswoman, related to him by blood on both his father's and his mother's side. And she, too, remained untouched by strangers, even when it became known that she was his wife.[85] But we should not rank Isaac above his father simply because he knew no woman other than his one wife. For there is no doubt that the merits of his father's faith and obedience were greater than his, inasmuch as God declares that it is for Abraham's sake that he does the good that he does for Isaac. *All the peoples of earth*, he says, *shall be blessed in your seed, because your father Abraham obeyed my voice and kept my precepts, my commandments, my statutes, and my laws* (Gn 26:4-5). And again, in another oracle he says, *I am the God of your father Abraham. Do not be afraid, for I am with you and I have blessed you, and I will multiply your seed for the sake of Abraham, your father.* (Gn 26:24)

What we should note, then, is how chastely Abraham acted, despite the fact that to some, who are without shame and who seek support from Sacred Scripture for their own indecency, he seems to have acted out of lust. And we should also learn from this that we should not compare people to each other on the basis of their individual good points but should rather take the whole picture into consideration in each case. For it can happen that one person has some feature of his life and

---

84. This understanding of the relationship of Jacob and Esau is found already at the beginning of the second century in *Epistle of Barnabas* 13.
85. See Gn 26:7-11.

character in which he surpasses another person and which far outweighs anything in which he is surpassed by the other. Consequently, on this true and sound basis for judgment, even though continence ranks higher than marriage, it is still true that a married person who has faith is better than a celibate person who does not. In fact, the person without faith is not only less praiseworthy but is especially despicable. Let us take it as given that both are morally good; even so, the married person who is fully faithful and fully obedient to God is unquestionably better than a celibate who is less faithful and less obedient. But, if everything else were equal, of course, who would hesitate to prefer the celibate to the married person?[86]

The Blessing of Jacob

37. So Isaac's two sons, Esau and Jacob, grew up together. The primacy of the older was transferred to the younger by a pact and agreement between them. This happened because the older immoderately desired the dish of lentils that the younger had prepared for his meal and, having given his oath, he sold his birthright to his brother for this price.[87] From this we learn that it is not the kind of food we eat that makes us blameworthy but rather unrestrained greed. Isaac was growing old, and his eyesight was dimmed with age. He wished to bless his older son, but, without knowing it, he blessed his younger son instead of the older brother. The older son was a hairy man; but the younger put himself under his father's hands with goatskins wrapped around himself, as if he were bearing the sins of another.[88] But, to keep us from thinking that Jacob's deceit was a fraudulent deceit — and, at the same time, to prompt us to look for the great mystery it represents — Scripture had earlier said, *Esau was a skillful hunter, a man of the fields; but Jacob was a simple man, living at home* (Gn 25:27).[89]

There are some among us who have translated this "without deceit" rather than *simple*. But, whether the Greek *aplastos* means "without deceit" or "simple" or — better yet — "without feigning," what deceit is there when a blessing is obtained by a man who is without deceit? What deceit is there in a simple man, what feigning is there in one who does not lie, unless this is a profound mystery of the truth? And what was the character of the blessing itself? Isaac said, *Ah, the smell of my son is like the smell of a plentiful field that the Lord has blessed. May God give you of the dew of heaven and of the plenty of the earth, and abundance of*

---

86. While maintaining the universal view on the superiority of virginity to marriage, Augustine is careful here to place virginity explicitly within the context of faith and to allow for the possibility of a practice of virginity that does not include faith.
87. See Gn 25:29-34.
88. See Gn 27:1-29. Goatskins symbolize sinfulness.
89. Augustine's best-known attempt to exculpate Jacob from deception, as here and in the following lines, occurs in *Against Lying* 10,24, where he famously observes, *Non est mendacium sed mysterium* ("It is not a lie but a mystery").

grain and wine. Let the peoples serve you and princes bow down to you. Be lord over your brother, and your father's sons shall bow down to you. Anyone who curses you shall be cursed, and anyone who blesses you shall be blessed. (Gn 27:27-29) Thus the blessing of Jacob foretells the proclamation of Christ to all peoples. And this is happening; this is being done.

Isaac is the law and the prophets, and Christ is blessed by them, even through the mouth of the Jews, as by one who does not know what he is doing, because the law and the prophets are themselves unknown to them. The world, like a field, is full of the sweet smell of the name of Christ. His is the blessing that is *of the dew of heaven* (Gn 27:28), that is, the showers of divine words. His is the blessing that is *of the plenty of the earth* (Gn 27:28), that is, the gathering of the peoples. His is *the abundance of grain and wine* (Gn 27:28), that is, the multitude which the grain and wine bring together in the sacrament of his body and blood.[90] He is the one whom the peoples serve, and to whom the princes bow down. He is the one who is lord over his brother, since his people rule over the Jews. He is the one to whom the sons of his father bow down, that is, the sons of Abraham according to faith, for he himself is also a son of Abraham according to the flesh. Anyone who curses him is cursed, and anyone who blesses him is blessed. Our Christ, I say, is blessed — that is, he is spoken of truthfully — even from the mouth of the Jews who, although in error, still recite the law and the prophets. And this is true despite the fact that they suppose that there is another who is blessed, one who is still awaited by those erring people.[91]

Take note: When the older son comes to ask for the promised blessing, Isaac is appalled, and he realizes that he has blessed one son in place of the other. He is astonished, and he asks who this person is, but he does not complain that he has been deceived. On the contrary, with the great mystery immediately revealed to him inwardly in his heart, he shows no indignation. Instead, he confirms the blessing. *Who was it, then*, he says, *who hunted game for me and brought it to me, and I ate of all of it before you came? And I blessed him, and blessed he shall be.* (Gn 27:33) Who would not expect to find the curse of an angry man here, if all this had taken place in the ordinary earthly way rather than by inspiration from above? These were real events, but real events with prophetic significance; events on earth, but prompted by heaven; events enacted by human beings, but under divine inspiration. If we were to explore their every detail, each pregnant with such profound mysteries, we would fill many volumes. But we must impose some reasonable limits on this work, and this compels us to move along to other topics.

---

90. I.e., the eucharist.
91. Augustine offers a lengthy interpretation of Isaac's blessing and the circumstances surrounding it in Sermon 4, where he notes (in section 24) that the entire event is susceptible of a christological interpretation.

Jacob and Joseph

38. Jacob was sent by his parents to Mesopotamia to take a wife there. His father sent him off with these words: *You shall not take a wife from the daughters of the Canaanites. Arise and go at once to Mesopotamia to the house of Bethuel, your mother's father, and take as wife from there one of the daughters of Laban, your mother's brother. And may my God bless you and increase and multiply you, and you shall become companies of peoples. And may he give to you the blessing of your father Abraham, to you and to your seed after you, so that you may inherit the land where you live, which God gave to Abraham.* (Gn 28:1-4) Here we now see that Jacob's seed was set apart from Isaac's other seed, which is descended from Esau. For, when it said, *In Isaac shall your seed be called* (Gn 21:12), this clearly referred to the seed belonging to the city of God, from which Abraham's other seed, which descended from the maidservant's son and which would descend from Keturah's sons, was set apart. At that point, however, there was still room for doubt as to whether that blessing pertained to both of Isaac's twin sons or only to one of them, and, if only to one, to which of the two. But this was made clear when Jacob was prophetically blessed by his father and was told, *And you shall become companies of peoples. And may he give to you the blessing of your father Abraham.* (Gn 28:3-4)

On his way to Mesopotamia, then, Jacob received an oracle in his sleep, about which Scripture says, *And Jacob left the well of the oath and went toward Haran, and he came to a place and slept there, for the sun had set. And he took one of the stones of the place and put it under his head, and he slept in that place and had a dream. And see, a ladder was set up on the earth, and its top reached to heaven, and the angels of God were ascending and descending on it. And the Lord stood above it, and said, I am the God of Abraham your father, and the God of Isaac. Do not be afraid. I will give the land on which you are sleeping to you and to your seed. And your seed shall be like the sands of the earth, and it shall spread out across the sea and into Africa and to the north and to the east.*[92] *And all the families of the earth shall be blessed in you and in your seed. And see, I am with you, and I will keep you wherever you go, and I will bring you back to this land, for I will not leave you until I have done all that I have told you. And Jacob awoke from his sleep, and said, Surely the Lord is in this place, and I did not know it. And he was afraid, and said, How terrifying is this place! This is none other than the house of God, and this is the gate of heaven. And Jacob stood up, and he took the stone that he had put under his head and set it up as a monument and poured oil on the top of it. And he called that place the House of God.* (Gn 28:10-19)

---

92. The Latin text of the Book of Genesis that Augustine knew gave the four points of the compass as cited here, including *across the sea* and *into Africa* as representative of the west and the south. The sea would have been the Mediterranean.

This was a prophetic act. Jacob did not pour oil over the stone as idolaters do, as though making the stone into a god; nor did he bow down to the stone or sacrifice to it. Rather, because Christ's name comes from "chrism," that is, from "anointing,"[93] his act was clearly a figure pointing to a great mystery. As for the ladder, we see that the Savior himself recalls it to mind for us in the Gospel. There he says of Nathaniel, *Here is truly an Israelite in whom there is no deceit* (Jn 1:47). And then, because Israel had seen this vision (for Israel and Jacob are one and the same), he adds in the same passage, *Amen, amen, I tell you, you shall see heaven opened and the angels of God ascending and descending on the Son of Man* (Jn 1:51).

Then Jacob went on to Mesopotamia to take a wife there. Scripture indicates, however, that he came to have four women from there, by whom he fathered twelve sons and one daughter, though he had felt no illicit desire for any of them. In fact he had come to take just one. But when another was intruded on him in her place, he did not send her away. For, without knowing who she was, he had sex with her during the night, and he did not want it to seem as though he had treated her as a plaything. At that time, for the sake of increasing the birthrate, the law did not prohibit having many wives, and so he also took the one woman to whom he had already pledged that he would marry her. Because she was barren, however, she gave her husband her maidservant in order that, by her, she herself might have children; and her older sister did the same, even though she had already had children, because she wanted more.[94] We do not read, however, that Jacob ever sought any women but the one, nor that he ever made use of any except for the purpose of fathering children. He kept his marriage vow, for he would not have done even this except that his wives, who had legitimate power over their husband's body,[95] demanded it of him. Thus he fathered twelve sons and one daughter by four women. Then he went to Egypt, on account of his son Joseph, who had been sold by his jealous brothers and taken there, where he had risen to great heights.[96]

39. As I said just previously, Jacob was also called Israel,[97] and the people descended from him mostly took this name. It is the name bestowed on him by the angel who wrestled with him on his return journey from Mesopotamia, and who clearly represented a type of Christ. For the fact that Jacob prevailed over him — just as the angel willed, of course, in order to prefigure a mystery — signifies the passion of Christ, in which the Jews seemed to prevail over him.[98] And yet

---

93. The Latin *chrisma*, used here, is a transliteration of the Greek word with the same meaning. Christ is "the anointed one."
94. See Gn 29:1-30.
95. See 1 Cor 7:4.
96. See Gn 46:1-7.
97. See above at XVI,38.
98. That the angel who fought Jacob was Christ is a commonplace in patristic literature. See Justin Martyr, *Dialogue with Trypho* 58, 126; Origen, *Select Passages from Genesis*, ad loc. (PG 12,128). But Augustine's understanding of the struggle between Jacob and the angel as a foreshadowing

Jacob obtained a blessing from the very angel whom he had overcome, and the bestowing of this name was the blessing, for "Israel" means "seeing God,"[99] which will be the reward of all the saints at the end. But the same angel also touched the one who appeared to prevail on the breadth of his thigh, and in this way he made him lame.[100] Thus, one and the same Jacob was both blessed and lamed. He was blessed in those from this same people who believed in Christ, and he was lamed in those who have not believed. For the breadth of the thigh represents the multitude of his race. And, in fact, it was of the majority of his stock that it was prophetically declared, *And they have limped away from their paths* (Ps 18:45)....

41. With respect to the Christian people, then, in whom the city of God is on pilgrimage on earth, if we look for the line leading to the flesh of Christ in the seed of Abraham, the sons of his concubines are set aside, and Isaac remains. And if we look for that line in the seed of Isaac, Esau, who is also Edom, is set aside, and Jacob remains, who is also Israel. And if we look for that line in the seed of Israel himself, the others are set aside, and it is Judah who remains, because Christ came from the tribe of Judah. And so let us listen to the blessing that Israel prophetically gave to Judah when, just before he died, he blessed his sons in Egypt: *Judah*, he said, *your brothers shall praise you. Your hands shall be on the neck of your enemies; your father's sons shall bow down to you. Judah is a lion's whelp. You have risen up, my son, from a shoot. You have lain down and slept like a lion, and like a lion's whelp. Who will rouse him up? A ruler shall not be lacking from Judah, nor a leader from his loins, until the things come that have been laid up for him, and he himself is the expectation of the peoples. Binding his colt to the vine, and his donkey's colt to the tendril, he shall wash his robe in wine and his garment in the blood of the grape. His eyes are dark with wine, and his teeth are whiter than milk.* (Gn 49:8-12)....

42. Thus Isaac's two sons, Esau and Jacob, present a figure of the two peoples, the Jews and the Christians (although, in fact, as far as descent in the flesh is concerned, it is not the Jews who come from the seed of Esau but the Idumeans, and it is not the Christian people who come from Jacob but rather the Jews, for the figure holds good only with respect to the declaration that *the older shall serve the younger* [Gn 25:23]). And this is also the case with regard to the two sons of Joseph, for the older is a type of the Jews, and the younger a type of the Christians. When Jacob blessed Joseph's sons, he placed his right hand on the younger, who was on his left, and his left hand on the older, who was on his right; and Joseph thought that this was a serious mistake, and he warned his father as if to correct his error

---

of Christ's suffering at the hands of the Jews is, if not unique to him, relatively unusual.
99. Although there are several possible meanings for the name "Israel," based on the Hebrew, "seeing God," which was embraced by many of the Fathers (e.g., Jerome, *Interpretation of Hebrew Names*, Exodus, s.v. Israel), does not seem to be one of them.
100. See Gn 32:24-32.

and show him which was the older.[101] But Jacob refused to change his hands, and said, *I know, my son, I know; he also shall become a people, and he also shall be great. But his younger brother shall be greater than he, and his seed shall become a multitude of peoples.* (Gn 48:19) Here again, then, it presents the two promises. For the one shall become *a people*, the other *a multitude of peoples*. What could be more evident than that, in the light of these two promises, both the people of Israel and the whole world are contained in Abraham's seed, the one according to the flesh and the other according to faith?

From Moses to David

43. After the death of Jacob and the death of Joseph, during the remaining 144 years until they went forth from the land of Egypt, this people grew in incredible numbers, even though they were ground down by terrible persecutions which at one point went so far as the slaughtering of the male children born to them, because the Egyptians were so dismayed and distressed by the extraordinary increase of these people.[102] At that time Moses was saved by stealth from those who were slaughtering the infants; and, because God was preparing to do great things through him, he was brought to the king's house. There he was cared for and adopted by the daughter of Pharaoh[103] (in Egypt, Pharaoh was the title of all their kings), and he grew up to be such a powerful man that he was the one who delivered that people, miraculously multiplied as they were, from the harsh and bitter yoke of servitude that they endured there. Or, rather, it was through him that God delivered them, just as he had promised to Abraham.

Earlier, it is true, Moses had fled from Egypt because, in defending an Israelite, he had killed an Egyptian, and he was afraid for his life.[104] But afterwards he was sent back by God,[105] and, in the power of God's spirit, he overcame the opposition of Pharaoh's magicians when they resisted him.[106] It was at this time that, through him, ten memorable plagues were inflicted on the Egyptians for refusing to let God's people go. Water was turned into blood; there were frogs, lice, and flies; their cattle died; and there were boils, hail, locusts, darkness, and the death of their first-born.[107] And when the Egyptians, broken by all these terrible plagues, finally let the Israelites go, they were themselves wiped out in the Red Sea as they pursued their former captives. For the sea divided to make a path for the fleeing Israelites, but the returning waves drowned the pursuing Egyptians.[108]

---

101. See Gn 48:8-18.
102. See Ex 1:7-22.
103. See Ex 2:1-10.
104. See Ex 2:11-15.
105. See Ex 3:9-10.
106. See Ex 7:8-8:19.
107. See Ex 7:14-12:29.
108. See Ex 14:5-30.

After this, the people of God spent forty years in the wilderness with Moses as their leader. It was during this time that the tabernacle of the testimony was given its name,[109] where God was worshiped with sacrifices that foretold things to come. This all happened, of course, after the law had been given on the mountain in awe and terror, for it was there that the divine presence was most clearly attested in wondrous signs and sounds.[110] This occurred shortly after the people had departed from Egypt and begun to live in the wilderness, on the fiftieth day after the paschal feast was celebrated with the sacrifice of a lamb.[111] This lamb is so obviously a type of Christ[112] — foretelling that he would pass over from this world to the Father through the sacrifice of his passion (for in Hebrew "pasch" means "passover"[113]) — that, when the new covenant was revealed, it was on the fiftieth day after Christ our Passover was sacrificed that the Holy Spirit came down from heaven.[114] And in the Gospel the Holy Spirit is called *the finger of God* (Lk 11:20) to remind us of that first foreshadowing event, for the tables of the law are also said to have been written *with the finger of God* (Ex 31:18).

After the death of Moses, Joshua the son of Nun ruled the people and brought them into the promised land and divided it among them.[115] These two wondrous leaders also waged wars with wondrous success, although God bears witness that their victories came to them not so much on account of the merits of the Hebrew people as on account of the sins of the peoples they defeated. After these two leaders, now that the people were settled in the promised land, there were judges.[116] Thus the first promise made to Abraham began to be fulfilled with regard to one people — that is, the Hebrew people — and with regard to the land of Canaan, although not yet with regard to all peoples or with regard to the whole earth. For that was to be fulfilled at Christ's coming in the flesh and not by the observance of the old law but rather by the faith of the Gospel. And this was prefigured in the fact that the people were led into the promised land not by Moses, who had received the law for the people on Mount Sinai, but by Joshua, whose name had even been changed at God's command so that he was called Jesus.[117] In the time of the judges, however, success and failure in war alternated according to the sins of the people and the mercy of God.

---

109. See Ex 25:9-22. "Tabernacle of the testimony": *tabernaculum testimonii*. This was more commonly known as the ark of the covenant.
110. See Ex 19:16-31:17.
111. See Ex 12:21-28.
112. On the rich christological symbolism of the paschal lamb see Jean Daniélou, *The Bible and the Liturgy* (Notre Dame, Ind.: University of Notre Dame Press, 1956) 162-176.
113. "Pasch...passover": *pascha...transitus*.
114. See Acts 2:1-4.
115. See Jos passim.
116. See Jg passim.
117. Joshua had been called Hoshea. See Nm 13:16. Joshua and Jesus are the same name, respectively, in Hebrew and Latin, and in Latin there is no distinction between the two. It is somewhat surprising that Augustine does not use the opportunity offered here to discuss how Joshua foreshadows Jesus, as in Justin Martyr, *Dialogue with Trypho* 113.132; Origen, *Homilies on Joshua* 1,1.

Here, then, we come to the time of the kings, of whom Saul was the first to reign. When he was repudiated[118] and fell in a disastrous battle,[119] and his whole line was rejected from the kingship, David succeeded to the kingdom, and Christ is called, in particular, the son of David.[120] David marks a turning point, and here, we might say, the people of God begins to come of age and to enter young adulthood.[121] From Abraham down to David this race had lived out, as it were, a kind of adolescence. For it was not without reason that the evangelist Matthew recorded the genealogy of Christ in such a way as to ascribe fourteen generations to this first period, namely, the period extending from Abraham down to David.[122] It is, of course, from adolescence that a man begins to be able to father children, and that is why his list of generations took its start from Abraham, who was appointed the father of nations when he received his new name.[123] Prior to Abraham, this race of the people of God was, so to speak, in its childhood, during the period extending from Noah down to Abraham himself, and that is why it was found to have its own language at this time, namely, Hebrew. For it is in childhood that a man begins to speak, after his infancy, which takes its name precisely from the fact that infants are unable to speak.[124] And this first age, the age of infancy, is sunk in oblivion, just as the first age of mankind was erased by the flood. For how many are there who can remember their own infancy?[125]

Thus, just as the previous book covered that first age in the course followed by the city of God, so the present book covers the second and the third ages; and in this third age, as indicated by the three-year-old heifer, the three-year-old female goat, and the three-year-old ram,[126] the yoke of the law was imposed, an abundance of sins appeared, and the earthly kingdom had its beginning. At the same time, however, there was no lack of spiritual people, who were sacramentally prefigured by the turtledove and the pigeon.[127]

---

118. See 1 S 15:10-34.
119. See 1 S 31:1-13.
120. See, e.g., Mt 1:1.
121. On the biblical ages discussed in the following lines see also above at XVI,24.
122. See Mt 1:2-6.
123. See Gn 17:5.
124. The Latin for "infant" is *infans*, meaning "not speaking." See also below at XXI,16.
125. See *Confessions* I,6,8.
126. See Gn 15:9 and above at XVI,24.
127. See ibid. and above at XVI,24. "Sacramentally prefigured": *figuratum est sacramentum*. The turtledove and the pigeon are "sacraments" — i.e., objects carrying a meaning beyond themselves — of the spiritual people of the Old Testament.

Study Questions for Book XVI

Augustine interprets the stories of Noah and the patriarchs as prophetic — in other words, as anticipating and foreshadowing later events in the life and death of Jesus Christ. Can such a figurative Christian reading of the Old Testament be maintained amid contemporary sensibilities to the problems inherent in supersessionism (that is, the conviction that the new covenant has superseded God's covenant with the Jews) and its theological variants?

Both Abraham and Isaac had presented their wives as their "sisters." Abraham and Jacob practiced polygamy. Augustine defends the patriarchs against accusations of lying and lust with interesting arguments to justify their choices. Is he proposing a kind of situation ethics? Does he discern the work of grace underneath ancient cultural practice and amid the difficult and dangerous situations faced by the patriarchs by focusing on their motivations?

In Augustine's account of the two cities' course through time, a political embodiment of the City of Man first emerges with his mention of Assyria, where "the dominion of the ungodly city prevailed (XVI,17)." In King David he sees the people of God emerge into "young adulthood," and in David he finds Christ prefigured. Is there a parallel between Assyria as symbolic of the City of Man and the Kingdom of David as symbolic of the City of God?

BOOK XVII

Book XVII follows the course of the city of God down to "the age of the prophets," which runs from Samuel to the birth of Christ. In that era, it singles out two episodes — first, the rejection of the priesthood of Eli and, second, the anointing of Saul as king, followed by his rejection and replacement by David — as events that foreshadow and thus prophetically anticipate the ultimate transformation of the priesthood and kingship in the coming of Christ, and the transition from the old covenant to the new. At the same time, on the level of prophecy in words rather than events, it identifies three types of prophecy — referring respectively to the earthly Jerusalem alone, to the heavenly Jerusalem alone, and to both at once — and presents extended interpretations of selected prophecies (which are quoted at length) taken from key prophetic figures, most especially David and Solomon, that point in various ways, some more openly and some more obscurely, to Christ and the Church. In this context, it insists on the exegetical rule that more obscure passages in a prophetic text are to be interpreted in the light of and in accord with plainer and more open ones. The book concludes by noting that, after the division of the Israelite kingdom into Israel and Judah, there was very little prophecy in either kingdom, or in the subsequent Babylonian captivity, or in the period following the Jews' return from captivity, although the division itself, as a prophetic event, foreshadowed the final division of the Jewish people into those who do and those who do not accept Christ.

1. As for the promises God made to Abraham — to whose seed, as we have learned, we owe both the Israelite people according to the flesh and all peoples according to faith, in accord with God's promise — the course of the city of God through the ages will indicate how these are being fulfilled. And, since the end of the previous book brought us down to the reign of David, we will now touch on what came after his reign so far as seems sufficient for the work we have undertaken.

The Age of the Prophets

The entire period that extends from the point at which the holy Samuel began to prophesy[1] down to the time when the people of Israel were taken as captives

---

1. See 1 S 3:19-20.

to Babylonia, and then down to the point at which, after the return of the Israelites seventy years later, the house of God was restored as prophesied by the holy Jeremiah,[2] constitutes the age of the prophets. Of course, we can — and not without reason — give the name of prophet both to the patriarch Noah himself, in whose time the whole earth was wiped out by the flood,[3] and to others before and after him, right down to the present era when there began to be kings among the people of God. For certain future events having to do with the city of God and with the kingdom of heaven were signified or foretold through them in one way or another, and in fact we read that several of them, such as Abraham and Moses, were expressly called prophets.[4] It remains true, however, that the period chiefly and principally termed "the days of the prophets" starts with the earliest prophecies of Samuel, who at God's command first anointed Saul as king[5] and then, when Saul was repudiated,[6] anointed David himself,[7] from whose stock all the following kings succeeded each other, so long as it was fitting for such a succession to last.

It would be an unending task, however, if I wanted to compile everything that the prophets foretold about Christ during this time, as the city of God was running its course and the generations of its members came and went, one dying out and the next coming to birth. This is due to the fact, first of all, that Scripture itself — which seems, in presenting its ordered account of the kings and their deeds and their fates, to have been chiefly concerned with historical accuracy in its narration of events — is found, when considered and interpreted with the help of God's Spirit, to be even more intent (or, certainly, no less intent) on foretelling things to come in the future than it is on relating things that happened in the past. And who, if he gave the matter even a little thought, could fail to see how laborious and interminable it would be to trace all this out and present it in full detail, not to mention how many volumes it would require? In addition, there is the fact that even the passages that unambiguously count as prophecies relating to Christ and the kingdom of heaven, which is the city of God, are so numerous that it would require a longer discussion to present them all than the scope of this work allows. If I can, therefore, I shall keep my pen firmly under control so that I say neither anything more nor anything less than is needed to bring this work to its completion, according to God's will.

2. In the previous book we said that two things were promised to Abraham from the start. The first was that his seed was going to possess the land of Canaan, and this was signified where Scripture said, *Go to the land that I shall show you, and I will make of you a great nation* (Gn 12:1). But the second, and by far the

---

2. See Jer 25:11-12.
3. See Gn 6:11-9:17.
4. For Abraham see Gn 20:7; for Moses see Dt 34:10.
5. See 1 S 10:1.
6. See 1 S 15:10-34.
7. See 1 S 16:13.

more important, concerned not his carnal but rather his spiritual seed, because of which he is the father not simply of the one Israelite people but of all the peoples that follow in the footsteps of his faith, and this promise begins with these words: *And in you all the tribes of the earth shall be blessed* (Gn 12:3). And we have shown by many testimonies that these two promises were kept in full measure. Thus, Abraham's seed according to the flesh — that is, the people of Israel — were now in the promised land and had now begun to rule there, not only by taking and holding the cities of their enemies but also by having kings. God's promises concerning this people, then, had already been fulfilled in large part — not only those made to the three patriarchs, Abraham, Isaac, and Jacob, and to others of their time, but also those made through Moses himself, through whom this same people was delivered from their Egyptian servitude, and through whom all the past promises were revealed in his time, when he led the people through the wilderness.

God's promise that the land of Canaan would extend from a certain river of Egypt all the way to the great river Euphrates,[8] however, was not fulfilled through the illustrious leader Joshua the son of Nun, who led that people into the promised land, defeated its inhabitants, divided it among the twelve tribes as God had commanded, and then died.[9] Nor was it fulfilled after him, during the whole period of the judges, even though it was no longer prophesied of the distant future but rather was expected to be fulfilled at any moment. This promise was fulfilled, however, through David and through his son Solomon, whose rule extended over all the area that had been promised, for they subdued all those lands and made them pay tribute.[10] Under these kings, therefore, Abraham's seed according to the flesh was so fully established in the promised land — that is, in the land of Canaan — that nothing of God's earthly promise remained to be fulfilled except that the Hebrew people should continue in this same land, secure and unshaken so far as temporal prosperity is concerned, through the successive generations of their posterity right down to the end of this mortal age, just so long as they obeyed the laws of the Lord their God. But, since God knew that they would not do this, he also made use of his temporal punishments both to train the few among them who remained faithful to him and to admonish those who were later going to be spread among all peoples. For it was right that those in whom he was going to fulfill his second promise, when the new covenant was revealed through the incarnation of Christ, should be admonished.

3. Thus, like the divine oracles granted to Abraham, Isaac, and Jacob, and like any other prophetic signs or sayings given in the earlier sacred writings, the rest of the prophecies, those given during the time of the kings, also refer partly to Abraham's people according to the flesh and partly to the seed of Abraham in

---

8. See Gn 15:18.
9. See Jos passim.
10. See 1 K 4:21.

which all peoples are blessed, as coheirs of Christ through the new covenant, for the sake of gaining eternal life and the kingdom of heaven. Partly, then, they refer to the maidservant whose children are born into servitude, that is, to the earthly Jerusalem, which is in servitude together with her children; and partly they refer to the free city of God, that is, the true Jerusalem, eternal in heaven, whose children are those who live according to God and are on pilgrimage here on this earth.[11] At the same time, however, there are some among these prophecies that we understand to refer to both at once, to the maidservant in their literal sense, and to the free woman in their figurative sense.

The Types of Prophecy

We find, then, that the sayings of the prophets are of three types: some have to do with the earthly Jerusalem, some have to do with the heavenly Jerusalem, and others have to do with both. I see, however, that I need to support what I say with examples. The prophet Nathan was sent to charge King David with a grievous sin and to foretell the future evils that would follow.[12] And who doubts that these statements and others like them referred to the earthly city, whether they were spoken publicly, that is, for the welfare and benefit of the people in general, or privately, as when someone receives divine words relating to his own affairs through which he learns something of the future for use in his temporal life? In contrast, when we read, *See, says the Lord, the days are coming when I will make a new covenant with the house of Israel and the house of Judah. It shall not be like the covenant that I made with their ancestors, when I took them by the hand to lead them out of the land of Egypt, for they did not continue in my covenant, and I despised them, says the Lord. But this is the covenant that I will make with the house of Israel after those days, says the Lord: I will put my laws in their minds, and I will write them on their hearts, and I will look to them, and I will be their God, and they shall be my people* (Jer 31:31-33), there is no doubt that this prophecy refers to the Jerusalem on high, whose reward is God himself and whose supreme and total good is to possess him and to be his.

But when Jerusalem is called the city of God, and it is prophesied that the house of God will be located there, this refers both to the earthly and to the heavenly Jerusalem. For we see that this prophecy was fulfilled when King Solomon built his celebrated Temple.[13] But this was not only a historical event in the earthly Jerusalem; it was also a figure of the heavenly Jerusalem. This third type of prophecy — in which the other two are, as it were, mixed and mingled together — is of great importance in the ancient canonical books that narrate historical events, and it has greatly exercised (and continues greatly to exercise) the abilities of those who study Sacred Scripture with the aim of discerning which of the things that we read were

---

11. See Gal 4:22-26.
12. See 2 S 12:1-14.
13. See 1 K 6:1-7:51.

foretold about and fulfilled in Abraham's seed according to the flesh were also things that allegorically signified something to be fulfilled in Abraham's seed according to faith. In fact, some have even thought that there is nothing that was prophesied or enacted in these books, or that was enacted without being prophesied, which does not carry some figurative significance that is to be referred to the heavenly city of God and to the children of that city who are pilgrims in this life.

If this is so, however, then the discourse of the prophets will be of only two types, not three; or, rather, this will be true of all the Scriptures that are included in the Old Testament. For, if whatever is said in the Old Testament about the earthly Jerusalem or in relation to it, and is fulfilled, also signifies something that refers to the heavenly Jerusalem and allegorically prefigures it, then there will be nothing in the Old Testament that refers only to the earthly Jerusalem. And, in that case, there will be only two kinds of prophecy, one referring to the free Jerusalem, and the other referring to both.

In my view, however, just as people are badly mistaken when they think that the events recorded in writings of this kind signify nothing more than the mere event itself, so people are far too rash when they insist that everything recorded there carries allegorical significance.[14] That is why I have said that the prophecies are of three types and not merely of two. In holding this view, however, I do not condemn those who have been able to devise a spiritual meaning for each historical event recorded there, just so long as, first of all, they preserve the truth of the history itself. On the other hand, with regard to any statements that cannot possibly apply to any historical event, whether divine or human, whether past or future, no person of faith can doubt that there must have been some good reason for making them. Anyone who could, would certainly interpret them in a spiritual sense; or, at the very least, he would grant that they should be interpreted in a spiritual sense by someone who can.

4. Thus, when the city of God had followed its course down to the period of the kings, it reached the point at which Saul was repudiated and David first took such a firm hold on the kingdom that, from then on, his descendants ruled in the earthly Jerusalem in enduring succession. Now, these events had figurative significance. For they signified and foretold something that must not be passed over in silence. They pointed to the change that was to take place in the future with respect to the two covenants, the old and the new, when the priesthood and the monarchy were transformed by the new and eternal priest and king who is Christ Jesus. For, when Eli the priest was rejected and Samuel was substituted for him in the service of God, functioning both as priest and as judge,[15] and when Saul was deposed and King David was established in the kingship,[16] these happenings prefigured the change I am talking about.

---

14. See Origen, *On First Principles* IV,3,5.
15. See 1 S 2:27-4:1.
16. See 1 S 16:1-13.

The Prophecy of Hannah, Mother of Samuel

And Samuel's mother Hannah, who first was barren and then rejoiced in fertility, seems to prophesy this very transformation when, in her delight, she pours forth her gratitude to the Lord and, after her child had been born and weaned, gives him back to God with the same devotion with which she had earlier made her vow. For she says, *My heart is strengthened in the Lord, my horn is exalted in my God. My mouth is enlarged over my enemies, I rejoice in your salvation. For no one is holy like the Lord, and no one is righteous like our God; no one but you is holy. Do not boast, and do not speak lofty words; let no arrogance come from your mouth. For the Lord is a God of knowledge, and a God who makes his own plans. He has made weak the bow of the mighty, and the weak are girded with strength. Those sated with bread have been reduced to want, and the hungry have passed over the earth. For the barren woman has given birth to seven, and she who has many children has been enfeebled. The Lord puts to death and brings to life, he brings down to hell and brings back again. The Lord makes poor and makes rich, he humbles and he exalts. He raises the poor from the dust and lifts the needy from the dunghill, to set him among the princes of the people and to make them inherit the seat of glory. He grants the vow to him who makes a vow, and he has blessed the years of the righteous, for it is not by his own strength that a man is powerful. The Lord shall make his adversary weak; holy is the Lord. Let not the prudent man glory in his prudence, nor let the powerful man glory in his power, nor let the rich man glory in his riches. But let him who glories glory in this: to understand and know the Lord, and to do justice and righteousness in the midst of the earth. The Lord has ascended into the heavens and has thundered; he himself shall judge the ends of the earth, for he is just, and he gives strength to our kings and shall exalt the horn of his anointed.* (1 S 2:1-10 LXX)

Are we really to suppose that these are simply the words of one insignificant woman giving thanks for the birth of her son? Are people's minds so turned away from the light of truth that they do not recognize that the words this woman poured forth go far beyond her own measure? Can anyone who is rightly moved by the things which have already begun to be fulfilled in this earthly pilgrimage fail to notice and see and recognize that through this woman (whose very name, Hannah, means "his grace"[17]) there speaks the Christian religion itself, the city of God itself, whose king and founder is Christ, and ultimately the grace of God itself? Through her, then, by the spirit of prophecy, there speaks the very grace of God, from which the proud are estranged so that they fall and by which the humbled are filled so that they rise — which was, in fact, the main theme resounding throughout her song of praise....

Let it be Christ's Church, then, *the city of the great king* (Ps 47:3; Mt 5:35), *full of grace* (Lk 1:28) and fruitful in offspring, that speaks the words that it knows

---

17. See Jerome, *Interpretation of Hebrew Names*, 1 Kingdoms, s.v. Anna. "His" implies "God's."

were prophesied of it so long ago through the mouth of this pious mother: *My heart is strengthened in the Lord, my horn is exalted in my God* (1 S 2:1 LXX). Her heart is truly strengthened, and her horn is truly exalted, for it is not in itself that her heart is strengthened and her horn exalted but rather in the Lord, her God. *My mouth is enlarged over my enemies* (1 S 2:1 LXX), because even in the grip of oppression *the word of God is not chained* (2 Tm 2:9), not even when its proclaimers are in chains. *I rejoice*, she says, *in your salvation* (1 S 2:1 LXX). This salvation is Christ Jesus, whom Simeon, as we read in the Gospel, took in his arms, an old man embracing a little child; and, recognizing him to be great, Simeon said, *Now, Lord, let your servant depart in peace, for my eyes have seen your salvation* (Lk 2:29-30). Therefore, let it be the Church that says, *I rejoice in your salvation, for no one is holy like the Lord, and no one is righteous like our God* (1 S 2:1-2 LXX), for he not only is holy but makes holy, and not only is righteous but makes righteous. *No one but you is holy* (1 S 2:2 LXX), for no one is made holy except by you. Then the passage continues, *Do not boast, and do not speak lofty words; let no arrogance come from your mouth, for the Lord is a God of knowledge* (1 S 2:3 LXX). He himself knows you, even when no one else does, *for, if anyone thinks he is something when he is nothing, he deceives himself* (Gal 6:3).

These things are said to the opponents of the city of God, who belong to Babylon, who presume on their own strength and glory in themselves, not in the Lord. Included among them are the Israelites according to the flesh, earthborn citizens of the earthly Jerusalem, who, as the Apostle says, *being ignorant of the righteousness of God* — that is, the righteousness given to man by God, who is alone righteous and alone makes righteous — *and seeking to establish their own* — that is, as if it were their own achievement, not God's gift — *have not submitted to God's righteousness* (Rom 10:3). For in their pride they imagine that they can please God by their own righteousness rather than by the righteousness of God, who is *a God of knowledge* and thus is also the judge of consciences, for he sees the thoughts that human beings have and knows that their thoughts are empty[18] if they come from themselves and not from him....

[The rest of chapter 4 continues the interpretation of Hannah's prophecy in 1 Samuel 2:3-10.]

...This was, then, the prophecy of Hannah, the mother of Samuel, a holy man and highly esteemed; and in him was prefigured the transformation of the old priesthood which has now been fulfilled, now that the woman who had *many children has been enfeebled* so that the barren woman who *gave birth to seven* might have a new priesthood in Christ.

---

18. See Ps 94:11.

The Transformation of the Priesthood: the Prophecy to Eli

5. But this transformation is expressed more clearly by the man of God who was sent to the priest Eli himself. Scripture does not tell us his name, but his office and ministry make it plain, beyond any doubt, that he was a prophet. For this is what Scripture says: *And a man of God came to Eli and said, Thus says the Lord, Truly, I revealed myself to the house of your father, when they were slaves in the house of Pharaoh, and I chose the house of your father out of all the tribes of Israel to serve as my priest, to go up to my altar, to burn incense, and to wear the ephod. And I gave to the house of your father all the offerings by fire of the children of Israel to be their food. Why, then, have you looked with insolent eye on my incense and my sacrifice and glorified your sons more than me, to bless the firstfruits of every offering in Israel in my sight? Therefore, thus says the Lord, the God of Israel, I declared that your house and the house of your father should walk before me forever. But now the Lord says, By no means, for I will glorify those who glorify me, and I will despise him who despises me. See, the days are coming when I will banish your seed and the seed of your father's house, and you shall not have an elder in my house all your days; and I will banish the male of your house from my altar, so that his eyes fail and his soul melts away. Every one of your house who survives shall die by the sword of men. And this shall be a sign to you, which shall come upon your two sons, Hophni and Phinehas: they shall both die on the same day. And I will raise up for myself a faithful priest, who does all that is in my heart and all that is in my mind; and I will build a sure house for him, and he shall walk before my anointed all his days. And it shall come to pass that everyone who is left in your house shall come to bow down to him for a piece of silver and shall say, Let me have a part in your priesthood, so that I may have bread to eat.* (1 S 2:27-36)

It is not the case that this prophecy, where the transformation of the old priesthood is announced with such clarity, may be said to have been fulfilled in Samuel. For, even though Samuel was not from a tribe other than the one that had been appointed by the Lord to serve the altar, still he was not one of the sons of Aaron, whose offspring had been set aside as those from whom priests should come.[19] As a consequence, in the event too there was a foreshadowing of the same transformation that was going to take place through Christ Jesus, and the prophecy itself pertained literally to the old covenant (with respect to the event) but figuratively to

---

19. See *Revisions* II,43(70),2, where Augustine corrects his text of *The City of God* for a second and final time (the first time with reference to X,8 above): "What was said of Samuel, 'He was not one of the sons of Aaron,' should instead have been 'He was not the son of a priest.' It was a more legitimate custom, in fact, for the sons of priests to succeed the dead priests. For Samuel's father is numbered among the sons of Aaron, but he was not a priest, nor is he [listed] among Aaron's sons as though he himself had begotten him, but he was like all of that people, who are called sons of Israel." Scripture does not in fact number Samuel's father Elkanah among the sons of Aaron.

the new (with respect to the words), for it signified by means of the event what was said to the priest Eli by means of the prophet's words. For in fact there were priests from Aaron's line in later times, such as Zadock[20] and Abiathar[21] during David's reign, and others after them, until the right time came for the transformation of the priesthood, foretold so long before, to be accomplished through Christ. But must not anyone who views the matter with the eyes of faith see that what was foretold has now been fulfilled? For now there is no tabernacle, no temple, no altar, and no sacrifice, and therefore there is no priest remaining for the Jews, despite the fact that they were commanded by God's law to appoint priests from Aaron's seed....

[The rest of chapter 5 continues the interpretation of the prophecy of the man of God sent to Eli in 1 Samuel 2:2-36.]

6. But, even though all this was foretold at that time in such profound terms and now shines forth with such obvious clarity, it is not without reason that a person might still feel moved to ask how we can be sure that everything whose coming was foretold in those books is actually going to come about. For one of the things that was declared by God in this passage clearly could not happen in fact — *that your house and the house of your father should walk before me forever* (1 S 2:30). For we see that that priesthood has been replaced, and there is no hope that what was promised to that house can ever be fulfilled, for what is now proclaimed as eternal is what succeeded it, after it was rejected and replaced. Anyone who says this, however, does not yet understand, or does not recollect, that the priesthood according to the order of Aaron was itself instituted as a kind of shadow of the eternal priesthood that was to come. Thus, when eternity was promised to it, it was not promised to the shadow or figure itself but rather to what was shadowed and prefigured by it. And so, to keep people from thinking that the shadow itself was going to endure, its replacement had to be prophesied as well.

The Transformation of the Kingship: Saul and Samuel

In the same way, the kingdom of Saul, who was himself repudiated and rejected, was the shadow of a future kingdom that was going to endure for all eternity. In fact, the oil with which he was anointed, by virtue of which he was called the anointed, must be taken in a mystical sense and must be understood as a great mystery.[22] David himself was so much in awe of this mystery in Saul's person that, with stricken heart, he trembled in fear when, while hiding in a cave that Saul

---

20. See 1 K 1:8.38.
21. See 2 S 15:24; 1 K 1:7; 2:26.
22. "Great mystery": *magnum sacramentum*. Similarly in the next few lines.

also entered to answer the call of nature, he sneaked up behind him and secretly cut off a tiny piece from his garment in order to have proof that he had spared Saul when he could have killed him.[23] David's aim was to remove from Saul's mind the suspicion due to which he was hunting down the holy David, thinking him to be his enemy. But David was terrified for fear that he might be guilty of having violated so great a mystery in Saul's person simply by touching his clothing in this way. For this is what Scripture says, *And David was stricken to the heart because he had cut off a corner of Saul's cloak* (1 S 24:5). And to the men who were with him, who were urging him to kill Saul since he had been given into his hands, David said, *The Lord forbid that I should do this thing to my lord, the Lord's anointed, to raise my hand against him, for he is the Lord's anointed* (1 S 24:6). Such great reverence was shown for this shadow of the future, however, not for its own sake but rather for the sake of what it prefigured.

Again, there is what Samuel said to Saul: *Because you have not kept my commandment, which the Lord commanded you, just as the Lord had once prepared your kingdom to last forever over Israel, now your kingdom shall not endure for you, and the Lord shall seek out for himself a man after his own heart, and the Lord shall command him to be a ruler over his people, because you have not kept what the Lord commanded you* (1 S 13:13-14). And again, we must not take this as if God had prepared Saul himself to rule forever and then refused to keep his promise after Saul sinned, for God certainly was not ignorant of the fact that Saul was going to sin. Rather, he had prepared Saul's kingdom as a prefiguration of the eternal kingdom. That is why he went on to say, *Now your kingdom shall not endure for you* (1 S 13:14). Thus, what was signified by his kingdom did endure and will endure, but it will not endure for him, because he himself was not going to rule forever. And neither were his offspring, so that it would not appear that the *forever* might be fulfilled through his descendants as they succeeded one another. *And the Lord*, he says, *shall seek out for himself a man* (1 S 13:14), here signifying either David or the *mediator of the new covenant* (Heb 9:15) himself, who was prefigured in the chrism with which both David himself and his descendants were anointed.[24] Of course, it is not that God did not know where the man was and so had to look for him. It is rather that, in speaking through a man, he speaks in the way we human beings speak, and it is precisely by speaking in our human way that he seeks us out. For we were already so thoroughly known not only to God the Father but also to his only-begotten Son, who came to seek what was lost,[25] that we were chosen in him even before the foundation of the world.[26]...

I have no doubt that what comes next is to be understood with reference to this distinction, *And Israel shall be divided in two* (1 S 15:28), that is, into the Israel that

---

23. See 1 S 24:3-4.
24. "Prefigured in the chrism" because both "Christ" and "chrism" have the same root.
25. See Lk 19:10.
26. See Eph 1:4.

is the enemy of Christ and the Israel that adheres to Christ, the Israel that belongs to the maidservant and the Israel that belongs to the free woman.[27] For these two peoples were at first together, just as Abraham still adhered to the maidservant until the barren woman, now made fertile by the grace of Christ, cried out, *Cast out the maidservant and her son* (Gn 21:10). We know, of course, that, due to Solomon's sin, Israel was divided in two during the reign of his son Rehoboam, and that the division persisted, with each part having its own kings,[28] until the whole people was overthrown with great devastation by the Chaldeans and carried away into captivity. But what did this have to do with Saul? For, if any such thing was to be threatened, the threat should properly have been addressed to David himself, since Solomon was his son. And at the present time the Hebrew people is not divided into two parts but is rather scattered indiscriminately across the earth in a single society of shared error. But the division with which God threatened the kingdom and people in the person of Saul, who personified them, was shown to be eternal and immutable by what came next: *And he shall not change his mind or repent, for he is not like a man, that he should repent, who issues a threat and does not stick to it* (1 S 15:29). That is, a man issues a threat and does not stick to it, but not God, who, unlike a man, does not repent. For, when we read that God repents, this only signifies a change in events, while the divine foreknowledge remains immutable. Thus, when it is said that God does not repent, the meaning is that he does not change.[29]

We see, then, that the divine sentence issued in these words with regard to this division of the people of Israel was completely indissoluble and wholly permanent. For any who have gone over to Christ from that people, or are now going over to Christ, or will go over to Christ, were not actually from that people according to God's foreknowledge, nor were they from them according to the one common nature of the human race. In fact, any Israelites who adhere to Christ and persevere in him will never be together with those Israelites who persist as his enemies to the end of this life; rather, they will remain forever divided by the division that is foretold here. For the old covenant *from Mount Sinai, bearing children for slavery* (Gal 4:24), is only of benefit because it points to the new. Otherwise, so long as Moses is read, a veil is placed over their hearts, but, when any of them go over to Christ, the veil is removed.[30] It is for this reason that the great prophet Samuel took the action he did in the period before he had anointed Saul as king. It was when he cried out to the Lord for Israel, and the Lord heard him; and, as he was offering a burnt offering, the foreigners drew near to attack the people of God, but the Lord thundered against them, and they were thrown into confusion, and they were routed before Israel.[31] Then Samuel took a stone and set

---

27. See Gal 4:22.
28. See 2 Chr 10.
29. See *Miscellany of Questions in Response to Simplician* II,2,4.
30. See 2 Cor 3:12-16.
31. See 1 S 7:7-11.

it up between the old and the new Mizpah and called it Ebenezer, which in Latin means "the stone of the helper," and he said, *To this point the Lord has helped us* (1 S 7:12). Mizpah means "watchfulness."[32] And "the stone of the helper" is the mediation of the savior, through whom one must go over from the old Mizpah to the new — that is, from the watchfulness that looks for false, carnal happiness in the carnal kingdom to the watchfulness that looks for the supremely true spiritual happiness in the kingdom of heaven. And, since there is nothing better than this, the Lord helps us *to this point*.

David, Solomon, and the Prophetic Anticipation of Christ

8. Because it is pertinent to our discussion, I see that I must now show what God promised to David himself, who succeeded Saul in the kingdom — a change that prefigured the ultimate change for the sake of which all these things were said and all these things were written under divine direction.

When much good fortune had come to David, he conceived the idea of building a house for God, namely, that Temple of extraordinary renown which was later constructed by his son King Solomon. While he was considering this, the word of the Lord came to Nathan the prophet for him to bring to the king. In Nathan's prophecy, after God had said that his house would not be built by David himself and that he had never, in all that time, commanded any of his people to build him a house of cedar, he said, *And now you shall say this to my servant David: Thus says the Lord almighty, I took you from the sheepfold to be a leader over my people, over Israel, and I have been with you wherever you went, and I have cut off all your enemies from before your face, and I have made a name for you like the name of the great ones who are over the earth. And I will appoint a place for my people Israel and will plant them, and they shall dwell apart and shall be troubled no more. And the son of iniquity shall not humiliate them any more, as he has done from the beginning, from the days when I appointed judges over my people Israel, and I will give you rest from all your enemies. And the Lord shall tell you, since you shall build a house for him. And, when your days are fulfilled, you shall sleep with your fathers, and I will raise up your seed after you, who shall come forth from your loins, and I will prepare his kingdom. He shall build me a house for my name, and I will guide his throne forever. I will be a father to him, and he shall be a son to me. And if he falls into iniquity, I will chasten him with the rod of men and with the blows of the sons of men, but I will not take away my mercy from him, as I took it away from those whom I put away from before my face. And his house shall be faithful, and his kingdom shall endure forever before me, and his throne shall be established forever.* (2 S 7:8-16).

---

32. See Jerome, *Interpretation of Hebrew Names*, 4 Kingdoms, s.v. Massephat. According to Jerome the word means "speculation or contemplation." The Hebrew meaning is "watchtower".

Anyone who thinks that this magnificent promise was fulfilled in Solomon is badly mistaken. He is only paying attention to *He shall build me a house* (2 S 7:13) (for Solomon did, in fact, build that most noble Temple), and he is not paying attention to *His house shall be faithful, and his kingdom shall endure forever before me* (2 S 7:16). Let him look, then, and see Solomon's house full of foreign women worshiping false gods and Solomon himself, who was formerly wise, now seduced by them into the same idolatry and brought low.[33] And let him not dare to suppose either that God was lying when he made this promise or that he was not capable of foreknowing that Solomon and his house would turn out this way. We should have no doubts about this, even if we did not see these things fulfilled in Christ our Lord, who came *from the seed of David according to the flesh* (Rom 1:3). Otherwise we might look fruitlessly and futilely for another, as do the carnal Jews. For they themselves understand full well that the son who — as they read in this passage — was promised to king David was not in fact Solomon; but they are so extraordinarily blind that even now, when the one who was promised has been made so completely obvious, they still profess to hope for another.

It is true, of course, that no insignificant image of what was to come was enacted in Solomon, in that he built the Temple, had peace in keeping with his name (for Solomon means "peaceable" in Latin[34]), and at the outset of his reign was wondrously worthy of praise. In his own person, however, although as a shadow of the future he foretold Christ's coming, he did not show forth Christ the Lord himself. Thus, certain things were written about Christ as if they were actually prophesied about Solomon, while in a way Holy Scripture, which prophesies by means of events as well as words, sketches in Solomon a figure of things to come. For, in addition to the books of sacred history where the story of his reign is told, Solomon's name is also inscribed in the title of the Seventy-first Psalm.[35] And in that Psalm so many things are said which could not possibly apply to him, but which apply to Christ the Lord as clearly as can be, that it becomes obvious that in Solomon a figure of some sort is represented, but in Christ the truth itself is presented. For example, the boundaries that enclosed Solomon's kingdom are well known, but in the Psalm (to mention nothing else) we read, *He shall have dominion from sea to sea and from the river to the ends of the earth* (Ps 72:8). And we see that this is fulfilled in Christ. For in fact his dominion took its beginning from the river where he was baptized by the same John who had already attested to him.[36]

It was there that he began to be acknowledged by disciples, who called him not only "teacher" but also "Lord."[37]...

---

33. See 1 K 11:4-8.
34. See Jerome, *Interpretation of Hebrew Names*, Matthew, s.v. Salomon.
35. The Seventy-first Psalm in Augustine's Latin version and in the Septuagint, but the Seventy-second in the Hebrew version.
36. See Mt 3:13-17 par. Although Augustine understands the river in question to be the Jordan, most modern commentators see it as the Euphrates, and some translations capitalize it — the River.
37. The same interpretation is given in *Exposition of Psalm* 71,11. On the titles of "teacher" and

[Chapters 9-13 continue the interpretation of Psalm 88 (89) as prophetic of Christ.[38]]

David's Prophecies of Christ and the Church: the Psalms

14. As the city of God ran its course through the ages, then, David first reigned in the shadow of what was to come, namely, in the earthly Jerusalem. Now David was a man skilled in song,[39] who loved the harmony of music not for vulgar pleasure but with a faithful will, and with that will he served his God, who is the true God, by mystically prefiguring a great thing. For the rational and measured arrangement of diverse sounds gives us an intimation of the unity of a well-ordered city, bound together in the variations of harmony.[40] In fact almost all his prophecy appears in Psalms, a hundred and fifty of which are included in what we call the Book of Psalms. Some people maintain that only those Psalms with his name in the title were actually composed by David. Again, there are others who hold that only those with *Of David* in the heading were composed by him, while those with *For David* in the title were composed by others, who adapted their work to his. But this opinion is refuted by the Savior's own voice in the Gospel, where he says that by the Spirit David himself called Christ his Lord.[41] For the Hundred and ninth Psalm[42] begins in this way: *The Lord said to my Lord, Sit at my right hand until I make your enemies your footstool* (Ps 110:1), and this Psalm certainly does not have *Of David* in the title but rather *For David*, as most do.

The view that seems most credible to me, however, is the view held by those who ascribe all one hundred and fifty Psalms to David's work.[43] In their opinion, he headed some Psalms with the names of other people, whose names represented something pertinent to the theme, but wanted the rest to have no one's name in the title, and it was the Lord who inspired him in this varied arrangement which, although enigmatic, is certainly not meaningless. Nor should anyone be moved to reject this view simply because the names of a few prophets who lived long after the time of King David happen to appear in the headings of certain Psalms in that

---

"Lord" see Jn 13:13.
38. The Eighty-eighth Psalm in Augustine's Latin version and in the Septuagint, but the Eightyninth in the Hebrew version.
39. For David as a lyre-player see 1 S 16:16-17.23; his skill in song is assumed from his supposed authorship of the Psalms.
40. Harmonious music often serves as an image of order in the world. See, e.g., Clement of Alexandria, *Protreptikos* 1; Athanasius, *Against the Nations* 42.
41. See Mt 22:43.
42. The Hundred and ninth Psalm in Augustine's Latin version and in the Septuagint, but the Hundred and tenth in the Hebrew version.
43. As is clear here, Augustine subscribes to a widespread but not unanimous opinion among early Christian authors in attributing all the Psalms to David.

book, or because the things said in these Psalms are presented as if spoken by those prophets themselves. For it was certainly not impossible for the prophetic Spirit to reveal these names of future prophets to King David as he was prophesying, so that he might prophetically sing something adapted to their person. It was in just this way, in fact, that, more than three hundred years beforehand, the rise and rule of King Josiah were revealed, along with his name, to another prophet, who also foretold Josiah's future deeds.[44]

15. Now, I see, it is expected that at this point in the book I shall indicate what David prophesied in the Psalms with regard to Christ and his Church. Even though I have already done this in the case of one Psalm, however, I am prevented from meeting this expectation not because there is too little material available but because there is too much. The need to avoid prolixity keeps me from taking up everything; but I am afraid that, if I select only some points, it will seem to those who know the material that I have omitted things that are even more necessary. Then, too, the testimony offered ought to be supported by the context of the whole Psalm, in order to show that, even if not everything in the Psalm supports the testimony, at least there is nothing that opposes it. Otherwise I might seem merely to be picking out individual verses on the topic I want, in the manner of a collection of quotations, as if I were taking excerpts from a long poem that turned out to have been written not on the relevant topic but on an entirely different subject.[45] To be able to show this, however, we would have to explicate the whole of each Psalm, and what a massive task this would be is indicated clearly enough both by the works of others and by my own, in which I have done just this.[46] Anyone who wishes to, and is able to, may read those works; and there he will discover how often and how much David, who was a prophet as well as a king, prophesied about Christ and his Church, that is, about the king and the city that he founded.

16. For, even though there may be open and explicit prophetic statements on a given topic, figurative expressions are invariably mingled with them, and it is these figurative expressions in particular that require the learned to take on the laborious task of explaining and expounding them for the benefit of those who are less quick-witted. All the same, some of these show us Christ and the Church at first glance, almost before they are spoken, despite the fact that there are things in them that remain to be explained at leisure, because they are less easy to understand....

---

44. See 1 K 13:2.
45. Augustine's emphasis on taking into consideration the context of a scriptural passage, in this case a Psalm, so that individual verses or phrases are not treated as discrete entities, runs counter to a certain tendency among many early Christian exegetes, who often ignored the context.
46. Augustine is referring to his monumental *Expositions of the Psalms*, the longest work under one title to have survived from Christian antiquity.

[The rest of chapter 16 and chapters 17-19 continue the interpretation of various Psalms as prophetic of Christ, including Psalms 45, 110, 22 and 41, among others.]

Solomon's Prophecies of Christ and the Church

20. Thus David reigned in the earthly Jerusalem, himself a son of the heavenly Jerusalem. He was highly praised by the divine testimony because his sins were overcome by such deep devotion through the saving humility of penitence that he certainly counts as one of those of whom he himself says, *Blessed are those whose iniquities are forgiven and whose sins are covered* (Ps 32:1). After him his son Solomon ruled over the whole of that same people; and Solomon, as I said earlier,[47] began to rule while his father was still alive. His rule had a good beginning but a bad ending. In fact "prosperity, which saps the spirits of the wise,"[48] did him more harm than his own wisdom did him good, even though his wisdom was praised far and wide at the time and is still memorable now and will be from now on. Solomon, too, is found to have prophesied in his books, three of which have been received into the authoritative canon — Proverbs, Ecclesiastes,[49] and the Song of Songs. But two others, one called Wisdom and the other Ecclesiasticus,[50] are customarily attributed to Solomon on account of a marked similarity of style. The more learned, however, have no hesitation in saying that they are not his. But, even so, the Church, and the western Church in particular, has received them as authoritative from early times.[51]

In one of these, called the Wisdom of Solomon, the passion of Christ is prophesied in the clearest possible terms. For it is certainly his impious killers who are there presented as saying, *Let us lie in wait for the righteous one, for he is displeasing to us and is opposed to our actions; he upbraids us for sins against the law and accuses us of sins against our training. He professes to have knowledge of God and calls himself the son of God. He has become to us a reproof of our thoughts. Just to see him is a burden to us, for his life is not like that of others and*

---

47. See above at XVII,8.
48. Sallust, *Catiline Conspiracy* 11.
49. Ecclesiastes is now sometimes known as Qoheleth (Qo).
50. Ecclesiasticus is now commonly known as Sirach (Sir).
51. In *Teaching Christianity* II,8,13 Augustine attributes both Wisdom and Ecclesiasticus to Jesus, son of Sirach, but in *Revisions* II,4 (31),2 he rejects the view that he was the author of Wisdom. As in the case of the authorship of the Book of Psalms and the Epistle to the Hebrews (see above at XVI,22), Augustine demonstrates his awareness of disputed authorship here, although it seems to have little or no bearing in his mind on the question of canonicity. A number of early Christian writers who commented on the issue, while conceding their edifying character, denied canonicity to Wisdom and Ecclesiasticus, among them Athanasius, Letter 39,7; Jerome, *Preface to the Books of Solomon*.

his ways stay unchanged. We are considered of no account by him, and he shuns our ways as unclean. He extols the last end of the righteous and prides himself on having God as his father. Let us see, therefore, if his words are true, and let us test what will happen to him, and we shall know what his last end will be. For if the righteous one is God's son, God will uphold him and will deliver him from the hands of his opponents. Let us interrogate him with insult and torture, so that we may find out how devout he is, and put his patience to the test. Let us condemn him to a most shameful death, for, according to his own statements, he will be cared for. These were their thoughts, but they went astray, for their own malice blinded them. (Wis 2:12-21)

Again, in Ecclesiasticus the future faith of the nations is foretold in this way: *Have mercy on us, God the ruler of all, and send the fear of you on all nations. Lift up your hand against foreign nations, and let them see your might. As you were sanctified in us before their eyes, so be magnified in them before our eyes, and let them know you as we have known you: that there is no God but you, O Lord.* (Sir 36:1-5) This prophecy, which was given in the form of a wish and a prayer, we see fulfilled through Jesus Christ.

Against our opponents, however, writings that are not included in the Jewish canon do not carry any great weight. But, in the case of the three books that everyone agrees are by Solomon and that the Jews accept as canonical, laborious explanation is required to show that anything found in them of this kind refers to Christ and the Church; and such an explanation, if we went into it here, would take us far beyond the due limits of this work....

Again, the Song of Songs gives expression to a kind of spiritual pleasure on the part of holy minds at the marriage of the king and queen of that city, that is, of Christ and the Church.[52] But this pleasure is covered over with allegorical veils, so that it may be desired all the more ardently and uncovered all the more joyfully, and so that the bridegroom may be revealed, to whom it is said in this same song, *Righteousness has loved you* (Song 1:4 LXX), and the bride also, who hears, *Love is in your delights* (Song 7:6). But, in our concern to bring this work to a close, we leave many things unmentioned.

Prophecy after Solomon

21. After Solomon the other kings of the Hebrews are found to have made hardly any prophecies at all through enigmatic aspects of their words or deeds that might refer to Christ and the Church, whether in Judah or in Israel. For the two parts of that people were called Judah and Israel after they were divided as a punishment inflicted by God on account of Solomon's offenses....

---

52. The christological-ecclesiological approach, which Augustine opts for here, is the oldest Christian method for interpreting the Song of Songs, traceable to Hippolytus's *Commentary on the Song of Songs*, produced in the early third century.

22. Jeroboam, the king of Israel, had a warped mind. He put no trust in God, despite the fact that he had found God to be true in promising and giving him his kingdom. He was afraid that, if his people went up to the Temple of God in Jerusalem (where, according to divine law, the entire nation was to go to offer sacrifice), they would be seduced away from him and would return to David's line as the royal stock. And so he instituted idolatry in his own kingdom, and, with horrendous impiety, he deceived the people of God, entangling both them and himself in the worship of images.[53] But God still did not cease to take every measure to admonish not only Jeroboam himself but also his successors and imitators in impiety, as well as the people in general, through the prophets. For it was at that time that there arose those great and celebrated prophets, Elijah and his disciple Elisha, who also performed many marvels. And it was at that time, too, that Elijah said, *Lord, they have killed your prophets; they have thrown down your altars; I alone am left, and they are seeking my life* (1 K 19:10.14), and God told him in response that there were seven thousand in Israel who had not bowed the knee to Baal.[54]

23. Similarly, in the kingdom of Judah, which belonged to Jerusalem, there was no lack of prophets in the times of the kings who succeeded Rehoboam, according as it pleased God to send prophets either to announce what was needed or to rebuke sins and enjoin righteousness. For in that kingdom also, although far less so than in Israel, kings arose who gravely offended God by their impieties, and these and people like them were punished with measured afflictions. In the case of Judah, however, there were also pious kings who are praised for their not inconsiderable merits. But in the case of Israel we read that all the kings were evil to a greater or lesser extent....

24. During the whole period following their return from Babylonia — after Malachi, Haggai, the Zechariah who prophesied then, and Ezra — the Jews had no prophets until the coming of the Savior. The only exceptions were another Zechariah, the father of John,[55] and his wife Elizabeth,[56] when Christ's birth was about to take place; and, after he was born, the aged Simeon[57] and Anna, a widow already in her old age;[58] and, last of all, John himself, who did not foretell Christ's future coming, since they were contemporaries and were both young men at the time. It was by prophetic knowledge, however, that John pointed out Christ when he was still unknown.[59] It is for this reason that the Lord himself says, *The prophets and the law prophesied down to John* (Mt 11:13). But the prophecies of these five are

---

53. See 1 K 12:25-33.
54. See 1 K 19:18.
55. See Lk 1:67.
56. See Lk 1:24.
57. See Lk 2:25-35.
58. See Lk 2:36-38.
59. See Jn 1:29-34.

known to us from the Gospel, where the virgin herself, the mother of the Lord, is found to have prophesied before John did.[60] The rejected Jews do not accept their prophecies, although the countless numbers of Jews who have come to believe in the Gospel do accept them. For this was the time when Israel was truly divided into two parts by the division that was foretold through Samuel the prophet to Saul the king as an immutable division.[61] But even the rejected Jews accept Malachi, Haggai, Zechariah and Ezra, considering them the last prophets received into divine authority. For they authored works which, like those of the very few others among all the multitude of prophets who wrote such works, have gained canonical authority. And I see that some of their predictions referring to Christ and the Church ought to be included in this work. But it will be more appropriate to take them up in the next book, with God's help, for we do not want to overburden this one, which is already so very long.

---

60. See Lk 1:46-55.
61. See 1 S 15:28.

Study Questions for Book XVII

Priesthood, prophecy and kingship: these three themes that Augustine explores in Book XVII continue to inform Christian theology. Priest, prophet and king are titles applied to Christ throughout the New Testament. Baptism initiates a Christian into these three roles by immersion into the mystery of Christ. Augustine presents these three elements in Hebrew Scripture as evolving and transforming in significant ways across Jewish history and in their Christian interpretation. How might each of these ancient roles be interpreted and realized in a post-Enlightenment, pluralistic world among those who aspire to live in the City of God today?

Augustine proposes Christian interpretations of the words and actions of various Hebrew priests and prophets, and especially of Kings David and Solomon. Centuries before Augustine, rabbinic scholars had been compiling thousands of pages of biblical instruction and commentary known as the Talmud. Using the method of comparative theology, might Augustine's Christian readings of Hebrew history and prophecy be studied alongside Jewish teaching in the Jerusalem and Babylonian Talmuds in ways that benefit both traditions?

BOOK XVIII

In Book XVIII, the longest of The City of God's twenty-two books, Augustine reverts to his tracing of the temporal course of the earthly city, which he had left off at Book XVI,11. After noting the source of division in human society, he proceeds by drawing chronological correlations between the rulers of earthly kingdoms on the one hand and eras and events in Israelite history on the other, focusing on Assyria (which he equates with Babylon) as the "first Rome" and Rome as the "second Babylon," but including various Greek and Latin kingdoms that would have been well-known to his readers. Within this framework he also indicates how the earthly kingdoms have made gods for themselves, primarily by elevating prominent human beings to divine status. Occasionally he devotes more extended attention to specific matters such as the naming of Athens, tales of human beings transformed into animals, and the Sibyl's prophecy of Christ. Then, starting at XVIII,27, he takes up a promise that he made at the end of Book XVII and provides an account of the Hebrew prophets, giving examples in each case of how their prophecies refer to Christ and the Church and concluding with the claim that prophetic wisdom is more ancient than the merely human wisdom of the Greeks and Egyptians and superior to that of the philosophers. In an extension of this history of prophecy, Augustine then discusses the Septuagint translation of the Hebrew Scriptures into Greek, its authoritative status over against other Greek and Latin translations, and its prophetic elements. Finally, he presents the human coming of Christ and the spread of the Church, in the face of both external and internal persecution, as the fulfillment of divine prophecy. Throughout much of Book XVIII Augustine relies heavily for his historical and chronological information on Eusebius of Caesarea's magisterial but often inaccurate Chronicles, as expanded and translated from Greek into Latin by Jerome.

1. I promised that, with the help of God's grace, I would refute the enemies of the city of God, who prefer their own gods to Christ its founder and who detest the Christians with a spite and malice that are far more destructive to themselves than to anyone else, and I did this in the first ten books. I also promised that I would then go on to write about the origin, the course, and the destined ends of the two cities, one of which is the city of God and the other the city of this world, in which the city of God dwells so far as its human element is concerned, but only as a pilgrim. With respect to the three parts of this last promise, I offered an account of the origins of the two cities in the four books following the tenth book; and then, in one book, the fifteenth of this work, I gave an account of the course that the two cities followed from the first man down to the flood. Again, from the flood down to Abraham, the two cities ran their course both in time and in our account; but, from Abraham down to the time of the Israelite kings, where we ended the sixteenth book, and then down to the coming of the Savior himself in the flesh, where the seventeenth book reaches its close, it is clear that my pen traced only the course of the city of God. In reality, however, this city did not run its course all alone in this world; rather, just as both cities began together, so both experienced the variations of time together in human history. I wrote as I did, however, so that the city of God might stand out the more clearly — without any opposing intrusion on the part of the other city — as it ran its course from the time when God's promises first began to be more open and apparent down to his birth from the virgin, in which the earlier promises were due to be fulfilled. For, up to the revelation of the new covenant, it ran its course not in broad daylight but in shadow. Now, therefore, I see that I must make up for my omission by giving an account of the course followed by that other city from the time of Abraham on down, and the account should at least be full enough to allow the reader to consider the contrast between the two cities.

The Divisions in Human Society

2. The society of mortals, then, was spread everywhere across the earth, and, despite all its different locations, it was still bound together by a kind of fellowship in one and the same nature, even though each group pursued its own advantage and followed its own desires. What people want, however, is never enough for anyone, or at least not for everyone, because they do not all want the same thing; and so human society is largely at odds with itself, and, whenever one part gains a position of strength, it oppresses another. For the vanquished submit to the victor, and they prefer to have peace and security at any price rather than power or even liberty.[1] And this is so universally true that it is a source of astonishment whenever anyone would rather die than lose his liberty. For, in almost all peoples, the voice of nature has somehow declared that those who suffer defeat should prefer to be subject to the victors than to be wholly eradicated by the devastation of war. And so it happened — although not apart from the providence of God, in whose power it lies to determine who falls under another's rule in war and who imposes his rule on others — that some peoples were endowed with kingdoms and some were subjected to the rule of others. But among the many kingdoms on earth into which the society that pursues earthly advantage and follows earthly desire has been divided — the society to which we give the all-embracing name of "the city of this world" — we see that two have come to stand out far more sharply than the rest: first that of the Assyrians, and then that of the Romans. These two are related

---

1. See Lucan, *Pharsalia* IV,577-579.

to and distinguished from each other in terms of both time and space. For, just as the one arose earlier and the other later, so the one arose in the east and the other in the west; and, finally, the beginning of the latter came immediately after the end of the former. And I would say that all other kingdoms and kings are like appendages of these.

Assyria as the "First Rome" and Rome as the "Second Babylon"

When Abraham was born in the land of the Chaldeans, then, Ninus was already ruling as the second king of the Assyrians, in succession to his father Bel, the first king of that kingdom.[2] At that time, there was also the extremely small kingdom of the Sicyonians,[3] and, because this kingdom was so ancient, Marcus Varro, a man of great learning in all fields, began his work *On the Race of the Roman People* with an account of it.[4] From the kings of Sicyon, he turns to the Athenians, and then to the Latins, and finally to the Romans. But the powers that he mentions prior to the founding of Rome are of little account in comparison with the kingdom of the Assyrians. This is true despite the fact that even the Roman historian Sallust admits that the Athenians gained the highest standing in Greece, although more in reputation than in reality. For in describing them he says, "The achievements of the Athenians, in my view, were great and glorious enough, but still rather less than their reputation suggests. But, because writers of great genius emerged in that city, the deeds of the Athenians are celebrated throughout the world as the greatest accomplishments. Thus the valor of those who performed these deeds is considered to equal the ability of writers of genius to praise them in words."[5] It is also true that this city won no little glory from literature and philosophy, for such studies flourished there to a remarkable degree. So far as imperial rule is concerned, however, there was no greater power in early times than that of the Assyrians, and none that extended so far and wide. In fact King Ninus, Bel's son, is reported to have subjugated all Asia as far as the borders of Lydia,[6] and Asia is counted as one of the three parts of the whole world, although in geographical extent it is actually found to cover half of the world.[7] The truth is that the only people in the regions of the east that Ninus did not bring under his rule were the Indians, and even they were attacked after his death by his wife Semiramis.[8] Thus, it came about that all the peoples and kings in those lands submitted to the rule and authority of the Assyrians and did whatever the Assyrians commanded them to do.

---

2. See above at XVI,17.
3. See ibid.
4. For Augustine's encomium of Varro's scholarship see above at VI,2. His work *On the Race of the Roman People* exists only in fragments.
5. *Catiline Conspiracy* 8.
6. See above at IV,6 and XVI,17.
7. See above at XVI,17.
8. See Eusebius, *Chronicles* I,15.

Abraham, then, was born in that kingdom, among the Chaldaeans, in the time of Ninus. But Greek history is much better known to us than Assyrian history, and those who have investigated the ancient origins of the race of the Roman people have traced a chronological sequence that runs through the Greeks to the Latins and then to the Romans, who themselves are also Latins. As a consequence, we must provide the names of the Assyrian kings, where necessary, in order to show how Babylon — the first Rome, as it were — runs its course along with the city of God on its pilgrimage in this world. At the same time, however, the points that we need to bring into this work for the sake of comparing the two cities — that is, the earthly and the heavenly — we should take rather from Greek and Latin history, in which Rome itself is like a second Babylon.[9]...

[The rest of chapter 2 and chapters 3-20 juxtapose the history of earthly kingdoms, especially Assyria, Greece and Troy, with Jewish history up to the end of Solomon's reign and the beginning of the two kingdoms of Israel and Judah.]

The End of Assyria and the Founding of Rome

21. After Aeneas, whom they made a god, Latium had eleven kings, none of whom was made a god. But Aventinus, the twelfth king after Aeneas, was struck down in battle and was buried on the hill which is still called by his name, and he was added to the number of the gods that people make for themselves. There are some, in fact, who were not willing to write that he was killed; instead, they claimed that he actually disappeared and that the hill was not named for him but rather was called the Aventine from the advent of birds.[10] After Aventinus no one else was made a god in Latium with the one exception of Romulus, the founder of Rome. Between Aventinus and Romulus, however, we find two kings, of whom the first — to grace him with a line from Virgil — was "the next, the famous Procas, the glory of the Trojan race."[11] And in his time, because Rome was already coming to birth, Assyria, that greatest of all kingdoms, reached the end of its long span. For its power passed to the Medes after some 1,305 years of rule, if we start our count from the time of Bel, who was the father of Ninus and who, as the first Assyrian king, was content with a small dominion there....

22. To make a long story short, Rome was founded as a second Babylon and as the daughter of the former Babylon, and it was through Rome that it pleased

---

9. See Rv 14:8.
10. "From the advent of birds": *ex adventu avium*. See Varro, *On the Latin Language* V,8. The Aventine is one of the seven famous hills of Rome.
11. *Aeneid* VI,767.

God to conquer the whole world, uniting it in the one society of Rome's republic and Rome's laws, and imposing peace throughout its length and breadth. For by now there were strong and powerful peoples, highly trained in arms, who would not submit easily and could only be conquered by appalling effort, at vast risk, and with no little devastation on both sides. In contrast, when the Assyrian kingdom subjugated almost all of Asia, even though this conquest was achieved by war, it could take place without much cruel and bitter warfare because the peoples were still unskilled in resistance and were not as numerous or as imposing. For, when Ninus subjugated all Asia except for India, not much more than a thousand years had passed since the vast and universal flood in which a mere eight human beings escaped in Noah's ark.[12] But Rome did not so quickly or so easily come to dominate all the many nations of both east and west that, as we see, are now under Roman rule. For Rome only grew little by little, and, whichever way it spread, it found robust and warlike peoples.

At the time of Rome's foundation, then, the people of Israel had lived in the promised land for 718 years. The first twenty-seven of these pertain to Joshua, the son of Nun, and the next 329 to the era of the judges. Then, from the point at which they first began to have kings, 362 years had passed. At that time there was a king in Judah, and it was Ahaz.[13] Or, on another reckoning, it was his successor, Hezekiah, who was an excellent and very devout king,[14] and it is generally agreed that he ruled in the time of Romulus. Meanwhile Hoshea had begun to rule over the part of the Hebrew people that was called Israel.[15]

Sibyline Prophecies of Christ

23. It was at this same time, some say, that the Erythraean Sibyl made her prophecies.[16] Varro maintains, however, that there were many Sibyls, not just one.[17] In any case, the Erythraean Sibyl certainly records some statements that manifestly refer to Christ. I first read these in a Latin translation, composed in bad Latin verse that did not scan — due, as I later found out, to the ineptitude of the translator, whoever he was. For once, when I was talking about Christ with Flaccianus, a distinguished man who was also proconsul and a person of ready eloquence and great learning,[18] he brought out a Greek manuscript, saying that it contained the poems of the Erythraean Sibyl. And he showed me that, in a certain passage of the manuscript, the order of the letters at the start of each line of verse

---

12. See Gn 6:11-8:19.
13. See 2 K 16:1-2.
14. See 2 K 18:1-8.
15. See 2 K 17:1.
16. The Erythraean Sibyl was associated with the Greek town of Erythrae and customarily uttered acrostic prophecies, as below.
17. Cited in Lactantius, *Divine Institutes* I,6.
18. Flaccianus is mentioned in Ammianus Marcellinus, *Roman History* XXVIII,6.

was so arranged that the letters spelled out the words ***IESOUS CHREISTOS THEOU UIOS SOTER***, which in Latin mean "Jesus Christ, Son of God, Savior."[19] These lines, whose initial letters give the meaning we have just noted, read as follows in a translation that someone has made which puts them into good Latin verse that does scan:

> **I**n sign of judgment, the earth shall be drenched with sweat.
> **E**ver more to reign, the future king shall come from heaven
> **S**o that he may, in person, judge the flesh and all the world.
> **O**ur God both unbelievers and believers then shall see,
> **U**plifted with the saints on high, as this age meets its end.
> **S**o shall the souls, enfleshed, be judged by him himself.
>
> **CH**oked in densest briars, all the world shall lie untilled;
> **R**ejected are the idols and all the wealth of men.
> **E**very land, and the sea and sky as well, shall be ablaze,
> **I**n fire seeking to destroy even the dreaded gates of hell.
> **S**alvation's light, in contrast, shall free the bodies of the saints,
> **T**hough the wicked shall burn in everlasting flames.
> **O**bscure and hidden acts shall be revealed, and every secret told.
> **S**o shall God expose the secrets of the heart to his bright light.
>
> **TH**en all shall weep and wail, and all shall gnash their teeth.
> **E**rased is the blazing of the sun, eradicated the chorus of the stars;
> **O**ur skies shall roll away, and the splendor of the moon go out;
> **U**p from below shall the valleys rise, and the hills shall be laid low,
>
> **U**ndoing any grandeur and all preeminence in the affairs of men.
> **I**n one flat plain the mountains lie; and the azure waters
> **O**f the sea shall cease; the very earth shall creak and break.
> **S**o, too, shall every spring and stream be quenched by fire.
>
> **S**orrowfully shall the trumpet then give out its sound, blaring
> **O**n high, bewailing all our wretched deeds and varied toils.
> **T**he gaping earth shall open up to show the vast abyss of hell.
> **E**ach king shall then be made to stand, each one before the Lord;
> **R**ivers of fire and brimstone shall flow from the sky like rain.[20]

In these Latin verses, no matter how well translated from the Greek, it was not possible to keep the full sense of the sequence of initial letters because, where

---

19. The spelling *Chreistos* differs from the usual *Christos*.
20. *Sibylline Oracles* VIII,217-243. The oracle is also quoted in its entirety, but with variant wording, in Constantine the Great, *Speech to the Assembly of the Saints* 18.

the letter *upsilon* occurred in the Greek, no Latin words could be found which begin with that letter and also fit the meaning. There are three lines for which this is true, the fifth, the eighteenth, and the nineteenth. Accordingly, if we link the letters at the beginning of each line but substitute the letter *upsilon* for the actual first letter of these three lines, as if it were really there, we get the five-word expression, "Jesus Christ, Son [of] God, Savior" — but only when the words are said in Greek, not in Latin.

Note also that there are twenty-seven lines in all, and twenty-seven is the cube of three. For three times three is nine; and, if nine is multiplied by three, making the figure three-dimensional instead of only two-dimensional, we arrive at twenty-seven. In addition, if you combine the initial letters of the five Greek words *Iesous CHreistos THeou Uios Soter* — which in Latin mean "Jesus Christ, Son of God, Savior" — you will get the Greek word *ichthus*, which means "fish,"[21] and in this word, understood mystically, we recognize Christ, in that he was able to stay alive (that is, without sin) in the abyss of this mortal existence, as in the depths of the sea. It is also noteworthy that this Sibyl — whether she is the Erythraean Sibyl or, as some prefer to believe, the Cumaean Sibyl — has nothing in her entire poem (of which these lines form only a tiny part) that refers to the worship of false or made-up gods. On the contrary, she speaks so strongly against such gods and against their worshipers that it seems as though she ought really to be included in the number of those who belong to the city of God.

Lactantius also includes in his work certain prophecies of the Sibyl about Christ, although he does not indicate which Sibyl he has in mind. I have thought it best, however, to connect the passages that he cited separately, as if the many brief statements he recorded made a single, continuous whole. "Afterwards," he says, "he will fall into the wicked hands of unbelievers, and they will strike God with their unclean hands and spit poisonous spittle from their impure mouths. But he will simply submit his back to their lashes. And he will receive their blows in silence, so that none may know that he came as the Word or know where he came from, and he will do this so that he may speak to those in hell and be crowned with a crown of thorns. They have given him gall for food and vinegar to drink; this is the inhospitable table they shall set out. For in your folly you have not recognized your God as he mocked the minds of mortals; instead, you have crowned him with thorns and mixed horrid gall for him. But the veil of the temple shall be torn asunder, and at midday the great darkness of night shall fall for three hours. And he shall fall asleep and lie in death for three days, and then he shall be the first to return from the lower regions and come forth into the light, showing the beginning of the resurrection to those called back from the dead."[22] Lactantius cited these Sibyline testimonies piecemeal, at intervals through his argument, as

---

21. Ichthus has been a word symbolic of Christ since at least the late second century. See Tertullian, *On Baptism* 1.
22. Cited in *Divine Institutes* IV,6.15.18.

the points that he meant to prove seemed to require. I have taken care, however, to present them without interruption in one connected sequence, marked off from each other only by capital letters (which copyists should not fail to preserve). But there are some who have written that the Erythraean Sibyl belonged not to the time of Romulus but rather to the time of the Trojan War....

[Chapters 24 – 26 trace the early rulers of Rome from Romulus until the Babylonian Captivity of the Jews. Chapters 27 – 36 highlight many Jewish prophecies that refer to the coming of Christ, and the call of the gentiles to faith in Christ. Representative passages from Isaiah, Micah, Jonah, Habakkuk, Jeremiah and Zephaniah are included here.]

29. The prophet Isaiah is not included in the book of the twelve prophets who are called "minor," since their discourses are short in comparison with those of the prophets who are called "major" because they composed lengthy works. Isaiah is one of the major prophets. Among the evils that Isaiah denounced, then, and the righteous acts that he prescribed, and the future evils that he foretold for a sinful people, he also prophesied much more than the others did concerning Christ and the Church, that is, concerning the king and the city that he founded; and, as a result, some have called him an evangelist rather than a prophet.[23] To keep this work within reasonable limits, however, I shall here consider just one of his many prophecies. Speaking in the person of God the Father, he says, *See, my servant shall understand, and he shall be exalted and shall be glorified greatly. Just as many shall be amazed at you, so shall your appearance be stripped of glory by men and your glory taken away by men. And as a result many nations shall marvel at him, and kings shall shut their mouths, for those to whom nothing was proclaimed about him shall see, and those who had heard nothing of him shall understand. Lord, who has believed what we have heard? And to whom has the arm of the Lord been revealed? We announced him in his presence as an infant, as a root in the thirsty ground; he has no form or glory. And we saw him, and he had no form or beauty; rather, his form was without honor, worse than any man's. He was a man beset with misfortunes, who knew how to bear infirmity. Because his face was turned away, he was dishonored and held of little account. He it is who bears our sins and suffers on our behalf, and yet we thought of him as a man caught in pain and misfortune and affliction. But he was wounded for our iniquities and made weak for our sins. Upon him was the chastisement that brings us peace, and by his bruises we were healed* (Is 52:13-53:5).... All this refers to Christ....

---

23. See Jerome, Letter 53,8; *Commentary on the Prophet Isaiah*, prologue.

30. The prophet Micah, representing Christ under the figure of a great mountain, says this: *In the last days, the mountain of the Lord shall be made manifest, set above the mountain peaks, and shall be raised up above the hills. And the peoples shall hasten to it, and many nations shall come and say, Come, let us go up to the mountain of the Lord and to the house of the God of Jacob, and he shall show us his way, and we will walk in his paths, for the law shall go forth out of Zion, and the word of the Lord out of Jerusalem. And he shall judge between many peoples and shall rebuke strong nations far away.* (Mic 4:1-3) This prophet also foretold the place in which Christ was born: *And you, Bethlehem, house of Ephrata, are very small to be among the thousands of Judah; from you shall come forth for me one who is to rule in Israel* (Mic 5:2)....

The prophet Jonah, in contrast, prophesied Christ not so much in words as in certain features of his experience. In fact, he prophesied far more clearly in this way than if with his voice he were crying out Christ's death and resurrection. For why else was he taken into the belly of the sea monster, and given back on the third day,[24] except to signify that Christ was going to return from the depths of hell on the third day?...

As for Habakkuk, to what else do we understand him to refer but the advent of Christ, who was to come, when he says, *And the Lord answered me and said, Write the vision plainly on a tablet so that one who reads these things may follow, for the vision still awaits its time, and it shall arise in the end, and not without purpose. If it delays, wait for it, for it shall surely come and shall not delay* (Hab 2:2-3)?

32. And again, in his prayer and song to whom but to the Lord Christ does Habakkuk say, *O Lord, I have heard your report, and I was afraid; O Lord, I have considered your works, and I was awestruck* (Hab 3:2)? For what is this but the inexpressible wonder of foreseeing a new and sudden salvation for men?...

33. Jeremiah is one of the major prophets like Isaiah, not one of the minor prophets like the others from whose writings I have now cited a number of passages. He prophesied at the time when Josiah was ruling in Jerusalem[25] and Ancus Marcius was ruling over the Romans, just before the captivity of the Jews; and, as we learn from his own writings, he continued to prophesy until the fifth month of their captivity.[26] Zephaniah, one of the minor prophets, is associated with him. For Zephaniah himself tells us that he prophesied in the days of Josiah,[27] although he does not say for how long. Jeremiah prophesied not only in the time of Ancus Marcius, then, but also in that of Tarquinius Priscus, whom the Romans had as their fifth king. For Tarquinius had already begun to rule when the captivity took place.

---

24. See Jon 1:17; 2:10.
25. See Jer 1:1-2.
26. See Jer 1:3.
27. See Zep 1:1.

Prophesying about Christ, Jeremiah says, *The breath of our mouth, the Lord Christ, has been taken captive in our sins* (Lm 4:20); in this way he briefly indicates both that Christ is our Lord and that he suffered for us.[28] Again, in another passage he says, *This is my God, and no other shall be compared to him. He found the whole way of prudence and gave it to his servant Jacob and to Israel his beloved; afterward he appeared on earth and conversed with men.* (Bar 3:36-37) Some people assign this testimony not to Jeremiah himself but to his scribe, who was called Baruch, but the more common opinion is that it belongs to Jeremiah.[29]

Again, the same prophet says this about Christ: *See, the days are coming, says the Lord, when I will raise up for David a righteous branch, and he shall reign as king and shall be wise and shall execute justice and righteousness in the land. In those days, Judah shall be saved and Israel shall live in safety. And this is the name which they shall call him: our righteous Lord.* (Jer 23:5-6) He also said this about the calling of the gentiles, which then lay in the future and we now see has been fulfilled: *O Lord, my God and my refuge in the day of evils, from the ends of the earth the peoples shall come to you and say, Truly, our fathers worshiped false images, and there is no profit in them* (Jer 16:19). But the same prophet also indicates that the Jews, by whom Christ was due to be killed, would not recognize him: *The heart is heavy in every way; and he is the man, and who recognizes him?* (Jer 17:9) Also from Jeremiah is the passage that I cited in the seventeenth book[30] about the new covenant, of which Christ is the mediator.[31] For it is Jeremiah who says, *See, the days are coming, says the Lord, when I will make a new covenant with the house of Jacob* (Jer 31:31), and the rest that we read there....

The Antiquity of Prophetic Wisdom

37. It was at the time of our prophets, whose writings had already come to the notice of nearly all peoples, and far more after the prophets, that the philosophers of the gentiles emerged, that is, philosophers who were actually called by this name, which began with Pythagoras of Samos, who first rose to prominence and gained recognition at the time when the Jews were delivered from their captivity.[32] All the more, then, are the other philosophers found to have lived after the prophets.[33] For Socrates himself, the Athenian, the teacher of all the most dis-

---

28. Here, as elsewhere, the term "Christ" translates the Hebrew and Greek words for "anointed." Here, as elsewhere, the term "Christ" translates the Hebrew and Greek words for "anointed."
29. The more common opinion was held as early as the second half of the second century, as witnessed in Irenaeus, *Against Heresies* V,35,1, where a long passage from Baruch is cited under the name of Jeremiah.
30. See above at XVII,3.
31. See Heb 9:15.
32. See above at VI,5 and VIII,2.
33. That the Old Testament prophets predated the Greek (and other) philosophers was an assertion of several early Christian writers. See Tatian, *Against the Greeks* 31-41; Tertullian, *Apology* 19.

tinguished philosophers of that time, and himself preeminent in the area that is called moral or practical philosophy, is found to come after Esdras in *The Chronicles*.[34] And it was not long afterwards that Plato was born, who would far surpass all the other disciples of Socrates.

Even if we add to these the earlier thinkers, who were not yet called philosophers — that is, the seven wise men and, after them, the natural philosophers who succeeded Thales and emulated him in their zeal for investigating the natural order, namely, Anaximander, Anaximenes, Anaxagoras, and a number of others who lived before Pythagoras first professed to be a philosopher[35] — it is still true that they do not predate the whole group of our prophets. For Thales — and all the rest came after him — is said to have gained prominence during the reign of Romulus, at the time when the river of prophecy burst forth from its fountain in Israel in those writings that would overflow the whole world. Thus, it is only the theological poets — Orpheus, Linus, Musaeus and any others there may have been among the Greeks — who are found to predate the Hebrew prophets whose writings we take as authoritative.

But not even the theological poets predated our Moses, a true theologian, who truly proclaimed the one true God, and whose writings now come first in the authoritative canon.[36] As a consequence, so far as the Greeks are concerned (in whose language the literature of this world has most flourished[37]), they have no reason to boast that their wisdom, if not superior to our religion, where true wisdom is found, at least seems to be more ancient. We must grant, however, that prior to Moses there was — certainly not in Greece but in barbarous nations such as Egypt — some learning that might be called the wisdom of these peoples. Otherwise, it would not be written in the holy books that *Moses was instructed in all the wisdom of the Egyptians* (Acts 7:22), as he undoubtedly was at the time when, born there and adopted and nurtured by Pharaoh's daughter,[38] he also received a liberal education. But not even the wisdom of the Egyptians could have predated the wisdom of our prophets, for Abraham, too, was a prophet. Besides, what wisdom could there have been in Egypt before Isis (whom, after her death, they thought they should worship as a great goddess) gave them the art of letters? But Isis is said to have been the daughter of Inachus, who first became king of the Argives at a time when we find that Abraham already had grandsons.

But Augustine does not claim here that the Greeks (or others) encountered the Hebrew prophets and acquired any of their learning from them, although above at VIII,11 he does not deny the possibility of their having been influenced by them through exposure to their writings.

34. See Eusebius, *Chronicles* II (PL 27,385-386).
35. See above at VIII,2-4.
36. Moses was the supposed author of the first five books of the Bible, the Pentateuch.
37. On the superiority of the Greek language see above at VIII,2.10.
38. See Ex 2:1-10.

38. But, to revert to far earlier times, our patriarch Noah obviously lived even before the great flood, and there is good reason to call him a prophet as well. For the ark that he built, and in which he and his household escaped,[39] was itself a prophecy of our times.[40] And what about Enoch, the seventh in descent from Adam?[41] Does not the canonical epistle of the apostle Jude tell us that he prophesied?[42] It is only because the writings of these men are so very ancient that they are not considered authoritative either by the Jews or by us. It is for this reason that it seemed better to count them as suspect, in order to make sure that no false writings were put forward as true. For there actually are some writings that are put forward as Noah's and Enoch's by people who are ready to believe anything they want.[43] But the purity of the canon has not accepted these works, not because the authority of these men, who were pleasing to God, is rejected but rather because the writings are not believed to be theirs.

Nor should it cause any surprise that writings put forward under a name of such antiquity are regarded as suspect. In fact, in the history of the kings of Judah and Israel itself, which contains events that we accept on the basis of the same canonical Scripture, there are many references to things that are not explicated there and are said to be found in other books that prophets wrote, and sometimes the actual names of those prophets are given.[44] But, even so, those books are not found in the canon that the people of God have accepted. I admit that the reason for this state of affairs escapes me, except that I presume that even those to whom the Holy Spirit undoubtedly revealed things that ought to fall under the authority of religion could well have written some works simply as men pursuing historical accuracy, but others as prophets writing under divine inspiration. And the two kinds of works were so distinct that it was thought that the first should be ascribed to the men themselves but the other to God speaking through them. Thus the former had to do with the increase of knowledge, the latter with the authority of religion, to which authority the canon is strictly limited. And outside the canon, even if some writings are now put forward under the names of true prophets, they have no value even for adding to the store of knowledge, because it is uncertain whether they were really written by the authors to whom they are ascribed. That is why we put no faith in them, and this is especially true of those in which we read things contrary to the faith of the canonical books, so that it is immediately apparent that they were not written by those prophets.

---

39. See Gn 6:11-8:19.
40. The ark was a common symbol of the Church. See above at XV,27.
41. See Gn 5:18-24.
42. See Jude 14-15.
43. Several apocryphal writings bearing the name of Enoch have survived.
44. Numerous titles of non-extant writings are mentioned in the canonical Scriptures, some of them supposedly of prophetic origin — e.g., *Chronicles of Samuel the Seer*, *Chronicles of Nathan the Prophet*, and *Chronicles of Gad the Seer* (see 1 Chr 29:29).

39. But we should not believe, as some have presumed, that it was only spoken Hebrew that was preserved by Heber (from whose name the word "Hebrews" is derived)[45] and came down from him to Abraham, while written Hebrew only began with the law that was given to Moses.[46] Rather, we should hold that the written language, together with its literature, was maintained through that succession of fathers. In fact, it was before the people had any knowledge of the written form of the law that Moses appointed some among them to preside over the teaching of writing. Scripture calls these men *grammatoeisagogoi*,[47] and in Latin they may be called "bringers of letters" or "introducers of letters" because, in a sense, they bring — that is, they introduce — letters into the minds of their pupils, or, rather, they introduce their pupils to letters.

With respect to the antiquity of its wisdom, therefore, let no nation presume to vaunt itself over our patriarchs and prophets, in whom divine wisdom was present. For not even Egypt, which has the habit of falsely and foolishly boasting about the antiquity of its learning, is found to predate the wisdom of our patriarchs with any sort of wisdom of its own. For no one will have the audacity to claim that the Egyptians became expert in their extraordinary learning before they learned their letters, that is, before Isis came and taught them their letters. And besides, what was that memorable learning of theirs, which is called wisdom, except for astronomy in particular[48] and other such disciplines that usually serve more to exercise human ingenuity than to illuminate the mind with true wisdom?

In fact, so far as philosophy is concerned, which claims to teach something that leads people to happiness, studies of that sort only came to prominence in those lands around the time of Mercury, whom they called Trismegistus.[49] That was, of course, long before the wise men and philosophers of Greece, but it was well after Abraham, Isaac, Jacob, and Joseph, and even well after Moses himself. For we find that it was at the time when Moses was born that Atlas lived, the great astronomer who was Prometheus's brother[50] and the maternal grandfather of the elder Mercury, and this Mercury Trismegistus was himself the grandson of the elder Mercury.

40. It is pointless, therefore, for some people to babble away in their unfounded presumption, claiming to have calculated that it was more than a hundred thousand years ago that Egypt came to understand the system of the stars. For in what books

---

45. See Gn 10:21-25.
46. See Ex 24:12. The verse says that God himself wrote the tablets of the law, giving rise to the notion that God was the author of written Hebrew.
47. See Ex 18:21.
48. By astronomy Augustine probably means astrology, of which, nor surprisingly, he takes a very dim view. See *Teaching Christianity* II,21,32-22,34.
49. The doctrine attributed to Trismegistus, usually called Hermes Trismegistus but here identified with a certain Mercury, is cited and analyzed at above at VIII,23-26.
50. See above at XVIII,8 and p. 286, note 37.

did they come up with that number, when they only learned their letters, thanks to the teaching of Isis, not much more than two thousand years ago? It is Varro who tells us this,[51] who is no minor authority in the field of history, and what he says is not out of line with the truth of the Divine Scriptures. For, since six thousand years have not yet passed from the time of the first man (who was called Adam), why should we not simply ridicule, rather than refute, people who try to persuade us to take such a different view of the passage of time, and one so contrary to this fully established truth?

Is there any narrator of past events whom we should trust more than one who also foretold future events that we now see before our very eyes? In fact, the very disagreement of historians among themselves gives us ample reason why we ought to believe the one who says nothing contrary to the divine history that we hold. Besides, when the citizens of the ungodly city, spread out through all the earth, read men of the greatest learning and see no reason to reject the authority of any of them, even when these men disagree with each other about events that are utterly remote from the memory of our present age, they find that they are left with no one in whom they ought to put more trust than any other. We, on the other hand, have the support of divine authority with regard to the history of our religion, and so we have no doubt that anything that opposes it is completely false, no matter what may otherwise be the case in secular writings which, whether true or false, provide nothing of any moment for living a righteous and happy life.[52]

The Superiority of Divine Wisdom over Human Philosophy

41. But, leaving aside the issue of historical knowledge, what about the philosophers themselves, from whom we digressed in order to take up the historical question? In pursuing their studies they seem to have worked with no other aim than to discover how we should shape our lives so as to attain happiness. Why is it, then, that disciples have disagreed with their teachers, and fellow-disciples have disagreed with each other, if not because they sought to do this as mere human beings relying only on the human senses and human reasoning? It is also possible, of course, that they were driven by sheer ambition for glory, each wanting to appear wiser and more acute than the other and not dependent on anyone else's views but rather to be the initiator of a teaching and a position of his own. At the same time, however, I grant that there were some, or even many, philosophers for whom it was genuine love of truth that led them to break with their teachers or their fellow disciples in order to fight for the truth as they saw it, whether actually true or not. But, even so, what does it matter where or how human wretchedness directs its efforts to attain happiness if divine authority does not lead the way?

---

51. See *On the Race of the Roman People*, fragment 12.
52. For a similar thought see *Teaching Christianity* II,42,63.

As for our authors — and it is not for nothing that the canon of Sacred Scripture is settled and limited to them — it is simply unthinkable that they should disagree among themselves in any respect. It is not without reason, then, that not just a few babblers, wrangling away in schools and lecture-halls, but a great many people of all sorts, both learned and unlearned, both in the country and in the cities, hold the belief that, when our authors wrote, God himself was speaking to them or through them. The authors themselves, of course, had to be few in number in order to keep what ought to be precious in religion from being cheapened at the hands of a mob. But it was also important that they not be so few that we would no longer marvel at their agreement. For, among the multitude of philosophers who left records of their teachings in their literary efforts, it is not easy to find any whose views completely agree. But it would take too long to prove this in the present work....

In the face of all these disagreements among the philosophers, and almost innumerable others, has any people or senate or public authority or high office in the ungodly city ever shown any interest in deciding among them, approving and accepting some, condemning and rejecting others? Instead, has not that city held in its lap — at random, in utter confusion, and without passing judgment — all these controversies among men whose differences are not about fields or houses or any financial matter but about the very things that determine whether our lives will be miserable or happy?

In that city, even if some of the things they said were true, they had exactly the same license to say things that were false, and it is not for nothing that such a city received the mystic name "Babylon." For Babylon means "confusion," as we remember saying before.[53] Nor does it make any difference to the devil, who is the king of that city, how they quarrel over their mutually contradictory errors, for they all equally belong to him by reason of their impiety in its many and varied forms.

In contrast, that nation, that people, that city, that republic, those Israelites, to whom the pronouncements of God were entrusted, definitely did not confuse false prophets with true or give them equal license. Rather, they acknowledged the prophets who were in accord with each other and did not disagree at all, taking them as the true authors of the sacred books. These were their philosophers, that is, their lovers of wisdom; these were their wise men, their theologians, their prophets, their teachers of integrity and piety. Anyone who thought and lived as they did thought and lived not according to men but according to God, who spoke through them. If sacrilege is forbidden there, it is God who has forbidden it. If it is said, *Honor your father and your mother* (Ex 20:12), it is God who has commanded it. If it is said, *You shall not commit adultery, You shall not kill, You shall not steal* (Ex 20:13-15), and other commandments of this sort, it was not human mouths but divine oracles that uttered them.

---

53. See above at XVI,4.

Some philosophers were able to catch a glimpse of truth amid all the false views they held, and in laborious arguments they attempted to make a persuasive case that God made this world and that he governs it with providential care. They urged the integrity of the virtues, love of country, loyalty in friendship, good works, and everything that pertains to good moral character. But they had no idea of the end to which all these are to be directed or of how they are to be directed to that end. In our city, however, it was by prophetic — that is, by divine — voices, although speaking through human beings, that these were commended to the people. They were not inculcated by any battle of arguments, and so anyone who came to know them dreaded to disregard what was not mere human ingenuity but were rather the very words of God.

The Translation of Hebrew Scripture into Greek: the Septuagint

42. Even one of the Ptolemies, the kings of Egypt, was eager to know and to have these sacred writings. For, with astonishing but short-lived power, Alexander of Macedon, also called "the Great," subjugated all Asia and in fact almost the entire world. He achieved his conquests partly by force of arms and partly by terror; and, among other parts of the east, he invaded and took Judea. At his death, however, his generals did not divide that vast empire peacefully among themselves and keep possession of it. Rather, they dissipated it in wars and reduced everything to devastation. It was then that the Ptolemies began to be the kings of Egypt, and the first of them, the son of Lagus, brought many captives from Judea into Egypt. But his successor, another Ptolemy, who is called Philadelphus, allowed all those who had been taken captive by his predecessor to return home as free men. What is more, he sent royal gifts to the Temple of God and requested that Eleazar, who was then the high priest, give him a copy of the Scriptures, for he had heard of their reputation as truly divine, and he wanted to have them in the widely celebrated library he had established. When the high priest sent him a copy in Hebrew, he then asked for translators, and seventy-two were provided, six from each of the twelve tribes, who were extremely learned in both languages, that is, in both Hebrew and Greek. It is their translation that is now customarily called the Septuagint.[54]

It is reported, in fact, that there was such wondrous, amazing, and obviously divine agreement in their translations that, even though each worked in a separate place (for it pleased Ptolemy to test their reliability in this way), they did not differ from one another in a single word, not even in the choice of a synonym with the same meaning. They did not even diverge in the order of the words. Rather, their translations were so perfectly at one that it was as if only one translator had been involved, for, in very truth, there was one Spirit present in them all. And the

---

54. The legend of the translation of the Septuagint, in large part as promoted by the so-called *Letter of Aristeas*, is recounted and taken as factual here. In contrast to the account below at XVIII,43, where seventy translators are mentioned, Augustine refers here to the variant number of seventy-two.

reason why they received such a wondrous gift from God was precisely so that the authority of those Scriptures might be presented not simply as that of human but rather as that of divine writings — which, in fact, they are — when the time came for them to benefit the gentiles who were going to believe (which, as we see, has already taken place).

43. There have also been others who translated those sacred discourses from Hebrew into Greek, including Aquila, Symmachus, and Theodotion; and, in addition, there is the translation whose author is unknown and which, for this reason, is simply called the "fifth" version without any translator's name.[55] But the Church has received the Septuagint as if it were the only translation, and it is the one that the Greek Christians use, most of them without knowing that there is any other. From the Septuagint a translation into Latin has been made, to which the Latin churches adhere,[56] and this remains true even though we now have the presbyter Jerome, a most learned man, and expert in all three languages, who translated these same scriptures into Latin not from the Greek but directly from the Hebrew.[57]

Despite the Jews' acknowledgement that Jerome's learned effort is reliable, however, and despite their insistence that the translators of the Septuagint went wrong in many places, the churches of Christ still maintain that no single translator is to be preferred to the authority of such a large group of men, all chosen for such an important task by Eleazer, who was then the high priest. For, even if it had not been clear that there was one undoubtedly divine Spirit present in them, and even if the seventy scholars had simply compared the words of their translations with each other, in ordinary human fashion, so that the version that prevailed was the version they all approved, it would still be true that no single translator should be preferred to them. But, since such a great mark of divinity did appear in them, any other reliable translator of these Scriptures from the Hebrew into any other language either agrees with the translators of the Septuagint or, if he appears not to agree, we must believe that the true prophetic depth lies with them. For the same Spirit that was in the prophets when they spoke these words was also in the seventy when they translated them, and that Spirit was perfectly able to say something different, by divine authority, as if the prophet himself had said both things,

---

55. Aquila's translation, dating to the early second century A.D., was a revision of the Septuagint that sought to bring it closer to the original Hebrew. Symmachus's translation dates to the late second century A.D. and was an attempt to render the Greek text in a more refined way. Theodotion made his translation toward the middle of the second century A.D. Of the so-called "fifth" translation, nothing more is known. All four were reproduced in Origen's monumental Hexapla, dating to the early third century and no longer extant. See Eusebius, *Ecclesiastical History* VI,16-17.
56. Augustine is probably indicating the version called the Itala, which he says in *Teaching Christianity* II,15,22 is superior to other Latin translations, all of which are often referred to together as the Old Latin (Vetus Latina).
57. Jerome's version, translated in the 380s, is known as the Vulgate (from *vulgatus*, meaning "common" or "popular"), which was universally adopted in the Latin West only after considerable initial reluctance, including on the part of Augustine. See Letters 71 and 75.

because it was the same Spirit that said both. And the Spirit could also have said the same thing in a different way so that, even if the words were not the same, the same meaning would still shine through for those who understood rightly; or the Spirit could both have omitted something and added something in order to show in this way, too, that the work was not due to slavish human rendering of word for word but rather to divine power filling and guiding the mind of the translator.[58]

There are some people who have supposed that the Greek manuscripts of the Septuagint translation should be corrected according to the Hebrew manuscripts. They have not dared, however, to remove anything that is found in the Septuagint but is lacking in the Hebrew. Instead, they have only added what is found in the Hebrew but not in the Septuagint, indicating the additions by means of certain signs in the shape of stars (called asterisks) placed at the start of the added verses. Similarly, they have indicated passages not appearing in the Hebrew but present in the Septuagint by placing horizontal strokes (like those used for ounces) at the start of those verses. And many manuscripts with these markings, including Latin manuscripts, are in wide circulation.

Unless we inspect both the Hebrew and the Greek copies, however, it is impossible to locate the passages that were neither omitted nor added but rather were expressed in different ways, whether they have different but not incompatible meanings, or whether they can be shown to express the same meaning in different forms. Thus, if — as we should — we see nothing in those Scriptures except what the Spirit of God has spoken through men, then whatever appears in the Hebrew texts but not in the Septuagint is something the Spirit of God did not want to say through the seventy translators but rather through the prophets themselves. And again, whatever is in the Septuagint but not in the Hebrew texts is something that the same Spirit preferred to say through the seventy translators rather than through the prophets themselves, thus showing that the translators were prophets as well, along with the prophets themselves. For, in exactly the same way, the Spirit said some things through Isaiah, some through Jeremiah, and still others through this prophet or that prophet; or the Spirit said the same thing in one way through one prophet and in another through another, just as the Spirit saw fit. Furthermore, whatever is found in both the prophets and the seventy translators is something that one and the same Spirit wanted to say through both, but in such a way that the former came first with their prophecies and the latter followed afterwards with their prophetic translation. For, just as the one Spirit of peace was in the prophets when they spoke the truth without disagreement, so the one Spirit was present in the translators when, without consulting each other, they translated the whole as if with one voice....

---

58. Augustine's reverence for the Septuagint, based on its legendary translation and its wide reception, allows him not only to accept its lack of consistency with the Hebrew original but even to argue that the inconsistency is inspired, as he also argues in *Teaching Christianity* II,15,22.

[Chapter 45 recounts Jewish history after the end of prophecy, through occupation by the Syrian Greeks, to the Roman conquest.]

The Coming of Christ in Fulfillment of Prophecy

46. During the reign of Herod in Judea,[59] then, and when, after the change in the republic's status, Caesar Augustus had become emperor[60] and brought peace to the world, Christ was born in Bethlehem of Judah in accord with the earlier prophecy.[61] Outwardly he was human, a man born from a human virgin; hiddenly he was God from God the Father. For this is what the prophet had foretold: *See, a virgin shall conceive in her womb and bear a son, and they shall call him Emmanuel, which means God with us* (Is 7:14; Mt. 1:23). And, in order to show himself as God, he performed many miracles, of which the scriptural Gospels contain as many as seemed sufficient to proclaim him. The first of these is that he was born in such a miraculous way, and the last is that he ascended into heaven with his body, which had itself been raised from the dead. But the Jews, who put him to death and would not believe in him (since it was necessary for him to die and rise again), suffered even more miserable devastation at the hands of the Romans. They were utterly uprooted from their kingdom, where they were already under the dominion of a foreign power, and were scattered through the world. In fact there is no place in the world where they are not present. Through their own Scriptures, then, they bear witness for us that we did not make up the prophecies about Christ. In fact a great many of them, reflecting on those prophecies both before his passion and most especially after his resurrection, have come to believe in him, and these are the Jews of whom it was foretold, *Though the number of the children of Israel were like the sand of the sea, a remnant of them shall be saved* (Is 10:22). The rest, however, were made blind, and of them it was foretold, *Let their table become a trap before them and a retribution and a stumbling block; let their eyes be darkened to keep them from seeing and their backs be always bent over* (Ps 69:22-23). Thus, when they do not believe our Scriptures, their own Scriptures, which they read with blind eyes,[62] are fulfilled in them. Someone might say, of course, that the Christians made up the prophecies about Christ that are cited under the name of the Sibyl or under the name of others — if any — who do not belong to the Jewish people. For us, however, the prophecies that come from the books of our enemies are enough, for we recognize that it is precisely for the sake of bearing this testimony, which they unwillingly provide for us sim-

---

59. See Mt 2:1.
60. See Lk 2:1.
61. See Mi 5:2.
62. See 2 Cor 3:15.

ply by having and preserving those books, that they were themselves scattered through all peoples, wherever the Church of Christ spreads.

For this very thing was itself prophesied in advance in the Psalms, which they also read, where it is written, *My God, his mercy shall go before me. My God has shown me with regard to my enemies: do not kill them, lest they some day forget your law; scatter them in your power* (Ps 59:10-11). Thus God has shown the Church the grace of his mercy with regard to her enemies the Jews, for, as the Apostle says, *Their sin is the salvation of the gentiles* (Rom 11:11). Thus the reason why God did not kill them — that is, the reason why he did not put an end to their being as Jews, despite the fact that they were conquered and oppressed by the Romans — is precisely so that they would not forget the law of God and, as a result, be unable to bear the testimony that we are discussing here. That is why it was not enough for the Psalm to say, *Do not kill them, lest they some day forget your law*, without also adding *scatter them* (Ps 59:11). For if the Jews, with the testimony that they bear from Scripture, were only in their own land and not everywhere, then the Church, which is everywhere, obviously could not have them as witnesses in all nations to the prophecies that were given in advance about Christ.

47. As a consequence, if it has come or should come to our attention that any foreigner — that is, anyone not born of Israel and not accepted by that people into the canon of Sacred Scripture — is read to have prophesied something about Christ, he can be cited by us as additional confirmation. It is not that we have need of any such outside testimony, even if it were lacking. It is rather that there is nothing inappropriate in believing that there were also people in other nations to whom this mystery was revealed and who were also driven to proclaim it. This is so regardless of whether they participated in the same grace from God or whether, quite apart from that grace, they were taught by evil angels — who, as we know, confessed Christ when he was present, even though the Jews did not acknowledge him.[63] For I do not think that even the Jews themselves dare to claim that, from the very beginning of Israel's line, after the rejection of his older brother,[64] no one other than the Israelites has ever belonged to God. It is quite true, of course, that there was no other people that could properly be called the people of God, but the Jews still cannot deny that there were also some people in other nations who belonged, not by earthly but by heavenly association, to the true Israelites who are citizens of the homeland above.[65] For, if they deny this, there is nothing easier than to refute them by referring to the holy and extraordinary man Job, who was neither a native-born Israelite nor a proselyte (that is, an outsider admitted into the people of Israel). He came rather from the race of Edom,[66] and that is where

---

63. See, e.g., Mt 8:29 par.; Mk 1:24.
64. I.e., Esau; see Gn 27:1-40.
65. A thought similar to that which Augustine develops here and in the following lines can be found in Justin Martyr, 1 *Apology* 46.
66. Job is said in Jb 1:1 to have come from Uz, which is identified with Edom in Lam 4:21.

he was born as well as where he died. But he is so highly praised in the divine discourses that no one of his time is his equal so far as righteousness and piety are concerned.[67] And, although we do not find his dates in *The Chronicles*, we gather from his book — which the Israelites accepted into their authoritative canon on its merits — that he came in the third generation after Israel.[68]

I have no doubt that it was due to divine providence that, by virtue of this one man, we know that there could also be people of other nations who lived according to God, were pleasing to him, and belonged to the spiritual Jerusalem. We should not believe, however, that this was granted to anyone to whom there was not revealed *the one mediator between God and man, the man Christ Jesus* (1 Tm 2:5), whose coming in the flesh was foretold to the saints of old, just as his having come was announced to us; and so the result is that, through him, one and the same faith leads to God all who are predestined for the city of God, the house of God, the temple of God. It remains possible, however, to suppose that any prophecies about the grace of God through Jesus Christ[69] that come from other sources were actually concocted by the Christians; and so there is no surer way of convincing outsiders, if they argue this point (and of making them ours, if they show good sense) than to cite the divine predictions about Christ that are written in the books of the Jews. It is, then, due to the expulsion of the Jews from their own homes and their dispersal throughout the entire world to bear this testimony that the Church has everywhere grown and increased....

The Spreading of the Church: Persecutions and Consolations

50. ... For the Church first spread out from Jerusalem, and, when a great many in Judea and Samaria had believed, it then went on to other peoples, as the Gospel was proclaimed by those whom Christ himself had prepared by his word, like lamps, and had set alight by the Holy Spirit. For he had said to them, *Do not fear those who kill the body but cannot kill the soul* (Mt 10:28), and, so that they would not be frozen with fear, they burned with the fire of love. Finally, the Gospel was proclaimed throughout the entire world, not only by those who had seen and heard Christ both before his passion and after his resurrection but also, after their death, by their successors, in the midst of dreadful persecutions, all sorts of torture, and the deaths of the martyrs. And God himself bore witness by signs and prodigies and various displays of power and by the gifts of the Holy Spirit, so that the peoples of the nations, believing in him who was crucified for their redemption, might venerate with Christian love the very blood of the martyrs that they had shed in devilish fury, and so that the rulers by whose laws the Church

---

67. See Jb 1:1; Ez 14:14.20; Jas 5:11.
68. Nothing in the Book of Job suggests this.
69. See Rom 7:25.

was being ravaged might savingly become subject to the very name that they had ruthlessly tried to erase from the face of the earth, and might begin to persecute the false gods for whose sake the worshipers of the true God had been persecuted before.

51. But when the devil saw that the temples of the demons were deserted and that all humanity was rushing to the name of the mediator who sets men free, he stirred up heretics who call themselves Christian but oppose Christian teaching. As if heretics could be contained indiscriminately in the city of God without any correction, in the same way that the city of confusion[70] indiscriminately contained philosophers who took different and mutually opposed positions! Thus, if anyone in the Church of Christ holds diseased and depraved opinions and, when corrected to bring him to sound and right views, resists and stubbornly refuses to revise his pernicious and deadly teachings but instead persists in defending them, he becomes a heretic; and, when he leaves the Church, he is counted among the enemies who put the Church to the test. Such people even turn out to benefit the true and catholic members of Christ by their very wickedness, for God puts even the evil to good use, and *all things work together for good for those who love God* (Rom 8:28). In fact all the Church's enemies, no matter how blinded by error or corrupted by malice, serve a useful purpose. If they have the power of inflicting bodily harm on the Church, they train it in patience; if they oppose it only by holding evil opinions, they train it in wisdom; and, in addition, whether it is with persuasive doctrine or with strict discipline that the Church addresses them, they train it in benevolence, or even in beneficence, so that even its enemies are loved.

Thus, even the devil, the prince of the ungodly city, is not allowed to do any harm to the Church when he stirs up his own vessels against the city of God on its pilgrimage here in this world. Beyond doubt, divine providence provides that city with both the consolation of prosperity, so that it is not broken by adversity, and the discipline of adversity, so that it is not corrupted by prosperity; and each is so tempered by the other that we recognize that the saying in the Psalm — *According to the multitude of my heart's sorrows, your consolations have cheered my soul* (Ps 94:19) — arises from no other source. And the words of the Apostle have the same basis: *Rejoicing in hope, patient in suffering* (Rom 12:12).

In fact no one should think that there is any time when another saying of the same teacher fails to apply: *All who want to live a godly life in Christ suffer persecution* (2 Tm 3:12). Even when those on the outside do not rage, and there appears to be, and really is, tranquility, which is a great consolation, especially to the weak, there are still some on the inside — indeed, there are many — who by their dissipated morals torment the hearts of those who live pious lives. They cause the name of "Christian" and "Catholic" to be blasphemed, and, the more precious this

---

70. I.e., Babylon, which means "confusion" and which symbolizes the earthly city. See above at XVI.4.

name is to those who want to live a godly life in Christ, the more deeply they are pained that, due to the wicked on the inside, it is less loved than the minds of the godly desire. And the heretics as well, since they are thought to have the Christian name and sacraments and Scriptures and creed, cause great pain in the hearts of the godly. For many who want to become Christians are compelled to hesitate due to the heretics' dissensions, and many revilers also find in them some ground for blaspheming the Christian name, since even the heretics are called Christians in one sense or another. It is due to these, and to other such depraved morals and human errors, that those who want to live a godly life in Christ suffer persecution, even when no one attacks or mistreats them in the body. For they suffer this persecution not in their bodies but in their hearts, and that is why the Psalm says *according to the multitude of my heart's sorrows* rather than "my body's."

At the same time, because the divine promises are considered immutable, and because the Apostle says, *The Lord knows those who are his* (2 Tm 2:19), *for those whom he foreknew he also predestined to be conformed to the image of his Son* (Rom 8:29), none of the elect can perish. And that is why the Psalm goes on to say, *Your consolations have cheered my soul.* In fact the very sorrow that strikes the hearts of the godly when they are persecuted by the misdeeds of evil or false Christians is actually of benefit to those who feel it. For it stems from a love due to which they do not want such people either to perish themselves or to be an obstacle to the salvation of others. Above all, great consolations come from the correction of these people, which flood the souls of the godly with a joy as great as were the sorrows that tormented them at the prospect that these people might be lost. And it is in this way that the Church runs its course on its pilgrimage in this world, in these evil days, amid the persecutions of the world and the consolations of God, not simply from the time of the bodily presence of Christ and his apostles but all the way from Abel himself, the first righteous man,[71] who was killed by his ungodly brother,[72] and ultimately on down to the end of this age.

The Persecutions of the Church

52. I certainly do not think, then, that we should be so rash as to say or believe what has seemed true and still seems true to some, that, until the time of Antichrist, the Church will suffer no further persecutions over and above the number it has already suffered — namely, ten — so that the eleventh and last persecution will come from Antichrist himself. They count Nero's persecution as the first, Domitian's as the second, Trajan's as the third, Antoninus's as the fourth, Severus's as the fifth, Maximinus's as the sixth, Decius's as the seventh, Valerian's as the eighth, Aurelian's as the ninth, and Diocletian's and Maximian's as the tenth.

---

71. See Mt 23:35. 72.
72. See Gn 4:8.

And they hold that, because there were ten plagues of Egypt before the people of God began their exodus from that country,[73] we should take this to mean that the last persecution — the persecution by Antichrist — will correspond to the eleventh plague, by which the Egyptians, in their hostile pursuit of the Hebrews, perished in the Red Sea while the people of God passed over on dry land.[74] In my view, however, those events in Egypt were not prophetic signs of these persecutions, despite the fact that those who think they were appear to have worked out exquisite and ingenious correlations between each of those plagues and each of these persecutions. They have done this, however, not by the Spirit of prophecy but rather by conjectures of the human mind, which sometimes attain the truth but sometimes go astray.[75]...

It seems to me that we should not set any limit on the number of persecutions that the Church must undergo for its testing and training. But, then again, it is no less rash to claim that there are going to be further persecutions by kings, apart from that final persecution about which no Christian is in doubt. As a consequence, I leave the matter undecided, neither supporting nor opposing either side but simply calling both sides back from the rash presumption of taking a stand on the issue.

53. Of course, Jesus himself will extinguish by his own presence that final persecution, which will be the work of Antichrist. For it is written that *he shall slay him with the breath of his mouth and shall annihilate him with the brightness of his coming* (2 Thes 2:8). Here people usually ask, "When will this happen?" But the question is wholly inappropriate. If it were any advantage for us to know this, who better to have told us than the master, God himself, when the disciples asked him? For they did not keep quiet about it when they were with him but asked him in person, *Lord, is this the time when you will restore the kingdom to Israel?* (Acts 1:6) But he replied, *It is not for you to know the times which the Father has put in his own power* (Acts 1:7). When they received this answer, obviously enough, they had not asked about the hour or the day or the year but about the time. It is to no avail, therefore, that we try to compute and determine the number of years that remain for this world, for we hear from the mouth of the Truth himself that it

---

73. See Ex 7:14-12:30.
74. See Ex 14:21-29.
75. Augustine seems to be addressing the elaborate scheme of Paulus Orosius in *Against the Pagans* VII,27, which posits the same ten persecutions and links them to the ten plagues, while reserving an eleventh persecution for the future, when the conquest of Antichrist will be comparable to the drowning of the Egyptians in the Red Sea. As Augustine points out in the following lines, the selection of these particular persecutions to the exclusion of others is quite arbitrary. Most historians would name those of Septimius Severus (beginning of the third century), Decius (early 250s) and Diocletian (beginning of the fourth century) as the most important, or even narrow that list to Decius and Diocletian. Ten persecutions are also singled out in Eusebius, *Chronicles* II (PL 27,454-496), which was quite likely a passage in that work with which Augustine was familiar, but they are not linked to the ten plagues.

is not for us to know this. All the same, some have claimed that there may be four hundred, others that there may be five hundred,[76] and still others that there may even be a thousand years to be completed between the Lord's ascension and his final coming. It would take too long to show how each of these groups supports its opinion, and in any case it is not necessary. For they are using human conjectures, and they offer nothing that is certain because it has the authority of canonical Scripture. And, in truth, when Christ says, *It is not for you to know the times which the Father has put in his own power,* he takes a load off the fingers of all those who are using them to make such calculations and tells them to let their fingers rest....

Now let us at last bring this book to a close. Up to this point, we have discussed and demonstrated, as far as seemed sufficient, the mortal course of the two cities, the heavenly and the earthly, which are mingled together from start to finish. One of them, the earthly city, has made for itself whatever false gods it wanted, creating them from anything at all, even from human beings, and serving them with sacrifices. The other, the heavenly city, which is on pilgrimage here on earth, does not make up false gods but is itself created by the true God and is itself his true sacrifice. Both alike make use of temporal goods, and both alike are afflicted by temporal evils.[77] But their temporal lives are directed by different faiths, different hopes, and different loves, until at last they are separated by the final judgment and each receives its own end, of which there is no end. It is these ends that we must now discuss.

---

76. Hippolytus, *Commentary on Daniel* IV,23-24, counts five hundred years from the birth of Christ to the end of time.

77. A similar idea, typical of early Christian apologetic literature, is expressed in *Letter to Diognetus* 5; Tertullian, *Apology* 42.

Study Questions for Book XVIII

Augustine, like other Christian, Jewish and pagan writers, made apologetic use of the pastiche of ancient poetic texts known as the Sibylline Oracles. Sibyls were prophetesses associated with holy sites throughout Italy, Greece, the Mideast and Asia Minor. During trances and frenzied states, they divined the meanings of current and future events. Does Augustine's appeal to these extra-biblical prophecies by women have any significance for his understanding of divine revelation?

We reach the fullest understanding of the Hebrew prophets, Augustine believed, when we interpret their writings as referring to Christ and the Church. Yet in *Teaching Christianity* he also insisted that all scriptural interpretation must ultimately lead to greater love of God and neighbor. Does his extensive and insistent effort to read all of the Old Testament in light of faith in Christ preclude a loving respect for contemporary Jewish readings of Scripture?

Augustine privileges the Greek translation of the Hebrew Scriptures known as the Septuagint, and he maintains its authoritative status over all other translations. Along with other Church Fathers, he considers the Septuagint to be divinely inspired. He argues that the 70 (or 72) translators, like the original biblical authors, were filled with the Holy Spirit, who guided their work. Even when their translation does not match the Hebrew text, "true prophetic depth lies with them" (XVIII,43). Does Augustine's teaching on this matter promote a locus of divine revelation that is separate from the historical events of salvation history?

BOOK XIX

Book XIX turns to the due ends of the two cities, the final or supreme good and the final or supreme evil. It starts with a brief sketch of Varro's account of possible philosophical positions on the issue and his presentation of his own view: the supreme good consists in a combination of the "primary goods of nature" and virtue. It then uses key features from Varro's analysis as markers in developing its counterargument. It insists that the final good, in which human happiness is achieved, is eternal life and that it cannot be found in this life. The "primary goods of nature," whether physical or mental, are all subject to various forms of misery and ailment; and virtue itself, precisely because it must constantly battle the vices, indicates how deeply this life is enmeshed in evil. The book gives special attention to the miseries of social existence at every level from the household to the universe at large; and, in this connection, it offers an extended consideration of peace, showing that earthly peace (in contrast to the eternal peace which is another name for the supreme good) is at best an accommodation of conflicting wills to each other in a fragile social and political order. Since the heavenly city, during its earthly pilgrimage, also needs a stable social order, it too makes use of this earthly peace. Here the question of the definition of a republic, left unfinished in Book II, reemerges, and the present book argues that, without justice, there can be no "people" according to Cicero's definition, and so there can be no "common good of a people," that is, no republic. The true "common good" of the people is only to be found, then, where there is justice as seen in the proper ordering of the body to the soul and the soul to the true God, and the full realization of this justice comes in the eternal life of the heavenly city with God. In contrast, the supreme evil, which is the due end of the earthly city, is eternal death, understood as an eternal state of torment in an unending war of passion against the will within the self.

The Ends of the Two Cities: the Supreme Good and the Supreme Evil

1. I see, then, that I must next discuss the due ends of these two cities, the earthly and the heavenly. And first I have to set out, so far as the scheme of this work allows, the arguments by which mortals have tried to contrive happiness for themselves in the midst of all the unhappiness of this life. I do this in order to make clear how different their empty views are both from our hope, which God has given us, and from the reality itself,[1] the true happiness which God will give us; and I shall proceed not only by appealing to divine authority but also, for the sake of unbelievers, by appealing to reason as far as possible.

Now, the philosophers have engaged in much and many-sided debate about the supreme ends of good and evil, and they have given this question their fullest attention in an effort to discover what it is that makes a person happy. For our final good is that for the sake of which other things are to be desired, while it is itself to be desired for its own sake; and the final evil is that for the sake of which other things are to be avoided, while it is itself to be avoided for its own sake. Thus, when we speak of the "end" of good in this context, we do not mean "end" in the sense that the good is finished and gone, so that it no longer exists; rather, we mean "end" in the sense of the culmination in which the good is brought to its full realization, so that it is wholly fulfilled. And again, when we speak of the "end" of evil, we do not mean "end" in the sense that evil ceases to exist but rather "end" in the sense of the culmination to which evil leads in doing its harm. These two ends, therefore, are the supreme good and the supreme evil. Now, as I have said, those who have devoted themselves to the pursuit of wisdom in the midst of the vanity of this world have worked hard to discover what each of these is and to attain the supreme good in this life while avoiding the supreme evil. And, although they have gone wrong in various ways, the limits imposed by nature kept them from veering too far from the path of truth. Thus, there are none who did not locate the ultimate good and the ultimate evil either in the soul or in the body or in both together. Starting from this threefold classification of general positions, Marcus Varro, in his work *On Philosophy*, identified by subtle and diligent analysis such a large variety of views that, by bringing certain distinctions to bear, he easily reached a total of two hundred and eighty-eight philosophical sects — not sects already in existence but possible schools of thought.[2]

Varro: Possible Positions on the Supreme Good

To show this briefly, I need to begin with the fact that in the above-mentioned book Varro himself observes and posits that there are four things which human beings seek naturally, that is, without a teacher, without the aid of instruction, without conscious effort, and without acquiring the art of living (which is called virtue and which, beyond doubt, is learned). These four are pleasure, by which bodily sense is moved with delight; repose, the state in which a person feels no bodily distress; the combination of these (which Epicurus nevertheless calls by the one name of pleasure[3]); or, comprehensively, the primary goods of nature, which include the first three in addition to others, whether in the body

---

1. "Hope...reality": *spes...res*. A frequent wordplay in Augustine. See also below at XIX,20.
2. Varro's text no longer exists and its contents are known only from *The City of God*.
3. See *Letter to Menoeceus*, cited in Diogenes Laertius, *Lives of Eminent Philosophers* X,128-132.

(such as the integrity of its members and its health and wellbeing) or in the mind (such as the abilities, small or great, which are found in the innate capacities of human beings). Now, these four — pleasure, repose, the combination of these, and the primary goods of nature — are in us in such a way that either virtue (which teaching implants in us at a later point) is to be sought for their sake, or they are to be sought for the sake of virtue, or both they and virtue are to be sought, each for its own sake. Thus we get twelve sects, since each of the first four is tripled by means of this consideration.

Once I have demonstrated this point in one case, it will not be difficult to see it in each of the others. Since, therefore, bodily pleasure may either be subordinated to virtue of mind, or preferred to virtue of mind, or set on the same plane with it, we get a threefold division of sects. Bodily pleasure is subordinated to virtue when it is brought into the service of virtue. For example, it belongs to the office of virtue both to live for one's country and to produce sons for the sake of one's country, neither of which can be done without bodily pleasure. For it is impossible to eat and drink (in order to live) or to have sexual intercourse (in order to generate children) without bodily pleasure. On the other hand, when bodily pleasure is preferred to virtue, it is sought for its own sake, and it is believed that virtue should be brought into the service of bodily pleasure. It is believed, that is, that the only point of virtue is to gain or to sustain bodily pleasure. This is certainly a deformed kind of life, where virtue becomes the slave of domineering pleasure (although in fact this should not be called virtue at all), but, even so, this horrible and degrading view has some philosophers who support and defend it.[4] Again, pleasure is set on the same plane with virtue when neither is sought for the sake of the other but both are sought, each for its own sake. Thus, pleasure gives us three sects, depending on whether it is subordinated to virtue, preferred to virtue, or set on the same plane with virtue; and, in exactly the same way, repose, the combination of pleasure and repose, and the primary goods of nature are each found to give rise to three sects. According as human opinions vary, each of these ends is sometimes subordinated to virtue, sometimes preferred to virtue, and sometimes set on the same plane with virtue. And so we reach a total of twelve sects.

But this number is itself doubled when a further distinction is brought into play, namely, social life. Anyone who follows any of these twelve sects does so either for his own sake alone or for the sake of others as well, for whom he is obligated to will the same good that he wills for himself. Thus, there are twelve sects of those who suppose that whichever view they take is to be held for the sake of oneself alone, and twelve others of those who maintain that this philosophy or that philosophy should be held not only for one's own sake but also for the sake of others, whose good they seek just as much as their own. And these twenty-four sects are again doubled, to make forty-eight, when a distinction drawn from the New Academy is introduced. On the one hand, a person may hold and defend the

---

4. E.g., Aristippus. See ibid. II,65-104.

views of any one of those twenty-four sects as being certain (in the same way that the Stoics defended their claim that the human good, by which a person attains happiness, consists only of virtue of soul[5]). But, on the other hand, someone else may hold his views as uncertain (in the way that the New Academics defended views that to them seemed not certain but still probable[6]). Thus, we get twenty-four sects made up of those who maintain that their views are to be followed as certain, because they are true, and another twenty-four made up of those who maintain that their views are to be followed, even though they are uncertain, because they are probable. Again, because one person who follows any one of these forty-eight sects may adopt the mode of life of most other philosophers, but another may adopt the mode of life of the Cynics,[7] the number is again doubled on the basis of this distinction, and we get ninety-six sects. And, finally, each of these sects can be followed and upheld either by people who love the life of leisured retirement, like those who only wanted and valued being free to study their sect's teachings; or by those who love the active life, like those who, while engaged in philosophy, were still fully occupied with the administration of the republic and governing human affairs; or by those who love a combination of both forms of life, like those who have alternately devoted themselves to learned leisure on the one hand and to necessary business on the other. And, on the basis of this distinction, the number of sects can again be tripled, getting us up to two hundred and eighty-eight sects.

Varro's Position on the Supreme Good and the Life of Happiness

I have set out these points from Varro's book as briefly and as clearly as I could, expressing his views in my own words. Now, he goes on to refute all these sects but one, which he wants to be that of the Old Academy. This sect was founded by Plato and continued down to Polemo, who was, after Plato, the fourth head of the school which was then called the Academy.[8] Varro wants it to appear that this school held its doctrines as certain; and, on this basis, he distinguishes it from the New Academy, which holds that all things are uncertain and which began with Arcesilaus, Polemo's successor. Varro also considers this sect — that is, the Old Academy — to have been as free from error as it was from doubt. It would take too long to follow out Varro's argument in all its detail, but his reasoning should not be wholly omitted.

First, then, he removes all the distinctions which multiplied the number of sects, and the reason he thinks that these distinctions should be taken away is that they have nothing to do with the issue of the supreme good. In his opinion, no position should be called a philosophical sect unless it differs from the others

---

5. See above at IX,4.
6. See *Answer to the Academics* II,5,11-6,15.
7. As explained later in this section, Cynicism is characterized less by philosophical ideals than by style of life; what one ate or how one dressed, for example, was a matter of indifference.
8. The writings of Polemo, or Polemon (died c. 270 B.C.), have not survived. See Diogenes Laertius, *Lives of Eminent Philosophers* IV,16-20.

in having a distinctive view of the supreme good and supreme evil. For there is no reason to pursue philosophy except in order to be happy, and what makes for human happiness is precisely the ultimate good. There is no reason to pursue philosophy, therefore, except the supreme good, and so a sect which does not have its own distinctive view of the ultimate good should not to be called a philosophical sect at all. When, therefore, it is asked whether the wise man ought to embrace the social life, so that he wants and cares about the supreme good, which makes a person happy, as much for his friend as for himself, or whether he does what he does solely for the sake of his own happiness alone, this is not a question about the ultimate good itself. Rather, it is only a question about including or not including a companion to participate in that good with oneself, and doing so not for one's own sake but for the sake of the companion, so that one rejoices as much in one's companion's good as one does in one's own. Again, if it is asked, with regard to the New Academy, to which all things are uncertain, whether this is the view we ought to take of the matters that philosophy should deal with or whether, like other philosophers, we ought to hold them as certain, this is not a question about what should be pursued as the ultimate good. Instead, the question is whether or not we should have doubts about the truth of the good it seems we should pursue. In other words, to put it more plainly, the question is whether the supreme good is to be pursued in such a way that the one pursuing it should say that it is true, or rather in such a way that the one pursuing it should say that it seems true to him, even though it may possibly be false. In either case, however, one and the same good is being pursued. Again, with regard to the distinction which has to do with the customs and mode of life of the Cynics, what is at issue is not the ultimate good. Rather, what is at issue is whether the person pursuing the true good — whatever it is that may seem true to him and rightly to be pursued — ought to follow those customs and that mode of life. There were, after all, people who pursued different ultimate goods (some pursued virtue, and some pleasure) but still adopted the same customs and the same mode of life as the Cynics, and so they were all called Cynics. Thus, whatever it is that distinguishes the Cynics from other philosophers, it obviously makes no difference with regard to their choice of and support for the good by which they sought to gain happiness. For, if it did make any difference, the same mode of life would require pursuit of the same end, and a different mode of life would exclude pursuit of the same end.

2. Again, in the matter of those three kinds of life — one spent not in mere idleness but in leisured contemplation of the truth or leisured inquiry into the truth, another spent in the business of managing human affairs, the third in a combination of both — when it is asked which of these should be chosen, the supreme good itself is not at issue. At issue is only which of these three makes it either difficult or easy to attain or retain the ultimate good. When a person achieves the supreme good, it at once makes him happy; but no one is immediately made happy simply by living a life of educated leisure or of public business or of both by turns. For many can live in any one of these three ways and still go wrong in seeking the supreme good that brings human happiness.

Thus, the question of the ultimate good and evil — the question which makes a philosophical sect a sect in its own right — is one thing, and the questions of the social life, the doubtfulness of the Academy, the food and dress of the Cynics, and the three kinds of life (the leisured, the active, and the combination of the two) are quite another. None of these involves any points of dispute about the supreme good and evil. Now, it was by using these four distinctions — that is, the social life, the New Academy, the Cynics, and the three kinds of life — that Marcus Varro arrived at his two hundred and eighty-eight sects (plus any others that could be added by similar calculations). Accordingly, once he removed them all on the grounds that they have nothing to do with the issue of the ultimate good to be pursued, and so give us nothing that either is or should be called a sect, he dropped back to those twelve sects in which what is at issue is the human good (the attainment of which brings happiness) in order to show that one of them is true, the others false. For, if the distinction based on the three kinds of life is taken away, two-thirds of the total are eliminated, and ninety-six sects remain. Again, if the distinction drawn from the Cynics is taken away, that number is reduced by half, which leaves forty-eight. And, if we exclude the distinction drawn from the New Academy, again only half remain, that is, twenty-four sects. Similarly, if we exclude the distinction which he brought in concerning the social life, only twelve sects remain — the number which that distinction had doubled, to make twenty-four.

As for the remaining twelve, then, nothing can be said against taking them as genuine sects, for their point of inquiry is in fact nothing other than the ultimate good and evil. And further, once you discover the ultimate good, you immediately have the ultimate evil as its contrary. Now, to get these twelve sects, four things are each multiplied by three: pleasure, repose, the combination of both, and the primary goods of nature, which Varro calls "innate goods." These four are each sometimes subordinated to virtue, so that they appear worthy of being sought not for their own sake but for the sake of their role in serving virtue. They are each sometimes preferred to virtue, so that virtue is considered necessary not for its own sake but simply for the sake of acquiring and holding onto them. And they are each sometimes put on the same plane as virtue, so that it is believed that both they and virtue are to be sought, each for its own sake. In this way the number four is tripled, and we get twelve sects. From these four things, however, Varro subtracts three, namely, pleasure and repose and the combination of both. He does this not because he rejects them but because the primary goods of nature already include both pleasure and repose. What need is there, then, to turn these two into three — that is, two when pleasure and repose are sought separately, each apart from the other, and a third when both are sought at the same time — especially when the primary goods of nature already include both of these and many other things as well? For Varro, then, there are only three sects that must be examined with care to see which should be chosen in preference to the others. For sound reason does not allow more than one to be true, whether it is one of these three or some other not included among them, as we shall see later on. In the meantime, however, let us set out as briefly and clearly as we can how Varro chooses one of the three. And there are three sects because either the primary goods of nature are to be sought for the sake of virtue, or virtue is to be sought for the sake of the primary goods of nature, or both virtue and the primary goods of nature are to be sought, each for its own sake.

3. Here, then, is how Varro tries to convince us as to which of these three sects is the one that is true and to be followed. First, since the ultimate good that philosophy seeks is not that of a tree or of an animal or of God but of human beings, he holds that we must start by asking what human beings themselves are. He maintains that, in human nature, there are two elements, body and soul, and he has no doubt that, of these two, the soul is the better and far and away the more excellent. But is the soul by itself the human being, so that the body is only related to the man as a horse to its rider? For the rider is not both the man and the horse but only the man, and he is called a rider only because he is related to the horse in a certain way. Or is the body by itself the human being, standing in some such relation to the soul as that of a cup to the drink it contains? For it is not the cup and the drink together that are called the cup, but only the cup itself — even though it is called a cup precisely because it is meant to hold a drink. Or, again, is it neither the soul by itself nor the body by itself that is the human being, but rather both at once, the soul and the body each being a part, but the whole requiring both if it is to be a human being? It is in this sense that we call two horses harnessed together a pair. The near horse and the off horse are both parts of the pair, but, no matter how they are connected to each other, we do not call either one of them a pair by itself but only both at once.

Of these three possibilities, Varro chose the third and concluded that a human being is neither the soul by itself nor the body by itself but the soul and the body together. Therefore, he says, the ultimate human good, which makes a human being happy, consists in the goods of both, that is, of both the soul and the body. As a consequence, he holds that the primary goods of nature are to be sought for their own sake, and so is virtue, which teaching implants in us as the art of living and which is the most excellent of all the goods of the soul. Accordingly, when this virtue — that is, the art of conducting one's life — takes its place with the primary goods of nature, which were present prior to virtue (and in fact were present prior to any teaching whatsoever), it seeks all of these for their own sake, and, at the same time, it also seeks itself for its own sake. Thus, virtue makes use of all these, and also of itself, to the end that it may delight in and enjoy them all. This enjoyment may be greater or less, according as each of these goods is itself greater or less. But virtue still rejoices in them all, although, if necessity requires, it may disdain some of the lesser ones for the sake of gaining or keeping greater ones. Of all these goods, however, whether of the soul or of the body, there is absolutely none that virtue ranks above itself. For it is virtue that makes right use both of itself and of the other goods that make for human happiness. And, where virtue itself is lacking, no matter how many other goods are present, they are of no good to the one whose goods they are, and in fact they should not really be called his "goods" at all, for they cannot possibly be of use to one who uses them wrongly.

This, then, is the human life that is properly called happy — the life that enjoys both virtue and the other goods of soul and body without which virtue cannot exist. But, if a life also enjoys any or many of those other goods without which virtue can exist, it is happier still; and, if it enjoys all goods, so that no good whether of soul or of body is lacking to it, it is happiest of all. For life is not identical with virtue, since not every life counts as virtue but only a life lived wisely. And there can, of course, be life of some sort without any virtue at all, even though it is impossible for virtue to exist without any life at all. I might say the same of memory and reason and any other such human faculties. For these are present prior to teaching, but without them there can be no teaching; and without them, therefore, neither can there be virtue, which is certainly learned through teaching. But to run well, to be beautiful in body, to prevail by great strength, and other things of this sort can obviously be present without virtue, just as virtue can be present without them. But they are goods all the same, and, according to these philosophers, virtue loves even these goods for their own sake and uses and enjoys them in a way that accords with virtue.

This happy life, these philosophers claim, is also social; it loves the good of friends for its own sake in the same way that it loves its own good, and, for their own sake, it wants for them precisely what it wants for itself. And this is true whether these are friends at home, such as one's spouse and children and other members of one's household; or friends in the place where one lives, such as a city, as are those called one's fellow-citizens; or friends in the world at large, as are those united with us by common membership in human society; or friends in the very universe itself, which is collectively called heaven and earth, as are those whom they call gods and want to count as a wise man's friends but whom we more usually call angels. In addition, they deny that there is any room for doubt with regard to the ultimate good and its opposite, the ultimate evil; and this, they assert, is what distinguishes them from the New Academy. Nor does it make any difference to these philosophers whether anyone who pursues philosophy adopts the Cynics' dress and diet or some other mode of life in seeking the ends which they hold to be true. Finally, with regard to those three kinds of life — the leisured, the active, and the combination of both — they insist that they prefer the third. Varro asserts that the Old Academy held and taught these things, and he bases his claim on the authority of Antiochus, Cicero's teacher and his own (although, in fact, Cicero seems to think that, on many points, Antiochus was more a Stoic than a follower of the Old Academy).[9] But what does that matter to us? For we ought to judge on the basis of the facts themselves rather than setting any great store on knowing what anyone else has thought about them.

---

9. Antiochus of Ascalon (c. 159-c. 86 B.C.) was a Greek philosopher whose lectures Cicero followed in Rome and to whom he often referred in his writings.

The Supreme Good and the Supreme Evil according to the City of God: Eternal Life and Eternal Death

4. If, then, we are asked what the city of God would respond when questioned on each of these points, and, first, what view it holds about the ultimate good and evil, its response will be that eternal life is the ultimate good and eternal death the ultimate evil, and that to attain the one and avoid the other we must live rightly. That is why Scripture says, *The just person lives by faith* (Rom 1:17). For we do not yet see our good, and, as a consequence, we must seek it by believing. Nor is it in our power to live rightly by our own efforts unless we are helped in believing and praying by the one who gave us the very faith by which we believe that we must have his help.

Happiness, the Supreme Good, Cannot Be Found in this Life

But those who have imagined that the ultimate good and evil are to be had in this life, whether they place the ultimate good in the body or in the soul or in both together — or, to speak more explicitly, whether they place it in pleasure or in virtue or in both of these, or in repose or in virtue or in both of these, or in the combination of pleasure and repose or in virtue or in both of these, or in the primary goods of nature or in virtue or in both of these — have wanted, with astonishing folly, to be happy in this life and to become happy by their own efforts. The Truth scoffed at these people in the words of the prophet, *The Lord knows the thoughts of men* (Ps. 94:11)— or, as the apostle Paul cites this passage, *The Lord knows the thoughts of the wise, that they are folly* (1 Cor 3:20).

For who, no matter how wonderful the flow of his eloquence, can find words to portray the miseries of this life?[10] Cicero lamented them as best he could in his *Consolation* on the death of his daughter,[11] but what did his best amount to? When, where, and how can what are called the primary goods of nature be so securely possessed in this life that they are not tossed about by uncertain chance? Is there any pain, the contrary of pleasure, or any distress, the contrary of repose, that cannot strike the wise man's body? The amputation or crippling of his limbs destroys his physical wellbeing, deformity ruins his beauty, sickness his health, weakness his strength, torpor or listlessness his mobility. And is there any one of these that is not perfectly capable of attacking the flesh of the wise man? The posture and movement of the body, when attractive and fitting, are numbered among the primary goods of nature. But what if some dire disease causes the limbs to shake with a tremor? What if a person's spine is so bent over that he drags his hands on the ground, making him a kind of human quadruped? Will this not put an end to all the beauty and grace of the body's posture and movement?

---

10. Augustine discusses the miseries of this life again below at XXII,22.
11. This work, written to memorialize Cicero's daughter Tullia, is no longer extant.

And what about the innate goods, as they are called, of the mind itself? The two ranked highest are sensation and intellect, because they are the ones that enable us to comprehend and perceive the truth. But how much sensation remains, and what kind, if a person becomes deaf and blind (to say nothing of other possibilities)? And where do reason and intelligence withdraw, where do they slumber, when a person is driven mad by some disease? The insane say and do all sorts of absurd things at odds with, or rather directly contrary to, their own good intentions and character; and, when we consider this or see it with our own eyes, if we are serious about it, we can hardly hold back our tears, or perhaps cannot hold them back at all. And what shall I say about people who suffer attacks from demons? Where does their own intelligence lie hidden and buried while the malign spirit makes use of their soul and body for its own purposes? And who has any certainty that this evil cannot strike the wise man in this life? Again, what sort of perception of the truth do we have in this flesh, and how much, when, as we read in the truth-bearing Book of Wisdom, *The corruptible body weighs down the soul, and this earthly habitation presses down on the mind that thinks many things* (Wis 9:15)? And again, with regard to the drive or impulse to action (if this is the right way to designate in Latin what the Greeks call *horme*)— for they count this, too, among the primary goods of nature — is it not this very impulse that produces, when sensation is deranged and reason asleep, those pitiable motions and actions of the insane that horrify us so?

The Struggle of the Virtues against the Vices: Temperance, Prudence, and Justice

And what about virtue itself, which is not one of the primary goods of nature, since it comes in later, brought in by teaching? Even though it claims the topmost place among human goods, what is its role here in this world but to do perpetual battle against the vices — and these not external but internal, not other people's but clearly our own? This is especially true of the virtue which the Greeks call *sophrosyne* and the Latins call temperance, which reins in the desires of the flesh to keep them from gaining the consent of the mind and drawing it into every sort of degrading act.[12] For it is certainly not true that there is no vice, when, as the Apostle says, *The desires of the flesh oppose the spirit* (Gal 5:17). To this vice, however, there is an opposing virtue, when, as the same Apostle says, *The desires of the spirit oppose the flesh, for these two are opposed to each other so that you do not do what you will to do* (Gal 5:17). But what is it that we will to achieve when we will to be made perfect by the ultimate good, unless it is precisely that the desires of the flesh should not oppose the spirit and that we should not have this vice in us for the desires of the spirit to oppose? But, since we are unable to achieve this in

---

12. This begins a brief discussion of the four so-called cardinal virtues — temperance, prudence, justice and fortitude.

this present life, no matter how much we may will it, we can at least see to it, with God's help, that we do not give in to the desires of the flesh that oppose the spirit or allow the spirit to be overcome, and that we are not drawn into committing sin by our own consent. God forbid, then, that we should imagine, so long as we are caught up in this internal warfare, that we have attained the happiness we wish to reach by our victory. And who is so fully wise that he no longer has to engage in any struggle against his fleshly desires?

What of the virtue called prudence? Does it not take all the vigilance that prudence can muster to distinguish the good from the evil, so that no error creeps in as we try to pursue the one and avoid the other? Thus, prudence itself bears witness that we dwell in the midst of evils and that there are evils dwelling in us. For prudence teaches us that it is evil to consent to the desire to sin and good not to consent to the desire to sin. But neither prudence, which teaches us not to consent to evil, nor temperance, which keeps us from consenting to evil, has the effect of removing that evil from this life.

What of justice, whose function is to assign to each his due — as a result of which a certain just order is established in man himself, so that the soul is set under God, and the flesh is set under the soul, and thus both the soul and the flesh are set under God? Does not justice, in performing this very function, show that it is still laboring at its task rather than resting because its task is done? For the less the soul focuses on God in all its thinking, the less it is set under God, and the more the flesh's desires oppose the spirit, the less the flesh is set under the soul. And so, as long as we have in us this infirmity, this plague, this torpor, how can we dare to claim that we are already saved? And, if we are not saved, how can we dare to claim that we are already happy with that ultimate happiness?

Fortitude and the Question of Suicide

Then there is the virtue called fortitude. No matter how much wisdom it is coupled with, however, it bears the most evident witness to human evils, for it is precisely these evils that it is compelled to endure with patience. It is astonishing to me that the Stoic philosophers have the gall to argue that these evils are not really evils. For at the same time they admit that, if these evils become so severe that a wise man could not or should not endure them, he would be compelled to put himself to death and take leave of this life.[13] These men, who suppose that the supreme good is to be found in this life and imagine that they can attain happiness by their own efforts, are so stupefied with pride that their wise man (as they describe him in their incredible folly)— even if he goes blind, deaf, and dumb; even if he is disabled in limb and tortured with pain; even if he is stricken with every other evil that can be described or imagined, so that he is compelled to put

---

13. The issue of suicide, which is discussed here, is treated at greater length above at I,17-27.

himself to death — feels no shame in calling this life, set in the midst of these evils, a happy life.[14] What a happy life! It seeks death's help to bring about its own end! If it is really a happy life, let the wise man remain in it. How can those things not be evils when they vanquish the good of fortitude and compel that same fortitude not only to give in to them but even to become so delirious that, at one and the same time, it both calls this life happy and insists that the wise man should flee from it. Who is so blind as not to see that, if this life is happy, it is not a life one ought to flee from? But their admission that it should be fled from is an open expression of weakness. Is there any reason, then, why they should not also give up their stiff-necked pride and go on to admit that this life is actually wretched? Was it out of patience, I ask you, that Cato killed himself, or out of impatience? For he would not have done this if he had not been so impatient that he could not endure Caesar's victory.[15] Where, then, was his fortitude? It clearly gave in; it clearly succumbed; it clearly was so thoroughly defeated that it forsook, abandoned, and fled from this "happy life." Or was it no longer a happy life? In that case it was wretched. How, then, were those things not evils which made his life wretched and made it something to flee from?

Those who admitted, therefore, that these things are evils, as did the Peripatetics[16] and the Old Academy (the sect that Varro defends), speak in a more acceptable way. But even they fall into astonishing error, when they argue that in the midst of these evils — even if they are so severe that a person who suffers them is right to flee from them by self-inflicted death — this life is still happy. "The torments and agonies of the body," Varro says, "are evils; and, the worse they are, the more evil they are. To be free of them, one should flee from this life." "From which life?" I ask. "From this life," he asserts, "which is weighed down by such evils." Is it definitely happy, then — this life in the midst of the very same evils on account of which you say that we ought to flee from it? Or do you call it happy, rather, precisely because it is permissible for you to escape these evils by death? What if, by some divine judgment, you had to remain in these evils and were not permitted to die or ever allowed to exist without them? Surely in that case, at least, you would say that such a life was miserable. What keeps it from being miserable, then, is the fact that it is quickly abandoned, since, if it lasted forever, even you yourself would consider it miserable! What keeps it from being miserable, then, is the fact that, since the misery does not last long, it should apparently not count as misery — or, what is even more absurd, the fact that, since the misery does not last long, it should be called happiness!

What tremendous power there is in these evils, which compel a man — and, according to these philosophers, even a wise man — to rob himself of the very fact

---

14. See Cicero, *Tusculan Disputations* IV,4,7-38,84.
15. Cato the Younger (95-46 B.C.), after having opposed Julius Caesar both politically and militarily, committed suicide rather than live under Caesar's rule. On the events surrounding his suicide see Plutarch, *Lives*, Cato the Younger 66-70.
16. I.e., members of the school founded by Aristotle.

that he is a man! For they say, and say rightly, that the first and greatest urging of nature, so to speak, is that a man should be at one with himself and therefore should instinctively flee from death, that he should be so thoroughly a friend to himself that he vehemently wishes and desires to be alive, a living being, and to stay alive in this conjunction of body and soul.[17] What tremendous power there is in these evils, which overthrow this natural impulse, in virtue of which we use our every strength and effort to avoid death — and overthrow it so completely that what was once avoided is now chosen and desired and, if it cannot come in any other way, is inflicted on a man by the very man himself! What tremendous power there is in these evils, which make fortitude a murderer — if in fact it should still be called fortitude when it is so completely defeated by these evils that it is not only unable to safeguard, through patience, the person whom, as a virtue, it is supposed to rule and protect but is itself compelled to put him to death. It is true, of course, that the wise man ought to bear even death with patience, but the death he ought to bear with patience is death that comes from some other source. If, however, he is compelled — as these philosophers claim — to inflict death on himself, surely they must admit that the things which compel him to commit this act are not only evils but are in fact unbearable evils.

The life, therefore, which is weighed down by the burden of such great and severe evils, or is subject to the chance that such great and severe evils might afflict it, should by no means be called happy. And it would not be called happy if the people who say this, when they are defeated by sound reasoning, would just condescend to give in to the truth in their search for the happy life, just as, when they are defeated by the growing press of evils, they give in to unhappiness in their self-inflicted death. In that case they would not imagine that there is any rejoicing in the ultimate good to be had here in this mortal condition. In this condition the very virtues themselves — than which nothing better or more beneficial is found in man here on earth — attest all the more clearly to its miseries precisely because they are our best helps against its perils, hardships, and pains. In fact, if they are true virtues, which can only be present in those who have true godliness, they make no claim to be able to guard the people in whom they are present from suffering misery. What they do claim is that human life, which is compelled to be miserable by all the terrible evils of this age, is happy by reason of hope for the age to come, just as it is also saved by hope. For how can a life be happy which is not yet saved? That is why the apostle Paul — speaking not of people who had no prudence or patience or temperance or justice but rather of those who live according to true piety and whose virtues are therefore true virtues — says, *For we are saved by hope. But hope that is seen is not hope. For why would a person hope for what he already sees? But, if we hope for what we do not see, then we look forward to it with patience.* (Rom 8:24-25) Just as it is by hope that we are saved, therefore, so it is by hope that we are made happy; and, just as we do not yet possess salvation

---

17. See Cicero, *On the Ends of the Good and the Evil* III,5,16; V,9,24.

in the present but look forward to salvation in the future, so we do not yet possess happiness in the present but look forward to happiness in the future, and we do this *with patience*. For we are in the midst of evils, which we ought patiently to endure until we attain those goods where everything will afford us inexpressible delight and there will be nothing left that we have to endure. Such is the salvation which, in the world to come, will itself also be our ultimate good. But these philosophers refuse to believe in this happiness because they do not see it; and precisely for this reason they try to contrive for themselves, here in this life, an utterly false happiness based on a virtue which is as fraudulent as it is arrogant.

The Miseries of Social Life: the Household and the City

5. The philosophers also hold that the life of the wise man is social, and this is a view that we much more fully approve. For we now have in hand the nineteenth book of this work on the city of God, and how could that city either make its start or proceed on its course or reach its due end if the life of the saints were not social? But who could possibly enumerate all the grinding evils with which human society abounds here in this mortal condition? Who is adequate to weigh them all up? These people should listen to a character in one of their own comedies, who expresses what everyone thinks and agrees with: "I took a wife. What misery I found! Children were born. More cares!"[18] What about the tribulations of love, listed off by that same Terence: "Injuries, suspicions, hostilities and war, then peace again."[19] Have these tribulations not filled up human affairs everywhere we look? Do we not find them, as often as not, even in the case of honorable love between friends? Are not human affairs everywhere full of these evils? We count injuries, suspicions, hostilities and war as certain evils. But we count peace as no more than an uncertain good, for we do not know the hearts of those with whom we wish to be at peace, and, even if we could know their hearts today, we still would not know what they might be like tomorrow.[20] Again, who usually are — or ought to be — more friendly with each other than those who live in the same household? But who feels secure about this, when such terrible evils so often arise from the secret treacheries of people who live together? And the sweeter the peace that was thought to be true — when it was actually no more than a clever disguise — the more bitter these treacheries are. That is why Cicero's words touch all our hearts so deeply that they compel us to weep: "There are no more insidious treacheries than those which hide behind a pretense of friendliness or under the name of kinship. For you can easily steer clear of an open enemy, simply by being

---

18. Terence, *Adelphoi* 867-868.
19. *Eunuch* 59-61.
20. See Letter 73,3,6-10, addressed to Jerome, in which Augustine alludes poignantly to the erstwhile friendship of Jerome and Rufinus of Aquileia, shattered by a dispute over Origen, and expresses the same sentiments.

on guard, but this hidden evil, being internal and domestic, not only arises but even overwhelms you before you so much as have a chance to detect and expose it."[21] That is also why it is with such deep sadness of heart that we hear the divine saying, *And one's foes will be the members of one's own household* (Mt 10:36). For, even if someone is strong enough to bear these evils with composure or alert enough to guard against the plots of false friendship with prudence and foresight, it is still true that, if he himself is good, he cannot help but feel terrible pain at the evil of his betrayers when he discovers just how evil they are. And this is so whether they were always evil and merely pretended to be good or whether they underwent some change from goodness to their subsequent malice. And, if not even the home is safe, our common refuge amid the evils of mankind, what of the city? The larger the city, the more its forum teems with lawsuits, both civil and criminal, and this is true even when a city is not disturbed by the turbulence, or more often the bloodshed, of sedition and civil war. For cities may sometimes be free from such events, but they are never free from the risk of them.

6. What about the verdicts pronounced by men on men, which no city can do without, no matter how fully at peace it is? How miserable, how lamentable we consider them to be, such as they are! For those who judge obviously cannot see into the consciences of those whom they judge. As a result, they are often compelled to seek the truth by torturing innocent witnesses in a case that has nothing to do with them.[22] And what about torture applied to a person in his own case? The question here is whether or not he is guilty. But he is tortured even if he is innocent; and so, for a crime that is uncertain, he suffers an all too certain punishment — not because he is found to have committed the crime but because it is not known that he did not commit it. For this reason the ignorance of the judge is most often a calamity for the innocent. And what is still more intolerable — and still more to be lamented and, if only it were possible, to be washed away in a flood of tears — is the fact that, when the judge tortures the accused in order to keep from unknowingly putting an innocent person to death, it may happen that, as a result of his wretched ignorance, he puts to death, both tortured and innocent, the very person whom he had tortured in order to keep from putting an innocent person to death. For if, following the wisdom of these philosophers, the accused chooses to flee from this life rather than to endure those torments any longer, he admits that he committed a crime he did not commit. And, when he has been condemned and put to death, the judge still does not know whether it was a guilty or an innocent man that he put to death, even though the very reason he tortured him was to keep from unknowingly putting an innocent man to death. Thus, he has both tortured an innocent man in order to learn the truth and put him to death without learning it.

---

21. See *Against Verres* II,1,15.
22. While lamenting the necessity of torture in the following lines, Augustine does not denounce it as an immoral practice.

In the midst of these dark shadows of the social life, will the wise man serve as a judge or will he shrink from doing so? Clearly he will serve. The claim of human society, which he finds it unthinkable to ignore, constrains him and draws him to this duty. For he does not find it unthinkable that innocent witnesses are tortured in cases that have nothing to do with them, or that the accused are very often overcome by the force of pain and make false confessions and are punished despite their innocence. Nor does he find it unthinkable that, even if not sentenced to death, they very often die under torture or due to torture, or that those who bring charges — moved, perhaps, by the desire to benefit society by seeing to it that crimes do not go unpunished — are sometimes themselves condemned by an unknowing judge in cases where witnesses lie and the guilty man himself adamantly refuses to crack under torture and confess, so that the plaintiffs are unable to prove their charges even though the charges are true. He does not count all these grievous evils as sins, for the wise judge does not do these things from any will to inflict harm but rather from the inescapable necessity of ignorance — but also, however, because human society demands it, due to the inescapable necessity of judging. All this certainly shows, therefore, the human misery of which I am speaking, although not any malice on the part of the wise man serving as judge. But, since it is due to the inescapable necessity of ignorance and the inescapable necessity of judging that he tortures the innocent or punishes the innocent, is it not enough for him that he is not counted guilty? Must he also be counted happy? How much more perceptive it would be, how much more worthy of a human being, for him to recognize the human misery laid bare by those necessities, to detest that misery's grip on him, and, if he is devout in his wisdom, to cry out to God, *Deliver me from my necessities* (Ps 25:17)!

The Miseries of Social Life: the World

7. After the city or town comes the world, which the philosophers posit as the third level of human society. They start with the household, go from there to the city, and come finally to the world. And the world, like a confluence of waters, is the more full of dangers due to its greater size. In the first place, the diversity of languages estranges people from each other. If two people meet, neither knowing the other's language, and are compelled by some necessity to stay together rather than moving on, it is easier for dumb animals, even if of different species, to associate together than it is for these people, even though they are both human beings. For, when people cannot communicate their thoughts to each other, because of nothing more than the diversity of their languages, their likeness of nature is of so little use in bringing them together that a man would rather be with his dog than with a foreigner. It is true enough that, for the sake of social peace, the imperial city has taken pains to impose on her subjugated peoples not only her yoke but also her language, so that there is not only no lack of interpreters but even an abundant supply. But at what a cost this was achieved: all those terrible wars, all that human slaughter, all that human bloodshed!

Those wars themselves are now over, but there is still no end to the misery of their evils. For, although there was not and is not any lack of enemy foreign nations, against which wars have always been waged and are still being waged, yet the very extent of the empire has given birth to even worse kinds of wars, namely, social and civil. By these the human race is even more miserably battered, either because the wars are actually being fought for the sake of eventual peace or because people are living in fear that war may break out again. If I wanted to describe, with words worthy of the reality, these many evils, these manifold disasters, these harsh and dire necessities, even though I could not possibly measure up to the reality itself, when would my discourse ever come to an end?

But the wise man, they say, will wage just wars. Surely, however, if he remembers that he is a human being, it is far more true that he will grieve at being faced with the necessity of waging just wars. If they were not just, he would not have to wage them, and so there would be no wars for the wise man. For it is the iniquity of the opposing side that imposes on the wise man the obligation of waging just wars; and this iniquity should certainly be lamented by human beings, even if no necessity of waging war arises from it, for the very reason that it is the iniquity of human beings. Let everyone, therefore, who reflects with sorrow on such vast, such horrendous, such savage evils as these, acknowledge our misery. And, if anyone suffers such evils, or even just thinks about them, without anguish of soul, he is even more miserable, for it is only because he has lost all human feeling that he thinks himself happy.

8. In the miserable circumstances of this life it often happens that we believe an enemy is actually a friend or that a friend is actually an enemy. But, if we do not fall prey to this ignorance, akin to madness, what greater consolation do we have in this human society, riddled with errors and anxieties, than the unfeigned faith and mutual love of true and good friends? The more friends we have, however, and the more places we have them in, the more widespread is our fear that some evil may happen to them out of all the accumulated evils of this world. Not only are we anxious lest they be afflicted by famine or war or disease or captivity (fearing that in slavery they may undergo sufferings more terrible than we can imagine), but also, with a far more bitter fear, we are anxious lest their friendship turn into betrayal, malice, and villainy. And, when such a thing does happen — and the more friends we have, the more often it happens — and comes to our knowledge, who but the one who has had this experience can really know the burning pain that scorches our heart? In fact we would rather hear that our friends were dead, although we also could not hear this without grief.

For, if their life delighted us with the comforts of friendship, how could it possibly happen that their death would bring us no sadness?[23] Anyone who forbids

---

23. See Augustine's description of his own reaction to the death of a young friend, and his later regret at having been so inconsolable, in *Confessions* IV,4,7-7,12.

such sadness must forbid, if he can, all friendly conversation; he must ban or banish all mutual affection; he must with unfeeling savagery sever the bonds of all human relationships; or else he must stipulate that they are only to be used in such a way that the soul gets no pleasure from them. But, if this is utterly impossible, how could it be that the death of a person whose life was sweet to us should not be bitter to us? This is why the grief of a heart that is not inhuman is like a wound or a sore, for whose healing we offer our kind words of consolation. Nor should we think that there is no healing involved just because, the more refined a soul is, the more quickly and easily it is healed.

Thus, even though the life of mortals is pained, sometimes more gently, sometimes more harshly, by the death of those most dear to us, and especially of those whose responsibilities are essential to human society, we would still rather hear of, or even see, the death of those whom we love than hear or see that they have fallen away from faith or virtue, that is, that they have died in their very soul.

The earth is full of this vast store of evils. That is why Scripture says, *Is not human life on earth a trial?* (Job 7:1 LXX) And that is why the Lord himself says, *Woe to the world because of stumbling blocks* (Mt 18:7); and again, *Because iniquity has abounded, the love of many shall grow cold* (Mt 24:12). As a result, we feel thankful at the death of good people who are our friends, for, even though their death saddens us, it at least offers us this more certain consolation: that they have been spared the evils by which, in this life, even good persons are either crushed or corrupted or put at risk of both.

The Miseries of Social Life: the Angels and the Demons

9. Then there is the society of the holy angels.[24] The philosophers who wanted to claim that the gods are our friends placed this on a fourth level, moving up from the earth to the universe at large so as to include, in some sense or other, even heaven itself. In this case it is certainly true that we have no fear that such friends will ever sadden us by dying or by becoming depraved. The angels, however, do not mingle with us on the familiar footing that human beings do, and this in itself is one of the tribulations of this life. Furthermore, as we read, Satan sometimes transforms himself into an angel of light[25] in order to tempt those who need this sort of training or who deserve to be deceived in this way. God's great mercy is needed, therefore, to keep anyone from supposing that he has good angels as friends when he actually has evil demons as false friends, and thus to keep him from suffering harm at the hands of these enemies. For, the more sly and deceitful they are, the more harm they do. And what is it that makes God's great mercy so

---

24. See *Teaching Christianity* I,30,31-33, where Augustine asserts that angels may be understood to be neighbors, as the term is used in Mt 22:39 par.
25. See 2 Cor 11:14.

necessary if it is not the great human misery which is so encumbered with ignorance that it is easily taken in by the demons' dissembling? In fact it is absolutely certain that the philosophers of the ungodly city who claimed that the gods were their friends had actually fallen into the hands of the malign demons to whom that city is totally subject and with whom it will endure eternal punishment. For the character of the beings who are worshiped in that city is made quite clear by the sacred — or, rather, the sacrilegious — rites by which its citizens suppose that they are to be worshiped and by the obscene shows, celebrating their crimes, by which its citizens suppose that they are to be propitiated. For the demons themselves are the ones who authorized and exacted all these vile indecencies.

10. But not even holy and faithful worshipers of the one true God are safe from the deceits and the many temptations of the demons. For, in this place of infirmity and in these evil days, anxiety on this score is not without its uses; it leads them to seek with more fervent longing that state of security where peace is completely full and assured. There the gifts of nature — that is, the gifts bestowed on our nature by the creator of all natures — will be not only good but also eternal, and this will be true not only for the soul, which is healed by wisdom, but also for the body, which will be renewed by resurrection. There the virtues will not do battle against any vices or against any evils at all but will have eternal peace as the reward of victory, a peace which no adversary will ever disturb. For this is the ultimate happiness, this the final perfection, which will have no end to bring it to an end. Here on earth, it is true, we are called happy when we have peace — the little peace, that is, which it is possible to have here on earth in living a good life. But this happiness is found to be sheer misery when compared to the happiness that we call ultimate. Thus, when we mortals, if we live rightly, have such peace as it is possible for human beings to have in mortal affairs, virtue makes right use of its goods; and, when we do not have that peace, virtue makes good use even of the evils a person suffers. But virtue is true virtue only when it directs all the goods of which it makes good use, and directs all that it does in making good use of both goods and evils, and directs itself as well, to the end where our peace will be so unsurpassed that it could not possibly be better or greater.

The Meanings of Peace

11. We may say of peace, then, as we have said of eternal life, that it is our ultimate good, and we may say this most especially because of what is said to the city of God (which is the subject of this very toilsome discourse of ours) in the holy Psalm: *Praise the Lord, O Jerusalem; praise your God, O Zion. For he has strengthened the bars of your gates; he has blessed your children within you; he has made your borders peace.* (Ps 147:12-14) For, when the bars of her gates are strengthened, then no one will enter her, nor will anyone go out from her. Thus, we should understand here that her borders are that final peace which I am now trying to set forth. For, as I have also said before, this city's mystic name, Jerusalem, means "vision of peace."[26]

But, since the term "peace" is also often used in relation to merely mortal affairs, where there obviously is no eternal life, I have preferred to call the ultimate end of this city, the end where its supreme good will be found, eternal life rather than peace. Of this end the Apostle says, *But now, having been set free from sin and made servants of God, you have your fruit in sanctification, and the end is eternal life* (Rom 6:22). On the other hand, those who are not familiar with Sacred Scripture may presume that the life of the wicked is also eternal life. They may think this because, even according to some of the philosophers, the soul is immortal;[27] or they may think this because, even according to our own faith, the punishment of the ungodly is endless. After all, how could the ungodly go through torments for all eternity if they did not live for all eternity? Consequently, in order that everyone might more easily understand what we mean, we really ought to call the end of this city, in which it will gain its supreme good, either "peace in life eternal" or "eternal life in peace." For peace is such a great good that, even in earthly and mortal affairs, no other word evokes more gratitude, nothing else is desired more intensely, and, in short, nothing better can possibly be found. And, if I choose to linger on the subject a little longer, I shall not, I think, be imposing any burden on my readers, both because peace is the ultimate end of the city we are discussing and because of the very sweetness of peace itself, which is dear to all.

The Universal Desire for Peace

12. Anyone who, with me, makes even a cursory examination of human affairs and our common human nature will realize how sweet peace is. For, just as there is no one who does not wish to have joy, neither is there anyone who does not wish to have peace. In fact, even those who want war want nothing other than victory; what they desire, then, in waging war is to achieve peace with glory. What is victory, after all, but the subjugation of those fighting against us? And, when this is achieved, there will be peace. It is with the aim of peace, therefore, that wars are waged, even when they are waged by men who are eager to exercise the martial virtues in command and in battle. It is plain, then, that peace is the desired end of war. For everyone seeks peace, even in making war, but no one seeks war by making peace. Even those who want to disrupt the state of peace they currently have do not despise peace; rather, they want that peace to be changed for one they like better. What they want, therefore, is not no peace but rather the peace that

---

26. See *Exposition of Psalm* 64,2. The Hebrew does not seem to allow for this understanding, although it had some currency among both Jewish and early Christian writers. See Jerome, *Interpretation of Hebrew Names*, Galatians, s.v. Jerosolyma. "Foundation of peace" may be the most likely meaning.
27. See Plato, *Phaedrus* 245b-246a; *Meno* 81c; Plotinus, *Enneads* IV,3,5.

they wish to have. And, even if they separate themselves from others by sedition, they cannot achieve their aim unless they maintain some sort of peace with their co-conspirators and confederates. Even robbers, in order to assault the peace of others both more ferociously and more safely, want to have peace with their own comrades.

Even in the case of a single bandit, who is so powerful on his own and so cautious about going in with others that he will not ally himself with anyone at all but rather works entirely alone, lying in wait, overwhelming his victims, and taking his booty from those he has overpowered and killed, it is still true that he maintains at least a shadow of peace with those whom he cannot kill and from whom he wishes to conceal his deeds. And in his own home, surely, he takes pains to be at peace with his wife and children and other members of his household. No doubt, in fact, he takes delight in having them serve his every beck and call. For, if this does not happen, he is outraged. He rebukes and punishes, and, if necessary, he even takes harsh measures to impose on his household a peace which he believes cannot exist unless all the other members of the same domestic society are subject to one master — who, in his own home, is himself. Thus, if he were offered the servitude of a larger group — of a city, say, or of a whole people — who would serve him in the same way he wishes to be served at home, he would no longer lurk in hiding like a robber but would exalt himself like a king for all to see.[28] But exactly the same avarice and malice would still remain in him. All men desire, then, to have peace with their own subjects, whom they want to live according to their dictates. And, if they can, they even want to make those on whom they wage war their subjects and to impose on them the laws of their own peace.

But let us imagine such a creature as poetry and fable portray, a creature so anti-social and wild that people have preferred to call him not human but half-human.[29] Even though his kingdom was the solitude of an ominous cave; even though his wickedness was so singular that he was given a name reflecting this fact (for the Greek word for "evil" is *kakos*, which is what he was called); even though he had no wife with whom to exchange expressions of love, no children to play with when they were little or to govern as they grew older, and no friends with whom to enjoy conversation, not even his father Vulcan (the only respect, but not an insignificant one, in which he was happier than his father was that he did not beget any monster such as himself); and, even though he gave nothing to anyone but rather took what he wanted from everyone he could whenever he could, it is still true that in his own solitary cave ("the floor of which," as it is described, "was always warm with fresh kill"[30]), all he wanted was a peace in which no one would trouble him and no violence, or fear of violence, from any side would disturb his quiet. Beyond this, he desired to be at peace with his own body; and, so far as he

---

28. See above at IV,4 for the exchange between Alexander the Great and an anonymous pirate.
29. For the story of Cacus, who is described in the following lines, see Virgil, *Aeneid* VIII,193-279.
30. Ibid. VIII,195-196.

had this, all was well with him. His limbs obeyed his commands, and, when his mortal nature rebelled against him out of need and stirred up the sedition of hunger with its threat of separating and excluding the soul from the body, he acted with all possible speed to pacify that nature: he plundered, he killed, he devoured. Thus, for all his cruelty and savagery, he was, by these cruel and savage means, solicitous of the peace of his life and of his wellbeing. And so, if he had only been willing to have the same peace with others that he was determined to have in his cave and with himself, he would not be called evil or monstrous or half-human. Or, if it was actually his bodily appearance and his belching of black flames that scared away human companions, perhaps it was not the desire to do harm that made him so savage but rather the need to preserve his own life. But perhaps he never existed at all or, more probably, was not anything like what poetic fantasy describes. For, if Cacus had not been painted so black, Hercules would have gotten too little praise.[31] As in the case of many figments of the poets' imagination, then, we should give no credence to the existence of such a man or, better, such a half-man.

For even the most savage wild animals, from whom Cacus drew a part of his wildness (for he was also called half-wild[32]), preserve their own kind by a sort of peace: they mate, they reproduce, they give birth, they nurse and nourish their young. And this is true even when, as in most cases, they are antisocial and solitary — that is, like lions, wolves, foxes, eagles, and owls, rather than like sheep, deer, doves, starlings, or bees.[33] For what tigress does not purr softly over her young and caress them with her ferocity kept at peace? What kite, no matter how solitary in hovering over its prey, does not couple with its mate, build a nest, keep the eggs warm, feed the chicks, and maintain with the mother of the family, as it were, as peaceful a domestic society as he can? How much the more, then, is a human being drawn by the laws of his nature, so to speak, to be social and to maintain peace with all human beings, so far as it lies in his power? Even the wicked wage war to ensure the peace of their own people and would want, if they could, to make all men their own, so that all men and all things might serve one master. But how could this happen unless they all consented to that master's peace, either out of love or out of fear?

And so pride is a perverse imitation of God. For it hates a society of equals under God and instead wishes to impose its own domination on its fellows in place of God's rule. Therefore, it hates the just peace of God and loves its own unjust peace. But it is quite impossible for it not to love some kind of peace. No one's vice is so completely contrary to nature that it destroys even the last vestiges of nature.

Thus, anyone who knows enough to prefer right to wrong and the well-ordered to the perverse sees that, in comparison to the peace of the just, the peace of the

---

31. I.e., for slaying him. See ibid. VIII,247-279.
32. See ibid VIII,267.
33. The same distinction between solitary and social animals is made above at XII,22.

unjust ought not to be called peace at all.[34] But even what is perverted must of necessity be at peace in or from or with some part of the order of things in which it exists or of which it consists. Otherwise it would not exist at all. If someone hangs upside down, for example, the position of his body and the arrangement of his limbs are certainly perverted. What nature requires to be above is actually below, and what nature intends to be below is actually above. This perversity disturbs the peace of the flesh and therefore puts it under stress. But, even so, the soul is at peace with its body and is concerned for its wellbeing, and that is why the person feels pain. But, even if the soul is driven out of the body by its distress and leaves the body behind, what is left is still not without a kind of peace among its parts, so long as the structure of the limbs remains, and that is why there is still someone hanging there. And, because the earthly body pulls down toward the earth and pulls against the chain that holds it up, it tends toward the position of its own peace, and, by the voice of its own weight, so to speak, it begs for a place where it may find rest. Even now, then, when it is lifeless and wholly without sensation, it does not depart from the peace that is natural to its ordered place, either when it holds to or when it tends toward that peace. For if treatments and preservatives are applied, which keep the corpse's form from disintegrating and dissolving, a kind of peace still joins one part to another and holds the whole mass in its earthly place, its fitting place, and therefore its place of peace.[35]

But, if no preservative treatment is applied and the body is simply left to nature's course, there is for a while a kind of tumult of exhalations that are disagreeable and offensive to our senses (for it is this that we smell in cases of such decay). This lasts until the body merges with the elements of the world and, little by little, particle by particle, is dispersed into their peace. In this process, however, nothing whatsoever falls outside the laws of the supreme creator and ruler by whom the peace of the universe is arranged and directed. For, even if tiny animals are born in the carcass of a larger animal, all those little bodies, by the same law of the creator, serve their little souls in the peace of their wellbeing; and even if the flesh of dead animals is devoured by other animals — no matter where it is taken, no matter what it is mixed with, no matter what it is transformed and changed into — it still finds itself under the same laws, which are spread out through all things for the wellbeing of each mortal species, matching, in peace, what is suitable with what is suitable.

---

34. At this point, and continuing on to section 20, the discussion of peace gradually develops into a discussion of order as well, which had been debated at length at the beginning of Augustine's career in *Order*, especially at I,3,6-8; II,4,11-5,14.
35. See *Confessions* XIII,9,10 for a meditation on place and peace.

Peace and Order

13. The peace of the body is, then, the properly ordered arrangement of its parts; the peace of the irrational soul is the properly ordered satisfaction of the appetites; the peace of the rational soul is the properly ordered accord of cognition and action; the peace of body and soul together is the properly ordered life and wellbeing of a living creature; peace between mortal man and God is properly ordered obedience, in faith, under eternal law; peace among men is the properly ordered concord of mind with mind; the peace of a household is the properly ordered concord, with respect to command and obedience, of those who are living together; the peace of a city is the properly ordered concord, with respect to command and obedience, of its citizens; the peace of the heavenly city is perfectly ordered and wholly concordant fellowship in the enjoyment of God and of each other in God. The peace of all things is the tranquility of order,[36] and order is the arrangement of things equal and unequal that assigns to each its due place.

Therefore, the wretched — since, insofar as they are wretched, they are certainly not at peace — lack the tranquility of order, which is free of all disturbance. Even in their very wretchedness, however, they do not and cannot fall outside the reach of order, for their wretchedness itself is just and deserved. They are obviously not united with the blessed, but it is precisely by the law of order that they are set apart from them. And, when they are free of disturbance, they are adapted to their circumstances with at least some degree of suitability, and, as a result, there is in them at least something of the tranquility of order, and therefore at least something of peace. But they are still wretched simply because, although they are to some degree free of care and pain, they are not in the place where they ought to be wholly without care or pain. And they would be still more wretched if there were no peace at all between them and the law by which the natural order is directed. For, when they are in pain, their peace is disturbed because of the part in which they feel pain, but there is still peace in the part in which no pain burns and the bodily structure itself is not dissolved. Just as there can be life without pain, therefore, but no pain without at least some degree of life, so there can be peace without war but no war without at least some degree of peace. This is due not to the nature of war itself but to the fact that it is waged by or within persons who are in some sense natural beings, for they would not exist at all if they did not subsist by virtue of some sort of peace.

There is, then, a nature in which there is no evil and in which in fact it is impossible for evil to exist, but it is not possible for there to be a nature in which there is no good. Not even the nature of the devil himself is evil, insofar as it is a

---

36. This thumbnail definition of peace as the tranquility of order has achieved classic status. See, e.g., Thomas Aquinas, *Summa Theologiae* II-II, q. 29, a. 1.

nature.[37] It is perversity that makes it evil. Thus, he did not stand in the truth,[38] but he did not escape the judgment of the truth. He did not remain in the tranquility of order, but even so he did not evade the power of the orderer. The goodness of God, which is his with respect to his nature, does not remove him from the justice of God, by which he is ordained for punishment. Nor does God punish the good which he created but rather the evil which the devil committed. For God does not take away all that he gave to that nature. Rather, he removes something and, at the same time, he leaves something, so that there is something left to feel pain over what is taken away. And this very pain attests both to the good that was taken away and to the good that was left, for, if no good had been left, there could be no pain over the good that was lost. A person who sins is even worse if he rejoices in the loss of righteousness; but a person in torment, even if he gains no good from it, at least feels pain at the loss of salvation. And since both righteousness and salvation are good, and since we ought to feel pain rather than joy at the loss of any good (as long as there is no greater good compensating for the loss, as, for instance, righteousness of soul is a greater good than health of body), it is obviously more fitting for the unjust to feel pain in punishment than to feel joy in sin. Thus, just as feeling joy in sin due to the good that one has forsaken is evidence of an evil will, so feeling pain in punishment due to the good that one has lost is evidence of a good nature. For anyone who feels pain at the lost peace of his nature feels this due to some remnant of that peace by virtue of which his nature still shows its care for itself. In the final punishment, then, it is right that, in their torments, the wicked and the ungodly should lament the loss of their natural goods, knowing that those goods were taken from them by the supremely just God, whom they despised when he was their supremely generous benefactor.

God is, therefore, the supremely wise creator and the supremely just orderer of all natures. He established the mortal human race as earth's highest ornament, and he bestowed on human beings certain goods suited to this life, namely, a temporal peace appropriate to the brief measure of a mortal life, consisting in bodily health and soundness, and the society of one's own kind, as well as whatever is necessary to maintain or recover this peace (such as those things which are readily and conveniently on hand for our senses — light, speech, air to breathe, water to drink — and whatever is suited to feeding, clothing, healing, and adorning the body). He did this, however, on the wholly just condition that any mortal who makes right use of such goods, which are meant to serve the peace of mortals, will receive fuller and better goods, namely, the peace of immortality and the glory and honor appropriate to it, in an eternal life meant for the enjoyment of God and of one's neighbor in God, but that anyone who uses them wrongly will not receive these eternal goods and in fact will lose those temporal goods.

---

37. See the more extended discussion on the devil above at XI,13-15.
38. See Jn 8:44.

Earthly Peace and Eternal Peace

14. In the earthly city, then, all use of temporal things is directed to the enjoyment of earthly peace; in the heavenly city, in contrast, it is directed to the enjoyment of eternal peace. Thus, if we were no more than irrational animals, we would seek nothing more than the properly ordered arrangement of the body's parts and the satisfaction of the appetites, that is, nothing more than the comfort of the body and a good supply of pleasures, so that the peace of the body might promote the peace of the soul. For, if the peace of the body is lacking, the peace of the irrational soul is also impeded, because it cannot achieve the satisfaction of its appetites. Together, however, these two kinds of peace promote the peace which the soul and the body have with each other, that is, the peace of properly ordered life and wellbeing. For, just as animals show their love for the body's peace by fleeing pain and their love for the soul's peace by pursuing pleasure in order to meet the demands of their appetites, so they indicate clearly enough, by fleeing death, how much they love the peace by which soul and body are harmoniously united with each other.

But, because man has a rational soul, he subordinates everything that he has in common with the beasts to the peace of the rational soul, and this is so that he may picture something with the mind and act in accord with what he has pictured so as to bring about that properly ordered accord of cognition and action which we have called the peace of the rational soul. And for this reason he should will to be neither distressed by pain nor disturbed by desire nor dissolved by death, so that he may arrive at some useful knowledge and may shape his life and moral character in accord with that knowledge. But because, in his very eagerness for knowledge, he may fall into some deadly error due to the weakness of the human mind, he has need of divine guidance, which he may obey with certainty, and divine help, so that he may obey it freely. And further, so long as he is in this mortal body, he is on pilgrimage far from God, and he walks by faith, not by sight.[39] That is why he directs all these forms of peace, whether of the body or of the soul or of both together, to the peace which mortal man has with the immortal God, so that he may have a properly ordered obedience, in faith, under eternal law.

Now, since God, our teacher, teaches two chief precepts, love of God and love of neighbor,[40] in which man finds three things to love — God, himself, and his neighbor; and since one who loves God does not go wrong in loving himself, it follows that he also wants his neighbor to love God, since he is commanded to love his neighbor as himself.[41] And so he wants this for his wife, for his children, for his entire household, and for anyone else he can, and he wants his neighbor to

---

39. See 2 Cor 5:6-7.
40. See Mt 22:36-40 par.
41. Ideas similar to those expressed in the following lines are developed more fully in *Teaching Christianity* I,22,20-29,30.

have the same concern for him, if he happens to be in need of it. As a result, he will be at peace with all men, so far as it is in his power, with that peace among men which is the properly ordered concord of man with man; and this concord's order is, first, to harm no one and, second, to help anyone that one can. First of all, then, his care will be for his own people, for, by the order of nature or of human society itself, he obviously has a readier and more immediate opportunity to care for them.[42] That is why the Apostle says, *Anyone who does not provide for his own, and especially for the members of his household, has denied the faith and is worse than an unbeliever* (1 Tm 5:8). It is here, therefore, that domestic peace takes its rise, that is, the properly ordered concord, with respect to command and obedience, of those who are living together. For it is those who exercise care that give the commands, as husbands to wives, parents to children, and masters to servants, and it is those who are cared for that obey, as wives their husbands, children their parents, and servants their masters. In the household of the just person who lives by faith[43] and is still on pilgrimage far from the heavenly city, however, even those who give commands are at the service of those whom they appear to command.[44] For they do not give their commands out of any desire for domination but rather out of dutiful concern for others, not out of any pride in ruling but rather out of compassion in providing for others.

Sin and Slavery

15. This is what the order of nature prescribes; this is the way God created man. For he said, *Let him have dominion over the fish of the sea and the birds of the air and every creeping thing that creeps on the earth* (Gn 1:26). He did not want a rational creature, made in his own image,[45] to have dominion except over irrational creatures — not man over man but man over beasts. That is why the first righteous men were established as shepherds of flocks rather than as kings of men,[46] so that in this way, too, God might indicate what the order of created beings requires and what the fault of sinners demands. For we recognize it is on sinners that the condition of slavery is justly imposed.[47] That is why we do not read of any slave in Scripture until the just man Noah[48] punished his son's sin with

---

42. On the proper order of caring for others see ibid. I,28,29.
43. See Rom 1:17.
44. See Mt 20:25-26 par. Augustine touches on this theme with respect to the relationship between bishops and their flocks in Sermons 340,1; 340A,1-3.
45. See Gn 1:26.
46. See Gn 4:2.
47. As becomes clearer from what follows, Augustine does not intend to say that a particular slave's sinfulness is responsible for the fact that he is enslaved but rather that the very existence of slavery is the result of human sinfulness in general. As with his discussion of torture above at XIX,6, Augustine regrets the existence of slavery but does not denounce it.
48. See Gn 6:9.

this designation.[49] His son deserved the name, then, not by nature but by fault. In Latin, the origin of the word for "slaves" is believed to stem from the fact that those who might have been killed under the laws of war were instead sometimes preserved by the victors and became slaves; thus they were called slaves due to the fact that they were preserved.[50] But even this does not hold good apart from the just deserts of sin. For, even when a just war is waged, the opposing side is fighting in defense of its sin; and every victory, even when it goes to the wicked, is a humiliation imposed on the vanquished by divine judgment either to correct or to punish their sins. Daniel, a man of God, is a witness on this score: when he was taken captive, he confessed his own sins and the sins of his people to God, and in devout sorrow he testified that this was the cause of his captivity.[51] The first cause of slavery, therefore, is sin, with the result that man is made subject to man by the bondage of this condition, which can only happen by the judgment of God, in whom there is no unrighteousness and who knows how to assign different punishments according to the merits of the offenders. As the Lord on high says, *Everyone who commits sin is a slave of sin* (Jn 8:34). Thus, although there are many godly men who are the slaves of unrighteous masters, this does not mean that the masters they serve are themselves free men, *for a person is a slave to whatever masters him* (2 Pt 2:19). Clearly it is a happier lot to be enslaved to a man than to be enslaved to lust; in fact it is the very lust for domination itself, to mention no others, that ravages the hearts of mortals by exercising the most savage kind of domination over them. And, within that order of peace by which some men are subject to others, while humility is beneficial to those who serve, pride is harmful to those who rule.

By nature, then, as God first created man, no one is a slave either to man or to sin. But it is also true that the punishment of slavery is ordained by precisely the same law which commands that the natural order is to be preserved and forbids it to be disturbed, for, if nothing had been done in violation of that law, there would be nothing for the punishment of slavery to keep under constraint. It is for this reason that the Apostle admonishes slaves to be subject to their masters and to serve them from the heart with a good will,[52] so that, if they cannot be freed by their masters, they can at least make their own slavery free in a sense, that is, by serving their masters not with cunning fear but with faithful love, until all unrighteousness passes away, all human rule and power are brought down,[53] and God is all in all.[54]

---

49. See Gn 9:25-26, where Canaan, the son of Ham, is called a slave.
50. "Slaves...preserved": *servi...servando*. Augustine's etymology is incorrect.
51. See Dn 9:3-19.
52. See Eph 6:5-8; Col 3:22-24; Tit 2:9-10.
53. See 1 Cor 15:24.
54. See 1 Cor 15:28.

16. Thus, even though our righteous fathers had slaves, and even though they managed their domestic peace in such a way as to distinguish between the status of their children and the condition of their slaves with regard to temporal goods, they still showed equal affection in their care for all the members of their household with regard to the worship of God,[55] in whom we are to place our hope for eternal goods. This is what the order of nature prescribes, with the result that this is the origin of the name *paterfamilias*,[56] which is now so widely and commonly used that even those who rule unjustly delight to be called by the name.[57] But the true fathers of their families are those who are just as much concerned for all in their households as they are for their children when it comes to worshiping God and living worthily of him. They desire and pray that they will all come to the heavenly home where the duty of commanding mortals will no longer be necessary, because the duty of caring for others will no longer be needed when they have all attained the happiness of that immortality. Until that home is reached, however, fathers have a greater obligation to put up with being masters than slaves do to put up with being slaves.

If anyone in the household disrupts domestic peace by his disobedience, he is corrected by word or blow or some other just and legitimate kind of punishment, to the extent that human society allows. This is, however, for the benefit of the person corrected, and its aim is that he may be brought back into line with the peace from which he had broken away. For, just as there is nothing kind about helping a person if it causes him to lose a greater good, neither is there anything blameless about sparing a person if it allows him to fall into graver evil. To be blameless, then, we are obliged not only to do no evil to a person but also to restrain him from sin or to punish his sin, either so that the one who is punished may be corrected by his experience or so that others may be deterred by his example.

Since, therefore, a man's household ought to be the beginning, or a small part, of the city, and since every beginning is directed to some end appropriate to its own kind, and since every part is directed to the integrity of the whole of which it is a part, it seems to follow clearly enough that domestic peace is directed to civic peace; that is, the properly ordered concord, with respect to command and obedience, of those who are living together is directed to the properly ordered concord, with respect to command and obedience, of citizens. So it is that the father of a family should draw his precepts from the law of the city, and he should so rule his household by those precepts that it is fully in accord with the peace of the city.

---

55. See, e.g., Ex 12:44.
56. I.e., "father of the family" or "head of the household." *Familia*, often translated as "family," had a broader connotation in Roman society than it does today and could include all the members of a household.
57. See Seneca, Letter 47,14.

Earthly Peace and the Two Cities

17. But a household of people who do not live by faith pursues an earthly peace based on the goods and advantages of this temporal life. In contrast, a household of people who live by faith looks to the eternal goods which are promised for the future. It makes use of earthly and temporal things like a pilgrim. It is not captivated by them, nor is it deflected by them from the path that leads toward God, but it is sustained by them so that it may more easily bear the burdens of the corruptible body that weighs down the soul[58] and may at least keep those burdens from getting any worse. Thus, use of the things necessary to this mortal life is common to both kinds of people and to both kinds of household, but each uses them for its own very different end.

So also the earthly city, which does not live by faith, seeks an earthly peace, and it establishes a concord of command and obedience among its citizens in order to bring about a kind of accommodation among human wills with regard to the things that pertain to this mortal life. And the heavenly city — or, rather, that part of it which is on pilgrimage in this mortal existence and which lives by faith — must of necessity make use of this peace as well, at least until this mortal existence, for which such peace is necessary, passes away. Consequently, for as long as it leads its pilgrim life as a captive, so to speak, in the earthly city, even though it has already received the promise of redemption and the gift of the Spirit as a pledge of that redemption, it does not hesitate to obey the laws of the earthly city, by which the things needed for sustaining this mortal life are administered. For, since this mortal existence is common to both cities, its obedience serves to maintain a concord between the two with regard to the things that pertain to our mortal life.

But the earthly city has included among its members certain wise men whose views the divine teaching rejects, and these thinkers, due either to their own surmise or to demonic deception, believed that there are many gods whose favor must be gained in human affairs and that various matters fall under the various areas of responsibility that these gods are presumed to have. Thus, the body falls to one god, the mind to another; and, within the body itself, the head falls to one god, the neck to another, and each of the other parts to other gods. Similarly, within the mind, native intelligence falls to one god, learning to another, anger to another, and desire to another. And so on with regard to all the things that bear on our lives: livestock fall to one god, grain falls to another, wine to another, oil to another, woods to another, money to another, navigation to another, wars and victories to another, marriage to another, birth and fertility to another, and so on and so forth.[59] In contrast, the heavenly city knew that the one God is alone to be

---

58. See Wis 9:15.
59. See Book VII passim.

worshiped, and it insisted with faithful devotion that only this God is to be served with the service which in Greek is called *latreia* and which is due only to God.

As a result of this difference, it has been impossible for the heavenly city to have laws of religion in common with the earthly city. Instead, it has of necessity had to dissent from the earthly city at this point and to become an annoyance to those who think differently. As a result it has had to endure their wrath, their hatred, and the assaults of their persecutions, except when it turned back the minds of its foes, sometimes due to their fear of its sheer numbers and always due to God's aid.

So long as this heavenly city is a pilgrim on earth, then, it calls forth citizens from all peoples and gathers together a pilgrim society of all languages. It cares nothing about any differences in the manners, laws, and institutions by which earthly peace is achieved or maintained. But it does not rescind or abolish any of these; rather, it preserves and follows them, provided only that they do not interfere with the religion which teaches that we are to worship the one supreme and true God,[60] for, however different they may be in different nations, they all aim at one and the same thing — earthly peace. Thus, even the heavenly city makes use of earthly peace during its pilgrimage, and, so far as sound piety and religion allow, it defends and seeks an accommodation among human wills with regard to the things that pertain to humanity's mortal nature. At the same time, however, it directs this earthly peace toward the heavenly peace which is so truly peace that, strictly speaking, it alone is to be considered and called the peace of the rational creature, namely, a perfectly ordered and wholly concordant fellowship in the enjoyment of God and of each other in God. When we reach this peace, our life will not be mortal but rather fully and definitely alive, and our body will not be the animal body which, so long as it is corrupted, weighs down the soul,[61] but rather the spiritual body, in need of nothing and wholly subject to the will. So long as the heavenly city is on pilgrimage, it has this peace in faith, and by this faith it lives justly when it directs toward the attainment of this peace every good act it performs for God and — since the life of a city is most certainly social — for neighbor.

The Issues of Certainty and Style of Life

18. As for the distinction which Varro ascribes to the New Academy, that all things are uncertain,[62] the city of God abhors such doubt as madness. With regard to things it apprehends by mind and reason, it has fully certain knowledge, even

---

60. For the same thought see above at XIV,1. This toleration of — or indifference to — diversity in secular matters is consonant with Augustine's attitude toward certain ecclesiastical customs, provided only that the divine law be obeyed. See Letter 54,2,2-7,10.
61. See Wis 9:15.
62. See above at XIX,1.

though that knowledge is circumscribed due to the corruptible body which weighs down the soul,[63] for, as the Apostle says, *We know in part* (1 Cor 13:9). In every case, too, it trusts the evidence of the senses, which the mind uses by means of the body, for anyone who thinks that the senses are never to be trusted is miserably mistaken. It also believes in the Holy Scriptures, both Old and New, which we call canonical, from which comes the very faith by which the just person lives[64] and by which we walk — without doubting — as long as we are on pilgrimage and away from the Lord.[65] As long as this faith is sound and certain, however, we may, without ground for reproach, have doubts about certain things which we have not perceived by sense or reason, which have not been made clear to us through canonical Scripture and which have not come to our knowledge through witnesses whom it would be absurd not to believe.

19. It makes no difference to the heavenly city what mode of dress or manner of life is adopted by one who follows the faith that leads to God, just so long as it is not contrary to the divine precepts. Consequently it does not compel those philosophers of theirs, when they become Christian, to change either their dress or their customary diet; it only compels them to change their false doctrines. Thus, it does not care at all about the distinction which Varro drew from the Cynics,[66] provided that it involves nothing indecent or intemperate. As for the three kinds of life — the leisured, the active, and the combination of both — it is true that anyone, so long as his faith is sound, can lead his life and attain to eternal rewards in any one of them. It does matter, however, what he holds back in his love of truth and what he pays out in the duty of charity. No one ought to be so completely at leisure that in his leisure he takes no thought for serving his neighbor, nor should anyone be so fully active that he makes no room for the contemplation of God. In the leisured life it is not inert idleness that ought to delight but rather the seeking or the finding of truth, so that each makes progress in this respect and no one jealously keeps from others what he finds. And in the active life it is not honor or power in this life that ought to be prized, since everything under the sun is vanity;[67] instead, what ought to be prized is the task accomplished by means of that honor and power, just so long as the task is accomplished rightly and helpfully, so that it truly contributes to the wellbeing of those set under us. This is what accords with God, as we have discussed above, and it is for this reason that the Apostle says, *Anyone who desires the episcopate desires a good work* (1 Tm 3:1). He wanted to explain what *episcopate* means, for it is the name of a task, not an honor. It is a Greek word, and it derives from the fact that a person who is set over others superintends them, that is, bears the responsibility of caring for them. For *skopos* means "intention," and

---

63. See Wis 9:15.
64. See Rom 1:17.
65. See 2 Cor 5:6.
66. See above at XIX,1.
67. See Qo 1:14.

so, if we wish, we may translate *episkopein* into Latin as "superintend." Thus, a person who loves being preeminent rather than helpful should understand that he is no bishop. No one, therefore, is barred from eagerness to know the truth, which is what makes the leisured life praiseworthy. But it is not seemly to seek out a high position, without which no people can be governed, even if that position is held and administered in a seemly fashion.

It is the love of truth, then, that seeks holy leisure, and it is the drive of love that takes on righteous activity. If no one imposes that burden on us, we ought to devote our free time to discerning and contemplating the truth, but, if that burden is imposed on us, we must accept it due to the drive of love. Even then, however, delight in the truth should by no means be abandoned, lest its pleasure be taken from us and that drive leave us swamped.

20. The supreme good of the city of God is, then, eternal and perfect peace, not the peace through which mortal men pass on their way from birth to death but rather the peace in which they remain as immortals and no longer suffer any adversity at all. Who, therefore, would deny that this is the supremely blessed life? Or who would not judge that, in comparison with it, the life which we lead here on earth, no matter how filled it may be with the goods of soul and body and external things, is utterly miserable? Nevertheless, if anyone uses this life in such a way that he directs it to that other life as the end which he loves with ardent intensity and for which he hopes with unwavering faithfulness, it is not absurd to call him happy even now, although happy in that hope rather than in this reality.[68] Without that hope, in fact, this reality is only a false happiness and a great misery. For it does not make use of the true goods of the soul, because no wisdom is true wisdom if it does not direct its intention — in everything that it discerns with prudence, bears with fortitude, constrains with temperance, and distributes with justice — to the end where God will be all in all[69] in assured eternity and perfect peace.

The Definition of a Republic

21. Here, then, is the place for me to fulfill, as briefly and as clearly as I can, the promise I made in the second book of this work.[70] There I promised to show, according to the definitions Scipio uses in Cicero's book, *The Republic*, that there never was a Roman republic. For, in brief, he defines a republic as "the common good of a people."[71] But, if this definition is true, there never was a Roman republic, because it never was "the common good of a people," which is the definition Scipio wanted to use for a republic. For he defined "a people" as "a multitude joined

---

68. "Hope...reality": *spe...re.*
69. See 1 Cor 15:28.
70. See above at II,21.
71. *Republic* I,39.

together by a common sense for what is right and a community of interest."[72] And in the course of the discussion he explains what he means by "a common sense for what is right," showing on this basis that a republic cannot be maintained without justice. Thus, where there is no true justice there can be no right. For what is done rightly is obviously done justly, while what is not done justly cannot possibly be done rightly. Thus, unjust human institutions should neither be called nor be considered right, for even the philosophers say that right is what flows from the fount of justice,[73] and they insist that it is false to say, as some wrongheaded thinkers do, that right is in fact the interest of the stronger.[74]

Where there is no true justice, then, there can be no gathering of persons "joined together by a common sense for what is right," and therefore there can be no people according to the definition used by Scipio and Cicero. And, if there is no people, there is no "common good of a people" but only of a multitude of some sort that is not worthy of the name "people." Thus, if a republic is "the common good of a people," and if a group which is not "joined together by a common sense for what is right" is not a people, and if there is no right where there is no justice, it follows beyond any doubt that where there is no justice there is no republic. Furthermore, justice is the virtue which gives to each his due. What sort of justice is it, then, that takes a person away from the true God and gives him over to demons? Is this to count as giving to each his due? Are we going to call a person unjust if he takes a piece of property away from the one who bought it and gives it to someone else who has no legal claim to it, but call a person just if he takes himself away from the Lord God who made him and instead serves evil spirits?

Now, in that same work, *The Republic*, an exceedingly strong and forceful argument is put forth on behalf of justice and against injustice. But first an argument was mounted on the side of injustice against justice, and the claim was made that without injustice it is impossible for a republic to stand and to be governed. It was taken as the strongest point in this argument that it is unjust for men to serve other men who hold dominion over them, but, unless an imperial city, the head of a great republic, takes up precisely this injustice, it cannot rule its provinces. But the response on the side of justice was that in fact this is just, because servitude is in the interest of such people; and, when it is established in the right way, it is established in their interest, that is, when its establishment takes the freedom to do harm away from the wicked. In that case, the subjugated people will be better off precisely because they were worse off before they were subjugated. And here a notable example was brought in, as if drawn from nature, to confirm this reasoning: "Why is it that God rules man, the soul rules the body, and reason rules the sensual desires and the other vice-ridden parts of the soul?"[75] By this example it

---

72. Ibid.
73. "Right...justice": *ius...iustitiae*.
74. See Plato, *Republic* 338c.
75. Cited also in *Answer to Julian* IV,12,61, where Augustine says that the quotation is taken from

was shown plainly enough that servitude is beneficial for some, and that in fact serving God is beneficial to all.

For, when it serves God, the soul rules the body rightly, and in the soul itself the reason that is subject to God as Lord rightly rules sensual desire and the other vices. When a person does not serve God, then, what justice are we to think there is in him? For, when the soul does not serve God, it can by no means rule the body justly, nor can reason rule the vices justly. And, if there is no justice in such a person, it is beyond doubt that there is no justice in a human gathering that is made up of such persons. Here, then, there is nothing of that "common sense for what is right" which makes a human multitude into a people, whose common good is called a republic. And what shall I say about that "community of interest" by virtue of which, according to this same definition, a human gathering is also called a people? If you look closely, in fact, you will see that nothing is in the interest of those who live impiously, as do all those who do not serve God but rather serve demons, who are all the more ungodly in that they want sacrifices made to them as gods, when in fact they are nothing but unclean spirits. But I think that what we have already said about a "common sense for what is right" is enough to make it clear that, by this definition, no people in which there is no justice may properly be called a republic.[76]

Justice and the True God: against Porphyry

And, if they claim that it was not unclean spirits that the Romans served in their republic but good and holy gods, must we repeat all over again the very same things we have already said so often, so very often? For how could anyone, after reading the earlier books of this work up to this point, still doubt that the Romans served evil and impure demons, unless, of course, he is just exceedingly stupid or obnoxiously argumentative? But, to say nothing of the kind of gods the Romans worshiped with their sacrifices, it is written in the law of the true God, *Whoever sacrifices to any gods but to the Lord alone shall be destroyed* (Ex 22:20). It is quite clear, then, that the one who gave this command, and backed it with such a dire threat, did not want us to sacrifice to any gods at all, whether good or evil.

22. Now, it could be said in reply, "Who is this God, and how is he shown worthy to be the one whom the Romans ought to have obeyed, worshiping no other god but him with their sacrifices?" But anyone still asking who this God is must be utterly blind! He is the very God whose prophets foretold the things that we now see with our own eyes. He is the very God from whom Abraham received

---

the third book of *The Republic*; the passage is known only from Augustine's citation.
76. At this point Augustine interrupts his discussion on the nature of a republic with a lengthy digression on the true God and Porphyry's understanding of him. The discussion is resumed below at XIX,24.

the answer, *In your seed all peoples shall be blessed* (Gn 22:18). And this is exactly what took place in Christ, who sprang from Abraham's seed according to the flesh. Even those who have remained hostile to his name acknowledge this, whether they like it or not. He is the very God whose divine Spirit spoke through the men whose prophecies, fulfilled in the Church that we now see spread through the whole world, I cited in the preceding books.[77] He is the very God who Varro, the most learned of the Romans, thought was Jupiter, although he did not know what he was saying.[78] I still thought it worth noting, however, that a man of such learning found that he could neither consider this God non-existent nor reduce him to insignificance but rather believed him to be the same as the supreme god. Finally, he is the very God who Porphyry, the most learned of the philosophers,[79] although the most bitter enemy of the Christians, acknowledges is a great god, even according to the oracles of those he takes to be gods.[80]

23. In the book that he calls *Philosophy from Oracles*,[81] in which he collects and compiles supposedly divine oracular responses on matters related to philosophy, Porphyry says (to use his own words, although translated from Greek into Latin), "To someone who inquired what god he should appease in order to recall his wife from Christianity, Apollo[82] gave this response in verse." Then come these words, as if from Apollo himself: "You would be more able, perhaps, to inscribe letters on water or to spread light wings and fly through the air like a bird than to recall a defiled and ungodly wife to her senses. Let her go on as she likes, persevering in her empty delusions and singing laments for a god who died in his own delusions, condemned by right-thinking judges and executed in full public view by the worst sort of ironbound death." Then, following these verses from Apollo (here translated into Latin prose), Porphyry goes on to say, "In these verses Apollo made it clear that the views of the Christians are incurable, saying that the Jews uphold God better than they do." See how, in demeaning Christ, he gives preference to the Jews over the Christians, asserting that it is the Jews who uphold God. For he explains the verses of Apollo, where the god says that Christ was killed by right-thinking judges, as if Christ actually deserved to be punished and as if those judges actually were just in their judgment. But as to what Apollo's lying seer said about Christ and Porphyry believed, or perhaps what the seer did not really say but Porphyry himself simply invented, that is their business. We

---

77. See above at Books XV-XVIII.
78. For Augustine's summary of Varro's view of God (although Jupiter is not mentioned) see above at IV,31.
79. Porphyry (234-c. 305) was one of the greatest Neoplatonic philosophers and a notable adversary of the Christian religion. He is cited at length above at X,9-32.
80. See *On Abstinence from Eating Animals* II,37.
81. The work has not survived in its entirety but exists in fragments, many of them in *The City of God*. It may be identical with Porphyry's *On the Return of the Soul*. See John J. O'Meara, *Porphyry's Philosophy from Oracles in Augustine* (Paris: Etudes Augustiniennes, 1959).
82. Apollo was the god who uttered oracles at Delphi in Greece.

shall see shortly, however, how consistent Porphyry is with himself or, rather, how consistent he makes those oracles of his with each other.

Here, at any rate, he says that the Jews, as upholders of God, judged rightly in determining that Christ should be tortured by the worst kind of death. Porphyry himself, therefore, bears witness to the God of the Jews, and so Porphyry should have listened when he said, *Whoever sacrifices to any god but to the Lord alone shall be destroyed*. But let us come to more obvious matters; let us hear how great Porphyry says the God of the Jews is. For example, when he asked Apollo which is better, word (that is, reason) or law, he says that Apollo "gave this response in verse." And then he adds Apollo's verses, from which I have selected these as sufficient for our purposes: "In God, the begetter, and the king before all things, before whom tremble heaven and earth, and the sea and the hidden places of the underworld, and from whom the very divinities themselves shrink in dread, whose law is the Father, whom the holy Hebrews greatly honor." In this oracle from his own god Apollo, Porphyry says that the God of the Hebrews is so great that the very divinities themselves shrink from him in dread. And, since it is this very God who said, *Whoever sacrifices to any gods but to the Lord alone shall be destroyed*, I am surprised that Porphyry himself did not shrink from him in dread and was not terrified of being destroyed for sacrificing to other gods.

But this philosopher also has some good things to say about Christ. It is as if he had forgotten that insult of his which we just mentioned, or as if his gods had said nasty things about Christ in their sleep but when awake recognized that he was good and gave him the praise he deserved. For Porphyry says, as if about to announce something marvelous and incredible, "What we are about to say will certainly seem beyond belief to some. For the gods have declared that Christ was most pious and has been made immortal, and that they think of him with favor; but the Christians, they say, are defiled and polluted and entangled in error, and they utter many such blasphemies against them." He then gives examples of supposed oracles in which the gods blaspheme the Christians and goes on to say, "But to those who inquired whether Christ was God, Hecate[83] replied, 'You know that the soul goes on after the body, but when it is cut off from wisdom it always errs. That soul is the soul of a man of outstanding piety; they worship it because the truth is alien to them.'" And, after citing the words of this supposed oracle, he adds his own comments: "Thus Hecate said that he was a most pious man and that his soul, like those of other pious men, was deemed worthy of immortality after death, and the Christians in their ignorance worship his soul. And to those who inquired, 'Why, then, was he condemned?' the goddess replied with this oracle: 'The body, of course, is always faced with debilitating torments, but the souls of the pious take their seat in heaven. But that soul gave to other souls the fatal gift of entanglement in error; these were souls to whom the fates had not granted that they

---

83. The goddess Hecate was the daughter of Perses and Asteria and had a wide range of powers.

should acquire the gifts of the gods or have knowledge of immortal Jupiter. It is for this reason, then, that they are hated by the gods: because to those who were not fated to know God or to receive the gifts of the gods this man gave the fatal gift of entanglement in error. He himself, however, was pious, and, like other pious men, he passed into heaven. And so you shall not blaspheme him but shall rather pity the madness of men. On his account they face a present and precipitous danger.'" Who, then, is so dull-witted as not to understand that these oracles were either invented by a devious man, the worst enemy of the Christians, or were the responses of unclean demons with a similar purpose? In praising Christ, of course, what they really want is to convince people that they are telling the truth in demeaning Christians and so, if possible, to close off the way of eternal salvation by which one becomes Christian. They obviously assume that it is no drawback to their malicious and multifarious cunning if they are believed when they praise Christ, just so long as they are also believed when they demean Christians. Their purpose is to ensure that the person who believes them on both counts will praise Christ but have no wish to become a Christian; and so, even though he praises Christ, he will not be delivered by Christ from the domination of these demons. This is especially true because anyone who believes in the Christ they proclaim will not be a true Christian but rather a Photinian heretic[84] — that is, one who acknowledges Christ as a man but does not acknowledge him as God and therefore cannot be saved by him and cannot avoid or escape from the snares of those lying demons. For our part, we cannot approve either of Apollo's demeaning of Christ or of Hecate's praising of him. Apollo would have it believed that Christ was an unrighteous man, since he says that he was put to death by right-thinking judges; Hecate would have it believed that he was the most pious of men, but only a man. In both cases, however, the intent is the same: to keep people from wanting to be Christian, for, unless people become Christian, they cannot be delivered from the demons' power.

But this philosopher, or, rather, any persons who believe in such so-called oracles against the Christians, must first, if they can, find a way to make Apollo and Hecate consistent with each other in what they say about Christ, so that either both condemn him or both praise him. Even if they were able to do this, however, we ourselves would still turn our backs on deceitful demons, whether demeaning Christ or praising him. But, when their own god and goddess contradict each other about Christ, the one demeaning and the other praising him, people who take a sound view of the matter will not put any stock in their blasphemies against the Christians.

---

84. So called after Photinus, a mid-fourth-century bishop of Sirmium who, among his other unorthodoxies, held that Christ was a mere man. He is closely associated with Paul of Samosata, a bishop of Antioch, who preceded him by nearly a century, because they believed many of the same things. See *Heresies* 44-45. Augustine mentions Photinus in *Confessions* VII,19,25 and indicates that, before he embraced orthodox Christianity, he was drawn to Photinianism.

In fact when Porphyry (or Hecate), in praising Christ, declares that he gave himself to Christians as a fatal gift entangling them in error, he also lays bare — so he thinks — the causes of that same error. But before I set out these causes in his own words, I first ask, If Christ gave Christians this fatal gift of entanglement in error, did he give it willingly or unwillingly? If willingly, how could he be just? If unwillingly, how could he be blessed? But now let us hear the causes of that error. "There are in a certain place," Porphyry says, "very small earthly spirits, subject to the power of evil demons. The wise men of the Hebrews (one of whom was this Jesus, as you have heard from the oracles of Apollo, quoted above) barred religious men from these foul demons and lesser spirits and forbade them to pay them any attention, telling them rather to venerate the celestial gods and most especially to venerate God the father. But the gods also teach this, and we have shown previously how they admonish the mind to turn to God and command it to worship him everywhere. But uninstructed and irreligious natures, who were not fated to obtain gifts from the gods or to have any conception of immortal Jupiter, paying no attention to the gods or to divine men, rejected all the gods; and, far from hating these forbidden demons, they revered them. Although they make a show of worshiping God, they do not do the things by which alone God is adored. For in fact God, as the father of all, is in need of nothing, but it is a benefit to us when we adore him by means of justice, chastity, and the other virtues, making our very life itself a prayer to him by imitating and seeking to know him. For seeking to know him purifies us, and imitation of him deifies us by shaping our disposition to reflect his."

Porphyry certainly did well in proclaiming God as father and in stating the mode of life by which he is to be worshiped; and the prophetic books of the Hebrews are full of such precepts, where the life of holy men is enjoined or praised. But his errors or slanders in speaking of the Christians are everything that the demons (whom he imagines to be gods) would want. It is not difficult, after all, to recall the shameful obscenities enacted in the theaters and temples at the behest of the gods; nor is it difficult, in contrast, to note what is read, said, and heard in the churches, and what is offered to the true God. And so it is not difficult to understand where moral character is built up and where it is brought down to ruin! Who but a diabolical spirit could have told Porphyry, or inspired in him, such a baseless and obvious lie as that the Christians revere, instead of hating, the demons whose worship was forbidden by the Hebrews? In fact the God whom the wise men of the Hebrews worshiped forbids sacrifice even to the holy angels and powers of God in heaven, whom we venerate and love, here in this mortal pilgrimage of ours, as our most blessed fellow citizens. For in God's law, which he gave to his Hebrew people, he declares with thunder and menace, *Whoever sacrifices to any gods shall be destroyed* (Ex 22:20). Now, someone might think that this command applies only to the foul demons and the earthly spirits whom Porphyry calls lesser or minor spirits. For even these are called gods in Sacred Scripture — not gods of the Hebrews, of course, but gods of the gentiles, as the seventy translators[85] make clear in one of the Psalms, where they say, *For all the gods of the peoples are demons* (Ps 96:5). To keep anyone from thinking, then, that sacrifice is forbidden only to these demons but is permitted to all or some of the heavenly beings, the command immediately adds, *but to the Lord alone* (Ex 22:20), that is, to the Lord only. I add this to make sure that no one presumes that *to the Lord alone* means "to the Lord, the Sun";[86] that this is not the meaning is easy to see from the Greek version of the Scriptures.

Thus, the God of the Hebrews, to whom even this preeminent philosopher gives such impressive testimony, gave the law to his Hebrew people, written in Hebrew, a law neither obscure nor unknown but rather spread abroad among all peoples. And in this law it is written, *Whoever sacrifices to any gods but to the Lord alone shall be destroyed*. What need is there, then, to hunt for more passages on this matter in his law and his prophets? In fact, there is no need at all to hunt for them, for the passages are not obscure or rare; there is not even any need to collect and cite the obvious and frequent passages in which it is made clearer than day that the true and supreme God wants there to be no sacrifice whatsoever to any but to himself alone. We have this one passage, spoken briefly but grandly, with menace but with truth, by the God whom their most learned thinkers proclaim so well. Let it be heard, let it be feared, let it be fulfilled, lest destruction come down on the disobedient. *Whoever sacrifices to any god*, he says, *but to the Lord alone shall be destroyed*. This is not because the Lord is in need of anything but because it is to our benefit to belong to him. For it is to him that the psalmist sings in the Hebrews' sacred writings, *You are my God, for you do not need my goods* (Ps 16:2). And we ourselves — that is, his own city — are his best and most noble sacrifice, and it is the mystery of this sacrifice that we celebrate in our offerings, which are known to the faithful, as we discussed in the previous books.[87] For it was announced by divine oracles through the Hebrew prophets that the sacrificial victims which the Jews used to offer were going to cease, and that from the rising of the sun to its setting the peoples were going to offer one sacrifice,[88] as we see happening now; and we have already selected a sufficient number of these oracles and presented them at various points throughout this work.

Thus, true justice is found where the one supreme God rules an obedient city, so that there is no sacrifice but to him alone, and where, in consequence, the soul rules the body in all who belong to that city and obey God, and reason faithfully rules the vices in lawful order. Consequently, just as a single just person lives by

---

85. I.e., of the Septuagint.
86. "To the Lord alone...to the Lord, the Sun": *Domino soli...Dominum solem*. The Latin word for "alone" (*solus*) could in an instance such as this be taken for the word "sun" (*sol*), since the dative case of both words is identical, i.e., *soli*. The sun was almost universally worshiped in antiquity and in Rome, as the god Sol, was often identified with Apollo/Phoebus.
87. See above at X,6.20.
88. See Mal 1:11; Ps 113:3.

the faith that works through love,[89] so does the whole company and people of the just. This is the love by which a person loves God as God ought to be loved, and his neighbor as himself.[90] But where there is no such justice, there clearly is no company of persons joined by a common sense for what is right and by a community of interest. And (assuming that this is the true definition of a people) where this is missing, there certainly is no people. And therefore there is no republic, for, where there is no people, there is no common good of a people.

An Alternate Definition of a People

24. But if a people is defined in another way — if we say, for instance, that a people is a multitude of rational beings joined together by common agreement on the objects of their love — then it is clear that to discover the character of any people we should take a close look at what it loves. No matter what it loves, however, if it is an assembled multitude, not of animals but of rational creatures, and is joined together by common agreement on the objects of its love, it is not absurd to call it a people, and it is clear that, the better the objects of its love, the better the people, and the worse the objects of its love, the worse the people. According to this definition of ours, the Roman people is a people, and its common good is without doubt a republic. As to what that people loved in its first days and what it subsequently came to love, and as to the moral decline by which it fell into bloody seditions and finally into the Social and Civil Wars, thus violating and corrupting the bond of concord which is, so to speak, the health of a people, history bears witness to all this, and we have provided many examples on this score in the previous books.[91] I do not claim on this account, however, that the Roman people is not a people, or that its common good is not a republic, given that there remains some sort of assembled multitude of rational creatures joined together by a common agreement on the objects of their love. I would have it understood, however, that what I have said about Rome's people and republic I also say and maintain about those of the Athenians and any other Greeks, about those of the Egyptians, about the former Babylon of the Assyrians, and about those of any other people, when they exercised imperial rule, great or small, in their republics. For in general the city of the ungodly is not ruled by God and is not obedient to him in offering sacrifice only to him, and in that city, as a consequence, the soul does not rightly and faithfully rule the body, nor does reason the vices. And so it lacks true justice.

25. For, no matter how laudably the soul may appear to rule the body and reason the vices, if the soul and reason do not themselves serve God as God himself has taught that he is to be served, they do not rule the body and the vices rightly at all.

---

89. See Gal 5:6.
90. See Mt 22:37-39 par.
91. See above at Books II-III.

What kind of ruler of the body and the vices can the mind be if it does not know the true God and, instead of being subject to his rule, is prostituted to the corrupting influence of the most vicious demons? In fact the very virtues which the mind imagines that it has, and by which it rules the body and the vices for the sake of gaining or keeping whatever is the object of its desire, are themselves vices, and not virtues at all, if the mind does not direct them to God. Some people suppose that the virtues are true and authentic when they are directed to themselves alone and are not sought for the sake of anything beyond themselves.[92] But even then they are puffed up and proud, and so they are not to be counted as virtues but rather as vices. For, just as what causes the flesh to live does not come from the flesh but is rather above it, so what causes a person to live blessedly does not come from the person but is rather above him. And this is true not only of human beings but also of every heavenly dominion and power whatsoever.

Earthly Peace and the City of God

26. Accordingly, just as the life of the flesh is the soul, so the blessed life of human beings is God, of whom the Hebrews' Sacred Scripture says, *Blessed is the people whose God is the Lord* (Ps 144:15). Wretched, therefore, is the people that is alienated from God. But even this people loves a kind of peace of its own, which is not to be despised. It will not have that peace in the end, because it does not make good use of it prior to the end. In the meantime, however, it is beneficial to us, too, that this people should have its peace in this life, for, as long as the two cities are intermingled, we also make use of the peace of Babylon. And this is true even though the people of God are so fully set free from Babylon by faith that during this meantime they are no more than pilgrims in its midst. But, because we do make use of the peace of Babylon, the Apostle admonished the Church to pray for its kings and for all in high positions[93] and went on to say, *so that we may live a quiet and tranquil life with all godliness and love* (1 Tm 2:2). And when the prophet Jeremiah foretold the captivity that was to come for the ancient people of God and commanded them, by divine inspiration, to go obediently into Babylon, serving their God by means of this very patience and endurance, he also admonished them on his own to pray for Babylon, *because in its peace is your peace* (Jer 29:7) He was referring, of course, to the temporal peace which, in this meantime, is common to the good and the evil alike.

27. The peace that is proper to us, in contrast, we both have now with God through faith and shall have for all eternity with God through sight.[94] But the peace that we have here, whether the peace common to both the good and the evil

---

92. This was part of the Stoic understanding of virtue, summarized in Seneca, Letter 66.
93. See 1 Tim 2:1-2.
94. See 2 Cor 5:7.

or the peace proper to us alone, is a solace for wretchedness rather than the joy of blessedness. Our justice, too, although it is true justice because it is directed to the true supreme good, is such that in this life it consists in the forgiveness of sins rather than in the perfection of virtue. The prayer of the whole city of God that is on pilgrimage here on earth bears witness to this point. In all its members it cries out to God, *Forgive us our debts, as we also forgive our debtors* (Mt 6:12). But this prayer has no efficacy for those whose faith is without works and dead;[95] it only has efficacy for those whose faith works through love.[96] Prayer of this kind is needed by the righteous because, in this mortal condition and in this corruptible body which weighs down the soul,[97] even though their reason is subject to God, it still does not perfectly rule the vices. For, although reason does indeed rule the vices, it by no means rules them without struggle and resistance on their part. And, in this place of weakness, even if reason fights well or goes on to dominate these enemies by defeating and subduing them, something still creeps in which leads into sin, if not by immediate action, then at least by unconsidered talk or fleeting thought.

As long as it is necessary to rule the vices, then, there is no full and complete peace. This is true both because our battle against the resisting vices is full of peril and because our triumph over defeated vices is still far from secure and effortless; it is only with an anxious and care-filled rule that we manage to hold them down. We live, then, in the midst of all these trials, which have been succinctly summarized in the divine discourse where it says, *Is not human life on earth a trial?* (Jb 7:1) And who will presume that he is living in such a way that he has no need to say to God, *Forgive us our debts* (Mt 6:12)? Only an arrogant person would be so presumptuous, not someone who is truly great but someone puffed up and bloated with pride, who is justly resisted by the one who pours out his grace on the humble. That is why it is written, *God resists the proud but gives grace to the humble* (Jas 4:6).

In this life, therefore, justice is only present in each person when the person is obedient to God's rule, when the mind rules the body, and when reason rules the vices, even when they fight against its rule by subduing or resisting them. Justice is only present when it is from God himself that the person seeks both the grace for meritorious works and the forgiveness for sins, and when he gives full thanks to God for the benefits he receives. In that final peace, however, to which this justice should be directed, and for the attaining of which it should be maintained, our nature will be healed by immortality and incorruption. Then it will have no vices, and there will be nothing at all, whether in ourselves or in anyone else, that fights against us. Thus, there will be no need for reason to rule the vices, because there will be no vices. But God will rule the person, the soul will rule the body,

---

95. See Jas 2:17.26.
96. See Gal 5:6.
97. See Wis 9:15.

and the delight and ease with which we obey in that final peace will be as great as the happiness with which we live and reign in it. There, for each and every one of us, this will last for all eternity, and its lasting for all eternity will be completely certain and totally assured; and so the peace of this blessedness, or the blessedness of this peace, will be the supreme good.

The Supreme Evil: Eternal Misery

28. For those who do not belong to the city of God, in contrast, there will be eternal misery. This misery is also called the second death,[98] because the soul cannot be said to be alive at that point, since it will be alienated from God, and neither can the body, since it will be subject to eternal torments. And so this second death will be all the harsher, precisely because it cannot come to an end in death. Now, just as misery is the opposite of happiness, and death the opposite of life, it seems that war is the opposite of peace. There is good reason, then, to ask what and what sort of war can be seen in the final state of the wicked in contrast to the peace we have proclaimed and praised in the final state of the good. But anyone who puts this question should take note of what it is that is so harmful and destructive in war, and he will see that it is nothing other than the opposition and conflict of things with each other. What more grievous and bitter war, then, can be imagined than a war in which the will is so deeply opposed to passion and passion so deeply opposed to the will that their hostility cannot be ended by victory on either side, or a war in which the force of pain conflicts so powerfully with the very nature of the body that neither can give in to the other? In this life, when such conflict occurs, either pain wins and death snuffs out all feeling, or nature wins and health takes away the pain. In the life to come, however, the pain persists to inflict torment, and nature endures to feel the pain. Neither one comes to an end, and so the punishment does not come to an end either.

These, then, are the final ends of the good and the evil, the one to be sought and the other to be avoided. And, since it is as the result of a judgment that the good will pass over to the one and the evil pass over to the other, I shall discuss this judgment, as far as God grants, in the following book.

---

98. See Rv 2:11; 20:6.14; 21:8. For a brief discussion of the second death see above at XIII,2.

Study Questions for Book XIX

There is today what one might call an "existential realism" among people of good will who do not believe in God or in an afterlife. They accept a "good enough" happiness that accommodates human expectations to the finality of death. Might Varro's approach, elaborating the goods of nature and extolling the virtue of the soul, serve as a contemporary articulation of such "good enough" happiness?

Augustine describes earthly peace as an accommodation of wills in conflict with each other within a fragile social and political order. The City of God needs that temporary social and political order to continue on its journey through this world to eternal peace and happiness. For Christians who serve in public office or work for social justice, what balance should there be between achieving compromise among partisan factions and political bodies and promoting Christian ideals that are based on faith in God and the equality of all persons?

Augustine defines a people as "a multitude of rational beings joined together by common agreement on the objects of their love." The goodness of a republic can be determined by an examination of the objects which a people love, values on which they have agreed, and ends for which they have organized and strive. The best republic includes among its love, values and ends the worship of the true God. Is this an argument for theocracy?

BOOK XX

Book XX argues that there will be a day of judgment at which the good and the evil are finally and irrevocably separated and assigned to their respective ends and that it will be accompanied by a bodily resurrection of some to eternal happiness and of others to eternal punishment. Since these topics lie beyond the reach of human reason, the argument relies on the testimony of Scripture, whose authority and reliability are rooted in and secured by the truthfulness of God. Following the order of dignity rather than that of chronology, the book presents testimonies taken first from the New and then from the Old Testament. (Particularly noteworthy in this context is the detailed treatment, covering chapters 7 to 17, of a lengthy passage from the Book of Revelation, which rarely received such extended attention in the early Church.) Within the framework of this argument, the book also notes the difference between God's final and manifest judgment and the judging in which God engages all along but in which the divine justice is often hidden from human understanding; draws a distinction between the first resurrection, the resurrection of the soul from the death of sin to life in faith, and the second resurrection, the resurrection of the body in which it is restored to the soul either for eternal happiness or for eternal punishment; provides a non-millenarian interpretation of the binding and releasing of the devil, the coming of Antichrist, and the thousand-year reign of the saints with Christ; defines the sense in which the world will perish at the end; touches on the return of Elijah and his role in leading those Jews who will be saved to the recognition of Christ; shows how the Old Testament points specifically to the coming of Christ as judge, indicating that the one who was judged as man will return to judge as man; and, finally, gives a summary listing of the events that will be associated with the last judgment in the order in which Augustine believes that they will occur.

1. Since, as far as God himself grants, we are now going to talk about the day of God's final judgment and to affirm it over against the ungodly and unbelievers, we should first lay down — as the foundation of the building, so to speak — the testimonies of Divine Scripture. Those who refuse to accept these testimonies try to counter them with false and fallacious little ventures of human reasoning. To this end, either they contend that the evidence taken from Sacred Scripture has some other meaning or they deny altogether that its statements are divinely inspired. For I do not suppose that any mortal man who understands these statements as they were spoken, and believes that they were spoken by the supreme and true God through holy souls, would not accept and consent to them, whether he openly acknowledges this or, due to some fault, is ashamed or afraid to admit it, or even, with a stubbornness close to insanity, insists on defending with all the pugnacity he can muster what he knows and believes to be false against what he knows and believes to be true.[1]

The Day of Judgment

The whole Church of the true God holds, confesses and professes that Christ is going to come from heaven to judge the living and the dead,[2] and this is what we call the final day of divine judgment, that is, the end time. For it is not certain how many days this judgment will take, but anyone who reads the Sacred Scriptures, no matter how carelessly, knows that they customarily use the word "day" to mean "time." Furthermore, when we speak of the day of God's judgment, we add the word "last" or "final." For God is judging now, and he has been judging from the very beginning of the human race, when he expelled the first human beings from paradise and barred them from the tree of life because of the great sin that they committed.[3] In fact God undoubtedly judged even before that, when he did not spare the angels who sinned, whose prince, after bringing ruin on himself, also brought ruin on men in his envy. Nor is it apart from his profound and just judgment that the life of demons in this heaven of air and the life of men here on earth is utter misery, choked with errors and sufferings. But, even if no one had sinned, God would not have sustained the whole rational creation in eternal blessedness, clinging to him without wavering as its Lord, apart from his good and righteous judgment.

And not only does he pass judgment universally on the whole race of demons and men, consigning them to misery as what they deserve for their first sins; he also judges the particular acts that individuals perform by free choice of the will. For even the demons pray not to be tormented, and it is certainly not without justice that they are either spared or else tormented for their wickedness in each case. Human beings, too, are punished by God for their actions, often openly, always hiddenly, whether in this life or after death, although no man acts rightly unless he is helped by divine aid, and no man or demon acts wickedly unless permitted to do so by that same completely righteous divine judgment. For, as the Apostle says, *There is no unrighteousness in God* (Rom 9:14); and, as he says elsewhere, *His judgments are inscrutable and his ways past finding out* (Rom 11:33).

---

1. At the very end of this book, below at XX,30, as though reprising his initial assertions on the topic, Augustine returns to the theme of the truthfulness of Scripture over against the vanity of human argumentation.
2. See 2 Tm 4:1. Augustine's choice of words ("The whole Church...confesses and professes...") suggests a reference to the relevant article of the creed.
3. See Gn 3:22-24.

In this book, therefore, I shall discuss, so far as God grants, not those first judgments, nor those intervening judgments, but the last judgment itself, when Christ will come from heaven to judge the living and the dead. It is this, in fact, that is properly called the day of judgment, because at that point there will be no room for ignorant complaints about why this unjust person is happy or that just person unhappy. For it will then be wholly clear that all the good, and only the good, have true and full happiness, and that all the evil, and only the evil, have merited and utter unhappiness.

God's Inscrutable Justice

2. In the meantime, however, we are learning both to bear without distress the evils that the good also suffer and not to attach much importance to the goods that the evil also acquire. And so, even in cases in which the divine justice is not apparent, divine teaching works to our good. For we do not know by what judgment of God this good person is poor or that evil person rich. We do not know why this person is joyful when it seems to us that he ought to be tormented with grief for his wanton ways, or why that person is consumed with grief when his praiseworthy life convinces us that he ought to have joy. We do not know why an innocent person leaves the courtroom not only not vindicated but actually condemned, either done in by the judge's injustice or undone by a mass of false evidence; nor do we know why, in contrast, his wicked adversary scoffs at him, going away not only unpunished but fully vindicated. We do not know why an irreligious person lives in the best of health, or why a religious person wastes away in sickness. We do not know why young men in perfect health are robbers, or why infants, who could not hurt anyone, even by a word, are afflicted by all sorts of dreadful diseases. We do not know why a person who contributes usefully to human affairs is snatched away by premature death, or why someone who, to our eyes, ought never to have been born lives on beyond all expectation. We do not know why a person whose life is rife with crimes is exalted with honors, or why a person who is above reproach is left in dark obscurity. And who could collect, who could enumerate, all the other examples of this kind of thing?

Now, if such cases just showed some consistency in their very absurdity, so that in this life — in which, as the sacred Psalm says, *man has become like vanity; his days pass away like a shadow* (Ps 144:4)— only the wicked received the transitory goods of this earth and only the good suffered its evils, it would be possible to ascribe all this to the righteous and even benign judgment of God. Then, it would seem, those who were not going to attain the eternal goods which make men happy were either being deluded by temporal goods in punishment for their malice or else, by God's mercy, were being consoled by them; and it would seem, too, that those who were not going to suffer eternal torments were either being afflicted by temporal evils for whatever sins they had committed, no matter how small, or else were being trained by them in order to fill out their virtues. As it is, however, not only do good people suffer evils and evil people enjoy goods, which seems unjust, but it is also true that, more often than not, evil things come to evil people, and good things fall to good people; and so the judgments of God are all the more inscrutable, and his ways all the more past finding out.

Thus, even though we do not know by what judgment God — in whom there is the highest power, the highest wisdom, the highest justice, and no weakness, no rashness, no injustice at all — causes or allows these things to happen, it is still salutary for us to learn not to attach much importance to either the goods or the evils that we see are common to the good and the evil alike, but rather to seek those goods which are proper to the good alone and especially to shun those evils which are proper to the evil alone. But, when we arrive at that judgment of God, whose time is properly called *the day of judgment*,[4] and sometimes *the day of the Lord*,[5] it will be clear that God's judgments are perfectly righteous, not only all the judgments that he will give then but also all the judgments that he has given from the beginning and all the judgments that he is still going to give up to that time. On that day, too, it will be made manifest how it happens, by the righteous judgment of God, that so many, and in fact almost all, of the righteous judgments of God are now hidden from the senses and the minds of mortals. What is not hidden from the faith of the godly in this matter, however, is that what is hidden is righteous.

[Chapters 3 – 29 review and interpret biblical passages that refer to the last judgment, the millenium, the resurrection of the dead and persecution under the anti-christ. Representative passages are included here.]

Testimonies to the Last Judgment from Scripture

4. I have undertaken, then, to set out the testimonies from Holy Scripture for this last judgment of God, and these are to be chosen first from the books of the New Testament and then from the Old. For, although the Old Testament is earlier in time, the New should be ranked ahead of it in dignity, since the Old Testament is the herald of the New. The testimonies from the New Testament will be presented first, therefore, and those from the Old will then be brought in to make our proof the more firm....

---

4. See, e.g., Mt 10:15.
5. See, e.g., Is 13:6; 1 Thes 5:2. This is by far the more common usage of the two.

Testimonies from the Gospel of Matthew: Judgment and Resurrection

5. Thus, the Savior himself, when he rebuked the cities which had not believed in him despite the fact that he did great works of power in them, compared them unfavorably to foreign cities, saying, *But I tell you, on the day of judgment it shall go easier for Tyre and Sidon than it shall for you* (Mt 11:22). A little later he says to another city, *But I tell you that on the day of judgment it shall go easier for the land of Sodom than it shall for you* (Mt 11:24). Here he is obviously predicting that a day of judgment will come. And in another place he says, *The people of Nineveh shall rise up at the judgment with this generation and shall condemn it, because they repented at the preaching of Jonah, and see, something greater than Jonah is here. The queen of the South shall rise up at the judgment and shall condemn it, because she came from the ends of the earth to hear the wisdom of Solomon, and see, something greater than Solomon is here.* (Mt 12:41-42) We learn two things from this passage: that there is a judgment to come, and that it will come together with the resurrection of the dead. For, when he said what he said about the Ninevites and the queen of the South, he was obviously talking about people who are dead, yet he foretold that they would rise up at the day of judgment. And when he said, *and they shall condemn it*, he did not mean that these people would themselves do the judging but rather that, in comparison with them, others would justly be condemned....

Testimonies from the Gospel of John: the First and the Second Resurrection

The evangelist John is the one who tells us most clearly that Christ foretold that the judgment would come at the resurrection of the dead. First he said, *For the Father judges no one but has given all judgment to the Son, so that all may honor the Son just as they honor the Father. Anyone who does not honor the Son does not honor the Father who sent him.* (Jn 5:22-23) Then he immediately added, *Amen, amen, I tell you that anyone who hears my word and believes him who sent me has eternal life and does not come under judgment but has passed from death to life* (Jn 5:24). Note that he said here that those who believe in him do not come under judgment. How is it, then, that they will be separated from the evil and stand at his right hand, unless in this passage he used *judgment* to mean condemnation? It is in this sense, then, that those who hear his word and believe the one who sent him do not come under judgment. They do not come under judgment as condemnation.

6. Then he goes on to say, *Amen, amen, I tell you that the hour is coming and now is when the dead shall hear the voice of the Son of God, and those who hear shall live. For, just as the Father has life in himself, so he has granted the Son also to have life in himself.* (Jn 5:25-26) Here he is not yet speaking of the second resurrection, that is, the resurrection of the body, which will come at the end. He is speaking, rather, of the first resurrection, which comes now. In fact it is precisely to distinguish the first resurrection from the second that he says, *The hour is coming and now is* (Jn 5:25). This is not the resurrection of the body but rather of the soul. Souls have a death of their own, in ungodliness and sin, and it is in this sense that the people are dead of whom the Lord says, *Let the dead bury their dead* (Mt 8:22), that is, let those who are dead in soul bury those who are dead in body. Thus, it is with respect to those who are dead in soul due to their impiety and iniquity that he says, *The hour is coming and now is when the dead shall hear the voice of the Son of God, and those who hear shall live* (Jn 5:25). By *those who hear* he means those who obey, believe, and persevere to the end. And in this case he made no distinction between the good and the evil. For it is good for everyone to hear his voice and to come alive by passing over to the life of godliness from the death of ungodliness....

Thus, anyone who does not wish to be condemned in the second resurrection should rise in the first. For *the hour is coming and now is when the dead shall hear the voice of the Son of Man, and those who hear shall live*; that is, they will not come under condemnation, which is called the second death. This is the death into which — after the second resurrection, which is the future resurrection of the body — all those will be hurled who do not rise up in the first resurrection, which is the resurrection of the soul. *For the hour is coming when all who are in their graves shall hear his voice and shall come forth* (Jn 5:28-29)....

And in what follows Christ teaches us why it is that not all will live. *Those who have done good*, he says, *to the resurrection of life* (Jn 5:29); these are the ones who will live. *And those who have done evil to the resurrection of judgment* (Jn 5:29); these are the ones who will not live, because they are the ones who are going to die the second death. They have done evil because their lives have been evil, and their lives have been evil because they did not rise in the first resurrection, the resurrection of the soul, which now is, or because, after they had risen, they did not endure until the end. There are, then, two regenerations, of which I have already spoken above: one takes place in faith and happens now through baptism; the other takes place in the flesh and will happen when the flesh attains immortality and incorruption through the great and last judgment. And so also there are two resurrections: the first resurrection, which happens now and is the resurrection of the soul, which keeps it from coming to the second death, and the second resurrection, which does not happen now but will happen at the end of the world, which is not the resurrection of the soul but of the body, and which, at the last judgment, will send some into the second death and others into the life that has no death.

Testimonies from the Book of Revelation: the Binding of the Devil for a Thousand Years

7. John the evangelist also spoke of these two resurrections in the book called The Apocalypse. But he spoke of them in such a way that some of us Christians have misunderstood the first resurrection; and, beyond that, it has even been turned into ridiculous fables. In the book just mentioned, then, the apostle John says, *And I saw an angel coming down from heaven, holding in his hand the key to the bottomless pit and a chain. And he took hold of the dragon, that ancient serpent, who is also named the devil and Satan, and bound him for a thousand years, and threw him into the pit, and shut and sealed it over him, so that he would no longer deceive the nations until the thousand years were ended. After that he must be released for a little while. And I saw thrones and those seated on them, and judgment was given. And the souls of those who were slain for their testimony to Jesus and for the word of God, and any who had not worshiped the beast or its image and had not received its mark on their foreheads or their hands, reigned with Jesus a thousand years, but the rest of them did not come to life until the thousand years were ended. This is the first resurrection. Blessed and holy are those who have a part in this first resurrection. Over these the second death has no power, but they shall be priests of God and of Christ, and they shall reign with him a thousand years.* (Rv 20:1-6) On the basis of this passage some have gotten the idea that the first resurrection will happen in the future and will be a bodily resurrection. Among other things they found the number of a thousand years particularly striking, as if it were right for the saints to have a kind of sabbath for all that time, that is, a holy rest after all the labors of the six thousand years from the time that man was created and then, due to his great sin, was expelled from the felicity of paradise into the toils of this mortal existence. Since Scripture says, *With the Lord one day is like a thousand years, and a thousand years are like one day* (2 Pt 3:8), they imagine that, at the end of the six thousand years, there is to follow a final thousand years as a kind of sabbath, just as, at the end of six days, there follows a seventh or sabbath day, and they suppose that the saints will rise again precisely to celebrate this sabbath.

We could put up with this view if it involved only the belief that the delights of the saints during that sabbath were going to be spiritual delights due to the presence of the Lord. In fact, I myself once held this opinion.[6] But, since they claim that those who are going to rise again will spend their rest in extravagant carnal feasts, in which the vast amounts of food and drink will not only go beyond all moderation but will exceed the very bounds of belief itself, only carnal people could possibly believe such a thing. Those who are spiritual, however, call people who believe such things by the Greek word "chiliasts," and, using the Latin equivalent, we can label them "millenarians."[7] It would take too long to refute them point by point, but we ought at least to show how this passage of Scripture is actually to be understood.

---

6. See Sermon 259,2.
7. The terms come from each language's word for "thousand." Millenarianism, more or less materially understood, was widely espoused in the first two centuries of Christianity but continued to have currency until at least the fifth century, as Augustine's concern suggests. Probably the most notorious example of a materially extravagant understanding occurs in the early-second-century Papias, Fragment 1, cited by Irenaeus, to buttress his own views on the topic, in *Against Heresies* V,33-36. See also Lactantius, *Divine Institutes* VII,23-24.

The Lord Jesus Christ himself says, *No one can enter a strong man's house and take away his goods unless he first binds the strong man* (Mk 3:27). By the *strong man* he means us to understand the devil, because the devil was able to take humanity captive. The *goods* which Christ was going to take away are the people whom the devil held in his possession because of their various sins and iniquities but who were going to become believers in him. Thus the reason why, in the Apocalypse, the apostle saw *an angel descending from heaven, holding in his hand the key to the bottomless pit and a chain* (Rv 20:1), was precisely in order that this *strong man* might be bound. *And he took hold*, he says, *of the dragon, that ancient serpent, who is also named the devil and Satan, and bound him for a thousand years* (Rv 20:2); that is, he checked and constrained his power so as to keep him from seducing and gaining possession of those who were going to be set free.

Now, the thousand years, so far as I can see, can be understood in two ways. First, it may mean that all this is taking place in the final thousand years, that is, in the sixth millennium (as though in the sixth day), the last stretches of which are now in the process of unrolling, and then there will follow a sabbath which has no evening; that is, there will follow the repose of the saints which has no end.[8] In this case it would be the last part of this millennium (or day), the part that remains up to the end of the world, which he called a thousand years, using the figure of speech in which a part is signified by the whole. Alternatively, he may have used the thousand years to stand for all the years of the present age, using a perfect number to designate the whole of time. For the number one thousand represents the cube of the number ten. Ten times ten makes a hundred, a square, but still only a plane figure. To give it height and make it a solid, the one hundred is again multiplied by ten, which gives us a thousand. Furthermore, the number one hundred is itself sometimes used to represent totality, as when the Lord promised anyone who left everything and followed him that he would *receive a hundredfold* (Mt 19:29) in this world; and the Apostle explains this, in a way, when he says, *as having nothing, and yet possessing everything* (2 Cor 6:10), since still earlier it had already been said, *The whole world is the wealth of the faithful man* (Prv 17:6 LXX). And, if a hundred is used to represent totality, does not a thousand represent totality even better, since it is not just ten squared but ten cubed to make a solid figure? Thus, when the Psalm says, *He has been mindful of his covenant forever, the word which he commanded for a thousand generations* (Ps 105:8), there is no better way to understand this than to interpret *for a thousand generations* to mean "for all generations."

And he threw him into the pit (Rv 20:3); that is, he threw the devil into the pit. Here *pit* signifies the innumerable multitudes of the ungodly, whose hearts are sunk deep in malignity against the Church of God. It is not that the devil was not in them before, but he is now said to have been thrown into the pit because,

---

8. This is Augustine's own position. See below at XXII,30.

when he is excluded from believers, he begins to take possession of the ungodly all the more fully. For the person who is not only estranged from God but also has an irrational hatred for God's servants is all the more fully possessed by the devil. *And shut and sealed it over him, so that he would no longer deceive the nations until the thousand years were ended* (Rv 20:3). The meaning of *and he shut it over him* is that he put a prohibition on the devil to keep him from being able to get out, that is, from being able to transgress what was forbidden to him. And the addition of the words *he sealed it* seems to me to signify that God wanted who belongs to the devil's party and who does not to remain hidden. For, in this world, in very fact, this is hidden from us, because it is uncertain whether anyone who now seems to stand is going to fall and whether anyone who now seems to be fallen is going to rise.[9]

Bound and imprisoned by this decree, then, the devil is prohibited and prevented from deceiving those nations which belong to Christ but which he had earlier deceived and held in his grip. For God *chose* those nations *before the foundation of the world* (Eph 1:4), to deliver them from the power of darkness and to bring them into the kingdom of his beloved Son,[10] as the Apostle says. For who among the faithful does not know that even now the devil deceives nations and draws them down with him into eternal punishment, although not those nations predestined to eternal life? Nor should anyone be troubled by the fact that the devil often deceives even those who have already been regenerated in Christ and are walking in the ways of God. For *the Lord knows those who are his* (2 Tm 2:19), and the devil deceives none of these into eternal damnation. For it is as God that the Lord knows them, not as a man. Nothing is hidden from God, not even the future. A man, in contrast, sees a person only as he is at present — if he can really be said to see a person at all, when he does not see into the person's heart — but does not see even himself well enough to know what sort of person he will be in the future. The devil was bound and shut up in the bottomless pit, then, so that he would no longer deceive the nations which make up the Church, the nations which he had previously deceived and held in his grip before they were the Church. For what the passage says is not "so that he would not deceive anyone"; what it says is rather *so that he would no longer deceive the nations* — by which it undoubtedly means the Church — *until the thousand years were ended*, that is, either what remains of the sixth day (which consists of a thousand years) or all the years still to come up to the end of the world.

Nor are these words — *so that he would no longer deceive the nations until the thousand years were ended* — to be understood as if they mean that afterwards he is going to deceive precisely the nations which make up the predestined Church, that is, the nations that he was previously prevented from deceiving because he was bound and imprisoned. Rather, it may be that they represent a figure of speech

---

9. See 1 Cor 10:12.
10. See Col 1:13.

which is often found in Scripture, as in the Psalm, *So our eyes look to the Lord our God, until he has mercy upon us* (Ps 123:2), for this certainly does not mean that, after God has had mercy, the eyes of his servants will no longer look to the Lord their God. Or it may be that the proper word order is this: *And he shut and sealed it over him until the thousand years were ended.* In this case the inserted phrase — *so that he would no longer deceive the nations* — functions in such a way that it is actually to be understood separately and outside the surrounding word order, as if it were added at the end. Thus, the whole sentence would read: *And he shut and sealed it over him until the thousand years were ended, so that he would no longer deceive the nations*; that is, he shut it over him until the thousand years were ended for the express purpose that he would no longer deceive the nations at all.

8. *After that,* John says, *he must be released for a little while* (Rv 20:3). Now, if the binding and shutting up of the devil means that he is unable to deceive the Church, does it follow that his release will mean that he can? By no means! For he will never deceive the Church that was predestined and chosen *before the foundation of the world*, the Church of which it is said, *The Lord knows those who are his* (2 Tm 2:19). And yet that Church will be here even during the time when the devil is to be released, just as it was here from the moment it was established and will be here at all times; it is here in its members who, in being born, replace those who die. For a little later John says that, when the devil has been released, he will deceive the nations throughout the whole world and will lead them into war against the Church, and the number of its enemies will be as the sands of the sea.[11] *And they went up*, he says, *over the breadth of the earth and surrounded the camp of the saints and the beloved city, and fire came down out of heaven from God and consumed them. And the devil who had deceived them was thrown into the lake of fire and sulfur, where the beast and the false prophet were, and they shall be tormented day and night for ever and ever.* (Rv 20:9-10) In this passage John is already referring to the last judgment. I thought it should be cited now, however, lest anyone should imagine that, during the little while when the devil will be released, the Church will not be here on this earth, either because the devil will not find it here when he is released or because he will destroy it when he persecutes it in every conceivable way.

The devil is bound, then, for the entire period covered by this book, that is, from the first coming of Christ to the end of the world, which will be his second coming. The fact that he is bound does not mean, however, that it is only for the interval called *a thousand years* that he will not deceive the Church, for neither will he deceive the Church after he is released. But if his being bound means that he is not able or is not permitted to deceive the Church, what else could his release mean except that he is now able, or is now permitted, to do this? God forbid that this should be so! What the binding of the devil means, rather, is that he is

---

11. See Rv 20:7-8.

not permitted to exert his full power of temptation, whether by force or by guile, to deceive people into his own party either by compelling them with violence or by duping them with illusion. For, if he were permitted to do this for such a long time and while many are so weak, he would bring down a great number of the faithful — precisely those to whom God does not wish this to happen — or would keep them from believing at all. And it was to prevent him from doing this that the devil was bound.

The Releasing of the Devil

But, when the *little while* comes, he will be released. For we read that for three years and six months he and his nations will rage with all their powers.[12] The people against whom he is to do battle, however, will be the kind of people who cannot be vanquished by his dreadful assault or by his cunning plots. Moreover, if he were never released, his malign power would not be made fully manifest, and the unwavering faith and endurance of the holy city would not be fully proved. In short, it would not be fully clear how the Almighty would turn such great evil on the devil's part to such good use. For God does not wholly keep him from putting the saints to the test — even though God did throw him out from their inner man, where faith in God is lodged — so that they may profit from the devil's outward attack. God also bound the devil in those who take his part, so that he might not, by expressing and exerting all his malice, bar the way to countless weak persons by whom the Church was to be increased and filled up, some going to believe, some already believing, either by scaring the former away from the faith of godliness or by shattering the faith of the latter. At the end, however, God will release him so that the city of God may see what a mighty foe it has overcome with the great glory of its redeemer, its helper, its deliverer....

The Thousand-Year Reign of the Saints

9. In the interim, while the devil is bound for a thousand years, the saints reign with Christ, also for a thousand years;[13] and these thousand years are no doubt to be understood in the same way, that is, as the time since Christ's first coming. This reign is, of course, quite different from the kingdom of which Christ will say at the end, *Come, you who are blessed of my father, inherit the kingdom prepared for you* (Mt 25:34). But his saints — to whom he says, *Behold, I am with you until the end of the world* (Mt 28:20)— are reigning with him even now, although in another and far lesser sense. If this were not so, the Church obviously would not be called his kingdom, or the kingdom of heaven, here and now in the present. For it is clearly during this period that the scribe... *who brings out of his treasure*

---

12. See Rv 11:2; 12:6; 13:5.
13. See Rv 20:4.

things new and old (Mt 13:52) is trained in the kingdom of God. And it is from the Church that the reapers are going to gather the tares which Christ allowed to grow together with the wheat until the harvest, as he explains when he says, *The harvest is the end of the age, and the reapers are the angels. Just as the tares are collected and burned up with fire, so shall it be at the end of the age. The Son of Man shall send his angels, and they shall collect out of his kingdom all occasions of sin.* (Mt 13:39-41) Can occasions of sin be gathered from the kingdom in which there are no occasions of sin? Therefore, it must be from this kingdom of his, that is, from the Church, that they are gathered.[14]

Again, he says, *Whoever breaks one of the least of these commandments and teaches others to do the same shall be called least in the kingdom of heaven, but whoever does them and teaches others to do the same shall be called great in the kingdom of heaven* (Mt 5:19). He speaks of both as being in the kingdom of heaven, both the one who does not do the commandments that he teaches (for *break* means "not to keep, not to do") and the one who does the commandments and teaches others to do the same. But the former he calls *least* and the latter *great*.... Accordingly, the Church as it is now includes both sorts of people; but, when only the second sort is included, that is, the Church as it will be when there are no evil persons in it.

Even now, therefore, the Church is the kingdom of Christ and the kingdom of heaven, and so even now the saints reign with him, although not in the same sense in which they will ultimately reign. The tares, however, do not reign with him, even though they are growing in the Church along with the wheat. For the ones who reign with him are the ones who do what the Apostle says, *If you have risen with Christ, seek the things that are above, where Christ is, seated at the right hand of God. Seek the things that are above, not the things on earth.* (Col 3:1-2) He also says of such people that their orientation is to heaven.[15] In short, the ones who reign with him are the ones who are in his kingdom in such a way that they themselves are his kingdom. But, not to mention anything else, how can those people be Christ's kingdom who, although they are included in it until all occasions of sin are gathered out of his kingdom at the end of the world, seek their own things[16] there and not the things of Jesus Christ?

It is about this kingdom at war, then, that The Apocalypse is speaking in the passage which we are considering. It is there that there is still conflict with the enemy, and there that we sometimes battle against the vices when they oppose us and sometimes rule them when they yield to us, until we come to that most peaceful kingdom where we shall reign without any enemy. And it is also speaking about

---

14. His reflection on Mt 13:39-41 obliges Augustine to come to the conclusion that the Church on earth must be identified with the kingdom of heaven in its earthly condition and also that the earthly manifestation of the kingdom must allow for the presence of sinners.
15. See Phil 3:20.
16. See 1 Cor 13:5.

the first resurrection which now is. And, after saying that the devil is bound for a thousand years and afterwards is released for a little while, John then gives a brief summation of what the Church does, or what is done in the Church, during those thousand years: *And I saw thrones and those seated on them, and judgment was given* (Rv 20:4). No one should think that this refers to the last judgment. Rather, we should understand that it refers to the thrones of the leaders and to the leaders themselves by whom the Church is now governed. And it seems that there is no better way of understanding the judgment that was given than the passage that says, *Whatever you bind on earth shall be bound in heaven, and whatever you loose on earth shall be loosed in heaven* (Mt 18:18). That is why the Apostle says, *For what have I to do with judging those outside? Is it not those who are inside that you are to judge?* (1 Cor 5:12)

And, John says, *the souls of those who were slain for their testimony to Jesus and for the word of God*; this goes together with what he is about to say: *reigned with Jesus a thousand years* (Rv 20:4). He is speaking about the souls of the martyrs whose bodies have not yet been restored to them. For the souls of the devout dead are not separated from the Church, which is even now the kingdom of Christ. Otherwise we would not commemorate them at the altar of God when we partake of the body of Christ,[17] nor would it be of any benefit to flee to Christ's baptism in times of danger, lest this life end without baptism, or to flee to reconciliation if one has been separated from that body due to the discipline of penance[18] or to a bad conscience. For why are these things done if not because the faithful, even when they have died, are members of Christ? Thus, their souls, although not yet reunited with their bodies, still reign with him while these thousand years run their course. That is why we read in another passage from the same book, *Blessed are the dead who die in the Lord. From now on, says the Spirit, may they rest from their labors, for their deeds follow them.* (Rv 14:13) Thus the Church now first reigns with Christ in both the living and the dead. *For*, as the Apostle says, *this is why Christ died, that he might be the Lord of both the living and the dead* (Rom 14:9). Only the souls of the martyrs are mentioned, because it is the dead who fought for the truth even to the point of death that are most especially the ones who reign. But, taking the part for the whole, we understand full well that the rest of the dead also belong to the Church, which is the kingdom of Christ....

10. ...Now, after it says, *Over these the second death has no power*, it goes on to say, *but they shall be priests of God and of Christ, and they shall reign with*

---

17. See Sermon 172,2, where Augustine says that the whole Church observes the custom of mentioning the names of the dead during the eucharistic liturgy.
18. In the early Church what has come to be known as the sacrament of penance, or reconciliation, could only be carried out once in a person's lifetime, and while it was being carried out, perhaps over the course of several months or even longer, the penitent was deprived of the eucharist. The process, as practiced in third-century North Africa (and not significantly changed by Augustine's time), is described in Tertullian, *On Penitence* 9-11.

him a thousand years (Rv 20:6). Clearly, this does not refer only to bishops and presbyters, who are now properly called priests in the Church.[19] Rather, just as we call all Christians "christs" by virtue of their mystical anointing,[20] so we call all Christians "priests" because they are all members of the one priest. That is why the apostle Peter says that they are *a holy people, a royal priesthood* (1 Pt 2:9). Although only briefly and in passing, John clearly intimates here that Christ is God. For he says that they are *priests of God and of Christ*, that is, of the Father and the Son. It was, however, in the form of a servant[21] and as the Son of Man that Christ was made a *priest forever after the order of Melchizedek* (Ps 110:4). But I have already discussed this point more than once in this work.[22]...

The Last Judgment, the Second Resurrection, and the Book of Life

14. After the mention of the final persecution, John briefly summarizes all that the devil and the enemy city, along with its prince, are going to suffer at what is now the last judgment. For he says, *And the devil who had deceived them was thrown into the lake of fire and sulfur, where the beast and the false prophet were, and they shall be tormented day and night for ever and ever* (Rv 20:10). The beast... can rightly be understood as the ungodly city itself, and the false prophet is either Antichrist or the image, that is, the pretence [of false Christians]. After this John gives a summary account of the last judgment itself, which will come at the second resurrection of the dead, the resurrection of the body, telling us how it was revealed to him: *And I saw a great white throne and the one who sat on it, from whose face heaven and earth flee away, and no place is found for them* (Rv 20:11).... For, in fact, once the judgment is accomplished, this heaven and this earth will cease to exist, and a new heaven and a new earth will come into being. It is not by its utter destruction, however, but rather by its transmutation that this world will pass away. That is why the Apostle says, *For the figure of this world is passing away. I want you to be free from anxieties.* (1 Cor 7:31-32) It is the figure, then, and not the nature that is passing away.

Thus, after John had said that he saw one sitting on the throne from whose face heaven and earth flee away, which will happen after the judgment, he went on

---

19. "Bishops...presbyters...priests": *episcopis...presbyteris...sacerdotes*. It seems (although it is not entirely clear) that Augustine is saying that both bishops and presbyters are properly referred to as *sacerdotes*, which in the Western Church in the first two or three centuries was a term that tended to be applied to bishops alone. Regarding the influential case of Cyprian, see Maurice Bévenot, "Did Cyprian Refer to Presbyteri as Sacerdotes?" in *Journal of Theological Studies* 30 (1979) 423, which answers in the negative. The Latin text of Rv 20:6, in any event, demands that the term not be restricted to clerics, whether bishops or presbyters, but be applied to all Christians.
20. "Christs...anointing": *christos...chrisma*.
21. See Phil 2:7.
22. See above at X,3.20.

to say, *And I saw the dead, great and small, and books were opened. And another book was opened, which is the book of each person's life. And the dead were judged according to their works on the basis of what was written in the books.* (Rv 20:12) He said that books were opened, and a book, but he does not conceal from us what sort of book this is: *which is*, he tells us, *the book of each person's life.* Thus, the first books he mentioned must be understood as the sacred books, both the Old Testament and the New Testament, which were opened to show what God has ordered us to do as his commandments, and in the book *which is the book of each person's life* it is shown which of these each person has or has not done. If we think of this book in a material sense, who could possibly estimate its size or its length, or how much time it would take to read a book in which the entire life of every person is written? Or will there be as many angels present as there are human beings, so that each person will hear his life recounted by the angel assigned to him? In that case there will not be one book for all but a separate book for each person. But this passage of Scripture clearly wants it to be understood that there is only one book, for it says, *And another book was opened.* We must take the view, then, that there is a certain divine force by which all a person's deeds, both good and evil, will be recalled to his memory and mentally reviewed with astonishing speed, so that each person's knowledge will accuse or excuse his conscience,[23] and so all and each will be judged at the same time. And this divine force is called a book, no doubt, because in it we read, in a sense, everything it causes us to remember....

15. ...This book is not a reminder to God, to keep him from making a mistake through forgetfulness. Rather, it signifies the predestination of those to whom eternal life will be given. For it is not that God has no knowledge of them and has to read this book to find out who they are. Rather, his foreknowledge of them, which cannot possibly be mistaken, is itself the book of life in which they are written, that is, are known beforehand.

16. Having finished with the judgment he foretold for the wicked, it remains for John to speak also of the good. First he explained what the Lord put briefly: *And these shall go into eternal punishment* (Mt 25:46); now he goes on to explain the words that follow: *But the righteous into eternal life* (Mt 25:46). *And I saw,* he says, *a new heaven and a new earth. For the first heaven and the first earth have passed away, and the sea is no more.* (Rv 21:1) This will happen in the order which he had already indicated by way of anticipation, when he said that he had seen the one who sat on the throne, *from whose face heaven and earth flee away.* For, once those who are not written in the book of life have been judged and thrown into eternal fire (and no one, I suppose, knows what kind of fire this will be, or where in the world or the universe it will be located, unless perhaps there is someone to whom the divine Spirit has made this known), then the figure of this world will pass away in a conflagration of this-worldly fires, just as the flood happened in an

---

23. See Rom 2:15.

inundation of this-worldly waters. In that this-worldly conflagration, as I say, the qualities of the corruptible elements which were suited to our corruptible bodies will wholly perish in the burning, and by a miraculous transformation their very substance will take on the qualities appropriate to immortal bodies. As a result, the world, now renewed for the better, will be fit and suited for persons who have themselves been renewed for the better, even in their flesh.

As for the statement, *and the sea is no more*, I do not find it easy to say whether the sea will be dried up by that intense heat or whether it will itself be changed for the better. We read that there will be a new heaven and a new earth, but I do not recall having read anything anywhere about a new sea, except, perhaps, what is found in this same book: *a sea of glass, as it were, like crystal* (Rv 4:6). In that passage, however, John was not speaking of the end of the world, nor does it seem that he was speaking of the sea in any literal sense but rather of *a sea, as it were*. But prophetic speech loves to mingle figurative with literal expressions and, in this way, to veil its meaning to some extent; and so in the present case it could be that, in saying that *the sea is no more*, he is speaking of the sea of which he had just said, *And the sea gave up the dead that were in it*. For then this age, the turbulent and stormy age of mortal life, will be no more; and so it is this age that the word *sea* indicates, in a figurative sense.

The New Jerusalem

17. *And I saw*, John says, *a great city, the new Jerusalem, coming down out of heaven from God, prepared as a new bride adorned for her husband. And I heard a great voice from the throne saying, See, the dwelling of God is with men, and he shall dwell with them, and they shall be his people, and God himself shall be with them. And he shall wipe every tear from their eyes, and death shall be no more, nor mourning, nor weeping, nor shall there be any pain at all, for the former things have passed away. And the one who was seated on the throne said, See, I make all things new.* (Rv 21:2-5) This city is said to come down out of heaven because the grace by which God made it is heavenly. That is why God also says to it through Isaiah, *I am the Lord who makes you* (Is 45:8 LXX). And this city has been coming down out of heaven from its very beginning, from the time when the number of its citizens began to increase in this present age by the grace of God, which comes from above through the washing of regeneration[24] in the Holy Spirit sent down out of heaven. But, by God's judgment through his son Jesus Christ (which will be the last judgment), its splendor will shine out by God's gift with a clarity so bright and so new that no traces of the old will remain. And even our bodies will pass from their old corruption and mortality into a new incorruption and immortality....

---

24. See Tit 3:5.

In this book called The Apocalypse many things are said obscurely in order to exercise the mind of the reader,[25] but there are a few things in it that are put clearly so that, in their light, the rest can be searched out with hard work. This is chiefly because John repeats the same things in many different ways, so that he seems to be speaking of different matters when in fact it turns out on investigation that he is speaking of the same matters in different ways. But when he says, *He shall wipe every tear from their eyes, and death shall be no more, nor mourning, nor crying, nor shall there be any pain at all*, it is as plain as day that he is speaking of the world to come and of the immortality and eternity of the saints, for only then and only there will these things be no more. And if we find this obscure, we should not expect to read anything clear at all in Sacred Scripture!...

Testimonies from the Apostle Paul: the Coming of Antichrist

19. I see that there are many passages in the Gospels and the apostolic writings about this last divine judgment that I have to leave out in order to keep this volume from running on too long. But I must not omit what the apostle Paul writes to the Thessalonians: *As to the coming of our Lord Jesus Christ and our being gathered together to him, we beg you, brothers, not to be quickly shaken in mind or alarmed, either by spirit or by word, or by a letter as though from us, as if the day of the Lord were at hand. Let no one deceive you in any way, for that day shall not come unless the apostate comes first and the man of sin is revealed, the son of perdition who opposes and exalts himself above all that is called God or is worshiped, so that he may take his seat in the temple of God, showing himself as if he were God. Do you not remember that these things were told to you when I was still with you? And now you know what is holding him back, so that he may be revealed when his time comes. For the mystery of iniquity is already at work. Only let the one who is now holding keep on holding, until he is taken from our midst, and then the iniquitous one shall be revealed, whom the Lord Jesus shall slay with the breath of his mouth and shall annihilate by the brightness of his coming. The coming of the iniquitous one is in accord with the working of Satan, with all power and signs and lying wonders and every deception of iniquity for those who are perishing, because they did not receive love of the truth so that they might be saved. For this reason God shall send them the workings of error, so that they may believe a lie, and all may be judged who did not believe the truth but consented to iniquity.* (2 Thes 2:1-12)

There is no doubt that it was about Antichrist that Paul said these things, and specifically that the day of judgment, which he here calls *the day of the Lord*, will not come unless there first comes the one whom he calls *the apostate* — apostate,

---

25. It was a widespread view, repeated often by Augustine, that scriptural obscurity was intended to exercise the reader. See *Teaching Christianity* II,6,7-8; IV,6,9; Letter 137,18. See also Origen, *Against Celsus* III,45.

that is, from the Lord God. And, if this name can rightly be used of all the ungodly, how much more of him! It is uncertain, however, in which temple he is going to take his seat, whether in the ruins of the temple built by Solomon or in the Church. For the Apostle certainly would not call the temple of any idol or demon *the temple of God*. For this reason, some hold that in this passage Antichrist means not the prince himself but rather his whole body as it were, that is, the multitude of people who belong to him, along with their prince himself.[26] And they think it would be more correct if the Latin said, as the Greek does, not *in the temple of God* but "as the temple of God," as if he were himself the temple of God, that is, the Church. It is in this sense, for instance, that we say that someone "sits as a friend," meaning "like a friend," or any other instances in which we customarily use expressions of this sort.

And now you know what is holding him back — that is, you know what is restraining him, what is causing his delay — *so that he may be revealed when his time comes* (2 Thes 2:6). Here, since he said that they already knew, Paul did not want to state this openly. And that is why we, who do not know what they knew, are not able to discover what the Apostle meant, even when we work at it, no matter how much we desire to do so, especially because what he says next makes his meaning even more obscure. For what does this mean: *For the mystery of iniquity is already at work. Only let the one who is now holding keep on holding, until he is taken from our midst, and then the iniquitous one shall be revealed* (2 Thes 2:78)? As for me, I admit that I simply do not know what he is talking about. I shall at least mention, however, the conjectures that I have been able to hear or to read.

Some people suppose that this refers to the Roman empire and that the apostle Paul did not want to write openly about it for fear of incurring the charge of wishing ill to the Roman empire at a time when people hoped it would be eternal. In this view, when he said, *For the mystery of iniquity is already at work* (2 Thes 2:7), he meant this to be understood as a reference to Nero, whose deeds already seemed like those of Antichrist.[27] And so some people speculate that Nero himself is going to rise again and will be Antichrist. Others even think that Nero was not killed but rather was secretly taken away, so that it would look as though he had been killed, and is living in hiding.[28] They believe that he is still in the full vigor of his age at the time he supposedly died and that he will stay in hiding until, *when his time comes*, he will be revealed and restored to his kingdom.[29] For my part, however, I am astonished at the extraordinary presumption of those who hold this opinion.

---

26. This collective understanding of Antichrist can be found in Tertullian, *Prescription against Heretics* 4; Tychonius, *Book of Seven Rules* 7 ("The devil and his body") (PL 18,55-66). Augustine was familiar with Tychonius's work and summarized it in *Teaching Christianity* III,30,42-37,56.
27. See Jerome, *Commentary on Daniel* 11:30: "Many of our people think that, on account of the vastness of his savagery and wickedness, Domitius Nero was Antichrist."
28. See Dio Chrysostom, *Discourse* 21,9-10.
29. See Suetonius, *Lives of the Twelve Caesars*, Nero 57.

On the other hand, when the Apostle says, *Only let the one who is now holding keep on holding, until he is taken from our midst* (2 Thes 2:7), it is not absurd to believe that this does refer to the Roman empire, as if Paul were saying, "Only let the one who reigns keep on reigning, until he is taken from our midst," that is, until he is removed from our midst. *And then the iniquitous one shall be revealed* (2 Thes 2:8): here no one doubts that Antichrist is signified. There are others, however, who think that the phrases *you know what is holding him back* and *the mystery of iniquity* simply refer to the wicked and the imposters who are in the Church until they become so numerous that they make up a great people for Antichrist; and this, they contend, is the *mystery of iniquity* because it seems to be hidden from our eyes. They think, too, that the Apostle is exhorting the faithful to persevere tenaciously in the faith that they hold, when he says, *Only let the one who is now holding keep on holding, until he is taken from our midst*, that is, until the mystery of iniquity, which is now hidden, departs from the midst of the Church. For they are of the opinion that John the evangelist is referring to this same mystery in his epistle, when he says, *Children, it is the last hour, and, as you have heard that Antichrist is going to come, even now there are many antichrists. From this we know that it is the last hour. They went out from us, but they did not belong to us. For, if they had belonged to us, they would have remained with us.* (1 Jn 2:18-19) Thus, they say, just as many heretics — whom John calls many antichrists — departed from the midst of the Church prior to the end, during the hour which he calls *the last hour*, so at that time all will depart who belong not to Christ but rather to that last Antichrist, who will then be revealed.

Thus one person makes one conjecture about the obscure words of the Apostle and another makes another. What is not in doubt, however, is that Paul said that Christ will not come to judge the living and the dead unless his adversary, Antichrist, comes first to deceive those who are dead in soul, although the very fact that they are deceived by him is a function of the judgment of God that is now hidden from us. For, as it is said, *the coming of the iniquitous one is in accord with the working of Satan, with all power and signs and lying wonders and every deception of iniquity for those who are perishing, because they did not receive love of the truth so that they might be saved* (2 Thes 2:9-10). At that time Satan will be released, and through that Antichrist he will work, marvelously but mendaciously, with all his power. It is a common matter of doubt whether these are called *signs and lying wonders* because the devil will deceive mortal senses by means of phantasms, so that he seems to do what he does not actually do, or because, even though they are true wonders, they will draw people into a lie since, not knowing the devil's power, they will believe that such works could only have been done by divine agency, especially at the time when the devil will have acquired such power as he never had before. After all, when fire fell from heaven and consumed the vast household and the vast flocks of holy Job at a stroke, and a whirlwind rushed in and destroyed his house and killed his children, these were no phantasms. But they were still the work of Satan, to whom God had given this power.[30]

Why these are called lying signs and wonders will be made clear, rather, at that time itself. No matter which of these is the reason, however, the people who are deceived by these signs and wonders will be the people who deserve to be deceived by them, *because*, as he says, *they did not receive love of the truth so that they might be saved* (2 Thes 2:10). And the Apostle did not hesitate to go on to say, *For this reason, God shall send them the workings of error, so that they may believe a lie* (2 Thes 2:11). It is God who will send this, because it is God who by his own just judgment permits the devil to do these things, although the devil is himself acting on the basis of his own wicked and malicious intent. *So that all may be judged*, he says, *who did not believe the truth but consented to iniquity* (2 Thes 2:12). Thus, having been judged, they will be deceived; and, having been deceived, they will be judged. But, having been judged, they will be deceived by virtue of those judgments of God, both hiddenly just and justly hidden, by which he has never ceased to judge since the rational creature first began to sin. And, having been deceived, they will be judged at that last and manifest judgment through Christ Jesus, who will judge most justly, even though he himself was most unjustly judged.

Paul on the Resurrection of the Dead

20. But the Apostle says nothing here about the resurrection of the dead. In his first epistle to these same people,[31] however, he writes, *We do not want you to be uninformed, brothers, about those who are asleep, so that you may not grieve as others do who have no hope. For, if we believe that Jesus died and rose again, even so, through Jesus, God shall bring with him those who have fallen asleep. For this we declare to you by the word of the Lord, that we who are alive, who are left until the coming of the Lord, will not precede those who have fallen asleep. For the Lord himself, with a cry of command and with the voice of the archangel and with the sound of the trumpet of God, shall descend from heaven, and the dead in Christ shall rise first. Then we who are alive, who are left, will be caught up in the clouds together with them to meet Christ in the air, and so we will be with the Lord forever.* (1 Thes 4:13-17) These words of the Apostle show most clearly that there will be a resurrection of the dead when Christ comes — when he comes, that is, to judge the living and the dead....

But how this is going to happen is something we can now only guess at with our feeble little reasoning powers; it is only when it actually happens that we shall be able to know. If we wish to be Christians, however, we must believe that

---

30. See Jb 1:12-19.
31. I.e., the Thessalonians.

there is certainly going to be a resurrection of the dead, in the flesh, when Christ comes to judge the living and the dead, and the fact that we are unable to understand perfectly how this resurrection will actually take place in no way means that our faith is empty on this score.

But now, as we promised above, we need to show — as far as seems sufficient — what the ancient prophetic books foretold about this last judgment of God, and it will not be necessary, I think, to expound and explain these passages at any great length if the reader simply takes the trouble to make use of the help provided by the passages we have already set forth.

Testimonies from the Prophet Isaiah: the Separate Ends of the Good and the Evil

21. The prophet Isaiah says,... *Thus says the Lord, Behold, I will flow down on them like a river of peace, and like a torrent overflowing the glory of the nations. Their children shall be carried on their shoulders and shall be comforted on their knees. As one whom his mother comforts, so will I comfort you, and you shall be comforted in Jerusalem, and you shall see, and your heart shall rejoice, and your bones shall rise up like the grass* (Is 66:12-14)....

By *Jerusalem* here we should understand not the Jerusalem which is in servitude with her children but rather the Jerusalem which is, according to the Apostle, the free woman, our mother, eternal in heaven.[32] There, after the toils of the anxieties and cares of this mortal existence, we shall be comforted like her little children carried on her shoulders and on her knees. For that unaccustomed bliss will support us, like new and inexperienced children, with the most tender of helping hands. There we shall see, and our heart will rejoice. Isaiah does not explicitly tell us what we shall see, but what else can he mean but God, so that the Gospel's promise may be fulfilled in us, *Blessed are the pure in heart, for they shall see God* (Mt 5:8)? And we shall see, too, all that we do not now see but believe, all that we can now only conceive according to the measure of our human capacity, which falls incomparably short of what the reality actually is. *And you shall see*, he says, *and your heart shall rejoice* (Is 66:14). Here you believe; there you will see.

Because he said, *And your heart shall rejoice*, he then adds, *and your bones shall rise up like the grass* (Is 66:14). Here he touches on the resurrection of the body, as if supplying an omission, in order to keep us from thinking that the blessings of Jerusalem pertain only to the spirit. For the resurrection of the body will not take place after we have seen; rather, it is after the resurrection of the body has taken place that we shall see. For he had already spoken of the new heaven and the new earth when he was describing, often and in many different ways, the things

---

32. See Gal 4:24-26.

which are promised to the saints at the end. *There shall be,* he had said, *a new heaven and a new earth, and the former things shall not be remembered or come to mind, but they shall find joy and exultation in it. See, I will make Jerusalem an exultation and my people a joy, and I will exult in Jerusalem and rejoice in my people, and the sound of weeping shall no longer be heard in her* (Is 65:17-19), and so on through the rest of the passage, which some try to apply to life in the flesh during those thousand years. In the usual prophetic manner, however, figurative and literal expressions are mingled here, so that sober attentiveness may, by useful and salutary labor, arrive at the spiritual meaning. In contrast, carnal indolence or the slowness of the uninstructed and untrained mind is content with the literal meaning that lies on the surface and presumes that there is no more inward meaning to be sought. But I have said enough about the words of the prophet written prior to the passage we have been concerned with....

Testimonies from the Psalms:
the Perishing of the World and Christ's Coming as Judge

24. Many passages in the Psalms speak of the last judgment, but for the most part only briefly and in passing. Yet I am certainly not going to leave out what is said there, with complete clarity, about the end of this world: *In the beginning, Lord, you laid the foundation of the earth, and the heavens are the work of your hands. They shall perish, but you endure; they shall all grow old like a garment, and you shall change them like clothing, and they shall be changed; but you are the same, and your years shall not fail* (Ps 102:25-27). Why is it that Porphyry, even though he praises the Hebrews for their piety in worshiping a God who is great and true and terrible even to the divinities themselves, charges the Christians with utter folly on the basis of oracles from those very gods of his, because they claim that this world is going to perish?[33] See what the Scriptures of the Hebrews' piety say to the very God before whom, as this philosopher admits, the divinities themselves shrink in dread: *The heavens are the work of your hands. They shall perish* (Ps 102:25-26)....

Testimonies from Malachi:
the Purification of the Saints and Their Pure Offering to God

25. The prophet Malachiel or Malachi, who is also called "Angel,"[34] is held by some to be Ezra the priest (Jerome says that this is the opinion of the Hebrews[35]),

---

33. See above at XIX,23.
34. "Malachi" means "my messenger" in Hebrew, and the Greek word for "messenger" is *angelos* ("angel"). "Malachiel" means "messenger of God."
35. See *Commentary on Malachi*, preface.

the author of certain other writings that have been accepted into the canon. He gives this prophecy about the last judgment: *See, he comes, says the Lord almighty, and who will endure the day of his coming, or who can bear to look at him? For he comes like a refiner's fire and like a fuller's herb, and he shall sit, refining and purifying them like silver and gold, and he shall purify the sons of Levi and shall pour them out like gold and silver. And they shall offer sacrifices to the Lord in righteousness, and the sacrifice of Judah and Jerusalem shall be pleasing to the Lord, as in the days of old and as in former years. And I will come to you in judgment, and I will be a swift witness against sorcerers, and against adulterers, and against those who swear falsely in my name, and against those who cheat hired workers of their wages, and against those who use their power to oppress widows and afflict orphans and pervert judgment with regard to the stranger and who do not fear me, says the Lord almighty. For I am the Lord your God, and do not change. (Mal 3:1-6)*

From what he says here it seems quite clear that in that judgment there will be a kind of purgatorial punishment for some. For what else can it mean when he says, *Who will endure the day of his coming, or who can bear to look at him? For he comes like a refiner's fire and like a fuller's herb, and he shall sit, refining and purifying them like silver and gold, and he shall purify the sons of Levi and pour them out like gold and silver* (Mal 3:2-3)? Isaiah, too, says something similar: *The Lord shall wash away the filth of the sons and daughters of Zion and shall cleanse the blood from their midst by a spirit of judgment and a spirit of burning* (Is 4:4), unless perhaps we should say that they are cleansed of their filth, and in a certain sense purified, when the evil are separated from them by penal judgment. In that case the separation and condemnation of the evil serves as the purgation of the good, since from then on they will live without any intermingling with such people. But when Malachi says, *And he shall purify the sons of Levi and pour them out like gold and silver, and they shall offer sacrifices to the Lord in righteousness, and the sacrifice of Judah and Jerusalem shall be pleasing to the Lord* (Mal 3:34), he clearly indicates that the ones who will be purified are the very ones who will then be pleasing to the Lord in their righteous sacrifices. They themselves will be cleansed of their unrighteousness, on account of which they were previously displeasing to God. And once they have been purified, they themselves will be offerings of full and perfect righteousness. For what can such persons offer that is more acceptable to God than themselves? But this question of purgatorial punishments must be postponed to another time for more detailed discussion.[36]...

29. After he had admonished them to remember the law of Moses — for he foresaw that for a long time to come they would still not interpret it in a spiritual sense as they should — he immediately went on to say, *And see, I will send you*

---

36. See below at XXI,13-14.

Elijah the Tishbite, before the great and luminous day of the Lord comes. He shall turn the heart of a father to his son and the heart of a man to his neighbor, lest I come and smite the earth to its depths. (Mal 4:5-6) It is very often on the lips and in the hearts of the faithful that in the last time, before the judgment, this great and wonderful prophet Elijah will expound the law to the Jews and that they will come to believe in the true Christ, that is, in our Christ. And it is not without reason that we hope that he himself will come before the Savior comes as judge,[37] for it is not without reason that we believe that he is still alive. In fact, as Sacred Scripture most clearly attests, he was caught up from this human world in a fiery chariot.[38] When he comes, then, he will interpret in a spiritual sense the law which the Jews now understand only in a carnal sense, and so *he shall turn the heart of a father to his son* (Mal 4:6), that is, the heart of fathers to their sons (for the translators of the Septuagint used the singular in place of the plural). And the meaning is that the sons, that is, the Jews, will understand the law in the same way that their fathers, that is, the prophets, including Moses himself, understood it. For the heart of fathers will be turned to their sons when the fathers' understanding is presented to their sons for their understanding, *and the heart of sons to their fathers* (Mal 4:6) when the former consent to the views of the latter. Here the Septuagint says *the heart of a man to his neighbor* (Mal 4:6), for fathers and sons are obviously neighbors to each other....

How the Old Testament Points to Christ as Judge

30. There are many other testimonies to the last judgment of God in Divine Scripture, but it would take too long for me to collect them all. Let it suffice, therefore, that we have proved that it was foretold in both the New and the Old Testaments. But the Old Testament does not express as clearly as the New that the judgment is going to take place through Christ, that is, that Christ is going to come from heaven as judge. For, when the Lord God says in the Old Testament that he will come, or it is said of the Lord God that he will come, people do not understand that, as a consequence, Christ is meant. For *the Lord God* can mean the Father or the Son or the Holy Spirit. But this is not a point that we can leave unsupported.

In the first place, then, we need to show how Jesus Christ speaks in the prophetic books as the Lord God, and yet it is quite clear that Jesus Christ is the one speaking. On this basis it will be possible to see that, even where this is not as clear, Jesus Christ is still the one meant when it says that the Lord God will come for that last judgment. There is a passage in the prophet Isaiah which shows clearly what I am talking about. For God says through the prophet, *Listen to me, Jacob and Israel, whom I call. I am the first, and I am forever, and my hand laid the foundation of*

---

37. See Mt 11:13-14, where Jesus says that Elijah has already come in the person of John the Baptist.
38. See 2 K 2:11.

the earth, and my right hand established the heavens. I will call them, and they shall stand together, and they shall all be gathered together and shall hear. Who has declared these things to them? For love of you, I did your will on Babylon, that I might take away the seed of the Chaldeans. And I have spoken and I have called; I have brought him and have made his way prosperous. Draw near to me and hear this. From the beginning I have not spoken in secret; when they came about, I was there. And now the Lord God has sent me, and his Spirit. (Is 48:12-16) Clearly it is Christ himself who is speaking here as the Lord God, but we would not have understood that it was Jesus Christ if he had not added, *And now the Lord God has sent me, and his Spirit* (Is 48:16). For he said this according to the form of a servant,[39] using the past tense to represent a future reality, just as we read in the same prophet, *He was led as a lamb to the slaughter* (Is 53:7). He did not say "will be led" but used the past tense of the verb for an event that was going to take place in the future. And prophecy regularly speaks in this way.[40]

There is another passage, in Zechariah, which plainly shows that the Almighty sent the Almighty, and who can the sender and the sent be if not God the Father and God the Son? For it is written, *Thus says the Lord almighty, After the glory he has sent me to the nations that plundered you, for one who touches you touches, as it were, the pupil of his eye. See, I will lift up my hand against them, and they shall become plunder for those who had served them, and you shall know that the Lord almighty has sent me.* (Zec 2:8-9) Take note: the Lord almighty says that he was sent by the Lord almighty. Who would dare to think that anyone but Christ was speaking here — speaking, that is, to the lost sheep of the house of Israel. For he says in the Gospel, *I was sent only to the lost sheep of the house of Israel* (Mt 15:24), whom he compared here to the pupil of God's eye, on account of God's deep feeling of love for them. After all, the apostles themselves were sheep of this kind.[41] But after the glory — that is, after the glory of his resurrection, for the evangelist says that, prior to his resurrection, *Jesus was not yet glorified* (Jn 7:39)— he was also sent to the nations in the persons of his apostles, and so what we read in the Psalm was fulfilled, *You shall deliver me from the contradictions of the people; you shall set me at the head of the nations* (Ps 18:43). Thus those who had plundered the Israelites, and whom the Israelites had served when they were subject to the gentiles, were not merely to be plundered in turn but were themselves to become the plunder of the Israelites. For this is what Christ had promised to the apostles, when he said, *I will make you fishers of men* (Mt 4:19); and to one of them he said, *From now on you shall be catching men* (Lk 5:10). The nations were to become plunder, then, but in a good sense, like goods taken from that strong man after he was bound more securely.[42]

---

39. See Phil 2:7.
40. Biblical Hebrew has no future tense and regularly uses the imperfect tense (*praeteritum tempus*) to express the future.
41. See Mt 26:31 (citing Zec 13:7) par.
42. See Mt 12:29.

Again, speaking through the same prophet, the Lord says, *And it shall be on that day that I will seek to destroy all the nations that come against Jerusalem, and I will pour out a spirit of grace and mercy on the house of David and on the inhabitants of Jerusalem, and they shall look on me because they reviled me, and they shall mourn for him as for their dearest, and they shall grieve as for an only-begotten son* (Zec 12:9-10). Now, to whom but God does it belong to destroy all the nations that are hostile to the holy city of Jerusalem and *come against* it, that is, are opposed to it, or, as others translate, "come upon it," that is, come upon it in order to subject it to themselves? And to whom but God does it belong to pour out *a spirit of grace and mercy on the house of David* and on the inhabitants of that same city? Clearly these things belong to God, and it is in the person of God as the speaker that they are announced through the prophet. And yet Christ shows that he is himself the God who does these obviously great and divine things, for he goes on to say, *And they shall look on me because they reviled me, and they shall mourn for him as for their dearest* (or *their beloved*), *and they shall grieve as for an only-begotten son* (Zec 12:10). For on that day, when they see him coming in his majesty and recognize him whom, at his first coming in humility, they mocked in their ancestors, the Jews (including even those who are going to receive a spirit of grace and mercy) will certainly grieve over having reviled Christ in his passion. Their ancestors themselves, however, the authors of that terrible impiety, will see Christ when they rise again, but only for their punishment, no longer for their correction. They are not the ones, then, to whom we should understand this passage to refer where it says, *And I will pour out a spirit of grace and mercy on the house of David and on the inhabitants of Jerusalem, and they shall look on me because they reviled me* (Zec 12:10). It is referring rather to their descendants, who at that time are going to believe, thanks to Elijah. But, just as we say to the Jews, "You killed Christ," even though it was actually their ancestors who did this, so also the Jews will grieve for having done in a sense what was actually done by those from whose line they descended. Thus, even though they will have received *a spirit of grace and mercy* and, as believers, will not be condemned along with their progenitors, they will still grieve as if they themselves had done what their ancestors did. Their grief, then, will stem not from criminal guilt but from a feeling of devotion.[43]

It is true that, where the translators of the Septuagint said, *And they shall look on me because they reviled me*, the Hebrew itself is translated this way, *And they shall look on me whom they pierced*. And the word *pierced* is obviously a clearer

---

43. From what Augustine says here, it is unclear whether he held that Jews who converted to Christianity were not responsible for what their ancestors did, although they could still be told that "you killed Christ" and would grieve over their ancestors' crime as if they themselves had committed it, or whether he believed that they were in fact responsible but were nonetheless forgiven. On Augustine's attitude toward the Jews, which was more tolerant than that of many of his contemporaries, see Paula Frederiksen, *Augustine and the Jews: A Christian Defense of Jews and Judaism* (New York: Doubleday, 2008).

indication of Christ crucified. But in fact the reviling which the Septuagint translators preferred to insert here was not lacking at any point in the whole passion of Christ. For they reviled him when he was arrested,[44] when he was bound,[45] when he was judged,[46] when he was clothed in humiliating garments to shame him,[47] when he was crowned with thorns,[48] when he was struck on the head with a reed,[49] when he was mockingly adored on bended knee,[50] when he was carrying his own cross,[51] and even while he was hanging on the tree.[52] Thus, it is not by following just one translation or the other, but rather by joining them together so as to include both *they reviled him* and *they pierced him*, that we come most fully to recognize the truth of the Lord's passion.

When, therefore, we read in the prophetic writings that God is going to come to carry out the last judgment, even if no other indication is given, we ought to understand that Christ is the one who will come, simply because the judgment itself is mentioned. For, even though the Father will judge, he will judge through the coming of the Son of Man. The Father himself, in his own manifest presence, *judges no one but has given all judgment to the Son* (Jn 5:22), who will be manifested as a man when he comes to judge, just as he was a man when he came to be judged. For who else is it of whom God speaks through Isaiah, under the name of Jacob and Israel, from whose line of descent he took his body? Here is what the passage says: *Jacob is my servant, I will uphold him; Israel is my chosen one, my soul has embraced him. I have given my spirit to him; he shall bring forth judgment to the nations. He shall not cry out, nor cease, nor shall his voice be heard outside. He shall not break a bruised reed, and he shall not quench the smoking flax, but he shall bring forth judgment in truth. He shall shine and shall not be broken until he sets judgment in the earth, and in his name the nations shall put their hope.* (Is 42:1-4) The names *Jacob* and *Israel* are not found in the Hebrew, but the Septuagint translators undoubtedly wanted to prompt us as to how we should understand the phrase, *my servant*, which is found in the Hebrew. This phrase is used on account of the form of a servant[53] in which the Most High showed himself in utter humility. And so, to signify Christ, the translators inserted the name of the very man from whose line of descent he took that form of a servant.

The Holy Spirit was given to him, and this was demonstrated, as the Gospel reports, by the appearance of a dove.[54] He brought forth judgment to the nations

---

44. See Mt 26:50 par.
45. See Mt 27:2 par.
46. See Mt 27:11-26 par.
47. See Mt 27:28 par.
48. See Mt 27:29 par.
49. See Mt 27:30 par.
50. See Mt 27:29 par.
51. See Mt 27:31-32 par.
52. See Mt 27:39-44 par.
53. See Phil 2:7.
54. See Mt 3:16 par.

in that he foretold the future judgment, which was hidden from the nations. In his meekness he did not cry out, but neither did he cease to proclaim the truth. His voice was not heard, and is not heard, outside, because he is not obeyed by those who are outside, cut off from his body. He did not break or quench the Jews themselves, his persecutors, who were compared to a bruised reed due to their loss of integrity and to smoking flax due to their loss of light; rather, he spared them, since he had not yet come to judge them but to be judged by them. He brought forth judgment in truth by proclaiming to them the time when they are to be punished if they persist in their wickedness. His face shone on the mountain,[55] and his fame in all the world. He was not broken or crushed, because neither in himself nor in his Church has he yielded to his persecutors and ceased to exist. And therefore what his enemies said, and still say, has not happened: *When will he die and his name perish?* (Ps 41:5)

Nor will it happen *until he sets judgment in the earth* (Is 42:4). See, the hidden thing that we were looking for has here been made clear. For this is the last judgment, which he will set on the earth when he himself comes from heaven, the one in whom we already see fulfilled the last phrase of this prophecy: *And in his name the nations shall put their hope* (Is 42:4). In the light of this fact, which certainly cannot be denied, let that also be believed which only brazen impudence would deny. For who could have hoped for this outcome? Not only we ourselves but even those who are still unwilling to believe in Christ now see it fulfilled, and, because they cannot possibly deny it, they gnash their teeth and melt away. Who, I say, could have hoped that the nations were going to put their hope in the name of Christ at the time when he was arrested, bound, scourged, mocked, and crucified, and when even the disciples themselves had lost the hope which they had begun to have in him? What a mere single thief on a cross hoped for then,[56] nations spread far and wide across the earth hope for now; and, lest they die an eternal death, they are marked with the sign of the very cross on which he died.[57]

The Events of the Last Judgment

No one, therefore, denies or doubts that there will be a last judgment through Jesus Christ as foretold by these sacred writings — no one, that is, except people who, due to their incredible animosity or their sheer blindness, do not believe these writings, even though they have now demonstrated their truth to the whole world. At that judgment, then, or close to it, we have learned that the following

---

55. See Mt 17:2.
56. See Lk 23:42-43.
57. Augustine is almost certainly referring to the signing of the cross on the forehead, possibly with blessed oil, made either during a person's candidacy for baptism or during baptism itself. See Leonel L. Mitchell, *Baptismal Anointing* (London: SPCK, 1966) 82-85. Although Augustine is somewhat reticent about the details of the baptismal rituals, Ambrose describes baptism in detail, as he celebrated it in Milan, and mentions such a signing in *On the Sacraments* VI,2.

things are going to happen: Elijah the Tishbite will come, the Jews will believe, Antichrist will persecute, Christ will judge, the dead will rise, the good will be separated from the evil, and the conflagration and renewal of the world will take place. All of these things, we must believe, are going to happen. But how they are going to take place, and in what order, is something that the experience of the actual events will teach us then far more fully than any human intelligence can grasp them now. My own view, however, is that they are going to happen in the order in which I have listed them.

Two books pertinent to our task remain if, with God's help, we are to complete what we have promised. One of these will deal with the punishment of the evil, the other with the happiness of the righteous. In these books, so far as God grants, we shall in particular refute the human arguments by which some wretched people, who think themselves wise, seem to gnaw away at the divine prophecies and promises and to deride as false and ridiculous the nourishment of our salutary faith. But those who are wise according to God hold that the strongest argument for all the things that seem incredible to human beings and yet are contained in Holy Scripture, whose truth has now been upheld in so many ways, is the sheer truthfulness and omnipotence of God. They take it as certain that God could by no means have lied in Scripture and that he is fully able to do what, to the unbeliever, is impossible.

Study Questions for Book XX

The Day of Judgment is attested to by the authority of Scripture and is beyond human reason. Yet Augustine's sweeping review of scriptural texts on this topic involves both a penetrating analysis of their meaning and an inventive narrative constructed out of his analysis. Is Book XX a good example of faith and reason as two complementary ways of knowing?

One of the titles or roles of Christ in the New Testament is that of Judge. What relationship do you see between Christ as Judge, so prominent in Book XX, and other titles of Christ favored by Augustine, such as, for example, Physician, Way, Shepherd and Mediator?

The images, persons and events described in the Book of Revelation and elaborated by Augustine are a Scripture-based affirmation of the "ends" of the two cities. Our decisions during this life, as citizens of the City of God or of the City of Man, have real and ultimate consequences. Do contemporary readings of the Book of Revelation based on historical-critical methods undercut the power of Augustine's hortatory passion regarding final judgement?

BOOK XXI

Book XXI discusses the eternal punishment of those who are condemned at the last judgment. It begins by offering a brief justification for taking up the punishment of the damned before turning to the eternal happiness of the blessed. The book then divides into two parts. In the initial part Augustine seeks to vindicate the notion of eternal bodily punishment first by arguing that the body can survive forever in fire; then, by indicating that the body can feel pain eternally without dying, especially since the soul, which is, after all, the real seat of pain, is immortal and therefore does not die, and the body will then be connected to the soul in such a way that the connection cannot be broken by death; and, finally, by noting that there are any number of natural wonders (many of which are so familiar to us that we no longer wonder at them) which show that divine power can do things that appear to be contrary to nature (but only appear to be, since it is actually the divine will that determines the order of nature) and ultimately can change a thing in such a way as to introduce properties that did not originally belong to it, including the bodily property of surviving in eternal torment. To these points the book appends brief considerations of the purgatorial nature of some punishments, the mode in which the demons feel the pain of material fire, and the justice of the correlation of temporal sin with eternal punishment (it is not the time it takes to commit a sin, but rather its gravity, that justifies eternal punishment). In the second part of the book Augustine addresses various views — which he holds to be erroneous — that all or some human beings will, on one basis or another, ultimately be released by divine mercy from the eternal punishment to which they were condemned at the last judgment. In responding to these views he argues first of all that Scripture makes it clear that eternal punishment means an eternal punishment that is not abrogated or abbreviated by any working of divine mercy (otherwise the eternality of eternal happiness would also be put in question); that participation in the sacraments, perseverance in the Catholic Church, and performing works of mercy do not by themselves guarantee ultimate release from eternal punishment (and thus provide a license to sin) without the love of Christ that is expressed in striving to live virtuously; that the intercession of the saints no longer applies in the case of those who, after death, have lost the opportunity for repentance; and, lastly, that, while Scripture speaks of a purgatorial fire that purifies some either in this life or after death, it is not to be identified with the eternal fire of eternal punishment.

1. In this book — as best we can with God's help — we need to discuss more fully the kind of punishment that is in store for the devil and all who belong to him when the two cities, the city of God and the city of the devil, reach their due ends through Jesus Christ our Lord, the judge of the living and the dead. I have preferred to follow this order, leaving the felicity of the saints for later, because, although both the damned and the saved will then be united with their bodies, it seems more incredible that bodies should continue to exist in eternal torments than that they should endure, without any pain at all, in eternal blessedness. Thus, a demonstration that such punishment should not be considered incredible will be a great help to me. It will make it much easier for people to accept the future immortality of the body, free from all affliction, in the case of the saints....

The Body and Eternal Fire

2. What can I point to, then, to convince the incredulous that it is possible for human bodies, endowed with soul and life, not only to exist forever without being dissolved by death but also to endure amid the torments of eternal flames? Such people refuse to let us simply ascribe this to the sheer power of the Almighty.[1] Instead, they insist that we persuade them with some example. We might reply that there are animals which are certainly subject to corruption, because they are mortal, but which live in the midst of flames; or, again, we might note that there is a species of worm found in the gushing water of hot springs — springs so hot that no one can touch them without burning himself — which not only lives there without any harm but cannot live anywhere else.[2] If we cite such cases, however, they refuse to believe us unless we show them the thing itself; and, even if we can produce an instance before their very eyes, or at least cite fully reliable witnesses, they contend, with the same disbelief, that these are not actually examples of the point in question. These animals, they argue, do not live forever and, what is more, they live in that intense heat without feeling pain. In fact, they claim, far from being in torment, these animals actually thrive in these conditions, which suit their nature — as if it were not even more incredible for them to thrive under such conditions than for them to be in torment! It is amazing to feel pain in the midst of fire and yet to live, but it is still more amazing to live in fire and yet to feel no pain. And, if people are ready to believe the latter, why not the former as well?

---

1. See, e.g., the pagan Celsus, cited in Origen, *Against Celsus* V,14, who both denies the possibility that the body can be everlasting and decries the argument which he says Christians commonly resort to when they are obliged to explain their position, namely, that "anything is possible to God."
2. For another such example see Pliny, *Natural History* XI,42,119. This is the first of a series of examples, continued in sections 4-5 below, of things animate and inanimate possessing unusual properties, mostly having to do with fire.

The Issue of Eternal Pain

3. But there is no body, they claim, which is able to feel pain but cannot die. And how do we know this? Who is certain that it is not in their bodies that the demons feel pain when they confess that they are afflicted with terrible torments? And, if they reply that there is no earthly body (that is, no solid and visible body) or, to put it in a word, no flesh, that is able to feel pain and yet unable to die, what are they saying? They are merely stating what people conclude on the basis of bodily sensation and experience. For the only flesh that they know is mortal flesh, and the whole basis of their reasoning is simply their presumption that what they have not experienced must be impossible. But what kind of reasoning is it to make pain an argument for death when it is actually an indication of life? Even if we have our doubts about whether it is possible to live forever, it is still absolutely certain that anything that feels pain is alive and that there can be no feeling of pain except in something alive. It is necessarily true, then, that anyone feeling pain is alive; but it is not necessarily true that every case of pain kills even these mortal bodies of ours, which are certainly going to die sooner or later. The reason why some pain causes death is that the soul is connected to this body in such a way that, in the face of extreme pain, it withdraws and departs. For the structure of the limbs and vital parts is so weak that it cannot endure the shock that causes great or extreme pain. But in the life to come the soul will be connected to such a body and will be connected to it in such a way that, just as no length of time will dissolve the connection, neither will any form of pain break the connection. Accordingly, even if there is now no sort of flesh which can both suffer the feeling of pain and yet not suffer death, there will then be flesh of a sort that does not exist now — just as there will then be death of a sort that does not exist now. For it is not that there will be no death; it is rather that there will be eternal death, when the soul, not having God, will be able neither to live nor to escape bodily pain by dying. The first death expels the soul from the body against its will; the second death compels the soul to stay in the body against its will. What is common to both deaths is that, in relation to its body, the soul suffers what it does not will.

Those who argue against us pay great attention to the fact that there is no flesh at present that can feel pain but cannot die. They pay no attention at all, however, to the fact that there is something greater than the body: it is perfectly clear that the soul itself, by whose presence the body lives and is governed, can both feel pain and not die. Here, then, we have something that both has the sensation of pain and yet is immortal. And this characteristic, which we know to be present now in the souls of all, will then be present in the bodies of the damned as well.

If we consider the matter more closely, however, we shall see that pain, which is said to belong to the body, actually pertains to the soul. For it is the soul, not the body, that feels pain, even when the reason for its pain stems from the body, in that it feels pain where the body is hurt. Thus, just as we say that bodies feel and bodies are alive, even though it is only due to the soul that the body has sensation and life, so also we say that bodies feel pain even though, apart from the soul, there can be no bodily pain. The soul, then, feels pain together with the body at the point where something happens to put it in pain; and the soul feels pain on its own, even though it is in the body, when it is saddened by some cause, even when the cause is invisible, but the body itself is not injured. The soul also feels pain even when it is not present in a body, for the rich man was certainly feeling pain in hell when he said, *I am in torment in this flame* (Lk 16:24). The body, on the other hand, feels no pain when the soul is not present; and, even when the soul is present, it still does not feel pain on its own apart from the soul. Thus, if we take the argument from pain to death as correct — that is, the argument that what can feel pain can die — death would then belong more to the soul than to the body, since pain itself belongs more to the soul than to the body. But since, in fact, that which is more able to feel pain cannot possibly die, is there any reason why we should believe that the bodies of the damned, because they are going to be in pain, are therefore also going to die?

It is true that the Platonists have claimed that the soul's fears and desires, griefs and joys, stem from these earthly bodies and death-bound members. Echoing their claim, Virgil says, "From these" — that is, from the death-bound members of the earthly body — "they have their fears and desires, their griefs and joys."[3] In the twelfth book of this work, however, we proved to the Platonists that, according to their own view, even after souls have been purged of every stain from the body, they still have a fatal desire due to which they begin once again to want to return to bodies.[4] And, where there can be desire, there obviously can be pain. In fact, frustrated desire — frustrated either because it does not get what it wants or because it loses what it had obtained — turns into pain. Therefore, if the soul — which is the only or at least the chief subject of pain — has its own kind of immortality, the fact that the bodies of the damned are going to feel pain certainly does not entail that they are going to be able to die. Besides, if it is bodies that cause souls to feel pain, why is it that they cannot inflict death on souls as well as pain, unless it simply does not follow that what causes pain also causes death? Why is it so incredible, then, that fire can inflict pain on the bodies of the damned, but not death, in exactly the same way that bodies cause souls to feel pain but do not compel them to die? Pain, therefore, is no argument that what feels pain is necessarily going to die.

The Issue of Survival in Eternal Fire: Natural Wonders and the Power of God

4. According to the works of those who have closely investigated the natural history of animals, the salamander lives in fire;[5] and certain well-known mountains

---

3. See *Aeneid* VI,733.
4. This is discussed not in the twelfth book but at XIV,3.5.
5. See Pliny, *Natural History* X,86,188; *Physiologus* 47.

in Sicily have seethed with flames from time immemorial and right down to the present, and yet they remain whole.[6] These examples provide sufficiently reliable witness that not everything that burns is consumed, and the soul itself shows that not everything that can feel pain is also able to die. Why, then, are we still asked to give examples in support of our teaching? Why is it so incredible to think that the bodies of people suffering eternal punishment do not lose their souls in the fire but instead burn without disintegrating and feel pain without perishing? After all, the substance of the flesh will then be endowed with precisely this quality, bestowed on it by the One who has given such marvelous and various qualities to innumerable things we see every day that, because we have become so used to them all, we no longer marvel at them. Who but God, the creator of all things, has given the flesh of the peacock the property of not rotting after death? When I first heard this, it seemed incredible to me. One day in Carthage, however, I was served a roast peacock, and I ordered that a suitable portion be carved from its breast and set aside. After an interval of some days, long enough for any other kind of cooked meat to have gone bad, it was brought out and presented without any offensive odor at all. It was put back again, and more than thirty days later it was found to be in the same state. And it was still the same after a year, except that the meat had become slightly more shriveled and dry.

Again, who gave straw such cooling power that it keeps snow that is covered with it from melting, and such warming power that it ripens green apples? And who can explain the marvels of fire itself? Whatever it burns, it blackens, but fire itself is bright. Fire itself has the most beautiful color, but it discolors almost everything it engulfs and embraces, and it turns bright coals into the ugliest ash. But this is no absolute rule. On the contrary, stones that are baked in a glowing fire turn white; and, even though the fire is actually red and the stones become white, it remains true that what is white coheres with light, just as what is black coheres with darkness. Thus, when fire burns wood to bake stones, it has contrary effects, but it does not have them in contrary objects. For, even though stones and wood are different, they are not contraries, like white and black. But the fire produces one of these colors in the stones, the other in the wood, its bright flame brightening the former and darkening the latter, although it would have no effect at all on the stones if it were not alive in the wood.

Again, is it not astonishing that charcoal is so brittle that the lightest blow shatters it and the slightest pressure crumbles it, but so durable that no moisture can erode it and no passage of time wear it away? It is so durable, in fact, that people who set up boundary stones make a practice of spreading charcoal under them in order to refute any litigant who might appear, no matter how much later, and claim that the fixed stone is not actually a boundary stone. What is it that enables charcoal to endure so long without damage when it is buried in damp earth where wood simply rots away? What but fire itself, which brings everything to destruction?

---

6. The most famous of these, active both in Augustine's time and at present, are Mounts Etna and Stromboli.

Let us also consider the marvels of lime. Apart from the fact that it becomes white in fire, which turns other things black (a point about which we have already said enough), it also absorbs fire into itself from fire in some mysterious way. While itself remaining a lump cold to the touch, it stores the fire so deep within that it is in no way apparent to our senses. But, as we learn from experience, the fire turns out to be slumbering within the lime even though it is unseen. This is why we call it "quicklime," as if the hidden fire were an invisible soul quickening a visible body. But the truly extraordinary thing is that it is precisely when this fire is quenched that it is kindled. For, to release the hidden fire, the lime is poured into water, or water is poured over it; and, though it was cold before, it is now made hot by the very thing that otherwise makes all hot things turn cold. Thus, as the lump of lime is breathing its last, so to speak, the departing fire, once hidden, now makes its appearance; and, from that point on, the lime is so cold in its death that adding water will no longer set it burning again, and what we once called "quicklime" we now call "extinct" or "slaked" lime. Is there anything that could possibly seem to add to this marvel? And yet there is more. For if you use not water but oil — which, unlike water, is fuel for fire — the lime does not grow hot, no matter whether the oil is poured over the lime or the lime is poured into the oil. If we have read or heard of this marvel in relation to some Indian stone, which we were unable to experience for ourselves,[7] surely we would either consider it an outright lie or, at the least, be very much surprised. But, when daily examples of these things meet our eyes, we take no account of them, not because they are any the less wondrous but simply because they are so commonplace. In fact we even cease to marvel at many of the wonders that come from India itself, a region remote and distant from us, once they have been brought back for us to wonder at.

There are many among us who have diamonds, especially goldsmiths and jewelers; and this stone, we are told, cannot be overcome by iron or fire or any other force except goat's blood.[8] But are those who already have and know diamonds ever as astonished at their power as those to whom that power is shown for the first time? People who have not actually seen its power may not believe it at all; or, if they do believe it, they marvel at something beyond their own experience. And, if they do happen to experience it, they still marvel at something that they find so unfamiliar. But repeated experience will gradually eliminate any stirring of wonder.

We know that the lodestone has the marvelous power to attract iron.[9] When I first saw it, I was utterly amazed. I saw an iron ring lifted up and held suspended by a stone. Then, as if the stone had imparted its own power to the ring it lifted up, sharing its power with it, this ring was put near another and lifted it up. As the

---

7. Pliny devotes *Natural History* XXXVII to stones, and in several places he refers to Indian stones. Augustine does not have a particular one in mind but mentions "some Indian stone" as an example of something exotic.
8. See ibid. XXXVII,15,55-61; *Physiologus* 49.
9. The lodestone, or magnet, is discussed in Pliny, *Natural History* XXXVII,15,61, where Pliny contrasts it with the diamond, as Augustine does below.

first ring clung to the stone, so the second ring clung to the first. And in the same way a third ring was added, and then a fourth. And now there was a kind of chain hanging down, with the rings joined together, not internally by an interlocking of their circles but externally by simply touching each other. Who would not be astounded at this power in a stone, which was not only present in the stone itself but was also transmitted through so many suspended rings, linking them together by invisible bonds?

But far more astonishing is what I learned about this stone from my brother and fellow bishop, Severus of Milevis.[10] He told me that once, when he was dining at the house of Bathanarius, the former count of Africa,[11] he himself saw Bathanarius bring out a lodestone, hold it under a silver dish, and place a piece of iron on the dish. Then, as he moved his hand under the dish, holding the stone, the iron was moved about in the same pattern on top of the dish. There was no effect at all on the silver in between, while the stone was being moved very quickly back and forth underneath it by the man and the iron was being pulled around on top of it by the stone.

I have related something I saw for myself, and I have related something I heard from someone I believed as fully as if I had seen it myself. Let me now report what I have also read about the magnet. When a diamond is placed next to it, it does not attract iron; and, if it has already attracted it, it drops it as soon as the diamond comes near. India sends us these stones, but, if we are already ceasing to marvel at magnets now that they have become familiar to us, how much more must that be true of the people who send them to us, since these stones are so common for them? Perhaps they regard magnets in the same way that we regard lime. In an astonishing way, lime grows hot in water, which usually extinguishes fire, and stays cold in oil, which usually fuels fire. But, just because this is so commonplace for us, we do not marvel at it at all.

5. In spite of all this, when we proclaim the divine miracles either of the past or of the future, which there is no way to enable unbelievers to experience for themselves, they demand that we give them a rational account of these things. And, since we cannot provide one, inasmuch as these are things that exceed the powers of the human mind, they presume that what we say is false. Let them provide, then, a rational account of all the wondrous things that we can see or do see. And, if they recognize that this is beyond human capacity, they should admit that the bare fact that a rational account cannot be provided for something does not mean that it did not happen or that it will not happen, given that there are all these things which are equally inexplicable.

There are a great many such things recorded in books; they are not over and done with but remain to this day, each in its place, and anyone who wants and is able to go to the right place will discover whether they are true....

---

10. Severus was a friend of Augustine's who died c. 426. See especially Letters 109-110.
11. Bathanarius was count of Africa from 401 until his death in 408.

Let unbelievers give a rational account of them if they can, since they are unwilling to put any credence in Divine Scripture. Their only basis for thinking that these writings are not divine is that they include unbelievable things, like the matter we are now discussing. Reason, they insist, will not admit that flesh can burn and not be consumed or that it can feel pain and not die. What great reasoners these people are, able to give a rational account of all the things that are universally agreed to be marvels! Well, then, let them give a rational account of just the very few that we have cited. We have no doubt that, if they did not know about these already, and if we said they were going to happen, they would be even less willing to believe in them than they are now to believe what we say is going to occur at a point in the future. Which of them would believe us if, instead of saying that there will be living human bodies that are always going to burn and feel pain but are never going to die, we were to say that in the world to come there will be salt that fire causes to melt as in water but that water causes to crackle as in fire; or that there will be a spring whose water gets so hot in the cold of night that no one can touch it and so cold in the heat of day that no one can drink it; or that there will be a stone which with its own heat burns the hand of anyone holding it tight, or a stone which, once set alight, cannot be extinguished at all, or any of the other things that I have listed, while omitting countless others?

If we were to say that such things as these will exist in the world to come, and if they were to respond incredulously, "If you want us to believe these things, give us a rational account of each of them," we would have to admit that we could not — simply because our feeble, mortal powers of reasoning are defeated by these and other similar wondrous works of God. As far as we are concerned, however, it is a fixed point of reason that it is not without reason that the Almighty does the very things for which the weak human mind can provide no reason. In many cases, of course, it is uncertain to us what God's will is; but this at least is completely certain — that nothing which God wills is impossible for him. And what he declares we believe, for we cannot believe either that he is powerless or that he is a liar. As for those who belittle our faith and demand rational explanations, what do they have to say about things like these, for which human reason can give no rational account but which plainly exist and seem to run counter to the very rational order of nature itself?...

6. ...How much more, then, is God able to do things which are incredible to unbelievers but easy for his power. He is, after all, the one who created the power of stones and other things, and who created the ingenuity of the people who use that power in wondrous ways. He is the one who created the angels with natures more powerful than all living things on earth. His marvelous power surpasses all marvels, as does his wisdom in working, commanding, and permitting; and the use to which he puts all things is as marvelous as his creation of them.

7. Why, then, would God not have the power both to make the bodies of the dead rise again and to cause the bodies of the damned to be tormented by eternal fire? He is the one who created a world full of innumerable marvels in the heavens, on earth, in the air, and in the waters; and of course the world itself is without doubt a greater and more outstanding miracle than all the wonders with which it is filled. The people with whom, or rather against whom, we are engaged also believe that there is a God who created the world, and they believe that there are gods created by him through whom he governs the world. Either they do not deny — or they go further and openly proclaim — that there are powers in the world that work miracles either on their own initiative, or as requested in some rite or ceremony, or by magic. But, when we call their attention to some marvelous property in other things which are neither rational animals nor spirits endowed with any kind of reason, like the few that I have listed, their usual reply is, "That's a natural property; their nature just is that way; that's how their own natures work." Thus the whole reason why flame causes Agrigentine salt to melt, while water causes it to crackle, is that this is its nature.[12] In fact, however, this seems to be entirely contrary to nature, which has assigned not to fire but to water the power to dissolve salt, and to fire, not water, the power to make something burn. All the same, they say, it is the natural property of *this* salt to be affected in the opposite way. And the same reason is also given for the Garamantine spring, where a single flow is cold by day and hot by night, with both properties harmful to the touch.[13] And likewise for that other spring, which is cold to the touch and extinguishes lighted torches like other springs, but unlike others — and astonishingly — also sets extinguished torches alight.[14] And likewise for the asbestos stone which, even though it has no fire of its own, still burns so strongly once it has been set alight from some outside source that it cannot be put out.[15]... In each case, even though some unusual power contrary to nature seems to be involved, they still have no other reason to offer except to say that this is their nature.

Their reason is certainly brief, I admit, and an adequate answer. But, since God is the author of natures, why are they unwilling to let us give a stronger reason when — in response to their demand that we give them a reason for something that they refuse to believe because they consider it impossible — we answer that this is the will of almighty God? And the reason why God is called "almighty" is precisely that he is able to do whatever he wills. He was able to create any number of things that would certainly be thought impossible if they were not shown to us or reported, still today, by reliable witnesses — including not only things completely unknown to us but also the very well-known cases that I have cited above. As for marvels that have no witness other than the authors in whose books we read about them, who were not taught by divine inspiration and so could, perhaps, have fallen prey to human error, anyone is free to disbelieve them without blame.

---

12. See Pliny, *Natural History* XXXI,41,85.
13. See ibid. V,5,36.
14. See ibid. II,106,222.
15. See ibid. XXXVII,54, 146.

Nor do I want anyone to believe rashly all the marvels I have cited myself. In fact I am not so fully convinced of them myself that I have no doubts in my mind, except in the case of those that I have experienced for myself and that it is easy for anyone to experience for himself....

My aim has been to show how many such things are recorded in the writings of their own authors, things that many of them believe even when no rational account of them is provided. They, in contrast, do not deign to believe us when we say that almighty God is going to do things that lie beyond their experience and exceed the reach of their senses, even when a rational account has been given. For what better and stronger reason can be given for such things than to state that the Almighty is able to do them, and to maintain that he is going to do the things which we read that he foretold, since he foretold them in the very writings where he foretold many other things that he is already proved to have done? He is certainly going to do what they think is impossible, because he foretold that he was going to do it, just as he promised that unbelieving nations would believe unbelievable things and then made that promise come true.

The Issue of the Nature and Properties of Human Flesh

8. They may argue, however, that the reason they do not believe what we say about human bodies burning forever without dying is that the nature of human bodies is known to be very differently constituted. Therefore, they may claim, we cannot use the same reason that they gave for those marvels of nature. We can't say, "That's a natural property; their nature just is that way"; and the reason why we can't is that we know this is not in fact the nature of human flesh. But we have an answer to their argument that is based on our sacred books: human flesh was constituted in one way prior to sin (that is, it was constituted in such a way that it was possible for it never to suffer death), but in another way after sin (that is, as it is known in the tribulations of this mortal life, where it is not possible for it to maintain perpetual life).[16] And it will be constituted in yet another way in the resurrection of the dead, when its constitution will again be different from the one known to us now. But they do not believe these writings, where we read what man was like when he lived in paradise and how far he then was from the necessity of death. If they did believe them, we would not be debating with them at such laborious length about the future punishment of the damned! And so we shall have to produce something from the writings of their most learned author[17] to show that it is possible for a thing to become different from what it was formerly known to be as determined by its nature.

---

16. See Gn 2:17.
17. Varro is occasionally referred to by Augustine as the most learned Roman authority, especially above at III.4 and VI,2.

There is a passage in Marcus Varro's *On the Race of the Roman People* which I shall quote exactly as it appears in his work: "There occurred a wondrous portent in the sky. Castor writes that this extraordinary portent occurred when the brilliant star Venus, which Plautus calls 'Vesperugo'[18] and Homer 'Hesperos,'[19] changed its color, size, shape, and course, which is something that has never happened before or since. The prominent mathematicians Adrastus of Cyzicus and Dion of Neapolis reported that this happened in the reign of King Ogygus."[20] A great author like Varro obviously would not have called this a portent if it had not seemed contrary to nature, and in fact we say that all portents are contrary to nature. But they are not. For how can anything that happens by God's will be contrary to nature, when the will of such a great creator simply *is* the nature of each created thing? A portent, therefore, does not happen contrary to nature but contrary to what we know of nature....

As far as the knowledge of nature is concerned, therefore, the unbelievers should not allow themselves to get lost in some self-created fog — as if nothing could possibly occur in a given object by divine agency except what they know of that object's nature through their own human experience. Even the commonplaces of nature are no less wondrous, and they would be astonishing to all who consider them, were it not for the fact that we humans only marvel at marvels that are rare. For who, on rational reflection, would not see how extraordinary it is that, given the countless numbers of human beings and their great similarity in nature, each individual has his own individual appearance? If they were not so much like each other, they would not be distinguished as a species from other animals; and, if they were not so unlike each other, no individual would be distinguishable from other human beings. The very people whom we acknowledge to be alike, therefore, we find to be different. But consideration of the difference is more marvelous, since their common nature seems properly to require that they be alike. And yet, because it is the rare that we consider marvelous, we are far more astonished when we find two people so exactly alike that we always or often have trouble telling them apart....

Therefore, just as it was not impossible for God to institute the natures that he willed, neither is it impossible for God to change the natures that he instituted into whatever he wills....

The Worm and the Fire: Eternal Punishment of Both Body and Soul

9. The upshot is that what God said through his prophet about the eternal punishment of the damned is certainly going to come true: *Their worm shall not*

---

18. See *Amphitruo* I,275.
19. See *Iliad* X,318.
20. *On the Race of the Roman People*, fragment 6. Adrastus of Cyzicus and Dion of Naples are otherwise unknown; Ogygus, or Ogyges, was a mythical king of ancient Greece.

die, and *their fire shall not be quenched* (Is 66:24). To reinforce the point even more strongly, the Lord Jesus spoke of the bodily members that cause a person to stumble — using those members to indicate the people that a person loves as he loves his own right hand — and prescribed that they be cut off: *It is better for you to enter into life maimed than to have two hands and go to Gehenna, to the unquenchable fire, where their worm does not die and the fire is not quenched* (Mk 9:43-44). Similarly he said of the foot, *It is better for you to enter into eternal life lame than to have two feet and be thrown into the Gehenna of unquenchable fire, where their worm does not die and the fire is not quenched* (Mk 9:45-46). And he spoke no differently of the eye: *It is better for you to enter into the kingdom of God with one eye than to have two eyes and be thrown into the Gehenna of fire, where their worm does not die and the fire is not quenched* (Mk 9:47-48). It did not bother him at all to use the same words three times over in the same passage.[21] Who would not be terrified at this repetition, and at the threat of this punishment, coming with such vehemence from the divine mouth itself?

But some people want both of these — that is, both the fire and the worm — to refer to the punishment not of the body but of the soul. They claim that those who will be separated from the kingdom of God, because they repented too late and thus uselessly, will burn with anguish of soul; and so they contend that "fire" could not unsuitably be used for this burning anguish, as in the passage where the Apostle says: *Who is made to stumble, and I do not burn?* (2 Cor 11:29) They also hold that the worm should be understood in the same way. For, they say, it is written, *Like a moth in a garment and a worm in wood, so does grief torment a person's heart* (Prv 25:20). In contrast, those who do not doubt that both soul and body will be punished in that punishment maintain that the body is burned by fire but that the soul is gnawed, in a sense, by the worm of grief. Yet even if this is a more plausible suggestion — for it is certainly absurd to think that either the body or the soul will then be free of pain — I still find it easier to hold that both *worm* and *fire* refer to the body than that neither does. And in my view the reason why Divine Scripture does not specifically mention the soul's pain in using these terms is that it is understood to follow (even if it is not explicitly stated) that, when the body is in so much pain, the soul will also be tortured by fruitless repentance. In fact in the Old Testament we read, *The punishment of the flesh of the ungodly is fire and worm* (Sir 7:17). It would have been shorter to say, "The punishment of the ungodly...." Why, then, did it say *the flesh of the ungodly* if not because both — that is, both fire and worm — will be the punishment of the flesh? Perhaps, however, it chose to speak of the punishment of the flesh because it is for living according to the flesh that a person is punished; for it is living according to the flesh that leads to the second death, as the Apostle indicated when he said, *For, if you live according to the flesh, you shall die* (Rom 8:13).

---

21. But the repetition of verses 44 and 46, which are identical with verse 48 (*where their worm does not die...*), is not attested in the most important ancient manuscripts.

Each may choose the view he prefers, either assigning the fire to the body and the worm to the soul, the one literally and the other figuratively, or assigning both to the body in the literal sense. For in any case I have already given previously an adequate argument that it is possible for animate beings to stay alive even in flames — burning without being consumed, feeling pain without dying — through a miracle of the almighty creator. Anyone who denies that this is possible for God does not realize who it is that brings about anything in all of nature that he marvels at. For it is God himself who made all the marvels in this world that we have mentioned, both great and small, as well as innumerable others that we have not mentioned; and it is God himself who included them in this world, itself a unique miracle and the greatest of them all. Let each choose, then, whichever of the two explanations he prefers, whether he wishes to hold that the worm pertains literally to the body or to hold that it pertains to the soul in a sense transferred from the corporeal to the incorporeal realm. Which of these is actually true the event itself will quickly make clear. At that point, however, the saints' knowledge will be such that they have no need of experience to learn about those punishments. Rather, the wisdom that they have then will be full and perfect; and it will suffice by itself to know this also. For now we know in part, until the perfect comes. Under no circumstances, however, should we believe that those future bodies will be such that they feel no pain from the fire.

[Chapter 10 addresses the question of how material fire can be punishment for Evil Spirits.]

The Issue of the Just Correlation of Temporal Sin and Eternal Punishment

11. Some of those against whom we are defending the city of God may consider it unjust for anyone to be condemned to eternal punishment for sins that, no matter how grave, took only a moment to commit — as if any law, to be just, had to match carefully the length of anyone's punishment to the length of time it took him to commit the crime!...

But, if a temporal sin is punished with an eternal punishment, they ask, how can what your Christ said be true: *The measure you give will be the measure you get back* (Lk 6:38)?[22] What they fail to notice is that the measure was said to be the same not by virtue of an equal length of time but by virtue of a reciprocation of evil. In short, one who does evil suffers evil. Alternatively, Christ's statement can be taken to refer specifically to the matter about which the Lord was speaking at the time, that is, to judging and condemning. Accordingly, anyone who judges

---

22. This question is also discussed in Letter 102,22-27.

and condemns unjustly, if he is justly judged and condemned, receives back the same measure (although not the same thing) that he gave. For he gave judgment, and he received judgment; and, although the condemnation he gave was unjust, the condemnation he received was just.

12. But eternal punishment seems harsh and unjust to human sensibilities because, in the infirmity of our death-bound senses, we lack any sense for that highest and purest wisdom by which we might recognize how great a crime was committed in mankind's first transgression. The more man was enjoying God, the greater was his impiety in turning away from God; and the one who destroyed in himself a good which might have been eternal made himself worthy of an eternal evil. As a result, the whole mass of mankind is condemned.[23] For the one who first sinned was punished together with all humanity, which was in him as in a root, and the result is that no one may be released from this just and deserved punishment except by merciful and undeserved grace. Thus, the human race is divided in two: in some the power of merciful grace is shown, in others the power of just retribution. Both could not be demonstrated in all. For, if all remained under the penalty of just damnation, the mercy of grace would appear in none; and again, if all were brought over from darkness to light, the truth of retribution would appear in none. But many more are left under retribution than are brought over to mercy,[24] in order to demonstrate in this way what was due to all. And, even if this due punishment were imposed on all, no one could justly complain about the justice of God's retribution; but, because so many are delivered from it, we have every reason to give great thanks for the free gift of God's deliverance.

The Issue of Remedial or Purgatorial Punishment

13. The Platonists, of course, although they want to maintain that no sins go unpunished, still insist that all punishments are meant to serve remedial purposes, whether they are imposed by human or divine laws, and whether they are imposed in this life or after death — after death, that is, either in cases when a person escapes punishment in this life or in cases when a person does receive punishment in this life but is not reformed by it....

Now, we grant that even in this mortal life some punishments are purgatorial. They are not purgatorial, of course, for those whose life is either not made better by them or is instead made worse by them; but they are purgatorial for those who are corrected and reformed under their constraints. All other punishments, however, whether temporal or eternal (depending on how each person is to be treated by divine providence), are imposed either for sins, whether past sins or sins in which

---

23. "The whole mass of mankind is condemned": *est universa generis humani massa damnata.* See also above at XIV, 26 and and XV,1.21.
24. The same pessimism as to the number of the saved appears in *Enchiridion* 24,97.

a person is still living, or to exercise a person's virtues and make them known, and they are imposed through men or through angels, whether good or evil.... As for temporal punishments, some suffer them only in this life, others after death, and still others both in this life and after death, but always prior to the final and most severe judgment. Nor does everyone who undergoes temporal punishments after death come under the eternal punishments which will follow that judgment. For, as we have already said, there are some for whom what is not forgiven in this world will be forgiven in the world to come, and these will not be punished in the eternal punishment of the world to come.[25]

All Human Life on Earth is a Trial

14. There are only a very few, however, who suffer no punishments at all in this life but only after it. Still, we ourselves have known and heard of some people who reached the decrepitude of old age without experiencing even the slightest touch of illness and who led completely peaceful lives. And yet this whole mortal life is itself a punishment, since it is all a trial, as Holy Scripture declares where it is written, *Is not human life on earth a trial?* (Jb 7:1 LXX) For folly and ignorance themselves are no small punishments, and we rightly judge that they are to be shunned — so much so that boys are compelled by punishments full of pain to learn trades or letters.[26] And the very learning to which they are driven by these punishments is itself so much a punishment to them that they often prefer enduring the punishments by which they are compelled to learn rather than the learning itself. If offered the choice between dying and becoming a child again, who would not recoil in horror and immediately choose death? The fact that an infant begins this life not with laughter but with tears amounts to an unwitting prophecy of the evils the child has entered.[27]...

15. As for the *heavy yoke* that is imposed *on the sons of Adam from the day they leave their mother's womb to the day they are buried in the mother of all* (Sir 40:1), even this evil turns out to be something of a marvel. It prompts us to live soberly and to understand that, due to the first and terrible sin committed in paradise, this life has been made penal for us, and to recognize that the provisions of the new covenant refer only to our new inheritance in the world to come. In this world we have received a pledge of that inheritance, and in its own time we shall receive the reality of which this is the pledge. For the present, however, let us walk in hope and, as we make progress from day to day, let us put the deeds of the

---

25. See Mt 12:32 par.
26. The classic text in Augustine on the difficulties of childhood, especially in terms of schooling (about which he is sometimes quite passionate), as expressed here, is *Confessions* I,9,14-15. See also *Christian Discipline* 11,12.
27. The same observation, that children are born crying, is made in Ephrem, *Hymns on Paradise* V,14.

flesh to death by the Spirit.[28] For *the Lord knows those who are his* (2 Tm 2:19), and *all who are led by the Spirit of God are sons of God* (Rom 8:14), which they are, however, by grace, not by nature. For there is only one Son of God by nature, and he in his compassion became a son of man for our sake so that we, who are by nature sons of man, might by grace become sons of God through him. Remaining immutable in himself, he took our nature on himself so that, in our nature, he might take us to himself. Holding fast to his own divinity, he participated in our infirmity so that we, changed for the better, might lose our condition of sin and mortality by participating in his immortality and righteousness and might preserve the good he accomplished in our nature, perfected by the supreme good in the goodness of his nature. For, just as we fell into this terrible evil through one man who sinned, so it is through one man who justifies[29] — and him God — that we shall attain that sublime good. But no one should feel confident that he has passed over from one condition to the other until he has reached the place where there will be no more temptation, until he has gained the peace that he seeks in the many and varied combats of this present warfare, in which the flesh lusts against the spirit and the spirit against the flesh.[30]

The Warfare of Flesh against Spirit and of Spirit against Flesh

There would never have been any such warfare if human nature had, by free choice, continued in the uprightness in which it was created. But now the nature which did not want to have peace with God in happiness is at war with itself in unhappiness. Yet, even though it is miserable to be in this evil condition, it is still better than our prior condition in this life.[31] For it is certainly better to struggle against the vices than it is to be governed by the vices without any struggle at all. Better war with the hope of eternal peace than captivity without any thought of release! We yearn, of course, to be free from this warfare; and, kindled by the fire of divine love, we burn to attain the fully ordered peace where, in unshakable stability, the lower is made subject to the higher in us. But even if — God forbid! — there were no hope of attaining this great good, we still ought to prefer to remain in the distress of struggle rather than simply allowing the vices to exercise dominion over us without resisting them at all.

---

28. See Rom 8:13.
29. See Rom 5:12.15.
30. See Gal 5:17.
31. "Our prior condition in this life" (*priora vitae huius*), as becomes apparent from the succeeding lines, is a state in which there is no struggle between virtue and vice and where vice simply governs. It is a state equivalent to infancy and childhood, according to Augustine's scheme of the moral ages of man that he deploys here and elsewhere and that he also links to three periods in the history of humankind — before the law, under the law and under grace (*ante legem*, *sub lege* and *sub gratia*). See *Miscellany of Eighty-three Questions* 66,3-6.

16. But God's mercy toward the vessels of mercy[32] which he has prepared for glory is so great that even the first age of man (that is, infancy) which gives in to the flesh without any struggle — as long as the child has received the sacraments of the mediator[33] and so has been transferred from the power of darkness into the kingdom of Christ,[34] even if the child dies at this early age — is not only not destined for eternal punishment but will not even undergo any purgatorial punishments after death. And the same is true of the second age of man, called childhood, where reason has not yet taken up the battle and thus falls prey to virtually all the delights of the vices. For, even though this age has the power of speech and thus seems to have gone beyond infancy,[35] its mind is still too weak to take in what is commanded. In both infancy and childhood, then, spiritual regeneration by itself is enough to keep the child from being harmed after death by the contract with death that carnal generation involves. But, once people reach the age when they understand the commandments and can put themselves under the sway of the law, they must take up the war against the vices and fight strenuously to keep from being led into sins that bring them to damnation. If the vices have not yet grown strong by regular victory, it is easier to vanquish them and make them submit; but, if they have become accustomed to conquer and rule, they are only overcome with great labor and difficulty.

It is only by delight in true righteousness that the vices are overcome in truth and sincerity, and it is faith in Christ that brings this delight. For, if the law's command is present but the Spirit's help is absent, then, due to the law's prohibition itself, the desire to sin grows and conquers, and so the guilt of transgression is added as well. Sometimes, it is true, open and obvious vices are overcome by other deep-hidden vices which are thought to be virtues; but in these cases it is actually pride that rules, along with a kind of ruinous, exalted self-satisfaction.[36] Thus we should only consider the vices overcome when they are overcome by love for God. Only God himself gives this love, and he gives it only through the mediator between God and men, the man Christ Jesus,[37] who became a participant in our mortality in order to make us participants in his divinity.

Only a very few, however, are so fortunate that from the onset of adolescence they commit no sins worthy of damnation (whether shameful acts, or actual crimes, or the error of some abominable impiety) but rather, by the Spirit's lavish generosity, vanquish everything that might have gained mastery over them through delight

---

32. See Rom 9:23.
33. I.e., baptism; the plural "sacraments" refers to the various rituals that formed part of baptism.
34. See Col 1:13.
35. "Speech...infancy": *fari...infantiam*. Augustine is alluding to the etymology of the word "infancy" (*infantia*), meaning "not speaking." See also above at XVI,43.
36. Similarly, Augustine says above at V,13 that the noble Romans of antiquity suppressed the more crass vices for the sake of the vice of the love of praise, or vainglory, which is closely related to pride.
37. See 1 Tm 2:5.

in the flesh. A great many, in contrast, once they have received the law's precept, are first overcome by the strength of the vices and made into transgressors of the law, and only then do they flee to grace for help. And with grace's help, having set their minds under God and thus over the flesh, they may become victors by bitter repentance and more strenuous battle. Thus, anyone who wants to escape everlasting punishment needs not only to be baptized but also to be justified in Christ, and so to pass over in truth from the devil to Christ. As for purgatorial punishments, however, he should not imagine that they will have any place following that last and terrible judgment. But, even so, it is certainly not to be denied that the eternal fire itself will be milder for some and harsher for others, according to their differing merits (although, in this case, all their merits will be evil), either because its intensity and heat will vary according to the punishment each deserves or because, although the fire itself will burn equally, it will not be felt with equal painfulness.

The Question of Divine Mercy and Eternal Punishment: Erroneous Views

17. I see that I must now turn to certain merciful persons among us and engage them peaceably in debate. They are unwilling to believe that punishment will be eternal either for all of the people whom the supremely just judge will judge worthy of hell or at least for some of them. Instead, they hold that the damned are to be set free from hell at the end of a fixed period of time, which will be longer or shorter depending on the extent of each person's sin.[38] In this regard, Origen carried mercy to yet greater lengths.[39] He believed that even the devil himself and his angels, after enduring the harsher and longer-lasting punishments which they deserve, are to be released from these torments and joined with the holy angels. But the Church — and not without reason — has condemned him for this and many other views,[40] and especially for his notion that there is a ceaseless alternation between blessedness and misery, an unending back-and-forth from the one to the other at fixed intervals lasting for epochs. In making this claim, however,

---

38. This view is presented and answered in *Enchiridion* 29,112-113.
39. Augustine is referring here and in what follows to the doctrine of the *apokatastasis* ("restoration" in Greek), which Origen explains most succinctly in *On First Principles* I,6 and which refers to the restoration of rational creatures, whether all or merely some, to a state of bliss with God that was lost in a primordial fall. It implies in other words that, at least for some rational creatures, hell is not eternal. Whether Origen actually taught the salvation of the devil himself has been debated at length but seems doubtful. See Henri Crouzel, *Origen*, trans. by A. S. Worrall (San Francisco: Harper and Row, 1989) 20-21, 262-265. Were Origen to have in fact suggested the possibility of the devil's redemption, he would not have been the only one in Christian antiquity. See Gregory of Nyssa, *Great Catechism* 26; Sulpicius Severus, *Life of Saint Martin* 22. Origen's supposed teaching on the non-eternity of heaven is included in a list of his erroneous opinions compiled by Jerome in Letter 92,2. Augustine also criticizes Origen above at XI,23.
40. Augustine is not referring here to the sort of formal ecclesiastical condemnation that Origen's teachings (or what were thought to be his teachings) ultimately underwent at the Councils of Constantinople in 543 and 553 but rather to a condemnation expressed by individuals such as Methodius of Olympus, Jerome, Theophilus of Alexandria and others.

Origen lost the very point that seemed so merciful. He posited true miseries for the saints, to pay the penalty of their sins, but he gave them only a false happiness; that is, the happiness he gave them lacks true and secure joy in eternal good untouched by any fear of loss.

Quite different, however, is the error about mercy that we are speaking of here. It is the error, based on human sentiment, of those who suppose that the misery of the people condemned in the final judgment will be temporal but that the happiness of all who are sooner or later set free will be eternal. If this view is good and true because it is merciful, then the more merciful it is, the better and more true it will be. Let the fountain of mercy be extended and deepened, then, so that it sets even the lost angels free, at least after some vast number of long ages. Why, after all, should this fountain flow to all human nature but immediately run dry when it reaches the angelic nature? Even so, these people do not dare to extend the reach of their mercy so far that it finally comes to include the liberation of the devil himself. If anyone did dare to do this, he would certainly outdo all others in mercy. But the more it seemed to him that he was thinking mercifully, the more it would actually turn out that he was monstrously and perversely in error over against the righteous words of God.

18. There are even some people — and I myself have met and talked with people of this kind — who seem to venerate Holy Scripture but live deplorable lives; and, when they plead their own cause, they ascribe far more mercy to God toward humanity than do those I have just mentioned. They assert that what was divinely foretold is true: evil and faithless people are worthy of punishment, but, when it comes to judgment, mercy will prevail. For, they claim, the merciful God will forgive them in response to the prayers and intercessions of his saints. For, if the saints prayed for them even when face to face with their hostility, how much more will they pray for them when they see them lying prostrate in humble supplication. It is beyond belief, they insist, that the saints will lose their bowels of compassion just when they attain the fullest and most perfect holiness, and that those who prayed for their enemies when they themselves were not without sin will refuse to pray for their suppliants when they no longer have any sin at all. And it is inconceivable that God will refuse to listen to so many of his children — and such outstanding children — when he finds that there is nothing in their supreme holiness to impede their prayer....

But even the people who hold this view do not extend their opinion to include the liberation of the devil and his angels or to exempt them from condemnation. Their human mercy is touched only by human beings; and, more specifically, they are pleading their own cause. Presuming on God's supposedly universal mercy for all mankind, they promise themselves a false impunity for their abandoned morals. But they are surpassed in their proclamation of God's mercy by those who extend the promise of this impunity even to the prince of demons and his retinue.

19. Again, there are others who at least do not promise liberation from eternal punishment to all people but only to those who have been washed with the baptism of Christ and who partake of his body, no matter how badly they live or what heresy or impiety they fall into. The basis for their view is that Jesus said, *This is the bread that has come down from heaven, so that if anyone eats of it he shall not die. I am the living bread that has come down from heaven. Whoever eats of this bread shall live forever.* (Jn 6:50-51) It necessarily follows, they claim, that these people will be delivered from eternal death and will eventually be brought to eternal life.

20. And again, there are some who promise this not to all who have the sacrament of Christ's baptism and of his body but only to Catholics, even if they live badly. For they have eaten Christ's body not merely in the sacrament but in reality itself, because they have been incorporated into his body, about which the Apostle says, *We who are many are one bread, one body* (1 Cor 10:17).[41] Thus, even if they later fall into some heresy, or even into pagan idolatry, they will not die for all eternity but at some point will attain eternal life simply because they received Christ's baptism and ate Christ's body in the body of Christ, that is, in the Catholic Church. All their impiety, no matter how great, will not be enough to make their punishment eternal, but only long-lasting and severe.

21. Further, on the basis of the passage that says, *The one who perseveres to the end shall be saved* (Mt 24:13), some make this promise only to those who persevere in the Catholic Church, even if they lead evil lives in it.[42] They will be saved through fire; that is, they will be saved by virtue of the foundation of which

---

41. "Not merely in the sacrament but in reality itself": *non solo sacramento sed re ipsa*. In the context of presenting an argument here that he disagrees with, which is that it is sufficient to be a Catholic Christian who has received the eucharist in order to be saved, irrespective of one's moral life, Augustine makes a distinction between receiving the eucharist merely sacramentally and receiving it "in reality itself." He had used the same distinction previously at X,5, in a similar setting, when he distinguished between sacrifices and the things that the sacrifices signified (*sacrificia...res...significatas*), i.e., between physical signs and inner realities, or between liturgical externalities and their spiritual effects. Augustine's theology in this respect is neatly summarized in Sermon 272: "The reason that these things are called sacraments is that in them one thing is seen, another is to be understood. What can be seen has a bodily appearance, what is to be understood provides spiritual fruit." Only Catholic Christians eat Christ's body both sacramentally and really. Other Christians, such as the schismatic Donatists (whom Augustine does not mention by name but whom he almost certainly had in mind), eat Christ's body "merely in the sacrament"; i.e., because of their lack of faith, evidenced by their non-adherence to the Catholic Church, they partake only of the physical sign but not of the inner reality. Yet even Catholics themselves must live upright lives in order to partake of the eucharist both sacramentally and really, rather than merely sacramentally, as immoral Catholics do who, because of their sinful lives, are no longer members of Christ and hence of his Church. From Augustine's distinction between *sacramentum* and *res* there developed the well-known and still useful distinction made by Scholastic theologians, who spoke in terms of the sacrament by itself (*sacramentum tantum*), the reality by itself (*res tantum*), and the reality and the sacrament together (*res et sacramentum*).
42. This view, elaborated in what follows, is presented and answered in *Enchiridion* 18,67-69; *Faith and Works* 15,24-16,30 (repeated in *Eight Questions of Dulcitius* 1,2-9).

the Apostle says, *For no one can lay any foundation other than the one that has been laid, which is Christ Jesus. Now, if anyone builds on the foundation with gold, silver, precious stones, wood, hay, straw — the work of each shall be made manifest; for the day shall disclose it, because it shall be revealed with fire, and the fire shall prove what sort of work each has done. If the work that anyone has built on it endures, he shall receive a reward. But if anyone's work is burned up, he shall suffer loss; he himself shall be saved, but only as through fire.* (1 Cor 3:11-15) Accordingly, they say, the Catholic Christian — whatever sort of life he leads — has Christ as his foundation, a foundation that no heresy can claim, since heresy is cut off from the unity of Christ's body; and therefore, they argue, even if the Catholic Christian leads an evil life, like one who builds with wood, hay, or straw, he will be saved through fire. That is, he will be set free after he has gone through the pains of the fire by which the evil will be punished at the last judgment.

22. I have also found that there are some people who think that the only ones who are going to burn in eternal punishment are those who neglect to do worthy works of mercy to atone for their sins.[43] For, according to the apostle James, *Judgment shall be without mercy to anyone who has shown no mercy* (Jas 2:13). Hence, they say, anyone who has shown mercy — even if he has not changed his life for the better but has lived wickedly and deplorably in the midst of all his works of mercy — will be judged with mercy; and, as a result, he will either be condemned to no punishment at all or will ultimately be set free from his condemnation after some set period of time, whether short or long.... When, with God's help, I have responded to all these mistaken opinions, I shall bring this book to its close.

Reply to Error: the Devil and His Angels Will Suffer Eternal Punishment

23. First of all, we need to ask and learn why the Church has not been able to tolerate the argument of people who promise purgation or pardon to the devil, even if only after the most severe and prolonged punishment. It is not that all those holy men, learned in the sacred writings of both the Old and the New Testament, were unwilling to grant purification, along with the blessedness of the kingdom of heaven, to angels of any kind and in any number after they had gone through punishments of any kind and any number. It is rather that they recognized that they could not cancel or weaken the divine sentence which the Lord foretold that he was going to pronounce at the judgment: *Depart from me, you accursed, into eternal fire, which is prepared for the devil and his angels* (Mt 25:41). Here he makes it very clear that the devil and his angels are going to burn in eternal fire. Again, it is

---

43. "Works of mercy": *elemosynas*, often translated as "almsgiving," which Augustine understands very broadly and does not restrict to money given to the needy. The view that the practice of mercy would be sufficient for salvation, irrespective of other aspects of a Christian's life, is presented and answered in *Enchiridion* 19,70-20,77.

written in The Apocalypse: *The devil who had deceived them was thrown into the lake of fire and sulfur, where the beast and the false prophet were, and they shall be tormented day and night forever* (Rv 20:10). The first passage has *eternal*, the second *forever*, and Scripture customarily uses these words for the sole purpose of signifying what has no end in time. No other more just or manifest reason can be found, therefore, for the fixed and immovable conviction of true godliness that the devil and his angels will never return to the righteousness and life of the saints: Scripture, which deceives no one, states that God did not spare them and in fact has already condemned them to be thrown into the lower regions for the meantime and held in prisons of darkness for punishment at the last judgment. And then eternal fire will receive them, in which they will be tormented forever.

Reply to Error: Eternal Punishment is Eternal

But, if this is so, how can we say that all people, or even that some people, will be released from the eternity of this punishment — no matter how long they suffer before being released — without immediately undercutting the faith by which we believe that the demons' punishment is going to be eternal? If all or some of those to whom it will be said, *Depart from me, you accursed, into eternal fire, which is prepared for the devil and his angels*, are not going to be in that fire forever, do we have any reason to believe that the devil and his angels are going to be there forever? Or is the sentence that God pronounces on the evil, both humans and angels alike, going to turn out to be true for the angels but false for human beings? Only if human conjecture outweighs God's own words could that be true. But that cannot be right, and so those who desire to avoid eternal punishment should obey the divine command while there is still time, rather than arguing against God....

Reply to Error: the Intercession of the Saints and the Prayers of the Church

24. This argument also holds good against those who, in pleading their own cause, try to oppose God's words on the pretext of a greater mercy. They argue that God's words are true in the sense that people deserve to suffer the things which God said they would suffer, but not in the sense that they are actually going to suffer them. Instead, they say, God will pardon people in response to the prayers of his saints, who will then pray all the more earnestly for their enemies because they will undoubtedly be more holy then; and, in addition, the prayers of those who will then have no sin at all will be even more effective and even more worthy of being heard by God. But in that case why would the saints not pray also — in their most perfect holiness and with their wholly pure and merciful prayers, which have the power to obtain every request — on behalf of the angels for whom eternal fire is prepared, praying that God mitigate his sentence, change it for the better, and exempt them from that fire?...

But, if the Church could know people well enough to be certain about which ones, although still present in this life, have been predestined to go into eternal fire with the devil, she would no more pray for those people than she does for the devil himself. Because she does not have this certainty about anyone, however, she prays for all her strictly human enemies while they remain in the body. But her prayers are not always heard. For they are heard only when she prays for people who, even if they oppose the Church, are predestined to have her prayers heard on their behalf and to become her sons. But, if anyone remains impenitent at heart until he dies and is never converted from an enemy to a son, the Church does not continue to pray for him — that is, for the spirit of such a person — after he has died. Why not? Because anyone who was not brought over to Christ while he was in the body is now counted as a member of the devil's party.

Thus, the reason why the Church will not pray then for the human beings who are due to be punished in eternal fire is the same reason why it does not pray, either now or then, for the evil angels. And it is also the reason why, although she does pray for human beings, she does not pray, even now, for the unbelieving and irreligious dead. The prayer of the Church, or of certain godly persons, is in fact heard on behalf of some of the dead, but only on behalf of those who were reborn in Christ and who did not live their lives in the body either so badly that they are judged unworthy of such mercy or so well that they are found to have no need of it…. In this light it would be exceedingly presumptuous to say that the punishment of those about whom God said that they would go into eternal punishment will not be eternal punishment — and on the basis of this presumption to make people also feel despair or doubt about the eternality of eternal life itself.

[The rest of chapter 24 and all of chapter 25 rebuke four more errors concerning God's mercy and human sinfulness.]

Reply to Error: Who It Is That Is Saved as through Fire

26. But Catholic Christians, they argue, have Christ as their foundation; and they have not departed from unity with him, no matter how bad the life they have built on this foundation, like wood, hay, or straw.[44] As a consequence, they claim, right faith — by virtue of which Christ is their foundation — will eventually be able to save them from the everlastingness of that fire, although not without loss, due to the fact that the things which they built on that foundation will be burned….

---

44. See 1 Cor 3:11-12. What follows offers a tentative justification for the existence of what has come to be known as purgatory. Perhaps Augustine was familiar with Ambrose, *Explanation of Psalm* 36,26, where a similar argument is made.

We shall find out who can be saved through fire if we first find out what it is to have Christ as one's foundation. To do this as quickly as possible, let us see what the image itself implies: In a building nothing comes before the foundation. Therefore, anyone who has Christ in his heart in the sense that he puts nothing earthly or temporal before him, not even things that are lawful and permitted, has Christ as his foundation. On the other hand, if he does put such things before Christ, even if he seems to have the faith of Christ, Christ is not in him as his foundation; instead, for him, these things come before Christ. And, if he scorns the precepts of salvation and commits unlawful acts, he is convicted all the more of putting Christ not first but last. In choosing to fulfill his own shameful desire in direct opposition to what Christ commands and permits, he has put the Christ who commands and permits last. Thus, if any Christian loves a prostitute and, cleaving to her, becomes one body with her,[45] he no longer has Christ as his foundation. In contrast, if anyone loves his own wife, and loves her in accord with Christ,[46] who can doubt that Christ is his foundation? Even if he loves her according to this world, carnally, in the disease of lust, like the gentiles who do not know God, the Apostle still permits this — or rather Christ permits it through the Apostle — as a concession.[47] Consequently, even such a man as this can have Christ as his foundation. As long as he does not put any such affection and pleasure before Christ, Christ is his foundation, even if he builds with wood, hay, or straw, and for this reason he will be saved through fire. The fire of tribulation will burn up such delights and earthly loves, which, because of the marital bond, do not deserve condemnation. To this fire belong bereavements and any other calamities which snatch these pleasures from us. This kind of building will bring loss to the person who builds it, because he will not get to keep what he built on its foundation and because he will be tormented by the loss of things he rejoiced to enjoy. But through this fire he will be saved by virtue of his foundation because, even if he were forced by a persecutor to choose whether he preferred these things to Christ, he would not put them before Christ....

Only those on Christ's left will be thrown into the eternal fire, in final and everlasting damnation. This other fire, however, also proves those on Christ's right hand.[48] It will prove some of them without burning up and consuming what they are found to have built on Christ, their foundation. Others it will prove in another way; that is, it will burn up what they have built, and as a result they will suffer loss. But they will themselves be saved because with surpassing love they have held fast to Christ as their firm and fixed foundation. And, if they are going

---

45. See 1 Cor 6:16.
46. See Eph 5:25.
47. See 1 Cor 7:6. Augustine considered marital intercourse for the sake of sexual pleasure, rather than for begetting children, to be a sin, although not a grave one; he saw the very fact that Paul made a "concession" as proof of its sinfulness. See *Enchiridion* 21,78; *The Excellence of Marriage* 6,6; *Marriage and Desire* I,15,17; *Answer to the Two Letters of the Pelagians* III,5,14.
48. See Mt 25:31-46.

to be saved, then they are obviously going to stand at Christ's right hand; and with the others they will hear him say, *Come, you who are blessed by my Father, take possession of the kingdom prepared for you.* They are not going to stand at his left hand, where the people will stand who are not going to be saved and who are therefore going to hear him say, *Depart from me, you accursed, into eternal fire.* In fact no one will be saved from that eternal fire, because all of them will go into eternal punishment, where their worm does not die and their fire is not quenched.[49] By that fire they will be tormented day and night forever.[50]

There is an interval, however, between the death of this body and the coming of the last day of condemnation and reward, which will follow the resurrection of the body; and some people say that during this interval the spirits of the dead suffer in fire. This fire, they claim, is of a kind that is not felt by those whose morals and whose loves, during their life in this body, did not build with wood, hay, and straw that must be consumed. But others, who brought this kind of building with them, do feel it. Whether only after death, or both before and after death, or before death in order to avoid it after death, they experience the fire of transitory tribulation which burns up anything that, although pardoned from damnation, is still a concern of this world.

I do not argue against this view, for perhaps it is true. In fact it is possible that the very death of the flesh, which resulted from the commission of the first sin, is part of this tribulation; and so it is possible that each person experiences the time after death according to the building he had built....

Reply to Error: the Issue of Works of Mercy

27. It remains to reply to the people who say that the only ones who are going to burn in eternal fire are those who neglect to do worthy acts of mercy for their sins. These people cite what is said by the apostle James: *Judgment shall be without mercy to anyone who has shown no mercy* (Jas 2:13). Therefore, they claim, anyone who shows mercy will be judged with mercy, even if he does not correct his abandoned morals but lives wickedly and deplorably despite his works of mercy. Such a person, they say, will either not be condemned at all or will be released from final damnation after some period of time. For this reason they hold that Christ will make the division between those on his right and those on his left on the sole basis of their love for or neglect of works of mercy, sending the former into his kingdom and the latter into eternal punishment. They maintain that daily sins, which they never cease to commit, no matter how many or how great these sins are, can be forgiven by virtue of acts of mercy, and to support this view they try to bring in the prayer that the Lord himself taught us as a witness in their

---

49. See Is 66:24.
50. See Rv 20:10.

favor. For, they say, just as there is no day when Christians do not say this prayer, neither is there a daily sin of any sort that is not forgiven by this prayer — when we also say, *Forgive us our debts* — just so long as we take care to do what follows, *as we forgive our debtors* (Mt 6:12). For, they point out, the Lord did not say, "If you forgive others their sins, your Father will forgive you your little daily sins"; he simply said, "Your Father will forgive you your sins."[51] Thus, no matter how many or how great the sins are, even if they are committed daily and even if the sinner does not change his life for the better and forsake his sins, they can still be forgiven — so these people presume — due to the mercy we show in not denying forgiveness to others....

The daily prayer which Jesus himself taught us (which is why it is called the Lord's Prayer) does of course wipe out our daily sins when we daily say, *Forgive us our debts*, and when we not only say but actually do what follows, *as we also forgive our debtors*. But we say this because we have committed sins; we do not say it in order to be able to commit sins because we have said it. By this prayer the Savior wanted to show us that, no matter how righteously we may live in the darkness and infirmity of this life, we are never without sins that we should pray to have forgiven, and that we must forgive those who sin against us if we want to be forgiven ourselves. Thus, when the Lord says, *If you forgive people their sins, your Father will also forgive you your sins* (Mt 6:14), he does not mean that, trusting in this prayer, we should feel safe in committing daily acts of evil whether because our position of power means that we have no need to fear the laws of men or because our clever cunning means that we can deceive men themselves. He means rather that we should learn from this prayer not to imagine that we are without sins, even if we are free of crimes.[52] For God also gave exactly the same admonition to the priests of the old law, when he commanded them to offer sacrifice first for their own sins and then for the sins of the people.[53]

For we must pay close attention to the exact words of our great teacher and Lord. He does not say, "If you forgive people their sins, your Father will also forgive you your sins, no matter what they are." He simply says *your sins*. In fact he was teaching a daily prayer, and he was teaching it to disciples who were already justified. What does *your sins* mean, then, but "the sins which not even you who are justified and sanctified will be able to avoid"? The people who want to find in this prayer an opportunity to commit evils every day assert that, because the Lord did not say, "He will forgive you your small sins" but simply *your sins*, he also meant to include great sins. But we in contrast take into account the character of the people to whom he was speaking; and, when we hear *your sins*, we have to

---

51. See Mt 6:14.
52. "Sins...crimes": *peccatis...criminibus*. It is unclear whether Augustine is distinguishing between what would eventually come to be called "venial" and "mortal" sins, as is suggested by what he says later in the section, or whether he is distinguishing between sins (however serious they may be) that are not crimes under civil law and sins that are.
53. See Heb 7:27.

think that he meant only small sins, because the sins of such people were no longer great sins. And in any case those great sins themselves — from which we must turn away by wholly changing our way of life for the better — are not forgiven those who say this prayer unless they actually do what it says: *As we also forgive our debtors.* For, if the smallest sins, from which not even the life of the righteous is free, are only remitted on this condition, it is all the more true that people who are entangled in a multitude of great crimes, even if they have now ceased to commit them, receive no pardon if they inexorably refuse to forgive others for the sins they have committed against them. For, as the Lord says, *But if you do not forgive people, neither will your Father forgive you* (Mt 6:15)....

As for those who are received by those righteous persons into eternal habitations, it must be stated that they are not endowed with such moral character that the life they lead can be enough to deliver them without the support of the saints; and so in their case mercy triumphs all the more over judgment. But on the other hand we should not think that this means that any wholly wicked person, without ever changing his life to the good or at least to the tolerable, will be received into eternal habitations simply because he has helped the saints with the mammon of unrighteousness, that is, with ill-gotten money or riches. After all, even if honestly acquired, these are still not true riches but only what iniquity counts as riches. For iniquity knows nothing of the true riches in which those of the righteous abound who receive others into eternal habitations. There is, then, a certain type of life which is not so evil that those who live it cannot be helped in gaining the kingdom of heaven by generosity in almsgiving, by which they support the righteous in their poverty and make friends who will receive them into eternal habitations; but neither is this type of life so good that by itself it is enough to attain such a great beatitude, if those who live it do not obtain mercy through the merits of those whom they have made their friends....

It is very difficult, however, to discover what this type of life is, and very risky to define what the sins are that impede us from reaching the kingdom of God but still win pardon through the merits of holy friends. I have given a lot of thought to the issue, but so far, at least, I have been unable to come to any conclusion. Perhaps the matter is hidden from us precisely in order to keep us from slacking off in our eagerness to make progress toward avoiding all sins. For, if people knew what the sins are, or what kinds of sins they are, for which we should seek and hope for the intercession of the saints, even if the sins persist and are not uprooted by progress toward a better life, then human sloth would happily wrap itself up in these sins and would give no thought at all to unwrapping itself from their entanglements by pursuit of virtue. Instead, it would only seek to be delivered by the merits of others, from whom it had made friends for itself with the mammon of unrighteousness by being generous in almsgiving. As it is, however, as long as we remain ignorant of the type of iniquity which, even if we persist in it, is only venial, we are certainly more vigilant in our eagerness to advance toward the better by praying and striving; nor do we spurn efforts to make the saints our friends by means of the mammon of unrighteousness.

This deliverance, whether it happens by virtue of a person's own prayers or by virtue of the intercession of the saints, means that the person is not sent into eternal fire. It does not mean that, after being sent into eternal fire, he will be rescued from it after some period of time, no matter how long that period may be. There are some people who imagine that what Scripture says about the good soil bringing forth abundant fruit, some thirtyfold, some sixtyfold, some a hundredfold,[54] should be understood to mean that the saints, according to the diversity of their merits, will deliver others, some delivering thirty people, some sixty, some a hundred. But even these people usually presume that this will happen on the day of judgment, not after the judgment. As far as their view is concerned, however, someone who saw how perverse it is for people to promise themselves impunity on the ground that everyone seems to gain deliverance in this way is said to have made a particularly telling reply. Instead, he remarked, we should lead good lives so that we may be included among those who are going to be interceding for the deliverance of others. Otherwise there may be so few intercessors that each will soon reach his limit of thirty, or sixty, or a hundred; and as a consequence a great many will be left behind who cannot be rescued from punishment by their intercession. And among these, of course, may be found anyone who has the empty temerity to promise himself the hope of being the fruit that someone else brings forth.

This will suffice as my response to those who do not reject the authority of the Sacred Scriptures that we have in common but who mistakenly interpret them to mean that what is going to occur is not what Scripture actually says but rather what they themselves want. And, having given this response, we bring this book to a close, just as we promised we would.

---

54. See Mt 13:8 par.

Study Questions for Book XXI

Contemporary theories of the conservation of matter, the complexities of matter-energy conversion, the origins and destinies of the universe, and other scientific discoveries all impinge on a twenty-first-century reading of Augustine's explanations of both purgatorial and eternal punishment. On the other hand, his insistence on the unimagined and unimaginable possibilities of the divine prerogative finds some consonance in the ever-unfolding horizons of scientific imagination to which physics and the other sciences invite us. Do Augustine's Scripture-based teachings on the punishments of the afterlife still have salvific value?

Augustine makes a tentative argument — "some people say" (XXI,26) — for what the Catholic Church calls purgatory. How much does Scripture factor into his observations on this matter?

From chapter 17 on, Augustine constrains divine mercy with a many-sided insistence on the importance of human responsibility. Do you find a dogmatic or a pastoral motivation, or both motivations, behind his arguments in these pages?

BOOK XXII

Book XXII presents the eternal blessedness of the city of God following the last judgment. It opens with brief references to the creation and fall of angels and humans, the immutability of the divine will, and the fulfillment of the divine promise, topics which form the backdrop to the discussion. From that point on, it falls — like Book XXI — into roughly two parts. The first part argues for the resurrection of the body against the objections of the philosophers, especially the Platonists, that an earthly body cannot be elevated to heavenly status. If the resurrection of the body seems incredible, it is supported by two further "incredible things" which cannot be denied, namely, that the world (as God foretold) has come to believe in it; and that the world has come to believe through a small group of unimportant and uneducated men, the apostles, whose persuasiveness can only be explained by the fact that it was backed by divine power. That power was evident in the miracles performed by the apostles themselves, and it is still evident in the miracles of the present, performed at the shrines and through the relics of the martyrs, whose faith itself bears witness to the resurrection. In response to various derisory questions about the resurrection posed by objectors, the first part of the book argues further that the resurrected body will have the form that all the raised had (or would have had if they had lived that long) at the "peak of youth." It will be a body without defects (thus, since female sex is not a defect, women will be raised with female, not male, bodies); and not a hair of the head will perish, although the material of the body may be redistributed, and some material may be added, in order to attain the beauty of the "peak of youth." The second part of the book turns to the eternal happiness of the redeemed. To enhance its picture of the life to come, it starts by rehearsing the miseries of the present life, both those common to the good and the evil alike and those unique to the good, who must do constant battle against the pull of the vices. On the other hand, it catalogues some of the great goods of this life and asks what the gifts of the life to come will be like, given that the consolations of the present life are so marvelous. Against Porphyry, the book insists that the soul, to attain happiness, has no need to flee all bodies. Instead, it will be restored to its own body, now made spiritual in the sense that it is fully conformed to the spirit, but still a body. How will the saints be occupied in the life to come? Purified in heart, they will see God. This point leads to a discussion of whether (and, if so, how) the saints will see God not only by the spirit but also with the eyes of the spiritual body. In any case, the saints will be in perfect peace. The desires of the flesh will no longer be at war with the desires of the spirit, and so they will be wholly free to love God. They will remember but will no longer feel the evils that they had suffered, and so their gratitude to God will be undiminished. And their life will be one in which they will unendingly see, love, and praise God. This will be their end without end.

1. As we promised in the previous book, this book — the last of the whole work — will contain a discussion of the eternal blessedness of the city of God. This city is not called eternal because it lasts a very long time, for ages and ages, but will eventually come to an end. It is called eternal, rather, in the sense in which it is written in the Gospel, *Of his kingdom there shall be no end* (Lk 1:33). Nor is it eternal in the sense that it has a mere outward appearance of perpetuity in that some of its members die and disappear while others arise to replace them, like an evergreen tree where the same green foliage seems to persist, when in fact leaves wither and fall away but others emerge to preserve the apparent density of its growth. Rather, all its citizens will be immortal, its human members attaining what the angels never lost. God, the most omnipotent creator of this city, will bring this about. He has promised it, and he cannot lie; and, to show his good faith, he has already done many things that he promised as well as many that he did not.

He is the one who in the beginning created the world,[1] full of all good things, both visible and intelligible; and in it he established nothing better than the spirits to whom he gave intelligence. These he made apt for contemplating him and capable of apprehending him; and he bound them together in one society, which we call the holy and supernal city, in which, for these spirits, God himself is the reality by which they are sustained and made blessed — their common life and food, as it were. On this same intellectual nature he bestowed free choice such that, if it willed, it might forsake God — might forsake, that is, its own happiness — with misery as the immediate consequence. And, even though he foreknew that some angels in their pride would will to be self-sufficient as the source of their own happiness and would forsake their great good, he did not take this power from them, for he judged it better and more powerful to bring good even out of evil than not to allow evil to exist.[2]

In fact there would have been no evil at all if this mutable nature — although good and created by the supreme God, the immutable good, who made all things good — had not made evil for itself by sinning. Its sin, however, is itself the evidence which proves that as a nature it was created good. For if it were not itself a great good (although not equal to the creator), its forsaking of God, as its light, could not have been its evil. Blindness is a defect of the eye, but it is the very thing which indicates that the eye was created for seeing light; and so, by its very defect, the

---

1. See Gn 1:1.
2. The same thought is expressed in *The Literal Meaning of Genesis* XI,9,12.

member capable of perceiving light is shown to be more excellent than the other bodily members, since there is no other reason that lack of light should be a defect in the eye. In the same way the nature which once enjoyed God shows by its very defect that it was created excellent, since the reason for its misery is precisely that it does not enjoy God.

God imposed on the angels who fell by their own volition the supremely just punishment of eternal unhappiness; and to all the rest of the angels who stood firm in the highest good he granted as their reward for standing firm the sure knowledge that they would remain with him without end. God also made man himself upright, with the same freedom of choice — an animal of the earth, to be sure, but worthy of heaven if he clung to his creator; and similarly, if he forsook God, the immediate consequence would be a misery suited to a nature of his kind. Again, even though God foreknew that man was going to sin by forsaking God in transgressing his law, he did not take away man's power of free choice, for he foresaw at the same time what good he would himself bring out of man's evil. For, from man's rightly and justly condemned mortal progeny, God is gathering together by his grace a people so great that, from it, he will fill and replenish the place left by the fallen angels.[3] As a result, the beloved and supernal city will not be cheated out of its due number of citizens, and it may even rejoice in a still more abundant number of them.

The Will of God and the Fulfillment of the Divine Promise

2. The wicked, of course, do many things that are contrary to God's will. But his wisdom and his power are so great that in fact all the things that seem opposed to his will actually tend toward the outcomes and ends which he himself foreknew to be good and just. Accordingly, when God is said to change his will — when, for example, he becomes angry at those to whom he was previously gentle — it is they who change rather than God; and they find him "changed," so to speak, in the way that they experience him. Similarly, to injured eyes the sun "changes" and somehow becomes harsh rather than mild, irritating rather than delightful, even though the sun in itself remains just the same as it was before. We also call "God's will" the will that God brings about in the hearts of those who obey his commandments; it is this will of which the Apostle says, *For it is God who works in you both to will...* (Phil 2:13). Similarly, it is not only the justice by which God himself is just that is called "God's justice" but also the justice which he brings about in the person who is justified by him. So also the law is called "God's law" when it is actually the law of human beings, although given by God. For it was obviously to human beings that Jesus said, *It is written in your law* (Jn 8:17); but in another passage we read, *The law of his God is in his heart* (Ps 37:31). According to the will that

---

3. For the idea that human beings are destined to replace the fallen angels see Origen, *Homily on Ezekiel* 13,2. See also *Enchiridion* 9,29;16,61-62.

God works in human beings, he is also said to will what he does not himself will but causes his people to will, just as he is said to know what he causes to be known by people who did not know it before. For, when the Apostle says, *But now that you know God, or rather are known by God* (Gal 4:9), it would be abhorrent for us to believe that God only then came to know those whom, in fact, he foreknew before the foundation of the world.[4] Rather, he is said to have then come to know what in actuality he then caused to be known. But I remember having discussed these ways of speaking already in earlier books.[5] It is, then, according to this sense of "God's will" — the sense in which we say that God wills what he causes others to will, to whom the future is not known — that he wills many things and yet does not do them.

For God's saints, with a holy will inspired by him, will many things to happen, and yet they do not happen. For example, they offer reverent and holy prayers for certain people, and yet God does not do what they pray for, even though by his Holy Spirit he himself caused them to have this will to pray. Thus when, in accord with God, the saints will and pray that someone may be saved, we can say by virtue of this way of speaking that God wills it, and yet he does not do it. What we mean is that God wills this in the sense that he causes the saints to will it. But, according to God's own will, which, like his foreknowledge, is eternal, he has already accomplished everything he has willed, both in heaven and on earth, and not only things past or present but also things future. Before the time comes at which he willed something to happen, a time which he foreknew and arranged before all time, we say, "It will happen *when* God wills." And, if we do not know when or even whether it will happen, we say, "It will happen *if* God wills." But this does not mean that God will then have a new will which he did not have before; it means rather that what has been prepared in his immutable will from all eternity will then take place....

The Miracle of the World's Belief in the Resurrection

5. This might once have been incredible, but the world has now come to believe that Christ's earthly body was taken up into heaven. Both learned and unlearned have now come to believe in the resurrection of the flesh and its ascension into heavenly abodes; and only a very few remain, whether learned or unlearned, who find it mystifying. If what all these people believe is credible, let those who do not believe it recognize how stupid they are; and, if it is incredible, surely it is also incredible that what is incredible has come to be so widely believed.[6] Here,

---

4. See 1 Pt 1:20.
5. See above at XI,8; XV,25; XVI,5.32.
6. Augustine's argument here and in what follows recalls Tertullian's famous words in *On the Flesh of Christ* 5, where he refers to some of the seeming contradictions of Christ's life ("It is not shameful, because it is something that one must be ashamed of.... It is entirely believable, because it is unfitting.... It is a certainty, because it is impossible"), which have often been

then, are two incredible things — namely, the resurrection of our body to eternity and the world's belief in something so incredible — and it was the same God who foretold that both were going to happen before either had actually taken place.[7]

We see that one of the two incredible things has already happened: the world believes what used to be incredible. Why, then, should we despair of the one that remains? What was once incredible — that the world would believe something so incredible — has happened. Why should what the world once believed incredible not happen too? After all, both of these incredible things, one of which we see and the other of which we believe, were foretold in the same writings through which the world has come to believe.

And the way in which the world came to believe, if we stop to think about it, turns out to be even more incredible. For Christ sent only a few fishermen out on the sea of this world with the nets of faith, men with no education in the liberal arts, completely untaught in the doctrines of pagan thought, not trained in grammar, not equipped with dialectic, not swollen with rhetoric.[8] It was in this way that Christ caught all those fish of every kind and even — more wonderful still, because more rare — some of the philosophers themselves. And so, if you please — or, rather, because it ought to please — we can add a third incredible thing.

Now we have three incredible things, and yet all three have actually happened. It is incredible that Christ rose in the flesh and ascended with his flesh into heaven. It is incredible that the world has come to believe something so incredible. It is incredible that a few obscure men, of no standing and with no education, were able to be so effective in persuading the world, including even the learned, of something so incredible. Of these three, the people we are debating refuse to believe the first; they are compelled to grant the second; and they can find no way to account for the second unless they believe the third. The resurrection of Christ and his ascension into heaven with the flesh in which he rose again are obviously now proclaimed and believed the whole world over. If it is not credible, why is it now believed throughout the world? If many noble, eminent, and learned people had reported that they saw this happen and had taken pains to spread the news of what they saw, it would be no wonder that the world believed them; in fact it would be perverse to refuse to believe witnesses such as these. But if — and this is the truth of the matter — the world believed a few obscure men of no importance and no learning who reported in speech and writing what they had seen, why are the

---

reduced to *credo quia absurdum* ("I believe because it is absurd"). The resemblance, however, is illusory: whereas Tertullian is flouting the conventions of logic for effect, Augustine is arguing that Christianity is all the more believable for having overcome the obstacles that he names.

7. See Mt 16:21 par.; 26:13.
8. Grammar, dialectic and rhetoric were the first three of the so-called liberal disciplines and the ones that were probably the most esteemed in the Roman world. See *Order* II,12,35-13,38. Augustine's mention of them in this context suggests a certain skepticism regarding the prestige that they enjoyed. That the gospel succeeded in being spread throughout the world by unlettered fishermen, despite all odds, is noted elsewhere in early Christian literature. See Origen, *Against Celsus* I,62.

few who remain so persistent and obstinate in not believing what the whole world now believes? The world has believed a tiny number of obscure, unimportant, unlearned men precisely because divinity has made itself even more miraculously convincing by using such contemptible witnesses. For the eloquence that made them persuasive in what they said was the eloquence not of words but rather of miraculous works. Those who had not seen Christ rise in the flesh and ascend with his flesh into heaven believed the men who told of seeing it because they not only spoke of it but also performed miraculous signs. They knew that these were men of only one language, or at most two, and suddenly they heard them miraculously speaking in the tongues of all peoples.[9] They saw a man who had been lame from the time when he was still nursing at his mother's breast stand up whole, after forty years, at the word of these men, spoken in Christ's name.[10] They saw handkerchiefs taken from the bodies of these men prove effective in healing the sick.[11] They saw countless people suffering from various diseases, all laid in a row along the street where these men were going to pass, so that their shadows might fall across them as they walked by;[12] and, for the most part, they saw the sick immediately restored to health. They saw many other astonishing things done by these men; and, finally, they even saw them raise the dead.[13]

If our opponents concede that these things actually occurred, as we read that they did, then just look how many incredible things we can now add to our first three. To get them to believe just one incredible thing — what we are told about the resurrection of the flesh and its ascension into heaven — we heap up the testimony of many incredible things; and yet, due to their terrible obstinacy, we still cannot bend these unbelievers to belief. But, if they refuse to believe that Christ's apostles really did work these miracles to convince people to believe in their preaching of Christ's resurrection and ascension, they still leave us with this one great miracle — that the whole world has come to believe it without any miracles at all. And that one miracle is enough for us!...

Miracles of the Present

8. Why is it, people ask, that the miracles which you say happened then do not still happen now?[14] I could reply, of course, that, before the world believed,

---

9. See Acts 2:4-11.
10. See Acts 3:1-10; 4:22.
11. See Acts 19:12.
12. See Acts 5:15.
13. See Acts 9:36-41; 20:9-12.
14. Augustine answers the same question in *True Religion* 25,47, written in 390, by saying that, were miracles to have continued up to his own time, people would have grown used to them and they would have become meaningless. He qualifies this opinion in *Revisions* I,13,7 by referring to contemporary miracles of which he is aware. See also ibid. I,14,5.

miracles were necessary in order to bring the world to believe. Now, however, anyone who still seeks marvels to make himself believe is himself a great marvel, since he does not believe at a time when the whole world believes. In asking their question, however, their real aim is to lead people to believe that the miracles of the past did not happen either. How is it, then, that Christ is now celebrated everywhere with such deep faith for having been taken up into heaven with his flesh? How is it that, in educated times which reject everything that could not actually be true, the world has so miraculously come to believe incredible things without any miracles at all? Or are they going to say, after all, that these things were credible, and that is the reason why they were believed? But, in that case, why do they not themselves believe?

Here, then, is our argument in brief: *either* a number of incredible things — which, although incredible, did happen and were seen — brought about faith in an incredible thing that was not seen, *or* the thing was actually so credible that it needed no miracles in order to be convincing, and that fact in itself refutes their incredulity. I only say this, however, to rebut these nonsensical people. For we cannot deny that many miracles have in fact occurred which attest to the one, great, and saving miracle of Christ's ascension into heaven with the flesh in which he rose again. They are all written in the same supremely truthful books, both the miracles that were done and the belief for the sake of which they were done. They became known in order to generate faith, and through the faith which they generated they are becoming still more widely known. They are read among the peoples so that they may be believed, and yet they would not be read among the peoples unless they had already been believed.

And, indeed, even now miracles are being worked in Christ's name, either through his sacraments or through the prayers or relics of his saints. But these miracles have not been brought to light with the same bright renown that has made the others so widely known. For the canon of Sacred Scripture, which has rightly been brought to a close, causes the earlier miracles to be recited everywhere and to stick in everyone's memory. But these recent miracles are barely known to all the residents of the city or the district where they are performed. All too often they are known only to a very few, and the rest have no knowledge of them at all, especially if the city is a large one. And when they are told to other people in other places — despite the fact that they are reported by Christian believers to Christian believers — there is no authority with the weight of Scripture to back them up and ensure that they are believed without doubt or difficulty.

A miracle which took place in Milan while I was there, when a blind man regained his sight, was able to become widely known because Milan is a great city and because the emperor was there at the time. In addition, the event was witnessed by an immense crowd that was gathering to see the bodies of the martyrs Protasius and Gervasius (which had been lost and were completely unknown until they were discovered due to a revelation to Bishop Ambrose in a dream). It was there that the blind man's long-standing darkness was dispelled and he saw the light of day.[15]

At Carthage, in contrast, who but a very few know of the healing of Innocentius, a former advocate of the vice-prefecture?[16] I myself was present at the event and saw it with my own eyes. For when my brother Alypius[17] and I came from across the sea[18] — we were not yet priests then but were already in God's service — Innocentius had received us, since he and his entire household were deeply religious; and we were staying with him at the time. He was under the care of physicians for fistulas, of which he had quite a number, complexly entangled, in the rectum and the lower parts of his body. The doctors had already operated on him and were treating what remained with the remedies of their art. In the operation he had suffered acute and prolonged pain. But one of the many abscesses had eluded the doctors; they should have opened it with the knife, but it was so well hidden that they could not reach it. At last all the abscesses which they had opened were cured; only this one remained, and all the work they devoted to it was of no use. Innocentius's suspicions were aroused by the delay, and he was terribly afraid that they would have to operate again.

Another doctor, his household physician, had predicted this. They had not allowed this doctor to be present for the first operation, not even just to watch to see how it was done, and Innocentius was so angry at his prediction that he had thrown him out of the house and had barely taken him back. Now Innocentius burst out with the question, "Are you going to cut me again? Am I going to find that the fellow you wouldn't even allow to watch has the last word?" They only belittled the other physician as lacking any skill and soothed the man's fear with fair words and promises. Many more days passed, and still nothing that they did was of any use at all. The doctors, however, continued to stand by their promise to close the abscess by means of their remedies without resorting to the knife. They also called in another physician, highly praised in that art, an old man called Ammonius, who was still alive at the time. Ammonius examined the place and promised just what the others had promised on the grounds of their attentiveness and skill. Reassured by this man's authority, Innocentius, as if already cured, gleefully made fun of his household physician for having predicted that a second operation would be needed.

Then what? After that, so many days of useless efforts went by that the doctors, exhausted and bewildered, had to admit that there was no way he could be

---

15. See *Confessions* IX,7,16; Paulinus, *Life of St. Ambrose* 14.
16. This Innocentius is unknown apart from what is told of him here, but he was one of several wealthy and influential benefactors who befriended Augustine over the course of his life. The miracle that Augustine records must have taken place c. 388.
17. Alypius (died c. 430) was the bishop of Thagaste and one of Augustine's closest friends; he is described at length in *Confessions* VI,7,11-10,16.
18. Augustine crossed the Mediterranean from Italy to North Africa in 388 and settled in Thagaste.

cured without the knife. He was terrified; he turned pale, thrown into turmoil by his overwhelming fear; and, when he had pulled himself together and could finally speak, he ordered them to go away and never come near him again. Worn out with weeping, and now driven by necessity, he could think of nothing else to do but to send for a certain Alexandrian who was regarded at the time as a marvelous surgeon and have him do what, in his anger, he refused to let the others do. But, when the Alexandrian came and, with his artist's eye, saw in the scars all the work the other physicians had put in, he acted as an honest man: he persuaded Innocentius that the doctors who had worked so hard for him, and whose work he had himself inspected with admiration, should have the satisfaction of completing his cure. He added that it was quite true that no cure was possible without another operation but that it would violate his integrity to steal the credit for their labor, by doing the little that remained to be done, from men whose supremely skillful work, diligence, and carefulness he had seen and admired in examining the scars. Accordingly, they were restored to favor, and it was agreed that the Alexandrian would stand by while the others opened with a scalpel the abscess which was now reckoned, by common consent, to be incurable in any other way. The operation itself was put off until the following day. But, when the doctors had left, there arose such lamentation in the house, due to the master's terrible distress, that it was like the mourning at a funeral, and we could hardly restrain it.

Certain holy men visited Innocentius each day — Saturninus of blessed memory, who was at that time bishop of Uzalis, the priest Gulosus, and the deacons of the church of Carthage. Among these — and the only one still active in affairs — was Aurelius, now a bishop, whom I must name with all due honor.[19] I have often spoken with him about this event as we were recalling the wondrous works of God, and I found that he remembered very well what I am describing. When these holy men visited Innocentius that evening, as was their custom, he begged them to be good enough to come next morning to be present not for his suffering but for his funeral. For, as a result of his earlier pain, he was gripped by such fear that he had no doubt that he was going to die at the doctors' hands. They comforted him and urged him to trust in God and submit to God's will like a man. Then we started to pray; and, while, in the customary way, we were kneeling and bowing to the ground, he threw himself down, as if someone had knocked him flat by force, and began to pray. Who could convey in words the way in which he prayed — the emotion, the mental turmoil, the flood of tears, the groans and sobs that shook his every limb and almost cut off his breath! Whether the others continued to pray without being distracted by all this, I do not know. I only know that I could not pray at all. I only said, briefly, in my heart, "Lord, what prayers of your people do you hear if you don't hear these?" For it seemed to me that nothing could be added to his prayer except for him to breathe his last in praying. We rose and, after receiving the bishop's blessing, departed. Innocentius implored the holy men to be there the next morning, and they exhorted him to keep up his spirits.

---

19. Aurelius, a close collaborator of Augustine, was bishop of Carthage from c. 392 to 430.

The dreaded day dawned; the servants of God[20] were there, as they had promised they would be; the physicians came in; everything the occasion required is made ready; the terrifying instruments are brought out; and all are in stunned suspense.[21] While those with the most influence raise Innocentius's failing spirits with words of comfort, his limbs are arranged on the couch, ready for the surgeon's hands. The knots of the bandages are untied; the place is laid bare. The physician examines it and, knife at the ready, looks carefully for the abscess to be cut open. He searches with his eyes and feels with his fingers; he tries everything — and he finds a perfectly firm scar! No words of mine can capture the joy and praise and thanksgiving to the merciful and almighty God which poured forth, with tears of gladness, from everyone's lips. This is a scene to be imagined, not described....

[Twelve more healing miracles are named: of cancer, gout, paralysis, epilepsy and demonic possession.]

But there is one miracle that took place among us which, although no greater than the others I have mentioned, was so renowned and celebrated that I imagine there is no one in Hippo who did not either see it or hear about it, and certainly no one who could possibly forget it. There was a family of ten, seven brothers and three sisters, from Caesarea in Cappadocia.[22] They were not undistinguished among their fellow citizens, but they had been cursed by their mother, who had recently before been left destitute by their father's death and was terribly bitter about some wrong which they had done her. As a result they were put under such a ferocious divine punishment that they all shook with a horrible trembling of their limbs. In this loathsome condition, unable to bear the stares of their fellow citizens, they wandered over virtually the whole Roman world in whatever direction each decided to go. Two of them came to our city, a brother and sister, Paulus and Palladia, who were already well known in many other places, due to widespread reports of their misery. They arrived some fifteen days before Easter, and they visited the church daily — and, in it, the shrine of the most glorious Stephen[23] — praying that God might now be appeased and restore their former health. Both there and wher-

---

20. "The servants of God": *servi Dei*. As he does also in Letter 20,2, Augustine is referring to himself and Alypius by this title, which describes persons who set themselves apart in some way to lead more intensely Christian lives.
21. It is noteworthy that apparently the operation — on what seems to have been a deeply embedded anal fistula — was going to be performed in the presence of numerous onlookers. At this point Augustine's narrative switches from the past to the present tense in order to heighten the suspense.
22. Caesarea was the administrative capital of the region of Cappadocia, in what is now east-central Turkey. The two members of the family who wandered from there to Hippo, as Augustine relates, traveled a great distance.
23. The relics of St. Stephen were discovered in Palestine in 415 and from there were disseminated

ever they went, they attracted the stares of the whole city. Some, who had seen them elsewhere and knew what caused their tremors, told the story to others whenever they could.

Easter arrived, and on the morning of the Sunday itself, when a large crowd was already present, the young man was praying while clinging to the railings of the holy place where the martyr's relics were kept. Suddenly he fell flat on his face and lay there, looking for all the world as if he were sleeping, but no longer trembling as the two usually did when asleep. Everyone was astonished. Some were terrified, others moved to pity. Some wanted to lift him up; others said not to and urged that it would be better to wait and see what happened next. And then he stood up. Because he had been cured, he was no longer trembling; and he stood there, safe and sound, looking back at all the people looking at him.

Who could keep from praising God? The whole church was filled with cries of thanksgiving. They ran to me where I was sitting, just waiting for the procession to begin. They rushed in, one after the other, each telling as new what the one before had just said; and, as I was joyfully offering my own silent thanks to God, the young man himself came in with several others. He bowed to my knees, then straightened up for my kiss. We processed in to the people; the church was full; it rang with shouts of joy: "Thanks be to God! Praise be to God!" No one was silent; the cries came from all sides. I greeted the people, and again they cried out with even more fervent shouts. When at last it was quiet, the appointed passages from Divine Scripture were read. But, when we reached the place for my sermon, I said only a few words, appropriate to the occasion and suited to the sheer delight of our rejoicing. I allowed them to reflect on God's eloquence in this divine work, so to speak, rather than to hear it. The man ate with us and told us in detail the whole calamitous story of his brothers and sisters and his mother. And so, on the following day, after the sermon, I promised that a report of his story would be written up the next day to be read to the people. When the reading took place, on the third day after Easter Sunday, I had the brother and sister stand on the steps of the apse while the report of them was read out, just below the place where I give my sermons.

The whole congregation, men and women alike, stared at the one standing there without any hint of abnormal movement and the other trembling in every limb. And, by looking at his sister, those who had not seen it already now grasped what the divine mercy had done for him. In his case they saw what they should give thanks for; and in hers they saw what they should pray for. Meanwhile, once the reading of the report was finished, I instructed them to withdraw from the people's stares; and I had begun to discuss the whole case somewhat more fully when, all of a sudden, while I was speaking, new cries of thanksgiving were heard from the martyr's shrine. Those who were listening to me turned away and began

---

throughout the Mediterranean world, including Hippo. See Sermons 314-324.

to run to the spot. For the sister, when she came down from the steps where she had been standing, had gone over to pray at the martyr's shrine; and, as soon as she touched the railings, she also fell down as if asleep and then stood up healed. While I was asking what had happened to cause that joyful uproar, they came back with her into the basilica where I was, leading her — now healed — from the martyr's shrine. And then such a shout of wonder went up from both men and women that it seemed impossible that the ongoing cries and tears would ever end. She was led to the place where, just a little before, she had stood trembling. Those who had then mourned that she remained unlike her brother now rejoiced to see her like him; and they realized that, even though they had not yet poured out their prayers for her, their antecedent wish had still been heard in an instant. They exulted in praising God, in shouts without words, a noise so loud that my ears could hardly bear it. And what was in the hearts of these exulting people but the very faith in Christ for which Stephen's blood had been shed?[24]

---

24. This final miracle story of the series gives us an insightful glimpse into the liturgical and devotional life of Hippo in Augustine's day. The setting is Easter Sunday to Tuesday, perhaps in 425, in the cathedral of Hippo, which was the site of a shrine to Saint Stephen. As Augustine prepares in the sacristy on Easter Sunday to celebrate the eucharist he is informed of a young man's miraculous public healing, which has taken place at the shrine. He and his ministers then process into the body of the church, accompanied by the shouts of the crowd, who are enthused by the miracle. He greets the people, and the shouting resumes. At last he obtains silence and the Scriptures are read. Rather than giving a sermon of the sort that would be expected on Easter Day, Augustine speaks very briefly about the miracle (Sermon 320). On Easter Monday Augustine speaks yet more briefly (Sermon 321) and promises that a report (*libellus*) of the miracle will be read the following day. On Easter Tuesday Augustine gives a short introduction to the report, in which he asks the young man and his sister, who suffered from the same affliction as her brother but had not yet been healed, to stand on the steps of the apse "just below the place where I give my sermons." Then the young man reads the report. (Both the introduction and the report are counted as Sermon 322.) Following the report it seems from what happens next that the sister goes to the shrine, and perhaps her brother accompanies her. Meanwhile Augustine comments on some of the siblings' background, on devotion to the relics of Saint Stephen, and on another healing that had taken place at another shrine (Sermon 323). As he is speaking the sister is suddenly healed and brought back to the apse. The congregation breaks into shouts, and Augustine quickly concludes his sermon. Finally Sermon 324, given on Easter Wednesday, is a relatively brief continuation of Sermon 323. In none of these five sermons, at least as they have been handed down to us, does Augustine so much as mention Easter. These two miracles — one on Easter Sunday itself and the second on Easter Tuesday — and the congregation's response to them seem together to have overwhelmed the celebration of the greatest feast of the liturgical year, and Augustine accepts this and addresses his people on what clearly mattered to them at the moment. The account of the miracles in *The City of God* and what we learn from Sermons 320-323 (and elsewhere) suggest both that Augustine's congregation was an excitable one and that he was skilled at adapting to and even controlling that excitement; we learn from other early Christian sermons that it was not all that unusual for church congregations to be spontaneous in expressing themselves and that successful preachers could accept and direct their moods. Augustine's liturgical flexibility included arranging for the reading, during the Tuesday eucharist, of an account of the first of the miracles; in other words, following a practice that was recent in North Africa (and that he mentioned shortly before in this section that he had introduced in Hippo), he inserted a non-liturgical element into the liturgy. Finally, as for the liturgy itself, we read of a procession, a greeting followed by readings from Scripture and then, as expected,

The Witness of the Martyrs

9. To what do all these miracles attest but the very faith which proclaims that Christ rose in the flesh and ascended into heaven with his flesh? For the martyrs themselves were martyrs — that is, witnesses[25] — to this faith. In giving their witness they endured the world's fiercest hostility and cruelty, and they overcame the world not by fighting back but by dying. For the sake of this faith they died, and now they are able to obtain these wonders from the Lord for whose name they were killed.[26] For the sake of this faith their wondrous patience came first, so that the extraordinary power in these miracles might come after. For, if the resurrection of the flesh to eternal life has not already happened in Christ and if it is not going to happen as Christ foretells and as the prophets foretold who foretold Christ, how is it that the dead, who were killed for the very faith that proclaims this resurrection, are able to do such wondrous things? It may be that God works these miracles himself, through himself alone, in the wondrous manner in which the eternal effects its work in time. It may be that he works them through his servants. And, when he works through his servants, it may be that he works some miracles through the spirits of the martyrs, just as he works some through persons still in the body; or it may be that he works all of them through the angels, over whom he has invisible, incorporeal, and immutable command — in which case what the martyrs are said to do is actually done only at their prayer and intercession, not by any act of their own; or it may be that God works some in these ways but others in ways that mortals simply cannot comprehend at all. Whatever the case may be, however, these miracles all bear witness to the faith which proclaims the resurrection of the flesh to eternal life....

Questions about the Character of the Resurrected Body

12. The Platonists often go over our view in great detail, and then they mock our belief that the flesh will be raised by asking questions such as whether aborted fetuses will rise again. Or, because the Lord says, *Amen, I say to you, not a hair of your head shall perish* (Lk 21:18), they ask whether all will be equal in stature and strength or whether there will be differences in bodily size. If their bodies are going to be equal in size, how can it be that aborted fetuses (assuming that they do in fact rise again) are going to have a bodily bulk that they never had before?[27]

---

the sermon. There is no mention of a penitential rite or a collect between the greeting and the readings. This fragmentary depiction of the first part of the eucharistic liturgy in Hippo is all the more precious for being a relative rarity in Augustine's writings.

25. The word "martyr" derives from the Greek word for "witness."
26. Note that Augustine does not take into account saints who were not martyrs; the cult of nonmartyrs was only in its infancy at the time.
27. On the resurrection of unborn children see *Enchiridion* 23,85-86.

Or, if they are not going to rise again (since they were not actually born but merely spilled out), they shift their question to the case of infants and ask how they are going to acquire a bodily measure which, as we plainly see, they lack when they die at this early age. After all, we are certainly not going to deny that infants will rise again; if they are capable of being born, they are capable of being reborn. Then, further, they ask how people will come to be equal in bodily size. For, if everyone is going to be as large and as tall as the largest and tallest people were here on earth, their question has to do not only with infants but with virtually everyone: if each person is going to receive back what he had here on earth, where is the surplus going to come from to make up for the size that he lacked here on earth?

On the other hand, the Apostle says that we are all going to come *to the measure of the age of the fullness of Christ* (Eph 4:13), and he also refers to those *whom he predestined to be conformed to the image of his Son* (Rom 8:29). If this means that all the human bodies in Christ's kingdom will have the shape and size of Christ's own body, they argue, then something will have to be subtracted from the size and height of the body in many cases. And, if some portion of the body's size is in fact going to perish, what will be left of the claim that *not a hair of your head shall perish*? Furthermore, with regard to the hair itself, it can be asked whether everything the barber has clipped off will be restored.[28] And, if it is going to be restored, who would not be horrified at such ugliness? For it would seem that the same thing would necessarily have to follow with regard to fingernails and toenails as well: everything clipped off in grooming the body would have to be restored. And in that case what will have happened to the bodily beauty which certainly ought to be greater in immortality than it could possibly be in this corruption? But, if all this is not restored, then it perishes. And in that case, they ask, how can it be true that not a hair of one's head will perish? They make a similar argument with regard to thinness and fatness. If all are going to be equal, then it obviously is not true that some will be thin and others fat. Something, therefore, will have to be added to some and something taken away from others; and as a result there will not be a restoration of what was there before. Instead, in some cases there will be an addition of what was not there before, and in others a subtraction of what was there before.

They are quite distressed, too, with regard to the issue of the decay and dissolution of dead bodies: one is changed into dust, another evaporates into the air; some are consumed by beasts, some by fire; some perish by shipwreck or drown in some other way, so that their flesh rots and dissolves into liquid. They do not believe that all these bits can be gathered up and made whole again as flesh. They also call attention to every sort of physical abnormality and defect, whether due to accident or to birth. With horror and derision they list off monstrous births and

---

28. On the disposition of hair and fingernails at the resurrection see ibid. 23,89.

BOOK XXII 531

demand to know what the resurrection will mean for each of these deformities.[29] If we say that nothing of this sort returns to the human body, they imagine that they can refute our response by referring to the wounds with which we proclaim that the Lord Christ rose from the dead. Among all the questions they ask, however, the most difficult one is this: if one person, driven by famine, eats the flesh of another to get sustenance, to whose body will that flesh be restored? It was obviously converted into the flesh of the one who kept himself alive by means of such food, and it filled in the loss made obvious by his emaciated state. Will it return, then, to the person who first had it, or will it return instead to the one whose flesh it later became? They put this question in order to mock our belief in the resurrection. For their part, however, all they have to offer is either, like Plato, to promise the human soul alternating states of true unhappiness and false happiness[30] or, like Porphyry, to acknowledge that, after cycling over and over again through different bodies, the soul finally ends its miseries and never goes back to them — not, however, by gaining an immortal body but rather by entirely fleeing the body.[31]

Response to the Questions

13. With God's mercy providing help to my efforts, let me respond to these objections from their side which, as I have presented them, seem to tell against me.

As to aborted fetuses, because they were alive in the womb, they also died there. I do not dare, however, either to affirm or to deny that they will rise again. Still, if they are not excluded from the number of the dead, I do not see why they should not be included in the resurrection of the dead. For either not all the dead will rise again, and some human souls that once had human bodies, even if only in their mothers' wombs, will be without bodies in eternity; or, if all human souls are going to receive their own bodies back at the resurrection — no matter where they first lived in the body and then departed from it when it died — I find no way to deny that even those who died in their mother's womb will be included in the resurrection of the dead. Whichever view one takes, however, what I am now going to say about infants who have actually come to birth must be understood to apply to aborted fetuses as well, if they do in fact rise again.

14. What, then, are we to say about infants? What can we say except that they are not going to rise again in the tiny bodies in which they died but instead are going to receive — immediately, and by a miraculous work of God — the bodies that otherwise would have come to them more slowly over time? When the Lord says that *not a hair of your head shall perish*, he obviously affirms that nothing which was once present will be missing, but he does not deny that something

---

29. On the resurrection of deformities see ibid. 23,87.
30. See *Phaedrus* 246d-249d. See also above at XII,21.
31. An opinion frequently cited by Augustine. See above at X,29; XII,27; and below at XXII,26.

once missing can then be present. The dead infant lacked the completed size of its body, for even a complete infant lacks the complete bodily size which, once reached, means that his stature can grow no further. Everyone has this measure of completeness, of course, in the sense that they are conceived and born with it. But they have it in principle, not in actual mass, in the same way that all the body's members are already latently present in the seed, despite the fact that some — such as teeth and the like — are still missing at birth. In virtue of this principle, which is implanted in each person's bodily matter, what is not yet present — or rather, what is latent but will with time come to be, or rather will make its appearance — seems somehow already to be woven into him. In this sense, then, the infant who is going to be short or tall is, in fact, already short or tall. And, in accord with this principle, we have no reason to fear any bodily deficit in the resurrection of the body....

15. ...We can only conclude, then, that each will receive his own bodily measure, either the size that he had in youth, if he died an old man, or the size that he would have had in youth, if he died before then. As for what the Apostle said about *the measure of the age of the fullness of Christ*, either we must take it to have a different meaning — namely, that the measure of Christ's age will be completed when the full number of all his members among the Christian people is added to him as head — or, if the Apostle was in fact speaking of the resurrection of the body, we should take it to mean that the bodies of the dead will rise neither older nor younger than their youthful form but at precisely the age and vigor that we know Christ attained here on earth. For even the most learned men of this world have set the peak of youth at about thirty years of age; and, once youth has reached the limit of its proper span, from that point on a person is already declining into a debilitating and burdensome old age.[32] The Apostle was referring, then, not to the measure of the body or to the measure of the stature but *to the measure of the age of the fullness of Christ*....

Thus, all will rise with a body of the size that they had, or would have had, at the peak of youth. But it would be no hindrance if, instead, the body's form were that of infancy or old age, just so long as no weakness either of mind or of body itself remained. Consequently, even if someone insists that each person will rise again with the same kind of body in which he died, there is no need to do battle with him in a tiresome round of arguments and counter-arguments.

The Resurrection of Women's Bodies

17. Because Scripture says, *Until we all come to complete manhood, to the measure of the age of the fullness of Christ* (Eph 4:13) and *conformed to the image*

---

32. Varro, who was one of Augustine's authorities, considered the period from one's thirtieth to one's forty-fifth year as youth, which was followed by the gradual onset of old age. See Censorinus, *On One's Natal Day* 14.

of the Son of God, some people believe that women will not rise again with their female sex; instead, they claim, all will rise as males,[33] because God made only the man from clay[34] but the woman from the man.[35] But the more sensible view, it seems to me, is the one held by those who do not doubt that both sexes will rise again.[36] For then there will be no lust, which is the cause of shame. Before they sinned they were naked, and the man and the woman were not ashamed.[37] All faults will be removed from those bodies, but their nature will be preserved. And female sex is not a fault but rather a matter of nature, and it will then be exempt from intercourse and childbirth. The female organs will still be present. Now, however, they will be accommodated not to their former use but to a new beauty which will not excite the lustful desire of the beholder, for there will be no lust. Instead, they will evoke praise for the wisdom and compassion of God, who both created what was not and freed what he created from corruption....

The woman, therefore, is just as much God's creation as is the man. But, by her being made from the man, human unity was commended to us;[38] and by her being made in this way, as I said, Christ and the Church were prefigured. Thus the one who established the two sexes will restore them both....

The Meaning of Complete Manhood

18. Again, with regard to the Apostle's statement that we shall all come to *complete manhood,* we need to take the whole context of the saying into account. The passage reads as follows: *He who descended is the same one who ascended above all the heavens, so that he might fill all things. And he himself gave some to be apostles, some to be prophets, some to be evangelists, some to be pastors and teachers, in order to perfect the saints for the work of ministry, for the building up of the body of Christ, until we all come to the unity of faith and the knowledge of the Son of God, to complete manhood, to the measure of the age of the fullness of Christ.*

---

33. See Jerome, *Commentary on the Epistle to the Ephesians* 5:29.
34. See Gn 2:7.
35. See Gn 2:21-22.
36. The present section is important in understanding Augustine's view of women. To summarize that view: being a woman is a matter of nature and not of vice; women's bodies will emphatically remain distinctly feminine and not become masculine at the resurrection; and, when Scripture uses what is normally the exclusively masculine form *vir,* it can often be understood inclusively to indicate both men and women. But this rather positive assessment of the feminine does not represent the whole of Augustine's attitude toward women and must be supplemented by other texts. For a brief overview of the subject see Allan D. Fitzgerald, *Augustine through the Ages: An Encyclopedia* (Grand Rapids: Eerdmans, 1999) 887-892.
37. See Gn 2:25.
38. See above at XII,22.

From him the whole body, linked and joined together in every act of providing for itself, with each part functioning in its measure, promotes the body's growth in building itself up in love (Eph 4:10-13.16). Here we see what *complete manhood* means: it is the head and the body, the latter consisting of all its members, whose number will be completed in its own time....

But, even if *complete manhood* is meant be understood as a reference to the form in which each person will rise again, what keeps us from understanding woman to be included when man is named, taking "man" to mean "human being"?[39] That is its meaning in the saying, *Blessed is the man who fears the Lord* (Ps 112:1), which clearly includes the women as well as the men who fear the Lord.

Further Responses to Questions about the Resurrected Body

19. Now, what reply shall I give with regard to the hair and fingernails? Once it is clear that the reason why nothing is going to perish from the body is to ensure that there will be no deformity in the body, it is simultaneously clear that any mass that would have caused a deformity will be restored to the body, but not to the places where it would disfigure the form of its members. Think of it this way: if a pot made from clay were reduced back to the original lump of clay and then remade, so that the whole new pot contained the whole lump of clay, it would not be necessary for the specific part of the clay that formed the old handle to go into the new handle or for the clay that made up the old base to make up the new base. All that would actually be required would be that all of the old clay would be used to form all of the new pot, that is, that exactly the same clay would be reused to make the whole new pot with none left over.[40] Thus, if cut hair and trimmed nails will cause a deformity if they are restored to their proper places, they will not be restored to those places. But they will not perish at the resurrection. Rather, by virtue of the mutability of matter, they will return to the same flesh and will have a place in the body, but with the due proportion of the parts kept intact....

As a consequence, neither fat people nor thin people should have any fear that at the resurrection they will be other than they would have chosen to be here on earth, if only they had been able to choose. All bodily beauty is a matter of the symmetry of the parts,[41] together with a certain attractiveness of color. When the parts are out of symmetry, however, there is something that grates on our nerves, either because it is misshapen, or because it is too small, or because it is too large. But there will be no deformity due to lack of symmetry among the parts. Anything misshapen will be set right; anything smaller than is fitting will be supplemented

---

39. "Man...human being": *virum...homine*.
40. See *Enchiridion* 23,89. The same example appears in a slightly different context in Gregory of Nyssa, *Great Catechism* 8.
41. See above at V,11 and XI,22.

BOOK XXII   535

from resources known to the creator; and anything larger than is fitting will be removed, but with the integrity of the material preserved. And how overwhelming the attractive color will be where *the righteous will shine like the sun in the kingdom of their Father* (Mt 13:43)!...

20. As for bodies that have been consumed by wild beasts or by fire, or that have collapsed into dust and ashes or dissolved into liquid or evaporated into the air, it is sheer absurdity to think that the creator's omnipotence is not able to bring them all back, reviving them and restoring them to life. It is sheer absurdity to think that anything hidden from our senses could be so deeply concealed in some secret recess of nature that it would also elude the knowledge or escape the power of the creator of all. When Cicero, their great author, wanted to define God as precisely as he could, he said, "God is a kind of mind, unfettered and free, set apart from all materiality and mortality, perceiving all things and moving all things, while itself endowed with eternal motion."[42] He found this definition in the teachings of the greatest philosophers. To speak in their terms, then, how can anything lie hidden from the one who perceives all things, or irrevocably escape the one who moves all things?

And it is on this basis, too, that we must respond to the question that seems more difficult than all the rest: When the flesh of a dead person also becomes the flesh of another, living person, to which of the two will it be restored in the resurrection? For, if a person, wasted and driven by hunger, eats a dead human being — an evil which has actually happened, as both ancient history and the unhappy experience of our own times teach us[43] — could anyone argue with truth and reason that everything he eats is digested and passed through the bowel without any of it being changed and converted into the flesh of the eater? The very fact that the person was emaciated, but now is not, shows clearly enough what he gained by such food.

But the points I have already made should be sufficient to solve this problem as well. For all the flesh that hunger stripped away from the person who was starving has plainly evaporated into the air; and, as we said, almighty God is perfectly able to bring back what has fled in this way. That flesh, therefore, will be restored to the person in whom it first began to be human flesh. For it must be regarded as borrowed, so to speak, by the one who ate it; and, like another person's money, it must be repaid to the one from whom it was borrowed. And, as for the person who was wasted by hunger, his own flesh will be restored to him by the one who is able to bring back even what has evaporated. Even if it had completely perished, so that none of its material remained in any of nature's hiding places, the Almighty would still restore it from any source he chose. The Truth said that *not a hair of*

---

42. *Tusculan Disputations* I,27,66.
43. Cannibalism is reported in 2 K 6:28-29. Jerome, Letter 127,12, speaks of cannibalism during Alaric's pillage of Rome in 410. Both are cases of mothers eating their children. See also below at XXII.22.

your head shall perish, and so it would be absurd to suppose that, even though not one hair of the head can perish, all that flesh could have perished because it was eaten away and consumed by hunger.

Now that we have considered and addressed all these concerns to the best of our ability, the upshot is that, at the resurrection of the flesh to eternity, the body will have the size and dimensions which, by the principle implanted in each, it had reached or would have reached at the peak of youth. It will also have the beauty that stems from having the appropriate proportions preserved in all its members. And if, for the sake of preserving this beauty, something is taken away from the unseemly size concentrated in one part of the body and redistributed throughout the whole — so that it does not perish, and at the same time the harmony of the parts is everywhere preserved — it is not absurd for us to believe that some of this material could be added to the body's stature. For in that way material that would have no beauty at all if it were all concentrated in one enormous part of the body is redistributed in such a way that the beauty of all parts of the body is preserved. Alternatively, if it is argued that each person will rise with the same bodily stature with which he died, there is no need to put up a pugnacious resistance to this claim, provided that there will be no deformity, no infirmity, no sluggishness, no corruption, nor anything else unsuited to the kingdom in which the sons of the resurrection and of the promise will be equal to the angels of God,[44] if not in body or in age, most certainly in felicity.

21. Anything that has perished from the living body, then, or from the corpse after death, will be restored; and, together with what remained in the tomb, it will rise again, changed from the oldness of the animal body to the newness of the spiritual body, and clothed with incorruption and immortality. Even if, by some dire chance or by enemy savagery, the whole body is utterly ground to dust, and even if the dust has been dispersed on the winds or in the waters so that, as far as possible, the body has completely ceased to exist, it still cannot in any way elude the creator's omnipotence, and it is still true that not one hair of its head will perish. Thus, the spiritual flesh will be subject to the spirit, but it will still be flesh, not spirit, just as the carnal spirit was itself subject to the flesh but was still spirit....

But, since we do not yet have any experience of what the grace of the spiritual body is or of how great it will be, it would, I fear, be rash to make any pronouncements about it.

The Gift of the Life to Come

For the sake of praising God, however, we must not keep silent about the joy of our hope, and from the inmost heart of an ardent holy love it was said, *Lord, I*

---

44. See Lk 22:30.

have loved the beauty of your house (Ps 26:8). With God's help, then, let us offer a conjecture, trying to infer as best we can from the gifts he bestows on good and evil alike in this troubled life how great the gift will be that we have not yet experienced and that we certainly have no power to describe as it deserves. I say nothing of the time when God made man upright; I say nothing of the happy life of the married couple in the abundance of paradise. That happy life was so brief that it did not even last long enough for their children to experience it. But even in this life, which we know and are still in and whose trials — or, rather, whose one long trial — we never cease to endure (no matter how long we are in this life, and no matter how much progress we make), who can tell of the marks of God's goodness toward the human race?

The Evils of this Life

22. From its very beginning, this life itself — if we can call it life, when it is full of so many and such dire evils — bears witness that the whole progeny of mortals has been condemned. What else is indicated by the terrible depth of ignorance from which springs all the error that holds the sons of Adam captive in a dark vale, from which no one can be delivered without toil, pain, and fear? What else is indicated by love for so many futile and harmful things — from which come gnawing cares, passions, griefs, fears, insane joys, discords, disputes, wars, intrigues, angers, enmities, deceit, flattery, fraud, theft, rapine, perfidy, pride, ambition, envy, murder, parricide, cruelty, savagery, wickedness, lasciviousness, insolence, shamelessness, lewdness, fornication, adulteries, incest, and so many other unnatural and impure acts of both sexes which it is indecent even to mention, sacrileges, heresies, blasphemies, perjuries, oppressions of the innocent, slanders, cheatings, prevarications, false testimony, unjust judgments, acts of violence, robberies, and any other evils that do not immediately come to mind but are never far from this life of ours?[45] These are, of course, the works of evil men, but they stem from that root of error and perverted love with which every son of Adam is born.[46] For who does not know what a great ignorance of truth, already manifest in infancy, and what an overflow of misdirected desire, first putting in its appearance in childhood, characterize each person coming into this life?[47] The result is that, if left to live as he likes and to do whatever he wants, he falls into all — or at least into many — of the crimes and shameful acts which I have listed and which I could not list.

---

45. This is almost certainly the longest catalogue of sins to have come down to us from Christian antiquity. Much shorter predecessors to it can be found, e.g., in Rom 1:29-31; Eph 5:19-21; *Didache* 5; Melito of Sardis, *On the Pasch* 49-53.
46. Augustine is referring to original sin.
47. On the role of ignorance and desire in human misery see also *Enchiridion* 8,24.

The divine governance, however, does not wholly abandon the condemned, and God does not hold back his mercies in anger.[48] Prohibition and instruction keep watch, in the very senses of humankind, against the dark shadows with which we are born, and they resist their attacks. But even prohibition and instruction are full of toil and pain. For what is the meaning of all the threats we invoke to restrain the willfulness of little children? What is the point of the tutors, the teachers, the rod, the strap, the cane, the discipline with which, Holy Scripture says, the sides of the beloved child must be beaten,[49] lest he grow up untamed and, once hardened, can barely be tamed, or perhaps not at all?[50] Why do we have all these punishments if not to overcome ignorance and to rein in misdirected desire, the evils with which we come into this world? Why does it take effort to remember, but no effort to forget? Why does it take effort to learn, but no effort to remain ignorant? Why does it take effort to be active, but no effort to do nothing? Is it not clear from all this which way our vitiated nature is inclined and prone to take, as if pulled by its own weight, and how much help it needs in order to be delivered from that tendency? Idleness, apathy, indolence, indifference are clearly vices that shun effort, since effort itself, even useful effort, is a punishment.

Besides the punishments of childhood, without which children cannot learn what their elders want them to — although they hardly ever want them to learn anything useful — there are also all the many and severe punishments that afflict humanity in general. These punishments pertain not to the malice and iniquity of the wicked but simply to the common condition and shared misery of all. Who could possibly list them in any one discourse? Who could possibly grasp them in any one sequence of thought? What fear and distress come from bereavement and mourning, from loss and condemnation, from deception and lying, from false suspicions, and from all the violent crimes and villainous actions of others? At their hands we often suffer pillage and enslavement, chains and prison, exile and torture, limbs hacked off and senses eradicated, oppression of the body to gratify the obscene lust of the oppressor, and any number of other horrors. And what about the fear and distress that arise from the innumerable accidents that threaten the body from without — heat and cold, tempests, downpours, floods, lightning, thunder, hail, thunderbolts, earthquakes and chasms opening in the earth, being crushed by collapsing buildings, injuries from frightened or even vicious domestic animals, all the poisons in plants, waters, air, or beasts, the painful or even fatal bites of wild animals, the madness which comes from a rabid dog (so that even this animal, usually so gentle and friendly to its master, is sometimes more strongly and sharply feared than a lion or a serpent) and which drives the person it infects so mad with its deadly contagion that he is more feared by his parents, wife, and

---

48. See Ps 77.9.
49. See Sir 30:12.
50. On the physical punishments meted out to schoolchildren see *Confessions* I,9,14-15; *On Christian Discipline* 11,12.

children than is any wild beast? What evils seafarers suffer, as do those who travel by land! Who goes anywhere without the likelihood of unexpected accidents? A man going home from the forum with perfectly sound limbs fell, broke his leg, and died from the injury. What seems safer than to be sitting down? But Eli the priest fell out of his chair and died.[51] Farmers — and in fact everyone — are fearful about all sorts of accidents to their crops, from the sky and the earth, or from harmful animals. Once the grain is gathered and stored, they usually feel secure. And yet, as we know, in some cases a sudden flood has put the farmers to flight and swept the finest harvest out of the barns and carried it away.

Can anyone rely on his own innocence to protect him against the myriad assaults of demons? In fact, to keep us from doing this, the demons sometimes assail even baptized infants (and nothing is more innocent than a baptized infant!) so viciously that, by God's permission of such things, we are shown in their case, more than any other, just how deeply we are to lament the calamity of this life and to desire the happiness of the life to come. Then again, there are so many evils of disease that arise from the very body itself that not even the books of the physicians can cover them all; and in most or virtually all cases the remedies and medicines are pure torment themselves, so that people are only delivered from a painful end by a painful cure. Has not fierce heat driven thirsty people to such desperation that they drink human urine, and even their own? Has not hunger driven them to such desperation that they cannot keep themselves from eating human flesh — and not just eating people they happened to find already dead but even people they themselves killed for the purpose, and not just eating some stranger or other but even mothers eating their own children in an incredible cruelty caused by their frenzy of hunger? Finally, there is sleep itself, which is rightly termed rest but is often made restless by dreams. Who can describe in words how it alarms the wretched soul and its senses with horrible (although illusory) terrors, which it somehow represents and presents so vividly that we cannot tell them apart from what is real? In the case of certain diseases or poisons, even people who are awake are desperately distressed by such false visions; and sometimes malignant demons, with their various modes of trickery, deceive even the healthy with visions of this sort. Even when they cannot win people over to their side, they still like to play tricks on their senses from the simple desire to get them to believe what is false.

This life is so wretched that it is like a sort of hell, and nothing delivers us from it but the grace of Christ the savior, our God and our Lord.[52] In fact the very name "Jesus" means "savior";[53] and, most of all, he saves us from a life after this one that is even more wretched than this one, an eternal life that is not life but death. In this life, although there is the great consolation of cures that come through holy objects or saintly persons, even these benefits are not always granted to those who

---

51. See 1 S 4:18.
52. See Rom 7:24-25.
53. See Mt 1:21.

ask, lest we seek religion for the sake of these benefits. Instead, we should seek religion for the sake of that other life where there will be no evils at all; and grace helps the good in the midst of the evils of this life precisely so that, the more faithful they are, the more they will be able to endure these evils with a brave heart.

The learned of this world claim that the true philosophy, which Cicero says that the gods have given only to a certain few, is also a help on this score. He maintains that the gods have never given, nor could they ever give, any greater gift than this to human beings.[54] To this extent even our opponents are compelled to admit, in a way, that divine grace is needed in order to gain not just any philosophy but the true philosophy. But, if the true philosophy, our one help against the miseries of this life, has been divinely given only to a few, this also shows quite clearly that the generality of mankind has been condemned to pay the penalty of these miseries. And since, by their own admission, there is no greater divine gift than this, we must also believe that it is given by no other god than the one of whom they themselves — who worship many gods — say there is none greater.

The Struggles of the Righteous: the Battle against the Vices

23. In addition to the evils of this life that are common to the good and the evil alike, the righteous also face certain struggles of their own: they do battle against the vices, and they lead their lives in the midst of the temptations and dangers of that sort of combat. For — although sometimes more violently, sometimes more mildly — the desires of the flesh never cease to oppose the spirit or the desires of the spirit to oppose the flesh, and so we cannot do the things that we want,[55] ridding ourselves entirely of all evil desire. Instead, as far as possible with God's help, we can only subdue evil desire by denying it our consent....

In the kingdom where we shall dwell forever with immortal bodies, we shall face no battles and have no debts. We would never have had any of these, at any time or any place, if our nature had remained upright as it was created. As it is, however, our present conflict, in which we are put in such danger, and from which we yearn to be delivered in final victory, belongs to the evils of this life; and, on the evidence of all its many and great evils, we prove that this life is a life under condemnation.

The Goods of this Life

24. This human wretchedness is, then, a punishment for which the justice of God deserves praise. We must also consider, however, the fact that the goodness of

---

54. See *On the Ends of the Good and the Evil* V,21,58.
55. See Gal 5:17.

the same God, who governs and guides all he created, has filled this misery with many kinds of goods. First of all, even after sin God did not choose to revoke the blessing he had pronounced before sin, *Increase and multiply and fill the earth* (Gn 1:28). The fruitfulness that he had given continued in the condemned stock; and even the blemish of sin, which also imposed the necessity of death on us, could not take away the wondrous power of seed — or, rather, the still more wondrous power by which seed is produced, a power that is inscribed on and in a way woven into human bodies. And in this river or torrent of the human race, so to speak, there are two currents flowing at once, the evil current derived from its first parent and the good current conferred by its creator. The original evil has two aspects, sin and punishment; and the original good has two different aspects, propagation and conformation. For our present purposes, however, we have already said enough about the two evils, one stemming from our own audacity (that is, sin) and the other from God's judgment (that is, punishment). Here I have undertaken to talk about the goods which God has conferred, and is still conferring even now, on this vitiated and condemned nature of ours. For in condemning our nature he did not take away everything that he had given; otherwise our nature would not exist at all. Nor did he remove our nature from his own power, even when he subjected it to the devil for its punishment; for he has not put even the devil himself beyond the reach of his rule. In fact the nature of the devil only subsists because God — who supremely exists, and who causes everything to exist that has any existence at all — causes it to subsist.

As we said, then, two goods flow from God's goodness, as from a kind of fountain, even into a nature that has been vitiated by sin and condemned to punishment. The first, propagation, God bestowed by the blessing he gave during the initial works of creation[56] from which he rested on the seventh day;[57] but the second, conformation, he bestows in the ongoing work which he continues right up to the present.[58] In fact, if God were to withdraw his efficacious power from things, they would not be able to go on and fill out their allotted spans in their own measured motions. They would not even remain in the state in which they were created. Thus, God created man in such a way that he added to him a kind of fertility by which he might propagate other human beings, producing in them the same possibility — but not necessity — of propagating others. God has, at his will, taken this fertility from certain people, leaving them sterile. But, once he gave it to the first couple by his general blessing,[59] he has never taken it from humanity at large. Even though the power of propagation was not taken away by sin, however, it is not now what it would have been if no one had sinned. Because man, placed in honor, fell and became like the beasts,[60] he breeds like the beasts.

---

56. See Gn 1:28.
57. See Gn 2:2.
58. See Jn 5:17.
59. See Gn 1:28.
60. See Ps 49:12.20.

But, even so, a certain spark of reason, by virtue of which he was made in the image of God,[61] has not been wholly extinguished in him.

If conformation were not added to propagation, however, propagation by itself would not lead to the forms and modes of each species. For, if human beings had not had sexual intercourse, and if God had still wished to fill the earth with human beings, he could have created them all in the same way he created the first man, without the mating of husband and wife. At the same time, even when humans have sex, they cannot produce offspring without God's creative power. Thus, just as the Apostle says of the spiritual instruction by which a person is formed in piety and righteousness, *Neither the one who plants nor the one who waters is anything, but God who gives the growth* (1 Cor 3:7), so we could also say here, "Neither the one who has intercourse nor the one who gives the seed is anything, but God who gives the form. Nor is the mother who conceives, carries, bears, and nurses the child anything, but God who gives the growth." For it is God himself, by the ongoing work which he continues right up to the present, who causes seeds to unfold their innate patterns and to evolve from certain hidden and invisible folds into the visible forms of the beauty that we see. It is God himself who wondrously joins and unites the incorporeal and the corporeal nature, the one in command and the other subject to it, and makes a living being. This work of his is so great and marvelous — not only in the case of man, who is a rational animal and consequently more excellent and outstanding than all earthly creatures, but even in the case of the tiniest little fly — that it astonishes the mind of any who consider it well, and it calls forth praise of the creator.

It is God himself, then, who has given the human soul a mind. In the infant, reason and intelligence are asleep, so to speak, as if they were not there at all. But they are ready to be roused and to go forth as the infant grows older, and so they become capable of knowledge and learning and suited for perceiving the truth and loving the good. Thanks to this capacity, the mind may drink in wisdom and be endowed with the virtues; and with the virtues — with prudence, with fortitude, with temperance, and with justice[62] — it can fight against errors and against the other implanted vices, and it can vanquish them by desiring nothing but the supreme and immutable good. And, even if it does not do this, who can adequately say or conceive how great a good the very capacity for such goods is, which is divinely established in the rational nature? Who can adequately say or conceive what a marvelous work of the Almighty this is?

For, quite apart from the arts of living well and attaining eternal happiness — which are called virtues and are given only by the grace of God, which is in Christ, to the sons of the promise and of the kingdom — there are the many and wonderful arts discovered by human ingenuity, some serving our needs, some serving our

---

61. See Gn 1:27.
62. These are the four so-called cardinal virtues.

pleasures. Even when it turns its desire to superfluous or, worse, to dangerous and harmful things, this extraordinary power of mind and reason shows what a great good it has by virtue of its nature, the good that enables it to discover, to learn, and to practice such arts. What wonderful, what astonishing heights human industry has reached in producing clothing and buildings! What progress it has made in agriculture and navigation! What artistry it has contrived and achieved in making pottery of all sorts, as well as in the varieties of sculpture and painting! What wonders it has devised to perform and present in the theaters, sheer marvels to those who see them, beyond belief to those who only hear about them! What a variety of ingenious methods it has invented for capturing, killing, and taming irrational animals! And against human beings themselves, so many kinds of poison, weaponry, and instruments of war! How many medicines and remedies it has detected for preserving and restoring our mortal health! How many seasonings and condiments it has discovered to please the palate! What a multitude and variety of signs for expressing thoughts and persuading others, among which words and writings hold the chief place! What ornaments of rhetoric, and what an abundant diversity of poems to delight the mind! What musical instruments and modes of singing it has thought up to charm the ear! What skill in measurement and number! How acutely it has come to grasp the motions and order of the stars! What enormous knowledge it has accumulated about the things of this world! Who could possibly describe all this, especially if we wished not to gather it all up in one heap but to dwell on each instance individually? Finally, who could adequately take the measure of the sheer ingenuity philosophers and heretics display in defending even errors and falsehood? For we are now speaking about the nature of the human mind with which this mortal life is adorned, not about the faith or the way of truth by which that immortal life is attained. And, since the creator of this wonderful nature is none other than the true and supreme God, who governs and guides all that he created and who possesses supreme power and supreme justice, surely it would never have fallen into its present miseries and would not be destined to pass on from them to eternal miseries — excepting only those who will be saved — unless there had first come some great sin in the first man, from whom all the rest have sprung.

How fully God's goodness appears in the human body itself, even though it shares mortality with the beasts and turns out to be weaker than many of them! How fully the providence of the great creator is evident! Are not the sense organs and the other parts of the body so arranged, and the form, shape, and stature of the whole body so disposed, as to indicate that it was made to serve the rational soul? For man was not created with his face pointing down to the ground, like the animals that lack reason. Instead the form of his body is erect; it faces up toward heaven, admonishing him to take thought for the things that are above.[63] Note

---

63. See *On Genesis: A Refutation of the Manicheans* I,17,28; *Miscellany of Eighty-three Questions* 51,3.

also the wonderful mobility given to the tongue and to the hands, apt for speaking and writing and suited, too, for accomplishing so many arts and offices. Does not this mobility show us quite clearly what kind of soul the body has been joined to, what kind of soul it is meant to serve?

Setting aside the requirements of function, the interrelationship of all the parts of the body is so harmonious, and so beautiful in its symmetries, that one hardly knows which counted for more in creating the body, utility or beauty. Certainly, we see nothing which was created in the body for the sake of utility that does not also have a place in its beauty. And this would be all the more clear to us if we knew the measured proportions by which all the parts are joined and adapted to each other. Perhaps human ingenuity could trace out these proportions, if it made the effort, for the parts which are prominent on the surface of the body. But, as for what is hidden and removed from sight, such as the intricate network of veins and nerves and internal organs and the secrets of the vital parts, no one can make headway here. Certain diligent but cruel physicians, known as anatomists, have dissected the bodies of the dead, or even the bodies of the dying, while they were still in the hands of the surgeon who was cutting into and examining them. In this way they have pried inhumanely into all the secrets of human bodies in order to learn more about their diseases and how to cure them. But as to the proportions of which I am speaking — on which the adaptation (what the Greeks call the *harmonia*) of the whole body, inside and out, is based, as in the case of a musical instrument — what shall I say? No one has been able to discover what no one has had the boldness to look for. But, if these proportions could also be known for the internal organs, which certainly make no show of beauty, their rational beauty would give us such delight that we would prefer it to every visible shape that pleases only the eyes. For it is the mind itself, which uses the eyes, that would delight in their beauty.

There are some things that are positioned in the body in such a way that they have only beauty but no use. A man's chest has nipples, for example, and his face has a beard. The fact that the beard is meant not for protection but as a male adornment is made clear by the smooth faces of women who, as weaker, are obviously the ones who ought to be better protected. Thus, if there is no member of the body — at least among those we can see, where there is no room for doubt — that is only useful without being beautiful, and, if there are some members of the body that have only beauty and no use, I think it is easy to see that, in the creation of the body, dignity took precedence over the necessities of use. After all, these necessities are going to pass away, and the time is going to come when we shall enjoy each other's beauty for itself alone, utterly without lust. And this in particular should lead us to praise the creator, to whom it is said in the Psalm, *You are clothed with praise and with beauty* (Ps 104:1).

And what words could possibly convey all the rest of creation's beauty and utility, which the divine generosity has granted to man to behold and to use, even though he has been condemned and cast down into all the toils and miseries of this life? Consider the multiform and variegated beauty of sky and earth and sea; the sheer abundance and marvelous splendor of light itself; the sun, the moon, the stars; the deep shade of woods; the colors and odors of flowers; the variety and number of chattering and bright-colored birds; the diverse species of so many and such wonderful animals, among which the smallest attract the greatest admiration (for we are more amazed at the work of tiny ants and bees than at the vast bodies of whales). Consider also the grand spectacle of the sea. It clothes itself with different colors like garments, sometimes green (and this in many shades), sometimes purple, sometimes blue. And what a delightful sight it is when the sea is storm-tossed, a sight made all the more appealing because it charms the onlooker without heaving and shaking him about like a sailor! Think of all the food that is everywhere on hand to keep us from hunger! Think of the diversity of flavors that give food its savor, a diversity spread out before us by the riches of nature rather than sought out by the art and the labor of cooks! Think of the aids to preserving or recovering good health that are found in so many things! How welcome is the alternation of day and night! How enticing is the coolness of the breeze! Think of all the materials we have from plants and animals for making clothes! Who could possibly list everything? Take only the items that I have gathered up here, so to speak, in a bundle: if I wanted to untie the bundle and unwrap it in order to discuss each detail of each item, what a delay it would cost me! And all these are only the consolations for the wretched and condemned, not the rewards for the blessed.

The Goods of the Life to Come

But if the consolations are so many, so varied, and so great, what will the rewards be? What will God give to those whom he has predestined to life, if he has given all this even to those whom he has predestined to death? What good things will he provide in the future life of happiness for those on whose behalf, in this life of misery, he willed his only-begotten Son to endure such terrible evils, including even death itself? Speaking of those predestined for that kingdom, the Apostle says, *He who did not spare his own Son but gave him up for all of us, will he not also give us, with him, all things?* (Rom 8:32) When this promise is fulfilled, what shall we be? What shall we be like? What good things are we going to receive in that kingdom, since we have already received Christ's death for us in pledge of them? What will man's spirit be like when it no longer has any vice at all, when it is not subject to vice, when it does not give in to vice, when it no longer has to strive against vice, no matter how laudably, but is perfect in virtue and fully at peace? How great, how lovely, how certain will be its knowledge of all things, without error and without effort, when it drinks in God's wisdom at its very source, with supreme happiness and with no difficulty at all! What will the body be like, when it is wholly subject to the spirit and made so fully alive by the spirit that it will need no other nourishment? For it will not be an animal body but a spiritual body, having the substance of flesh, of course, but without any carnal corruption.

Against Philosophical Objections to the Resurrection of the Body

25. Outstanding philosophers do not disagree with us regarding the goods of the soul which it will enjoy in perfect blessedness after this life. They do, however, argue against the resurrection of the flesh, and they deny it as far as they can....

26. Porphyry tells us that for the soul to be happy it must flee all bodies. Thus, it does no good to say that the body will be incorruptible if the soul will not be happy unless it makes its escape from all bodies. I have already discussed this objection as far as necessary in the thirteenth book.[64] Here I am only going to repeat one point from that discussion: let Plato, their teacher, amend his own writings and say that their gods, in order to be happy, are going to flee from their bodies, that is, are going to die. For he said that they were enclosed in celestial bodies, but he also said that the god by whom they were made promised them immortality in order to quiet their anxiety; that is, he promised that they would remain forever in those same bodies not by virtue of their own nature but by virtue of his overriding purpose.[65] In the same place he also overthrows the claim of those who say that the reason we should not believe in the resurrection of the flesh is that it is impossible. In fact, when the uncreated god promised immortality to the gods he had created, he said quite plainly that he would do what is impossible. Here is what he said, as Plato puts it: "Because you had a beginning, it is not possible for you to be immortal and indissoluble. Nevertheless, you will not be dissolved, nor will any fate of death destroy you or prove more powerful than my purpose, which secures your perpetuity more surely than do the bodies to which you have been bound."[66] Unless those who hear these words are not only stupid but deaf, they cannot possibly doubt that, according to Plato, what is impossible was promised to the created gods by the god who created them. For, when he says, "It is not possible for you to be immortal, but by my will you will be immortal," what is he saying but "What it is impossible for you to be is exactly what, by my doing, you will be"?

Thus, the one who, according to Plato, promised to do what is impossible, will raise up the flesh, making it incorruptible, immortal, and spiritual. When we proclaim that God — who, even according to Plato, does the impossible — is going to do this, why do they still proclaim that what God promised is impossible, especially when the whole world has believed the promise of the God who himself promised that the world would believe? For souls to be happy, then, they do not need to flee from all bodies but rather to receive an incorruptible body. And in what incorruptible body would it be more appropriate for them to rejoice than the same body in which they groaned when it was corruptible? For in that case they

---

64. See above at XIII,16-17.
65. See *Timaeus* 41c.
66. *Timaeus* 41b. This is a portion of a larger citation that appears above at XIII,16.

will not feel the dread desire that Virgil, following Plato,[67] ascribed to them when he said that "they begin to desire a return to bodies."[68] And the reason they will have no desire to return to bodies is that they will have the very bodies they would otherwise want to return to; and they will have them in such a way that they will never lose them and will never be parted from them for even the briefest moment by any kind of death.

27. If Plato and Porphyry had been able to exchange with each other some of the assertions that each made separately, they might both have become Christians. Plato stated that souls cannot exist for eternity without bodies. That is why he said that even the souls of the wise, after some indefinitely long period of time, will return to bodies.[69] Porphyry, on the other hand, claimed that the fully purified soul, once it has returned to the father, will never again return to the evils of this world.[70] Thus, if Plato had provided Porphyry with the truth that he saw — namely, that even the fully purified souls of the just and the wise are going to return to human bodies — and if Porphyry had provided Plato with the truth that he saw — namely, that holy souls are never going to return to the miseries of the corruptible body — they would each have made their claims not separately but together, each holding both truths. And in that case I think they would have seen what follows — *both* that souls return to bodies *and* that they receive the kind of bodies in which they may live in happiness and immortality. For, according to Plato, even holy souls will return to human bodies; and, according to Porphyry, holy souls will not return to the evils of this world. Therefore, let Porphyry say with Plato, "They will return to bodies," and let Plato say with Porphyry, "They will not return to evils." Then they will be in agreement that souls return to bodies, but to bodies in which they will suffer no evils. And these bodies will be none other than the bodies that God promises when he says that blessed souls will live for all eternity with their own eternal flesh. For, so far as I can see, both Plato and Porphyry would now readily grant us this — that anyone who acknowledges that the souls of the holy are going to return to immortal bodies would also permit them to return to their own bodies, in which they endured the evils of this world and in which they devoutly and faithfully worshiped God in order to be free from these evils....

28. ...Therefore, if Plato and Porphyry — or, rather, any of their admirers who are still alive — agree with us that holy souls are going to return to bodies (as Plato holds), but are not going to return to any evils (as Porphyry says), with the consequence that (as the Christian faith foretells) they will receive the kind of bodies in which they can live happily for all eternity without any evil, then let

---

67. Augustine may be referring to *Phaedrus* 249a-b.
68. *Aeneid* VI,751. See also above at X,30.
69. See *Phaedo* 81e-82a.
70. See *Letter to Marcella* 33.

them also take from Varro the assertion that the soul returns to the same body in which it lived before. Then they will have solved the whole question of the flesh's resurrection to eternity for themselves!

The Eternal Life of the Saints: the Vision of God

29. Now, so far as God grants his help, let us see how the saints will be occupied in their immortal and spiritual bodies, when their flesh is no longer living carnally but now spiritually. To tell the truth, however, I do not know what their activity, or rather their rest and repose, will be like. I have never seen it with my bodily senses; and, if I should say that I have seen it with my mind, that is, with my understanding, what does our understanding amount to, and how far can it take us, in relation to such excellence? Then, as the Apostle says, there will be *the peace of God which surpasses all understanding* (Phil 4:7). And whose understanding does he mean if not ours, and perhaps even that of the holy angels? It certainly does not surpass God's understanding! If the saints are going to live in the peace of God, then, they are clearly going to live in the peace *which surpasses all understanding*. It obviously surpasses our understanding; there is no doubt of that. If it also surpasses the angels' understanding — and the one who said *all understanding* seems not to have made an exception even of them — then we have to take this saying to mean that neither we nor any of the angels can know the peace of God, whereby God himself is at peace, as God knows it. And so it *surpasses all understanding* except, of course, his own.

But, because we have also been made partakers in his peace according to our capacity, we too know supreme peace in ourselves, among ourselves, and with him, insofar as what is supreme is possible for us. Similarly, the holy angels know it according to their capacity. At present, however, human beings know it only to a far lower degree, no matter how outstanding they are in mental progress. For we must keep in mind how great a man it was who said, *For we know only in part, and we prophesy only in part, until that which is perfect comes* (1 Cor 13:9) and *Now we see in a mirror dimly, but then face to face* (1 Cor 13:12). This is how the holy angels see already. The holy angels are also called our angels. For we have been rescued from the power of darkness, have received the pledge of the Spirit, and have been transferred to the kingdom of Christ,[71] and so we have already begun to belong to the angels with whom we shall share the holy and most delightful city of God, about which we have now written so many books. Thus, the angels, who are God's angels, are also our angels in the same way that Christ is both God's Christ and our Christ. They are God's because they did not abandon God, and they are ours because they have begun to have us as their fellow citizens. The Lord Jesus said, *See that you do not despise one of these little ones. For I tell you*

---

71. See Col 1:13.

that in heaven their angels always see the face of my Father who is in heaven. (Mt 18:10) As they see, then, we also shall see. But we do not yet see in this way....

Will the Saints See God with the Eyes of the Spiritual Body?

Consequently, when I am asked what the saints' activity in the spiritual body will be, I do not say what I already see. I say only what I believe, in keeping with what I read in the Psalm, *I believed, and therefore I have spoken* (Ps 116:10 LXX). And so I say that the saints are going to see God in the body.[72] But whether they will see him by means of the body — as we now see the sun, the moon, the stars, the sea, the earth, and the things on earth — is no small question. For, on the one hand, it is hard to say that the saints will then have bodies of such a kind that they will not be able to close and open their eyes whenever they want; but, on the other, it is even harder to say that anyone who shuts his eyes there will stop seeing God.

The prophet Elisha, although absent in body, saw his servant Gehazi receiving gifts given to him by Naaman the Syrian, whom the prophet had healed from the deformity of leprosy; and all the while the servant supposed that his wicked act was hidden because his master was not there to see it.[73] How much the more, then, will the saints in their spiritual bodies see all things, not only when their eyes are closed but even when they are not bodily present!...

Even in this life, therefore, where the prophetic gift of men with miraculous powers can only be compared to the future life as a child is compared to an adult, Elisha still saw his servant receiving gifts when he himself was far away. Does it make sense, then, to think that — once the perfect has come and the corruptible body no longer weighs down the soul[74] but is incorruptible and offers no impediment at all — the saints will need bodily eyes to see what they are going to see, especially when the absent Elisha had no need of bodily eyes to see his servant?... Even so, however, the bodily eyes will also be in their place and have their function, and the spirit will make use of them through the spiritual body. For the fact that the prophet did not need his bodily eyes to see his absent servant does not mean that he did not use them to see things present, even though, if he closed his eyes, he could have seen them by the spirit in the same way that he saw absent things when he was not there himself. It would be completely wrong, then,

---

72. Augustine also deals with the question of the vision of God in Letters 147 (*On Seeing God*) and 148. In Letter 147,23,53-54 he concludes that bodily eyes could not see the divinity, and he looks forward to further research regarding what precisely bodily eyes might be able to see in the resurrection. According to *Revisions* II,41(68), the results of that research are found in the present section of *The City of God*, where Augustine displays a certain openness to the possibility that bodily eyes could somehow see God, although he acknowledges that Scripture does not support such a possibility.
73. See 2 K 5:19-27.
74. See Wis 9:10.

to say that in the life to come the saints will not see God when they have their eyes closed, for they will always see him with the spirit.

But will they also see with their bodily eyes when they have them open? That is the question. If the eyes of the spiritual body, even as spiritual, can see no more than the eyes we have now, there is no doubt that God cannot be seen with them. They will have a far different power, then, if they are to see the incorporeal nature which is not contained in any place but is wholly present everywhere....

What we do not see with our bodily eyes, however, is life itself, separate from the body. Consequently, it is possible, and in fact highly probable, that in the world to come we will see the corporeal bodies of the new heaven and the new earth[75] in such a way that, wherever we look, we shall see God with brilliant clarity, everywhere present and governing all things, including bodily things — seeing him both through the bodies we shall be wearing and through the bodies we shall be looking at. It will not be as it is now. Now the invisible things of God are understood through the things he has made;[76] now they are seen in a mirror dimly and only in part;[77] now the faith by which we believe counts more for us than the sight of bodily things that we perceive with our bodily eyes. Even in this life, however, as soon as we catch sight of the people among whom we live — living people, showing vital motion — we not merely believe but actually see that they are alive. Even though we cannot see their life apart from their bodies, we do see it in their bodies, by means of our bodies, with no room for any doubt whatsoever. And in the same way, in the life to come, wherever we look with the spiritual eyes of our bodies, we shall, even by means of our bodies, behold the incorporeal God ruling all things.

It is possible, then, that God will be seen in this way due to the fact that the eyes will then have some excellence similar to that of the mind, by which they will even be able to discern an incorporeal nature. It is difficult, however, or even impossible to support this view with any examples or testimonies from Divine Scripture. Alternatively — and this is easier to grasp — God will be known to us in such a conspicuous way that we shall each see him by the spirit in ourselves, in each other, in himself, in the new heaven and the new earth, and in every created thing that will then exist; and, at the same time, by the body we shall each see him in every body, wherever the eyes of the spiritual body are directed with their penetrating gaze. Our thoughts, too, will then lie open to each other; for the words of the Apostle will be fulfilled, who, after saying, *Do not pronounce judgment before the time*, immediately added, *until the Lord comes, who shall bring to light the hidden things of darkness and shall make manifest the thoughts of the heart, and then each one shall have praise from God* (1 Cor 4:5).[78]

---

75. See Is 65:17; 66:22; 2 Pt 3:13; Rv 21:1.
76. See Rom 1:20.
77. See 1 Cor 13:12.
78. See Letter 92,2; *Enchiridion* 32,121.

The Felicity of the Saints: Seeing, Loving, and Praising God

30. How marvelous that felicity will be, where there will be no evil, where no good will be hidden from sight, where all our time will be given to praising God, who will be all in all![79] For I do not know what else we shall be doing when our activity will neither be halted by idleness nor driven by need. And I am guided, too, by the holy canticle, where I read or hear, *Blessed are those who dwell in your house; they shall praise you for ever and ever* (Ps 84:4).

All the members and organs of the incorruptible body, which we now see assigned to the various functions that the necessities of life require of them, will contribute to praising God; for then there will be no such necessities but only full, certain, secure, and eternal felicity. All the proportions of bodily harmony, of which I have already spoken[80] and which are now hidden from us, will no longer be hidden. Distributed through all the parts of the body, within and without, they — along with all the other great and wondrous things that will then be seen — will set rational minds on fire with praise for such a great artist from sheer delight in their rational beauty.

What the movements of such bodies will be in the world to come I am not rash enough to try to describe. In fact I cannot even imagine it. But their motion and their rest, like their form itself, will be fitting, for nothing unfitting will be there at all. Where the spirit wills, it is certain, there the body will instantaneously be; nor will the spirit will anything which could possibly be unfitting either for the spirit or for the body. True glory will be there, for no one will be praised in error or in flattery; true honor, for honor will be denied to no one who is worthy and will be awarded to no one who is unworthy, nor will anyone who is unworthy aspire to it, since only the worthy are permitted to be there; and true peace, for no one will suffer opposition either from himself or from others.

The reward of virtue will be God himself, who gave the virtue and who promised himself to it, and than whom there can be nothing better or greater. When he said through the prophet, *I will be their God, and they shall be my people* (Lv 26:12), what did he mean but "I will be their fulfillment; I will be all that people rightly desire — life, health, sustenance, plenty, glory, honor, peace, and all good things"? This is also the right way to understand what the Apostle says, *That God may be all in all* (1 Cor 15:28). He will be the end of our desires: he will be seen without end, loved without satiation, and praised without weariness. And this gift, this feeling, this activity, like eternal life itself, will be shared by all.

---

79. This final chapter of *The City of God*, which begins with the Latin words *Quanta erit illa felicitas*, must have been the inspiration for the twelfth-century theologian Peter Abelard's celebrated Saturday vespers hymn, *O quanta qualia*, which repeats several of the chapter's themes and images.

80. See above at XXII,24.

But who could possibly imagine, much less describe, the grades of honor and glory there will be then, in proportion to the merits deserving of reward? It is not to be doubted, however, that there will be such distinctions. And the blessed city will also see this great good in itself — that no inferior will envy any superior any more than the other angels envy the archangels. No one will wish to be what he has not been given to be, but will be linked by a bond of the utmost peace and concord to the one to whom this has been given — just as, in the body, the finger does not wish to be the eye, since the structure of the body contains both members in peace.[81] Thus, some will have lesser gifts than others, but they will also have the gift of not wanting more.

Sin will no longer be able to give them any delight, but this does not mean that they will have no free will.[82] On the contrary, it will be all the more free, because it will have been so completely set free from delight in sinning that it will take unfailing delight in not sinning. The initial free will, given to man when he was first created righteous, was able not to sin, but it was also able to sin. In contrast, the final free will will be more powerful than the first in that it will not be able to sin, but this will be due to God's gift, not to any capacity of its own nature. For it is one thing to be God and quite another to participate in God. God is by nature unable to sin, but one who participates in God receives it from God that he is unable to sin. In addition, there was a gradation in the divine gift that had to be preserved: man was first given a freedom of will by virtue of which he would be able not to sin, and he was ultimately given a freedom of will by virtue of which he would not be able to sin. The former was suited to acquiring merit, the latter is suited to receiving reward. But, because man's nature sinned when it was able to sin, it is delivered by a more generous gift of grace, so that it may be led to the liberty in which it is unable to sin. For, just as the first immortality, which Adam lost by sinning, consisted in being able not to die and the final immortality will consist in not being able to die, so the first free will consisted in being able not to sin and the final free will will consist in not being able to sin. Thus, it will be just as impossible then to lose the will to godliness and justice as it is impossible now to lose the will to happiness. For in sinning we lost our hold on both godliness and happiness, but, when we lost happiness, we obviously did not lose the will to happiness. Then, too, God himself certainly cannot sin. But does that mean we should deny that he has free will?

In the heavenly city, then, there will be freedom of will, one freedom in all and indivisible in each. It will be freed from all evil and filled with all good, enjoying without fail the delight of eternal joys; and it will have no memory of faults or punishments. It will not, however, have forgotten its own liberation, and so it will

---

81. See 1 Cor 12:14-26.
82. The same considerations on sin, the inability to sin, the maintenance of free will, death and the inability to die, as discussed in what follows, are expressed in *Enchiridion* 28,104-105; *Rebuke and Grace* 12,33-34.

not be ungrateful to its liberator. As a matter of rational knowledge, then, it will even remember its past evils; but as a matter of felt experience it will not remember them at all — in the same way that a highly skilled physician knows virtually all the diseases of the body as they are known to his art but is ignorant of most of them as they are actually felt in the body, since he has not suffered them himself.

There are, then, two kinds of knowledge of evils, one by virtue of which they are not hidden from the mind's grasp, another by virtue of which they are ingrained in felt experience. Indeed, all the vices are known in one way through the teachings of wisdom, and in quite another through the wicked life of the fool. Similarly, there are two ways of forgetting evils. The person who has education and learning forgets them in one way, the person who has actually experienced and suffered them forgets them in another way — the former when he disregards his knowledge, the latter when he is no longer in misery. It is according to this second kind of forgetting that the saints will have no memory of past evils. For they will now be free from all evils, and they will be completely erased from their feelings. By the great power of knowledge that they will have, however, they will be aware not only of their own past misery but also of the eternal misery of the damned. Otherwise — if they were to have no knowledge at all that they were once in misery — how, as the Psalm says, will they sing the Lord's mercies forever?[83] Nothing will give more joy to that city than this song to the glory of the grace of Christ, by whose blood we are delivered.[84]

Then the words of the Psalm will be fulfilled, *Be still and see that I am God* (Ps 46:10). This will truly be the supreme sabbath, the sabbath which has no evening, the sabbath which the Lord stamped with his approval in the first works of creation, where we read, *And on the seventh day God rested from all his works that he had done. And God blessed the seventh day and sanctified it, because on it he rested from all his works that he had begun to do.* (Gn 2:2) For we shall ourselves be the seventh day, when we have been made full by his blessing and made new by his sanctification. Then we shall be still and see that he is God; then we shall see that he is what we ourselves wanted to be, when we fell away from him, listening to what we heard from the seducer, *You shall be like gods* (Gn 3:5), and deserting the true God, who would have made us gods by participation in him, not by desertion of him. For what have we done without him except to waste away in his wrath? But, when we are made new by him and are perfected by his greater grace, we shall be still for all eternity and shall see that he is God, and by him we shall be filled when he is all in all.[85]

For it is only when we have come to understand that our good works are actually his, not ours, that they are credited to us so that we may attain this sabbath.

---

83. See Ps 89:1.
84. See Rv 5:9.
85. See 1 Cor 15:28.

If we ascribe them to ourselves, they will be servile works,[86] and it is said of the sabbath, *You shall do no servile work* (Dt 5:14). For the same reason it is also said through the prophet Ezekiel, *And I gave them my sabbaths as a sign between me and them, so that they might know that I am the Lord, who sanctifies them* (Ezk 20:12). We shall know this perfectly when we are perfectly still and see perfectly that he is God.

This sabbath will stand out more clearly if we enumerate the ages, as if they were days, according to the divisions of time that we see represented in Scripture, for we shall find that it is the seventh age.[87] The first age, counted as the first day, extends from Adam to the flood, and the second from the flood to Abraham. These two are equal not in length of time but in number of generations, for each turns out to contain ten generations. From Abraham down to the coming of Christ, by the reckoning of the evangelist Matthew, there are three ages, each extending across fourteen generations — one from Abraham to David, the second from David to the exile to Babylon, and the third from the exile to Babylon down to Christ's birth in the flesh.[88] These make five ages in all. The sixth age is now in progress, but it is not to be measured by any set number of generations, for Scripture says, *It is not for you to know the times that the Father has put in his own power* (Acts 1:7). After this sixth age God will rest, as on the seventh day; and he will cause this same seventh day — the day that we ourselves shall be — to rest in him.[89] It would take too long, however, to discuss each of these ages in detail now. It is enough simply to point out that this seventh age will be our sabbath, and its end will not be an evening but rather the Lord's Day, as an eighth and eternal day, consecrated by Christ's resurrection, and prefiguring the eternal rest not only of the spirit but also of the body. There we shall be still and see, see and love, love and praise. Behold what will be in the end without end! For what else is our end but to reach the kingdom that has no end?

It seems to me that, with God's help, I have now paid my debt with this huge work. May those who think it too small or too large forgive me; and may those who think it sufficient give joyful thanks not to me but, with me, to God. Amen. Amen.

---

86. I.e., works done for pay or for a reward.
87. The division of history into six (or seven) ages, as follows, is frequent in Augustine. See *On Genesis: A Refutation of the Manicheans* 1,23,35-40; *Miscellany of Eighty-three Questions* 58,2; *Instructing Beginners in Faith* 17,28-22,39; *The Trinity* IV,4,7.
88. See Mt 1:17.
89. See *Confessions* XIII,36,51-37,52.

Study Questions for Book XXII

Book XXII opens with a reprise of the fateful origins of the City of Man: the prideful, free-will decisions of the evil angels and of Adam and Eve. Likewise, this final crescendo of Augustine's long and challenging text affirms the eternal, omnipotent will of God that works mysteriously throughout creation, undeterred by human or angelic failing. What has been the role of free will throughout Augustine's analyses of the two cities?

The difficulties of his own life, the sufferings of his people, and the political and social turmoil of the Late Roman Empire are all evident in Augustine's realistic appraisal of the human condition. Yet Augustine's words also rise in poetic affirmations of the unassailable goodness of creation, and in profound gratitude for God's gift of embodied human experience. Does the physicality of Augustine's description of eternal life and the vitality of the risen bodies of men and women bear any significance for sacramental theology?

The philosophy of the Platonists had opened Augustine's mind when he was a young man in Milan and was an important part of his journey toward conversion. He continued his dialogue with Platonic thought throughout his life, critiquing it in light of faith and Scripture but valuing its contributions to Christian thinking. What is the significance of the prominent place of Porphyry in Book XXII?

THE COMPLETE WORKS OF ST. AUGUSTINE
A Translation for the 21st Century

Part I — Books

Autobiographical Works

The Confessions (I/1)
  cloth, 978-1-56548-468-9
  paper, 978-1-56548-445-0
  pocket, 978-1-56548-154-1
  Mobile App for iOS & Android available

Revisions (I/2)
  cloth, 978-1-56548-360-6

Dialogues I (I/3) forthcoming

Dialogues II (I/4) forthcoming.

Philosophical-Dogmatic Works

The Trinity (I/5)
  cloth, 978-1-56548-610-2
  paper, 978-1-56548-446-7

The City of God 1-10 (I/6)
  cloth, 978-1-56548-454-2
  paper, 978-1-56548-455-9

The City of God 11-22 (I/7)
  cloth, 978-1-56548-479-5
  paper, 978-1-56548-481-8

On Christian Belief
  cloth, 978-1-56548-233-3
  paper, 978-1-56548-234-0

Pastoral Works

Marriage and Virginity (I/9)
  cloth, 978-1-56548-104-6
  paper, 978-1-56548-222-7

Morality and Christian Asceticism (I/10)
  forthcoming

Exegetical Works

Teaching Christianity (I/11)
  (On Christian Doctrine)
  cloth, 978-1-56548-048-3
  paper, 978-1-56548-049-0

Responses to Miscellaneous Questions (I/12)
  cloth, 978-1-56548-277-7

On Genesis (I/13)
  cloth, 978-1-56548-175-6
  paper, 978-1-56548-201-2

Writings on the Old Testament (I/14)
  cloth, 978-1-56548-557-0

New Testament I and II (I/15 and I/16)
  cloth, 978-1-56548-529-7
  paper, 978-1-56548-531-0

The New Testament III (I/17) forthcoming

Polemical Works

Arianism and Other Heresies (I/18)
  cloth, 978-1-56548-038-4

Manichean Debate (I/19)
  cloth, 978-1-56548-247-0

Answer to Faustus, a Manichean (I/20)
  cloth, 978-1-56548-264-7

Donatist Controversy I (I/21) forthcoming

Donatist Controversy II (I/22) forthcoming

Answer to the Pelagians (I/23)
  cloth, 978-1-56548-092-6

Answer to the Pelagians (I/24)
  cloth, 978-1-56548-107-7

Answer To The Pelagians (I/25)
  cloth, 978-1-56548-129-9

Answer to the Pelagians (I/26)
  cloth, 978-1-56548-136-7

Part II — Letters

Letters 1-99 (II/1)
  cloth, 978-1-56548-163-3

Letters 100-155 (II/2)
  cloth, 978-1-56548-186-2

Letters 156-210 (II/3)
  cloth, 978-1-56548-200-5

Letters 211-270 (II/4)
  cloth, 978-1-56548-209-8

Part III — Homilies

Sermons 1-19 (III/1)
  cloth, 978-0-911782-75-2

Sermons 20-50 (III/2)
  cloth, 978-0-911782-78-3

Sermons 51-94 (III/3)
  cloth, 978-0-911782-85-1

Sermons 94A-150 (III/4)
  cloth, 978-1-56548-000-1

Sermons 151-183 (III/5)
  cloth, 978-1-56548-007-0

Sermons 184-229 (III/6)
cloth, 978-1-56548-050-6

Sermons 230-272 (III/7)
cloth, 978-1-56548-059-9

Sermons 273-305A (III/8)
cloth, 978-1-56548-060-5

Sermons 306-340A (III/9)
cloth, 978-1-56548-068-1

Sermons 341-400 (III/10)
cloth, 978-1-56548-028-5

Sermons Newly Discovered Since 1990 (III/11)
cloth, 978-1-56548-103-9

Homilies on the Gospel of John 1-40 (III/12)
cloth, 978-1-56548-319-4
paper, 978-1-56548-318-7

Homilies on the Gospel of John (41-124) (III/13) forthcoming

Homilies on the First Letter of John (III/14)
cloth, 978-1-56548-288-3
paper, 978-1-56548-289-0

Expositions of the Psalms 1-32 (III/15)
cloth, 978-1-56548-126-8
paper, 978-1-56548-140-4

Expositions of the Psalms 33-50 (III/16)
cloth, 978-1-56548-147-3
paper, 978-1-56548-146-6

Expositions of the Psalms 51-72 (III/17)
cloth, 978-1-56548-156-5
paper, 978-1-56548-155-8

Expositions of the Psalms 73-98 (III/18)
cloth, 978-1-56548-167-1
paper, 978-1-56548-166-4

Expositions of the Psalms 99-120 (III/19)
cloth, 978-1-56548-197-8
paper, 978-1-56548-196-1

Expositions of the Psalms 121-150 (III/20)
cloth, 978-1-56548-211-1
paper, 978-1-56548-210-4

**Essential Texts
Created for Classroom Use**

Augustine Catechism: Enchiridion on Faith Hope and Love
paper, 978-1-56548-298-2

Essential Expositions of the Psalms
paper, 978-1-56548-510-5

Essential Sermons
paper, 978-1-56548-276-0

Instructing Beginners in Faith
paper, 978-1-56548-239-5

Monastic Rules
paper, 978-1-56548-130-5

Prayers from The Confessions
paper, 978-1-56548-188-6

Selected Writings on Grace and Pelagianism
paper, 978-1-56548-372-9

Soliloquies: Augustine's Inner Dialogue
paper, 978-1-56548-142-8

Trilogy on Faith and Happiness
paper, 978-1-56548-359-0

E-books Available
*Essential Sermons, Homilies on the First Letter of John, Revisions,
The Confessions, Trilogy on Faith and Happiness, The Trinity,
The Augustine Catechism: The Enchiridion on Faith, Hope and Love.*

Custom Syllabus
Universities that wish to create a resource that matches their specific needs using selections from any of the above titles should contact New City Press.

Free Index
A free PDF containing all of the **Indexes** from *The Works of Saint Augustine, A Translation for the 21st Century* published by NCP is available for download at www.newcitypress.com.

New City Press — The Works of Saint Augustine Catalog
For a complete interactive catalog of *The Works of Saint Augustine, A Translation for the 21st Century* go to New City Press website at: www.newcitypress.com

Electronic Editions
InteLex Corporation's Past Masters series encompasses the largest collection of full-text electronic editions in philosophy in the world. The Past Masters series, which includes *The Works of Saint Augustine, A Translation for the 21st Century*, published by New City Press, supports scholarly research around the world and is now being utilized at numerous research libraries and academic institutions. The Works of Saint Augustine (Fourth release), full-text electronic edition, is available for subscription from InteLex. The Fourth release includes all 41 of the published volumes as of May 2016. For more information, visit: http://www.nlx.com/home.

About the Augustinian Heritage Institute
In 1990, the Augustinian Heritage Institute was founded by John E. Rotelle, OSA to oversee the English translation of *The Works of Saint Augustine, A Translation for the 21st Century*. This project was started in conjunction with New City Press. At that time, English was the only major Western language into which the Works of Saint Augustine in their entirety had not yet been attempted. Existing translations were often archaic or faulty and the scholarship was outdated. These new translations offer detailed introductions, extensive critical notes, both a general index and scriptural index for each work as well as the best translations in the world.

The Works of Saint Augustine, A Translation for the 21st Century in its complete form will be published in 49 volumes. To date, 42 volumes have been published.

New City Press

About New City Press
New City Press is one of more than 20 publishing houses sponsored by the Focolare, a movement founded by Chiara Lubich to help bring about the realization of Jesus' prayer: "That all may be one" (John 17:21). In view of that goal, New City Press publishes books and resources that enrich the lives of people and help all to strive toward the unity of the entire human family. We are a member of the Association of Catholic Publishers.

Free Index to *The Works of Saint Augustine*
Download a PDF file that provides the ability to search all of the available indexes from each volume published by New City Press.

Visit http://www.newcitypress.com/index-to-the-works-of-saintaugustine-a-translation-for-the-21st-century.html for more details.